The Works of
William James

Supervised by a team of scholars, each a specialist in his field, *The Works of William James* fills the long-standing need for an authoritative, standard edition of the philosopher's works. The General Editor and supervisor of the project is Frederick Burkhardt. Mr. Burkhardt, formerly a professor of philosophy and then a college president, is President Emeritus of the American Council of Learned Societies. The Textual Editor, Fredson Bowers, Linden Kent Professor of English, Emeritus, at the University of Virginia, is in charge of the establishment of the text and its production according to standards of the Center for Editions of American Authors. Gold Medalist of the Bibliographical Society, Fellow of the American Academy of Arts and Sciences, and Corresponding Fellow of the British Academy, Mr. Bowers is the author of two books on the theory and practice of textual criticism and editor of several multivolume critical editions. Ignas K. Skrupskelis, the Associate Editor, contributes the substantive notes. He is Professor of Philosophy at the University of South Carolina and has conducted extensive research in the James collection.

The Works of William James

Editors
Frederick H. Burkhardt, General Editor
Fredson Bowers, Textual Editor
Ignas K. Skrupskelis, Associate Editor

Advisory Board

Max H. Fisch	Eugene T. Long
John J. McDermott	Edward H. Madden
Maurice Mandelbaum	H. S. Thayer

*This edition of the Works of William James
is sponsored by the American Council of
Learned Societies*

This volume is edited by
Frederick H. Burkhardt
Fredson Bowers
Ignas K. Skrupskelis

Introduction by
John J. McDermott

William James in 1894–95?

photograph by Mrs. Montgomery Sears; courtesy Houghton Library, Harvard University

Essays in Philosophy

William James

HARVARD UNIVERSITY PRESS

Cambridge, Massachusetts
and London, England

1978

Copyright © 1978 by the President and Fellows of Harvard College

All rights reserved

Printed in the United States of America

CENTER FOR EDITIONS OF
AMERICAN AUTHORS

AN APPROVED TEXT

MODERN LANGUAGE
ASSOCIATION OF AMERICA

®

Library of Congress Cataloging in Publication Data
James, William, 1842–1910.
Essays in philosophy.
(The works of William James)
Includes bibliographical references and index.
1. Philosophy—Addresses, essays, lectures.
I. Burkhardt, Frederick Henry, 1912–
II. Bowers, Fredson Thayer.   III. Skrupskelis,
Ignas K., 1938–   IV. Title.
B945.J23E66   100   77–27361
ISBN 0–674–26712–5

Foreword

Essays in Philosophy is the fifth volume to be published in THE WORKS OF WILLIAM JAMES. It follows the editorial policy established for the edition as a whole in its inaugural volume, *Pragmatism*. Briefly stated, that policy has as its object to provide the reader with an authoritative text based on the principles of modern textual criticism. These principles, and the techniques involved in the preparation of such a text, are set forth in the Note on the Editorial Method.

The edition seeks to present James's writings in the form that represents as closely as possible his final intentions, with such additional material as will make his text understandable in terms of its background and references, and by relating it to pertinent manuscript material in the substantial collection of James papers in the Houghton Library at Harvard University. While no attempt is made to provide any interpretation of James's philosophy, the editors have sought to provide a dependable foundation for scholarly work of the future.

The text of the essays has been established by Fredson Bowers, Linden Kent Professor of English, Emeritus, at the University of Virginia, the Textual Editor of the WORKS. Professor Bowers has also provided a history of the text and the authority of its source documents, together with a textual apparatus that will enable scholars to reconstruct the documents used in the editing. The Associate Editor, Professor Ignas K. Skrupskelis of the University of South Carolina, is responsible for the section of reference Notes to the text and for the General Index. In addition, he contributed to the documentation of the publishing history.

The Advisory Board of scholars listed in the front matter was appointed by the American Council of Learned Societies, which sponsors this edition of the WORKS. The editors have had the benefit of general policy guidance and many specific suggestions from the members of the Board—one of whom, Professor John J. McDermott of Texas A&M University, deserves special thanks for writing the Introduction to *Essays in Philosophy*.

This volume brings together twenty-one essays that William James wrote for various professional and popular publications between 1876 and 1910. Several of them are well known to students of James as being of particular importance in the development of his thought: for example, "Remarks on Spencer's Definition of Mind as Correspondence," "The Sentiment of Rationality," and "The Knowing of Things Together." Each contains seminal ideas that recur in his later works in revised and expanded form.

In the aggregate this collection includes James's philosophic writings apart from those which he himself assembled and published in books such as *The Will to Believe*, *Pragmatism*, and *The Meaning of Truth*. It should be said, however, that there is a degree of arbitrariness involved in the selection. Philosophy in James's time, and certainly in his own mind, was not a field of inquiry separated by clear lines of demarcation from other subject matters, such as psychology or religion. In assembling this volume the editors have taken philosophy in a narrower sense, more consonant with current practice. Forthcoming volumes will bring together essays in psychology, in religion and morality, and in psychic research.

The editors have reserved two essays for publication in other volumes. One is "Philosophical Conceptions and Practical Results," which James first published in 1898 and which has already appeared as an appendix to *Pragmatism* in the present edition of the WORKS, because its text formed the basis of Lecture III of that volume. Moreover, "The Pragmatic Method" in the present volume is a condensed and revised version of it. The other essay, "Rationality, Activity and Faith," which was first printed in the *Princeton Review* in 1882, was largely incorporated in the much-revised "Sentiment of Rationality" that James put together for *The Will to Believe*. The passages that James did not utilize will be reprinted in Appendix II of that forthcoming volume so that the whole essay may be reconstructed without difficulty. ("The

Sentiment of Rationality" reprinted in the present volume is in its original unreworked form.)

It remains for the editors to acknowledge their indebtedness to the individuals and institutions that have helped make this volume possible.

The National Endowment for the Humanities has generously provided funds for the editorial work on this and other volumes of the WORKS. The Endowment has also helped with the cost of publishing *Essays in Philosophy* by permitting the use of funds it had granted to the American Council of Learned Societies to pay for the preparation of camera-ready copy of the end matter. Dr. Ronald Berman, as Chairman of the Endowment, and Dr. George F. Farr, Jr., of its Division of Research Grants, have been consistently encouraging and supportive of the entire project.

Mr. Alexander James and Dr. William Bond of the Houghton Library have granted permission to use and reproduce both printed and manuscript texts in the James Collection at Harvard University. The members of the staff of the Houghton Reading Room have been unfailingly helpful and patient in making the James Papers available to the editors.

The University of South Carolina, which cooperated in the planning of the edition as a whole, has continued to provide research assistance and working space to the Associate Editor.

The Department of Manuscripts and University Archives of Cornell University granted permission to quote from letters in the Frank Thilly Papers relevant to James's "Preface to Paulsen's *Introduction to Philosophy.*"

The Hoose Library of Philosophy at the University of Southern California kindly furnished the editors with the texts and permission to print four letters and one postcard from William James to W. T. Harris concerning the publication of "The Sentiment of Rationality" and "Remarks on Spencer's Definition of Mind as Correspondence."

Mr. J. R. Kantor, University Archivist at the University of California, Berkeley, provided useful information about the typed manuscript of the lecture "Philosophical Conceptions and Practical Results," which James delivered at Berkeley in 1898 and which forms the basis of the text of "The Pragmatic Method" in the present volume.

The Manuscripts Division of the Stanford University Libraries provided the letters from James to F. C. S. Schiller that were used in editing the essays on "Bradley or Bergson?" and "The Chicago School."

A letter from James to James McKeen Cattell related to "Bradley or Bergson?" was made available by the Library of Congress.

The Columbia University Libraries provided James's correspondence with F. J. E. Woodbridge concerning "The Pragmatic Method" and "A Suggestion about Mysticism," and a letter relating to "Bradley or Bergson?" from the *Journal of Philosophy, Psychology, and Scientific Methods.*

The British Library, Bodleian Library, and London Library made their collections of English editions of James's works available to the editors.

Signora Anna Casini, granddaughter of Giovanni Papini, kindly sent the editors copies of all of James's letters to him.

Professor G. Thomas Tanselle of the University of Wisconsin examined the volume for the seal of the Center for Editions of American Authors.

Mrs. Audrone Skrupskelis assisted the Associate Editor in searching for James's quotations and bibliographical references.

Finally, Mrs. Anne Quigley, Chief Research Assistant to the Textual Editor, and her staff, Mrs. Mary Mikalson, Mrs. Elizabeth M. Berkeley, Mr. Richard Rainville, and Miss Janice Cauwels, performed with great skill the work involved in preparing the manuscript for publication.

Frederick H. Burkhardt

Contents

Contents

Introduction
by
John J. McDermott

Few philosophers have written with the verve and elegance of William James. The essays, reviews, and occasional pieces that grace this volume reveal many of James's life-long interests, and his style throughout is engaging and personal. In alternating moods he is witty, acerbic, compassionate, and polemical. What is striking about these essays is that despite their topicality, they often have a contemporary message. In the opening piece, "The Teaching of Philosophy in Our Colleges," written more than a century ago, James laments the existence of those students who leave college "rather dampened and discouraged than stimulated by the lifeless discussions and flabby formulas they have had to commit to memory" (*EP*, p. 3).[1] Thirty years later, in 1906, James returns to the theme in his commentary on Giovanni Papini:

Our university seminaries (where so many bald-headed and bald-hearted young aspirants for the Ph.D. have all these years been accustomed to bore one another with the pedantry and technicality, formless, uncircumcised, unabashed and unrebuked, of their 'papers' and 'reports') are bearing at last the fruit that was to be expected, in an almost complete blunting of the literary sense in the more youthful philosophers of our land (*EP*, p. 145).

These are strong words and they make fledgling readers of James uncomfortable about their ability to write philosophy that is tech-

[1] References to *Essays in Philosophy*, designated in these pages as *EP*, are to the present volume. References to *Pragmatism, The Meaning of Truth, Essays in Radical Empiricism, A Pluralistic Universe*, and *The Will to Believe* are to this edition of THE WORKS OF WILLIAM JAMES. All other references to James's work are to first printings.

nically sound and yet free of aridity. I do not think that James's style can be emulated, or for that matter should be emulated. Yet even the occasionally more technical piece in this volume, such as "Remarks on Spencer's Definition of Mind as Correspondence," has James press upon us not only the possibility but the importance of stylistic clarity and felicitous use of language. Whatever may be the evaluation of James's thought in the long run, it can be said with confidence that he is unfailingly interesting.

Before we isolate some important themes in these essays, it will be helpful to comment on the organization of the present volume. James never published a book entitled *Essays in Philosophy*, nor for that matter did he publish books entitled *Essays in Religion and Morality* or *Essays in Psychology*, which are to be two subsequent volumes in this edition of the WORKS. Arrangement of the essays according to disciplines gives rise to the danger that the interdisciplinary character of James's thought may be somewhat obscured. James did not honor hard and fast distinctions among philosophy, psychology, and religion, but regarded each of them as names given to varieties of human behavior and patterns of inquiry. Indeed, the range of James's writings in any given year shows a bewildering array of interests. In 1876, for example, he wrote reviews and notes on biology, physiology, philosophy, the teaching of philosophy, vivisection, the theory of color, and the writings of Bain, Renouvier, and Renan. Until his death in 1910, barely a year went by in which his writing did not reflect a similar catholicity of interest. And it must be granted that the interplay of his many and varied interests is crucial to a full understanding of his thought. On the other hand, a merely chronological arrangement of these varied essays would have made it difficult for the reader to follow the ways in which James developed the basic themes in each of the fields that engaged his attention. As a compromise it was decided to arrange the essays by fields, but to publish them in chronological order within each field, so that the student of the WORKS might read all that James wrote, including unpublished material, year by year, as well as in the more conventional way, volume by volume.

The unity of the volume at hand lies in the function of recurrent themes rather than in any systematic continuity. In date of publication, the essays span thirty-four years, from 1876 to 1910, with more than half written in the last decade of James's life. The essay entitled "A Pluralistic Mystic," written as a testament to the unsung thinker Benjamin Paul Blood, was the last writing that James prepared for publication. Four of the essays included in this volume are essential to the canon of James's mature philosophical work. They are "Remarks on Spencer's Definition of Mind as Correspondence" (1878), "The Sentiment of Rationality" (1879), "The Knowing of Things Together" (1895), and "The Pragmatic Method" (1904). Although only a paragraph long, the two entries in Baldwin's *Dictionary of Philosophy and Psychology* (1902) on "Pragmatism" and "Experience" are clear anticipations of James's later position on those important terms. His controversial doctrine of the "Will to Believe" is clearly foreshadowed in "Quelques Considérations sur la méthode subjective" (1878), and his long-standing interest in psychic states and mysticism is given personal dimension by his autobiographical reports in "A Suggestion about Mysticism" (1910). The remainder of the pieces introduce the reader to many of the philosophers whose thought occupied James, leading to either polemics or praise, the most noteworthy being the judicious but devastating review of Herbert Spencer's work and the perceptive assessment of the influence of John Dewey and the importance of his work at the University of Chicago in 1903.

The first piece in this volume, "The Teaching of Philosophy in Our Colleges," is a response to an open letter written to the *Nation* by G. Stanley Hall in 1876. Hall criticized the comparative neglect of philosophy in American colleges and especially the dependence of philosophical teaching on "theological considerations."[2] In a companion piece James writes to the *Nation* and agrees with Hall, although he points to the renascence of philosophical study at Harvard College. Two aspects of James's response are of interest in the present discussion. First, as seen from the text cited above on the lifelessness of philosophical teaching, James has already introduced a major strand of his pedagogy. No matter how difficult the problem under consideration, he refuses to banish wit and imagination from discussions of philosophical and psychological problems. Second, in this early formal statement of the nature of philosophical inquiry James shows that he has already developed pragmatic sensibility, a foreshadowing of his later pragmatism. He writes, "One can never deny that philosophic study means the habit of always seeing an alternative, of not taking the usual for granted, of making conventionalities fluid again, of imagining foreign states of mind"

2 *The Letters of William James* (Boston: Atlantic Monthly Press, 1920), I, 189.

(*EP*, p. 4). This attitude of openness to the future and a willingness to change his mind becomes in James's later language an awareness of *consequences* and an affirmation of the hypothetical character of even our most trusted beliefs.

Two years after his comment on the teaching of philosophy, in 1878, James published his first substantial piece on matters philosophical, "Remarks on Spencer's Definition of Mind as Correspondence." Although at the time James was teaching physiology and psychology at Harvard and did not become Assistant Professor of Philosophy until 1880, his writing had taken on a philosophical cast. In the piece just discussed, on the teaching of philosophy, he had written of the academic disciplines that "all branches must be taught from the first in a philosophic manner, must be saturated with the liberal spirit, for any good to be effected" (*EP*, p. 5). Accordingly, James analyzes Spencer's *Principles of Psychology* within the context of his emerging philosophical concerns.

James takes as his task a criticism of Spencer's contention that the whole of mental evolution can be explicated by the formula that accounts for the *"adjustment of inner to outer relations"* (*EP*, p. 7). His first complaint is that Spencer considers only the phenomena of cognition and omits "all sentiments, all æsthetic impulses, all religious emotions and personal affections" (*EP*, p. 8). Put differently, James holds that Spencer, like some nineteenth-century anthropologists such as E. B. Tylor, falls prey to what is now called the genetic fallacy. James cites Tylor as saying, to that effect, "Whatever throws light on the origin of a conception throws light on its validity" (*EP*, p. 9). James's major objection to this position of Spencer is that it eliminates the active role of the human organism in the mental action. This in turn leads to the introduction of one of James's most important and influential themes, that of interest. In a somewhat ironic statement James maintains that "interests are the real *a priori* element in cognition" (*EP*, p. 11n). Interests must be "awakened" before the notice of outer, environing relations takes place. And James makes it clear also that the individual is a "social being" and thus "the interests of his fellow are a part of his environment" (*EP*, p. 13). After an extended further analysis of Spencer's definition of correspondence, James again introduces the theme of implication and consequence. He holds that in the last analysis our theories must pass the test of what "works best" (*EP*,

p. 21).[3] For James the knower is not a passive witness to a simply existing order. We are in the dark about the ultimate nature of reality and about the nature of our own activities. Both reality and our interests are coercive of each other, and the nature of thought is to be worked out within the framework of that tension. James then concludes his essay on Spencer with a statement that proves to be characteristic of his future epistemology. "By its very essence, the reality of a thought is proportionate to the way it grasps us. Its intensity, its seriousness—its interest, in a word—taking these qualities, not at any given instant, but as shown by the total upshot of experience" (*EP*, p. 21).

It is noteworthy that James's essay on Spencer, too little acknowledged as one of the founding statements of pragmatism, was published the same year as Peirce's important paper "How to Make Our Ideas Clear." In addition to its criticism of Spencer, this essay should also be read as a trenchant critique of British empiricism, especially with regard to the correspondence theory of truth reigning at the time.

In 1878, the year of his essay on Spencer, James published "Quelques Considérations sur la méthode subjective." Although he acknowledges the significance of the objective method of science, James denies that it can ever act as an unvarying rule of method. "Rejeter rigoureusement la méthode subjective partout où la vérité existe en dehors de mon action et se détermine avec certitude indépendamment de tout ce que je peux désirer ou craindre, rien de plus sage" (*EP*, p. 24). The problem arises with that class of "facts" which are not established before action. He gives as an example the need to leap over a chasm on an alpine ascent. Should I have confidence in my ability and strength to accomplish this, I am thereby aided to do what I might not otherwise be able to do. On the other hand, hesitation over my ability to accomplish this leap may well be the decisive element in bringing about a failure otherwise avoidable. Belief or nonbelief in ability constitutes for James a preliminary condition of the act itself. Then, in a passage that anticipates a theme to be found in the later and more famous setting of his essay on "The Will to Believe," James writes: "Il y a donc des cas où *une*

---

[3] The term "works" has long been a subject of controversy in the secondary literature pertaining to James. For a clarification of James's meaning of "works," see H. S. Thayer's Introduction to *The Meaning of Truth* in the Works, pp. xxxi–xlii.

croyance crée sa propre vérification. Ne croyez pas, vous aurez raison; et, en effet, vous tomberez dans l'abîme. Croyez, vous aurez encore raison, car vous vous sauverez. Toute la différence entre les deux cas, c'est que le second vous est fort avantageux" (*EP*, p. 24).

James's statement that there are some cases in which belief can create its own verification is modest enough, but as readers of the literature on James are well aware, that contention unloosed a spate of criticism over the years.[4] Suffice it to say that whatever other philosophical difficulties attend James's position, naiveté is not one of them. As early as 1868, when James was recovering from a period of severe personal depression and affirming his individuality and creative power, he nonetheless wrote: "My belief, to be sure, *can't* be optimistic—but I will posit life (the real, the good) in the self-governing *resistance* of the ego to the world. Life shall [be built in] doing and suffering and creating."[5]

James was not a fideist. Faith is not belief in something about which we are certain. Rather, belief for James was an energizing, a probe, a sally forth with risk acknowledged. As he puts it epistemically in the essay on the subjective method, "Au résumé *foi* et *working hypothesis* sont ici la même chose" (*EP*, p. 29). Actually, if we follow James through his later interest in psychical research and speculative cosmology, it could be said that for him the direction of human life itself was profoundly hypothetical, inevitably subject to novelty and chance.

In 1879 James published one of his most significant essays, "The Sentiment of Rationality." James sets his task as an analysis of why philosophers philosophize. As in the earlier piece on the subjective method, he criticizes the view that philosophy functions only on behalf of a dispassionate concern for the formal truths of an objective order of reality. In this essay James concentrates on the psychological dimensions of the activity of philosophizing. Subsequently, in 1882, he concerned himself with the ethical aspects of this question in an essay entitled "Rationality, Activity and Faith."

In theoretical terms, James sees the philosophical quest as one that seeks a "conception." And on that issue he is very explicit.

---

[4] An analysis of the critical response to James's "Will to Believe" essay can be found in Edward H. Madden's Introduction to *The Will to Believe and Other Essays in Popular Philosophy* in the WORKS.

[5] *Letters*, I, 148.

What now is a *conception*? It is a *teleological instrument*. It is a partial aspect of a thing which *for our purpose* we regard as its essential aspect, as the representative of the entire thing (*EP*, p. 34).[6]

James then proceeds to move through a series of presentations, representing philosophers and philosophical positions over a vast range of importance and interest. (James's justly praised tolerance of other thinkers and his catholicity of interest often do him a disservice. He is notorious at failing to sort out the thinker and thoughts that have staying power from those he just happens upon.) Despite the rush of names, from Eduard von Hartmann to Spencer or from Hume to the anatomist Jules Luys, the villain is apparent. James's long-standing *bête noire* has surfaced; it is *monism*.

The craving for Monism at any cost is the parent of the entire evolutionist movement of our day, so far as it pretends to be more than history. The [Spencerian] Philosophy of Evolution tries to show how the world at any given time may be conceived as absolutely identical, except in appearance, with itself at all past times. What it most abhors is the admission of anything which, appearing at a given point, should be judged essentially other than what went before (*EP*, p. 37).

Even when James adds another basic attitude to philosophizing, that of the passion to distinguish, his description is strikingly like that of the simplicity of monism. Those who wish to distinguish, to be clear, and are dead set against a vapid principle of unity, nonetheless have a "dislike of blurred outlines, of vague identifications" (*EP*, p. 37). In a word, James at this time in his life has developed a resistance to those philosophical approaches which set out primarily to get things straight and in so doing ignore the consequences of the concessions necessary to such an end. James flails away at both the attitudes in question, simplicity and clearness, but it is not always clear what he is doing, for at this point he has no distinctive metaphysics of his own. His position appears to be an ordinary variety of realism, stressing both the need to unify and the need to distinguish.

6 James never abandons this position. Indeed, he later offers a more extreme version of it, as when he writes, "*The only meaning of essence is teleological, and that classification and conception are purely teleological weapons of the mind.*" *The Principles of Psychology* (Boston: Henry Holt, 1890), II, 335.

The truly wise man will take the phenomenon in its entirety and permanently sacrifice no one aspect to another. Time, place, and relations differ, he will freely say; but let him just as freely admit that the quality is identical with itself through all these differences. Then if, *to satisfy the philosophic interest*, it becomes needful to conceive this identical part as the essence of the several entire phenomena, he will gladly call them one; whilst if some other interest be paramount, the points of difference will become essential and the identity an accident. Realism is eternal and invincible in this phenomenal sense (*EP*, p. 51).

On a closer look at this text, however, we find that James has stressed the philosophical "interest." Contrary to the attitudes of simplicity and clarity, James has set the stage for the development of his own metaphysical position. The most telling statement of his "interest" is found in his *Psychology* [Briefer Course], where he writes, "It is, the reader will see, the reinstatement of the vague and inarticulate to its proper place in our mental life which I am so anxious to press on the attention."[7] James's fidelity to the vague and inarticulate in his analysis of human knowing finally led him to cut between the passion for the simple and the passion for the clear and thereby to develop a relational metaphysics.

In 1893 James wrote two communications to *Mind* as part of his continued polemical dispute with F. H. Bradley. The bibliographical sources and some of the relevant texts in this dispute are provided in the Notes to the present volume. The issue in question in these two pieces is ostensibly "resemblance," but a wider knowledge of the Bradley-James conflict shows that what is involved is the status of relations. James asks rhetorically of Bradley, "Why need we insist that the 'relations' between the terms, the likenesses and differences themselves, must be engendered by such an impossible summation or synthesis?" (*EP*, p. 68). The synthesis to which James is objecting derives from his rejection of what he takes to be the Hegelian penchant for taking the world as *All-einheit*, that is, from a single rather than from a multiple point of view. James's original opponent in this connection was his colleague Josiah Royce, for whom single ideas were but fragments unless they were grasped as part of an infinite system. Whether Bradley's view was the same as this early position of Royce is a disputed question, and James himself is not always sure just where Bradley stands. In fact, after

[7] *Psychology* [Briefer Course] (Boston: Henry Holt, 1892), p. 165.

severely criticizing Bradley in these two brief rejoinders, James concludes the second by saying, "*I* never meant to go beyond psychology; and on that relatively superficial plane I now confidently greet Mr. Bradley, no longer as the foe which by a mere verbal ambiguity he has seemed, but as a powerful and welcome ally" (*EP*, p. 70).

James's remark about proceeding from the superficial plane of psychology gives away too much, which unfortunately is not an unusual stylistic characteristic of his. This is evident in the fact that it is in an essay devoted to "psychology" that James prepares the way for his own doctrine of relations, which was the focal point of his later attack on Bradley. The reference here is to James's important essay of 1884, "On Some Omissions of Introspective Psychology," where he defends the position that every relation is just as much a matter of direct, particular experience as the poles of the relationship. This position was repeated in the chapter on "The Stream of Thought" in *The Principles of Psychology* and finally became the cornerstone of his radical empiricism.[8] Bradley was right to chastise James in this early phase of their dispute, because James was unclear about the alternatives to the position he criticized. On the other hand, although James can say that we do not know how the quality of a relation of likeness "makes itself," he had already given considerable thought to that question independent of his conflict with Bradley. Readers of the present volume should consider these two pieces on Bradley as being merely an entry into one of the most significant and elegant philosophical disputes of the last hundred years.

In 1894 James delivered the President's Address to the American Psychological Association and it was published one year later. By that time James was an influential figure in psychology, having published his massive and brilliant two-volume study, *The Principles of Psychology*, in 1890. Although his more distinctively philosophical work was not as extensive as the *Principles*, by 1895 he had begun to set out the fundamental direction of his philosophy. In addition to the essays discussed above, James had also published "The Dilemma of Determinism" in 1884 and "On the Function of Cognition" in 1885. The latter essay clarified James's basic epistemological leanings and is noteworthy for its distinction between

---

8 The genesis of James's radical empiricism and the dispute with Royce and Bradley is discussed in my Introduction to *Essays in Radical Empiricism* in the WORKS, pp. xiii–xxv.

knowledge-by-acquaintance and knowledge-about. In other terms, James writes of this distinction as that between percepts and concepts.

A percept knows whatever reality it directly or indirectly operates on and resembles; a conceptual feeling, or thought, knows a reality, whenever it actually or potentially terminates in a percept that operates on or resembles that reality, or is otherwise connected with it or with its context.[9]

James repeats this distinction in "The Knowing of Things Together," where he writes, "There are two ways of knowing things, knowing them immediately or intuitively, and knowing them conceptually or representatively" (*EP*, p. 73). James denies any "inner mystery" in the process of knowing things representatively, for "*to know an object is here to lead to it through a context which the world supplies*" (*EP*, p. 74). The case of "immediate or intuitive acquaintance" is quite different. Taking as his example a piece of white paper that we now see, and abstracting it from every other event as if it were itself the universe, James contends that "the paper seen and the seeing of it are only two names for one indivisible fact which, properly named, is *the datum, the phenomenon, or the experience*" (*EP*, p. 75). In James's view, knowledge-by-acquaintance is defined by an identity of mental content and object. James's use of the term "identical" in this context seems misleading, for he is actually describing the "passing moment," the ever-present transition and active fringes that characterize our experience, taken both as object and as content.

James is convinced that thought and thing are but two names for either of the "two great associative systems, that of the experiencer's mental history, or that of the experienced facts of the world" (*EP*, p. 75n). He does admit, however, that it is very difficult to trace "the particular *conditions* whereby we know particular things together" (*EP*, p. 78). He surveys a series of competing approaches to this problem, singling out such types as the physiological, psychological, animistic, and transcendental. As expected, he finds them wanting for one reason or another. He then closes this essay with a criticism of his previous judgment, found in the *Principles*, that psychology should not concern itself with "the whole business of ascertaining

[9] *The Meaning of Truth*, Works, pp. 27–28.

how we come to know things together or to know them at all" (*EP*, p. 87). James feared that such a quest would generate "unsafe hypotheses" and dilute the "scientific" character of psychology. The position he takes in 1895 is reflective of his conviction that "no conventional restrictions *can* keep metaphysical and so-called epistemological inquiries out of the psychology-books" (*EP*, p. 88). What is more, psychology must seek to understand "that altogether unique kind of complexity in unity which mental states involve" (*EP*, p. 89). James himself was to devote much of his own energy to that problem in his *Essays in Radical Empiricism* and *A Pluralistic Universe*.

The next six pieces are comparatively brief, although not without interest. The first is a "Preface" to Friedrich Paulsen's *Introduction to Philosophy*, published in 1895. James wrote a number of such prefaces and they are invariably elegant. He praises Paulsen's attempt to forge continuity between philosophy and life and his ability to avoid the "besetting sin of philosophers," which James holds to be "the absolutism of their intellects" (*EP*, p. 93). In passing, he reminds us that "no philosophy can be more than an hypothesis" (*EP*, p. 93). Following the preface to Paulsen's book we find two entries written for James Mark Baldwin's *Dictionary of Philosophy and Psychology*, published in 1902. The first one is entitled "Pragmatism." James's controversial book *Pragmatism* was not published until 1907, but he had long been interested in the problems central to a pragmatic epistemology. In 1898 he published an important essay in this vein, "Philosophical Conceptions and Practical Results." At that time he referred his readers back to the paper of Charles S. Peirce, in the *Popular Science Monthly* of January 1878. James sums up Peirce's principles of pragmatism as follows:

To attain perfect clearness in our thoughts of an object, then, we need only consider what effects of a conceivably practical kind the object may involve—what sensations we are to expect from it, and what reactions we must prepare. Our conception of these effects, then, is for us the whole of our conception of the object, so far as that conception has positive significance at all.[10]

In the definition for Baldwin's *Dictionary* James uses the term "consequences" instead of "effects," and in so doing stresses the

[10] *Pragmatism*, WORKS, p. 259.

active, even constitutive, function of conceptions. Consequences, for James, do not refer simply to that which comes after, as in serial fashion, but denote also those results, often novel, which accrue because we can act out the conception beyond the bounds of its original, defined meaning. This change widens considerably James's earlier version of Peirce and throws into relief a fundamental strand of his own later pragmatism.

James's second entry in Baldwin's *Dictionary* is devoted to "Experience," definitely the most important single concern in his philosophy. Despite the brevity of this entry, James manages to put his finger on what is to become the point of departure for his later philosophy of pure experience. He takes a stand against the dualistic position that divides experience into objective and subjective aspects. He writes that "if experience be used with either an objective or a subjective shade of meaning, then question-begging occurs, and discussion grows impossible" (*EP*, p. 95). It is on behalf of such a position that James is forced to account for cognition in other than the traditional relationships between subject and object. James's reflection on this matter reaches its climax in 1904 with his contention that consciousness is a function rather than an entity and that "thought" and "thing" are what we *do* to experience and not what we *find* in experience.[11]

I turn now to James's writings on the thought of Herbert Spencer, occasioned by Spencer's death in 1903. From our present vantage point it is difficult to realize that Spencer was an enormously influential thinker in the last half of the nineteenth century. Like the writings of John Fiske, who also published voluminously, Spencer's work has all but disappeared from view and these days he is rarely taken seriously as a philosopher. This was not yet the case in James's time, even though a decline in his reputation was soon to set in. In the two pieces on Spencer included in this volume, "Herbert Spencer Dead" and "Herbert Spencer," James has already pointed out the severe weaknesses in his work. Yet we should not forget that James himself was at one time very taken with Spencer. He began reading him as a young man in 1860, and as late as 1878 James was using Spencer's *Principles of Psychology* in a philosophy course at Harvard College. That was also the year James

---

[11] Both the epistemological and metaphysical dimensions of the nature of experience are considered in detail in James's essays, "Does 'Consciousness' Exist?" and "A World of Pure Experience." See *Essays in Radical Empiricism*, Works, pp. 3–44.

published his essay on "Spencer's Definition of Mind." An important reason for Spencer's influence was his ability to appeal to two completely different, perhaps contrary, types of readers. On the one hand, he defended a radical individualism, clearly identified with the tradition of English liberty. On the other hand, he was a spokesman for a deterministic pattern of social evolution. Those who believed that, as individuals, we can do nothing to effect social amelioration, followed Spencer. So too did those who believed that individuals were masters of their fate and should not brook any interference. James is aware of this tension in Spencer's thought and refers to his simultaneous dependence on both the "English ideal of individual liberty" and on the "theory of universal evolution" as an instance of the ambiguity in his fundamental position.

In Mr. Spencer's heroic defence of individualism against socialism and the general encroachment of the state there is a similar seeming incoherence, so marked that one cannot help suspecting his thought to have started from two independent foci, and to be faithful to two ideals (*EP*, p. 99).

The two essays here in question contain many criticisms of isolated positions taken by Spencer, criticisms interestingly first raised to James by C. S. Peirce (*EP*, p. 116). More devastating, however, is James's overall assessment of Spencer's method, which he regards as procrustean. He writes that Spencer has little "*desultory* curiosity. . . . His facts, in short, seem all collected for a purpose; those which help the purpose are never forgotten, those which are alien to it have never caught his eye" (*EP*, p. 98). For all that, James is not without generosity and apologizes for finding so much fault with Spencer.

Misprised by many specialists, who carp at his technical imperfections, he has nevertheless enlarged the imagination, and set free the speculative mind of countless doctors, engineers, and lawyers, of many physicists and chemists, and of thoughtful laymen generally. He is the philosopher whom those who have no other philosopher can appreciate (*EP*, p. 115).

There is historical irony in the fact that much of the same kind of praise has been suggested with respect to James himself.

The remaining piece of the six here under discussion is James's response to the publication of *Studies in Logical Theory* by John Dewey and his colleagues at the University of Chicago. James is extremely prescient in his commentary on this book, singling out the strength of Dewey's position and predicting the kind of problems that Dewey and Mead would have to work out if their philosophical approach were to prevail. Further, he correctly points to a serious omission in the program of the Chicago writers, that is, the absence of a "cosmology," which for James means that they have failed to give a "positive account of the order of physical fact, as contrasted with mental fact" (*EP*, p. 105). In the ensuing years, James himself was to work out a fuller version of this statement by developing a concern for the extensive reaches of consciousness, beyond our common observations and beyond the strictures of the science of his time. In *A Pluralistic Universe* he attempts to overcome the distinction between "mental" and "physical" fact by positing as a possibility "the compounding of consciousness" (*PU*, pp. 83–100). In that work, James goes so far as to write:

The believer finds that the tenderer parts of his personal life are continuous with a *more* of the same quality which is operative in the universe outside of him and which he can keep in working touch with, and in a fashion get on board of and save himself, when all his lower being has gone to pieces in the wreck. In a word, the believer is continuous, to his own consciousness, at any rate, with a wider self from which saving experiences flow in (*PU*, p. 139).

Dewey was always wary of such speculation, especially in its religious formulation, and despite the extremely wide range of his philosophical interests, never addressed that area of human experience in much detail.

Perhaps the reason James was able to arrive at such a clear and decisive version of Dewey's position is that it so strongly resembled his own evolving thought. He cites Dewey as holding to only a "functional" difference between fact and theory. "What is fact for one epoch, or for one inquirer, is theory for another epoch or another inquirer. It is 'fact' when it functions steadily; it is 'theory' when we hesitate" (*EP*, pp. 104–105). He sees correctly that the term "situation" is crucial to the understanding of Dewey's thought. Dewey, like James, holds that there is a "grain" in things, which we ignore at our peril, but they also agree that this grain "creates itself from situation to situation, so the truth creates itself *pari passu*"

(*EP*, p. 105). Finally, James attributes to Dewey a position which he later formulates, in virtually the same language, as the "generalized conclusion" to his doctrine of radical empiricism. James says of Dewey that he holds there to be "no eternally standing system of extra-subjective verity to which our judgments, ideally and in advance of the facts, are obliged to conform" (*EP*, p. 105). James's version of this position occurs in the Preface to *The Meaning of Truth*. "The directly apprehended universe needs, in short, no extraneous trans-empirical connective support, but possesses in its own right a concatenated or continuous structure."[12]

I do not want to give the impression that James and Dewey had identical positions in all areas of their thought. In addition to the absence of Dewey's "cosmology," James had a deeper sense of the idiosyncratic dimensions of personal life. Dewey, on the other hand, cast his thinking in terms of a more profound awareness of the irreducibly social matrix of all of our activities, and his sense of social and political issues was far more sophisticated than that of James. Still, the similarities in their philosophical attitudes clearly outweigh the dissimilarities and the extensive influence of James on Dewey has not been sufficiently appreciated. The most immediate way to discern this is to read James's *Essays in Radical Empiricism* and then proceed to the essays in Dewey's *Influence of Darwin on Philosophy and Other Essays in Contemporary Thought*.[13] Dewey's book focuses on the same themes as James's, takes fundamentally the same position, and could readily have had the same title. James predicts a great future for the philosophy of Dewey, as he did for that of Henri Bergson. Like Bergson, Dewey's future was deeply dependent on what he had learned from James, as he significantly admits when he dedicates the *Studies in Logical Theory* to James and cites the "preeminent obligation" of the Chicago School to his work.

Although the next essay in this collection is dated 1904, it can be traced back to 1898. "The Pragmatic Method" is a slightly revised version of "Philosophical Conceptions and Practical Results" and was republished in the *Journal of Philosophy, Psychology, and*

12 *The Meaning of Truth*, WORKS, p. 7.
13 *The Influence of Darwin on Philosophy and Other Essays in Contemporary Thought* (New York: Henry Holt, 1910). The most important essays in this book were published from 1905 until 1907, just after James published his journal articles on radical empiricism, from 1904 until 1905.

Scientific Methods because of the flurry of interest directed at that time to allied themes. In one sense, "The Pragmatic Method" is still vintage James and presents positions that he continued to hold. I caution the reader, however, to realize that in 1904 James was developing a far more complex and philosophically sophisticated version of his thought. In the first place, he was just beginning to work out his radical empiricism as the significant metaphysical context for his pragmatism. Second, he was preparing lectures on pragmatism to be given at Chicago, Wellesley, and Glenmore in 1905, themselves preparatory to his more extensive treatment, published as *Pragmatism*, in 1907. Given that "The Pragmatic Method" does not reflect James's more mature thinking on pragmatism, the focus here will be on those aspects of the essay which remain as strands in his fundamental attitude toward philosophy.

The key to this essay, and to most of James's thought, is his linking of inquiry to conduct. In that context, James proposes what he modestly calls a "simple test" to evaluate the nature of "philosophical disputes."

There can *be* no difference which doesn't *make* a difference—no difference in abstract truth which does not express itself in a difference of concrete fact, and of conduct consequent upon the fact, imposed on somebody, somehow, somewhere and somewhen (*EP*, p. 125).

To prove his point, James poses the following hypothetical situation. "Let us . . . assume," he writes, "that the present moment is the absolutely last moment of the world, with bare nonentity beyond it, and with no hereafter for either experience or conduct" (*EP*, p. 125). In such a situation, the question of whether God or matter is the producer of all reality offers us an "idle and insignificant alternative" (*EP*, p. 125). Given the contrary supposition, however, that the world does have a future, James then argues that the alternative of whether God or matter is the ultimate principle of explanation takes on extreme significance. In sustaining this contention, James makes it clear that his notion of God is one continuous with the religious tradition, rather than with that of the "systematic theologians" for whom he has nothing but contempt.[14]

---

[14] James's interest in religious experience as opposed to theology and absolute idealism was not simply a passing concern. In 1901, three years after the original publication of this essay, he finished his Gifford Lectures on *The Varieties of Religious*

Their orthodox deduction of God's attributes is nothing but a shuffling and matching of pedantic dictionary-adjectives, aloof from morals, aloof from human needs, something that might be worked out from the mere word 'God' by a logical machine of wood and brass as well as by a man of flesh and blood (*EP*, p. 132).

After several pages of attack on the theologians, James shifts the venue of his argument to the metaphysical arena, raising there the ancient problem of the one and the many. His position is basically the same as the one directed to theology, for he repeats the pragmatic maxim and asks what difference accrues if we take one or the other as our principle of accountability. At this point the absolute idealists, such as Josiah Royce, replace the theologians as the opponent. Against them James raises the banner of the English-speaking philosophers, and in a series of some precipitous and rather startling generalizations he lists Locke, Berkeley, Hume, Stewart, Brown, James Mill, John Stuart Mill, Bain, and Peirce as having the right approach. To this highly dubious historical assessment he adds an outrageous cameo version of Kant, whom he refers to as a "mere curio," and whose bequest is judged to be neither original nor indispensable. Despite the suddenness and ahistorical character of these judgments, James's fundamental point is well taken. The empiricist tradition, in fact, does lean to some version of the pragmatic maxim. As stated by James in this essay, it has to do with asking oneself, of any conception, the following questions. "What is it *known as*? In what facts does it result? What is its *cash-value* in terms of particular experience? and what special difference would come into the world according as it were true or false?" (*EP*, p. 137). James later changed his mind on the merits of some of the above philosophers, but he remained true to the maxim as here expressed.

Of the remaining seven pieces in this volume, five are comparatively slight in scope and have to do with James's response to the thought of one or more of his contemporaries. The other two are fairly substantial contributions to James's experience and reflection relative to mysticism. I shall treat the five period pieces as a

---

Experience. In a letter of April 13, 1900, to Miss Frances R. Morse, he spoke of the lectures as an attempt "to defend (against all the prejudices of my 'class') 'experience' against 'philosophy' as being the real backbone of the world's religious life." *Letters*, II, 127.

cluster, then close with some remarks about James's fascination with unusual psychic experiences.

James's "Preface" to Harald Höffding's *Problems of Philosophy*, published in an American edition of 1906, illustrates anew his generosity and also his considerable reputation in the eyes of European thinkers of his time. James not only wrote the Preface to a book with which he was only in partial sympathy, but as the Notes in this volume attest, he extensively revised the English translation. Höffding, of course, was a far more competent historian of modern philosophy[15] than James could ever hope to be, yet he lacked an equal philosophical originality. In his Preface James indicated his opinion of Höffding in saying that while he was one who had "the *manner* of a rationalistic professor of Philosophy," he was at the same time able to "keep in touch with the temperament of concrete reality" (*EP*, p. 141). This in turn led James to speak of Höffding's "critical" as opposed to "absolute" monism, a term that one would expect James to reject out of hand. This is especially true since his subsequent description of Höffding's "critical" monism was strikingly reminiscent of a position held by the young Royce and rejected by James. In short, I advise the reader that the last place to look for James's position is in his commentaries on other thinkers, particularly those for whom he has a fraternal affection. I shall return to this later in my remarks about James's comparison of Bradley and Bergson.

I come next to James's piece on "G. Papini and the Pragmatist Movement in Italy," published in the *Journal of Philosophy, Psychology, and Scientific Methods* in 1906. This is James at his most distinctive, lending his by then significant international reputation to a struggling group of maverick Italian philosophers with whom he found himself in sympathy. (Parenthetically, it should be mentioned that James's international reputation stemmed in part from his mastery of European languages. Unlike most of his generation, and for that matter ours as well, James was polylingual; fluent in French, German, and Italian, he was also able to speak Spanish and Portuguese.)

James was particularly attracted to Papini because of his style, brash and "promethean," which contrasted favorably in his opin-

[15] See Harald Höffding, *A History of Modern Philosophy*, 2 vols. (London: Macmillan, 1900).

ion with the academic and "uncouth" phrasing of his American students and colleagues. He rightfully sensed that Papini had a pragmatic attitude and a belief in pluralism. James was extremely pleased with the openness of the Italian pragmatists to the possibility of novelty and with their stress on the multiplicity of options available to human decision.

Pragmatism, according to Papini, is thus only a collection of attitudes and methods, and its chief characteristic is its armed neutrality in the midst of doctrines. It is like a corridor in a hotel, from which a hundred doors open into a hundred chambers. In one you may see a man on his knees praying to regain his faith; in another a desk at which sits some one eager to destroy all metaphysics; in a third a laboratory with an investigator looking for new footholds by which to advance upon the future. But the corridor belongs to all, and all must pass there. Pragmatism, in short, is a great *corridor-theory* (*EP*, p. 146).[16]

Despite his linguistic and cultural familiarity with Italy, James did not grasp the larger setting that produced Italian pragmatism. Papini's favorite phrase, *Il crepuscolo*, is reminiscent of Nietzsche and portends a political and religious antiestablishment position far beyond James's own intentions. Fortunately James did not live to see pragmatism, albeit distorted beyond belief, as one of the sources to which Mussolini appealed in formulating his doctrine of fascism.[17] This historical distortion does warn us, however, that the pragmatic maxim as directed to decisions that reflect our social responsibilities must be developed with a sophistication equivalent to its concern for consequences attendant upon individual action. John Dewey was to see this dimension of pragmatism more clearly than did James.

In "The Mad Absolute," James's response to Willard Clark Gore's defense of the absolute as the acme of sanity finds him re-

[16] James's remark about the "open-doors" of the "corridor-theory" was not casual. He wrote to his sister, Alice James, a description of his new summer home in Chocorua, New Hampshire, by saying "Oh, it's the most delightful house you ever saw; has 14 doors all opening outside." Alice replied in her *Diary* that "his brain isn't limited to 14, perhaps unfortunately." Gay Wilson Allen, *William James—A Biography* (New York: Viking Press, 1967), p. 286.

[17] For a discussion of Mussolini's misuse of James's pragmatism, see Ralph Barton Perry, *The Thought and Character of William James* (Boston: Little, Brown, 1935), II, 575–579.

turning again to an attack on monism. The argument is a mental-health version of the ancient conflict that proceeded from the attempt to account for the existence of evil in a world created by God. If God is infinite and good, why and how does evil exist? James's version by analogy asks if the absolute is sane, why and how is it that we are mad, given that the very intelligibility of our being is inextricably tied to that same absolute? James claims that the only way out of this dilemma takes the direction of the hypothesis of a world consciousness, examined inductively.

In James's view, this approach *may* lead to a position whereby human consciousness is continuous with a vast but finite world consciousness, a position that possibly obviates the thorny distinction between an infinite God and a finite world. In the "Mad Absolute" essay he is extremely vague about his own thoughts on the matter and cites Fechner as the only one who has done any elaborate work on this question, although in 1909 James himself was to devote many of his lectures on *A Pluralistic Universe* to similar problems.

The year 1910 was the last of James's life. The present volume contains four publications from that year. The first is another response to F. H. Bradley, entitled "Bradley or Bergson?" Typical of James's writings on Bradley, the piece gives the initial impression that the two men agree fundamentally, with only semantic difficulties to be clarified. This initial impression, however, never seems to hold up, for as James proceeds with his analysis, he inevitably points to some unbridgeable chasm between their views. It is significant that Bradley's response to James is usually the reverse of this procedure; he starts with severe criticism and then praises James for coming close to his own position.[18]

James contends that Bradley joins Henri Bergson in contradicting the idealist position that feelings are "woven into continuity by the various synthetic concepts which the intellect applies" (*EP*, p. 151). According to James, this is acceptable; but then, unfortunately, Bradley does not take the route of Bergson, which is to affirm the primacy of perception over conception. Rather, in what James describes as the "thin watershed" that exists between life and philosophy, he affirms that Bradley chooses philosophy. Of Bradley, he writes:

[18] See F. H. Bradley, *Essays on Truth and Reality* (Oxford: Clarendon Press, 1914), pp. 142–158.

Forward, forward, let us range! He makes the desperate transconceptual leap, assumes *beyond* the whole ideal perspective an ultimate 'suprarelational' and transconceptual reality in which somehow the wholeness and certainty and unity of feeling, which we turned our backs on forever when we committed ourselves to the leading of ideas, are supposed to be resurgent in transfigured form; and shows us as the only authentic object of philosophy, with its 'way of ideas,' an absolute which 'can be' and 'must be' and therefore 'is.' 'It *shall* be' is the only candid way of stating its relation to belief; and Mr. Bradley's statement comes very near to that (*EP*, p. 154).

James then cites Bergson as the thinker who takes us "into the valley where the green pastures and the clear waters always were" (*EP*, p. 155). His brief description of Bergson's position, however, is more James than it is Bergson. Perhaps it is because of long frustration with Bradley that James invokes Bergson as the one who will set it all straight. It is true that in his book *Essai sur les données immediates de la conscience*, published in 1889, Bergson parallels much of James's thought on the meaning of time in the flow of human consciousness. But Bergson, contrary to James, was extremely wary of the reductionistic possibilities of psychophysics and therefore never developed a radically empirical metaphysics in which matter and mind were functionally rather than ontologically distinct. And he never gave to the "feelings of relation" the status accorded them by James, preferring rather to present his position in the more traditional terms of interaction found, for example, in the concluding lines of *Matière et mémoire*: "L'esprit emprunte à la matière les perceptions d'où il tire sa nourriture, et les lui rend sous forme de mouvement, où il a imprimé sa liberté."[19]

Even granted that James was often more generous to other thinkers than they perhaps deserved, his frequent and lavish praise of Bergson seems to be excessive. At one point in 1907 James wrote of Bergson's *Creative Evolution* that it was "the absolutely *divinest* book on philosophy ever written up to this date."[20] This is not the place for a full discussion of the important question whether James or Bergson can claim priority in the development of their philosophies of consciousness. Ralph Barton Perry takes the questionable position, without adequate argumentation, that they were developed independently of each other, whereas Théodore Flournoy

[19] Henri Bergson, *Oeuvres* (Paris: Presses Universitaires de France, 1959) p. 378.
[20] Perry, *Thought and Character*, II, 604.

believes that James was the originator and Bergson the less original.[21] Aside from that dispute, Flournoy was perceptive about James's proclivity to give away his own claim to originality.

Apropos Bergson, it always amuses me to see your admiration of his writings. It is not that I do not appreciate them and the magic of their style; but you make me think of a rich proprietor who does not even surmise all that he possesses and who falls into a swoon before jewels which a clever goldsmith has stolen from him and has simply disguised by means of a new and glittering setting. (This is between ourselves.)[22]

The last of the five period pieces under consideration, "A Great French Philosopher at Harvard," was written on the occasion of a visit by Emile Boutroux to Harvard as a guest of the Hyde Foundation. James, lamenting the fact that so few students and faculty attended the lectures, criticizes the narrowness of graduate education in America, which tends to close off students from a wider world.

Our young fogies in the graduate schools continue working for their Ph.D. examinations by moving, like Faust's Wagner, "von Buch zu Buch," "von Blatt zu Blatt," and remain for the most part quite unconscious that an opportunity has been lost to them (*EP*, p. 167).

In the case of Boutroux, the students had lost the opportunity to meet a man who combined extraordinary learning with simplicity and felicity of style. No polemicist, Boutroux is thought by James to be a fount of both pragmatism and Bergsonism. He cites in that connection the important contribution of Boutroux's book of 1874, *De La Contingence des lois de la nature* (*EP*, p. 168). Associating Boutroux with the work of Peirce, Dewey, Schiller, Höffding, and Bergson, James holds that the philosopher's originality proceeds from "his firm grasp of the principle of interpreting the whole of nature in the light of that part of it with which we are most fully acquainted, namely, our own personal experience" (*EP*, p. 171).[23]

[21] See Perry, *Thought and Character*, II, 599–600, and Robert C. Le Clair, *The Letters of William James and Théodore Flournoy* (Madison: University of Wisconsin Press, 1966), p. 190.

[22] Le Clair, *Letters of James and Flournoy*, p. 215.

[23] It is noteworthy that Boutroux, in turn, had considerable admiration for James's work. See Emile Boutroux, *William James* (New York: Longmans, Green, 1912).

The remaining two essays in this volume relate to James's interest in mysticism and the expansion of consciousness. Both of them were published in 1910 and it is fitting that they close out his literary career. From his adolescence on, James was fascinated by unusual psychic states. As is well known, James experienced several "vastations," in which his hold on his personal identity was challenged. He was subject to depression and on several occasions experimented with hallucinogenic substances such as peyote and nitrous oxide gas, as agents of an "anaesthetic revelation." James was active in both the American and the British Society for Psychical Research and was especially concerned with the possibility of communication with the dead.[24] It is obvious that his interest in mysticism was not of a purely academic nature, despite his disclaimer on the opening page of "A Suggestion about Mysticism."

In more philosophical terms, James had an abiding interest in the activity of human consciousness. His distinctive version of consciousness, however, stressed opening to a "wider self from which saving experiences flow in."[25] In his last years James discussed consciousness as a "field," pulsating and providing alternating "thresholds" or "margins." He writes of the field of consciousness as follows:

The field is composed at all times of a mass of present sensation, in a cloud of memories, emotions, concepts, etc. Yet these ingredients, which have to be named separately, are not separate, as the conscious field contains them. Its form is that of a much-at-once, in the unity of which the sensations, memories, concepts, impulses, etc., coalesce and are dissolved. The present field as a whole came continuously out of its predecessor and will melt into its successor as continuously again, one sensation-mass passing into another sensation-mass and giving the character of a gradually changing *present* to the experience, while the memories and concepts carry time-coefficients which place whatever is present in a temporal perspective more or less vast. (*EP*, p. 158).

James then attempts to sustain his hypothesis by reporting four of his own personal experiences, each of which had the effect of "enlarging" his conscious field. The first three were intrusive and short-lived, whereas the fourth resulted from two dreams that

[24] See Gardner Murphy and Robert O. Ballou, eds., *William James on Psychical Research* (New York: Viking Press, 1960).
[25] *A Pluralistic Universe*, WORKS, p. 139.

yielded "the most intensely peculiar experience of my whole life" (*EP*, p. 160). Despite the intensity of these experiences and his "emotional conviction" of their importance, James is reluctant to conclude anything philosophically definite from them. He does warn us, nonetheless, that such experiences should not be dismissed, despite the contentions of the scientific establishment: "We know so little of the noetic value of abnormal mental states of any kind that in my own opinion we had better keep an open mind and collect facts sympathetically for a long time to come. We shall not *understand* these alterations of consciousness either in this generation or in the next" (*EP*, p. 165). It is not unimportant that our generation has heeded this advice and has begun to confront these experiences in an unprejudiced way and by the method of scientific inquiry.

The final essay in this book is, quite literally, the last writing that James did for publication. Its title, "A Pluralistic Mystic," refers to the person of Benjamin Paul Blood, in whom James finds an ability to bring together the usually disparate contentions of the pluralist and the mystic. It is not irrelevant that in 1910 such an approach reflected James's own position. The background to Blood's life and the development of his thought is provided in the extensive appended Notes in this volume.[26]

"A Pluralistic Mystic" is actually a collage of Blood's writings, interspersed with some passing commentary by James. In my judgment the main intention of this essay is to put Blood's writings before the knowledgeable readers of the *Hibbert Journal*, sponsored, as it were, by William James. In a way, this is a fitting final piece for James, in that all his life he had a special affection for the downtrodden, the unsung, and the unknown. It is also somewhat dramatic that the conclusion of this essay and of the book, as well as of James's literary career, ends with the word "farewell."

Let *my* last word, then, speaking in the name of intellectual philosophy, be *his* word:—"There is no conclusion. What has concluded, that we might conclude in regard to it? There are no fortunes to be told, and there is no advice to be given.—Farewell!" (*EP*, p. 190).

In this Introduction I have attempted to provide some continuity for these essays and to assist the reader in the location of those

---

[26] For a discussion of the relationship between James and Blood see Perry, *Thought and Character*, II, 553–560.

texts which most significantly tie into James's more extensive work. Each essay stands on its own as having a principle of coherence and an appropriate style, yet they are best appreciated when woven into the complete fabric of James's life and work. The following expression of one of James's most deeply felt and persistently held beliefs provides a clue to the proper interpretation of that work:

All neat schematisms with permanent and absolute distinctions, classifications with absolute pretensions, systems with pigeon-holes, etc., have this character [of bad taste]. All 'classic,' clean, cut and dried, 'noble,' fixed, 'eternal,' *Weltanschauungen* seem to me to violate the character with which life concretely comes and the expression which it bears of being, or at least of involving, a muddle and a struggle, with an 'ever not quite' to all our formulas, and novelty and possibility forever leaking in.[27]

[27] Perry, *Thought and Character*, II, 700.

Essays in Philosophy

The Teaching of Philosophy in Our Colleges

We print in another column an interesting letter on this subject from a correspondent, with whom, it is needless to say, we fully agree. The evil he deplores has been, and still is, a real one. The philosophical teaching, as a rule, in our higher seminaries is in the hands of the president, who is usually a minister of the Gospel, and, as he more often owes his position to general excellence of character and administrative faculty than to any speculative gifts or propensities, it usually follows that "safeness" becomes the main characteristic of his tuition; that his classes are edified rather than awakened, and leave college with the generous youthful impulse, to reflect on the world and our position in it, rather dampened and discouraged than stimulated by the lifeless discussions and flabby formulas they have had to commit to memory. In Germany, as if by a sort of compensation for the long political enslavement of the country, philosophic speculation has gone on as a rule without any reference to its ecclesiastical consequences. In England and this country, on the contrary, whilst speculation on political and practical matters has been free as air, metaphysical thought has always been haunted by the consciousness of the religious orthodoxy of the country, and either assiduously sought to harmonize itself therewith, or, if sceptical in character, it has been trammelled and paralyzed and made petty by the invidious presence of this polemic bias. The form of philosophic problems and discussions, in short, is too apt to be *set* for us by the existence of the Church. England is just beginning to emerge from this condition; but until we are fully emancipated from the traditional college régime, no really able movement of philosophic thought can be hoped for among us.

Let it not be supposed that we are prejudging the question whether the final results of speculation will be friendly or hostile to the formulas of Christian thought. All we contend for is that we, like the Greeks and the Germans, should now attack things as if there were no official answer preoccupying the field. At present we are bribed beforehand by our reverence or dislike for the official answer; and the free-thinking tendency which the *Popular Science Monthly*, for example, represents, is condemned to an even more dismal shallowness than the spiritualistic systems of our textbooks of "Mental Science." We work with one eye on our problem, and with the other on the consequences to our enemy or to our law-giver, as our case may be; the result in both cases alike is mediocrity.

If the best use of our colleges is to give young men a wider open-ness of mind and a more flexible way of thinking than special tech-nical training can generate, then we hold that philosophy (taken in the broad sense in which our correspondent uses the word) is the most important of all college studies. However sceptical one may be of the attainment of universal truths (and, to make our position more emphatic, we are willing here to concede the extreme Posi-tivistic position), one can never deny that philosophic study means the habit of always seeing an alternative, of not taking the usual for granted, of making conventionalities fluid again, of imagining foreign states of mind. In a word, it means the possession of mental perspective. Touchstone's question, "Hast any philosophy in thee, shepherd?" will never cease to be one of the tests of a well-born nature. It says, Is there space and air in your mind, or must your companions gasp for breath whenever they talk with you? And if our colleges are to make men, and not machines, they should look, above all things, to this aspect of their influence. Here indeed lies the real interest of the question which is sure sooner or later to convulse the universities—the question whether Greek shall re-main obligatory or not. As philologic training, Greek is but a lan-guage among others. Its value to the universal college student lit-erally consists in its being a "humanity"—in its bringing him into contact with a different human life from that which he sees, but one whose eminent worth he must nevertheless acutely feel. Its function is what we have called philosophical as distinguished from technical. Teach all sciences in a liberal and philosophic manner, and Greek ceases to be indispensable. Teach Greek in a dry, grammatic fashion, and it becomes no better than Gothic. So that the decision of the Greek question depends on the decision of the philosophic question. "G. S. H." speaks of the "application of philosophical systems to history, politics, and law." We hope he does not mean that these should be taught separately from the ordinary historical, political, and legal courses. That would be building a house and getting a man from the city to come down and put on the "architecture" afterwards. All branches must be taught from the first in a philosophic manner, must be saturated with the liberal spirit, for any good to be effected.

As for philosophy, technically so called, or the reflection of man on his relations with the universe, its educational essence lies in the quickening of the spirit to its *problems*. What doctrines students take from their teachers are of little consequence provided they catch from them the living, philosophic attitude of mind, the independent, personal look at all the data of life, and the eagerness to harmonize them. Youth is certainly the time when the impulse to metaphysical reflection is in its flower—certain authors say it disappears after thirty. The "supposed unpopularity" of these studies alluded to by our correspondent is, we are convinced, a mistake, in spite of the dead teaching. We have been assured by the librarian of one of the largest of our college libraries that the metaphysical alcove there is twice as much visited as any other, and we are quite sure that this is the result of a perfectly normal law.

It is probable that the unfortunate condition of things which "G. S. H." and we alike regret is already on the eve of changing. Physical science is becoming so speculative and audacious in its constructions, and at the same time so authoritative, that all doctrines find themselves, willy-nilly, compelled to settle their accounts and make new treaties with it. Every newspaper and magazine overflows with symptoms of the new fermentation. *What, then, is man?* is once more a keen and urgent problem; the very atmosphere is pregnant with new-formed essays at its solution. The sleepiest doctor-of-divinity-like repose must soon be awakened at its teaching-desk, and, getting disquieted at the novel agitation around its throne, end by abdicating in favor of teachers of more

5

alert temperament. "The marvellous new developments in England and Germany," whatever their intrinsic worth may be, have at least enough momentum of prestige in the popular eye to effect this. It is more than doubtful whether Fechner's "psychophysic law" (that sensation is proportional to the logarithm of its stimulus) is of any great *psychological* importance, and we strongly suspect that Helmholtz's "unconscious inferences" are not the last word of wisdom in the study of perception; but because these things are very difficult and very "scientific," people who do not understand them will remain persuaded that they are of portentous moment, and will mistrust all teachers who have not swallowed and assimilated them. There is indeed something touching in the helpless way in which Fechner's law is beginning to be hawked about, as it were, in popular philosophic literature, by writers who do not know in the least what to do with it, but who evidently feel persuaded that somehow or other it must be of tremendous import. But be these discoveries important or not important, the fact that they involve a change in the method and *personnel* of philosophic study is unshaken. To criticise these "new developments" at all, one must have gone through a thorough physiological training. And accordingly, we find Leipzig, now the foremost university in Germany, calling the eminent physiologist Wundt to fill its principal philosophic chair; and a metaphysician like Dr. McCosh writing, in a chapter on the future of his favorite study: "The metaphysician must enter the physiological field. He must, if he can, conduct researches; he must at least master the ascertained facts. He must not give up the study of the nervous system and brain to those who cannot comprehend any thing beyond . . . their senses."

In short, philosophy, like Molière, claims her own where she finds it. She finds much of it to-day in physics and natural history, and must and will educate herself accordingly. Young men who aspire to professorships and who will bear this in mind will, we are sure, before many years find a number of vacant places calling for their peculiar capacity. Meanwhile, when we find announced that the students in Harvard College next year may study any or all of the following works under the guidance of different professors—Locke's *Essay*, Kant's *Kritik*, Schopenhauer and Hartmann, Hodgson's *Theory of Practice*, and Spencer's *Psychology*—we need not complain of *universal* academic stagnation, even to-day.

Remarks on Spencer's Definition of Mind as Correspondence

As a rule it may be said that, at a time when readers are so over-whelmed with work as they are at the present day, all purely criti-cal and destructive writing ought to be reprobated. The half-gods generally refuse to go, in spite of the ablest criticism, until the gods actually *have* arrived; but then, too, criticism is hardly needed. But there are cases in which every rule may be broken. "What!" exclaimed Voltaire, when accused of offering no substitute for the Christianity he attacked, *"je vous délivre d'une bête féroce, et vous me demandez par quoi je la remplace!"* Without comparing Mr. Spencer's definition of Mind either to Christianity or to a *"bête féroce,"* it may certainly be said to be very far-reaching in its con-sequences, and, according to certain standards, noxious; whilst probably a large proportion of those hard-headed readers who sub-scribe to the *Popular Science Monthly* and *Nature*, and whose sole philosopher Mr. Spencer is, are fascinated by it without being in the least aware what its consequences are.

The defects of the formula are so glaring that I am surprised it should not long ago have been critically overhauled. The reader will readily recollect what it is. In part III of his *Principles of Psy-chology*, Mr. Spencer, starting from the supposition that the most essential truth concerning mental evolution will be that which allies it to the evolution nearest akin to it, namely, that of Life, finds that the formula *"adjustment of inner to outer relations,"*

which was the definition of life, comprehends also "the entire process of mental evolution." In a series of chapters of great apparent
thoroughness and minuteness he shows how all the different grades
of mental perfection are expressed by the degree of extension of
this adjustment, or, as he here calls it, "correspondence," in space,
time, speciality, generality, and integration. The polyp's tentacles
contract only to immediately present stimuli, and to almost all
alike. The mammal will store up food for a day, or even for a sea-
son; the bird will start on its migration for a goal hundreds of
miles away; the savage will sharpen his arrows to hunt next year's
game; while the astronomer will proceed, equipped with all his
instruments, to a point thousands of miles distant, there to watch,
at a fixed day, hour, and minute, a transit of Venus or an eclipse
of the Sun.

The picture drawn is so vast and simple, it includes such a multitude of details in its monotonous frame-work, that it is no wonder
that readers of a passive turn of mind are, usually, more impressed
by it than by any portion of the book. But on the slightest scrutiny
its solidity begins to disappear. In the first place, one asks, what
right has one, in a formula embracing professedly the "entire process of mental evolution," to mention only phenomena of cognition, and to omit all sentiments, all æsthetic impulses, all religious
emotions and personal affections? The ascertainment of outward
fact constitutes only one species of mental activity. The genus contains, in addition to purely cognitive judgments, or judgments of
the actual—judgments that things do, as a matter of fact, exist so
or so—an immense number of emotional judgments: judgments of
the ideal, judgments that things *should* exist thus and not so. How
much of our mental life is occupied with this matter of a better or
a worse? How much of it involves preferences or repugnances on
our part? We cannot laugh at a joke, we cannot go to one theater
rather than another, take more trouble for the sake of our own
child than our neighbor's; we cannot long for vacation, show our
best manners to a foreigner, or pay our pew rent, without involving in the premises of our action some element which has nothing
whatever to do with simply cognizing the actual, but which, out
of alternative possible actuals, selects one and cognizes that as the
ideal. In a word, "Mind," as we actually find it, contains all sorts
of laws—those of logic, of fancy, of wit, of taste, decorum, beauty,
morals, and so forth, as well as of perception of fact. Common sense

estimates mental excellence by a combination of all these standards, and yet how few of them correspond to anything that actually *is*—they are laws of the Ideal, dictated by subjective *interests* pure and simple. Thus the greater part of Mind, quantitatively considered, refuses to have anything to do with Mr. Spencer's definition. It is quite true that these ideal judgments are treated by him with great ingenuity and felicity at the close of his work— indeed, his treatment of them there seems to me to be its most admirable portion. But they are there handled as separate items having no connection with that extension of the "correspondence" which is maintained elsewhere to be the all-sufficing law of mental growth.

Most readers would dislike to admit without coercion that a law was adequate which obliged them to erase from literature (if by literature were meant anything worthy of the title of "mental product") all works except treatises on natural science, history, and statistics. Let us examine the reason that Mr. Spencer appears to consider coercive.

It is this: That, since every process grows more and more complicated as it develops, more swarmed over by incidental and derivative conditions which disguise and adulterate its original simplicity, the only way to discover its true and essential form is to trace it back to its earliest beginning. There it will appear in its genuine character pure and undefiled. Religious, æsthetic, and ethical judgments, having grown up in the course of evolution, by means that we can very plausibly divine, of course may be stripped off from the main stem of intelligence and leave that undisturbed. With a similar intent Mr. Tylor says: "Whatever throws light on the origin of a conception throws light on its validity." Thus, then, there is no resource but to appeal to the polyp, or whatever shows us the form of evolution just *before* intelligence, and what that, and only what that, contains will be the root and heart of the matter.

But no sooner is the reason for the law thus enunciated than many objections occur to the reader. In the first place, the general principle seems to lead to absurd conclusions. If the embryologic line of appeal can alone teach us the genuine essences of things, if the polyp is to dictate our law of mind to us because he came first, where are we to stop? He must himself be treated in the same way. Back of him lay the not-yet-polyp, and, back of all, the universal mother, fire-mist. To seek there for the reality, of course would reduce all thinking to nonentity, and, although Mr. Spencer would probably not regard this conclusion as a *reductio ad absurdum* of his principle, since it would only be another path to his theory of the Unknowable, less systematic thinkers may hesitate. But, waiving for the moment the question of principle, let us admit that relatively to *our* thought, at any rate, the polyp's thought is pure and undefiled. Does the study of the polyp lead us distinctly to Mr. Spencer's formula of correspondence? To begin with, if that formula be meant to include disinterested scientific curiosity, or "correspondence" in the sense of cognition, with no ulterior selfish end, the polyp gives it no countenance whatever. He is as innocent of scientific as of moral and æsthetic enthusiasm; he is the most narrowly teleological of organisms; reacting, so far as he reacts at all, only for self-preservation.

This leads us to ask what Mr. Spencer exactly means by the word correspondence. Without explanation, the word is wholly indeterminate. Everything corresponds in some way with everything else that co-exists in the same world with it. But, as the formula of correspondence was originally derived from biology, we shall possibly find in our author's treatise on that science an exact definition of what he means by it. On seeking there, we find nowhere a definition, but numbers of synonyms. The inner relations are "adjusted," "conformed," "fitted," "related," to the outer. They must "meet" or "balance" them. There must be "concord" or "harmony" between them. Or, again, the organism must "counteract" the changes in the environment. But these words, too, are wholly indeterminate. The fox is most beautifully "adjusted" to the hounds and huntsmen who pursue him; the limestone "meets" molecule by molecule the acid which corrodes it; the man is exquisitely "conformed" to the *trichina* which invades him, or to the typhus poison which consumes him; and the forests "harmonize" incomparably with the fires that lay them low. Clearly, a further specification is required; and, although Mr. Spencer shrinks strangely from enunciating this specification, he everywhere works his formula so as to imply it in the clearest manner.

Influence on physical well-being or survival is his implied criterion of the rank of mental action. The moth which flies into the candle, instead of away from it, "fails," in Spencer's words (vol. I, p. 409), to "correspond" with its environment; but clearly, in this sense, pure cognitive inference of the existence of heat after a perception of light would not suffice to constitute correspondence; while a moth which, on feeling the light, should merely vaguely fear to approach it, but have no proper image of the heat, would "correspond." So that the Spencerian formula, to mean anything definite at all, must, at least, be re-written as follows: "Right or intelligent mental action consists in the establishment, corresponding to outward relations, of such inward relations and reactions as will favor the survival of the thinker, or, at least, his physical well-being."

Such a definition as this is precise, but at the same time it is frankly teleological. It explicitly postulates a distinction between mental action pure and simple, and *right* mental action; and, furthermore, it proposes, as criteria of this latter, certain ideal ends—those of physical prosperity or survival, which are pure *subjective interests* on the animal's part, brought with it upon the scene and corresponding to no relation already there.[1] No mental action is right or intelligent which fails to fit this standard. No correspondence can pass muster till it shows its subservience to these ends. Corresponding itself to no actual outward thing; referring merely to a future which *may* be, but which these interests now say *shall* be; purely ideal, in a word, they judge, dominate, determine all correspondences between the inner and the outer. Which is as much as to say that *mere* correspondence with the outer world is a notion on which it is wholly impossible to base a definition of mental action. Mr. Spencer's occult reason for leaving unexpressed the most important part of the definition he works with probably

---

[1] These interests are the real *a priori* element in cognition. By saying that their pleasures and pains have nothing to do with correspondence, I mean simply this: To a large number of terms in the environment there may be inward correlatives of a neutral sort as regards feeling. The "correspondence" is already there. But, now, suppose some to be accented with pleasure, others with pain; that is a fact additional to the correspondence, a fact with no outward correlative. But it immediately orders the correspondences in this way: that the pleasant or interesting items are singled out, dwelt upon, developed into their farther connections, whilst the unpleasant or insipid ones are ignored or suppressed. The future of the Mind's development is thus mapped out in advance by the way in which the lines of pleasure and pain run. The interests precede the outer relations noticed. Take the utter absence of response of a dog or a savage to the greater mass of environing relations. How can you alter it unless you previously *awaken an interest*—i.e., produce a susceptibility to intellectual pleasure in certain modes of cognitive exercise? Interests, then, are an all-essential factor which no writer pretending to give an account of mental evolution has a right to neglect.

lies in its apparent implication of subjective spontaneity. The mind, according to his philosophy, should be pure product, absolute derivative from the non-mental. To make it dictate conditions, bring independent interests into the game which may determine what we shall call correspondence, and what not, might, at first sight, appear contrary to the notion of evolution which forbids the introduction at any point of an absolutely new factor. In what sense the existence of survival interest does postulate such a factor we shall hereafter see. I think myself that it is possible to express all its outward results in non-mental terms. But the unedifying look of the thing, its simulation of an independent mental teleology, seems to have frightened Mr. Spencer here, as elsewhere, away from a serious scrutiny of the facts. But let us be indulgent to his timidity, and assume that survival was all the while a "mental reservation" with him, only excluded from his formula by reason of the comforting sound it might have to Philistine ears.

We should then have, as the embodiment of the highest ideal perfection of mental development, a creature of superb cognitive endowments, from whose piercing perceptions no fact was too minute or too remote to escape; whose all-embracing foresight no contingency could find unprepared; whose invincible flexibility of resource no array of outward onslaught could overpower; but in whom all these gifts were swayed by the single passion of love of life, of survival at any price. This determination filling his whole energetic being, consciously realized, intensified by meditation, becomes a fixed idea, would use all the other faculties as its means, and, if they ever flagged, would by its imperious intensity spur them and hound them on to ever fresh exertions and achievements. There can be no doubt that, if such an incarnation of earthly prudence existed, a race of beings in whom this monotonously narrow passion for tribal self-preservation were aided by every cognitive gift, they would soon be kings of all the earth. All known human races would wither before their breath, and be as dust beneath their conquering feet.

But whether any Spencerian would hail with hearty joy their advent is another matter. Certainly Mr. Spencer would not; while the common sense of mankind would stand aghast at the thought of them. Why does common opinion abhor such a being? Why does it crave greater "richness" of nature in its mental ideal? Simply because, to common sense, survival is only one out of many interests—

primus inter pares, perhaps, but still in the midst of peers. What are these interests? Most men would reply that they are all that makes survival worth securing. The social affections, all the various forms of play, the thrilling intimations of art, the delights of philosophic contemplation, the rest of religious emotion, the joy of moral self-approbation, the charm of fancy and of wit—some or all of these are absolutely required to make the notion of mere existence tolerable; and individuals who, by their special powers, satisfy these desires are protected by their fellows and enabled to survive, though their mental constitution should in other respects be lamentably ill-"adjusted" to the outward world. The story-teller, the musician, the theologian, the actor, or even the mere charming fellow, have never lacked means of support, however helpless they might individually have been to conform with those outward relations which we know as the powers of nature. The reason is very plain. To the individual man, as a social being, the interests of his fellow are a part of his environment. If his powers correspond to the wants of this social environment, he may survive, even though he be ill-adapted to the natural or "outer" environment. But these wants are pure subjective ideals, with nothing outward to correspond to them. So that, as far as the individual is concerned, it becomes necessary to modify Spencer's survival formula still further, by introducing into the term environment a reference, not only to existent things, but also to ideal wants. It would have to run in some such way as this: "Excellence of the individual mind consists in the establishment of inner relations more and more extensively conformed to the outward facts of nature, and to the ideal wants of the individual's fellows, but all of such a character as will promote survival or physical prosperity."

But here, again, common sense will meet us with an objection. Mankind desiderate certain qualities in the individual which are incompatible with his chance of survival being a maximum. Why do we all so eulogize and love the heroic, recklessly generous, and disinterested type of character? These qualities certainly imperil the survival of their possessor. The reason is very plain. Even if headlong courage, pride, and martyr-spirit do ruin the individual, they benefit the community as a whole whenever they are displayed by one of its members against a competing tribe. "It is death to you, but fun for us." Our interest in having the hero as he is, plays indirectly into the hands of our survival, though not of his.

13

This explicit acknowledgment of the survival interests of the tribe, as accounting for many interests in the individual which seem at first sight either unrelated to survival or at war with it, seems, after all, to bring back unity and simplicity into the Spencerian formula. Why, the Spencerian may ask, may not all the luxuriant foliage of ideal interests—æsthetic, philosophic, theologic, and the rest—which co-exist along with that of survival, be present in the tribe and so form part of the individual's environment, merely by virtue of the fact that they minister in an indirect way to the survival of the tribe as a whole? The disinterested scientific appetite of cognition, the sacred philosophic love of consistency, the craving for luxury and beauty, the passion for amusement, may all find their proper significance as processes of mind, strictly so-called, in the incidental utilitarian discoveries which flow from the energy they set in motion. Conscience, thoroughness, purity, love of truth, susceptibility to discipline, eager delight in fresh impressions, although none of them are traits of Intelligence *in se*, may thus be marks of a general mental energy, without which victory over nature and over other human competitors would be impossible. And, as victory means survival, and survival is the criterion of Intelligent "Correspondence," these qualities, though not expressed in the fundamental law of mind, may yet have been all the while understood by Mr. Spencer to form so many secondary consequences and corollaries of that law.

But here it is decidedly time to take our stand and refuse our aid in propping up Mr. Spencer's definition by any further good-natured translations and supplementary contributions of our own. It is palpable at a glance that a mind whose survival interest could only be adequately secured by such a wasteful array of energy squandered on side issues would be immeasurably inferior to one like that which we supposed a few pages back, in which the monomania of tribal preservation should be the one all-devouring passion.

Surely there is nothing in the essence of intelligence which should oblige it forever to delude itself as to its own ends, and to strive towards a goal successfully only at the cost of consciously appearing to have far other aspirations in view.

A furnace which should produce along with its metal fifty different varieties of ash and slag, a planing-mill whose daily yield in shavings far exceeded that in boards, would rightly be pronounced inferior to one of the usual sort, even though more energy should be displayed in its working, and at moments some of that energy be directly effective. If ministry to survival be the sole criterion of mental excellence, then luxury and amusement, Shakespeare, Beethoven, Plato, and Marcus Aurelius, stellar spectroscopy, diatom markings, and nebular hypotheses are by-products on too wasteful a scale. The slag-heap is too big—it abstracts more energy than it contributes to the ends of the machine; and every serious evolutionist ought resolutely to bend his attention henceforward to the reduction in number and amount of these outlying interests, and the diversion of the energy they absorb into purely prudential channels.

Here, then, is our dilemma: One man may say that the law of mental development is dominated solely by the principle of conservation; another, that richness is the criterion of mental evolution; a third, that pure cognition of the actual is the essence of worthy thinking—but who shall pretend to decide which is right? The umpire would have to bring a standard of his own upon the scene, which would be just as subjective and personal as the standards used by the contestants. And yet some standard there must be, if we are to attempt to define in any way the worth of different mental manifestations.

Is it not already clear to the reader's mind that the whole difficulty in making Mr. Spencer's law work lies in the fact that it is not really a constitutive, but a regulative, law of thought which he is erecting, and that he does not frankly say so? Every law of Mind must be either a law of the *cogitatum* or a law of the *cogitandum*. If it be a law in the sense of an analysis of what we *do* think, then it will include error, nonsense, the worthless as well as the worthy, metaphysics, and mythologies as well as scientific truths which mirror the actual environment. But such a law of the *cogitatum* is already well known. It is no other than the association of ideas according to their several modes; or, rather, it is this association definitively perfected by the inclusion of the teleological factor of interest by Mr. Hodgson in the fifth chapter of his masterly *Time and Space*.

That Mr. Spencer, in the part of his work which we are considering, has no such law as this in view is evident from the fact that he has striven to give an original formulation to such a law in another part of his book, in that chapter, namely, on the associability of relations, in the first volume, where the apperception of times and places, and the suppression of association by similarity, are made to explain the facts in a way whose artificiality has puzzled many a simple reader.

Now, every living man would instantly define right thinking as thinking in correspondence with reality. But Spencer, in saying that right thought is that which conforms to existent outward relations, and this exclusively, undertakes to decide what the reality *is*. In other words, under cover of an apparently formal definition he really smuggles in a material definition of the most far-reaching import. For the Stoic, to whom *vivere convenienter naturæ* was also the law of mind, the reality was an archetypal Nature; for the Christian, whose mental law is to discover the will of God, and make one's actions correspond thereto, *that* is the reality. In fact, the philosophic problem which all the ages have been trying to solve in order to make thought in some way correspond with it, and which disbelievers in philosophy call insoluble, is just that: What is the reality? All the thinking, all the conflict of ideals, going on in the world at the present moment is in some way tributary to this quest. To attempt, therefore, with Mr. Spencer, to decide the matter merely incidentally, to forestall discussion by a definition—to carry the position by surprise, in a word—is a proceeding savoring more of piracy than philosophy. No, Spencer's definition of what we ought to think cannot be suffered to lurk in ambush; it must stand out explicitly with the rest, and expect to be challenged and give an account of itself like any other ideal norm of thought.

We have seen how he seems to vacillate in his determination of it. At one time, "scientific" thought, mere passive mirroring of outward nature, purely registrative cognition; at another time, thought in the exclusive service of survival, would seem to be his ideal. Let us consider the latter ideal first, since it has the polyp's authority in its favor: "We must survive—that end must regulate all our thought." The poor man who said to Talleyrand, "*Il faut bien que je vive!*" expressed it very well. But criticise this ideal, or transcend it as Talleyrand did by his cool reply, "*Je n'en vois pas la necessité,*" and it can say nothing more for itself. *A priori* it is a mere brute teleological affirmation on a par with all others. Vainly you should hope to prove it to a person bent on suicide, who has but the one longing—to escape, to cease. Vainly you would argue with a Buddhist or a German pessimist, for they feel the full im-

perious strength of the desire, but have an equally profound per-
suasion of its essential wrongness and mendacity. Vainly, too, would
you talk to a Christian, or even to any believer in the simple creed
that the deepest meaning of the world is moral. For they hold that
mere conformity with the outward—worldly success and survival—
is not the absolute and exclusive end. In the *failures* to "adjust"—
in the rubbish-heap, according to Spencer—lies, for them, the real
key to the truth—the sole mission of life being to teach that the
outward actual is not the whole of being.

And, now—if, falling back on the scientific ideal, you say that to
know is the one τέλος of intelligence—not only will the inimitable
Turkish cadi in Layard's Nineveh praise God in your face that he
seeks not that which he requires not, and ask, "Will much knowledge create thee a double belly?"—not only may I, if it please me,
legitimately refuse to stir from my fool's paradise of theosophy and
mysticism, in spite of all your calling (since, after all, your true
knowledge and my pious feeling have alike nothing to back them
save their seeming good to our respective personalities)—not only
this, but to the average sense of mankind, whose ideal of mental
nature is best expressed by the word "richness," your statistical
and cognitive intelligence will seem insufferably narrow, dry, tedious, and unacceptable.

The truth appears to be that every individual man may, if it
please him, set up his private categorical imperative of what rightness or excellence in thought shall consist in, and these different
ideals, instead of entering upon the scene armed with a warrant—
whether derived from the polyp or from a transcendental source—
appear only as so many brute affirmations left to fight it out upon
the chess-board among themselves. They are, at best, postulates,
each of which must depend on the general consensus of experience
as a whole to bear out its validity. The formula which proves to have
the most massive destiny will be the true one. But this is a point
which can only be solved *ambulando*, and not by any *a priori* definition. The attempt to forestall the decision is free to all to make,
but all make it at their risk. Our respective hypotheses and postulates help to shape the course of thought, but the only thing which
we all agree in assuming is, that thought will be coerced away from
them if they are wrong. If Spencer to-day says, "Bow to the actual,"
whilst Swinburne spurns "compromise with the nature of things,"
I exclaim, "*Fiat justitia, pereat mundus,*" and Mill says, "To hell

I will go, rather than 'adjust' myself to an evil God,'' what umpire can there be between us but the future? The idealists and the empiricists confront each other like Guelphs and Ghibellines, but each alike waits for adoption, as it were, by the course of events.

In other words, we are all fated to be, *a priori*, teleologists whether we will or no. Interests which we bring with us, and simply posit or take our stand upon, are the very flour out of which our mental dough is kneaded. The organism of thought, from the vague dawn of discomfort or ease in the polyp to the intellectual joy of Laplace among his formulas, is teleological through and through. Not a cognition occurs but feeling is there to comment on it, to stamp it as of greater or less worth. Spencer and Plato are *ejusdem farinæ*. To attempt to hoodwink teleology out of sight by saying nothing about it, is the vainest of procedures. Spencer merely takes sides with the τέλος he happens to prefer, whether it be that of physical well-being or that of cognitive registration. He represents a particular teleology. Well might teleology (had she a voice) exclaim with Emerson's Brahma:

> "If the red slayer think he slays,
>   Or if the slain think he is slain,
> They know not well the subtle ways
>   I keep, and pass, and turn again.
>
> * * * * * * * * * *
>
> "They reckon ill who leave me out;
>   When me they fly, I am the wings;
> I am the doubter and the doubt," etc.

But now a scientific man, feeling something uncanny in this omnipresence of a teleological factor dictating *how* the mind shall correspond—an interest seemingly tributary to nothing non-mental —may ask us what we meant by saying sometime back that in one sense it is perfectly possible to express the existence of interests in non-mental terms. We meant simply this: That the reactions or outward consequences of the interests could be so expressed. The interest of survival which has hitherto been treated as an ideal *should-be*, presiding from the start and marking out the way in which an animal must react, is, from an outward and physical point of view, nothing more than an objective future implication of the reaction (if it occurs) as an actual fact. If the animal's brain acts fortuitously in the right way, he survives. His young do the same.

The reference to survival in noway preceded or conditioned the intelligent act; but the fact of survival was merely bound up with it as an incidental consequence, and may, therefore, be called accidental, rather than instrumental, to the production of intelligence. It is the same with all other interests. They are pleasures and pains incidentally implied in the workings of the nervous mechanism, and, therefore, in their ultimate origin, non-mental; for the idiosyncrasies of our nervous centers are mere "spontaneous variations," like any of those which form the ultimate *data* for Darwin's theory. A brain which functions so as to insure survival may, therefore, be called intelligent in no other sense than a tooth, a limb, or a stomach, which should serve the same end—the sense, namely, of appropriate; as when we say "that is an intelligent device," meaning a device fitted to secure a certain end which we assume. If *nirvana* were the end, instead of survival, then it is true the means would be different, but in both cases alike the end would not precede the means, or even be coeval with them, but depend utterly upon them, and follow them in point of time. The fox's cunning and the hare's speed are thus alike creations of the non-mental. The τέλος they entail is no more an agent in one case than another, since in both alike it is a resultant. Spencer, then, seems justified in not admitting it to appear as an irreducible ultimate factor of Mind, any more than of Body.

This position is perfectly unassailable so long as one describes the phenomena in this manner from without. The τέλος in that case can only be hypothetically, not imperatively, stated: *if* such and such be the end, then such brain functions are the most intelligent, just as such and such digestive functions are the most appropriate. But such and such cannot be declared *as* the end, except by the commenting mind of an outside spectator. The organs themselves, in their working at any instant, cannot but be supposed indifferent as to what product they are destined fatally to bring forth, cannot be imagined whilst fatally producing one result to have at the same time a notion of a different result which should be their truer end, but which they are unable to secure.

Nothing can more strikingly show, it seems to me, the essential difference between the point of view of consciousness and that of outward existence. We can describe the latter only in teleological terms, hypothetically, or else by the addition of a supposed contemplating mind which measures what it sees going on by its private teleological standard, and judges it intelligent. But consciousness itself is not merely intelligent in this sense. It is *intelligent intelligence*. It seems both to supply the means and the standard by which they are measured. It not only *serves* a final purpose, but *brings* a final purpose—posits, declares it. This purpose is not a mere hypothesis—"*if* survival is to occur, then brain must so perform," etc.—but an imperative decree: "Survival *shall* occur, and, therefore, brain *must* so perform!" It seems hopelessly impossible to formulate anything of this sort in non-mental terms, and this is why I must still contend that the phenomena of subjective "interest," as soon as the animal consciously realizes the latter, appears upon the scene as an absolutely new factor, which we can only suppose to be latent thitherto in the physical environment by crediting the physical atoms, etc., each with a consciousness of its own, approving or condemning its motions.

This, then, must be our conclusion: That no law of the *cogitandum*, no norm-ative receipt for excellence in thinking, can be authoritatively promulgated. The only formal canon that we can apply to mind which is unassailable is the barren truism that it must think rightly. We can express this in terms of correspondence by saying that thought must correspond with truth; but whether that truth be actual or ideal is left undecided.

We have seen that the invocation of the polyp to decide for us that it is actual (apart from the fact that he does not decide in that way) is based on a principle which refutes itself if consistently carried out. Spencer's formula has crumbled into utter worthlessness in our hands, and we have nothing to replace it by except our several individual hypotheses, convictions, and beliefs. Far from being vouched for by the past, these are verified only by the future. They are all of them, in some sense, laws of the ideal. They have to keep house together, and the weakest goes to the wall. The survivors constitute the right way of thinking. While the issue is still undecided, we can only call them our prepossessions. But, decided or not, "go in" we each must for one set of interests or another. The question for each of us in the battle of life is, "Can we *come out* with it?" Some of these interests admit to-day of little dispute. Survival, physical well-being, and undistorted cognition of what is, will hold their ground. But it is truly strange to see writers like Messrs. Huxley and Clifford, who show themselves able to call most things in question, unable, when it comes to the interest of cognition, to touch it with their solvent doubt. They assume some mysterious imperative laid upon the mind, declaring that the infinite ascertainment of facts is its supreme duty, which he who evades is a blasphemer and child of shame. And yet these authors can hardly have failed to reflect, at some moment or other, that the disinterested love of information, and still more the love of consistency in thought (that true scientific *œstrus*), and the ideal fealty to Truth (with a capital T), are all so many particular forms of æsthetic interest, late in their evolution, arising in conjunction with a vast number of similar æsthetic interests, and bearing with them no *a priori* mark of being worthier than these. If we may doubt one, we may doubt all. How shall I say that knowing fact with Messrs. Huxley and Clifford is a better use to put my mind to than feeling good with Messrs. Moody and Sankey, unless by slowly and painfully finding out that in the long run it works best?

I, for my part, cannot escape the consideration, forced upon me at every turn, that the knower is not simply a mirror floating with no foot-hold anywhere, and passively reflecting an order that he comes upon and finds simply existing. The knower is an actor, and co-efficient of the truth on one side, whilst on the other he registers the truth which he helps to create. Mental interests, hypotheses, postulates, so far as they are bases for human action—action which to a great extent transforms the world—help to *make* the truth which they declare. In other words, there belongs to mind, from its birth upward, a spontaneity, a vote. It is in the game, and not a mere looker-on; and its judgments of the *should-be*, its ideals, cannot be peeled off from the body of the *cogitandum* as if they were excrescences, or meant, at most, survival. We know so little about the ultimate nature of things, or of ourselves, that it would be sheer folly dogmatically to say that an ideal rational order may not be real. The only objective criterion of reality is coerciveness, in the long run, over thought. Objective facts, Spencer's outward relations, are real only because they coerce sensation. Any interest which should be coercive on the same massive scale would be *eodem jure* real. By its very essence, the reality of a thought is proportionate to the way it grasps us. Its intensity, its seriousness—its interest, in a word—taking these qualities, not at any given instant, but as shown by the total upshot of experience. If judgments of the *should-be* are fated to grasp us in this way, they are what "correspond." The ancients placed the conception of Fate at the bottom of things—deeper than the gods themselves. "The fate of thought," utterly barren and indeterminate as such a formula is, is the only unimpeachable regulative Law of Mind.

Quelques Considérations sur la méthode subjective

AUX RÉDACTEURS DE LA *Critique philosophique*

Messieurs,

Depuis longtemps déjà, quand des idées noires, pessimisme, fatalisme, etc., me viennent obséder, j'ai l'habitude de m'en débarrasser par un raisonnement fort simple, et tellement d'accord avec les principes de la philosophie à laquelle votre revue est consacrée, que je m'étonne presque de ne l'avoir pas encore rencontré *totidem verbis* dans quelqu'un de vos cahiers hebdomadaires. J'ose vous le soumettre.

Il s'agit de savoir *si l'on est en droit de repousser une théorie confirmée en apparence par un nombre très-considérable de faits objectifs, uniquement parce qu'elle ne répond point à nos préférences intérieures.*

On n'a pas ce droit, nous disent les hommes qui cultivent aujourd'hui les sciences, ou du moins presque tous, et tous les positivistes. Repousser une conclusion par ce seul motif qu'elle contrarie nos sentiments intimes et nos désirs, c'est faire emploi de la méthode subjective; et la méthode subjective, à les en croire, est le péché originel de la science, la racine de toutes les erreurs scientifiques. Suivant eux, loin d'aller où le portent ses attraits, l'homme qui cherche la vérité doit se réduire à la simple condition d'instrument enregistreur, faire de sa conscience de savant une sorte de feuille blanche et de surface morte, sur laquelle la réalité extérieure viendrait se retracer sans altération ni courbure.

Je nie absolument la légitimité d'un tel parti pris chez ceux qui prétendent le poser en règle universelle de la méthode. Cette règle est bonne à appliquer à un ordre de recherches, mais elle est dénuée de valeur, elle est même absurde, dans un autre ordre de vérités à trouver. Rejeter rigoureusement la méthode subjective partout où la vérité existe en dehors de mon action et se détermine avec certitude indépendamment de tout ce que je peux désirer ou craindre, rien de plus sage. Ainsi, les faits acquis de l'histoire, les mouvements futurs des astres sont dès maintenant déterminés, soit qu'ils me plaisent ou non comme ils sont ou seront. Mes préférences ici sont impuissantes à produire ou à modifier les choses et ne pourraient qu'obscurcir mon jugement. Je dois résolument leur imposer silence.

Mais il est une classe de faits dont la matière n'est point ainsi constituée ou fixée d'avance,—des faits qui ne sont pas *donnés.*—Je fais une ascension alpestre. Je me trouve dans un mauvais pas dont je ne peux sortir que par un saut hardi et dangereux, et ce saut, je voudrais le pouvoir faire, mais j'ignore, faute d'expérience, si j'en aurai la force. Supposons que j'emploie la méthode subjective: je crois ce que je désire; ma confiance me donne des forces et rend possible ce qui, sans elle, ne l'eût peut-être pas été. Je franchis donc l'espace et me voilà hors de danger. Mais supposons que je sois disposé à nier ma capacité, par ce motif qu'elle ne m'a pas encore été démontrée par ce genre d'exploits: alors je balance, j'hésite, et tant et tant qu'à la fin, affaibli et tremblant, réduit à prendre un élan de pur désespoir, je manque mon coup et je tombe dans l'abîme. En pareil cas, quoi qu'il en puisse advenir, je ne serai qu'un sot si je ne crois pas ce que je désire, car ma croyance se trouve être une condition préliminaire, indispensable de l'accomplissement de son objet qu'elle affirme. Croyant à mes forces, je m'élance; le résultat donne raison à ma croyance, la *vérifie*; c'est alors seulement qu'elle *devient vraie*, mais alors on peut dire aussi qu'elle *était vraie*. Il y a donc des cas où *une croyance crée sa propre vérification*. Ne croyez pas, vous aurez raison; et, en effet, vous tomberez dans l'abîme. Croyez, vous aurez encore raison, car vous vous sauverez. Toute la différence entre les deux cas, c'est que le second vous est fort avantageux.

Dès que j'admets qu'une certaine alternative existe, et que

l'option pour moi n'est possible qu'à ce prix que je veuille fournir une contribution personnelle; dès que je reconnais que cette contribution personnelle dépend d'un certain degré d'énergie subjective, qui lui-même a besoin, pour se réaliser, d'un certain degré de foi dans le résultat, et qu'ainsi l'avenir possible repose sur la croyance actuelle, je dois voir en quelle absurdité profonde je tomberais en voulant bannir la méthode subjective, la foi de l'esprit. Sur l'existence actuelle de cette foi, la possibilité de l'avenir se fonde. Cette foi peut tromper, très-bien. Les efforts dont elle me rend capable peuvent ne pas aboutir à créer un ordre de choses qu'elle entrevoit et voudrait déterminer; voilà qui est dit. Eh bien! ma vie est manquée, c'est indubitable; mais la vie de M. Huxley, par exemple,—de M. Huxley, qui écrivait dernièrement: «Croire parce qu'on voudrait croire serait faire preuve de la dernière immoralité»,—cette vie ne serait-elle pas tout aussi manquée, s'il se trouvait par hasard que la croyance qu'il voudrait proscrire comme dénuée de garantie objective fût en définitive la vraie!

Le cas est toujours possible. Quoi qu'on fasse, en ce jeu qu'on appelle la vie, qu'on croie, qu'on doute, qu'on nie, on est également exposé à perdre. Est-ce une raison pour ne pas jouer? Non, évidemment; mais puisque ce qu'on perd est une quantité fixe (on ne fait après tout que payer de sa personne), c'est une raison de s'assurer, par tous les moyens légitimes qu'on a, qu'au cas que l'on gagne, le gain soit un maximum. Si, par exemple, on peut, en croyant, augmenter le grand bien qu'on poursuit, le prix possible, voilà une raison de *croire*.

Or, il en est précisément ainsi touchant plusieurs de ces questions universelles, qui sont les problèmes de la philosophie. Prenons celle du pessimisme. Sans être arrivé partout à l'état de dogme philosophique, comme nous le voyons en Allemagne, le pessimisme pose à tout penseur un sérieux problème: A quoi bon la vie? ou, comme on dit vulgairement, le jeu en vaut-il la chandelle? Si on prend parti pour la réponse pessimiste, que gagne-t-on à avoir raison? Pas grand'chose, assurément. Au contraire, on gagne un maximum, au cas qu'on ait raison en décidant en faveur de l'opinion qui tient que le monde est bon. Que pouvons-nous faire pour que ce monde soit bon? y contribuer de notre part; et comment une contribution minime peut-elle changer la valeur d'un total si grand? en ce qu'elle est d'une *qualité* incomparablement supérieure. Telle est la qualité des faits de la vie morale.

Soit M la masse des faits indépendants de moi, et soit r ma réaction propre, le contingent des faits qui dérivent de mon activité personnelle. M contient, nous le savons, une somme immense de phénomènes de besoin, misère, vieillesse, douleur, et de choses faites pour inspirer le dégoût et l'effroi. Il se pourrait alors que r se produisît comme une réaction du désespoir, fût un acte de suicide, par exemple, $M + r$, la totalité avec ce qui me concerne, représenterait donc un état de choses mauvais de tout point. Nul rayon dans cette nuit. Le pessimisme, dans cette hypothèse, se trouve parachevé par mon acte lui-même, dérive de ma croyance. Le voilà fait, et j'avais raison de l'affirmer.

Supposons, au contraire, que le sentiment du mal contenu dans M, au lieu de me décourager, n'ait fait qu'accroître ma résistance intérieure. Cette fois ma réaction sera l'opposé du désespoir; r contiendra patience, courage, dévouement, foi à l'invisible, toutes les vertus héroïques et les joies qui découlent de ces vertus. Or, c'est un fait d'expérience, et l'empirisme ne peut le contester, que de telles joies sont d'une valeur incomparable auprès des jouissances purement passives qui se trouvent exclues par le fait de la constitution de M telle qu'elle est. Si donc il est vrai que le bonheur moral est le plus grand bonheur actuellement connu; si, d'autre part, la constitution de M, par le mal qu'il contient et la réaction qu'il provoque, est la condition de ce bonheur, n'est-il pas clair que M est au moins *susceptible* d'appartenir au meilleur des mondes? Je dis *susceptible* seulement, parce que tout dépend du caractère de r. M en soi est ambigu, capable, selon le complément qu'il recevra, de figurer dans un pessimisme ou dans un optimisme moral.[1]

Il fera difficilement partie d'un optimisme, si nous perdons notre énergie morale; il *pourra* en faire partie, si nous la conservons. Mais comment la conserver, à moins de croire à la possibilité d'une réussite, à moins de compter sur l'avenir et de se dire: Ce monde *est bon*, puisque, au point de vue moral, il est *ce que je le fais*, et

---

[1] Il est clair qu'il ne faut pas donner ici à ce mot *optimisme* le sens qu'il a reçu par rapport aux questions de théodicée, ou celui qu'on y attache dans la philosophie de l'histoire: sens que résument les propositions: *Tout est bien, Tout est nécessaire*. Mais le *pessimisme* signifiant ci-dessus la doctrine du *Tout est mal*, on entend sans doute ici par l'*optimisme* non pas le *contraire logique*, mais simplement le *contradictoire logique* (pour employer les termes de l'École) de cette doctrine; à savoir non pas que tout est bien, mais qu'il est faux que tout soit mal, qu'*il* y a du bien, que le *monde peut être bon*. Au delà les questions subsistent. (Note de la *Critique philosophique*.)

que je le ferai bon? En un mot, comment exclure de la *connaissance* du fait la méthode subjective, alors que cette méthode est le propre instrument de la production du fait?

En toute proposition dont la portée est universelle, il faut que les actes du sujet et leurs suites sans fin soient renfermés d'avance dans la formule. Telle doit être l'extension de la formule $M + r$, dès qu'on la prend pour représenter le monde. Ceci posé, nos vœux, nos souhaits étant des coefficients réels du terme r, soit en eux-mêmes, soit par les croyances qu'ils nous inspirent ou, si l'on veut, par les hypothèses qu'ils nous suggèrent, on doit avouer que ces croyances engendrent une partie au moins de la vérité qu'elles affirment. Telles croyances, tels faits; d'autres croyances, d'autres faits. Et notons bien que tout ceci est indépendant de la question de la liberté absolue ou du déterminisme absolu. Si nos faits sont déterminés, c'est que nos croyances le sont aussi; mais déterminées ou non que soient ces dernières, elles sont une condition phénoménale nécessairement préalable aux faits, nécessairement constitutive, par conséquent, de la vérité que nous cherchons à connaître.

Voilà donc la méthode subjective justifiée logiquement, pourvu qu'on en limite convenablement l'emploi. Elle ne serait que pernicieuse, et il faut même dire immorale, appliquée à des cas où les faits à formuler ne renfermeraient pas comme facteur le terme subjectif r. Mais partout où entre un tel facteur, l'application en est légitime. Prenons encore ce problème pour exemple:

La nature intime du monde est-elle morale, ou le monde n'est-il qu'un pur fait, une simple existence actuelle? C'est au fond la question du matérialisme. Les positivistes objecteront qu'une question pareille est insoluble, ou même irrationnelle, attendu que la nature intime du monde, existât-elle, n'est pas un phénomène et ne peut en conséquence être vérifiée. Je réponds que toute question a un sens et se pose nettement, de laquelle résulte une claire alternative pratique, en telle sorte que, selon qu'on y réponde d'une manière ou d'une autre, on doive adopter une conduite ou une autre. Or, c'est le cas: le matérialiste et celui qui affirme une nature morale du monde devront agir différemment l'un de l'autre en bien des circonstances. Le matérialiste, quand les faits ne concordent pas avec ses sentiments moraux, est toujours maître de sacrifier ces derniers. Le jugement qu'il porte sur un fait, en tant que *bon* ou *mauvais*, est relatif à sa constitution psychique et en dépend; mais cette constitution n'étant elle-même qu'un fait et *une donnée*, n'est en soi ni bonne ni mauvaise. Il est donc permis de la modifier,—d'engourdir, par exemple, le sentiment moral à l'aide de toutes sortes de moyens,—et de changer ainsi le jugement, en transformant la donnée de laquelle il dérive. Au contraire, celui qui croit à la nature morale intime du monde, estime que les attributs de bien et de mal conviennent à tous les phénomènes et s'appliquent aux données psychiques aussi bien qu'aux faits relatifs à ces données. Il ne saurait donc songer, comme à une chose toute simple, à fausser ses sentiments. Ses sentiments eux-mêmes *doivent*, selon lui, être d'une manière et non d'une autre.

D'un côté donc, résistance au mal, pauvreté acceptée, martyre s'il le faut, la vie tragique, en un mot; de l'autre, les concessions, les accommodements, les capitulations de conscience et la vie épicurienne; tel est le partage entre les deux croyances. Observons seulement que leurs divergences ne se marquent avec force qu'aux moments décisifs et critiques de la vie, quand l'insuffisance des maximes journalières oblige de recourir aux grands principes. Là, la contradiction éclate. L'un dit: Le monde est chose sérieuse, partout et toujours, et il y a fondements pour le jugement moral. L'autre, le matérialiste, répond: Qu'importe comment je juge, puisque *vanitas vanitatum* est le fond de tout? Le dernier mot de la sagesse aux abois, pour celui-ci, c'est *anesthésie*; pour celui-là, *énergie*.

On voit que le problème a un sens, puisqu'il comporte deux solutions contradictoires dans la pratique de la vie. Comment savoir à présent quelle solution est la bonne? Mais comment un savant sait-il si son hypothèse est la bonne? Il la prend pour bonne et il procède aux déductions, il agit en conséquence de ce qu'il a posé. Tôt ou tard les suites de son activité le détromperont, si son point de départ a été pris faussement. N'en est-il pas ici de même? Nous avons toujours affaire à $M + r$. Si M, en sa *nature intime*, est moral et que r soit fourni par un matérialiste, ces deux éléments sont en désaccord et ils iront s'écartant de plus en plus l'un de l'autre. La même divergence devra s'accuser au cas que l'agent règle sa conduite sur la croyance que le monde est un fait moral, et que le monde, en réalité, ne soit qu'un fait brut, une somme de phénomènes tout matériels. Des deux parts, il y a attente trompée; d'où la nécessité d'hypothèses subsidiaires, et de plus en plus compliquées, comme celles dont l'histoire de l'astronomie nous fournit un exemple dans la multiplicité des épicycles qu'on dut imaginer pour faire cadrer les faits de mieux en mieux observés avec le système de Ptolémée. Si donc le partisan du monde moral, en sa croyance, s'est déterminé pour l'hypothèse fausse, il éprouvera une suite de mécomptes et n'arrivera pas définitivement à la paix du cœur; il restera inconsolé dans ses peines; son choix *tragique* ne sera pas justifié.

Dans le cas contraire, $M + r$ formant une harmonie et non plus un assemblage d'éléments disparates, le temps irait confirmant l'hypothèse, et l'agent qui l'aurait embrassée aurait toujours plus de raisons de se féliciter de son choix: il nagerait pour ainsi dire à pleines voiles dans la destinée qu'il se serait faite.

Le moyen est donc le même ici que dans les sciences, de prouver qu'une opinion est fondée, et nous n'en connaissons pas d'autre. Observons seulement que, selon les questions, le temps requis pour la vérification varie. Telle hypothèse, en physique, sera vérifiée au bout d'une demi-heure. Une hypothèse comme celle du transformisme demandera plus d'une génération pour s'établir solidement, et des hypothèses d'un ordre universel, telles que celles dont nous parlons, pourront rester sujettes au doute pendant bien des siècles encore. Mais en attendant il faut agir, et pour agir il faut choisir son hypothèse. Le doute même équivaut souvent à un choix actif. Du moment qu'on est obligé d'opter, il n'y a rien de plus rationnel que de donner sa préférence à celui des partis à prendre pour lequel on se sent le plus d'attrait, quitte ensuite à se voir démenti et condamné par la nature des choses si l'on a mal jugé. Au résumé *foi* et *working hypothesis* sont ici la même chose. Avec le temps, la vérité se dévoilera.

Je peux aller plus loin. Je demande pourquoi le matérialisme et la croyance en un monde moral ne seraient pas *l'un comme l'autre vérifiables* de la manière que je viens de dire? Qu'est-ce, en d'autres termes, qui empêche que M ne soit essentiellement ambigu et n'attende de son complément r la détermination ultime qui le fera ou rentrer dans un système moral ou se réduire à un système de faits bruts?

Le cas est concevable. Telle ligne peut faire partie d'un nombre infini de courbes, tel mot peut entrer dans beaucoup de phrases différentes. Si nous avions affaire à un cas de ce genre, il pourrait dépendre de r de faire pencher la balance en un sens ou en l'autre. Agissons, je suppose, en nous inspirant de la croyance en l'univers moral: cette vérité que le monde est chose très-sérieuse éclatera chaque jour davantage. Au contraire, agissons en matérialistes, et la suite des temps montrera de plus en plus que le monde est chose frivole et que *vanitas vanitatum* est bien le fond de tout. Ainsi le monde sera ce que nous le ferons.

Et qu'on ne me dise pas qu'une chose infime telle que *r* ne saurait changer du tout au tout le caractère de *M*, cette masse immense. Une simple particule négative renverse bien le sens des plus longues phrases! Si l'on avait à définir l'univers au point de vue de la sensibilité, il faudrait ne regarder qu'au seul règne animal, pourtant si pauvre comme fait *quantitatif*. La définition *morale* du monde pourrait dépendre de phénomènes plus restreints encore. Croyons à ce monde-là: les fruits de notre croyance remédieront aux défauts qui l'empêchaient d'être. Croyons qu'il n'est qu'une idée vaine, et en effet il sera vain. La méthode subjective est ainsi légitime en pratique et en théorie.

J'ai déjà remarqué qu'il n'était pas question de liberté absolue dans les exemples que j'ai pris. Cette liberté peut être ou n'être pas réellement. Mais si des actes libres sont possibles, ils peuvent se produire et devenir plus fréquents, grâce à la méthode subjective. En effet, la foi en leur possibilité augmente l'énergie morale qui les suscite. Mais parler de liberté dans la *Critique philosophique*, c'est porter de l'or en Californie. J'aime donc mieux finir et me résumer en disant que je crois avoir montré dans la méthode subjective autre chose que le procédé qualifié de honteux par un étrange abus de l'esprit soi-disant scientifique. Il faut passer outre à cette espèce de proscription, à ce veto ridicule qui, si nous voulions nous y conformer, paralyserait deux de nos plus essentielles facultés: celle de nous proposer, en vertu d'un acte de croyance, un but qui ne peut être atteint que par nos propres efforts, et celle de nous porter courageusement à l'action dans les cas où le succès ne nous est pas assuré d'avance.

Croyez, messieurs, à la sympathie très-particulière avec laquelle je suis, votre tout dévoué,

Wm. JAMES.

Harvard College, Cambridge (Mass.), États-Unis d'Amérique, 20 nov. 1877.

L'auteur du très-remarquable article qu'on vient de lire fait à la *Critique philosophique* beaucoup d'honneur en voulant bien s'étonner de ce qu'il n'a pas encore rencontré l'expression de ses propres pensées *totidem verbis* dans nos pages. Il est vrai qu'elles sont en tout conformes à la méthode criticiste et nous nous estimerions heureux de pouvoir les signer. Mais la manière dont elles sont présentées, la forme originale du raisonnement et la saveur à la fois délicate et forte des leçons données à la fausse science par un homme qui est fort au courant de la vraie, impriment un réel cachet de personnalité à cette justification de la «méthode subjective». Nous sommes bien sûrs que nos lecteurs seront de notre avis, dussent-ils faire leurs réserves sur un point ou sur un autre, ou plutôt réclamer des éclaircissements qui parfois ne seraient pas de trop. Quant à nous, nous ne manquerons pas de reprendre ce grand sujet et d'essayer d'ajouter aux ingénieuses démonstrations de M. Wm. James, quelques-uns des nombreux commentaires qu'elles sont de nature à appeler.

The Sentiment of Rationality

What is the task which philosophers set themselves to perform? And why do they philosophize at all? Almost everyone will immediately reply: They desire to attain a conception of the frame of things which shall on the whole be more rational than the rather fragmentary and chaotic one which everyone by gift of nature carries about with him under his hat. But suppose this rational conception attained by the philosopher, how is he to recognize it for what it is, and not let it slip through ignorance? The only answer can be that he will recognize its rationality as he recognizes everything else, by certain subjective marks with which it affects him. When he gets the marks he may know that he has got the rationality.

What then are the marks? A strong feeling of ease, peace, rest, is one of them. The transition from a state of puzzle and perplexity to rational comprehension is full of lively relief and pleasure.

But this relief seems to be a negative rather than a positive character. Shall we then say that the feeling of rationality is constituted merely by the absence of any feeling of irrationality? I think there are very good grounds for upholding such a view. All feeling whatever, in the light of certain recent psychological speculations, seems to depend for its physical condition not on simple discharge of nerve-currents, but on their discharge under arrest, impediment or resistance. Just as we feel no particular pleasure when we breathe freely, but a very intense feeling of distress when the respiratory motions are prevented; so any unobstructed tendency to action discharges itself without the production of much cogitative accompaniment, and any perfectly fluent course of thought awakens but little feeling. But when the movement is inhibited or when the thought meets with difficulties, we experience a distress which yields to an opposite feeling of pleasure as fast as the obstacle is overcome. It is only when the distress is upon us that we can be said to strive, to crave, or to aspire. When enjoying plenary freedom to energize either in the way of motion or of thought, we are in a sort of anæsthetic state in which we might say with Walt Whitman, if we cared to say anything about ourselves at such times, "I am sufficient as I am." This feeling of the sufficiency of the present moment, of its absoluteness—this absence of all need to explain it, account for it or justify it—is what I call the Sentiment of Rationality. As soon, in short, as we are enabled from any cause whatever to think of a thing with perfect fluency, that thing seems to us rational.

Why we should constantly gravitate towards the attainment of such fluency cannot here be said. As this is not an ethical but a psychological essay, it is quite sufficient for our purposes to lay it down as an empirical fact that we strive to formulate rationally a tangled mass of fact by a propensity as natural and invincible as that which makes us exchange a hard high stool for an arm-chair or prefer travelling by railroad to riding in a springless cart.

Whatever modes of conceiving the cosmos facilitate this fluency of our thought, produce the sentiment of rationality. Conceived in such modes Being vouches for itself and needs no further philosophic formulation. But so long as mutually obstructive elements are involved in the conception, the pent-up irritated mind recoiling on its present consciousness will criticize it, worry over it, and never cease in its attempts to discover some new mode of formulation which may give it escape from the irrationality of its actual ideas.

Now mental ease and freedom may be obtained in various ways. Nothing is more familiar than the way in which mere custom makes us at home with ideas or circumstances which, when new, filled the mind with curiosity and the need of explanation. There is no more

common sight than that of men's mental worry about things incongruous with personal desire, and their thoughtless incurious
acceptance of whatever happens to harmonize with their subjective ends. The existence of evil forms a "mystery"—a "problem":
there is no "problem of happiness." But, on the other hand, purely
theoretic processes may produce the same mental peace which custom and congruity with our native impulses in other cases give;
and we have forthwith to discover how it is that so many processes
can produce the same result, and how Philosophy, by emulating
or using the means of all, may attain to a conception of the world
which shall be rational in the maximum degree, or be warranted
in the most composite manner against the inroads of mental unrest
or discontent. Discarding for the present both custom and congruity, the present essay will deal with the theoretic way alone.

II

The facts of the world in their sensible diversity are always before
us, but the philosophic need craves that they should be conceived
in such a way as to satisfy the sentiment of rationality. The philosophic quest then is the quest of a conception. What now is a *conception*? It is a *teleological instrument*. It is a partial aspect of a
thing which *for our purpose* we regard as its essential aspect, as the
representative of the entire thing. In comparison with this aspect,
whatever other properties and qualities the thing may have, are unimportant accidents which we may without blame ignore. But the
essence, the ground of conception, varies with the end we have in
view. A substance like oil has as many different essences as it has uses
to different individuals. One man conceives it as a combustible, another as a lubricator, another as a food; the chemist thinks of it as a
hydro-carbon; the furniture-maker as a darkener of wood; the specu-
lator as a commodity whose market price to-day is this and to-
morrow that. The soap-boiler, the physicist, the clothes-scourer
severally ascribe to it other essences in relation to their needs.
Ueberweg's doctrine[1] that the essential quality of a thing is the
quality of most *worth*, is strictly true; but Ueberweg has failed to
note that the worth is wholly relative to the temporary interests of
the conceiver. And, even, when his interest is distinctly defined in

[1] *Logic*, English tr., p. 139.

34

his own mind, the discrimination of the quality in the object which has the closest connexion with it, is a thing which no rules can teach. The only *à priori* advice that can be given to a man embarking on life with a certain purpose is the somewhat barren counsel: Be sure that in the circumstances that meet you, you attend to the *right* ones for your purpose. To pick out the right ones is the measure of the man. "Millions," says Hartmann, "stare at the phenomenon before a *genialer Kopf* pounces on the concept."[2] The genius is simply he to whom, when he opens his eyes upon the world, the "right" characters are the prominent ones. The fool is he who, with the same purposes as the genius, infallibly gets his attention tangled amid the accidents.

Schopenhauer expresses well this ultimate truth when he says that Intuition (by which in this passage he means the power to distinguish at a glance the essence amid the accidents) "is not only the source of all knowledge, but is knowledge κατ᾽ ἐξοχήν . . . is real *insight . . . . Wisdom,* the true view of life, the right look at things, and the judgment that hits the mark, proceed from the mode in which the man conceives the world which lies before him . . . . He who excels in this talent knows the (Platonic) ideas of the world and of life. Every case he looks at stands for countless cases; more and more he goes on to conceive of each thing in accordance with its true nature, and his acts like his judgments bear the stamp of his insight. Gradually his face too acquires the straight and piercing look, the expression of reason, and at last of wisdom. For the direct sight of essences alone can set its mark upon the face. Abstract knowledge about them has no such effect."[3]

The right conception for the philosopher depends then on his interests. Now the interest which he has above other men is that of reducing the manifold in thought to simple form. We can no more say why the philosopher is more peculiarly sensitive to this delight, than we can explain the passion some persons have for matching colours or for arranging cards in a game of solitaire. All these passions resemble each other in one point; they are all illustrations of what may be called the æsthetic Principle of Ease. Our pleasure at finding that a chaos of facts is at bottom the expression of a single underlying fact is like the relief of the musician at resolving a confused mass of sound into melodic or harmonic order.

[2] *Philosophie des Unbewussten,* 2te Auflage, p. 249.
[3] *Welt als Wille u. Vorstellung,* II., p. 83.

The simplified result is handled with far less mental effort than the original data; and a philosophic conception of nature is thus in no metaphorical sense a labor-saving contrivance. The passion for parsimony, for economy of means in thought, is thus the philosophic passion *par excellence*, and any character or aspect of the world's phenomena which gathers up their diversity into simplicity will gratify that passion, and in the philosopher's mind stand for that essence of things compared with which all their other determinations may by him be overlooked.

More universality or extensiveness is then the one mark the philosopher's conceptions must possess. Unless they appear in an enormous number of cases they will not bring the relief which is his main theoretic need. The knowledge of things by their causes, which is often given as a definition of rational knowledge, is useless to him unless the causes converge to a minimum number whilst still producing the maximum number of effects. The more multiple are the instances he can see to be cases of his fundamental concept, the more flowingly does his mind rove from fact to fact in the world. The phenomenal transitions are no real transitions; each item is the same old friend with a slightly altered dress. This passion for unifying things may gratify itself, as we all know, at truth's expense. Everyone has friends bent on system and everyone has observed how, when their system has once taken definite shape, they become absolutely blind and insensible to the most flagrant facts which cannot be made to fit into it. The ignoring of data is, in fact, the easiest and most popular mode of obtaining unity in one's thought.

But leaving these vulgar excesses let us glance briefly at some more dignified contemporary examples of the hypertrophy of the unifying passion.

Its ideal goal gets permanent expression in the great notion of Substance, the underlying One in which all differences are reconciled. D'Alembert's often quoted lines express the postulate in its most abstract shape: "L'univers, pour qui sauroit l'embrasser d'un seul point de vue, ne seroit, s'il est permis de le dire, qu'un fait unique et une grande vérité." Accordingly Mr. Spencer, after saying on page 158 of the first volume of his *Psychology*, that no effort enables us to assimilate Feeling and Motion, they have nothing in common, cannot refrain on page 162 from invoking abruptly an "Unconditioned Being common to the two."

The craving for Monism at any cost is the parent of the entire evolutionist movement of our day, so far as it pretends to be more than history. The Philosophy of Evolution tries to show how the world at any given time may be conceived as absolutely identical, except in appearance, with itself at all past times. What it most abhors is the admission of anything which, appearing at a given point, should be judged essentially other than what went before. Notwithstanding the *lacunae* in Mr. Spencer's system; notwithstanding the vagueness of his terms; in spite of the sort of jugglery by which his use of the word "nascent" is made to veil the introduction of new primordial factors like consciousness, as if, like the girl in *Midshipman Easy,* he could excuse the illegitimacy of an infant, by saying it was a very little one—in spite of all this, I say, Mr. Spencer is, and is bound to be, the most popular of all philosophers, because more than any other he seeks to appease our strongest theoretic craving. To undiscriminating minds his system will be a sop; to acute ones a program full of suggestiveness.

When Lewes asserts in one place that the nerve-process and the feeling which accompanies it are not two things but only two "aspects" of one and the same thing, whilst in other passages he seems to imply that the cognitive feeling and the outward thing cognized (which is always other than the nerve-process accompanying the cognitive act) are again one thing in two aspects (giving us thereby as the ultimate truth One Thing in Three Aspects, very much as Trinitarian Christians affirm it to be One God in Three Persons), —the vagueness of his mode only testifies to the imperiousness of his need of unity.

The crowning feat of unification at any cost is seen in the Hegelian denial of the Principle of Contradiction. One who is willing to allow that A and not-A are one, can be checked by few farther difficulties in Philosophy.

III

But alongside of the passion for simplification, there exists a sister passion which in some minds—though they perhaps form the minority—is its rival. This is the passion for distinguishing; it is the impulse to be *acquainted* with the parts rather than to comprehend the whole. Loyalty to clearness and integrity of perception, dislike of blurred outlines, of vague identifications, are its char-

acteristics. It loves to recognize particulars in their full completeness, and the more of these it can carry the happier it is. It is the
mind of Cuvier *versus* St. Hilaire, of Hume *versus* Spinoza. It prefers any amount of incoherence, abruptness and fragmentariness
(so long as the literal details of the separate facts are saved) to a
fallacious unity which swamps things rather than explains them.

Clearness *versus* Simplicity is then the theoretic dilemma, and
a man's philosophic attitude is determined by the balance in him
of these two cravings. When John Mill insists that the ultimate
laws of nature cannot possibly be less numerous than the distinguishable qualities of sensation which we possess, he speaks in the
name of this æsthetic demand for clearness. When Prof. Bain says[4]:
—"There is surely nothing to be dissatisfied with, to complain of,
in the circumstance that the elements of our experience are, in the
last resort, two, and not one. . . . Instead of our being 'unfortunate'
in not being able to know the essence of either matter or mind—in
not comprehending their union; our misfortune would rather be
to have to know anything different from what we do know,"—he
is animated by a like motive. All makers of architectonic systems
like that of Kant, all multipliers of original principles, all dislikers
of vague monotony, whether it bear the character of Eleatic stag-
nancy or of Heraclitic change, obey this tendency. *Ultimate kinds*
of feeling bound together in harmony by laws, which themselves
are *ultimate kinds* of relation, form the theoretic resting-place of
such philosophers.

The unconditional demand which this need makes of a philosophy is that its fundamental terms should be representable. Phenomena are analyzable into feelings and relations. Causality is a
relation between two feelings. To abstract the relation from the
feelings, to unify all things by referring them to a first cause, and
to leave this latter relation with no term of feeling before it, is to
violate the fundamental habits of our thinking, to baffle the imagination, and to exasperate the minds of certain people much as everyone's eye is exasperated by a magic-lantern picture or a microscopic object out of focus. Sharpen it, we say, or for heaven's sake
remove it altogether.

The matter is not at all helped when the word Substance is
brought forward and the primordial causality said to obtain between this and the phenomena; for Substance *in se* cannot be di-

4 "On Mystery, etc." *Fortnightly Review*, Vol. IV. N.S., p. 394.

rectly imaged by feeling, and seems in fact but to be a peculiar form of relation between feelings—the relation of organic union between a group of them and time. Such relations, represented as non-phenomenal entities, become thus the *bête noire* and pet aversion of many thinkers. By being posited as existent they challenge our acquaintance but at the same instant defy it by being defined as noumenal. So far is this reaction against the treatment of relational terms as metempirical entities carried, that the reigning British school seems to deny their function even in their legitimate sphere, namely as phenomenal elements or "laws" cementing the mosaic of our feelings into coherent form. Time, likeness, and unlikeness are the only phenomenal relations our English empiricists can tolerate. One of the earliest and perhaps the most famous expression of the dislike to relations considered abstractedly is the well-known passage from Hume: "When we run over libraries, persuaded of these principles, what havoc must we make? If we take in our hand any volume; of divinity or school metaphysics, for instance; let us ask, *Does it contain any abstract reasoning concerning quantity or number?* No. *Does it contain any experimental reasoning concerning matter of fact and existence?* No. Commit it then to the flames: For it can contain nothing but sophistry and illusion."[5]

Many are the variations which succeeding writers have played on this tune. As we spoke of the excesses of the unifying passion, so we may now say of the craving for clear representability that it leads often to an unwillingness to treat any abstractions whatever as if they were intelligible. Even to talk of space, time, feeling, power, &c., oppresses them with a strange sense of uncanniness. Anything to be real for them must be representable in the form of a *lump*. Its other concrete determinations may be abstracted from, but its *tangible* thinghood must remain. Minds of this order, if they can be brought to psychologize at all, abound in such phrases as "tracts" of consciousness, "areas" of emotion, "molecules" of feeling, "agglutinated portions" of thought, "gangs" of ideas &c., &c.

Those who wish an amusing example of this style of thought should read *Le Cerveau* by the anatomist Luys, surely the very worst book ever written on the much-abused subject of mental physiology. In another work, *Psychologie réaliste*, by P. Sièrebois (Paris 1876), it is maintained that "our ideas exist in us in a molec-

5 *Essays*, ed. Green and Grose, II., p. 135.

ular condition, and are subject to continual movements. . . . Their mobility is as great as that of the molecules of air or any gas." When we fail to recall a word it is because our ideas are hid in some distant corner of the brain whence they cannot come to the muscles of articulation, or else "they have lost their ordinary fluidity." . . . "These ideal molecules are material portions of the brain which differs from all other matter precisely in this property which it possesses of subdividing itself into very attenuated portions which easily take on the likeness in form and quality of all external objects." In other words, when I utter the word "rhinoceros" an actual little microscopic rhinoceros gallops towards my mouth.

A work of considerable acuteness, far above the vulgar materialistic level, is that of Czolbe, *Grundzüge einer extensionalen Erkenntnisstheorie* (1875). This author explains our ideas to be extended substances endowed with mutual penetrability. The matter of which they are composed is "elastic like india-rubber." When "concentrated" by "magnetic self-attraction" into the middle of the brain, its "intensity" is such that it becomes conscious. When the attraction ceases, the idea-substance expands and diffuses itself into infinite space and so sinks from consciousness.

Again passing over these *quasi*-pathological excesses, we come to a permanent and, for our purpose, most important fact—the fact that many minds of the highest analytic power will tolerate in Philosophy no unifying terms but elements immanent in phenomena, and taken in their phenomenal and representable sense. Entities whose attributes are not directly given in feeling, phenomenal relations functioning as entities, are alike rejected. Spinozistic Substance, Spencerian Unknowable, are abhorred as unrepresentable things, numerically additional to the representable world. The substance of things for these clear minds can be no more than their common measure. The phenomena bear to it the same relation that the different numbers bear to unity. These contain no other matter than the repeated unit, but they may be classed as prime numbers, odd numbers, even numbers, square numbers, cube numbers, &c., just as truly and naturally as we class concrete things. The molecular motions, of which physicists hope that some day all events and properties will be seen to consist, form such an immanent unity of colossal simplifying power. The "infinitesimal event" of various modern writers, Taine for example, with its two "aspects," inner and outer, reaches still farther in the same direction. Writers of this class, if they deal with Psychology, repudiate the "soul" as a scholastic entity. The phenomenal unity of consciousness must flow from some element immutably present in each and every representation of the individual and binding the whole into one. To unearth and accurately define this phenomenal self becomes one of the fundamental tasks of Psychology.

But the greatest living insister on the principle that unity in our account of things shall not overwhelm clearness, is Charles Renouvier. His masterly exposition of the irreducible categories of thought in his *Essais de critique générale* ought to be far better known among us than it is. The onslaughts which this eminently clear-headed writer has made and still makes in his weekly journal, the *Critique philosophique,* on the vanity of the evolutionary principle of simplification, which supposes that you have explained away all distinctions by simply saying "they arise" instead of "they are," form the ablest criticism which the school of Evolution has received. Difference "thus displaced, transported from the *esse* to the *fieri*, is it any the less postulated? And does the *fieri* itself receive the least commencement of explanation when we suppose that everything which occurs, occurs little by little, by insensible degrees, so that, if we look at any one of these degrees, what happens does so as easily and clearly as if it did not happen at all? ... If we want a continuous production *ex nihilo*, why not say so frankly, and abandon the idea of a 'transition without break' which explains really nothing?"[6]

IV

Our first conclusion may then be this: No system of philosophy can hope to be universally accepted among men which grossly violates either of the two great æsthetic needs of our logical nature, the need of unity and the need of clearness, or entirely subordinates the one to the other. Doctrines of mere disintegration like that of Hume and his successors, will be as widely unacceptable on the one hand as doctrines of merely engulphing substantialism like those of Schopenhauer, Hartmann and Spencer on the other. Can we for our own guidance briefly sketch out here some of the conditions of most favorable compromise?

In surveying the connexions between data we are immediately

[6] *Critique philosophique,* 12 Juillet, 1877, p. 383.

struck by the fact that some are more intimate than others. Propositions which express those we call necessary truths; and with them we contrast the laxer collocations and sequences which are known as empirical, habitual or merely fortuitous. The former seem to have an *inward* reasonableness which the latter are deprived of. The link, whatever it be, which binds the two phenomena together, seems to extend from the heart of one into the heart of the next, and to be an essential reason why the facts should always and indefeasibly be as we now know them. "Within the pale we stand." As Lotze says[7]:—"The intellect is not satisfied with merely associated representations. In its constant critical activity thought seeks to refer each representation to the rational ground which conditions the alliance of what is associated and proves that what is grouped *belongs* together. So it separates from each other those impressions which merely coalesce without inward connexions, and it renews (while corroborating them) the bonds of those which, by the inward kinship of their content, have a right to permanent companionship."

On the other hand many writers seem to deny the existence of any such inward kinship or rational bond between things. Hume says: "All our distinct perceptions are distinct existences, and the mind never perceives any real connexion among distinct existences."[8]

Hume's followers are less bold in their utterances than their master, but throughout all recent British Nominalism we find the tendency to enthrone mere juxtaposition as lord of all and to make of the Universe what has well been styled a Nulliverse. "For my part," says Prof. Huxley, "I utterly repudiate and anathematise the intruder [Necessity]. Fact I know; and Law I know; but what is this Necessity, save an empty shadow of the mind's own throwing?"

And similarly J. S. Mill writes: "What is called explaining one law by another is but substituting one mystery for another, and does nothing to render the course of nature less mysterious. We can no more assign a *why* for the more extensive laws than for the partial ones. The explanation may substitute a mystery which has become familiar and has grown to seem not mysterious for one which is still strange. And this is the meaning of explanation in

7 *Mikrokosmus*, 2nd ed., I., p. 261.
8 *Treatise on Human Nature*, ed. T. H. Green, I., p. 559.

common parlance. . . . The laws thus explained or resolved are said to be *accounted for;* but the expression is incorrect if taken to mean anything more than what has been stated."[9]

And yet the very pertinacity with which such writers remind us that our explanations are in a strict sense of the word no explanations at all; that our causes never unfold the essential nature of their effects; that we never seize the inward reason why attributes cluster as they do to form things, seems to prove that they possess in their minds some ideal or pattern of what a genuine explanation would be like in case they should meet it. How could they brand our current explanations as spurious, if they had no positive notion whatever of the real thing?

Now have we the real thing? And yet may they be partly right in their denials? Surely both; and I think that the shares of truth may be easily assigned. Our "laws" *are* to a great extent but facts of larger growth, and yet things *are* inwardly and necessarily connected notwithstanding. The entire process of philosophic simplification of the chaos of sense consists of two acts, Identification and Association. Both are principles of union and therefore of theoretic rationality; but the rationality between things associated is outward and custom-bred. Only when things are identified do we pass inwardly and necessarily from one to the other.

The first step towards unifying the chaos is to classify its items. "Every concrete thing," says Prof. Bain, "falls into as many classes as it has attributes."[10] When we pick out a certain attribute to conceive it by, we literally and strictly identify it *in that respect* with the other concretes of the class having that attribute for its essence, concretes which the attribute recalls. When we conceive of sugar as a white thing it is *pro tanto* identical with snow; as a sweet thing it is the same as liquorice; *quâ* hydro carbon, as starch. The attribute picked out may be *per se* most uninteresting and familiar, but if things superficially very diverse can be found to possess it buried within them and so be assimilated with each other, "the mind feels a peculiar and genuine satisfaction. . . . The intellect, oppressed with the variety and multiplicity of facts, is joyfully relieved by the simplification and the unity of a great principle."[11]

Who does not feel the charm of thinking that the moon and the

[9] *Logic,* 8th ed., I., p. 549.
[10] *Ment. and Mor. Science,* p. 177.
[11] Bain, *Logic,* II., p. 120.

apple are, as far as their relation to the earth goes, identical? of knowing respiration and combustion to be one? of understanding that the balloon rises by the same law whereby the stone sinks? of feeling that the warmth in one's palm when one rubs one's sleeve is identical with the motion which the friction checks? of recognizing the difference between beast and fish to be only a higher degree of that between human father and son? of believing our strength when we climb or chop to be no other than the strength of the sun's rays which made the oats grow out of which we got our morning meal?

We shall presently see how the attribute performing this unifying function, becomes associated with some other attribute to form what is called a general law. But at present we must note that many sciences remain in this first and simplest classificatory stage. A classificatory science is merely one the fundamental concepts of which have few associations or none with other concepts. When I say a man, a lizard, and a frog are one in being vertebrates, the identification, delightful as it is in itself, leads me hardly any farther. "The idea that all the parts of a flower are modified leaves, reveals a connecting law, which surprises us into acquiescence. But now try and define the leaf, determine its essential characteristics, so as to include all the forms that we have named. You will find yourself in a difficulty, for all distinctive marks vanish, and you have nothing left, except that a leaf in the wider sense of the term is a lateral appendage of the axis of a plant. Try then to express the proposition 'the parts of the flower are modified leaves' in the language of scientific definition, and it reads, 'the parts of the flower are lateral appendages of the axis.' "[12] Truly a bald result! Yet a dozen years ago there hardly lived a naturalist who was not thrilled with rapture at identifications in "philosophic" anatomy and botany exactly on a par with this. Nothing could more clearly show that the gratification of the sentiment of rationality depends hardly at all on the worth of the attribute which strings things together but almost exclusively on the mere fact of their being strung at all. Theological implications were the utmost which the attributes of archetypal zoology carried with them, but the wretched poverty of these proves how little they had to do with the enthusiasm engendered by archetypal identifications. Take Agassiz's conception of class-characters, order-characters &c., as

[12] Helmholtz, *Popular Scientific Lectures*, p. 47.

"thoughts of God." What meager thoughts! Take Owen's archetype of the vertebrate skeleton as revealing the artistic temperament of the Creator. It is a grotesque figure with neither beauty nor ethical suggestiveness, fitted rather to discredit than honor the Divine Mind. In short the conceptions led no farther than the identification pure and simple. The transformation which Darwin has effected in the classificatory sciences is simply this—that in his theory the class-essence is not a unifying attribute pure and simple, but an attribute with wide associations. When a frog, a man and a lizard are recognized as one, not simply in having the same backbone, &c., but in being all offspring of one parent, our thought instead of coming to a standstill, is immediately confronted with further problems and, we hope, solutions. Who were that parent's ancestors and cousins? Why was he chosen out of all to found such an enormous line? Why did he himself perish in the struggle to survive? &c.

Association of class-attributes *inter se*, is thus the next great step in the mind's simplifying industry. By it Empirical Laws are founded and sciences, from classificatory, become explanatory. Without it we should be in the position of a judge who could only decide that the cases in his court belonged each to a certain class, but who should be inhibited from passing sentence, or attaching to the class-name any further notion of duty, liability, or penalty. This *coupling* of the class-concept with certain determinate *consequences* associated therewithal, is what is practically important in the laws of nature as in those of society.

When, for example, we have identified prisms, bowls of water, lenses and strata of air as distorting media, the next step is to learn that all distorting media refract light rays towards the perpendicular. Such additional determination makes a law. But this law itself may be as inscrutable as the concrete fact we started from. The entrance of a ray and its swerving towards the perpendicular, may be simply *associated* properties, with, for aught we see, no inwardly necessary bond, coupled together as empirically as the colour of a man's eyes with the shape of his nose.

But such an empirical law may have its terms again classified. The essence of the medium may be to retard the light-wave's speed. The essence (in an obliquely-striking wave) of deflection towards the perpendicular may be earlier retardation of that part of the wave-front which enters first, so that the remaining portion swings

45

round it before getting in. Medium and bending towards perpendicular thus coalesce into the one identical fact of retardation. This being granted gives an inward explanation of all above it. But retardation itself remains an empirical coupling of medium and light-movement until we have classified both under a single concept. The explanation reached by the insight that two phenomena are at bottom one and the same phenomenon, is rational in the ideal and ultimate sense of the word. The ultimate identification of the subject and predicate of a mathematical theorem, an identification which we can always reach in our reasonings, is the source of the inward necessity of mathematical demonstration. We see that the top and bottom of a parallelogram must be equal as soon as we have unearthed in the parallelogram the attribute that it consists of two equal, juxtaposed triangles of which its top and bottom form homologous sides—that is, as soon as we have seen that top and bottom have an identical essence, their length, as being such sides, and that their position is an accident. This criterion of identity is that which we all unconsciously use when we discriminate between brute fact and explained fact. There is no other test.

In the contemporary striving of physicists to interpret every event as a case of motion concealed or visible, we have an adumbration of the way in which a common essence may make the sensible heterogeneity of things inwardly rational. The cause is one motion, the effect the same motion transferred to other molecules; in other words, physics aims at the same kind of rationality as mathematics. In the second volume of Lewes's *Problems* we find this anti-Humean view that the effect is the "procession" of the cause, or that they are one thing in two aspects brought prominently forward.[13]

And why, on the other hand, do all our contemporary physical philosophers so vie with each other in the zeal with which they reiterate that in reality nerve-processes and brain-tremors "explain" nothing of our feelings? Why does "the chasm between the two classes of phenomena still remain intellectually impassable"?[14] Simply because, in the words of Spencer which we quoted a few pages back, feeling and motion have nothing whatever in common,

[13] This view is in growing favor with thinkers fed from empirical sources. See Wundt's *Physikalischen Axiome* and the important article by A. Riehl, "Causalität und Identität," in *Vierteljahrssch. f. wiss. Philos.* Bd. I., p. 365. The Humean view is ably urged by Chauncey Wright, *Philosophical Discussions*, N.Y. 1877, p. 406.

[14] Tyndall, *Fragments of Science*, 2nd ed., p. 121.

no identical essence by which we can conceive both, and so, as Tyndall says, "pass by a process of reasoning from one to the other." The "double-aspect" school postulate the blank form of "One and the Same Fact," appeal to the image of the circle which is both convex and concave, and think that they have by this symbolic identification made the matter seem more rational.

Thus then the connexions of things become strictly rational only when, by successive substitutions of essences for things, and higher for lower essences, we succeed in reaching a point of view from which we can view the things as one. A and B are concretes; *a* and *b* are partial attributes with which for the present case we conceive them to be respectively identical (classify them) and which are coupled by a general law. M is a further attribute which rationally explains the general law as soon as we perceive it to form the essence of both *a* and *b*, as soon as we identify them with each other through it. The softening of asphalt pavements in August is explained first by the empirical law that heat, which is the essence of August, produces melting, which is the essence of the pavement's change, and secondly this law is inwardly rationalized by the conception of both heat and melting being at bottom one and the same fact, namely, increased molecular mobility.

Proximate and ultimate explanations are then essentially the same thing. Classification involves all that is inward in any explanation, and a perfected rationalization of things means only a *completed* classification of them. Everyone feels that all explanation whatever, even by reference to the most proximate empirical law, does involve something of the essence of inward rationalization. How else can we understand such words as these from Prof. Huxley? "The fact that it is impossible to comprehend how it is that a physical state gives rise to a mental state, no more lessens the value of our [empirical] explanation in the latter case, than the fact that it is utterly impossible to comprehend how motion is communicated from one body to another, weakens the force of the explanation of the motion of one billiard ball by showing that another has hit it."[15]

To return now to the philosophic problem. It is evident that our idea of the universe cannot assume an inwardly rational shape until each separate phenomenon is conceived as fundamentally identical with every other. But the important fact to notice is that in the

[15] "Modern 'Symposium.'" *Nineteenth Century.* Vol. I., 1877.

steps by which this end is reached the really rationalizing, pregnant moments are the successive steps of conception, the moments of picking out essences. The association of these essences into laws, the empirical coupling, is done by nature for us and is hardly worthy to be called an intellectual act; and on the other hand the coalescence-into-one of all items in which the same essence is discerned, in other words the perception that an essence whether ultimate, simple and universal, or proximate and specific, is identical with itself wherever found, is a barren truism. The living question always is, Where *is* it found? To stand before a phenomenon and say *what* it is; in other words to pick out from it the embedded character (or characters) also embedded in the maximum number of *other* phenomena, and so identify it with them—here lie the stress and strain, here the test of the philosopher. So we revert to what we said far back: the genius can do no more than this; in Butler's words—

> "He knows *what's what*, and that's as high
> As metaphysic wit can fly." [16]

[16] This doctrine is perfectly congruous with the conclusion that identities are the only propositions necessary *à priori*, though of course it does not necessarily lead to that conclusion, since there may be in things elements which are not simple but bilateral or synthetic, like straightness and shortness in a line, convexity and concavity in a curve. Should the empiricists succeed in their attempt to resolve such Siamese-twin elements into habitual juxtapositions, the Principle of Identity would become the only *à priori* truth, and the philosophic problem like all our ordinary problems would become a question as to facts: *What* are these facts which we perceive to exist? Are there any existing facts corresponding to this or that conceived class? Lewes, in the interesting discussion on necessary and contingent truth in the Prolegomena to his *History* and in Chap. XIII. of his first *Problem*, seems at first sight to take up an opposite position, in that he maintains our commonly so-called contingent truths to be really necessary. But his treatment of the question most beautifully confirms the doctrine I have advanced in the text. If the proposition "A is B" is ever true, he says it is so necessarily. But he proves the necessity by showing that what we mean by A is its essential attribute *x*, and what we mean by B is again *x*. Only *in so far* as A and B are identical is the proposition true. But he admits that a fact sensibly just like A may lack *x*, and a fact sensibly unlike B may have it. In either case the proposition, to be true, must change. The contingency which he banishes from propositions, he thus houses in their terms; making as I do the act of conception, subsumption, classification, intuition, naming, or whatever else one may prefer to call it, the pivot on which thought turns. Before this act there is infinite indeterminateness—A and B may be anything. After the act there is the absolute certainty of truism—all *x*'s are the same. *In* the act—is A, *x*? *is* B, *x*? or not?—we have the sphere of truth and error, of living experience, in short, of Fact. As Lewes himself says: "The only necessity is that a thing is what it is; the only contingency is that our proposition may not state what the thing is" (*Problems*, Vol. I., p. 395).

We have now to ask ourselves how far this identification may be legitimately carried and what, when perfected, its real worth is. But before passing to these further questions we had best secure our ground by defending our fundamental notion itself from nominalistic attacks. The reigning British school has always denied that the same attribute *is* identical with itself in different individuals. I started above with the assumption that when we look at a subject with a certain purpose, regard it from a certain point of view, some one attribute becomes its essence and identifies it, *pro hac vice*, with a class. To this James Mill replies: "But what is meant by a mode of regarding things? This is mysterious; and is as mysteriously explained, when it is said to be the taking into view the particulars in which individuals agree. For what is there, which it is possible for the mind to take into view, in that in which individuals agree? Every colour is an individual colour, every size is an individual size, every shape is an individual shape. But things have no individual colour in common, no individual shape in common, no individual size in common; that is to say, they have neither shape, colour, nor size in common. What, then, is it which they have in common, which the mind can take into view? Those who affirmed that it was something, could by no means tell. They substituted words for things; using vague and mystical phrases, which, when examined, meant nothing";[17] the truth being according to this heroic author, that the only thing that can be possessed in common is a name. Black in the coat and black in the shoe agree only in that both are named black—the fact that on this view the *name* is never the same when used twice being quite overlooked. But the blood of the giants has grown weak in these days, and the nominalistic utterances of our contemporaries are like sweet-bells jangled, sadly out of tune. If they begin with a clear nominalistic note, they are sure to end with a grating rattle which sounds very like *universalia in re*, if not *ante rem*. In M. Taine,[18] who may

[17] *Analysis*, Vol. I., p. 249.

[18] How can M. Taine fail to have perceived that the entire doctrine of "Substitution" so clearly set forth in the nominalistic beginning of his brilliant book is utterly senseless except on the supposition of realistic principles like those which he so admirably expounds at its close? How *can* the image be a useful substitute for the sensation, the tendency for the image, the name for the tendency, unless sensation, image, tendency and name be *identical* in some respect, in respect namely of function,

fairly be included in the British School, they are almost *ante rem.* This *bruit de cloche fêlée,* as the doctors say, is pathognomonic of the condition of Ockham's entire modern progeny.

But still we may find expressions like this: "When I say that the sight of any object gives me the *same* sensation or emotion to-day that it did yesterday, or the *same* which it gives to some other person, this is evidently an incorrect application of the word *same;* for the feeling which I had yesterday is gone never to return. . . . Great confusion of ideas is often produced, and many fallacies engendered, in otherwise enlightened understandings, by not being sufficiently alive to the fact (in itself not always to be avoided), that they use the same name to express ideas so different as those of identity and undistinguishable resemblance."[19]

What are the exact facts? Take the sensation I got from a cloud yesterday and from the snow to-day. The white of the snow and that of the cloud differ in place, time and associates; they agree in quality, and we may say in origin, being in all probability both produced by the activity of the same brain tract. Nevertheless, John Mill denies our right to call the quality the same. He says that *it* essentially differs in every different occasion of its appearance, and that no two phenomena of which it forms part are really identical even as far as *it* goes. Is it not obvious that to maintain this view he must abandon the phenomenal plane altogether? Phenomenally considered, the white *per se is* identical with itself wherever found in snow or in cloud, to-day or to-morrow. If any nominalist deny the identity I ask him to point out the difference. *Ex hypothesi* the qualities are sensibly indistinguishable, and the only difference he can indicate is that of time and place; but these are not differences in the quality. If our quality be not the same with itself, what meaning has the word "same"? Our adversary though silenced may still grudge assent, but if he analyze carefully the grounds of this reluctance he will, I think, find that it proceeds from a difficulty in believing that the *cause* of the quality can be just the same at different times. In other words he abandons altogether the platform of the sensible phenomenon and ascends

---

of the relations they enter into? Were this realistic basis laid at the outset of Taine's *De l'Intelligence,* it would be one of the most consistent instead of one of the most self-contradictory works of our day.

19 J. S. Mill, *Logic,* 8th ed., I., p. 77.

into the empyrean, postulating some inner noumenal principle of *quality* + *time* + *place* + *concomitants*. The entire group being never twice alike, of course this ground, or being *in se*, of the quality must each time be distinct and, so to speak, personal. This transcendental view is frankly avowed by Mr. Spencer in his *Psychology*, II., p. 63—(the passage is too complex to quote); but all nominalists must start from it, if they think clearly at all.[20]

We, who are phenomenists, may leave all metaphysical entities which have the power of producing whiteness to their fate, and content ourselves with the irreversible *datum* of perception that the whiteness after it *is* manifested is the same, be it here or be it there. Of all abstractions such entities are the emptiest, being ontological hypostatizations of the mere susceptibility of being distinguished, whilst this susceptibility has its real, nameable, phenomenal ground all the while, in the time, place, and relations affected by the attribute considered.

The truly wise man will take the phenomenon in its entirety and permanently sacrifice no one aspect to another. Time, place, and relations differ, he will freely say; but let him just as freely admit that the quality is identical with itself through all these differences. Then if, *to satisfy the philosophic interest*, it becomes needful to conceive this identical part as the essence of the several entire phenomena, he will gladly call them one; whilst if some other interest be paramount, the points of difference will become essential and the identity an accident. Realism is eternal and invincible in this phenomenal sense.

We have thus vindicated against all assailants our title to consider the world as a matter susceptible of rational formulation in the deepest, most inward sense, and not as a disintegrated sandheap; and we are consequently at liberty to ask· (1) Whether the mutual identification of its items meet with any necessary limit; and (2) What, supposing the operation completed, its real worth and import amount to.

---

[20] I fear that even after this some persons will remain unconvinced, but then it seems to me the matter has become a dispute about words. If my supposed adversary, when he says that different times and places prevent a quality which appears in them from ever being twice the same, will admit that they do not make it in any conceivable way *different*, I will willingly abandon the words "same" and "identical" to his fury; though I confess it becomes rather inconvenient to have no single positive word left by which to indicate complete absence of difference.

VI

In the first place, when we have rationally explained the connexion of the items A and B by identifying both with their common attribute x, it is obvious that we have really explained only so much of these items as *is x*. To explain the connexion of choke-damp and suffocation by the lack of oxygen is to leave untouched all the other peculiarities both of choke-damp and of suffocation, such as convulsions and agony on the one hand, density and explosibility on the other. In a word, so far as A and B contain l, m, n and o, p, q, respectively in addition to x, they are not explained by x. Each additional particularity makes its distinct appeal to our rational craving. A single explanation of a fact only explains it from a single point of view.[21] The entire fact is not accounted for until each and all of its characters have been identified with their likes elsewhere. To apply this now to universal formulas we see that the explanation of the world by molecular movements explains it only so far as it actually *is* such movements. To invoke the "Unknowable" explains only so much as is unknowable; "Love" only so much as is love; "Thought" so much as is thought; "Strife" so much as is strife. All data whose actual phenomenal quality cannot be identified with the attribute invoked as Universal Principle, remain outside as ultimate, independent *kinds* or *natures*, associated by empirical laws with the fundamental attribute but devoid of truly rational kinship with it. If A and B are to be *thoroughly* rationalized together, l, m, n and o, p, q, must each and all turn out to be so many cases of x in disguise. This kind of wholesale identification is being now attempted by physicists when they conceive of all the ancient, separate Forces as so many determinations of one and the same essence, molecular mass, position and velocity.

Suppose for a moment that this idea were carried out for the physical world,—the subjective sensations produced by the different

---

[21] In the number of the *Journal of Speculative Philosophy* for April 1879, Prof. John Watson most admirably asserts and expresses the truth which constitutes the back-bone of this article, namely that every manner of conceiving a fact is relative to some interest, and that there are no absolutely essential attributes—every attribute having the right to call itself essential in turn, and the truth consisting of nothing less than all of them together. I avow myself unable to comprehend as yet this author's Hegelian point of view, but his pages 164 to 172 are a most welcome corroboration of what I have striven to advance in the text.

molecular energies, colour, sound, taste, &c., &c., the relations of likeness and contrast, of time and position, of ease and effort, the emotions of pain and delight, in short, all the mutually irreducible categories of mental life, would still remain over. Certain writers strive in turn to reduce all these to a common measure, the primordial unit of feeling, or infinitesimal mental event which builds them up as bricks build houses. But this case is wholly different from the last. The physical molecule is conceived not only as having a being *in se* apart from representation, but as being essentially of representable kind. With magnified perceptions we should actually see it. The mental molecule, on the other hand, has by its very definition no existence except in being felt, and yet by the same definition never is felt. It is neither a fact in consciousness nor a fact out of consciousness, and falls to the ground as a transcendental absurdity. Nothing could be more inconclusive than the empirical arguments for the existence of this noumenal feeling which Taine and Spencer draw from the sense of hearing.

But let us for an instant waive all this and suppose our feelings reduced to one. We should then have two primordial natures, the molecule of matter and the molecule of mind, coupled by an empirical law. Phenomenally incommensurable, the attempt to reduce them to unity by calling them two "aspects" is vain so long as it is not pointed out who is there *adspicere*; and the *Machtspruch* that they are expressions of one underlying Reality has no rationalizing function so long as that reality is confessed unknowable. Nevertheless the absolute necessity of an identical substratum for the different species of feeling on the one hand, and the genera feeling and motion on the other, if we are to have any evolutionary *explanation* of things, will lead to ever renewed attempts at an atomistic hylozoism. Already Clifford and Taine, Spencer, Fechner, Zöllner, G. S. Hall, and more besides, have given themselves up to this ideal.

But again let us waive this criticism and admit that even the chasm between feeling and motion may be rationally bridged by the conception of the bilateral atom of being. Let us grant that this atom by successive compoundings with its fellows builds up the universe; is it not still clear that each item in the universe would still be explained only as to its general *quality* and not as to its other particular determinations? The particulars depend on the exact number of primordial atoms existing at the outset and their

exact distances from each other. The "universal formula" of Laplace which Du Bois-Reymond has made such striking use of in
his lecture *Ueber die Grenzen des Naturerkennens*, cannot possibly get along with fewer than this almost infinite number of data.
Their homogeneity does not abate their infinity—each is a separate
empirical fact.

And when we now retract our provisional admissions, and deny
that feelings incommensurable *inter se* and with motion can be possibly unified, we see at once that the reduction of the phenomenal
Chaos to rational form must stop at a certain point. It is a limited
process,—bounded by the number of elementary attributes which
cannot be mutually identified, the specific *qualia* of representation,
on the one hand, and, on the other, by the number of entities
(atoms or monads or what not) with their complete mathematical
determinations, requisite for deducing the fulness of the concrete
world. All these irreducible data form a system, no longer phenomenally rational, *inter se*, but bound together by what are for
us empirical laws. We merely find the system existing as a matter
of fact, and write it down. In short, a plurality of categories and an
immense number of primordial entities, determined according
to these categories, is the minimum of philosophic baggage, the
only possible compromise between the need of clearness and the
need of unity. All simplification, beyond this point, is reached
either by throwing away the particular concrete determinations of
the fact to be explained, or else it is illusory simplification. In the
latter case it is made by invoking some sham term, some pseudo-
principle, and conglomerating it and the data into one. The principle may be an immanent element but no true universal: Sensation,
Thought, Will are principles of this kind; or it may be a transcendent entity like Matter, Spirit, Substance, the Unknowable, the
Unconscious, &c.[22] Such attempts as these latter do but postulate
unification, not effect it; and if taken avowedly to represent a mere
claim, may be allowed to stand. But if offered as actual explanations, though they may serve as a sop to the rabble, they can but
nauseate those whose philosophic appetite is genuine and entire.
If we choose the former mode of simplification and are willing to
abstract from the particulars of time, place and combination in the

---

[22] The idea of "God" in its popular function is open to neither of these objections,
being conceived as a phenomenon standing in causal relation to other phenomena.
As such, however, it has no unifying function of a properly *explanatory* kind.

concrete world, we may simplify our elements very much by neglecting the numbers and collocations of our primordial elements and attending to their qualitative categories alone. The system formed by these will then really rationalize the universe so far as its qualities go. Nothing can happen in it incommensurable with these data, and practically this abstract treatment of the world as quality is all that philosophers aim at. They are satisfied when they can see it to be a place in which none but these qualities appear, and in which the same quality appears not only once but identically repeats itself. They are willing to ignore, or leave to special sciences the knowledge of what times, places and concomitants the recurring quality is likely to affect. The *Essais de critique générale* of Renouvier form, to my mind, by far the ablest answer to the philosophic need thus understood, clearness and unity being there carried each to the farthest point compatible with the other's existence.

VII

And now comes the question as to the worth of such an achievement. How much better off is the philosopher when he has got his system than he was before it? As a mere phenomenal system it stands between two fires. On the one hand the unbridled craver of unity scorns it, as being incompletely rational, still to a great extent an empirical sand-heap; whilst on the other the practical man despises its empty and abstract barrenness. All it says is that the elements of the world are such and such and that each is identical with itself wherever found; but the question: Where is it found? (which is for the practical man the all-important question about each element) he is left to answer by his own wit. Which, of all the essences, shall here and now be held the essence of this concrete thing, the fundamental philosophy never attempts to decide. We seem thus led to the conclusion that a system of categories is, on the one hand, the only possible philosophy, but is, on the other, a most miserable and inadequate substitute for the fulness of the truth. It is a monstrous abridgment of things which like all abridgments is got by the absolute loss and casting out of real matter. This is why so few human beings truly care for Philosophy. The particular determinations which she ignores are the real matter exciting other æsthetic and practical needs, quite as potent and authoritative as hers. What does the moral enthusiast care for philosophical ethics? Why does the *Æsthetik* of every German philosopher appear to the artist like the abomination of desolation? What these men need every moment is a particular counsel, and no barren, universal truism.

"Grau, theurer Freund, ist alle Theorie
Und grün des Lebens goldner Baum."

The entire man, who feels all needs by turns, will take nothing as an equivalent for Life but the fulness of living itself. Since the essences of things are as a matter of fact spread out and disseminated through the whole extent of time and space, it is in their spread-outness and alternation that he will enjoy them. When weary of the concrete clash and dust and pettiness, he will refresh himself by an occasional bath in the eternal spring, or fortify himself by a daily look at the immutable Natures. But he will only be a visitor, not a dweller in the region; he will never carry the philosophic yoke upon his shoulders, and when tired of the gray monotony of her problems and insipid spaciousness of her results, will always escape gleefully into the teeming and dramatic richness of the concrete world.

So our study turns back here to its beginning. We started by calling every concept a teleological instrument (*supra* p. 319 [*ed.*, 34.19–26]). No concept can be a valid substitute for a concrete reality except with reference to a particular interest in the conceiver. The interest of theoretic rationality, the relief of identification, is but one of a thousand human purposes. When others rear their heads it must pack up its little bundle and retire till its turn recurs. The exaggerated dignity and value that philosophers have claimed for their solutions is thus greatly reduced. The only virtue their theoretic conception need have is simplicity, and a simple conception is an equivalent for the world only so far as the world is simple; the world meanwhile, whatever simplicity it may harbor, being also a mightily complex affair. Enough simplicity remains, however, and enough urgency in our craving to reach it, to make the theoretic function one of the most invincible and authoritative of human impulses. All ages have their intellectual populace. That of our own day prides itself particularly on its love of Science and Facts and its contempt for all metaphysics.

Just weaned from the Sunday-school nurture of its early years, with the taste of the catechism still in its mouth, it is perhaps not surprising that its palate should lack discrimination and fail to recognize how much of ontology is contained in the "Nature," "Force" and "Necessary Law," how much mysticism in the "Awe," "Progress" and "Loyalty to Truth" or whatever the other phrases may be with which it sweetens its rather meager fare of fragmentary physiology and physics. But its own inconsistency should teach it that the eradication of music, painting and poetry, games of chance and skill, manly sports and all other æsthetic energies from human life, would be an easy task compared with that suppression of Metaphysics which it aspires to accomplish. Metaphysics of some sort there must be. The only alternative is between the good Metaphysics of clear-headed Philosophy and the trashy Metaphysics of vulgar Positivism. Metaphysics, the quest of the last clear elements of things, is but another name for thought which seeks thorough self-consistency; and so long as men must think at all, some will be found willing to forsake all else to follow that ideal.

VIII

Suppose then the goal attained. Suppose we have at last a Metaphysics in which clearness and unity join friendly hands. Whether it be over a system of interlocked elements, or over a substance, or over such a simple fact as "phenomenon" or "representation," need not trouble us now. For the discussion which follows we will call the result the metaphysical Datum and leave its composite or simple nature uncertain. Whichever it be, and however limited as we have seen be the sphere of its utility, it satisfies, if no other need, at least the need of rationality. But now I ask: Can that which is the ground of rationality in all else be itself properly called rational? It would seem at first sight that in the sense of the word we have hitherto alone considered, it might. One is tempted at any rate to say that, since the craving for rationality in a theoretic or logical sense consists in the identification of one thing with all other outstanding things, a unique datum which left nothing else outstanding would leave no play for further rational demand, and might thus be said to quench that demand or to be rational *in se*. No *otherness* being left to annoy the mind we should sit down at peace.

In other words, just as the theoretic tranquillity of the boor results from his spinning no further considerations about his chaotic universe which may prevent him from going about his practical affairs; so any brute datum whatever (provided it were simple and clear) ought to banish mystery from the Universe of the philosopher and confer perfect theoretic peace, inasmuch as there would then be for him absolutely no further considerations to spin.

This in fact is what some persons think. Prof. Bain says: "A difficulty is solved, a mystery unriddled, when it can be shown to resemble something else; to be an example of a fact already known. Mystery is isolation, exception, or it may be apparent contradiction; the resolution of the mystery is found in assimilation, identity, fraternity. When all things are assimilated, so far as assimilation can go, so far as likeness holds, there is an end to explanation; there is an end to what the mind can do, or can intelligently desire. . . . The path of science, as exhibited in modern ages, is towards generality, wider and wider, until we reach the highest, the widest laws of every department of things; there explanation is finished, mystery ends, perfect vision is gained."

But unfortunately this first answer will not hold. Whether for good or evil, it is an empirical fact that the mind is so wedded to the process of seeing an *other* beside every item of its experience, that when the notion of an absolute datum which is all is presented to it, it goes through its usual procedure and remains *pointing* at the void beyond, as if in that lay further matter for contemplation. In short, it spins for itself the further positive consideration of a Nonentity enveloping the Being of its datum; and as that leads to no issue on the further side, back recoils the thought in a circle towards its datum again. But there is no logical identity, no natural bridge between nonentity and this particular datum, and the thought stands oscillating to and fro, wondering "Why was there anything but nonentity? Why just this universal datum and not another? Why anything at all?" and finds no end, in wandering mazes lost. Indeed, Prof. Bain's words are so untrue that in reflecting men it is just when the attempt to fuse the manifold into a single totality has been most successful, when the conception of the universe as a *fait unique* (in D'Alembert's words) is nearest its perfection, that the craving for further explanation, the ontological θαυμάζειν arises in its extremest pungency.

As Schopenhauer says, "The uneasiness which keeps the never-resting clock of metaphysics in motion, is the consciousness that the non-existence of this world is just as possible as its existence."[23]

The notion of Nonentity may thus be called the parent of the philosophic craving in its subtlest and profoundest sense. Absolute existence is absolute mystery. Although *selbstständig*, it is not *selbstverständlich*; for its relations with the Nothing remain unmediated to our understanding. One philosopher only, so far as I know, has pretended to throw a logical bridge over this chasm. Hegel, by trying to show that Nonentity and Being as actually determined are linked together by a series of successive identities, binds the whole of possible thought into an adamantine unity with no conceivable outlying notion to disturb the free rotary circulation of the mind within its bounds. Since such unchecked motion constitutes the feeling of rationality, he must be held, if he has succeeded, to have eternally and absolutely quenched all its logical demands.

But for those who, like most of us, deem Hegel's heroic effort to have failed, nought remains but to confess that when all has been unified to its supreme degree, (Prof. Bain to the contrary notwithstanding), the notions of a Nonentity, or of a possible Other than the actual, may still haunt our imagination and prey upon the ultimate data of our system. The bottom of Being is left logically opaque to us, a *datum* in the strict sense of the word, something which we simply come upon and find, and about which, (if we wish to act), we should pause and wonder as little as possible. In this confession lies the lasting truth of Empiricism, and in it Empiricism and imaginative Faith join hands. The logical attitude of both is identical, they both say there is a *plus ultra* beyond all we know, a womb of unimagined other possibility. They only differ in their sentimental temper: Empiricism says, "Into the *plus ultra* you have no right to carry your anthropomorphic affirmations"; Faith says, "You have no right to extend to it your denials." The mere ontologic emotion of wonder, of mystery, has in some minds such a tinge of the rapture of sublimity, that for this æsthetic reason alone, it will be difficult for any philosophic system completely to exorcise it.

In truth, the philosopher's logical tranquillity is after all in essence no other than the boor's. Their difference regards only the point at which each refuses to let further considerations upset

23 *Welt als Wille &c.*, 3 Auflage, I., p. 189.

the absoluteness of the data he assumes. The boor does so immediately, and is therefore liable at any moment to the ravages of many kinds of confusion and doubt. The philosopher does not do so till unity has been reached, and is therefore warranted against the inroads of *those* considerations—but only practically not essentially secure from the blighting breath of the *ultimate* "Why?" Positivism takes a middle ground, and with a certain consciousness of the beyond abruptly refuses by an inhibitory action of the will to think any further, stamps the ground and says "Physics, I espouse thee! for better or worse, be thou my absolute!"

The Absolute is what has not yet been transcended, criticized or made relative. So far from being something quintessential and unattainable as is so often pretended, it is practically the most familiar thing in life. Every thought is absolute to us at the moment of conceiving it or acting upon it. It only becomes relative in the light of further reflection. This may make it flicker and grow pale—the notion of nonentity may blow in from the infinite and extinguish the theoretic rationality of a universal datum. As regards this latter, absoluteness and rationality are in fact convertible terms. And the chief effort of the rationalizing philosopher must be to gain an absoluteness for his datum which shall be *stable* in the maximum degree, or as far as possible removed from exposure to those further considerations by which we saw that the vulgar *Weltanschauung* may so promptly be upset. I shall henceforward call the further considerations which may supervene and make relative or derationalize a mass of thought, the *reductive* of that thought. The reductive of absolute being is thus nonentity, or the notion of an *aliter possibile* which it involves. The reductive of an absolute physics is the thought that all material facts are representations in a mind. The reductive of absolute time, space, causality, atoms, &c., are the so-called antinomies which arise as soon as we think fully out the thoughts we have begun. The reductive of absolute knowledge is the constant potentiality of doubt, the notion that the next thought may always correct the present one—resulting in the notion that a noumenal world is there mocking the one we think we know. Whatever we think, some reductive seems in strict theoretic legitimacy always imminently hovering over our thought ready to blight it. Doubleness dismissed at the front door re-enters in the rear and spoils the rationality of the simple datum we flattered ourselves we had attained. Theoretically the task of the philosopher, if he cannot reconcile the datum with the reductive by the way of identification *à la* Hegel, is to exorcise the reductive so that the datum may hold up its head again and know no fear. Prof. Bain would no doubt say that nonentity was a pseud-idea not derived from experience and therefore meaningless, and so exorcise that reductive.[24] The antinomies may be exorcised by the distinction between potentiality and actuality.[25] The ordinary half educated materialist comforts himself against idealists by the notion that, after all, thought is such an obscure mystical form of existence that it is almost as bad as no existence at all, and need not be seriously taken into account by a sensible man.

If nothing else could be conceived than thoughts or fancies, these would be credited with the maximum of reality. Their reductive is the belief in an objective reality of which they are but copies. When this belief takes the form of the affirmation of a noumenal world contrasted with all possible thought, and therefore playing no other part than that of reductive pure and simple,—to discover the formula of exorcism becomes, and has been recognized ever since Kant to be, one of the principal tasks of philosophy rationally understood.

The reductive used by nominalists to discredit the self-identity of the same attribute in different phenomena is the notion of a still higher degree of identity. We easily exorcise this reductive by challenging them to show what the higher degree of sameness can possibly contain which is not already in the lower.

The notion of Nonentity is not only a reductive; it can assume upon occasion an exorcising function. If, for example, a man's ordinary mundane consciousness feels staggered at the improbability of an immaterial thinking-principle being the source of all things, Nonentity comes in and says, "Contrasted with me, (that is, considered simply as *existent*) one principle is as probable as another." If the same mundane consciousness recoils at the notion of providence towards individuals or individual immortality as involving, the one too infinite a subdivision of the divine atten-

---

[24] The author of *A Candid Examination of Theism* (Trübner, 1878) exorcises Nonentity by the notion of the all-excluding infinitude of Existence,—whether reasonably or not I refrain from deciding. The last chapter of this work (published a year after the present text was written), is on "the final Mystery of Things," and expresses in striking language much that I have said.

[25] See Renouvier: *Premier Essai.*

tion, the other a too infinite accumulation of population in the heavens, Nonentity says, "As compared with me all quantities are one: the wonder is all there when God has found it worth His while to guard or save a single soul."

But if the philosopher fails to find a satisfactory formula of exorcism for his datum, the only thing he can do is to "blink" the reductive at a certain point, assume the Given as his necessary ultimate, and proceed to a life whether of contemplation or of action based on that. There is no doubt that this half wilful act of arrest, this acting on an opaque necessity, is accompanied by a certain pleasure. See the reverence of Carlyle for brute fact: "There is an infinite significance in Fact." "Necessity," says a German philosopher,[26] and he means not rational but simply given necessity, "is the last and highest point that we can reach in a rational conception of the world. . . . It is not only the interest of ultimate and definitive knowledge, but also that of the feelings, to find a last repose and an ideal equilibrium, in an uttermost datum which can simply not be other than it is."

Such is the attitude of ordinary men in their theism, God's fiat being in physics and morals such an uttermost datum. Such also is the attitude of all hard-minded analysts and *Verstandesmenschen*. Renouvier and Hodgson, the two foremost contemporary philosophers, promptly say that of experience as a whole no account can be given, but do not seek to soften the abruptness of the confession or reconcile us with our impotence.

Such mediating attempts may be made by more mystical minds. The peace of rationality may be sought through ecstasy when logic fails. To religious persons of every shade of doctrine moments come when the world as it is seems so divinely orderly, and the acceptance of it by the heart so rapturously complete, that intellectual questions vanish, nay the intellect itself is hushed to sleep —as Wordsworth says, "Thought is not, in enjoyment it expires." Ontological emotion so fills the soul that ontological speculation can no longer overlap it and put her girdle of interrogation-marks around existence. Even the least religious of men must have felt with our national ontologic poet, Walt Whitman, when loafing on the grass on some transparent summer morning, that "Swiftly arose and spread around him the peace and knowledge that pass all the argument of the earth." At such moments of energetic liv-

26 Dühring: *Cursus der Philosophie*, Leipzig 1875, p. 35.

ing we feel as if there were something diseased and contemptible, yea vile, in theoretic grubbing and brooding. To feel "I *am* the truth" is to abolish the opposition between knowing and being.

Since the heart can thus wall out the ultimate irrationality which the head ascertains, the erection of its procedure into a systematized method would be a philosophic achievement of first-rate importance. As used by mystics hitherto it has lacked universality, being available for few persons and at few times, and even in these being apt to be followed by fits of "reaction" and "dryness"; but it may nevertheless be the forerunner of what will ultimately prove a true method. If all men could permanently say with Jacobi, "In my heart there is light," though they should for ever fail to give an articulate account of it, existence would really be rationalized.[27]

But if men should ever all agree that the mystical method is a subterfuge without logical pertinency, a plaster, but no cure, that the Hegelian method is fallacious, that the idea of Nonentity can therefore neither be exorcised nor identified, Empiricism will be the ultimate philosophy. Existence will be a brute Fact to which as a whole the emotion of ontologic wonder shall rightfully cleave, but remain eternally unsatisfied. This wonderfulness or mysteriousness will then be an essential attribute of the nature of things,

---

[27] A curious recent contribution to the construction of a universal mystical method is contained in the *Anæsthetic Revelation* by Benj. P. Blood (Amsterdam, N.Y., 1874). The author, who is a writer abounding in verbal felicities, thinks we may all grasp the secret of Being if we only intoxicate ourselves often enough with laughing-gas. "There is in the instant of recall from the anæsthetic stupor a moment in which the genius of being is revealed. . . . Patients try to speak of it but invariably fail in a lost mood of introspection. . . . But most will accept this as the central point of the illumination that sanity is not the basic quality of intelligence, . . . but that only in sanity is formal or contrasting thought, while the naked life is realized outside of sanity altogether. It is the instant contrast of this tasteless water of souls with formal thought as we *come to* that leaves the patient in an astonishment that the awful mystery of life is at last but a homely and common thing. . . . To minds of sanguine imagination there will be a sadness in the tenor of the mystery, as if the key-note of the universe were low—for no poetry, no emotion known to the normal sanity of man, can furnish a hint of its primeval prestige, and its all-but appalling solemnity; but for such as have felt sadly the instability of temporal things there is a comfort of serenity and ancient peace; while for the resolved and imperious spirit there are majesty and supremacy unspeakable." The logical characteristic of this state is said to be "an apodal sufficiency—to which sufficiency a wonder or fear of why it is sufficient cannot pertain and could be attributed only as an impossible disease or lack. . . . The disease of Metaphysics vanishes in the fading of the question and not in the coming of an answer."

and the exhibition and emphasizing of it will always continue to be an ingredient in the philosophic industry of the race. Every generation will produce its Job, its Hamlet, its Faust or its Sartor Resartus.

With this we seem to have exhausted all the possibilities of purely theoretic rationality. But we saw at the outset that when subjectively considered rationality can only be defined as perfectly unimpeded mental function. Impediments which arise in the purely theoretic sphere might perhaps be avoided if the stream of mental action should leave that sphere betimes and pass into the practical. The structural unit of mind is in these days, deemed to be a triad, beginning with a sensible impression, ending with a motion, and having a feeling of greater or less length in the middle. Perhaps the whole difficulty of attaining theoretic rationality is due to the fact that the very quest violates the nature of our intelligence, and that a passage of the mental function into the third stage before the second has come to an end in the *cul de sac* of its contemplation, would revive the energy of motion and keep alive the sense of ease and freedom which is its psychic counterpart. We must therefore inquire what constitutes the feeling of rationality in its *practical* aspect; but that must be done at another time and in another place.

NOTE.—This article is the first chapter of a psychological work on the motives which lead men to philosophize. It deals with the purely theoretic or logical impulse. Other chapters treat of practical and emotional motives and in the conclusion an attempt is made to use the motives as tests of the soundness of different philosophies.

Mr. Bradley on Immediate Resemblance

My agreement with Mr. Bradley that "the issue involved is one of very great and wide-reaching importance" must be my excuse for sending a word of comment on his paper in the January MIND. The text of his criticism is furnished by pp. 490–4, and 532–3 of vol. i. of my work *The Principles of Psychology*, and the exact question is this: Is the 'resemblance' which we predicate of two objects due in the last resort always to the operations on our mind of qualitatively identical elements contained in each? Or, may we, on the other hand, admit the existence, amongst our mind's objects, of qualities or natures which have no definite 'point' in common, but which we perceive to be, although numerically distinct, yet *like* each other in various degrees and ways? We so often discover later the exact point of resemblance in two composite objects which first struck us by their likeness as vague wholes, and we are so often able to name it as an identical portion in both, that the temptation to generalize lies very near; and we then say that there can nowhere be natures *immediately* like or unlike each other, and that every case of so-called similarity, even the simplest, must constitute a problem in analysis, which a higher discernment might solve. But since the higher discernment, methodically abandoned to this analytic quest, ought not to stop at any elements of which resemblance is simply affirmed (for the 'point' of this resemblance must then also be sought), it is obvious that the problem can only lead to one of two conclusions, either to

(1) The postulation of point after point, encapsulated within each other *in infinitum*, as the constitutive condition of the resemblance of any two objects; or to

(2) A last kind of element (if one could then say 'kind') of whose self-compoundings all the objects, and of whose diverse *numbers* in the objects, all the likeness and unlikeness in the world are made.

Of these two views of resemblance the former leads to a sort of Leibnitzian metaphysics, and the latter to what I call the Mind-dust theory.

My solution, or rather Stumpf's (for in my book I am but the humble follower of the eminent Munich psychologist), was to take neither of these objectionable alternatives, but (challenging the hasty hypothesis that composition must explain all) to admit

(3) That the last elements of things may differ variously, and that their 'kinds' and bare unmediated resemblances and contrasts may be ultimate data of our world as well as provisional categories of our perception.

Mr. Bradley is dissatisfied both with this thesis,[1] and with the arguments given in my book to support it. I care much more about the thesis than about the arguments, so I will spare the reader all cavil at my critic's treatment of the latter. In particular I abandon the *series*-business to his mercy, as being something inessential, for I am much more concerned with furthering understanding of the subject than with defending my own text.[2] As regards the thesis itself, Mr. Bradley quarrels greatly with the *simplicity of the elements* between which in the last resort it contends that bare unmediated resemblance may obtain. I did, it is true, assume in my text that the elements were simple, and I called them simple qualities, but I regard that as an entirely inessential point. So far as my

[1] Or have I made a gross blunder, and is he dissatisfied really not with 'simple resemblance' but only with 'resemblance between simples,' on which, as I presently explain, I do not insist?

[2] One misapprehension, however, I may complain of. Mr. Bradley seems to accuse me of believing that the 'points of resemblance' which form the ground of similarity must be 'separable' parts of the similar things. *Discernible* parts are all that the argument requires; and I surely never implied that the 'points' in question must be susceptible of physical isolation. The accusation is so absurd that I fear I have not understood Mr. Bradley's text.

thesis stands up for ultimate unmediated likeness as against likeness dependent on partially identical content, it makes no difference whether the last elements assumed to be like, be simple or complex. They must only not contain any identical point. In other words, complexes like *abc* and *def* might resemble each other by principle (3) as well as simple elements like *a* and *b*.

This clears up one confusion. But dire confusion still remains in my mind as to the rest of what Mr. Bradley may mean. He has a solution of his own which is like neither (1), (2), nor (3) as propounded above. He alludes to it abundantly, but dispenses himself from stating it articulately, or illustrating it by any example, because it proceeds from a principle which he imagines to be "the common property of philosophical students." Such oracular expression of opinion might fairly exempt one from the duty of nearer research, but the great debt I owe to Mr. Bradley's *Logic* makes me struggle in the hope of yet finding valuable truth. Mr. Bradley appears to hold that all likeness must be "in and through a particular point"—at least he says so on page 85. Now call the 'point' *m*, and the two like objects *a* and *b*. If the *m* in *a* were simply *like* the *m* in *b*, that would be that simple resemblance over again with which Mr. Bradley is not content. But if we suppose the two *m*'s to be alike by virtue of another 'point,' finer still, that leads to infinite regress; and that again I understand Mr. Bradley not to favor. It then would remain open to say that the two *m*'s in *a* and *b* are *identical* in nature and only numerically distinct. But here again pure identity displeases Mr. Bradley, whose great principle is that "our one chance lies in maintaining the vital, the inseparable, connexion at every point between identity and difference" (bottom of p. 88). Just how this principle works in the matter in question, Mr. Bradley does not divulge, and I wish that, instead of his pleasant irony about my familiarity with the dialectical method, he had himself given some exacter account. I have labored with the greatest good-will to reconstruct his thought, but feel wholly at sea with my results. If he means simply the Hegelian commonplace that since neither the abstract sameness nor the abstract otherness of two objects can constitute likeness between them, the likeness must seek in the 'synthesis' of the sameness with the otherness its only possible mode of realization, that seems but an excessively clumsy way of stating in terms of a *quasi*-miracle the very truth which Stumpf and I express by saying that likeness is an immediately ascertained relation. You cannot for ever analytically exhibit its *ground*, but must somewhere at last postulate it as there, as having already effected itself, you know not how. Nothing is gained for our understanding by presenting the process as a sort of juggler's trick, that, namely, of the seemingly impossible coalescence of two contradictory terms; and therefore I cannot believe that the subtle Mr. Bradley has anything as innocent as that in his mind. Perhaps what I write may draw him from his reserve!

Of course there is a familiar path open to those who believe that likeness must be "in and through a particular point," and who yet deny that the 'point' can be in two objects the *same*. They can call likeness an 'Antinomy'; saying that all likeness of wholes is conditioned on that of their metaphysical parts, but that unconditionally like parts are unattainable, however long one may seek. But this leaves both immediate likeness and apparent identity as ever-recurring categories in our thinking, never to be expelled from our empirical world, and I submit that Mr. Bradley has not yet shown these categories to be absurd. 'Antinomies' should surely not be multiplied beyond necessity. The qualities of the things of this world, the 'terms' between which likenesses and differences obtain, are not supposed to be engendered by the summation of a procession of still more inward qualities involved within each other in infinite regression, like the whirls of an endlessly converging spiral that never reaches its central point. Why need we insist that the 'relations' between the terms, the likenesses and differences themselves, must be engendered by such an impossible summation or synthesis? How quality logically *makes itself*, we do not know; and we know no more in the case of the quality of a relation of likeness, than in that of the quality of a sensational content.

Immediate Resemblance

May another word be permitted in reply to Mr. Bradley's second utterance on this subject, as possibly helping to clear up the dispute? My point of view was merely psychological in contending, as I did in my book, for the admission of immediate resemblance as an ultimate category of our perception, and of comparison as an ultimate function of our thought. The doctrine (made so plausible by familiar examples) that all resemblances must be analyzable into identities concealed under non-identities, I showed could not be extended to every imaginable case. Mr. Bradley now says that immediate resemblance without identity seems to him "sheer nonsense," and that to deny the principle of Identity is to destroy the world, and he challenges me again to "state the principle" on which I "object to identity." To which challenge I can only reply that to Identity as such I have no objection in the world, and am astonished that any one should suspect me of such an irrational aversion. Every act of reasoning, every bit of analysis, proves the practical utility and the psychological necessity of the assumption that identical characters may be 'encapsulated' in different things. But I say that there must be *some* things whose resemblance is *not* based on such discernible and abstractable identity. Now, the identity on which Mr. Bradley himself thinks that the resemblance between all things must be based is no such abstractable identity. It is not separable, it is not even discernible, he says, from difference.

It is only one aspect of an integral whole on which you may lay stress for a moment, but if you abstract it, or put it ideally in a box by itself, you make it self-inconsistent, or reduce it to nothing. But an 'identity' thus conceived is so different a thing from the stark self-sameness which 'identity' denotes in logic, that it seems unfortunate to describe it by the same name. The usual English name for that sort of identity between two things which you cannot abstract or distinguish from their difference is their 'resemblance.' So that Mr. Bradley now makes perfectly clear that in seeming to attack Prof. Stumpf's and my doctrine he is but reaffirming it under a changed name. When he insists that every resemblance must have for its inner ground an 'identity' thus complicatedly conceived, he is like a man who should say "every resemblance must have for its inner ground the resemblance itself." Why, such being the case, he should quarrel with me I cannot fathom: for this is exactly the opinion I have myself stood up for in all simple cases. Can it be the word 'simple' which has caused all the trouble?—for I believe that in my book I did heedlessly use the expression 'simple resemblance' in one place. But I never meant thereby to imply that the simplest phenomenon of resemblance might not seem, when contemplated long enough, fairly to curdle and swim with inner complexity, to embody inseparable oppositions, or whatever more of vital mystery any one may find. The simplest ideas, as I meant to use the word simple, begin to look the queerest when gazed at in this way. But such gazing is a 'metaphysical' occupation, in which we shall all indulge, I am sure, with the greatest profit, when Mr. Bradley's new book comes out. *I* never meant to go beyond psychology; and on that relatively superficial plane I now confidently greet Mr. Bradley, no longer as the foe which by a mere verbal ambiguity he has seemed, but as a powerful and welcome ally.

The Knowing of Things Together[1]

1 Read as the President's Address before the American Psychological Association at Princeton, December, 1894, and reprinted with some unimportant omissions, a few slight revisions, and the addition of some explanatory notes.

I

The nature of the synthetic unity of consciousness is one of those great underlying problems that divide the psychological schools. We know, say, a dozen things singly through a dozen different mental states. But on another occasion we may know the same dozen things together through a single mental state. The problem is as to the relation of the previous many states to the later one state. In physical nature, it is universally agreed, a multitude of facts always remain the multitude they were and appear as one fact only when a mind comes upon the scene and so views them, as when H–O–H appear as 'water' to a human spectator. But when, instead of extramental 'things,' the mind combines its own 'contents' into a unity, what happens is much less plain.

The matters of fact that give the trouble are among our most familiar experiences. We know a lot of friends and can think of each one singly. But we can also think of them together, as composing a 'party' at our house. We can see single stars appearing in succession between the clouds on a stormy night, but we can also see whole constellations of those stars at once when the wind has blown the clouds away. In a glass of lemonade we can taste both the lemon and the sugar at once. In a major chord our ear can single out the *c, e, g,* and *c'*, if it has once become acquainted with these notes apart. And so on through the whole field of our experience, whether conceptual or sensible. Neither common sense nor commonplace psychology finds anything special to explain in these facts. Common sense simply says the mind 'brings the things together,' and common psychology says the 'ideas' of the various things 'combine,' and at most will admit that the occasions on which ideas combine may be made the subject of inquiry. But to formulate the phenomenon of knowing things together thus simply as a combining of ideas, is already to foist in a theory about the phenomenon. Not so should a question be approached. The phenomenon offers itself, in the first instance, as that of *knowing things together*; and it is in those terms that its solution must, in the first instance at least, be sought.

'Things,' then; to 'know' things; and to know the 'same' things 'together' which elsewhere we knew singly—here, indeed, are terms concerning each of which we must put the question, 'What do we *mean* by it when we use it?'—that question that Shadworth Hodgson lays so much stress on, and that is so well taught to students, as the beginning of all sound method, by our colleague Fullerton. And in exactly ascertaining what we do mean by such terms there might lie a lifetime of occupation.

For we do mean something; and we mean something true. Our terms, whatever confusion they may connote, denote at least a fundamental fact of our experience, whose existence no one here present will deny.

II

What, then, do we mean by 'things'? To this question I can only make the answer of the idealistic philosophy. For the philosophy that began with Berkeley, and has led up in our tongue to Shadworth Hodgson, things have no other nature than thoughts have, and we know of no things that are not given to somebody's experience. When I see the thing white paper before my eyes, the nature of the thing and the nature of my sensations are one. Even if with science we supposed a molecular architecture beneath the smooth whiteness of the paper, that architecture itself could only be defined as the stuff of a farther possible experience, a vision, say, of certain vibrating particles with which our acquaintance with the paper would terminate if it were prolonged by magnifying artifices not yet known. A thing may be my phenomenon or some one else's; it may be frequently or infrequently experienced; it may be shared by all of us; one of our copies of it may be regarded as the original, and the other copies as representatives of that original; it may appear very differently at different times; but whatever it be, the stuff of which it is made is thought-stuff, and whenever we speak of a thing that is out of our own mind, we either mean nothing; or we mean a thing that was or will be in our own mind on another occasion; or, finally, we mean a thing in the mind of some other possible receiver of experiences like ours.

Such being 'things,' what do we mean by saying that we 'know' them?

There are two ways of knowing things, knowing them immediately or intuitively, and knowing them conceptually or representatively. Although such things as the white paper before our eyes can be known intuitively, most of the things we know, the tigers now in India, for example, or the scholastic system of philosophy, are known only representatively or symbolically.

Suppose, to fix our ideas, that we take first a case of conceptual knowledge; and let it be our knowledge of the tigers in India, as we sit here. Exactly what do we *mean* by saying that we here know the tigers? What is the precise fact that the cognition so confidently claimed is *known-as*, to use Shadworth Hodgson's inelegant but valuable form of words?

Most men would answer that what we mean by knowing the tigers is having them, however absent in body, become in some way present to our thought; or that our knowledge of them is known as presence of our thought to them. A great mystery is usually made of this peculiar presence in absence; and the scholastic philosophy, which is only common sense grown pedantic, would explain it as a peculiar kind of existence, called *intentional inexistence*, of the tigers in our mind. At the very least, people would say that what we mean by knowing the tigers is mentally *pointing* towards them as we sit here.

But now what do we mean by *pointing*, in such a case as this? What is the pointing known-as, here?

To this question I shall have to give a very prosaic answer—one that traverses the prepossessions not only of common sense and scholasticism, but also those of nearly all the epistemological writers whom I have ever read. The answer, made brief, is this: The pointing of our thought to the tigers is known simply and solely as a procession of mental associates and motor consequences that follow on the thought, and that would lead harmoniously, if followed out, into some ideal or real context, or even into the immediate presence, of the tigers. It is known as our rejection of a jaguar, if that beast were shown us as a tiger; as our assent to a genuine tiger if so shown. It is known as our ability to utter all sorts of propositions which don't contradict other propositions that are true of the real tigers. It is even known, if we take the tigers very seriously, as actions of ours which may terminate in directly intuited tigers, as they would if we took a voyage to India for the purpose of tiger-hunting and brought back a lot of skins of the striped rascals which we had laid low. In all this there is no self-transcendency in our mental images taken by themselves. They are one physical fact; the tigers are another; and their pointing to the tigers is a perfectly commonplace physical relation, if you once grant a connecting world to be there. In short, the ideas and the tigers are in themselves as loose and separate, to use Hume's language, as any two things can be; and pointing means here an operation as external and adventitious as any that nature yields.[2]

I hope you may agree with me now that in representative knowledge there is no special inner mystery, but only an outer chain of physical or mental intermediaries connecting thought and thing. *To know an object is here to lead to it through a context which the world supplies.* All this was most instructively set forth by our colleague Miller, of Bryn Mawr, at our meeting in New York last Christmas, and for re-confirming my sometime wavering opinion, I owe him this acknowledgment.[3]

Let us next pass on to the case of immediate or intuitive acquaintance with an object, and let the object be the white paper before our eyes. The thought-stuff and the thing-stuff are here indistin-

---

[2] A stone in one field may 'fit,' we say, a hole in another field. But the relation of 'fitting,' so long as no one carries the stone to the hole and drops it in, is only one name for the fact that such an act may happen. Similarly with the knowing of the tigers here and now. It is only an anticipatory name for a further associative and terminative process that may occur.

[3] See also Dr. Miller's article on Truth and Error, in the *Philosophical Review*, July, 1893.

guishably the same in nature, as we saw a moment since, and there is no context of intermediaries or associates to stand between and separate the thought and thing. There is no 'presence in absence' here, and no 'pointing,' but rather an allround embracing of the paper by the thought; and it is clear that the knowing cannot now be explained exactly as it was when the tigers were its object. Dotted all through our experience are states of immediate acquaintance just like this. Somewhere our belief always does rest on ultimate data like the whiteness, smoothness, or squareness of this paper. Whether such qualities be truly ultimate aspects of being or only provisional suppositions of ours, held-to till we get better informed, is quite immaterial for our present inquiry. So long as it is believed in, we see our object face to face. What now do we mean by 'knowing' such a sort of object as this? For this is also the way in which we should know the tiger if our conceptual idea of him were to terminate by having led us to his lair?

This address must not become too long, so I must give my answer in the fewest words. And let me first say this: So far as the white paper or other ultimate datum of our experience may be considered to enter also into some one else's experience, and we, in knowing it, are held to know it there as well as here; so far again as it may be considered to be a mere mask for hidden molecules that other now impossible experiences of our own might some day lay bare to view; so far it is a case of tigers in India again, for, the things known being absent experiences, the knowing can only consist in passing smoothly towards them through the intermediary context that the world supplies. But if our own private vision of the paper be considered in abstraction from every other event, as if it constituted by itself the universe (and it might perfectly well do so, for aught we can understand to the contrary), then the paper seen and the seeing of it are only two names for one indivisible fact which, properly named, is *the datum, the phenomenon, or the experience.* The paper is in the mind and the mind is around the paper, because paper and mind are only two names that are given later to the one experience, when, taken in a larger world of which it forms a part, its connections are traced in different directions.[4] *To know*

---

[4] What is meant by this is that 'the experience' can be referred to either of two great associative systems, that of the experiencer's mental history, or that of the experienced facts of the world. Of both of these systems it forms part, and may be

immediately, then, or intuitively, is for mental content and object to be identical. This is a very different definition from that which we gave of representative knowledge; but neither definition involves those mysterious notions of self-transcendency and presence in absence which are such essential parts of the ideas of knowledge, both of common men and of philosophers. Is there no experience that can justify these notions, and show us somewhere their original?

I think the mystery of presence in absence (though we fail to find it between one experience and another remote experience to which it points, or between the 'content' and 'object' of any one experience falsely rent asunder by the application to it of these two separate names) may yet be found, and found between the parts of a single experience. Let us look for it, accordingly, in its simplest possible form. What is the smallest experience in which the mystery remains? If we seek, we find that there is no datum so small as not to show the mystery. The smallest effective pulse of consciousness, whatever else it may be consciousness of, is also consciousness of passing time. The tiniest feeling that we can possibly have involves for future reflection two sub-feelings, one earlier and the other later, and a sense of their continuous procession. All this has been admirably set forth by Mr. Shadworth Hodgson,[5] who shows that there is literally no such datum as that

---

regarded, indeed, as one of their points of intersection. One might let a vertical line

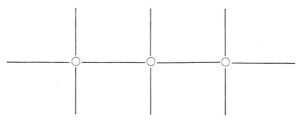

stand for the mental history; but the same object, O, appears also in the mental history of different persons, represented by the other vertical lines. It thus ceases to be the private property of one experience, and becomes, so to speak, a shared or public thing. We can track its outer history in this way, and represent it by the horizontal line. [It is also known representatively at other points of the vertical lines, or intuitively there again, so that the line of its outer history would have to be looped and wandering, but I make it straight for simplicity's sake.] In any case, however, it is the same *stuff* that figures in all the sets of lines.

[5] *Philosophy of Reflection*, Vol. I, p. 248 ff.

of the present moment, and no such content, and no such object, except as an unreal postulate of abstract thought. The *passing* moment is the only thing that ever concretely was or is or shall be; and in the phenomenon of elementary memory, whose function is to apprehend it, earlier and later are present to each other in an experience that feels either only on condition of feeling both together.

We have the same knowing together in the matter that fills the time. The rush of our thought forward through its fringes is the everlasting peculiarity of its life. We realize this life as something always off its balance, something in transition, something that shoots out of a darkness through a dawn into a brightness that we know to be the dawn fulfilled. In the very midst of the alteration our experience comes as one continuous fact. 'Yes,' we say at the moment of full brightness, *this* is what I meant. No, we feel at the moment of the dawning, this is not yet the meaning, there is more to come. In every crescendo of sensation, in every effort to recall, in every progress towards the satisfaction of desire, this succession of an emptiness and fulness that have reference to each other and are one flesh is the essence of the phenomenon. In every hindrance of desire the sense of an absent, which the only function of the present is to *mean*, is even more notoriously there. And in the movement of thoughts not ordinarily classed as involving desire, we have the same phenomenon. When I say *Socrates is mortal*, the moment *Socrates* is incomplete; it falls forward through the *is* which is pure movement, into the *mortal*, which is indeed bare mortal on the tongue, but for the mind, is *that mortal*, the *mortal Socrates*, at last satisfactorily disposed of and told off.

Here, then, inside of the minimal pulse of experience which, taken as object, is change of feeling, and, taken as content, is feeling of change, is realized that absolute and essential self-transcendency which we swept away as an illusion when we sought it between a content taken as a whole and a supposed objective thing outside. *Here in the elementary datum of which both our physical and our mental worlds are built, we find included both the original of presence in absence and the prototype of that operation of knowing many things together which it is our business to discuss.*[6] For

[6] It seems to me that we have here something like what comes before us in the psychology of space and time. Our original intuition of space is the single field of view; our original intuition of time covers but a few seconds; yet by an ideal piecing

the fact that past and future are already parts of the least experience that can really be, is just like what we find in any other case of an experience whose parts are many. Most of these experiences are of objects perceived to be simultaneous and not to be immediately successive as in the heretofore considered case. The field of view, the chord of music, the glass of lemonade are examples. But the gist of the matter is the same—it is always knowing-together. You cannot separate the consciousness of one part from that of all the rest. What is given is pooled and mutual; there is no dark spot, no point of ignorance; no one fraction is eclipsed from any other's point of view. Can we account for such a being-known-together of complex facts like these?

The general *nature* of it we can probably never account for, or tell how such a unity in manyness can be, for it seems to be the ultimate essence of all experience, and anything less than it apparently cannot be at all. But the particular *conditions* whereby we know particular things together might conceivably be traced, and to that humble task I beg leave to devote the time that remains.

III

Let me say forthwith that I have no pretension to give any positive solution. My sole ambition now is, by a little classification, to smooth the ground somewhat so that some of you, more able than I, may be helped to advance, before our next meeting perhaps, to results that I cannot obtain.

---

together and construction we frame the notions of immensity and eternity, and suppose dated events and located things therein, of whose actual intervals we grasp no distinct idea. So in the case before us. The way in which the constituents of one undivided datum drag each other in and run into one, saying *this* is what *that* means, gives us our original intuition of what knowing is. That intuition we extend and constructively build up into the notion of a vast tissue of knowledge, shed along from experience to experience until, dropping the intermediary data from our thought, we assume that terms the most remote still know each other, just after the fashion of the parts of the prototypal fact. Cognition here is only constructive, as we have already seen. But he who should say, arguing from its nature here, that it nowhere is direct, and seek to construct it without an originally given pattern, would be like those psychologists who profess to develop our idea of space out of the association of data that possess no original extensity. Grant the *sort* of thing that is meant by presence in absence, by self-transcendency, by reference to another, by pointing forward or back, by knowledge in short, somewhere in our experience, be it in ever so small a corner, and the construction of pseudo-cases elsewhere follows as a matter of course. But to get along without the real thing *anywhere* seems difficult indeed.

Now, the first thing that strikes us in these complex cases is that the condition by which one thing may come to be known together with other things is an *event*. It is often an event of the purely physical order. A man walks suddenly into my field of view, and forthwith becomes part of it. I put a drop of cologne-water on my tongue, and, holding my nostrils, get the taste of it alone, but when I open my nostrils I get the smell together with the taste in mutual suffusion. Here it would seem as if a sufficient condition of the knowing of (say) three things together were the fact that the three several physical conditions of the knowing of each of them were realized at once. But in many other cases we find on the contrary that the physical conditions are realized without the things being known together at all. When absorbed in experiments with the cologne-water, for example, the clock may strike, and I not know that it has struck. But again, some seconds after the striking has elapsed, I may, by a certain shifting of what we call my attention, hark back to it and resuscitate the sound, and even count the strokes in memory. The condition of knowing the clock's striking is here an event of the mental order which must be added to the physical event of the striking before I can know it and the cologne-water at once. Just so in the field of view I may entirely overlook and fail to notice even so important an object as a man, until the inward event of altering my attention makes me suddenly see him with the other objects there. In those curious phenomena of dissociation of consciousness with which recent studies of hypnotic, hysteric and trance-states have made us familiar (phenomena which surely throw more new light on human nature than the work of all the psycho-physical laboratories put together), the event of hearing a 'suggestion,' or the event of passing into trance or out of it, is what decides whether a human figure shall appear in the field of view or disappear, and whether a whole set of memories shall come before the mind together, along with its other objects, or be excluded from their company. There is in fact no possible object, however completely fulfilled may be the outer condition of its perception, whose entrance into a given field of consciousness does not depend on the additional inner event called attention.

Now, it seems to me that this need of a final inner event, over and above the mere sensorial conditions, quite refutes and disposes of the associationist theory of the unity of consciousness. By associationist theory, I mean any theory that says, either implicitly or explicitly, that for a lot of objects to be known together, it suffices that a lot of conscious states, each with one of them as its content, should exist, as James Mill says, 'synchronically.' Synchronical existence of the ideas does not suffice, as the facts we now have abundantly show. Gurney's, Binet's and Janet's proofs of several dissociated consciousnesses existing synchronically, and dividing the subject's field of knowledge between them, is the best possible refutation of any such view.

Union in consciousness must be *made* by something, must be brought about; and to have perceived this truth is the great merit of the anti-associationist psychologists.[7] The form of unity, they have obstinately said, must be specially accounted for; and the form of unity the radical associationists have as obstinately shied away from and ignored, though their accounts of those preliminary conditions that supply the matters to be united have never been surpassed. As far as these go, we are all, I trust, associationists, and reverers of the names of Hartley, Mill, and Bain.

Let us now rapidly review the chief attempts of the anti-associationists to fill the gap they discern so well in the associationist tale.

1. *Attention.*—Attention, we say, by turning to an object, includes it with the rest; and the naming of this faculty in action has by some writers been considered a sufficient account of the decisive 'event.'[8] But it is plain that the act of Attention itself needs a farther account to be given, and such an account is what other theories of the event implicitly give.

We find four main types[9] of other theory of how particular

---

[7] In this rapid paper I content myself with arguing from the experimental fact that something *happens* over and above the realization of sensorial conditions, wherever an object adds itself to others already 'before the mind.' I say nothing of the logical self-contradiction involved in the associationist doctrine that the two facts, 'A is known,' and 'B is known,' *are* the third fact, 'A + B are known together.' Those whom the criticisms already extant in print of this strange belief have failed to convince, would not be persuaded, even though one rose from the dead. The appeal to the actual facts of dissociation may make impression, however, even on such hardened hearts as theirs.

[8] It might seem natural to mention Wundt's doctrine of 'Apperception' here. But I must confess my inability to say anything about it that would not resolve itself into a tedious comparison of texts. Being alternately described as intellection, will, feeling, synthesis, analysis, principle and result, it is too 'protean' a function to lend itself to any simplified account at second hand.

[9] It is only for the sake of completeness that we need mention such notions of a sort of mechanical and chemical activity between the ideas as we find in Herbart, Steinthal and others. These authors see clearly that mere synchronical existence is

things get known together, a physiological, a psychological, an animistic, and a transcendentalist type. Of the physiological or 'psycho-physical' type many varieties are possible, but it must be observed that none of them pretends to assign anything more than an empirical law. A psycho-physical theory can couple certain antecedent conditions with their result; but an explanation, in the sense of an inner reason why the result should have the nature of one content with many parts instead of some entirely different nature, is what a psycho-physical theory cannot give.[10]

2. *Reminiscence.*—Now, empirically, we have learned that things must be known in succession and singly before they can be known together.[11] If A, B, and C, for example, were outer things that came for the first time and affected our senses all at once, we should get one content from the lot of them and make no discriminations. The content would symbolically point to the objects A, B, C, and eventually terminate there, but would contain no parts that were immediately apprehended as standing for A, B, and C severally. Let A, B, and C stand for pigments, or for a tone and its overtones, and you will see what I mean when I say that the first result on consciousness of their falling together on the eye or ear would be a single new kind of feeling rather than a feeling with three kinds of inner part. Such a result has been ascribed to a 'fusion' of the three feelings of A, B, and C; but there seems no ground for supposing that, under the conditions assumed, these distinct feelings have ever been aroused at all. I should call the

---

not combination, and attribute to the ideas dynamic influences upon each other; pressures and resistances according to Herbart, and according to Steinthal 'psychic attractions.' But the philosophical foundations of such physical theories have been so slightly discussed by their authors that it is better to treat them only as rhetorical metaphors and pass on. Herbart, moreover, must also be mentioned later, along with the animistic writers.

10 We find this impotence already when we seek the conditions of the passing pulse of consciousness, which, as we saw, always involves time and change. We account for the passing pulse, physiologically, by the overlapping of dying and dawning brain-processes; and at first sight the elements time and change, involved in both the brain-processes and their mental result, give a similarity that, we feel, might be the real reason for the psycho-physic coupling. But the moment we ask 'metaphysical' questions—"Why not each brain-process felt apart?—Why just this amount of time, neither more nor less?" etc., etc.—we find ourselves falling back on the empirical view as the only safe one to defend.

11 The latest empirical contribution to this subject, with which I am acquainted, is Dr. Herbert Nichols' excellent little monograph, *Our Notions of Number and Space*, Boston, Ginn & Co., 1894.

phenomenon one of *indiscriminate knowing together*, for the most we can say under the circumstances is that the content resembles somewhat each of the objects A, B, and C, and knows them each potentially, knows them, that is, by possibly leading to each smoothly hereafter, as we know Indian tigers even whilst sitting in this room.

But if our memory possess stored-up images of former A-s, B-s, and C-s, experienced in isolation, we get an altogether different content, namely, one through which we know A, B, and C together, and yet know each of them in discrimination through one of the content's own parts. This has been called a 'colligation' or *Verknüpfung* of the 'ideas' of A, B, and C, to distinguish it from the aforesaid fusion. Whatever we may call it, we see that its physiological condition is more complex than in the previous case. In both cases the outer objects, A, B, and C, exert their effects on the sensorium. But in this case there is a coöperation of higher tracts of memory which in the former case was absent. *Discriminative knowing-together, in short, involves higher processes of reminiscence.* Do these give the element of manyness, whilst the lower sensorial processes that by themselves would result in mere 'fusion,' give the unity to the experience? The suggestion is one that might repay investigation, although it has against it two pretty solid objections: first, that in man the consciousness attached to infra-cortical centres is altogether subliminal, if it exist; and, second, that in the cortex itself we have not yet discriminated sensorial from ideational processes. Possibly the frontal lobes, in which Wundt has supposed an *Apperceptionsorgan*, might serve a turn here. In any case it is certain that, into our present rough notions of the cortical functions, the future will have to weave distinctions at present unknown.

3. *Synergy.*—The theory that, physiologically, the oneness precedes the manyness, may be contrasted with a theory that our colleagues Baldwin and Münsterberg are at present working out, and which places the condition of union of many data into one datum, in the fact that the many pour themselves into one motor discharge. The motor discharge being the last thing to happen, the condition of manyness would physiologically here precede and that of oneness follow. A printed word is apprehended as one object, at the same time that each letter in it is apprehended as one of its parts. Our secretary, Cattell, long ago discovered that we

recognize words of four or five letters by the eye as quickly, or even more quickly, than we recognize single letters. Recognition means here the motor process of articulation; and the quickness comes from the fact that all the letters in the particular combination unhesitatingly coöperate in the one articulatory act. I suppose such facts as these to lie at the base of our colleagues' theories, which probably differ in detail, and which it would be manifestly unjust to discuss or guess about in advance of their completer publication. Let me only say that I hope the latter may not be long delayed.

These are the only types of physiological theory worthy of mention. I may next pass to what, for brevity's sake, may be called *psychological accounts* of the event that lets an object into consciousness, or, by not occurring, leaves it out. These accounts start from the fact that what figures as part of a larger object is often perceived to have relations to the other parts. Accordingly the event in question is described as an *act of relating thought*. It takes two forms.

4. *Relating to Self.*—Some authors say that nothing can enter consciousness except on condition that it be related to the self. Not *object*, but *object-plus-me*, is the minimum knowable.

5. *Relating to other Objects.*—Others think it enough if the incoming object be related to the other objects already there. To fail to appear related is to fail to be known at all. To appear related is to appear with other objects. If relations were correlates of special cerebral processes, the addition of these to the sensorial processes would be the wished-for event. But brain physiology as yet knows nothing of such special processes, so I have called this explanation purely psychological. There seem to be fatal objections to it as a universal statement, for the reference to self, if it exist, must in a host of cases be altogether subconscious; and introspection assures us that in many half-waking and half-drunken states the relations between things that we perceive together may be of the dimmest and most indefinable kind.

6. *The Individual Soul.*—So we next proceed to *the animistic account.* By this term I mean to cover every sort of individualistic soul-theory. I will say nothing of older opinions; but in modern times we have two views of the way in which the union of a many by a soul occurs. For Herbart, for example, it occurs because the soul itself *is* unity, and all its *Selbsterhaltungen* are obliged to

necessarily share this form. For our colleague Ladd, on the other hand, to take the best recent example, it occurs because the soul, which *is* a real unity indeed, furthermore performs a unifying *act* on the naturally separate data of sense—an act, moreover, for which no psycho-physical analogon can be found. It must be admitted that much of the reigning bias against the soul in so-called scientific circles is an unintelligent prejudice, traceable far more to a vague impression that it is a theological superstition than to exact logical grounds. The soul is an 'entity,' and, indeed, that worst sort of entity, a 'scholastic entity'; and, moreover, it is something to be damned or saved; so let's have no more of it! I am free to confess that in my own case the antipathy to the Soul with which I find myself burdened is an ancient hardness of heart of which I can frame no fully satisfactory account even to myself. I passively agree that if there were Souls that we could use as principles of explanation, the *formal* settlement of the questions now before us could run far more smoothly towards its end. I admit that a soul is a medium of union, and that brain-processes and ideas, be they never so 'synchronical,' leave all mediating agency out. Yet, in spite of these concessions, I never find myself actively taking up the soul, so to speak, and making it do work in my psychologizing. I speak of myself here because I am one amongst many, and probably few of us can give adequate reasons for our dislike. The more honor to our colleague from Yale, then, that he remains so unequivocally faithful to this unpopular principle! And let us hope that his forthcoming book may sweep what is blind in our hostility away.[12]

But all is not blind in our hostility. When, for example, you say that A, B, and C, which are distinct contents on other occasions, are now on this occasion joined into the compound content ABC

[12] I ought, perhaps, to apologize for not expunging from my printed text these references to Professor Ladd, which were based on the impression left on my mind by the termination of his *Physiological Psychology*. It would now appear from the paper read by him at the Princeton meeting, and his *Philosophy of Mind*, just published, that he disbelieves in the Soul of old-fashioned ontology; and on looking again at the *P. P.*, I see that I may well have misinterpreted his deeper meaning there. I incline to suspect, however, that he had himself not fully disentangled it when that work was written; and that between now and then his thought has been evolving somewhat as Lotze's did between his *Medical Psychology* and his *Metaphysic*. It is gratifying to note these converging tendencies in different philosophers; but I leave the text as I read it at Princeton, as a mark of what one could say not so very unnaturally at that date.

by a unifying act of the soul, you say little more than that now they *are* united, unless you give some hint as to *how* the soul unites them. When, for example, the hysteric women whom Pierre Janet has studied with such loving care, go to pieces mentally, and their souls are unable any longer to connect the data of their experience together, though these data remain severally conscious in dissociation, what is the condition on which this inability of the soul depends? Is it an impotence in the soul itself? or is it an impotence in the physiological conditions, which fail to stimulate the soul sufficiently to its synthetic task? The *how* supposes on the Soul's part a constitution adequate to the act. An hypothesis, we are told in the logic-books, ought to propose a being that has some other constitution and definition than that of barely performing the phenomenon it is evoked to explain. When physicists propose the 'ether,' for example, they propose it with a lot of incidental properties. But the soul proposed to us has no special properties or constitution of which we are informed. Nevertheless, since particular conditions do determine its activity, it must have a constitution of some sort. In either case, we ought to know the facts. But the soul-doctrine, as hitherto professed, not only doesn't answer such questions, it doesn't even ask them; and it must be radically rejuvenated if it expects to be greeted again as a useful principle in psychological philosophy. Here is work for our spiritualist colleagues, not only for the coming year, but for the rest of their lives.[13]

7. *The World-soul.*—The second spiritualist theory may be named as that of *transcendentalism*. I take it typically and not as set forth by any single author. Transcendentalism explains things by an over-soul of which all separate souls, sensations, thoughts,

---

[13] The soul can be taken in three ways as a unifying principle. An already existing lot of animated sensations (or other psychic data) may be simply *woven* into one by it; in which case the form of unity is the soul's only contribution, and the original stuff of the Many remains in the One as its stuff also. Or, secondly, the resultant synthetic One may be regarded as an immanent *reaction* of the Soul on the preëxisting psychic Many; and in this case the Soul, in addition to creating the new form, reproduces in itself the old stuff of the Many, superseding it for our use, and making it for us become subliminal, but not suppressing its existence. Or, thirdly, the One may again be the Soul's immanent reaction on a physiological, not on a mental, Many. In this case preëxisting *sensations or ideas* would not be there at all, to be either woven together or superseded. The synthetic One would be a primal psychic datum with parts, either of which might know the same object that a possible sensation, realized under other physiological conditions, could also know.

and data generally are parts. To be, as it would be known together with everything else in the world by this over-soul, is for transcendentalism the *true* condition of each single thing, and to pass into this condition is for things to fulfill their vocation. Such being known together, since it is the innermost reality of life, cannot on transcendentalist principles be explained or accounted for as a work wrought on a previous sort of reality. The monadic soul-theory starts with separate sensational data, and must show how they are *made* one. The transcendentalist theory has rather for its task to show how, being one, they can illusorily be made to appear separate. The problem for the monadic soul, in short, is that of unification, and the problem for the over-soul is that of insulation. The removal of insulating obstructions would sufficiently account for things reverting to their natural place in the over-soul and being known together. The most natural insulating or individualizing principle to invoke is the bodily organism. As the pipes of an organ let the pressing mass of air escape only in single notes, so do our brains, the organ pipes of the infinite, keep back everything but the slender threads of truth to which they may be pervious. As they obstruct more, the insulation increases, as they obstruct less it disappears. Now transcendental philosophers have as a rule not done much dabbling in psychology. But one sees no abstract reason why they might not go into psychology as fully as any one, and erect a psycho-physical science of the conditions of more separate and less separate cognition which would include all the facts that psycho-physicists in general might discover. And they would have the advantage over other psycho-physicists of not needing to explain the nature of the resultant knowing-together when it should occur, for they could say that they simply begged it as the ultimate nature of the world.

This is as broad a disjunction as I can make of the different ways in which men have considered the conditions of our knowing things together. You will agree with me that I have brought no new insight to the subject, and that I have only gossiped to while away this unlucky presidential hour to which the constellations doomed me at my birth. But since gossip we have had to have, let me make the hour more gossipy still by saying a final word about the position taken up in my own *Principles of Psychology* on the general question before us, a position which, as you doubtless remember, was so vigorously attacked by our colleague from the University of Pennsylvania at our meeting in New York a year ago.[14] That position consisted in this, that I proposed to simply eliminate from psychology 'considered as a natural science' the whole business of ascertaining *how* we come to know things together or to know them at all. Such considerations, I said, should fall to metaphysics. That we do know things, sometimes singly and sometimes together, is a fact. That states of consciousness are the vehicle of the knowledge, and depend on brain states, are two other facts. And I thought that a natural science of psychology might legitimately confine itself to tracing the functional variations of these three sorts of fact, and to ascertaining what determinate bodily states are the condition when the states of mind know determinate things and groups of things. Most states of mind can be designated only by naming what objects they are 'thoughts-of,' *i.e.*, what things they know.

Most of those which know compound things are utterly unique and solitary mental entities demonstrably different from any collection of simpler states to which the same objects might be singly known.[15] Treat them all as unique in entity, I said then; let their

[14] Printed as an article entitled 'The Psychological Standpoint,' in this REVIEW, Vol. I, p. 113. (March, 1894.)

[15] When they know conceptually they don't even remotely resemble the simpler states. When they know intuitively they resemble, sometimes closely, sometimes distantly, the simpler states. The sour and sweet in lemonade are extremely unlike the sour and sweet of lemon juice and sugar, singly taken, yet like enough for us to 'recognize' these 'objects' in the compound taste. The several objective 'notes' recognized in the chord sound differently and peculiarly there. In a motley field of view successive and simultaneous contrast give to each several tint a different hue and luminosity from that of the 'real' color into which it turns when viewed without its neighbors by a rested eye. The difference is sometimes so slight, however, that we overlook the 'representative' character of each of the parts of a complex content, and speak as if the latter were a cluster of the original 'intuitive' states of mind that, occurring singly, know the 'object's' several parts in separation. Prof. Meinong, for example, even after the true state of things had been admirably set forth by Herr H. Cornelius (in the *Vierteljahrschrift f. wiss. Phil.*, XVI, 404; XVII, 30), returns to the defence of the radical associationist view (in the *Zeitschrift f. Psychologie*, VI, 340, 417). According to him, the single sensations of the several notes lie unaltered in the chord-sensations; but his analysis of the phenomenon is vitiated by his non-recognition of the fact that the *same objects* (*i.e.*, the notes) *can be known* representatively through one compound state of mind, and directly in several simple ones, without the simple and the compound states having strictly anything in common with each other. In Meinong's earlier work, 'Ueber Begriff und Eigenschaften der Empfindung' (*Vierteljahrschrift*, Vol. XII), he seems to me to have hit the truth much better, when he says that the aspect *color*, *e.g.*, in a concrete sensation of *red*, is not

complexity reside in their plural cognitive function; and you have a psychology which, if it doesn't ultimately explain the facts, also does not, in describing them, make them self-contradictory (as the associationist psychology does when it calls them many ideas fused into one idea) or pretend to explain them (as the soul-theory so often does) by a barren verbal principle.

My intention was a good one, and a natural science infinitely more complete than the psychologies we now possess could be written without abandoning its terms. Like all authors, I have, therefore, been surprised that this child of my genius should not be more admired by others—should, in fact, have been generally either misunderstood or despised. But do not fear that on this occasion I am either going to defend or to re-explain the bantling. I am going to make things more harmonious by simply *giving it up*. I have become convinced since publishing that book that no conventional restrictions *can* keep metaphysical and so-called epistemological inquiries out of the psychology-books. I see, moreover, better now than then, that my proposal to designate mental states merely by their cognitive function leads to a somewhat strained way of talking of dreams and reveries, and to quite an unnatural way of talking of some emotional states. I am willing, consequently, henceforward that mental contents should be called complex, just as their objects are, and this even in psychology. Not because their parts are separable, as the parts of objects are; not because they have an eternal or quasi-eternal individual existence, like the parts of objects; for the various 'fields' of which they are parts are integers, existentially, and their parts only live as long as *they* live. Still, *in* them, we can call parts, parts.—But when, without circumlocution or disguise, I thus come over to your views, I insist that those of you who applaud me (if any such there be) should recognize the obligations which the new agreement imposes on yourselves. Not till you have dropped the old phrases, so absurd or so empty, of ideas 'self-compounding' or 'united by a spiritual principle'; not till you have in your turn succeeded in some such

---

an abstractable *part* of the sensation, but an *external relation of resemblance* between that sensation and other sensations to the whole lot of which we give the name of colors. Such, I should say, are the aspects of *c, e, g* and *c′* in the chord. We may call them *parts* of the chord if we like, but they are not *bits* of it, identical with *c*'s, *e*'s, *g*'s and *c′*'s elsewhere. They simply resemble the *c*'s, *e*'s, *g*'s and *c′*'s elsewhere, and know these contents or objects representatively.

long inquiry into conditions as the one I have just failed in; not till you have laid bare more of the nature of that altogether unique kind of complexity in unity which mental states involve; not till then, I say, will psychology reach any real benefit from the conciliatory spirit of which I have done what I can to set an example.

Preface to Paulsen's *Introduction to Philosophy*

It gives me great pleasure to be sponsor to our public for Professor Paulsen's *Introduction to Philosophy*. For many years past young Americans have brought back tales from Berlin University of the wide-spread interest in Philosophy which Professor Paulsen's lectures were arousing there and of the great influence of his *Introduction* over students not pursuing a technically philosophical career. Two years ago these introductory lectures were published in the form of the present book. Professor Paulsen is a farmer's son, was born in 1846 in Schleswig-Holstein, took his Ph.D. degree at Berlin in 1871, became Privat-docent in '75, extraordinary-professor in '77, and full professor in 1893. The temper of his mind is essentially ethical, and philosophy for him is nothing if it do not connect itself with active human ideals. His most important publications besides the present one are on Ethics and Pedagogics. His *History of German Universities* has just been translated into English by Professor E. D. Perry of Columbia College, and published by Macmillan, 1895. He writes a style of which even English readers must feel the euphony as well as admire the clearness, and which (unconsciously, no doubt, to the author) reveals his heart as much as it displays his technical mastery.

There have always been two ways of thinking about Nature. For Christianity, e.g., Nature is something opposed to the truer unseen world, a surface of recoil to which we must first die. For the more pantheistic systems the relation of Nature to the Unseen is not one of contrast but rather of less and more—there is but one world, partly seen and partly unseen, and its evolution is simple and direct. Now if we give the name of "naturalism" to any specimen of the latter way of thinking that also asserts the universality of mechanistic determination throughout the universe, the present *Introduction to Philosophy* may be briefly described as an attempt so to state naturalism as to make it harmoniously continuous with religious faith. Professor Paulsen does not believe in a philosophy that is only a "philosophy of the human mind." The philosophic aim until Locke's time was always to give as unified an account as possible of all existence in the heavens above and on the earth beneath; and our author thinks that Philosophy should never have taken anything less than this for her ideal task. On this view it is impossible to separate philosophy from the natural sciences. But the natural sciences left to themselves have more and more drifted towards an atomistic materialism. For atomistic materialism, however, the very existence of consciousness is inexplicable, and remains what has been called by one of Paulsen's colleagues an "absolute world-riddle." The notion that the spiritual must be something completely foreign to the primarily real, and its connection with the real an absolute enigma, is of course sufficient, as our author says, to stamp with inadequacy any theory that implies it. He accordingly substitutes for physical atomism an idealistic monism or modernized hylozoism which, being supported by inductive arguments, is, to say the least, as "scientific" an hypothesis. The universe on this view is animated or spiritual both in its parts and as a whole, and the nature of Being is most reasonably to be conceived everywhere after the analogy of our own immediately experienced life. In this latter, feeling and appetency are more primordial elements than conception and reasoning, so it is fair to suppose that the inner life of the infra-human parts of the world is of a more appetitive or conative sort, whilst the Soul of the larger totals (the globe which we inhabit and the starry heaven itself) involving our rational souls, as it does, also knows all that our reason lets us know and much more besides. Psycho-physical monism has had a number of advocates in recent years. I know none as persuasive as Paulsen; for his statement is untechnical, undogmatic, classical in expression, and absolutely sincere. I should go so far as to say that his exposition of the naturalistic view as a whole is by the superiority of its form calculated to supersede all previous general statements, and to serve as the standard text for criticism by those to whom for any reason the view itself is repugnant.

Passing now to the religious side of the book, there can be no "conflict" between science and religion for Professor Paulsen, for their diverse assertions about the world relate, he says, to entirely different aspects of its being. The task of science is to trace the facts, that of religion is to declare the system of values which they form, or to measure their teleological expressiveness. Religious faith, an utterance of something in us that is deeper than the intellect, insists that the facts not only exist, but have worth or import, and that the order of Nature which science ascertains and describes is *also* a moral order. Such faith does not (when taken in its essential purity) undertake to establish special facts at all, but only to affirm a special sort of significance for such facts as it finds. Whether facts that exist have significance or do not have it is something that cannot be proved or disproved by argument. If one *feels* the significance, it is there; but it can only be affirmed or denied dogmatically, as it were; so that religion and atheism stand opposite to each other not as theories, but rather as expressions of the will, and differing practical attitudes of men towards life. The essential religious affirmation, according to our author, is confidence that the soul of the world (whose existence has been inductively made probable) is *good*—in other words, that the vaster and more eternal sort of Fact is also the more perfect sort of being. The belief that this attitude of faith may be one's most important vital function is also an expression of the voluntary life, and not a theory that can be scientifically refuted. One's question towards it is rather the practical question: Shall I keep it? or be shamed out of it? or perhaps spontaneously give it up?

There is a class of minds to whom Professor Paulsen's system will seem intolerably *loose,* and on that account repugnant from beginning to end. The very charm and untechnicality of his style will be accounted a crime by readers who believe that only what is *streng wissenschaftlich* can be counted true. I myself should be glad to see the system *tightened* in certain places, and am personally doubtful of many propositions in which Professor Paulsen believes. All these defects, however, are minor matters in my eyes in comparison with the one immense merit of his work, which is its perfect candor and frank abandonment of dogmatic pretence. The besetting sin of philosophers has always been the absolutism of their intellects. We find an assumption that was the soul of Scholasticism, the assumption namely that anything that is necessary in the way of belief must be susceptible of articulate proof, as rampant as it ever was, in the irreligious agnosticism of to-day; and we find it moreover blossoming out into corollaries, as, for instance, that to believe anything without such proof is to be unscientific, and that to be unscientific is the lowest depth to which a thinking mind can fall. Now these assumptions necessarily make philosophy discontinuous with life, because biologically considered man's life consists for the most part in adjustments that are unscientific, and deals with probabilities and not with certainties. Professor Paulsen makes philosophy and life continuous again; so the pedants of both camps among us will unite in condemnation of his work. Life lies open, and the philosophy which their intellects desiderate must wear the form of a closed system. We need ever to be reminded afresh that no philosophy can be more than an hypothesis. As a great contemporary thinker, Renouvier, has said: "Toute philosophie qui ne tient pas compte avant tout des incertitudes, et des variations, et des contradictions de la philosophie, mais qui s'entretient dans l'illusion de les supprimer pour s'en affranchir, est, disons-le hautement, un pur enfantillage, auquel un homme ne doit plus s'arrêter."

I frankly confess that it is the anti-absolutism of Professor Paulsen that pleases me in him most. I have said nothing of the predominantly historic method of his exposition, which in the pages that follow is very happily and instructively carried out. Professor Thilly has well performed the translator's task, and I may say that I have been using advance sheets of the first three quarters of the translation as a text-book in one of my courses, and that, in a long experience as a teacher, it is one of the very few text-books about which I have heard no grumbling.

I should be glad if these introductory words of mine could procure for the *Introduction to Philosophy* a readier reception by American and English students.

"Pragmatism": from Baldwin's *Dictionary*

The doctrine that the whole 'meaning' of a conception expresses itself in practical consequences, consequences either in the shape of conduct to be recommended, or in that of experiences to be expected, if the conception be true; which consequences would be different if it were untrue, and must be different from the consequences by which the meaning of other conceptions is in turn expressed. If a second conception should not appear to have other consequences, then it must really be only the first conception under a different name. In methodology it is certain that to trace and compare their respective consequences is an admirable way of establishing the differing meanings of different conceptions.

(2) Psychic or mental: the entire process of phenomena, of present data considered in their raw immediacy, before reflective thought has analysed them into subjective and objective aspects or ingredients. It is the summum genus of which everything must have been a part before we can speak of it at all.

In this neutrality of signification it is exactly correlative to the word PHENOMENON (q. v.), meaning (4). If philosophy insists on keeping this term indeterminate, she can refer to her subject-matter without committing herself as to certain questions in dispute. But if experience be used with either an objective or a subjective shade of meaning, then question-begging occurs, and discussion grows impossible.

Herbert Spencer Dead

In the death of Mr. Herbert Spencer, England has to deplore the loss of one of the two or three most influential thinkers whom she has given to our generation. Influences can be measured in either of two ways, by their wide and immediate, or by their deep and remote effects. For wide and immediate influence, Spencer must come before even Darwin. Darwin's influence was primarily over technical circles, and the students whom he directly touched perhaps owed as much to his methods and theoretic temper as to his results. On the "Public" his influence has been remote. Of twenty educated men who think they know all "about" Darwinism, hardly one has read of it in the original. Spencer's influence, contrariwise, is not only wide but direct. Thousands of readers who are not technical students know him in the original; and to such readers he has given (what they care about far more than either method or theoretic temper) a simple, sublime, and novel system of the world, in which things fall into easy perspective relations, whose explanatory formula applies to every conceivable phenomenon, and whose practical outcome is the somewhat vague optimism which is so important a tendency in modern life. In this enormous popular success of Spencer's works the incomparable superiority of constructive over critical methods is shown. Half the battle is won already by the man who has a positive system to propound. *He* need not waste time in clearing away old views; his view simply makes others obsolete by the fact that it is there. And in award-ing "points" to the various candidates for immortality in the "Pantheon of Philosophy," few are entitled to a higher mark than Mr. Spencer on this score of positive and systematic form. What-ever greatness this quality imports—and surely it is as rare and great as any—belongs to Mr. Spencer in the fullest measure. Who, since he wrote, is not vividly able to conceive of the world as a thing evolved from a primitive fire mist, by progressive integra-tions and differentiations, and increases in heterogeneity and co-herence of texture and organization? Who can fail to think of life, both bodily and mental, as a set of ever-changing ways of meeting the "environment"? Who has not at some time suddenly grown grave at the thought that the parents' sinful or virtuous habits are inherited by the children, and destined to accumulate from gen-eration to generation whilst the race endures?

When one tries, however, to give a nearer account of Herbert Spencer's genius, and a more exact appraisal of his importance in the history of thought, one finds the task a hard one, so unique and idiosyncratic was the temperament of the man; and, with all the breadth of ground which his work covered, so narrow and angular was the outline which he personally showed. A pen like Carlyle's might convey a living impression of all the pluses and minuses which Mr. Spencer's character embodied, but a writer like the present critic must surely fail. Carlyle himself, indeed, had he ever tried the task, would have failed. With his so different temperament, the littlenesses of the personage would have tempted his descriptive powers exclusively, and the elements of greatness would have got scant justice from his pen. As a rule, all people in whom a genius like Carlyle's raises a responsive thrill find some-thing strangely exasperating in the atmosphere of Spencer's mind: it seems to them so fatally lacking in geniality, humor, pictur-esqueness, and poetry, and so explicit, so mechanical, so flat in the panorama which it gives of life. "The 'Arry of Philosophy" is a name which we have seen applied to Spencer by one critic of this sort. Another has likened him to a kind of philosophic sawmill, delivering, year in and out, with unvarying rectilinear precision, paragraph after paragraph, chapter after chapter, and book after book, as similar one to another as if they were so many wooden planks. Another still says that "his contact is enough to take the flavor out of every truth."

How inexhaustible are the varieties of human character! Every reader of Spencer can recognize the quality in him which provokes reactions such as these. Yet the fact remains that long before any of his contemporaries had seized its universal import, he grasped a great, light-giving truth—the truth of evolution; grasped it so that it became bone of his bone and flesh of his flesh, and with a pertinacity of which the history of successful thought gives few examples, had applied it to the whole of life, down to the minutest details of the most various sciences. And how, one may well ask, is profundity and the genuine "spirit of prophecy" ever to be shown in a man, if not by fruits like these? Moreover, although Spencer's intellect is essentially of the deductive and à priori order, starting from universal abstract principles and thence proceeding down to facts, what strikes one more than anything else in his writings is the enormous number of facts from every conceivable quarter which he brings to his support, and the unceasing study of minutest particulars which he is able to keep up. No "Baconian" philosopher, denying himself the use of à priori principles, has ever filled his pages with half as many facts as this strange species of à priorist can show. This unflagging and profuse command of facts is what gives such peculiar weightiness to Mr. Spencer's manner of presenting even the smallest topics. Some of his *Essays* have a really monumental character from this cause. 'Manners and Fashion,' 'The Origin of Laughter,' 'Illogical Geology,' and the reviews of 'Bain's Emotions and Will' and 'Owen's Archetype of the Vertebrate Skeleton,' immediately occur to the mind as examples. In all his writings on social morals, from *Social Statics* to *The Man versus the State*, the same quality is most impressively shown. Yet with this matchless knowledge of certain sets of facts, one may hear it plausibly argued that Spencer is not a "widely informed" man in the vulgar acceptation of the term. He shows, that is, small signs of *desultory* curiosity. His command, *e.g.*, of foreign languages is small, and in the history of philosophy he is obviously unversed. His facts, in short, seem all collected for a purpose; those which help the purpose are never forgotten, those which are alien to it have never caught his eye.

Mr. Spencer's attitude towards religion, again, is slightly paradoxical. Few men have paid it more sincere explicit respect; and the part called 'The Unknowable' of his *First Principles* celebrates the ultimate mysteriousness of things, and the existence of a Supreme Reality behind the veil, in terms whose emphatic character it is hard elsewhere to match. Yet on the whole he passes, and we imagine passes rightly, for an irreligious philosopher. His metaphysical "Absolute" is too ineffable to become active in the system; and an absolute Physics forthwith takes its place. The mystery of things, instead of being "omnipresent," is all neatly swept together into this one chapter, and then dismissed with an affectionate good-by; while all the particular mysteries which later present themselves are quickly explained away, Life being but complicated mechanism, and Consciousness only physical force "transformed," etc., etc. In Mr. Spencer's heroic defence of individualism against socialism and the general encroachment of the state there is a similar seeming incoherence, so marked that one cannot help suspecting his thought to have started from two independent foci, and to be faithful to two ideals. The first one was the old English ideal of individual liberty, culminating in the doctrine of *laissez faire*, for which the book *Social Statics*, published in 1851, was so striking a plea. The second was the theory of universal evolution, which seems to have taken possession of Mr. Spencer in the decade which ensued. The Spencerian law of evolution is essentially statistical. Its "integrations," "differentiations," etc., are names for describing results manifested in collections of units, and the laws of the latter's individual action are, in the main and speaking broadly, hardly considered at all. The fate of the individual fact is swallowed up in that of the aggregate total. And this is the impression (unless our memory betrays us) which Mr. Spencer's dealings with the individual man in society always gives us, so long as the general description of the process of evolution is what he has in hand. He denies free-will, as a matter of course; he despises hero worship and the tendency to ascribe social changes to individual initiative rather than to "general conditions," and in every way tends to minimize the particular concrete man. Society drags the unit along in its fatal tow. Yet in the political writings of Mr. Spencer, with their intense and absolute reliance on individuals, we find the very opposite of this. Deeper students than we are may see the point in his system where these two streams of tendency unite. To us they seem, not perhaps incompatible, but at least detached.

To the present critic, the ethical and political part of Mr. Spencer's writings seems the most impressive and likely to endure. The

Biology, the *Psychology*, the *Sociology*, even were they abler than they are, must soon become obsolete books; but the antique spirit of English individualism is a factor in human life less changeable than the face of the sciences, and such expressions of it as Spencer has given will probably long deserve to be read. The *Data of Ethics* is unquestionably the most valuable single part of the *Synthetic Philosophy*, not for the reason that it makes ethics for the first time "scientific" (although this was probably its chief merit in its author's eyes), but because it gives voice with singular energy to one man's ideals concerning human life. Ideals as manly, as humane, as broadly inclusive and as forcibly expressed are always a force in the world's destinies. The *Data of Ethics* will therefore long continue to be read.

The *Principles of Biology* and of *Psychology* are already somewhat out of date. Spencer's heroic attempts mechanically to explain the genesis of living forms are altogether too coarsely carried out in the former book; and the problems of reproduction and heredity are complicated to-day with elements of which he could know nothing when he wrote.

Of the *Psychology*, too, it may be said that not much remains that is of value beyond the general conception, supported by many applications, that the mind grew up in relation to its environment, and that the two cannot be studied apart—a conception that sounded decidedly more original in the '50s and '60s than it does now. The *Sociology* has probably a larger lease of life. It is more recent, and must long be valued as a vast collection of well-arranged anthropological facts. As a chapter in the *System of Philosophy*, its value is almost evanescent, for the author's habit of periodically pointing out how well the phenomena illustrate his law of evolution seems quite perfunctory and formal when applied to social facts, so strained and unnatural is it to conceive of these as mechanical changes in which matter is integrated and motion dispersed. It is probable—strange irony of fate!—that the book called *First Principles*, although from a strict point of view it is far more vulnerable than anything its author ever wrote, is the work by which the *Synthetic Philosophy* will remain best known to the reading world.

This, however, is very likely as it should be. A man like Spencer can afford to be judged, not by his infallibility in details, but by the bravery of his attempt. He sought to see truth as a whole. He brought us back to the old ideal of philosophy, which since Locke's time had well nigh taken flight, the ideal, namely, of a "completely unified knowledge," into which the physical and mental worlds should enter on equal terms. This was the original Greek ideal of philosophy, to which men surely must return. Spencer has been likened to Aristotle. But he presents far more analogies to Descartes, whose mechanical theory of evolution swept over his age as Spencer's sweeps over ours. And although Spencer can show no such triumphs of detail as Descartes's discoveries of analytical geometry, of dioptrics, of reflex action, and of perception by the eye, his moral character inspires an infinitely greater sympathy than that of the earlier philosopher. Descartes's life was absolutely egotistic, and he was basely servile to the powers that be. Mr. Spencer's faculties were all devoted to the service of mankind, and few men can have lived whose personal conduct unremittingly trod so close upon the heels of their ideal.

The Chicago School[1]

The rest of the world has made merry over the Chicago man's legendary saying that 'Chicago hasn't had time to get round to culture yet, but when she does strike her, she'll make her hum.' Already the prophecy is fulfilling itself in a dazzling manner. Chicago has a School of Thought!—a school of thought which, it is safe to predict, will figure in literature as the School of Chicago for twenty-five years to come. Some universities have plenty of thought to show, but no school; others plenty of school, but no thought. The University of Chicago, by its Decennial Publications, shows real thought and a real school. Professor John Dewey, and at least ten of his disciples, have collectively put into the world a statement, homogeneous in spite of so many coöperating minds, of a view of the world, both theoretical and practical, which is so simple, massive, and positive that, in spite of the fact that many parts of it yet need to be worked out, it deserves the title of a new system of philosophy. If it be as true as it is original, its publication

---

[1] 1. *Studies in Logical Theory*, John Dewey, with the coöperation of members and fellows of the Department of Philosophy. The Decennial Publications, second series. Volume XI., Chicago. The University of Chicago Press, 1903. 2. "The Definition of the Psychical," George H. Mead. 3. "Existence, Meaning, and Reality," A. W. Moore. 4. "Logical Conditions of a Scientific Treatment of Morality," John Dewey. 5. "The Relations of Structural and Functional Psychology to Philosophy," James Rowland Angell. Reprints from Volume III. of the first series of Decennial Publications. *ibid.*, 1903.

must be reckoned an important event. The present reviewer, for one, strongly suspects it of being true.

The briefest characterization is all that will be attempted here. Criticism from various quarters will doubtless follow, for about the new system as a bone of contention discussion is bound to rage.

Like Spencer's philosophy, Dewey's is an evolutionism; but unlike Spencer, Dewey and his disciples have so far (with the exception of Dewey's admirable writings on ethics) confined themselves to establishing certain general principles without applying them to details. Unlike Spencer, again, Dewey is a pure empiricist. There is nothing real, whether being or relation between beings, which is not direct matter of experience. There is no Unknowable or Absolute behind or around the finite world. No Absolute, cither, in the sense of anything eternally constant; no term is static, but everything is process and change.

Like Spencer, again, Dewey makes biology and psychology continuous. 'Life,' or 'experience,' is the fundamental conception; and whether you take it physically or mentally, it involves an adjustment between terms. Dewey's favorite word is 'situation.' A situation implies at least two factors, each of which is both an independent variable and a function of the other variable. Call them E (environment) and O (organism) for simplicity's sake. They interact and develop each other without end; for each action of E upon O changes O, whose reaction in turn upon E changes E, so that E's new action upon O gets different, eliciting a new reaction, and so on indefinitely. The situation gets perpetually 'reconstructed,' to use another of Professor Dewey's favorite words, and this reconstruction is the process of which all reality consists.

I am in some doubt as to whether, in the last resort, Dewey thinks monistically or pluralistically of this reality. He often talks of 'experience' in the singular as if it were one universal process and not a collective name for many particular processes. But all his special statements refer to particular processes only, so I will report him in pluralistic terms.

No biological processes are treated of in this literature, except as incidental to ethical discussion, and the ethical discussions would carry us too far afield. I will confine myself therefore to the psychological or epistemological doctrines of the school.

Consciousness is functionally active in readjustment. In perfectly 'adapted' situations, where adjustments are fluent and stereo-typed, it exists in minimal degree. Only where there is hesitation, only where past habit will not run, do we find that the situation awakens explicit thought. Thought is thus incidental to change in experience, to conflict between the old and new. The situation must be reconstructed if activity is to be resumed, and the rejudg-ing of it mentally is the reconstruction's first stage. The nucleus of the *Studies in Logical Theory* becomes thus an account of the judging process.

"In psychological terms, we may say, in explanation of the judg-ing process, that some stimulus to action has failed to function properly as a stimulus, and that the activity which was going on has thus been interrupted. Response in the accustomed way has failed. In such a case there arises a division in experience into sen-sation content as subject and ideal content as predicate. In other words, . . . upon failure of the accustomed stimulus to be adequate . . . activity ceases, and is resumed in an integral form only when a new habit is set up to which the new or altered stimulus is ade-quate. It is in this process of reconstruction that subject and predi-cate appear." The old subject (the *that* of the situation) stands for the interrupted habit, the new subject (the *that* with the new *what* added) stands for the new habit begun. The predicate is thus essen-tially hypothetical—the situations to which the use of it leads may have quickly to be reconstructed in turn. In brief, *S* is a stimulus intellectually irritating; *P* is an hypothesis in response; *SP* is a mental action, which normally is destined to lead or pass into action in a wider sense. The sense of 'objectivity' in the *S* emerges emphatically only when the *P* is problematic and the action un-defined. Then only does the *S* arrest attention, and its contrast with the self become acute. 'Knowing,' therefore, or the conscious relation of the object to the self, is thus only an incident in the wider process of 'adjustment,' which includes unconscious adjust-ments as well.

This leads Professor Dewey and his disciples to a peculiar view of 'fact.' What is a fact? A fact and a theory have not different na-tures, as is usually supposed, the one being objective, the other subjective. They are both made of the same material, experience-material namely, and their difference relates to their way of func-tioning solely. What is fact for one epoch, or for one inquirer, is theory for another epoch or another inquirer. It is 'fact' when it functions steadily; it is 'theory' when we hesitate. 'Truth' is thus in process of formation like all other things. It consists not in conformity or correspondence with an externally fixed archetype or model. Such a thing would be irrelevant even if we knew it to exist. Truth consists in a character inclosed within the 'situation.' Whenever a situation has the maximum of stability, and seems most satisfactory to its own subject-factor, it is true for him. If accused here of opening the door to systematic protagoreanism, Professor Dewey would reply that the concrete facts themselves are what keep his scepticism from being systematic in any practically objectionable sense. Experience is continually enlarging, and the object-factors of our situations are always getting problematic, making old truths unsatisfactory, and obliging new ones to be found. The object-factors moreover are common to ourselves and others; and our truths have to be mated with those of our fellow men. The real safeguard against caprice of statement and indetermination of belief is that there is a 'grain' in things against which we can't practically go. But as the grain creates itself from situation to situation, so the truth creates itself *pari passu*, and there is no eternally standing system of extra-subjective verity to which our judgments, ideally and in advance of the facts, are obliged to conform.

There are two great gaps in the system, which none of the Chicago writers have done anything to fill, and until they are filled, the system, as a system, will appear defective. There is no cosmology, no positive account of the order of physical fact, as contrasted with mental fact, and no account of the fact (which I assume the writers to believe in) that different subjects share a common object-world. These lacunæ can hardly be inadvertent—we shall doubtless soon see them filled in some way by one or another member of the school.

I might go into much greater technical detail, and I might in particular make many a striking quotation. But I prefer to be exceedingly summary, and merely to call the reader's attention to the importance of this output of Chicago University. Taking it *en gros*, what strikes me most in it is the great sense of concrete reality with which it is filled. It seems a promising *via media* between the empiricist and transcendentalist tendencies of our time. Like empiricism, it is individualistic and phenomenalistic; it places truth *in rebus*, and not *ante rem*. It resembles transcendentalism, on the other hand, in making value and fact inseparable, and in standing for continuities and purposes in things. It employs the genetic method to which both schools are now accustomed. It coincides remarkably with the simultaneous movement in favor of 'pragmatism' or 'humanism' set up quite independently at Oxford by Messrs. Schiller and Sturt. It probably has a great future, and is certainly something of which Americans may be proud. Professor Dewey ought to gather into another volume his scattered essays and addresses on psychological and ethical topics, for now that his philosophy is systematically formulated, these throw a needed light.

Herbert Spencer

"God moves in a mysterious way his wonders to perform." If the greatest of all his wonders be the human individual, the richness with which the specimens thereof are diversified, the limitless variety of outline, from gothic to classic or flowing arabesque, the contradictory nature of the filling, composed of little and great, of comic, heroic, and pathetic elements blended inextricably, in personalities all of whom can *go,* and go successfully, must surely be reckoned the supreme miracle of creative ingenuity. Rarely has Nature performed an odder or more Dickens-like feat than when she deliberately designed, or accidentally stumbled into, the personality of Herbert Spencer. Greatness and smallness surely never lived so closely in one skin together.

The opposite verdicts passed upon his work by his contemporaries bear witness to the extraordinary mingling of defects and merits in his mental character. Here are a few, juxtaposed:—

"A philosophic saw-mill."—"The most capacious and powerful thinker of all time."

"The ' 'Arry' of philosophy."—"Aristotle and his master were not more beyond the pygmies who preceded them than he is beyond Aristotle."

"Herbert Spencer's chromo-philosophy."—"No other man that has walked the earth has so wrought and written himself into the life of the world."

"The touch of his mind takes the living flavor out of everything."—"He is as much above and beyond all the other great philosophers who have ever lived as the telegraph is beyond the carrier pigeon, or the railway beyond the sedan chair."

"He has merely combined facts which we knew before into a huge fantastic contradictory system, which hides its nakedness and emptiness partly under the veil of an imposing terminology, and partly in the primeval fog."—"His contributions are of a depth, profundity, and magnitude which have no parallel in the history of mind. Taking but one—and one only—of his transcendent reaches of thought,—namely, that referring to the positive sense of the Unknown as the basis of religion,—it may unhesitatingly be affirmed that the analysis and synthesis by which he advances to the almost supernal grasp of this mighty truth give a sense of power and reach verging on the preternatural."

Can the two thick volumes of autobiography which Mr. Spencer leaves behind him explain such discrepant appreciations?[1] Can we find revealed in them the higher synthesis which reconciles the contradictions? Partly they do explain, I think, and even justify, both kinds of judgment upon their author. But I confess that in the last resort I still feel baffled. In Spencer, as in every concrete individual, there is a uniqueness that defies all formulation. We can feel the touch of it and recognize its taste, so to speak, relishing or disliking, as the case may be, but we can give no ultimate account of it, and we have in the end simply to admire the Creator.

Mr. Spencer's task, the unification of all knowledge into an articulate system, was more ambitious than anything attempted since St. Thomas or Descartes. Most thinkers have confined themselves either to generalities or to details, but Spencer addressed himself to everything. He dealt in logical, metaphysical, and ethical first principles, in cosmogony and geology, in physics, and chemistry after a fashion, in biology, psychology, sociology, politics, and æsthetics. Hardly any subject can be named which has not at least been touched on in some one of his many volumes. His erudition was prodigious. His civic conscience and his social courage both were admirable. His life was pure. He was devoted to truth and usefulness, and his character was wholly free from envy and malice (though not from contempt), and from the perverse egoisms that so often go with greatness.

[1] *An Autobiography.* By Herbert Spencer. New York: D. Appleton & Co. 1904.

Surely, any one hearing this veracious enumeration would think that Spencer must have been a rich and exuberant human being. Such wide curiosities must have gone with the widest sympathies, and such a powerful harmony of character, whether it were a congenital gift, or were acquired by spiritual wrestling and eating bread with tears, must in any case have been a glorious spectacle for the beholder. Since Goethe, no such ideal human being can have been visible, walking our poor earth.

Yet when we turn to the *Autobiography*, the self-confession which we find is this: An old-maidish personage, inhabiting boarding-houses, equable and lukewarm in all his tastes and passions, having no desultory curiosity, showing little interest in either books or people. A petty fault-finder and stickler for trifles, devoid in youth of any wide designs on life, fond only of the more mechanical side of things, yet drifting as it were involuntarily into the possession of a world-formula which by dint of his extraordinary pertinacity he proceeded to apply to so many special cases that it made him a philosopher in spite of himself. He appears as modest enough, but with a curious vanity in some of his deficiencies,—his lack of desultory interests, for example, and his nonconformity to reigning customs. He gives a queer sense of having no emotional perspective, as if small things and large were on the same plane of vision, and equally commanded his attention. In spite of his professed dislike of monotony, one feels an awfully monotonous quality in him; and in spite of the fact that invalidism condemned him to avoid thinking, and to saunter and potter through large parts of every day, one finds no twilight region in his mind, and no capacity for dreaminess or passivity. All parts of it are filled with the same noonday glare, like a dry desert where every grain of sand shows singly, and there are no mysteries or shadows.

"Look on this picture and on that," and answer how they can be compatible.

For one thing, Mr. Spencer certainly writes himself *down* too much. He complains of a poor memory, of an idle disposition, of a general dislike for reading. Doubtless there have been more gifted men in all these respects. But when Spencer once buckled to a particular task, his memory, his industry, and his reading went beyond those of the most gifted. He had excessive sensibility to stimulation by a challenge, and he had preëminent pertinacity.

When the notion of his philosophic system once grasped him, it seemed to possess itself of every effective fibre of his being. No faculty in him was left unemployed,—nor, on the other hand, was anything that his philosophy could contain left unstated. Roughly speaking, the task and the man absorbed each other without residuum.

Compare this type of mind with such an opposite type as Ruskin's, or even as J. S. Mill's, or Huxley's, and you realize its peculiarity. Behind the work of those others was a background of overflowing mental temptations. The men loom larger than all their publications, and leave an impression of unexpressed potentialities. Spencer tossed all his inexpressibilities into the Unknowable, and gladly turned his back on them forever. His books seem to have expressed all that there was to express in his character.

He is very frank about this himself. No *Sturm und Drang Periode,* no problematic stage of thought, where the burden of the much-to-be-straightened exceeds the powers of straightening.

When George Eliot uttered surprise at seeing no lines on his forehead, his reply was:—

"I suppose it is because I am never puzzled."—"It has never been my way," he continues, "to set before myself a problem and puzzle out an answer. The conclusions at which I have from time to time arrived, have not been arrived at as solutions of questions raised; but have been arrived at unawares—each as the ultimate outcome of a body of thoughts which slowly grew from a germ. Some direct observation, or some fact met with in reading, would dwell with me: apparently because I had a sense of its significance. . . . A week afterwards, possibly, the matter would be remembered; and with further thought about it, might occur a recognition of some wider application: new instances being aggregated with those already noted. Again after an interval," etc., etc. "And thus, little by little, in unobtrusive ways, without conscious intention or appreciable effort, there would grow up a coherent and organized theory" (vol. i, pages 462–464).

A sort of mill, this, wound up to grind in a certain way, and irresponsive otherwise.

"To apply day after day merely with the general idea of acquiring information, or of increasing ability, was not in me." "Anything like passive receptivity is foreign to my nature; and there results an unusually small tendency to be affected by others' thoughts. It seems as though the fabric of my conclusions had in all cases to be developed from within . . . . Material which could be taken in and organized so as to form part of a coherent structure, there was always a readiness to receive. But ideas and sentiments of alien kinds, or unorganizable kinds, were, if not rejected, yet accepted with indifference and soon dropped away." "It has always been out of the question for me to go on reading a book the fundamental principles of which I entirely dissent from. . . . I take it for granted that if the fundamental principles are wrong the rest cannot be right; and thereupon cease reading—being, I suspect, rather glad of an excuse for doing so." "Systematic books of a political or ethical kind, written from points of view quite unlike my own, were either not consulted at all . . . or else they were glanced at and thereafter disregarded" (vol. i, pages 215, 277, 289, 350).

There is pride rather than compunction in these confessions. Spencer's mind was so narrowly systematized, that he was at last almost incapable of believing in the reality of alien ways of feeling. The invariable arrogance of his replies to criticisms shows his absolute self-confidence. Every opinion in the world had to be articulately right or articulately wrong,—so proved by some principle or other of his infallible system.

He confesses freely his own inflexibility and censoriousness. His account of his father makes one believe in the fatality of heredity. Born of old nonconformist stock, the elder Spencer was a man of absolute punctuality. Always he would step out of his way to kick a stone off the pavement lest somebody should trip over it. If he saw boys quarreling he stopped to expostulate; and he never could pass a man who was ill-treating a horse without trying to make him behave better. He would never take off his hat to any one, no matter of what rank, nor could he be induced to address any one as "Esquire" or as "Reverend." He would never put on any sign of mourning, even for father and mother; and he adhered to one style of coat and hat throughout all changes of fashion. Improvement was his watchword always and everywhere. Whatever he wrote had to be endlessly corrected, and his love of detail led all his life to his neglecting large ends in his care for small ones. A good heart, but a pedantic conscience, and a sort of energetically mechanical intelligence.

Of himself Herbert Spencer says: "No one will deny that I am much given to criticism. Along with exposition of my own views there has always gone a pointing out of defects in those of others. And, if this is a trait in my writing, still more is it a trait in my conversation. The tendency to fault-finding is dominant—disagreeably dominant. The indicating of errors in thought and in speech made by those around, has all through life been an incurable habit —a habit for which I have often reproached myself, but to no purpose."

The *Autobiography* abounds in illustrations of the habit. For instance:—

"Of late I have observed sundry cases in which, . . . having found the right, people deliberately desert it for the wrong. . . . A generation ago salt-cellars were made of convenient shapes—either ellipses or elongated parallelograms: the advantage being that the salt-spoon, placed lengthwise, remained in its place. But, for some time past, fashion has dictated circular salt-cellars, on the edges of which the salt-spoon will not remain without skilful balancing: it falls on the cloth. . . . In my boyhood a jug was made of a form at once convenient and graceful. . . . Now, however, the almost universal form of jug in use, is a frustum of a cone, with a miniature spout. It combines all possible defects. When anything like full, it is impossible to pour out a small quantity without part of the liquid trickling down beneath the spout; and a larger quantity cannot be poured out without exceeding the limits of the spout and running over on each side of it. If the jug is half empty, the tilting must be continued for a long time before any liquid comes; and then, when it does come, it comes with a rush; because its surface has now become so large that a small inclination delivers a great deal. To all which add that the shape is as ugly a one as can well be hit upon. Still more extraordinary is the folly of a change made in another utensil of daily use"—and Spencer goes on to find fault with the cylindrical form of candle extinguisher, proving by a description of its shape that "it . . . squashes the wick into the melted composition: the result being that when, next day, the extinguisher is taken off, the wick, imbedded in the solidified composition, cannot be lighted without difficulty" (vol. ii, page 238).

The remorseless explicitness, the punctuation, everything, make these specimens of public fault-finding with what probably was the equipment of Mr. Spencer's latest boarding-house, sound like passages from *The Man versus the State*. Another example:—

"Playing billiards became 'my custom always of the afternoon.' . . . Those who confess to billiard-playing commonly make some kind of excuse. . . . It suffices for me that I like billiards, and the attainment of the pleasure given I regard as a sufficient motive. I have for a long time deliberately set my face against that asceticism which makes it an offence to do a thing for the pleasure of doing it; and have habitually contended that, so long as no injury is inflicted on others, nor any ulterior injury on self, and so long as the various duties of life have been discharged, the pursuit of pleasure for its own sake is perfectly legitimate and requires no apology. The opposite view is nothing else than a remote sequence of the old devil-worship of the barbarian; who sought to please his god by inflicting pains on himself, and believed his god would be angry if he made himself happy" (vol. ii, page 263).

The tone of pedantic rectitude in these passages is characteristic. Every smallest thing is either right or wrong, and if wrong, can be articulately proved so by reasoning. Life grows too dry and literal, and loses all aerial perspective at such a rate; and the effect is the more displeasing when the matters in dispute have a rich variety of aspects, and when the aspect from which Mr. Spencer deduces his conclusions is manifestly partial.

For instance, in his art-criticisms. Spencer in his youth did much drawing, both mechanical and artistic. Volume one contains a photo-print of a very creditable bust which he modeled of his uncle. He had a musical ear, and practiced singing. He paid attention to style, and was not wholly insensible to poetry. Yet in all his dealings with the art-products of mankind he manifests the same curious dryness and mechanical literality of judgment,—a dryness increased by pride in his nonconformity. He would, for example, rather give a large sum than read to the end of Homer's *Iliad*,—the ceaseless repetition of battles, speeches, and epithets like well-greaved Greeks, horse-breaking Trojans; the tedious enumeration of details of dresses, arms, and chariots; such absurdities as giving the genealogy of a horse while in the midst of a battle; and the appeals to savage and brutal passions, having soon made the poem intolerable to him (vol. i, page 300). Turner's paintings he finds untrue, in that the earth-region is habitually as bright in tone as the air-region. Moreover, Turner scatters his detail too evenly. In Greek statues the hair is falsely treated. Renaissance painting, even the best, is spoiled by unreal illumination, and non-rendering of reflected light in the shadows. Venetian gothic sins by meaningless ornamentation. St. Mark's Church may be precious archæologically, but is not æsthetically precious. Of Wagner's music he admires nothing but the skillful specialization of the instruments in the orchestra.

The fault-finding in all these cases rests on observation, true as far as it goes; but the total absence of genial relations with the entirety of the phenomenon discussed, the clutching at some paltry mechanical aspect of it that lends itself to reasoned proof by *a* plus *b*, and the practical denial of everything that only appeals to vaguer sentiment, show a mind so oddly limited to ratiocinative and explicit processes, and so wedded to the superficial and flagrantly *insufficient*, that one begins to wonder whether in the philosophic and scientific spheres the same mind can have wrought out results of extraordinary value.

Both "yes" and "no" are here the answer. Every one who writes books or articles knows how he must flounder until he hits upon the proper opening. Once the right beginning found, everything follows easily and in due order. If a man, however narrow, strikes, even by accident, into one of these fertile openings, and pertinaciously follows the lead, he is almost sure to meet truth on his path. Some thoughts act almost like mechanical centres of crystallization; facts cluster of themselves about them. Such a thought was that of the gradual growth of all things, by natural processes, out of natural antecedents. Until the middle of the nineteenth century no one had grasped it *wholesale*; and the thinker who did so earliest was bound to make discoveries just in proportion to the exclusiveness of his interest in the principle. He who had the keenest eye for instances and illustrations, and was least divertible by casual side-curiosity, would score the quickest triumph.

To Spencer is certainly due the immense credit of having been the first to see in evolution an absolutely universal principle. If any one else had grasped its universality, it failed at any rate to grasp him as it grasped Spencer. For Spencer it instantly became "the guiding conception running through and connecting all the concrete sciences" (vol. ii, page 196). Here at last was "an object at once large and distinct enough" to overcome his "constitutional idleness." "With an important and definite end to achieve, I could work" (vol. i, page 215). He became, in short, the victim of a vivid obsession, and for the first time in his life seems to have grown genuinely ambitious. Every item of his experience, small or great, every idea in his mental storehouse, had now to be considered with reference to its bearing on the new universal principle. On pages 194–199 of volume two he gives an interesting summary of the way in which all his previous and subsequent ideas moved into harmonious coördination and subordination, when once he had this universal key to insight. Applying it wholesale as he did, innumerable truths unobserved till then had to fall into his gamebag. And his peculiar trick, a priggish infirmity in daily intercourse, of treating every smallest thing by abstract law, was here a merit. Add his sleuthhound scent for what he was after, and his untiring pertinacity, to his priority in perceiving the one great truth, and you fully justify the popular estimate of him as one of the world's geniuses, in spite of the fact that the "temperament" of genius, so called, seems to have been so lacking in him.

In one sense, then, Spencer's personal narrowness and dryness were not hindering, but helping conditions of his achievement. Grant that a vast picture *quelconque* had to be made before the details could be made perfect, and a greater richness and receptivity of mind would have resulted in hesitation. The quality would have been better in spots, but the extensiveness would have suffered.

Spencer is thus the philosopher of vastness. Misprised by many specialists, who carp at his technical imperfections, he has nevertheless enlarged the imagination, and set free the speculative mind of countless doctors, engineers, and lawyers, of many physicists and chemists, and of thoughtful laymen generally. He is the philosopher whom those who have no other philosopher can appreciate. To be able to say this of any man is great praise, and gives the "yes" answer to my recent question.

Can the "no" answer be as unhesitatingly uttered? I think so, if one makes the qualitative aspect of Spencer's work undo its quantitative aspect. The lukewarm equable temperament, the narrowness of sympathy and passion, the fondness for mechanical forms of thought, the imperfect receptivity and lack of interest in facts as such, dissevered from their possible connection with a theory; nay, the very vividness itself, the keenness of scent and the pertinacity; these all are qualities which may easily make for second-rateness, and for contentment with a cheap and loosely woven achievement. As Mr. Spencer's *First Principles* is the book which more than any other has spread his popular reputation, I had perhaps better explain what I mean by criticising some of its peculiarities.

I read this book as a youth when it was still appearing in numbers, and was carried away with enthusiasm by the intellectual perspectives which it seemed to open. When a maturer companion, Mr. Charles S. Peirce, attacked it in my presence, I felt spiritually wounded, as by the defacement of a sacred image or picture, though I could not verbally defend it against his criticisms.

Later I have used it often as a textbook with students, and the total outcome of my dealings with it is an exceedingly unfavorable verdict. Apart from the great truth which it enforces, that everything has evolved somehow, and apart from the inevitable stimulating effect of any such universal picture, I regard its teachings as almost a museum of blundering reasoning. Let me try to indicate briefly my grounds for such an opinion.

I pass by the section on the Unknowable, because this part of Mr. Spencer's philosophy has won fewer friends than any other. It consists chiefly of a rehash of Mansel's rehash of Hamilton's *Philosophy of the Conditioned,* and that has hardly raised its head since John Mill so effectively demolished it. If criticism of our human intellectual constitution is needed, it can be got out of Bradley to-day better than out of Spencer. The latter's way of reconciling science and religion is, moreover, too absurdly *naïf.* Find, he says, a fundamental abstract truth on which they can agree, and that will reconcile them. Such a truth, he thinks, is that *there is a mystery.* The trouble is that it is over just such common truths that quarrels begin. Did the fact that both believed in the existence of the Pope reconcile Luther and Ignatius Loyola? Did it reconcile the South and the North that both agreed that there were slaves? Religion claims that the "mystery" is interpretable by human reason; "Science," speaking through Spencer, insists that it is not. The admission of the mystery is the very signal for the quarrel. Moreover, for nine hundred and ninety-nine men out of a thousand the sense of mystery is the sense of *more-to-be-known,* not the sense of a More, *not* to be known.

But pass the Unknowable by, and turn to Spencer's famous law of Evolution.

"Science" works with several types of "law." The most frequent and useful type is that of the "elementary law,"—that of the composition of forces, that of gravitation, of refraction, and the like. Such laws declare no concrete facts to exist, and make no prophecy as to any actual future. They limit themselves to saying that *if* a certain character be found in any fact, another character will co-exist with it or follow it. The usefulness of these laws is proportionate to the extent to which the characters they treat of pervade the world, and to the accuracy with which they are definable.

Statistical laws form another type, and positively declare something about the world of actuality. Although they tell us nothing of the elements of things, either abstract or concrete, they affirm that the resultant of their actions drifts preponderantly in a particular direction. Population tends toward cities; the working classes tend to grow discontented; the available energy of the universe is running down—such laws prophesy the real future *en gros*, but they never help us to predict any particular detail of it.

Spencer's law of Evolution is of the statistical variety. It defines what evolution means, and what dissolution means, and asserts that, although both processes are always going on together, there is in the present phase of the world a drift in favor of evolution. In the first edition of *First Principles* an evolutive change in anything was described as the passage of it from a state of indefinite incoherent homogeneity to a definite coherent heterogeneity. The existence of a drift in this direction in everything Mr. Spencer proves, both by a survey of facts, and by deducing it from certain laws of the elementary type, which he severally names "the instability of the homogeneous," "the multiplication of effects," "segregation," and "equilibration." The two former insure the heterogeneity, while "segregation" brings about the definiteness and coherence, and "equilibration" arrests the process, and determines when dissolutive changes shall begin.

The whole panorama is resplendent for variety and inclusiveness, and has aroused an admiration for philosophy in minds that never admired philosophy before. Like Descartes in earlier days, Spencer aims at a purely mechanical explanation of Nature. The knowable universe is nothing but matter and motion, and its history is nothing but the "redistribution" of these entities. The value of such an explanation for scientific purposes depends altogether on how consistent and exact it is. Every "thing" must be interpreted as a "configuration," every "event" as a change of configuration, every predicate ascribed must be of a geometrical sort.

Measured by these requirements of mechanics Spencer's attempt has lamentably failed. His terms are vagueness and ambiguity incarnate, and he seems incapable of keeping the mechanical point of view in mind for five pages consecutively.

"Definite," for example, is hardly a physical idea at all. Every motion and every arrangement of matter is definitely what it is,—a fog or an irregular scrawl, as much so as a billiard ball or a straight line. Spencer means by definiteness in a thing any character that makes it arrest our attention, and forces us to distinguish it from other things. The word with him has a human, not a physical connotation. Definite things, in his book, finally appear merely as *things that men have made separate names for,* so that there is hardly a pretense of the mechanical view being kept. Of course names increase as human history proceeds, so "definiteness" in things must necessarily more and more evolve.

"Coherent," again. This has the definite mechanical meaning of resisting separation, of sticking together; but Spencer plays fast and loose with this meaning. Coherence with him sometimes means *permanence in time,* sometimes such *mutual dependence of parts* as is realized in a widely scattered system of no fixed material configuration; a commercial house, for example, with its "travelers" and ships and cars.

An honestly mechanical reader soon rubs his eyes with bewilderment at the orgy of ambiguity to which he is introduced. Every term in Spencer's fireworks shimmers through a whole spectrum of meanings in order to adapt itself to the successive spheres of evolution to which it must apply. "Integration," for instance. A definite coherence is an Integration; and examples given of integration are the contraction of the solar nebula, the formation of the earth's crust, the calcification of cartilage, the shortening of the body of crabs, the loss of his tail by man, the mutual dependence of plants and animals, the growth of powerful states, the tendency of human occupations to go to distinct localities, the dropping of terminal inflexions in English grammar, the formation of general concepts by the mind, the use of machinery instead of simple tools, the development of "composition" in the fine arts, etc., etc. It is obvious that no one form of the motion of matter characterizes all these facts. The human ones simply embody the more and more successful pursuit of certain ends.

In the second edition of his book, Mr. Spencer supplemented

his first formula by a unifying addition, meant to be strictly mechanical. "Evolution," he now said, "is the progressive integration of matter and dissipation of motion," during which both the matter and the motion undergo the previously designated kinds of change. But this makes the formula worse instead of better. The "dissipation of motion" part of it is simple vagueness,—for what particular motion is "dissipated" when a man or state grows more highly evolved? And the integration of matter belongs only to stellar and geologic evolution. Neither heightened specific gravity, nor greater massiveness, which are the only conceivable integrations of matter, is a mark of the more evolved vital, mental, or social things.

It is obvious that the facts of which Spencer here gives so clumsy an account could all have been set down more simply. First there is solar, and then there is geological evolution, processes accurately describable as integrations in the mechanical sense, namely, as decrease in bulk, or growth in hardness. Then Life appears; and after that neither integration of matter nor dissipation of motion plays any part whatever. The result of life, however, is to fill the world more and more with things displaying *organic unity*. By this is meant any arrangement of which one part helps to keep the other parts in existence. Some organic unities are material,—a sea urchin, for example, a department store, a civil service, or an ecclesiastical organization. Some are mental, as a "science," a code of laws, or an educational programme. But whether they be material or mental products, organic unities must *accumulate*; for every old one tends to conserve itself, and if successful new ones arise they also "come to stay." The human use of Spencer's adjectives "integrated," "definite," "coherent," here no longer shocks one. We are frankly on teleological ground, and metaphor and vagueness are permissible.

This tendency of organic unities to accumulate when once they are formed is absolutely all the truth I can distill from Spencer's unwieldy account of evolution. It makes a much less gaudy and chromatic picture, but what there is of it is exact.

Countless other criticisms swarm toward my pen, but I have no heart to express them,—it is too sorry an occupation. A word about Spencer's conception of "Force," however, insists on being added; for although it is one of his most essential, it is one of his vaguest ideas.

Over all his special laws of evolution there reigns an absolutely general law, that of the "persistence of force." By this Spencer sometimes means the phenomenal law of conservation of energy, sometimes the metaphysical principle that the quantity of existence is unalterable, sometimes the logical principle that nothing can happen without a reason, sometimes the practical postulate that in the absence of any assignable difference you must call a thing the same. This law is one vast vagueness, of which I can give no clear account; but of his special vaguenesses "mental force" and "social force" are good examples. These manifestations of the universal force, he says, are due to vital force, and this latter is due to physical force, both being proportionate to the amount of physical force which is "transformed" into them. But what on earth is "social force"? Sometimes he identifies it with "social activity" (showing the latter to be proportionate to the amount of food eaten), sometimes with the work done by human beings and their steam-engines, and shows it to be due ultimately to the sun's heat. It would never occur to a reader of his pages that a social force proper might be anything that acted as a stimulus of social change,—a leader, for example, a discovery, a book, a new idea, or a national insult; and that the greatest of "forces" of this kind need embody no more "physical force" than the smallest. The measure of greatness here is the effect produced on the environment, not a quantity antecedently absorbed from physical nature. Mr. Spencer himself is a great social force; but he ate no more than an average man, and his body, if cremated, would disengage no more energy. The effects he exerts are of the nature *of releases,*—his words pull triggers in certain kinds of brain.

The fundamental distinction in mechanics between forces of push-and-pull and forces of release is one of which Mr. Spencer, in his earlier years, made no use whatever. Only in his sixth edition did he show that it had seriously arrested his attention. In biology, psychology, and sociology the forces concerned are almost exclusively forces of release. Spencer's account of social forces is neither good sociology nor good mechanics. His feeble grasp of the conception of force vitiates, in fact, all his work.

But the task of a carper is repugnant. The *Essays, Biology, Psychology, Sociology,* and *Ethics* are all better than *First Principles,* and contain numerous and admirable bits of penetrating work of detail. My impression is that, of the systematic treatises, the *Psychology* will rank as the most original. Spencer broke new ground here in insisting that, since mind and its environment have evolved together, they must be studied together. He gave to the study of mind in isolation a definitive quietus, and that certainly is a great thing to have achieved. To be sure he overdid the matter, as usual, and left no room for any mental structure at all, except that which passively resulted from the storage of impressions received from the outer world in the order of their frequency by fathers and transmitted to their sons. The belief that whatever is acquired by sires is inherited by sons, and the ignoring of purely inner variations, are weak points; but to have brought in the environment as vital was a master stroke.

I may say that Spencer's controversy over use-inheritance with Weismann, entered into after he was sixty, seems to me in point of quality better than any other part of his work. It is genuine labor over a puzzle, genuine research.

Spencer's *Ethics* is a most vital and original piece of attitude-taking in the world of ideals. His politico-ethical activity in general breathes the purest English spirit of liberty, and his attacks on over-administration and criticisms on the inferiority of great centralized systems are worthy to be the textbooks of individualists the world over. I confess that it is with this part of his work, in spite of its hardness and inflexibility of tone, that I personally sympathize most.

Looking back on Mr. Spencer as a whole, as this admirably truth-telling *Autobiography* reveals him, he is a figure unique for quaint consistency. He never varied from that inimitable blend of small and vast mindedness, of liberality and crabbedness, which was his personal note, and which defies our formulating power. If an abstract logical concept could come to life, its life would be like Spencer's,—the same definiteness of exclusion and inclusion, the same bloodlessness of temperament, the same narrowness of intent and vastness of extent, the same power of applying itself to numberless instances. But he was no abstract idea; he was a man vigorously devoted to truth and justice as he saw them, who had deep insights, and who finished, under terrible frustrations from bad health, a piece of work that, taken for all in all, is extraordinary. A human life is greater than all its possible appraisers, assessors, and critics. In comparison with the fact of Spencer's actual living, such critical characterization of it as I have been at all these pains to produce seems a rather unimportant as well as a decidedly graceless thing.

The Pragmatic Method[1]

The principle of pragmatism, as we may call it, may be expressed in a variety of ways, all of them very simple. In the *Popular Science Monthly* for January, 1878, Mr. Charles S. Peirce introduces it as follows: The soul and meaning of thought, he says, can never be made to direct itself towards anything but the production of belief, belief being the demicadence which closes a musical phrase in the symphony of our intellectual life. Thought in movement has thus for its only possible motive the attainment of thought at rest. But when our thought about an object has found its rest in belief, then our action on the subject can firmly and safely begin. Beliefs, in short, are really rules for action; and the whole function of thinking is but one step in the production of habits of action. If there were any part of a thought that made no difference in the thought's practical consequences, then that part would be no proper element of the thought's significance. Thus the same thought may be clad in different words; but if the different words suggest no different conduct, they are but outer accretions, and have no part in the thought's meaning. If, however, they determine conduct differ-

[1] The following address was originally delivered before the Philosophical Union of the University of California, on August 26, 1898, and was printed in *The University Chronicle* for September, 1898. It is reprinted here with a few omissions and with the author's consent, on account of its intimate relation to current discussions.— EDITOR.

ently, they are essential elements of the significance. Thus to develope a thought's meaning we need only determine what conduct it is fitted to produce; that conduct is for us its sole significance. And the tangible fact at the root of all our thought-distinctions, however subtle, is that there is no one of them so fine as to consist in anything but a possible difference of practice. To attain perfect clearness in our thoughts of an object, then, we need only consider what effects of a conceivably practical kind the object may involve —what sensations we are to expect from it, and what reactions we must prepare. Our conception of these effects, then, is for us the whole of our conception of the object, so far as that conception has positive significance at all.

This is the principle of Peirce, the principle of pragmatism. I think myself that it should be expressed more broadly than Mr. Peirce expresses it. The ultimate test for us of what a truth means is indeed the conduct it dictates or inspires. But it inspires that conduct because it first foretells some particular turn to our experience which shall call for just that conduct from us. And I should prefer to express Peirce's principle by saying that the effective meaning of any philosophic proposition can always be brought down to some particular consequence, in our future practical experience, whether active or passive; the point lying rather in the fact that the experience must be particular, than in the fact that it must be active.

To take in the importance of this principle, one must get accustomed to applying it to concrete cases. Such use as I am able to make of it convinces me that to be mindful of it in philosophical disputations tends wonderfully to smooth out misunderstandings and to bring in peace. If it did nothing else, then, it would yield a sovereignly valuable rule of method for discussion. Suppose, in fact, that there are two different philosophical definitions, or propositions, or maxims, or what not, which seem to contradict each other, and about which men dispute. If, by assuming the truth of the one, you can foresee no conceivable practical consequence to anybody at any time or place, which is different from what you would foresee if you assumed the truth of the other, why then the difference between the two propositions is no real difference—it is only a specious and verbal difference, unworthy of further contention. Both formulas mean radically the same thing, although they may say it in such different words. It is astonishing to see how many philosophical disputes collapse into insignificance the moment you subject them to this simple test. There can *be* no difference which doesn't *make* a difference—no difference in abstract truth which does not express itself in a difference of concrete fact, and of conduct consequent upon the fact, imposed on somebody, somehow, somewhere and somewhen. It is true that a certain shrinkage of values often seems to occur in our general formulas when we measure their meaning in this prosaic and practical way. They diminish. But the vastness that is merely based on vagueness is a false appearance of importance, and not a vastness worth retaining. The x's, y's and z's always do shrivel, as I have heard a learned friend say, whenever at the end of your algebraic computation they change into so many plain a's, b's and c's; but the whole function of algebra is, after all, to get them into that more definite shape; and the whole function of philosophy ought to be to find out what definite difference it will make to you and me, at definite instants of our life, if this world-formula or that world-formula be the one which is true.

If we start off with an impossible case, we shall perhaps all the more clearly see the use and scope of our principle. Let us therefore put ourselves, in imagination, in a position from which no forecasts of consequence, no dictates of conduct, can possibly be made, so that the principle of pragmatism finds no field of application. Let us, I mean, assume that the present moment is the absolutely last moment of the world, with bare nonentity beyond it, and with no hereafter for either experience or conduct.

Now I say that in that case there would be no sense whatever in some of our most urgent and envenomed philosophical and religious debates. The question, 'Is matter the producer of all things, or is a God there too?' would, for example, offer a perfectly idle and insignificant alternative if the world were finished and no more of it to come. Many of us, most of us I think, now feel as if a terrible coldness and deadness would come over the world were we forced to believe that no informing spirit or purpose had to do with it, but it merely accidentally had come. The actually experienced details of fact might be the same on either hypothesis, some sad, some joyous; some rational, some odd and grotesque; but without a God behind them, we think they would have something ghastly, they would tell no genuine story, there would be no speculation in those eyes that they do glare with. With the God, on the other hand, they would grow solid, warm, and altogether full of real significance.

But I say that such an alternation of feelings, reasonable enough in a consciousness that is prospective, as ours now is, and whose world is partly yet to come, would be absolutely irrational in a purely retrospective consciousness summing up a world already past. For such a consciousness, no emotional interest could attach to the alternative. The problem would be purely intellectual; and if unaided matter could, with any scientific plausibility, be shown to cipher out the actual facts, then not the faintest shadow ought to cloud the mind, of regret for the God that by the same ciphering would prove needless and disappear from our belief.

For just consider the case sincerely, and say what would be the *worth* of such a God if he *were* there, with his work accomplished and his world run down. He would be worth no more than just that world was worth. To that amount of result, with its mixed merits and defects, his creative power could attain, but go no farther. And since there is to be no future; since the whole value and meaning of the world has been already paid in and actualized in the feelings that went with it in the passing, and now go with it in the ending; since it draws no supplemental significance (such as our real world draws) from its function of preparing something yet to come;—why then, by it we take God's measure, as it were. He is the being who could once for all do *that*; and for that much we are thankful to him, but for nothing more. But now, on the contrary hypothesis, namely, that the bits of matter following their 'laws' could make that world and do no less, *should we not be just as thankful to them?* Wherein should we suffer loss, then, if we dropped God as an hypothesis and made the matter alone responsible? Where would the special deadness, 'crassness' and ghastliness come in? And how, experience being what it is once for all, would God's presence in it make it any more 'living,' any richer in our sight?

Candidly, it is impossible to give any answer to this question. The actually experienced world is supposed to be the same in its details on either hypothesis, "the same for our praise or blame," as Browning says. It stands there indefeasibly; a gift which can't be taken back. Calling matter the cause of it retracts no single one of the items that have made it up, nor does calling God the cause augment them. They are the God or the atoms, respectively, of just that and no other world. The God, if there, has been doing just what atoms could do—appearing in the character of atoms, so to speak—and earning such gratitude as is due to atoms, and no more. If his presence lends no different turn or issue to the performance, it surely can lend it no increase of dignity. Nor would indignity come to it were he absent, and did the atoms remain the only actors on the stage. When a play is once over, and the curtain down, you really make it no better by claiming an illustrious genius for its author, just as you make it no worse by calling him a common hack.

Thus if no future detail of experience or conduct is to be deduced from our hypothesis, the debate between materialism and theism becomes quite idle and insignificant. Matter and God in that event mean exactly the same thing—the power, namely, neither more nor less, that can make just this mixed, imperfect, yet completed world—and the wise man is he who in such a case would turn his back on such a supererogatory discussion. Accordingly, most men instinctively—and a large class of men, the so-called positivists or scientists, deliberately—do turn their backs on philosophical disputes from which nothing in the line of definite future consequences can be seen to follow. The verbal and empty character of our studies is surely a reproach with which you of the Philosophical Union are but too sadly familiar. A student said to me the other day, 'Words, words, words, are all that you philosophers care for.' We philosophers think it all unjust; and yet, if the principle of pragmatism be true, it is a perfectly sound reproach unless the metaphysical alternatives under investigation can be shown to have alternative practical outcomes, however delicate and distant these may be. The common man and the scientist can discover no such outcomes. And if the metaphysician can discern none either, the common man and scientist certainly are in the right of it, as against him. His science is then but pompous trifling; and the endowment of a professorship for such a being would be something really absurd.

Accordingly, in every genuine metaphysical debate some practical issue, however conjectural and remote, is involved. To realize this, revert with me to the question of materialism or theism; and place yourselves this time in the real world we live in, the world that has a future, that is yet uncompleted whilst we speak. In this unfinished world the alternative of 'materialism or theism?' is intensely practical; and it is worth while for us to spend some minutes of our hour in seeing how truly this is the case.

How, indeed, does the program differ for us, according as we consider that the facts of experience up to date are purposeless configurations of atoms moving according to eternal elementary laws, or that on the other hand they are due to the providence of God? As far as the past facts go, indeed there is no difference. These facts are in, are bagged, are captured; and the good that's in them is gained, be the atoms or be the God their cause. There are accordingly many materialists about us to-day who, ignoring altogether the future and practical aspects of the question, seek to eliminate the odium attaching to the word materialism, and even to eliminate the word itself, by showing that, if matter could give birth to all these gains, why then matter, functionally considered, is just as divine an entity as God, in fact coalesces with God, is what you mean by God. Cease, these persons advise us, to use either of these terms, with their outgrown opposition. Use a term free of the clerical connotations, on the one hand; of the suggestion of grossness, coarseness, ignobility, on the other. Talk of the primal mystery, of the unknowable energy, of the one and only power, instead of saying either God or matter. This is the course to which Mr. Spencer urges us at the end of the first volume of his *Psychology.* In some well-written pages he there shows us that a 'matter' so infinitely subtle, and performing motions as inconceivably quick and fine as modern science postulates in her explanations, has no trace of grossness left. He shows that the conception of spirit, as we mortals hitherto have framed it, is itself too gross to cover the exquisite complexity of nature's facts. Both terms, he says, are but symbols, pointing to that one unknowable reality in which their oppositions cease.

Throughout these remarks of Mr. Spencer, eloquent, and even noble in a certain sense, as they are, he seems to think that the dislike of the ordinary man to materialism comes from a purely aesthetic disdain of matter, as something gross in itself, and vile and despicable. Undoubtedly such an aesthetic disdain of matter has played a part in philosophic history. But it forms no part whatever of an intelligent modern man's dislikes. Give him a matter bound *forever* by its laws to lead our world nearer and nearer to perfection, and any rational man will worship that matter as readily as Mr. Spencer worships his own so-called unknowable power. It not only has made for righteousness up to date, but it will make for righteousness forever; and that is all we need. Doing practically all that a God can do, it is equivalent to God, its function is a God's function, and is exerted in a world in which a God would now be superfluous; from such a world a God could never lawfully be missed.

But *is* the matter by which Mr. Spencer's process of cosmic evolution is carried on any such principle of never-ending perfection as this? Indeed it is not, for the future end of every cosmically evolved thing or system of things is tragedy; and Mr. Spencer, in confining himself to the aesthetic and ignoring the practical side of the controversy, has really contributed nothing serious to its relief. But apply now our principle of practical results, and see what a vital significance the question of materialism or theism immediately acquires.

Theism and materialism, so indifferent when taken retrospectively, point, when we take them prospectively, to wholly different practical consequences, to opposite outlooks of experience. For, according to the theory of mechanical evolution, the laws of redistribution of matter and motion, though they are certainly to thank for all the good hours which our organisms have ever yielded us and for all the ideals which our minds now frame, are yet fatally certain to undo their work again, and to redissolve everything that they have once evolved. You all know the picture of the last foreseeable state of the dead universe, as evolutionary science gives it forth. I cannot state it better than in Mr. Balfour's words: "The energies of our system will decay, the glory of the sun will be dimmed, and the earth, tideless and inert, will no longer tolerate the race which has for a moment disturbed its solitude. Man will go down into the pit, and all his thoughts will perish. The uneasy consciousness, which in this obscure corner has for a brief space broken the contented silence of the universe, will be at rest. Matter will know itself no longer. 'Imperishable monuments' and 'immortal deeds,' death itself, and love stronger than death, will be as though they had never been. Nor will anything that *is* be better or be worse for all that the labour, genius, devotion, and suffering of man have striven through countless generations to effect."[2]

That is the sting of it, that in the vast driftings of the cosmic weather, though many a jeweled shore appears, and many an en-

2 *The Foundations of Belief*, p. 30.

129

chanted cloud-bank floats away, long lingering ere it be dissolved—even as our world now lingers, for our joy—yet when these transient products are gone, nothing, absolutely *nothing*, remains, to represent those particular qualities, those elements of preciousness which they may have enshrined. Dead and gone are they, gone utterly from the very sphere and room of being. Without an echo; without a memory; without an influence on aught that may come after, to make it care for similar ideals. This final wreck and tragedy is of the essence of scientific materialism as at present understood. The lower and not the higher forces are the eternal forces, or the last surviving forces within the only cycle of evolution which we can definitely see. Mr. Spencer believes this as much as anyone; so why should he argue with us as if we were making silly aesthetic objections to the 'grossness' of 'matter and motion'—the principles of his philosophy—when what really dismays us in it is the disconsolateness of its ulterior practical results?

No, the true objection to materialism is not positive but negative. It would be farcical at this day to make complaint of it for what it *is*, for 'grossness.' Grossness is what grossness *does*—we now know *that*. We make complaint of it, on the contrary, for what it is *not*—not a permanent warrant for our more ideal interests, not a fulfiller of our remotest hopes.

The notion of God, on the other hand, however inferior it may be in clearness to those mathematical notions so current in mechanical philosophy, has at least this practical superiority over them, that it guarantees an ideal order that shall be permanently preserved. A world with a God in it to say the last word, may indeed burn up or freeze, but we then think of him as still mindful of the old ideals and sure to bring them elsewhere to fruition; so that, where he is, tragedy is only provisional and partial, and shipwreck and dissolution not the absolutely final things. This need of an eternal moral order is one of the deepest needs of our breast. And those poets, like Dante and Wordsworth, who live on the conviction of such an order, owe to that fact the extraordinary tonic and consoling power of their verse. Here then, in these different emotional and practical appeals, in these adjustments of our concrete attitudes of hope and expectation, and all the delicate consequences which their differences entail, lie the real meanings of materialism and theism—not in hair-splitting abstractions about matter's inner essence, or about the metaphysical attributes of

God. Materialism means simply the denial that the moral order is eternal, and the cutting off of ultimate hopes; theism means the affirmation of an eternal moral order and the letting loose of hope. Surely here is an issue genuine enough, for anyone who feels it; and, as long as men are men, it will yield matter for serious philosophic debate. Concerning this question, at any rate, the positivists and pooh-poohers of metaphysics are in the wrong.

But possibly some of you may still rally to their defense. Even whilst admitting that theism and materialism make different prophecies of the world's future, you may yourselves pooh-pooh the difference as something so infinitely remote as to mean nothing for a sane mind. The essence of a sane mind, you may say, is to take shorter views, and to feel no concern about such chimaeras as the latter end of the world. Well, I can only say that if you say this, you do injustice to human nature. Religious melancholy is not disposed of by a simple flourish of the word insanity. The absolute things, the last things, the overlapping things, are the truly philosophic concern; all superior minds feel seriously about them, and the mind with the shortest views is simply the mind of the more shallow man.

However, I am willing to pass over these very distant outlooks on the ultimate, if any of you so insist. The theistic controversy can still serve to illustrate the principle of pragmatism for us well enough, without driving us so far afield. If there be a God, it is not likely that he is confined solely to making differences in the world's latter end; he probably makes differences all along its course. Now the principle of practicalism says that the very meaning of the conception of God lies in those differences which must be made in our experience if the conception be true. God's famous inventory of perfections, as elaborated by dogmatic theology, either means nothing, says our principle, or it implies certain definite things that we can feel and do at particular moments of our lives, things which we could not feel and should not do were no God present and were the business of the universe carried on by material atoms instead. So far as our conceptions of the deity involve no such experiences, so far they are meaningless and verbal,—scholastic entities and abstractions, as the positivists say, and fit objects for their scorn. But so far as they do involve such definite experiences, God means something for us, and may be real.

Now if we look at the definitions of God made by dogmatic

theology, we see immediately that some stand and some fall when treated by this test. God, for example, as any orthodox text-book will tell us, is a being existing not only *per se*, or by himself, as created beings exist, but *a se*, or from himself; and out of this 'aseity' flow most of his perfections. He is, for example, necessary; absolute; infinite in all respects; and single. He is simple, not compounded of essence and existence, substance and accident, actuality and potentiality, or subject and attribute, as are other things. He belongs to no genus; he is inwardly and outwardly unalterable; he knows and wills all things, and first of all his own infinite self, in one indivisible eternal act. And he is absolutely self-sufficing, and infinitely happy.—Now in which one of us practical Americans here assembled does this conglomeration of attributes awaken any sense of reality? And if in no one, then why not? Surely because such attributes awaken no responsive active feelings and call for no particular conduct of our own. How does God's 'aseity' come home to *you*? What specific thing can I do to adapt myself to his 'simplicity'? Or how determine our behavior henceforward if his 'felicity' is anyhow absolutely complete? In the '50's and '60's Captain Mayne Reid was the great writer of boys' books of out-of-door adventure. He was forever extolling the hunters and field-observers of living animals' habits, and keeping up a fire of invective against the 'closet-naturalists,' as he called them, the collectors and classifiers, and handlers of skeletons and skins. When I was a boy I used to think that a closet-naturalist must be the vilest type of wretch under the sun. But surely the systematic theologians are the closet-naturalists of the deity, even in Captain Mayne Reid's sense. Their orthodox deduction of God's attributes is nothing but a shuffling and matching of pedantic dictionary-adjectives, aloof from morals, aloof from human needs, something that might be worked out from the mere word 'God' by a logical machine of wood and brass as well as by a man of flesh and blood. The attributes which I have quoted have absolutely nothing to do with religion, for religion is a living practical affair. Other parts, indeed, of God's traditional description do have practical connection with life, and have owed all their historic importance to that fact. His omniscience, for example, and his justice. With the one he sees us in the dark, with the other he rewards and punishes what he sees. So do his ubiquity and eternity and unalterability appeal to our confidence, and his goodness banish our fears. Even attributes of less meaning to this present audience have in past times so appealed. One of the chief attributes of God, according to the orthodox theology, is his infinite love of himself, proved by asking the question, 'By what but an infinite object can an infinite affection be appeased?' An immediate consequence of this primary self-love of God is the orthodox dogma that the manifestation of his own glory is God's primal purpose in creation; and that dogma has certainly made very efficient practical connection with life. It is true that we ourselves are tending to outgrow this old monarchical conception of a deity with his 'court' and pomp—'his state is kingly, thousands at his bidding speed,' etc.—but there is no denying the enormous influence it has had over ecclesiastical history, nor, by repercussion, over the history of European states. And yet even these more real and significant attributes have the trail of the serpent over them as the books on theology have actually worked them out. One feels that, in the theologians' hands, they are only a set of dictionary-adjectives, mechanically deduced; logic has stepped into the place of vision, professionalism into that of life. Instead of bread we get a stone; instead of fish, a serpent. Did such a conglomeration of abstract general terms give really the gist of our knowledge of the deity, divinity-schools might indeed continue to flourish, but religion, vital religion, would have taken its flight from this world. What keeps religion going is something else than abstract definitions and systems of logically concatenated adjectives, and something different from faculties of theology and their professors. All these things are after-effects, secondary accretions upon a mass of concrete religious experiences, connecting themselves with feeling and conduct, that renew themselves *in saecula saeculorum* in the lives of humble private men. If you ask what these experiences are, they are conversations with the unseen, voices and visions, responses to prayer, changes of heart, deliverances from fear, inflowings of help, assurances of support, whenever certain persons set their own internal attitude in certain appropriate ways. The power comes and goes and is lost, and can be found only in a certain definite direction, just as if it were a concrete material thing. These direct experiences of a wider spiritual life with which our superficial consciousness is continuous, and with which it keeps up an intense commerce, form the primary mass of direct religious experience on which all hearsay religion rests, and which furnishes that notion of an ever-present

God out of which systematic theology thereupon proceeds to make capital in its own unreal pedantic way. What the word 'God' means is just those passive and active experiences of your life. Now, my friends, it is quite immaterial to my purpose whether you yourselves enjoy and venerate these experiences, or whether you stand aloof and, viewing them in others, suspect them of being illusory and vain. Like all other human experiences, they too certainly share in the general liability to illusion and mistake. They need not be infallible. But they are certainly the originals of the God-idea, and theology is the translation; and you remember that I am now using the God-idea merely as an example, not to discuss as to its truth or error, but only to show how well the principle of pragmatism works. That the God of systematic theology should exist or not exist is a matter of small practical moment. At most it means that you may continue uttering certain abstract words and that you must stop using others. But if the God of these particular experiences be false, it is an awful thing for you, if you are one of those whose lives are stayed on such experiences. The theistic controversy, trivial enough if we take it merely academically and theologically, is of tremendous significance if we test it by its results for actual life.

I can best continue to recommend the principle of practicalism to you by keeping in the neighborhood of this theological idea. I reminded you a few minutes ago that the old monarchical notion of the deity as a sort of Louis the Fourteenth of the Heavens is losing nowadays much of its ancient prestige. Religious philosophy, like all philosophy, is growing more and more idealistic. And in the philosophy of the Absolute, so called, that post-Kantian form of idealism which is carrying so many of our higher minds before it, we have the triumph of what in old times was summarily disposed of as the pantheistic heresy,—I mean the conception of God, not as the extraneous creator, but as the indwelling spirit and substance of the world. I know not where one can find a more candid, more clear, or, on the whole, more persuasive statement of this theology of Absolute Idealism than in the addresses made before this very Union three years ago by your own great California philosopher (whose colleague at Harvard I am proud to be), Josiah Royce. His contributions to the resulting volume, *The Conception of God*, form a very masterpiece of popularization. Now you will remember, many of you, that in the discussion that followed Professor Royce's address, the debate turned largely on the ideas of unity and plurality, and on the question whether, if God be One in All and All in All, 'One with the unity of a single instant,' as Royce calls it, 'forming in His wholeness one luminously transparent moment,' any room is left for real morality or freedom. Professor Howison, in particular, was earnest in urging that morality and freedom are relations between a manifold of selves, and that under the régime of Royce's monistic Absolute Thought 'no true manifold of selves is or can be provided for.' I will not go into any of the details of that particular discussion, but just ask you to consider for a moment whether, in general, any discussion about monism or pluralism, any argument over the unity of the universe, would not necessarily be brought into a shape where it tends to straighten itself out, by bringing our principle of practical results to bear.

The question whether the world is at bottom One or Many is a typical metaphysical question. Long has it raged! In its crudest form it is an exquisite example of the *loggerheads* of metaphysics. 'I say it is one great fact,' Parmenides and Spinoza exclaim. 'I say it is many little facts,' reply the atomists and associationists. 'I say it is both one and many, many in one,' say the Hegelians; and in the ordinary popular discussions we rarely get beyond this barren reiteration by the disputants of their pet adjectives of number. But is it not first of all clear that when we take such an adjective as 'One' absolutely and abstractly, its meaning is so vague and empty that it makes no difference whether we affirm or deny it? Certainly this universe is not the mere number One; and yet you can number it 'one,' if you like, in talking about it as contrasted with other possible worlds numbered 'two' and 'three' for the occasion. What exact thing do you *practically* mean by 'One,' when you call the universe One, is the first question you must ask. In what ways does the oneness come home to your own personal life? By what difference does it express itself in your experience? How can you act differently towards a universe which is one? Inquired into in this way, the unity might grow clear and be affirmed in some ways and denied in others, and so cleared up, even though a certain vague and worshipful portentousness might disappear from the notion of it in the process.

For instance, one practical result that follows when we have one thing to handle, is that we can pass from one part of it to another without letting go of the thing. In this sense oneness must be partly denied and partly affirmed of our universe. Physically we can pass continuously in various manners from one part of it to another part. But logically and psychically the passage seems less easy, for there is no obvious transition from one mind to another, or from minds to physical things. You have to step off and get on again; so that in these ways the world is not one, as measured by that practical test.

Another practical meaning of oneness is susceptibility of collection. A collection is one, though the things that compose it be many. Now, can we practically 'collect' the universe? Physically, of course we cannot. And mentally we cannot, if we take it concretely in its details. But if we take it summarily and abstractly, then we collect it mentally whenever we refer to it, even as I do now when I fling the term 'universe' at it, and so seem to leave a mental ring around it. It is plain, however, that such abstract noetic unity, as we may call it, is a very insignificant thing. Chaos, once named, has a noetic unity which seems to carry with it no further consequences at all.

Again, oneness may mean generic sameness, so that you can treat all parts of the collection by one rule and get the same results. It is evident that in this sense the oneness of our world is incomplete, for in spite of much generic sameness in its elements and items, they still remain of many irreducible kinds. You can't pass by mere logic all over the field of it.

Its elements have, however, an affinity or commensurability with each other, are not wholly irrelevant, but can be compared, and fit together after certain fashions. This again might practically mean that they were one *in origin*, and that, tracing them backwards, we should find them arising in a single primal causal fact. Such unity of origin would have definite practical consequences, would have them for our scientific life at least.

I can give only these hasty superficial indications of what I mean when I say that it tends to clear up the quarrel between monism and pluralism to subject the notion of unity to such practical tests. On the other hand, it does but perpetuate strife and misunderstanding to continue talking of it in an absolute and mystical way. I have little doubt myself that this old quarrel might be completely smoothed out to the satisfaction of all claimants, if only the maxim of Peirce were methodically followed here. The current monism on the whole still keeps talking in too abstract a way. It says the world must be either pure disconnectedness, no universe at all, or absolute unity. It insists that there is no stopping-place half way. Any connection whatever, says this monism, is only possible if there be still more connection, until at last we are driven to admit the absolutely total connection required. But this absolutely total connection either means nothing, is the mere word 'one' spelt long, or else it means the sum of all the partial connections that can possibly be conceived. I believe that when we thus attack the question, and set ourselves to search for these possible connections, and conceive each in a definite practical way, the dispute is already in a fair way to be settled beyond the chance of misunderstanding, by a compromise in which the Many and the One both get their lawful rights.

But I am in danger of becoming technical; so I must stop right here, and let you go.

I am happy to say that it is the English-speaking philosophers who first introduced the custom of interpreting the meaning of conceptions by asking what difference they make for life. Mr. Peirce has only expressed in the form of an explicit maxim what their sense for reality led them all instinctively to do. The great English way of investigating a conception is to ask yourself right off, 'What is it *known as*? In what facts does it result? What is its *cash-value* in terms of particular experience? and what special difference would come into the world according as it were true or false?' Thus does Locke treat the conception of personal identity. What you mean by it is just your chain of memories, says he. That is the only concretely verifiable part of its significance. All further ideas about it, such as the oneness or manyness of the spiritual substance on which it is based, are therefore void of intelligible meaning; and propositions touching such ideas may be indifferently affirmed or denied. So Berkeley with his 'matter.' The cash-value of matter is our physical sensations. That is what it is known as, all that we concretely verify of its conception. That therefore is the whole meaning of the word 'matter'—any other pretended meaning is mere wind of words. Hume does the same thing with causation. It is known as habitual antecedence, and tendency on our part to look for something definite to come. Apart from this practical meaning it has no significance whatever, and books about it may be committed to the flames, says Hume. Stewart and Brown, James Mill, John Mill, and Bain, have followed more or less consistently the same method; and Shadworth Hodgson has used it almost as explicitly as Mr. Peirce. These writers have many of them no doubt been too sweeping in their negations; Hume, in particular, and James Mill and Bain. But when all is said and done, it was they, not Kant, who introduced 'the critical method' into philosophy, the one method fitted to make philosophy a study worthy of serious men. For what seriousness can possibly remain in debating philosophic propositions that will never make an appreciable difference to us in action? And what matters it, when all propositions are practically meaningless, which of them be called true or false?

The shortcomings and the negations and baldnesses of the English philosophers in question come, not from their eye to merely practical results, but solely from their failure to track the practical results completely enough to see how far they extend. Hume can be corrected and built out, and his beliefs enriched, by using Humian principles exclusively, and without making any use of the circuitous and ponderous artificialities of Kant. It is indeed a somewhat pathetic matter, as it seems to me, that this is not the course which the actual history of philosophy has followed. Hume had no English successors of adequate ability to complete him and correct his negations; so it happened as a matter of fact that the building out of critical philosophy has mainly been left to thinkers who were under the influence of Kant. Even in England and this country it is with Kantian catch-words and categories that the fuller view of life is pursued, and in our universities it is the courses in transcendentalism that kindle the enthusiasm of the more ardent students, whilst the courses in English philosophy are committed to a secondary place. I cannot think that this is exactly as it should be. And I say this not out of national jingoism, for jingoism has no place in philosophy; or out of excitement over the great Anglo-American alliance against the world, of which we nowadays hear so much—though heaven knows that to that alliance I wish a God-speed. I say it because I sincerely believe that the English spirit in philosophy is intellectually, as well as practically and morally, on the saner, sounder and truer path. Kant's mind is the rarest and most intricate of all possible antique bric-a-brac museums; and connoisseurs and dilettanti will always wish to visit it and see the wondrous and racy contents. The temper of the dear old man about his work is perfectly delectable. And yet he is really—although I shrink with some terror from saying such a thing before some of you here present—at bottom a mere curio, a 'specimen.' I mean by this a perfectly definite thing: I believe that Kant bequeathes to us not one single conception which is both indispensable to philosophy and which philosophy either did not possess before him, or was not destined inevitably to acquire after him through the growth of men's reflection upon the hypotheses by which science interprets nature. The true line of philosophic progress lies, in short, it seems to me, not so much *through* Kant as *round* him to the point where now we stand. Philosophy can perfectly well outflank him, and build herself up into adequate fulness by prolonging more directly the older English lines.

Preface to Höffding's *Problems of Philosophy*

Professor Höffding of Copenhagen is one of the wisest, as well as one of the most learned of living philosophers. His *Psychology*, his *Ethics*, and his *History of Modern Philosophy* have made his name known and respected among English readers, though his admirable *Philosophy of Religion* still calls for a translator. The following little work is, so to speak, his philosophical testament. In it he sums up in an extraordinarily compact and pithy form the result of his lifelong reflections on the deepest alternatives of philosophical opinion. The work, to my mind, is so pregnant and its conclusions so sensible—or at least so in accordance with what I regard as sensible—that I have had it translated as a contribution to the education of our English-reading students.

Rationalism in philosophy proceeds from the whole to its parts, and maintains that the connection between facts must at bottom be intimate and not external: the universe is a Unit, and the parts of Being must be interlocked continuously. Empiricism, on the other hand, goes from parts to whole, and is willing to allow that in the end some parts may be merely added to others, and that what the word 'and' stands for may be a part of real Being as well as of speech. For radical rationalism, Reality in itself is eternally complete, and the confusions of experience are our illusion. For radical empiricism, confusion may be a category of the Real itself, and 'ever not quite' a permanent result of our attempts at thinking it out straighter. Professors of Philosophy are almost always rationalists; and the student, passing from the street into their lecture-rooms, usually finds a world presented to him, so abstract, pure, and logical, and perfect, that it is hard for him to see in it any resemblance of character to the struggling and disjointed sum of muddy facts which he has left behind him, outside.

Now the peculiarity of Professor Höffding is that whereas he has the *manner* of a rationalistic professor of Philosophy, being as abstract and technical in his style of exposition as any one can wish, his results, nevertheless, keep in touch with the temperament of concrete reality, and he allows that 'ever not quite' may be the last word of our attempts at understanding life rationally.

The word 'rationally' here denotes certain definite connections which Professor Höffding also sums up under the name of 'continuities.' He opposes to them the notion of the 'irrational,' as that residuum of crude or 'alogical' fact, '*mere*' fact, that may remain over when our attempts to establish logical continuity among things have reached their limit. The conjunction 'and' would be the only bond here between the continuous and the irrational portion of Reality. Professor Höffding is in short an empiricist and pluralist, although he prefers to call himself a 'critical Monist.' He means by the word 'critical,' here, to indicate that the continuity and unity of Reality are at no time complete, but may be yet in process of completion. Our thought, which is itself a part of Reality, is surely incomplete; but in endeavoring to make itself ever more continuous and to see the world as ever more rational, it works in the direction of more continuity; and the whole of Creation may analogously be in travail to get itself into an ever more continuous and rational form.

Empiricist matter presented in a rationalist's manner—this to my mind gives their distinction to the pages that follow. They form a *multum in parvo* so well calculated to impress and influence the usual rationalistic-minded student of philosophy, that I put them forth in English for his benefit.

It takes, I confess, some little knowledge of philosophic literature to appreciate the far-reaching significance of some of our author's paragraphs, and to distribute emphasis properly among them. They are too brief and abstract for the unguided beginner. For his benefit let me barely indicate some of the book's positions which seem to me particularly noteworthy.

I have spoken of the notion that since the world is incomplete anyhow, so far as our thought goes, it may also in other ways be only approaching perfection. Perfection, in other words, may not be eternal; rather are things working toward it as an ideal; and God himself may be one of the co-workers. Time, on this view, must be real, and cannot, Professor Höffding says, be banished, as ultra-rationalists pretend, from absolute reality.

With this general position goes what our author calls the 'dynamic' notion of Truth, as opposed to the 'static' notion. I should interpret this as equivalent to saying that 'knowledge' is a relation of our thinking activities to reality, and that those activities are 'truest' which *work* best—the term 'work' being taken in the widest possible number of senses. Thought is thus an instrument of adaptation to, and eventually of modification of, its objects. Its duty may, but need not always, be merely to copy the latter. In all this, Professor Höffding aligns himself with the 'economical' school of scientific logicians, and (if I mistake not) with the recent 'humanistic' and 'pragmatistic' literature of our own language.

Professor Höffding's 'critical' (as opposed to absolute) Monism means that although you cannot exhaustively account for any item of fact by referring to the whole of which it is a member, yet so much of *what we call* a fact consists of its relations to other facts, that we are equally unable to see any fact as wholly independent. The part in itself remains for us an *abstraction*, and from a whole which itself is for us a mere *ideal*. Neither is given in experience, nor can either be adequately supplied by our reason; so that, both above and below, thought fails to *continue*, and terminates against an 'irrational.' This in the end *may* mean that Being is really incomplete, in any sense in which our logic apprehends completeness.

No one better than Professor Höffding in these pages has shown how all our attempted definitions of the Whole of things, are made by conceiving it as analogous in constitution to some one of its parts which we treat as a type-phenomenon. No one has traced better the logical limitations of this sort of speculation. We never can absolutely prove its validity. We can only paint our more or less plausible pictures; and philosophy thus must always be something of an *art* as well as of a science.

The fundamental type-phenomenon is the fact that we can, to some degree at any rate, make things mentally *intelligible*. Being and our mental forms are thus *not incongruent*. And as our mental forms act in us as unifying forces, so we must suppose that the energy in Being that tends toward unity *in the thought-part of Being*, tends, by analogy, toward unity elsewhere also. This puts Professor Höffding in a general attitude of harmony with idealistic ways of thinking. But he still insists that Being can never be expressed in thought without some blind remainder.

In Ethics the same antinomy or conflict between part and whole occurs which we find in the other problems. The single act or agent must have independent value, yet must also be a means toward farther values. Neither from any whole or any parts concretely given can we deduce a continuous ethical system. Such a system is still a vacant abstraction; and both in Being and in concrete thinking the kingdom of goods must be regarded as still engaged in the making.

Our author's conception of religion is one of his best strokes, in my opinion. He defines it as a belief in the ultimate 'conservation of values,' or rather of what has value. This seems to me to cover more facts in the concrete history of human religions than any definition with which I am acquainted. Yet one easily sees how experience may change our ideas of what the most genuinely ideal values are; so the 'philosophy' of religion, less than any other philosophy perhaps, is entitled to become dogmatic. The belief in the conservation of values has itself a value, for it can give an energy to life. Being so vital a function, it will always be sure to find some form for itself functionally equivalent to the religions of the past, whether that form be called by the name of religion, or be called by some other name.

An unfinished world then, with all Creation, along with our thought, struggling into more continuous and better shape—such is our author's general view of the matter of Philosophy. I have doubtless emphasized the points that appealed most to my own personal interests. Others—and there are many which are fundamental—I must leave the reader to find out. I need only add that I have carefully revised the translation, and that (though it may not be elegant) it is, I believe, faithful to the author's meaning throughout.

G. Papini and the Pragmatist Movement in Italy

American students have so long had the habit of turning to Germany for their philosophic inspiration, that they are only beginning to recognize the splendid psychological and philosophical activity with which France to-day is animated; and as for poor little Italy, few of them think it necessary even to learn to read her language. Meanwhile Italy is engaged in the throes of an intellectual *rinascimento* quite as vigorous as her political one. Her sons still class the things of thought somewhat too politically, making partizan capital, clerical or positivist, of every conquest or concession, but that is only the slow dying of a habit born in darker times. The ancient genius of her people is evidently unweakened, and the tendency to individualism that has always marked her is beginning to mark her again as strongly as ever, and nowhere more notably than in philosophy.

As an illustration, let me give a brief account of the aggressive movement in favor of 'pragmatism' which the monthly journal *Leonardo* (published at Florence, and now in its fourth year) is carrying on, with the youthful Giovanni Papini tipping the wedge of it as editor, and the scarcely less youthful names of Prezzolini, Vailati, Calderoni, Amendola and others, signing the more conspicuous articles. To one accustomed to the style of article that has usually discussed pragmatism, Deweyism, or radical empiricism, in this country, and more particularly in this JOURNAL, the

Italian literature of the subject is a surprising, and to the present writer a refreshing, novelty. Our university seminaries (where so many bald-headed and bald-hearted young aspirants for the Ph.D. have all these years been accustomed to bore one another with the pedantry and technicality, formless, uncircumcised, unabashed and unrebuked, of their 'papers' and 'reports') are bearing at last the fruit that was to be expected, in an almost complete blunting of the literary sense in the more youthful philosophers of our land. Surely no other country could utter in the same number of months as badly written a philosophic mass as ours has published since Dewey's *Studies in Logical Theory* came out. Germany is not 'in it' with us, in my estimation, for uncouthness of form.

In this Florentine band of Leonardists, on the other hand, we find, instead of heaviness, length and obscurity, lightness, clearness and brevity, with no lack of profundity or learning (quite the reverse, indeed), and a frolicsomeness and impertinence that wear the charm of youth and freedom. Signor Papini in particular has a real genius for cutting and untechnical phraseology. He can write descriptive literature, polychromatic with adjectives, like a decadent, and clear up a subject by drawing cold distinctions, like a scholastic. As he is the most enthusiastic pragmatist of them all (some of his colleagues make decided reservations) I will speak of him exclusively. He advertises a general work on the pragmatist movement as in press; but the February number of *Leonardo* and the last chapter of his just published volume, *Il crepuscolo dei filosofi*,[1] give his program, and announce him as the most radical conceiver of pragmatism to be found anywhere.

The *Crepuscolo* book calls itself in the preface a work of 'passion,' being a settling of the author's private accounts with several philosophers (Kant, Hegel, Schopenhauer, Comte, Spencer, Nietzsche) and a clearing of his mental tables from their impeding rubbish, so as to leave him the freer for constructive business. I will only say of the critical chapters that they are strongly thought and pungently written. The author hits essentials, but he doesn't always cover everything, and more than he has said, either for or against, remains to be said about both Kant and Hegel. It is the preface and the final chapter of the book that contain the passion. The 'good riddance,' which is Papini's cry of farewell to the past of philosophy, seems most of all to signify for him a good-by to its

[1] Milano: Società Editrice Lombarda.

exaggerated respect for universals and abstractions. Reality for him *exists* only *distributively,* in the particular concretes of experience. Abstracts and universals are only instruments by which we meet and handle these latter.

In an article in *Leonardo* last year,[2] he states the whole pragmatic scope and program very neatly. Fundamentally, he says, it means an *unstiffening* of all our theories and beliefs by attending to their *instrumental* value. It incorporates and harmonizes various ancient tendencies, as

1. *Nominalism,* by which he means the *appeal to the particular.* Pragmatism is nominalistic not only in regard to words, but in regard to phrases and to theories.

2. *Utilitarianism,* or the emphasizing of practical aspects and problems.

3. *Positivism,* or the disdain of verbal and useless questions.

4. *Kantism,* in so far as Kant affirms the primacy of practical reason.

5. *Voluntarism,* in the psychological sense, of the intellect's secondary position.

6. *Fideism,* in its attitude towards religious questions.

Pragmatism, according to Papini, is thus only a collection of attitudes and methods, and its chief characteristic is its armed neutrality in the midst of doctrines. It is like a corridor in a hotel, from which a hundred doors open into a hundred chambers. In one you may see a man on his knees praying to regain his faith; in another a desk at which sits some one eager to destroy all metaphysics; in a third a laboratory with an investigator looking for new footholds by which to advance upon the future. But the corridor belongs to all, and all must pass there. Pragmatism, in short, is a great *corridor-theory.*

In the *Crepuscolo* Sig. Papini says that what pragmatism has always meant for him is the necessity of enlarging our means of action, the vanity of the universal as such, the bringing of our spiritual powers into use, and the need of making the world over instead of merely standing by and contemplating it. It *inspires human activity,* in short, differently from other philosophies.

"The common denominator to which all the forms of human life can be reduced is this: *the quest of instruments to act with,* or, in other words, *the quest of power.*"

[2] April, 1905, p. 45.

By 'action' Sig. Papini means any change into which man enters as a conscious cause, whether it be to add to existing reality or to substract from it. Art, science, religion and philosophy all are but so many instruments of change. Art changes things for our vision; religion for our vital tone and hope; science tells us how to change the course of nature and our conduct towards it; philosophy is only a more penetrating science. Tristan and Isolde, Paradise, Atoms, Substance, neither of them copies anything real; all are creations placed above reality, to transform, build out and interpret it in the interests of human need or passion. Instead of affirming with the positivists that we must render the ideal world as similar as possible to the actual, Sig. Papini emphasizes our duty of turning the actual world into as close a copy of the ideal as it will let us. The various ideal worlds are here because the real world fails to satisfy us. They are more adapted to us, realize more potently our desires. We should treat them as *ideal limits* towards which reality must evermore be approximated.

All our ideal instruments are as yet imperfect. Arts, religions, sciences, philosophies, have their vices and defects, and the worst of all are those of the philosophies. But philosophy can be regenerated. Since change and action are the most general ideals possible, philosophy can become a *'pragmatic'* in the strict sense of the word, meaning a *general theory of human action*. Ends and means can here be studied together, in the abstractest and most inclusive way, so that philosophy can resolve itself into a comparative discussion of all the possible programs for man's life when man is once for all regarded as a creative being.

As such, man becomes a kind of god, and where are we to draw his limits? In an article called 'From Man to God' in the *Leonardo* for last February Sig. Papini lets his imagination work at stretching the limits. His attempt will be called Promethean or bullfroggian, according to the temper of the reader. It has decidedly an element of literary swagger and conscious impertinence, but I confess that I am unable to treat it otherwise than respectfully. Why should not the divine attributes of omniscience and omnipotence be used by man as the pole-stars by which he may methodically lay his own course? Why should not divine *rest* be his own ultimate goal, rest attained by an activity in the end so immense that all desires are satisfied, and no more action necessary? The unexplored powers and relations of man, both physical and mental, are certainly enormous; why should we impose limits on them *a priori*? And, if not, why are the most utopian programs not in order?

The program of a Man-God is surely one of the possible great type-programs of philosophy. I myself have been slow in coming into the full inwardness of pragmatism. Schiller's writings and those of Dewey and his school have taught me some of its wider reaches; and in the writings of this youthful Italian, clear in spite of all their brevity and audacity, I find not only a way in which our English views might be developed farther with consistency—at least so it appears to me—but also a tone of feeling well fitted to rally devotees and to make of pragmatism a new militant form of religious or quasi-religious philosophy.

The supreme merit of it in these adventurous regions is that it can never grow doctrinarian in advance of verification, or make dogmatic pretensions.

When, as one looks back from the actual world that one believes and lives and moves in, and tries to understand how the knowledge of its content and structure ever grew up step by step in our minds, one has to confess that objective and subjective influences have so mingled in the process that it is impossible now to disentangle their contributions or to give to either the primacy. When a man has walked a mile, who can say whether his right or his left leg is the more responsible? and who can say whether the water or the clay is most to be thanked for the evolution of the bed of an existing river? Something like this I understand to be Messrs. Dewey's and Schiller's contention about 'truth.' The subjective and objective factors of any presently functioning body of it are lost in the night of time and indistinguishable. Only the way in which we see a new truth develop shows us that, by analogy, subjective factors must always have been active. Subjective factors thus are potent, and their effects remain. They are in *some* degree creative, then; and this carries with it, it seems to me, the admissibility of the entire Italian pragmatistic program. But, be the God-Man part of it sound or foolish, the Italian pragmatists are an extraordinarily well-informed and gifted, and above all an extraordinarily free and spirited and unpedantic, group of writers.

The Mad Absolute

Mr. Gore, in this JOURNAL for October 11, tries very neatly to turn Mr. Schiller's joke on the absolute against the joker, and I suppose that those whom the latter gentleman's jokes vex are correspondingly content.

But are the tables turned?

It is *we* in our dissociated, finite shapes who are mad, says Mr. Gore, and not the absolute. The absolute in its integrated shape is the very beau ideal of sanity, and in our own successful quest of it, he adds, lies our only hope of cure. Get confluent with one another, restore the original unbrokenness of our infinitely inclusive real self, and the universe will wake up well.

But in the name of all that's absolute how did it ever get so sick? That we finite subjects are sick we know well enough, and no philosophy beyond the plainest lessons of our finite experience is needed to teach us that more union among ourselves would be remedial. But if all these distracted persons of ours really signify the absolute in a state of madness, why, how or when did it get mad? If it was ever sane, its friends ought surely to explain. Moreover, in that case must it be supposed that we have once for all superseded and abolished its primal wholeness, or does the wholeness still obtain entire behind the scenes, coexisting with our fragmentary persons, and, like another Sally Beauchamp, knowing about us all the while we know so little about it?

If the former alternative be the true one, we are back in the time-process and the mystery of a fall, reedited in these days by Messrs. Renouvier and Prat. Mr. Gore's monist puts the case in time-form, as a dramatic event, and seems to adopt this horn of the dilemma. But another monist might consider this unorthodox, and insist that the absolute is 'timeless' and that it lives, Sally-like, alongside of our split-off selves.

But in this latter case what would be the significance of that re-union of these selves, from which, according to the absolutist philosophy, we are to hope for a cure? Is it to produce a second absolute, duplicating the first one? Or is it to be imagined as a reabsorption rather, with only the one indivisible primary absolute left? How ought we to conceive it at all? Reabsorption would seem inadmissible on absolutist principles. It would hardly go without the time-process; and would moreover be strongly suggestive of the cure of a disease *upon* the eternal absolute subject, much as an eruption may break out and be 'resolved' again upon one's skin. But the absolute can have no skin, no outside.

I doubt, therefore, whether Mr. Gore's monist has greatly helped his client's plight. Nor would it essentially mend matters for him simply to declare that the absolute is eternally three things—its pure identical self, the finite emanation or eruption and the re-absorption, all in one. And yet I believe that the path that Mr. Schiller and he have struck into is likely to prove a most important lead. The absolute is surely one of the great hypotheses of philosophy; it must be thoroughly discussed. Its advocates have usually treated it only as a logical necessity; and very bad logic, as it seems to me, have they invariably used. It is high time that the hypothesis of a world-consciousness should be discussed seriously, as we discuss any other question of fact; and that means inductively and in the light of all the natural analogies that can be brought to bear. No philosophy can ever do more than interpret the whole, which is unknown, after the analogy of some particular part which we know. So far, Fechner is the only thinker who has done any elaborate work of this kind on the world-soul question, although Royce deserves praise for having used arguments for analogy along with his logical proofs. I can not help thinking that Fechner's successors, if he ever have any, must make great use of just such cases as the one so admirably analyzed and told by Dr. Prince.[1]

1 Morton Prince, *The Dissociation of a Personality.*

Bradley or Bergson?

Dr. Bradley has summed up his *Weltanschauung* in last October's *Mind*, in an article which for sincerity and brevity leaves nothing to be desired. His thought and Bergson's run parallel for such a distance, yet diverge so utterly at last that a comparison seems to me instructive. The watershed is such a knife-edge that no reader who leans to one side or the other can after this plead ignorance of the motives of his choice.

Bradley's first great act of candor in philosophy was his breaking loose from the kantian tradition that immediate feeling is all disconnectedness. In his *Logic* as well as in his *Appearance* he insisted that in the flux of feeling we directly encounter reality, and that its form, as thus encountered, is the continuity and wholeness of a transparent much-at-once. This is identically Bergson's doctrine. In affirming the 'endosmosis' of adjacent parts of 'living' experience, the french writer treats the minimum of feeling as an immediately intuited much-at-once.

The idealist tradition is that feelings, aboriginally discontinuous, are woven into continuity by the various synthetic concepts which the intellect applies. Both Bradley and Bergson contradict this flatly; and although their tactics are so different, their battle is the same. They destroy the notion that conception is essentially a unifying process. For Bergson all concepts are discrete; and though you can get the discrete out of the continuous, out of the

151

discrete you can never construct the continuous again. Concepts, moreover, are static, and can never be adequate substitutes for a perceptual flux of which activity and change are inalienable features. Concepts, says Bergson, make things less, not more, intelligible, when we use them seriously and radically. They serve us practically more than theoretically. Throwing their map of abstract terms and relations round our present experience, they show its bearings and let us plan our way.

Bradley is just as independent of rationalist tradition, and is more thoroughgoing still in his criticism of the conceptual function. When we handle felt realities by our intellect they grow, according to him, less and less comprehensible; activity becomes inconstruable, relation contradictory, change inadmissible, personality unintelligible, time, space, and causation impossible—nothing survives the bradleyan wreck.

The breach which the two authors make with previous rationalist opinion is complete, and they keep step with each other perfectly up to the point where they diverge. Sense-perception first developes into conception; and then conception, developing its subtler and more contradictory implications, comes to an end of its usefulness for both authors, and runs itself into the ground. Arrived at this conviction, Bergson *drops* conception—which apparently has done us all the good it can do; and, turning back towards perception with its transparent multiplicity-in-union, he takes its data integrally up into philosophy, as a kind of material which nothing else can replace. The fault of our perceptual data, he tells us, is not of nature, but only of extent; and the way to know reality intimately is, according to this philosopher, to sink into those data and get *our sympathetic imagination to enlarge their bounds. Deep* knowledge is not of the conceptually mediated, but of the immediate type. Bergson thus allies himself with old-fashioned empiricism, on the one hand, and with mysticism, on the other. His breach with rationalism could not possibly be more thorough than it is.

Bradley's breach is just as thorough in its first two steps. The form of oneness in the flow of feeling is an attribute of reality which even the absolute must preserve. Concepts are an organ of misunderstanding rather than of understanding; they turn the 'reality' which we 'encounter' into an 'appearance' which we 'think.' But with all this anti-rationalist *matter*, Bradley is faithful to his anti-empiricist *manner* to the end. Crude unmediated feelings shall never form a part of 'truth.' "Judgment, on our view," he writes, "transcends and must transcend that immediate unity of feeling upon which it cannot cease to depend. Judgment has to qualify the Real ideally. . . . This is the fundamental inconsistency of judgment . . . . For ideas cannot qualify reality as reality is qualified immediately in feeling . . . . The reality as conditioned in feeling has been in principle abandoned, while other conditions have not been found."[1]

Abandoned in 'principle,' Mr. Bradley says; and, in sooth, nothing but a sort of religious principle against admitting 'untransformed' feeling into philosophy would seem to explain his procedure from here onwards. "At the entrance of philosophy," he says, "there appears to be a point where the roads divide. By the one way you set out to seek truth in ideas . . . . On this road what is sought is ideas, and nothing else is current. . . . If you enter here, you are committed to this principle. . . . [This] whole way doubtless may be a delusion, but, if you choose to take this way . . . no possible appeal to designation [*i.e.*, to feeling] in the end is permitted. . . . This I take to be the way of philosophy . . . . It is not the way of life or of common knowledge, and to commit oneself to such a principle may be said to depend upon choice. The way of life starts from, and in the end it rests on dependence upon feeling . . . . Outside of philosophy there is no consistent course but to accept the unintelligible . . . . For worse or for better the man who stands on particular feeling must remain outside of philosophy. . . . I recognise that in life and in ordinary knowledge one can never wholly cease to rest on this ground. But how to take over into ultimate theory and to use there this certainty of feeling, *while still leaving that untransformed*, I myself do not know. I admit that philosophy, as I conceive it, is onesided. I understand the dislike of it and the despair of it while this its defect is not remedied. But to remedy the defect by importing bodily into philosophy the 'this' and 'mine,' as they are felt, to my mind brings destruction on the spot."[2]

Mr. Bradley's 'principle' seems to be only that of doggedly following a line once entered on to the bitterest of ends. We encounter reality in feeling, and find that when we develope it into ideas

[1] *Mind,* October, 1909, p. 498.
[2] *Ibid.,* pp. 500–502.

it becomes more intelligible in certain definite respects. We then have 'truth' instead of reality; which truth, however, pursued beyond a certain practical point, develops into the whole bog of unintelligibilities through which the critical part of *Appearance and Reality* wades. The wise and natural course at this point would seem to be to drop the notion that truth is a *thoroughgoing* improvement on reality, to confess that its value is limited, and to hark back. But there is nothing that Mr. Bradley, religiously loyal to the direction of development once entered upon, will not do sooner than this. Forward, forward, let us range! He makes the desperate transconceptual leap, assumes *beyond* the whole ideal perspective an ultimate 'suprarelational' and transconceptual reality in which somehow the wholeness and certainty and unity of feeling, which we turned our backs on forever when we committed ourselves to the leading of ideas, are supposed to be resurgent in transfigured form; and shows us as the only authentic object of philosophy, with its 'way of ideas,' an absolute which 'can be' and 'must be' and therefore 'is.' 'It *shall* be' is the only candid way of stating its relation to belief; and Mr. Bradley's statement comes very near to that.

How could the elements of a situation be made more obvious? Or what could bring to a sharper focus the factor of personal choice involved?

The way of philosophy is not the way of life, Mr. Bradley admits, but for the philosopher, he continues, it seems to be *all there is*—which is like saying that the way of starvation is not the way of life, but to the starveling it is all there is. Be it so! Though what *obliges* one to become either such a philosopher or such a starveling does not clearly appear. The only motive I can possibly think of for choosing to be a philosopher on these painful terms is the old and obstinate intellectualist prejudice in favor of universals. They are loftier, nobler, more rational objects than the particulars of sense. In their direction, then, and away from feeling, should a mind conscious of its high vocation always turn its face. Not to enter life is a *higher vocation* than to enter it, on this view.

The motive is pathetically simple, and anyone can take it in. On the thin watershed between life and philosophy, Mr. Bradley tumbles to philosophy's call. Down he slides, to the dry valley of 'absolute' mare's nests and abstractions, the habitation of the fictitious suprarelational being which his will prefers. Never was there such a case of will-to-believe; for Mr. Bradley, unlike other anti-empiricists, deludes himself neither as to feeling nor as to thought: the one reveals for him the inner *nature* of reality perfectly, the other falsifies it utterly as soon as you carry it beyond the first few steps. Yet once committed to the conceptual direction, Mr. Bradley thinks we can't reverse, we can save ourselves only by hoping that the absolute will re-realize unintelligibly and 'somehow,' the unity, wholeness, certainty, etc., which feeling so immediately and transparently made us acquainted with at first.

Bergson and the empiricists, on the other hand, tumble to life's call, and turn into the valley where the green pastures and the clear waters always were. If in sensible particulars reality reveals the manyness-in-oneness of its constitution in so convincing a way, why then withhold, if you will, the name of 'philosophy' from perceptual knowledge, but recognize that perceptual knowledge is at any rate the *only complete kind of knowledge,* and let 'philosophy' in Bradley's sense pass for the onesided affair which he candidly confesses that it is. When the alternative lies between knowing life in its full thickness and activity, as one acquainted with its *me's* and *thee's* and *now's* and *here's,* on the one hand, and knowing a transconceptual evaporation like the absolute, on the other, it seems to me that to choose the latter knowledge merely because it has been named 'philosophy' is to be superstitiously loyal to a name. But if names are to be used eulogistically, rather let us give that of philosophy to the fuller kind of knowledge, the kind in which perception and conception mix their lights.

As one who calls himself a radical empiricist, I can find no possible excuse for not inclining towards Bergson's side. He and Bradley together have confirmed my confidence in non-'transmuted' percepts, and have broken my confidence in concepts down. It seems to me that their parallel lines of work have converged to a sharp alternative which now confronts everybody, and in which the reasons for one's choice must plainly appear and be told. Be an empiricist or be a transconceptualist, whichever you please, but at least say why! I sincerely believe that nothing but inveterate anti-empiricist prejudice accounts for Mr. Bradley's choice; for at the point where he stands in the article I have quoted, I can discover no sensible reason why he should prefer the way he takes.

If he should ever take it into his head to *revoke*, and drop into the other valley, it would be a great day for english thought. As Kant is supposed to have extinguished all previous forms of rationalism, so Bergson and Bradley, between them, might lay post-kantian rationalism permanently underground.

A Suggestion about Mysticism

Much interest in the subject of religious mysticism has been shown in philosophic circles of late years. Most of the writings I have seen have treated the subject from the outside, for I know of no one who has spoken as having the direct authority of experience in favor of his views. I also am an outsider, and very likely what I say will prove the fact loudly enough to readers who possibly may stand within the pale. Nevertheless, since between outsiders one is as good as another, I will not leave my suggestion unexpressed.

The suggestion, stated very briefly, is that states of mystical intuition may be only very sudden and great extensions of the ordinary 'field of consciousness.' Concerning the causes of such extensions I have no suggestion to make; but the extension itself would, if my view be correct, consist in an immense spreading of the margin of the field, so that knowledge ordinarily transmarginal would become included, and the ordinary margin would grow more central. Fechner's 'wave-scheme' will diagrammatize the alteration, as I conceive it, if we suppose that the wave of present awareness, steep above the horizontal line that represents the plane of the usual 'threshold,' slopes away below it very gradually in all directions. A fall of the threshold, however caused, would, under these circumstances, produce the state of things which we see on an unusually flat shore at the ebb of a spring-tide. Vast tracts usually covered are then revealed to view, but nothing rises more than a few inches above the water's bed, and great parts of the scene are submerged again whenever a wave washes over them.

Some persons have naturally a very wide, others a very narrow, field of consciousness. The narrow field may be represented by an unusually steep form of the wave. When by any accident the threshold lowers in persons of this type—I speak here from direct personal experience—so that the field widens and the relations of its centre to matters usually subliminal come into view, the larger panorama perceived fills the mind with exhilaration and sense of mental power. It is a refreshing experience; and—such is now my hypothesis—we only have to suppose it to occur in an exceptionally extensive form, to give us a mystical paroxysm, if such a term be allowed.

A few remarks about the field of consciousness may be needed to give more definiteness to my hypothesis. The field is composed at all times of a mass of present sensation, in a cloud of memories, emotions, concepts, etc. Yet these ingredients, which have to be named separately, are not separate, as the conscious field contains them. Its form is that of a much-at-once, in the unity of which the sensations, memories, concepts, impulses, etc., coalesce and are dissolved. The present field as a whole came continuously out of its predecessor and will melt into its successor as continuously again, one sensation-mass passing into another sensation-mass and giving the character of a gradually changing *present* to the experience, while the memories and concepts carry time-coefficients which place whatever is present in a temporal perspective more or less vast.

When, now, the threshold falls, what comes into view is not the next mass of *sensation*; for sensation requires new physical stimulations to produce it, and no alteration of a purely mental threshold can create these. Only in case the physical stimuli were already at work subliminally, preparing the next sensation, would whatever sub-sensation was already prepared reveal itself when the threshold fell. But with the memories, concepts, and conational states, the case is different. Nobody knows exactly how far we are 'marginally' conscious of these at ordinary times, or how far beyond the 'margin' of our present thought transmarginal consciousness of them may exist.[1] There is at any rate no definite bound set

[1] Transmarginal or subliminal, the terms are synonymous. Some psychologists deny the existence of such consciousness altogether (A. H. Pierce, for example, and Mün-

between what is central and what is marginal in consciousness, and the margin itself has no definite bound *a parte foris.* It is like the field of vision, which the slightest movement of the eye will extend, revealing objects that always stood there to be known. My hypothesis is that a movement of the threshold downwards will similarly bring a mass of subconscious memories, conceptions, emotional feelings, and perceptions of relation, etc., into view all at once; and that if this enlargement of the nimbus that surrounds the sensational present is vast enough, while no one of the items it contains attracts our attention singly, we shall have the conditions fulfilled for a kind of consciousness in all essential respects like that termed mystical. It will be transient, if the change of threshold is transient. It will be of reality, enlargement, and illumination, possibly rapturously so. It will be of unification, for the present coalesces in it with ranges of the remote quite out of its reach under ordinary circumstances; and the sense of *relation* will be greatly enhanced. Its form will be intuitive or perceptual, not conceptual, for the remembered or conceived objects in the enlarged field are supposed not to attract the attention singly, but only to give the sense of a tremendous *muchness* suddenly revealed. If they attracted attention separately, we should have the ordinary steep-waved consciousness, and the mystical character would depart.

Such is my suggestion. Persons who *know* something of mystical experience will no doubt find in it much to criticize. If any such shall do so with definiteness, it will have amply served its purpose of helping our understanding of mystical states to become more precise.

The notion I have tried (at such expense of metaphor) to set forth was originally suggested to me by certain experiences of my own, which could only be described as very sudden and incomprehensible enlargements of the conscious field, bringing with them a curious sense of cognition of real fact. All have occurred within the past five years; three of them were similar in type; the fourth was unique.

In each of the three like cases, the experience broke in abruptly

---

sterberg apparently). Others, *e.g.,* Bergson, make it exist and carry the whole freight of our past. Others again (as Myers) would have it extend (in the 'telepathic' mode of communication) from one person's mind into another's. For the purposes of my hypothesis I have to postulate its existence; and once postulating it, I prefer not to set any definite bounds to its extent.

upon a perfectly commonplace situation and lasted perhaps less than two minutes. In one instance I was engaged in conversation, but I doubt whether the interlocutor noticed my abstraction. What happened each time was that I seemed all at once to be reminded of a past experience; and this reminiscence, ere I could conceive or name it distinctly, developed into something further that belonged with it, this in turn into something further still, and so on, until the process faded out, leaving me amazed at the sudden vision of increasing ranges of distant fact of which I could give no articulate account. The mode of consciousness was perceptual, not conceptual—the field expanding so fast that there seemed no time for conception or identification to get in its work. There was a strongly exciting sense that my knowledge of past (or present?) reality was enlarging pulse by pulse, but so rapidly that my intellectual processes could not keep up the pace. The *content* was thus entirely lost to retrospection—it sank into the limbo into which dreams vanish as we gradually awake. The feeling—I won't call it belief—that I had had a sudden *opening*, had seen through a window, as it were, distant realities that incomprehensibly belonged with my own life, was so acute that I can not shake it off to-day.

This conviction of fact-revealed, together with the perceptual form of the experience and the inability to make articulate report, are all characters of mystical states. The point of difference is that in my case certain special directions only, in the field of reality, seemed to get suddenly uncovered, whereas in classical mystical experiences it appears rather as if the whole of reality were uncovered at once. *Uncovering* of some sort is the essence of the phenomenon, at any rate, and is what, in the language of the Fechnerian wave-metaphor, I have used the expression 'fall of the threshold' to denote.

My fourth experience of uncovering had to do with dreams. I was suddenly intromitted into the cognizance of a pair of dreams that I could not remember myself to have had, yet they seemed somehow to connect with me. I despair of giving the reader any just idea of the bewildering confusion of mind into which I was thrown by this, the most intensely peculiar experience of my whole life. I wrote a full memorandum of it a couple of days after it happened, and appended some reflections. Even though it should cast no light on the conditions of mysticism, it seems as if this record might be worthy of publication, simply as a contribution to the descriptive literature of pathological mental states. I let it follow, therefore, as originally written, with only a few words altered to make the account more clear.

"San Francisco, Feb. 14th 1906.—The night before last, in my bed at Stanford University, I woke at about 7.30 A.M., from a quiet dream of some sort, and whilst gathering my waking wits, seemed suddenly to get mixed up with reminiscences of a dream of an entirely different sort, which seemed to telescope, as it were, into the first one, a dream very elaborate, of lions, and tragic. I concluded this to have been a previous dream of the same sleep; but the apparent mingling of two dreams was something very queer, which I had never before experienced.

"On the following night (Feb. 12–13) I awoke suddenly from my first sleep, which appeared to have been very heavy, in the middle of a dream, in thinking of which I became suddenly confused by the contents of two other dreams that shuffled themselves abruptly in between the parts of the first dream, and of which I couldn't grasp the origin. Whence come *these dreams?* I asked. They were close to *me*, and fresh, as if I had just dreamed them; and yet they were far away *from the first dream*. The contents of the three had absolutely no connection. One had a cockney atmosphere, it had happened to some one in London. The other two were American. One involved the trying on of a coat (was this the dream I seemed to wake from?) the other was a sort of nightmare and had to do with soldiers. Each had a wholly distinct emotional atmosphere that made its individuality discontinuous with that of the others. And yet, in a moment, as these three dreams alternately telescoped into and out of each other, and I seemed to myself to have been their common dreamer, they seemed quite as distinctly *not* to have been dreamed in succession, in that one sleep. *When*, then? Not on a previous night, either. *When*, then? and *which* was the one out of which I had just awakened? *I could no longer tell*: one was as close to me as the others, and yet they entirely repelled each other, and I seemed thus to belong to three different dream-systems at once, no one of which would connect itself either with the others or with my waking life. I began to feel curiously confused and *scared*, and tried to wake myself up wider, but I seemed already wide-awake. Presently cold shivers of dread ran over me: *am I getting into other people's dreams?* Is this a 'telepathic' experience? Or an invasion of double (or treble) personality? Or is it a thrombus in a cortical artery? and the beginning of a general mental 'confusion' and disorientation which is going on to develop who knows how far?

"Decidedly I was losing hold of my 'self,' and making acquaintance with a quality of mental distress that I had never known before, its nearest analogue being the sinking, giddying anxiety that one may have when, in the woods, one discovers that one is really 'lost.' Most human troubles look towards a terminus. Most fears point in a direction, and concentrate towards a climax. Most assaults of the evil one may be met by bracing oneself against something, one's principles, one's courage, one's will, one's pride. But in this experience all was diffusion from a centre, and foothold swept away, the brace itself disintegrating all the faster as one needed its support more direly. Meanwhile vivid perception (or remembrance) of the various dreams kept coming over me in alternation. Whose? *whose?* WHOSE? Unless I can *attach* them, I am swept out to sea with no horizon and no bond, getting *lost.* The idea aroused the 'creeps' again, and with it the fear of again falling asleep and renewing the process. It had begun the previous night, but then the confusion had only gone one step, and had seemed simply curious. *This* was the second step—where might I be after a third step had been taken? My teeth chattered at the thought.

"At the same time I found myself filled with a new pity towards persons passing into dementia with *Verwirrtheit*, or into invasions of secondary personality. *We* regard them as simply *curious*; but what *they* want in the awful drift of their being out of its customary self, is any principle of steadiness to hold on to. We ought to assure them and reassure them that we will stand by them, and recognize the true self in them to the end. We ought to let them know that we are with *them* and not (as too often we must seem to them) a part of the world that but confirms and publishes their deliquescence.

"Evidently I was in full possession of my reflective wits; and whenever I thus objectively thought of the situation in which I was, my anxieties ceased. But there was a tendency to relapse into the dreams and reminiscences, and to relapse vividly; and then the confusion recommenced, along with the emotion of dread lest it should develop farther.

"Then I looked at my watch. Half past twelve! Midnight, therefore. And this gave me another reflective idea. Habitually, on going to bed, I fall into a very deep slumber from which I never naturally awaken until after two. I never awaken, therefore, from a midnight dream, as I did to-night, so of midnight dreams my ordinary consciousness retains no recollection. My sleep seemed terribly heavy as I woke to-night. Dream states carry dream memories—why may not the two succedaneous dreams (whichever two of the three *were* succedaneous) be memories of *twelve o'clock dreams of previous nights*, swept in, along with the just-fading dream, into the just-waking system of memory? Why, in short, may I not be tapping, in a way precluded by my ordinary habit of life, *the midnight stratum* of my past experiences?

"This idea gave great relief—I felt now as if I were in full possession of my *anima rationalis.* I turned on my light, resolving to read myself to sleep. But I didn't read, I felt drowsy instead, and, putting out the light, soon was in the arms of Morpheus.

"I woke again two or three times before daybreak with no dream-experiences, and finally, with a curious, but not alarming, confusion between two dreams, similar to that which I had had the previous morning, I awoke to the new day at seven.

"Nothing peculiar happened the following night, so the thing seems destined not to develop any further."[2]

The distressing confusion of mind in this experience was the exact opposite of mystical illumination, and equally unmystical

---

[2] I print the rest of my memorandum in the shape of a note:—

"Several ideas suggest themselves that make the observation instructive.

"First, the general notion, now gaining ground in mental medicine, that certain mental maladies may be foreshadowed in dream-life, and that therefore the study of the latter may be profitable.

"Then the specific suggestion, that states of 'confusion,' loss of personality, *apraxia*, etc., so often taken to indicate cortical lesion or degeneration of dementic type, may be very superficial functional affections. In my own case the confusion was *foudroyante* —a state of consciousness unique and unparalleled in my 64 years of the world's experience; yet it alternated quickly with perfectly rational states, as this record shows. It seems, therefore, merely as if the threshold between the rational and the morbid state had, in my case, been temporarily lowered, and as if similar confusions might be very near the line of possibility in all of us.

"There are also the suggestions of a telepathic entrance into some one else's dreams, and of a doubling up of personality. In point of fact I don't know now 'who' had those three dreams, or which one 'I' first woke up from, so quickly did they substitute themselves back and forth for each other, discontinuously. Their discontinuity was the pivot of the situation. My sense of it was as 'vivid' and 'original' an experience as anything Hume could ask for. And yet they kept telescoping!

"Then there is the notion that by waking at certain hours we may tap distinct strata of ancient dream-memory."

was the definiteness of what was perceived. But the exaltation of the sense of relation was mystical (the perplexity all revolved about the fact that the three dreams *both did and did not belong in the most intimate way together*); and the sense that *reality was being uncovered* was mystical in the highest degree. To this day I feel that those extra dreams were dreamed in reality, but when, where, and by whom, I can not guess.

In the *Open Court* for December, 1909, Mr. Frederick Hall narrates a fit of ether-mysticism which agrees with my formula very well. When one of his doctors made a remark to the other, he chuckled, for he realized that these friends "believed they saw real things and causes . . . . But they *didn't*; and I did. . . . I was where the causes *were* and to see them required no more mental ability than to recognize a color as blue . . . . The knowledge of how little [the doctors] actually did see, coupled with their evident feeling that they saw all there *was*, was funny to the last degree . . . . [They] knew as little of real causes as does the child who, viewing a passing train and noting its revolving wheels, supposes that they, turning of themselves, give to coaches and locomotive their momentum. Or imagine a man seated in a boat, surrounded by dense fog and out of the fog seeing a flat stone leap from the crest of one wave to another. *If he had always sat thus*, his explanations must be very crude as compared with those of a man whose eyes could pierce fog and who saw upon the shore the boy skipping stones. In some such way the remarks of the two physicians seemed to me like the last two 'skips' of a stone thrown from my side . . . . All that was essential in the remark I knew before it was made. Thus to discover, convincingly and for myself, that the things which are unseen are those of real importance, this was sufficiently stimulating."

It is evident that Mr. Hall's marginal field got enormously enlarged by the ether, yet so little defined as to its particulars that what he perceived was mainly the thoroughgoing causal integration of its whole content. That this perception brought with it a tremendous feeling of importance and superiority is a matter of course.

I have treated the phenomenon under discussion as if it consisted in the uncovering of tracts of *consciousness*. Is the consciousness already there waiting to be uncovered? and is it a veridical revelation of reality? These are questions on which I do not touch. In the subjects of the experience the 'emotion of conviction' is always strong, and sometimes absolute. The ordinary psychologist disposes of the phenomenon under the conveniently 'scientific' head of *petit mal*, if not of 'bosh' or 'rubbish.' But we know so little of the noetic value of abnormal mental states of any kind that in my own opinion we had better keep an open mind and collect facts sympathetically for a long time to come. We shall not *understand* these alterations of consciousness either in this generation or in the next.

A Great French Philosopher at Harvard

The Hyde lectureship, which has year after year brought to Harvard some splendid object-lesson of the way in which popular lectures may best be given, has never till this year taken a philosopher as its example-setter. This year we have been having Professor Emile Boutroux, and the occasion seems to me so well worthy of commemoration that I venture to set down a brief account of it for the *Nation's* readers.

The whole enterprise of international exchange of professors is still in its tentative infancy, and one may hear as many arguments against it as reasons for it. The Hyde foundation requires all lectures to be in the French tongue, and the first thing that has been disclosed is the appalling rarity of ability to understand spoken French, even in a centre of learning like Cambridge.

M. Boutroux's auditors this year should preëminently have been our students of philosophy; but, victims of the deplorable manner in which they have been taught foreign languages, hardly half a dozen of them have shown their faces. Few, even of our instructors, follow a French lecture easily—though many more can follow German—and what with "other engagements," and the terrors of the title, "Contingence et Liberté," of M. Boutroux's course, their number proved so small that the bulk of the audience consisted of world's people from Boston and elsewhere, including a good number of French visitors attracted, I am sure, less by the particular subject, than by the rare pleasure of hearing any intelligible discourse whatever in the language of the far-off native country.

It is obvious that the institution of professorial exchange needs overhauling. It ought to be a means of vital stimulation, of making our somewhat torpid youth aware of the presence of a wider world about them, human and social as well as intellectual. So far it has missed fire in this respect. Our young fogies in the graduate schools continue working for their Ph.D. examinations by moving, like Faust's Wagner, "von Buch zu Buch," "von Blatt zu Blatt," and remain for the most part quite unconscious that an opportunity has been lost to them.

M. Boutroux is one of the veterans of his country in the sphere of philosophy, and an extraordinarily influential personage in all academic lines of activity. Almost every philosopher of the younger generation has been his pupil; one finds him sitting as a judge at every *soutenance de thèse* for the doctorate in philosophy; he attends congresses; has been since its foundation *directeur* of the Institut Thiers, and is president this year of the Académie des Sciences Morales et Politiques, where he will shortly have to welcome Mr. Roosevelt as an *associé étranger*. He is a somewhat ascetic looking figure, with a very French and rather military physiognomy, but with the kindliest of manners, a power of extraordinarily clear statement, and, above all, a great air of simplicity and sincerity while lecturing.

M. Boutroux, like almost all his compatriots, thinks it no praise to say of a lecturer that "he talks like a book." German and Anglo-Saxon lecturers may talk like books, but the idea of a public lecture in France is different. It ought not to furnish information of details as a book does. It ought rather to confine itself to tracing perspectives, defining tendencies, bringing out contrasts, and summing up results. It ought, above all, to generalize and simplify, and it ought to avoid technicality of language. Needless to say that, for this task, complete mastery of the subject is an indispensable condition, and only the great masters have succeeded greatly as popular expositors. M. Boutroux's single lectures on Pascal and on Comte showed the breadth and simplicity which result from absolute mastery of a subject.

His continuous course, entitled "Contingence et Liberté," consisted of eight lectures, and the high originality of his position here is what, in my eyes, entitles his visit to notice beyond the immediate circle of his listeners. M. Boutroux is, by virtue of priority, the leader *de jure* of the reaction against the abstract, and in favor of the concrete point of view in philosophy, which in the last few years has got under full headway in all countries. The leader *de jure*, I say, meaning the historic leader or precursor, for the leadership in loudness has passed in England and this country to more strident voices, and in France to those more radically revolutionary in tone. Boutroux is above all a liberal, grants cheerfully to the opposing side what it can fairly claim, harbors no enmities, and makes no enemies, so that many a convert to "pragmatism" or to "Bergsonism" has remained ignorant that the ball was set rolling by his first publication, *La Contingence des lois de la nature*, away back in 1874. His freedom from polemic virulence, his indisposition to flourish a party flag, have kept his name more in the shade than has been just. The most important features of "pragmatism" and "Bergsonism" find clear expression in that early work. And the *Weltanschauung* of that work, matured and reinforced, but in no wise altered, was what this course of lectures reaffirmed. Deemed paradoxical when it first appeared, that *Weltanschauung* is now recognized as possibly discussable, to say the very least, and is evidently about to enter on a powerful career.

I can only sketch the essence of it briefly, without following the lecturer's own order, or going into any detail. The quickest way to get at the character of anything is to know what to contrast it with. The best term with which to contrast M. Boutroux's way of looking at the world is the "scholastic" way of taking it. When I say "scholastic," I don't use the word historically, but as commonsense uses it when it makes of it a reproach. In this sense scholasticism is found in science as well as in philosophy. It means the pretension to conceive things so vigorously that your definitions shall contain all that need be known about their objects. It means the belief that there is but one set of thoughts which absolutely tell the truth about reality, and it means the claim to possess those thoughts, or the more essential part of them. If the word "scholastic" be objected to, let the word "classic" be employed. M. Boutroux's bugbear would then be the classic spirit, and he might be treated as a "romantic" in philosophy.

H. Taine has attributed the misfortunes of France in the revolutionary and Napoleonic periods to the rule of the classic spirit, with its trust in immutable principles and rigorously logical applications; but Taine himself, so far as his general view of man and nature went, cherished classic ideals. If we look back to his time, we find a different idea of the meaning of "Science" from that which the best investigators have now come to believe in. Taine, Berthelot, Renan, and the other great influencers of public opinion during the Second Empire, thought of science as an absolute dissipator of the mysteries of nature. It stripped reality naked of disguise, revealed its intimate structure, was destined to found a new morality and to replace religion. Its votaries were to be the high priests of the future, and the destinies of our planet were to be committed to their keeping. John Fiske's favorite word "deanthropomorphization" serves as a good summary of this whole way of thinking.

Carried away by the triumphs of chemistry, physics, and mathematics, these men imagined that the frame of things was eternally and literally mechanical, and that truth was reached by abstracting from it everything connected with personality. Personal life is a mere by-product, it was said, and its categories, though we have to live in them practically, have no theoretic validity. At the present day, however, concepts like mass, force, inertia, atom, energy, are themselves regarded rather as symbolic instruments, like coördinates, curves, and the like, for simplifying our map of nature and guiding us through its jungle. But the whole undivided jungle, with our personal life and all, is the reality immediately given; and though it is given only in small bits at a time to any one, yet the whole content and quality of it is more completely real than that of any of those conceptual substitutes.

This was the central thesis of Professor Boutroux's lectures. Whereas the classic and scholastic tradition is that reality is above all the abstracted, simplified, and reduced, the inalterable and self-identical, the fatal and eternal, Boutroux took the diametrically opposite view. It is the element we wholly live in, it is what Plutarch's and Shakespeare's pages give us, it is the superabounding, growing, ever-varying and novelty-producing. Its real shape is biography and history, and its "categories," far from sterilizing our world for all purposes of living reason, keep fertilizing it infinitely. "Reason" is a term which Professor Boutroux rescues from its purely classic use of tracing identities, concealed or patent. It is for him the faculty of judgment in its widest sense, using sentiments and willingnesses, as well as concepts, as its premises, and abounding in power, as everything else does, the more abundantly it is exercised.

The practical gist of his whole contention was that reality means novelty, elementary and genuine, and not merely apparent. For the classic rationalism, elementary novelty would be synonymous with Absolute Chance at the heart of things, and that is inadmissible. "Pure irrationalism and sentimentalism" would then be the verdict on Professor Boutroux's *Weltanschauung*. But Boutroux is above all things a liberal and mediating mind, and loves not harsh oppositions. If novelties came abruptly "out of whole cloth" and juxtaposed themselves to the existent, like dominoes against dominoes in a game, the world would be as bad a field of rattling bones as the "irreducible" categories and concepts of classical philosophy make it. Not chance, therefore, but "contingency," is the idea which Professor Boutroux prefers to work with; and by contingency he means the element of spontaneity which characterizes concrete human life—where the consciousness of the present is ever of *many* future possibilities, and contains always enough causality for either of them, when realized, to be regarded as its natural effect. Which *shall* be realized is meanwhile uncertain until our living reason makes its choice. Ever something new, but never anything entirely new. No literal imitation like that which is postulated as the "uniformity of nature," yet always imitation in the midst of the variation; and an "order" unlike that "logical" order, where the same comes only from the same, and which is all that mathematical science can imagine—an order satisfying other kinds of demand, and yet not disappointing the intellectual demand that the effect shall in *some* way grow out of and continue all that went before it.

In this sense the entities of science, the molecules or energies, and the equations that express their laws, are previous in reality only in the way in which "grams" and "metres" are, or only as a statue is previous in its rock. The creative touch of human reason was needed in each case for the extrication; and that those particular creations resulted rather than a hundred others just as possible, is one of those selective interactions between living minds and their environment which can be "understood" when once it has occurred, but which no acquaintance with the previous conditions can show to an outsider that it was the sole thing possible.

Theories result from psychological variations, just as Roosevelts and Rockefellers result from biological variations. Both variations are adapted partly, and partly non-adapted. They change the world-situation and are changed by the world-situation; but the resultant new situation is always a unique one, and none but the agents of its production are in a position vitally to understand why or how it comes into being.

With such a view it would seem natural to interpret the non-human environment as enjoying also an interior life. Panpsychism of some kind, although the lecturer did not enter into that consequence, would seem, in other words, to be a rightful part of his system.

The great originality of M. Boutroux throughout all these years has been his firm grasp of the principle of interpreting the whole of nature in the light of that part of it with which we are most fully acquainted, namely, our own personal experience. The filling in of the picture will require endless research of detail, but the working direction, once given, cannot be easily forgotten; and it seems not unlikely that at a future not remote the whole earlier efforts to substitute a logical skeleton of as few "immutable" principles and relations as we can dissect out cleanly for the abounding richness and fertility of the reality we live in, and to call this skeleton the deeper truth, will seem an aberration. It is essentially a view of things from the outside, and knows nothing of how they *happen*. M. Boutroux has steadily called his generation to take the inside view of how things really happen.

Even less than I expected, have I followed his own order or language, but it is too late to re-write. Those readers who know something of present-day philosophy will recognize in my account the same call to return to the fulness of concrete experience, with which the names of Peirce, Dewey, Schiller, Höffding, Bergson, and of many minor lights are associated. It is the real empiricism, the real evolutionism, the real pluralism; and Boutroux (after Renouvier) was its earliest, as he is now its latest, prophet. It keeps us on cordial terms with natural life, and refuses to divorce our "philosophy" of men from the world of our bosoms and our business.

A Pluralistic Mystic

Not for the ignoble vulgar do I write this article, but only for those dialectic-mystic souls who have an irresistible taste, acquired or native, for higher flights of metaphysics. I have always held the opinion that one of the first duties of a good reader is to summon other readers to the enjoyment of any unknown author of rare quality whom he may discover in his explorations. Now for years my own taste, literary as well as philosophic, has been exquisitely titillated by a writer the name of whom I think must be unknown to the readers of this article; so I no longer continue silent about the merits of BENJAMIN PAUL BLOOD.

Mr. Blood inhabits a city otherwise, I imagine, quite unvisited by the Muses, the town called Amsterdam, situated on the New York Central Railroad. What his regular or bread-winning occupation may be I know not, but it can't have made him super-wealthy. He is an author only when the fit strikes him, and for short spurts at a time; shy, moreover, to the point of publishing his compositions only as private tracts, or in letters to such far-from-reverberant organs of publicity as the *Gazette* or the *Recorder* of his native Amsterdam, or the *Utica Herald*, or the *Albany Times*. Odd places for such subtile efforts to appear in, but creditable to American editors in these degenerate days! Once, indeed, the lamented W. T. Harris of the old *Journal of Speculative Philosophy* got wind of these epistles, and the result was a revision of some of them for that review ("Philosophic Reveries," 1889). Also a couple of poems were reprinted from their leaflets by the editor of *Scribner's Magazine* ("The Lion of the Nile," 1888, and "Nemesis," 1899). But apart from these three dashes before the footlights, Mr. Blood has kept behind the curtain all his days.[1]

The author's maiden adventure was the *Anæsthetic Revelation*, a pamphlet printed privately at Amsterdam in 1874. I forget how it fell into my hands, but it fascinated me so 'weirdly' that I am conscious of its having been one of the stepping-stones of my thinking ever since. It gives the essence of Blood's philosophy, and shows most of the features of his talent—albeit one finds in it little humor and no verse. It is full of verbal felicity, felicity sometimes of precision, sometimes of metaphoric reach; it begins with dialectic reasoning, of an extremely fichtean and hegelian type, but it ends in a trumpet-blast of oracular mysticism, straight from the insight wrought by anaesthetics—of all things in the world!—and unlike anything one ever heard before. The practically unanimous tradition of 'regular' mysticism has been unquestionably *monistic*; and inasmuch as it is the characteristic of mystics to speak, not as the scribes, but as men who have 'been there' and seen with their own eyes, I think that this sovereign manner must have made some other pluralistic-minded students hesitate, as I confess that it has often given pause to me. One cannot criticize the vision of a mystic—one can but pass it by, or else accept it as having some amount of evidential weight. I felt unable to do either with a good conscience until I met with Mr. Blood. His mysticism, which may, if one likes, be understood as monistic in this earlier utterance, develops in the later ones a sort of 'left-wing' voice of defiance, and breaks into what to my ear has a radically pluralistic sound. I confess that the existence of this novel brand of mysticism has made my cowering mood depart. I feel now as if my own pluralism were not without the kind of support which mystical corroboration may confer. Monism can no longer claim to be the only beneficiary of whatever right mysticism may possess to lend *prestige*.

This is my philosophic, as distinguished from my literary in-

---

[1] "Yes! Paul is quite a correspondent!" said a good citizen of Amsterdam from whom I inquired the way to Mr. Blood's dwelling many years ago, after alighting from the train. I had sought to identify him by calling him an 'author,' but his neighbor thought of him only as a writer of letters to the journals I have named.

terest, in introducing Mr. Blood to this more fashionable audience: his philosophy, however mystical, is in the last resort not dissimilar from my own. I must treat him by 'extracting' him, and simplify—certainly all too violently—as I extract. He is not consecutive as a writer, aphoristic and oracular rather; and being moreover sometimes dialectic, sometimes poetic, and sometimes mystic in his manner, sometimes monistic and sometimes pluralistic in his matter, I have to run my own risk in making him orate *pro domo meâ*, and I am not quite unprepared to hear him say, in case he ever reads these pages, that I have entirely missed his point. No matter; I will proceed.

I

I will separate his diverse phases and take him first as a pure dialectician. Dialectic thought of the hegelian type is a whirlpool into which some persons are sucked out of the stream which the straightforward understanding follows. Once in the eddy, nothing but rotary motion can go on. All who have been in it know the feel of its swirl—they know thenceforward that thinking unreturning on itself is but one part of reason, and that rectilinear mentality, in philosophy at any rate, will never do. Though each one may report in different words of his rotational experience, the experience itself is almost childishly simple, and whosoever has been there instantly recognizes other authentic reports. To have been in that eddy is a freemasonry of which the common password is a 'fie' on all the operations of the simple popular understanding.

In Hegel's mind the vortex was at its liveliest, and anyone who has dipped into Hegel will recognize Mr. Blood to be of the same tribe. "That Hegel was pervaded by the great truth," Blood writes, "cannot be doubted. The eyes of philosophy, if not set directly on him, are set towards the region which he occupied. Though he may not be the final philosopher, yet pull him out, and all the rest will be drawn into his vacancy."

Drawn into the same whirlpool, Mr. Blood should say. Nondialectic thought takes facts as singly given, and accounts for one fact by another. But when we think of "*all* fact," we see that nothing of the nature of fact can explain it, "for that were but one more added to the list of things to be accounted for.... The beginning of curiosity, in the philosophic sense," Mr. Blood again writes, "is the stare of being at itself, in the wonder why anything is at all, and what this being signifies. Naturally we first assume the void, and then wonder how, with no ground and no fertility, anything should come into it." We treat it as a positive nihility, "a barrier from which all our batted balls of being rebound."

Upon this idea Mr. Blood passes the usual transcendentalist criticism. There *is* no such separate opposite to being; yet we never think of being as such—of pure being as distinguished from specific forms of being—save as what stands relieved against this imaginary background. Being has no *outline* but that which non-being makes, and the two ideas form an inseparable pair. "Each limits and defines the other. Either would be the other in the same position, for here (where there is as yet no question of content, but only of being itself) the position is all and the content is nothing. Hence arose that paradox: 'Being is by nothing more real than not-being.' "

"Popularly," Mr. Blood goes on, "we think of all that is as having got the better of non-being. If all were not—*that*, we think, were easy: there were no wonder then, no tax on ingenuity, nothing to be accounted for. This conclusion is from the thinking which assumes all reality as immediately given, assumes knowledge as a simple physical light, rather than as a distinction involving light and darkness equally. We assume that if the light were to go out, the show would be ended (and so it would), but we forget that if the darkness were to go out, that would be equally calamitous. It were bad enough if the master had lost his crayon, but the loss of the blackboard would be just as fatal to the demonstration. Without darkness light would be useless—universal light as blind as universal darkness. Universal thing and universal no-thing were indistinguishable. Why, then, assume the positive, the immediately affirmative, as alone the ingenious? Is not the mould as shapely as the model? The original ingenuity does not show in bringing light out of darkness, nor in bringing things out of nothing, but in evolving, through the just opposition of light and darkness, this wondrous picture, in which the black and white lines have equal significance—in evolving from life and death at once, the conscious spirit. . . .

"It is our habit to think of life as dear, and of death as cheap (though Tithonus found them otherwise), or, continuing the simile of the picture, that paper is cheap while drawing is expensive; but the engraver had a different estimation in one sense, for all his labor was spent on the white ground while he left untouched those parts of the block which make the lines in the picture. If being and non-being are both necessary to the presence of either, neither shall claim priority or preference. Indeed, we may fancy an intelligence which, instead of regarding things as simply owning entity, should regard chiefly their background as affected by the holes which things are making in it. Even so, the paper-maker might see your picture as intrusive!"

Thus "does the negation of being appear as indispensable in the making of it." But to anyone who should appeal to particular forms of being to refute this paradox, Mr. Blood admits that "to say that a picture, or any other sensuous thing, is the same as the want of it, were to utter nonsense indeed: there is a difference equivalent to the whole stuff and merit of the picture; but in so far as the picture can be there for thought, as something either asserted or negated, its presence or its absence are the same and indifferent. By *its* absence we do not mean the absence of anything else, nor absence in general; and how, forsooth, does its absence differ from these other absences, save by containing a complete description of the picture? The hole is as round as the plug; and from our thought the 'picture' cannot get away. The negation is specific and descriptive, and what it destroys it preserves for our conception."

The result is that, whether it be taken generally or taken specifically, all that which *either is or is not* is or is not *by distinction or opposition.* "And observe the life, the process, through which this slippery doubleness endures. Let us suppose the present tense, that gods and men and angels and devils march all abreast in this present instant, and the only real time and date in the universe is now. And what *is* this instant now? Whatever else, it is *process—* becoming and departing; with what between? Simply division, difference; the present has no breadth, for if it had, that which we seek would be the middle of that breadth. There is no precipitate, as on a stationary platform, of the process of becoming, no residuum of the process of departing, but between the two is a curtain, *the apparition of difference,* which is all the world."

I am using my scissors somewhat at random on my author's paragraphs, since one place is as good as another for entering a ring by, and the expert reader will discern at once the authentic dialectic circling. Other paragraphs show Mr. Blood as more hegelian still, and thoroughly idealistic:—

"Assume that knowing is distinguishing, and that distinction is of difference; if one knows a difference, one knows it as of entities which afford it, and which also he knows; and he must know the entities and the difference apart—one from the other. Knowing all this, he should be able to answer the twin question, 'What is the difference *between sameness and difference?*' It is a 'twin' question, because the two terms are equal in the proposition, and each is full of the other. . . .

"Sameness has 'all the difference in the world'—from difference; and difference is an entity as difference—it being identically that. They are alike and different at once, since either is the other when the observer would contrast it with the other—so that the sameness and the difference are 'subjective,' are the property of the observer: his is the 'limit' in their unlimited field. . . .

"We are thus apprised that distinction involves and carries its own identity; and that ultimate distinction—distinction in the last analysis—is self-distinction—'self-knowledge,' as we realize it consciously every day. Knowledge is self-referred: to know is to know that you know, and to be known as well.

" 'Ah! but *both in the same time?*' enquires the logician. A subject-object knowing itself as a seamless unit, while its two items show a real distinction: this passes all understanding."

But the whole of idealism goes to the proof that the two sides *cannot* succeed one another in a time-process. "To say you know, and you know that you know, is to add nothing in the last clause; it is as idle as to say that you lie, and you know that you lie," for if you know it not you lie not.

Philosophy seeks to grasp totality, "but the power of grasping or consenting to totality involves the power of thought to make itself its own object. Totality itself may indeed be taken by the naïve intellect as an immediate topic, in the sense of being just an *object*, but it cannot be just that; for the knower, as other or opposite, would still be within that totality. The 'universe' by definition must contain all opposition. If distinction should vanish, what would remain? To what other could it change as a whole? How can the loss of distinction make a *difference?* Any loss, at its utmost, offers a new status with the old, but obviously it is too late now to efface distinction by a *change*. There is no possible conjecture, but such as carries with it the subjective that holds it; and when the conjecture is of distinction in general, the subjective fills the void with distinction of itself. The ultimate, ineffaceable distinction is self-distinction, self-consciousness. . . . 'Thou art the unanswered question, couldst see thy proper eye.' . . . The thought that must be is the very thought of our experience; the ultimate opposition, the to be *and* not to be, is personality, spirit—somewhat that is in knowing that it is, and is nothing else but this knowing in its vast relations.[2]

"Here lies the bed-rock; here the brain-sweat of twenty-five centuries crystallizes to a jewel five words long: 'THE UNIVERSE HAS NO OPPOSITE.' For here the wonder of that which is, rests safe in the perception that all things *are* only through the opposition which is their only fear."

"The inevitable generally," in short, is exactly and identically that which in point of fact is actually here.

This is the familiar nineteenth-century development of Kant's idealistic vision. To me it sounds monistic enough to charm the monist in me unreservedly. I listen to the felicitously-worded concept-music circling round itself, as on some drowsy summer noon one listens under the pines to the murmuring of leaves and insects, and with as little thought of criticism.

But Mr. Blood strikes a still more vibrant note: "No more can

---

2 "How shall a man know he is alive—since in thought the knowing constitutes the being alive, without knowing that thought (life) from its opposite, and so knowing both, and so far as being is knowing, being both? Each defines and relieves the other, each is impossible in thought without the other; therefore each has no distinction save as presently contrasting with the other, and each by itself is the same, and nothing. Clearly, then, consciousness is neither of one nor of the other nor of both, but a knowing subject perceiving them and itself together and as one. . . . So, in coming out of the anaesthetic exhilaration . . . we want to tell something; but the effort instantly proves that something will stay back and do the telling—one must utter one's own throat, one must eat one's own teeth, to express the being that possesses one. The result is ludicrous and astounding at once—astounding in the clear perception that this is the ultimate mystery of life, and is given you as the old Adamic secret, which you then feel that all intelligence must sometime know or have known; yet ludicrous in its familiar simplicity, as somewhat that any man should always perceive at his best, if his head were only level, but which in our ordinary thinking has grown into a thousand creeds and theories dignified as religion and philosophy."

be than rationally is; and this was always true. There is no reason for what is not; but for what there is reason, that *is* and ever was. Especially is there no becoming of reason, and hence no reason for becoming, to a sufficient intelligence. In the sufficient intelligence all things always are, and are rational. To say there is something yet to be which never was, not even in the sufficient intelligence wherein the world is rational and not a blind and orphan waif, is to ignore all reason. Aught that might be assumed as contingently coming to be could only have 'freedom' for its origin; and 'freedom' has not fertility or invention, and is not a reason for any special thing, but the very vacuity of a ground for anything in preference to its room. Neither is there in bare time any principle or originality whereby anything should come or go. . . .

"Such idealism inures greatly to the dignity and repose of man. No blind fate, prior to what is, shall necessitate that all first be and afterward be known, but knowledge is first, with fate in her own hands. When we are depressed by the weight and immensity of the immediate, we find in idealism a wondrous consolation. That alien positive, so vast and overwhelming by itself, reduces its pretensions when the whole negative confronts it on our side.[3] It matters little for its greatness when an equal greatness is opposed. When one remembers that the balance and motion of the planets are so delicate that the momentary scowl of an eclipse may fill the heavens with tempest, and even affect the very bowels of the earth—when we see a balloon, that carries perhaps a thousand pounds, leap up a hundred feet at the discharge of a sheet of note paper—or feel it stand deathly still in a hurricane, because it goes with the hurricane, sides with it, and ignores the rushing world below—we should realize that one tittle of pure originality would outweigh this crass objective, and turn these vast masses into mere breath and tissue-paper show."[4]

[3] Elsewhere Mr. Blood writes of the "force of the negative" thus:—"As when a faded lock of woman's hair shall cause a man to cut his throat in a bedroom at five o'clock in the morning; or when Albany resounds with legislation, but a little hen-pecked judge in a dusty office at Herkimer or Johnstown sadly writes across the page the word 'unconstitutional'—and the glory of the Capitol has faded."

[4] Elsewhere Blood writes:—"But what then, in the name of common sense, *is* the external world? If a dead man could answer he would say Nothing, or as Macbeth said of the air-drawn dagger, 'there is no such thing.' But a live man's answer might be in this way: What is the multiplication table when it is not written down? It is a necessity of thought; it was not created, it cannot but be; every intelligence which goes to it, and thinks, must think in that form or think falsely. So the universe is the static

But whose is the originality? There is nothing in what I am treating as this phase of our author's thought to separate it from the old-fashioned rationalism. There must be a reason for every fact; and so much reason, so much fact. The reason is always the whole foil and background and negation of the fact, the whole remainder of reality. "A man may feel good only by feeling better. . . . Pleasure is ever in the company and contrast of pain; for instance, in thirsting and drinking, the pleasure of the one is the exact measure of the pain of the other, and they cease precisely together—otherwise the patient would drink more. The black and yellow gonfalon of Lucifer is indispensable in any spiritual picture." Thus do truth's two components seem to balance, vibrating across the centre of indifference; "being and non-being have equal value and cost," and "mainly are convertible in their terms."[5]

This sounds radically monistic; and monistic also is the first account of the Ether-revelation, in which we read that "thenceforth each is all, in God. . . . The One remains, the many change and pass; and every one of us is the One that remains."

---

necessity of reason; it is not an object for any intelligence to find, but it is half object and half subject; it never cost anything as a whole; it never *was* made, but always *is* made, in the Logos, or expression of reason—the Word; and slowly but surely it will be understood and uttered in every intelligence, until he is one with God or reason itself. As a man, for all he knows, or has known, stands at any given instant the realization of only one thought, while all the rest of him is invisibly linked to that in the necessary form and concatenation of reason, so the man as a whole of exploited thoughts is a moment in the front of the concatenated reason of the universal whole; and this whole is personal only as it is personally achieved. This is the Kingdom that is 'within you,' and the *God* which 'no man hath seen at any time.' "

[5] There are passages in Blood that sound like a well-known essay by Emerson. For instance:—"Experience burns into us the fact and the necessity of universal compensation. The philosopher takes it from Heraclitus, in the insight that everything exists through its opposite; and the bummer comforts himself for his morning headache as only the rough side of a square deal. We accept readily the doctrine that pain and pleasure, evil and good, death and life, chance and reason, are necessary equations—that there must be just as much of each as of its other.

"It grieves us little that this great compensation cannot at every instant balance its beam on every individual centre, and dispense with an under dog in every fight; we know that the parts must subserve the whole; we have faith that our time will come; and if it comes not at all in this world, our lack is a bid for immortality, and the most promising argument for a world hereafter. 'Though He slay me, yet will I trust in Him.'

"This is the faith that baffles all calamity, and insures genius and patience in the world. Let not the creditor hasten the settlement; let not the injured man hurry toward revenge; there is nothing that draws bigger interest than a wrong, and to 'get the best of it' is ever in some sense to get the worst."

II

It seems to me that any transcendental idealist who reads this article ought to discern in the fragmentary utterances which I have quoted thus far, the note of what he considers the truer dialectic profundity. He ought to extend the glad hand of fellowship to Mr. Blood; and if he finds him afterwards palavering with the enemy, he ought to count him, not as a simple ignoramus or philistine, but as a renegade and relapse. He cannot possibly be treated as one who sins because he never has known better, or as one who walks in darkness because he is congenitally blind.

Well, Mr. Blood, explain it as one may, does turn towards the darkness as if he had never seen the light. Just listen for a moment to such irrationalist deliverances on his part as these:—

"Reason is neither the first nor the last word in this world. Reason is an equation; it gives but a pound for a pound. Nature is excess; she is ever-more, without cost or explanation.

> 'Is heaven so poor that *justice*
>   Metes the bounty of the skies?
> So poor that every blessing
>   Fills the debit of a cost?
> That all process is returning?
>   And all gain is of the lost?'

Go back into reason, and you come at last to fact, nothing more— a given-ness, a something to wonder at and yet admit, like your own will. And all these tricks for logicizing originality, self-relation, absolute process, subjective contradiction, will wither in the breath of the mystical fact—they will swirl down the corridors before the besom of the everlasting Yea."

Or again: "The monistic notion of a oneness, a centred wholeness, ultimate purpose, or climacteric result of the world, has wholly given way. Thought evolves no longer a centred whole, a One, but rather a numberless many, adjust it how we will."

Or still again: "The pluralists have talked philosophy to a standstill—Nature is contingent, excessive and mystical essentially."

Have we here contradiction simply, a man converted from one faith to its opposite? Or is it only dialectic circling, like the opposite points on the rim of a revolving disc, one moving up, one down, but replacing one another endlessly, while the whole disc never moves? If it be this latter—Mr. Blood himself uses the image—the dialectic is too pure for me to catch: a deeper man must mediate the monistic with the pluralistic Blood. Let my incapacity be castigated, if my 'Subject' ever reads this article, but let me treat him from now onwards as the simply pluralistic mystic which my reading of the rest of him suggests. I confess to some dread of my own fate at his hands. In making so far an ordinary transcendental idealist of him, I have taken liberties, running separate sentences together, inverting their order, and even altering single words—for all which I beg pardon; but in treating my author from now onwards as a pluralist, interpretation is easier, and my hands can be less stained (if they *are* stained) with exegetic blood.

I have spoken of his verbal felicity, and alluded to his poetry. Before passing to his mystic gospel, I will refresh the reader (doubtless now fatigued with so much dialectic) by a sample of his verse. "The Lion of the Nile" is an allegory of the "champion spirit of the world" in its various incarnations.
Thus it begins:—

> "Whelped on the desert sands, and desert bred
> From dugs whose sustenance was blood alone—
> A life translated out of other lives,
> I grew the king of beasts; the hurricane
> Leaned like a feather on my royal fell;
> I took the Hyrcan tiger by the scruff
> And tore him piecemeal; my hot bowels laughed
> And my fangs yearned for prey. Earth was my lair:
> I slept on the red desert without fear:
> I roamed the jungle depths with less design
> Than e'en to lord their solitude; on crags
> That cringe from lightning—black and blasted fronts
> That crouch beneath the wind-bleared stars, I told
> My heart's fruition to the universe,
> And all night long, roaring my fierce defy,
> I thrilled the wilderness with aspen terrors,
> And challenged death and life. . . ."

Again:

> "Naked I stood upon the raked arena
> Beneath the pennants of Vespasian,

While seried thousands gazed—strangers from Caucasus,
Men of the Grecian Isles, and Barbary princes,
To see me grapple with the counterpart
Of that I had been—the raptorial jaws,
The arms that wont to crush with strength alone,
The eyes that glared vindictive.—Fallen there,
Vast wings upheaved me; from the Alpine peaks
Whose avalanches swirl the valley mists
And whelm the helpless cottage, to the crown
Of Chimborazo, on whose changeless jewels
The torrid rays recoil, with ne'er a cloud
To swathe their blistered steps, I rested not,
But preyed on all that ventured from the earth,
An outlaw of the heavens.—But evermore
Must death release me to the jungle shades;
And there like Samson's grew my locks again
In the old walks and ways, till scapeless fate
Won me as ever to the haunts of men,
Luring my lives with battle and with love. . . ."

I quote less than a quarter of the poem, of which the rest is just as good, and I ask: Who of us all handles his english vocabulary better than Mr. Blood?[6]

His proclamations of the mystic insight have a similar verbal power:—

"There is an invariable and reliable condition (or uncondition) ensuing about the instant of recall from anaesthetic stupor to 'coming to,' in which the genius of being is revealed. . . . No words may express the imposing certainty of the patient that he is realizing the primordial Adamic surprise of Life.

---

[6] Or what thinks the reader of the verbiage of these verses?—addressed in a mood of human defiance to the cosmic Gods—

"Whose lightnings tawny leap from furtive lairs,
To helpless murder, while the ships go down
Swirled in the crazy stound, and mariners' prayers
Go up in noisome bubbles—such to *them*;—
Or when they tramp about the central fires,
Bending the strata with æonian tread
Till steeples totter, and all ways are lost,—
Deem they of wife or child, or home or friend,
Doing these things as the long years lead on
Only to other years that mean no more,
That cure no ill, nor make for use or proof—
Destroying ever, though to rear again."

"Repetition of the experience finds it ever the same, and as if it could not possibly be otherwise. The subject resumes his normal consciousness only to partially and fitfully remember its occurrence, and to try to formulate its baffling import,—with but this consolatory afterthought: that he has known the oldest truth, and that he has done with human theories as to the origin, meaning, or destiny of the race. He is beyond instruction in 'spiritual things.' . . .

"It is the instant contrast of this 'tasteless water of souls' with formal thought as we 'come to,' that leaves in the patient an astonishment that the awful mystery of Life is at last but a homely and a common thing, and that aside from mere formality the majestic and the absurd are of equal dignity. The astonishment is aggravated as at a thing of course, missed by sanity in overstepping, as in too foreign a search, or with too eager an attention: as in finding one's spectacles on one's nose, or in making in the dark a step higher than the stair. My first experiences of this revelation had many varieties of emotion; but as a man grows calm and determined by experience in general, so am I now not only firm and familiar in this once weird condition, but triumphant—divine. To minds of sanguine imagination there will be a sadness in the tenor of the mystery, as if the key-note of the universe were low, for no poetry, no emotion known to the normal sanity of man, can furnish a hint of its primeval prestige, and its all-but appalling solemnity; but for such as have felt sadly the instability of temporal things there is a comfort of serenity and ancient peace, while for the resolved and imperious spirit there are majesty and supremacy unspeakable. Nor can it be long until all who enter the anaesthetic condition (and there are hundreds every secular day) will be taught to expect this revelation, and will date from its experience their initiation into the Secret of Life. . . .

"This has been my moral sustenance since I have known of it. In my first printed mention of it I declared: 'The world is no more the alien terror that was taught me. Spurning the cloud-grimed and still sultry battlements whence so lately Jehovan thunders boomed, my gray gull lifts her wing against the nightfall, and takes the dim leagues with a fearless eye.' And now, after twenty-seven years of this experience, the wing is grayer, but the eye is fearless still, while I renew and doubly emphasize that declaration.

I know, as having known, the meaning of Existence: the sane centre of the universe—at once the wonder and the assurance of the
soul."

After this rather literary interlude I return to Blood's philosophy again. I spoke a while ago of its being an 'irrationalistic' philosophy in its latest phase. Behind every 'fact' rationalism postulates its 'reason.' Blood parodizes this demand in true nominalistic
fashion. "The goods are not enough, but they must have the invoice with them. There must be a *name*, something *to read*. I think
of Dickens's horse that always fell down when they took him out
of the shafts; or of the fellow who felt weak when naked, but
strong in his overcoat."—No bad mockery, this, surely, of rationalism's habit of explaining things by putting verbal doubles of them
beneath them as their ground!

"All that philosophy has sought as cause, or reason," he says,
"pluralism subsumes in the status and the given fact, where it
stands as plausible as it may ever hope to stand. There may be
disease in the presence of a question as well as in the lack of an
answer. We do not wonder so strangely at an ingenious and well-
set-up effect, for we feel such in ourselves; but a cause, reaching
out beyond the verge [of fact] and dangling its legs in nonentity,
with the hope of a rational foothold, should realize a strenuous
life. Pluralism believes in truth and reason, but only as mystically
realized, as lived in experience. Up from the breast of a man, up
to his tongue and brain, comes a free and strong determination,
and he cries, originally, and in spite of his whole nature and environment, 'I will.' This is the Jovian fiat, the pure cause. This is
reason; this or nothing shall explain the world for him. For how
shall he entertain a reason bigger than himself? . . . Let a man stand
fast, then, as an axis of the earth; the obsequious meridians will
bow to him, and gracious latitudes will measure from his feet."

This seems to be Blood's mystical answer to his own monistic
statement which I quoted above, that 'freedom' has no fertility,
and is no reason for any special thing.[7] "Philosophy," Mr. Blood

[7] I subjoin a poetic apostrophe of Mr. Blood's to freedom:
"Let it ne'er be known.
If in some book of the Inevitable,
Dog-eared and stale, the future stands engrossed

writes to me in a letter, "is past. It was the long endeavour to logicize what we can only realize practically or in immediate experience. I am more and more impressed that Heraclitus insists on the equation of reason and unreason, or chance, as well as of being and not-being, etc. This throws the secret beyond logic, and makes mysticism outclass philosophy. The insight that mystery—the MYSTERY—as such is final, is the hymnic word. If you

E'en as the past. There shall be news in heaven,
And question in the courts thereof; and chance
Shall have its fling, e'en at the [ermined] bench.

. . . .

Ah, long ago, above the Indian ocean,
Where wan stars brood over the dreaming East,
I saw, white, liquid, palpitant, the Cross;
And faint and far came bells of Calvary
As planets passed, singing that they were saved,
Saved from themselves: but ever low Orion—
For hunter too was I, born of the wild,
And the game flavor of the infinite
Tainted me to the bone—he waved me on,
On to the tangent field beyond all orbs,
Where form nor order nor continuance
Hath thought nor name; there unity exhales
In want of confine, and the protoplasm
May beat and beat, in aimless vehemence,
Through vagrant spaces, homeless and unknown.

. . . .

There ends One's empire!—but so ends not all;
One knows not all; my griefs at least are mine—
By me their measure, and to me their lesson;
E'en I am one—(poor deuce to call the Ace!)
And to the open bears my gonfalon,
Mine ægis, Freedom!—Let me ne'er look back
Accusing, for the withered leaves and lives
The sated past hath strewn, the shears of fate,
But forth to braver days.
                              O, Liberty,
Burthen of every sigh!—thou gold of gold,
Beauty of the beautiful, strength of the strong!
My soul forever turns agaze for thee.
There is no purpose of eternity
For faith or patience; but thy buoyant torch
Still lighted from the Islands of the Blest,
O'erbears all present for potential heavens
Which are not—ah, so more than all that are!
Whose chance postpones the ennui of the skies!
Be thou my genius—be my hope in thee!
For this were heaven: to be, and to be free."

use reason pragmatically, and deny it absolutely, you can't be beaten—be assured of that. But the *Fact* remains, and of course the Mystery."[8]

The "Fact," as I understand the writer here to mean it, remains in its native disseminated shape. From every realized amount of fact some other fact is *absent*, as being uninvolved. "There is nowhere more of it consecutively, perhaps, than appears upon this present page." There is, indeed, to put it otherwise, no more one all-enveloping fact than there is one all-enveloping spire in an endlessly growing spiral, and no more one all-generating fact than there is one central point in which an endlessly converging spiral ends. Hegel's "bad infinite" belongs to the eddy as well as to the line. "Progress?" writes our author. "And to what? Time turns a weary and a wistful face; has he not traversed an eternity? and shall another give the secret up? We have dreamed of a climax and a consummation, a final triumph where a world shall burn *en barbecue*; but there is not, cannot be, a purpose of eternity; it shall pay mainly as it goes, or not at all. The show is on; and what a show, if we will but give our attention! Barbecues, bonfires and banners? Not twenty worlds a minute would keep up our bonfire of the sun; and what banners of our fancy could eclipse the meteor pennants of the pole, or the opaline splendors of the everlasting ice? . . . Doubtless we *are* ostensibly progressing, but there have been prosperity and high-jinks before. Nineveh and Tyre, Rome, Spain and Venice also had their day. We are going, but it is a question of our standing the pace. It would seem that the news must become less interesting or tremendously more so—'a breath can make us, as a breath has made.'"

Elsewhere we read: "Variety, not uniformity, is more likely to be the key to progress. The genius of being is whimsical rather than consistent. Our strata show broken bones of histories all forgotten. How can it be otherwise? There can be no purpose of

---

[8] In another letter Mr. Blood writes:—"I think we are through with 'the Whole,' and with 'causa sui,' and with the 'negative unity' which assumes to identify each thing as being what it lacks of everything else. You can, of course, build out a chip by modelling the sphere it was chipped from;—but if it wasn't a sphere? What a weariness it is to look back over the twenty odd volumes of the *Journal of Speculative Philosophy*, and see Harris's mind wholly filled by that one conception of self-determination—everything to be thought as 'part of a system'—a 'whole' and 'causa sui.'—I should like to see such an idea get into the head of Edison or Geo. Westinghouse."

eternity. It is process all. The most sublime result, if it appeared as the ultimatum, would go stale in an hour—it could not be endured."

Of course from an intellectual point of view this way of thinking must be classed as scepticism. "Contingency forbids any inevitable history, and conclusions are absurd. Nothing in Hegel has kept the planet from being blown to pieces." Obviously the mystical 'security,' the 'apodal sufficiency' yielded by the anaesthetic revelation, are very different moods of mind from aught that rationalism can claim to father—more active, prouder, more heroic. From his ether-intoxication Blood may feel towards ordinary rationalists "as Clive felt towards those millions of Orientals in whom honour had no part." On page 6 [181], above, I quoted from his "Nemesis"—"Is heaven so poor that justice," etc. The writer goes on, addressing the goddess of 'compensation' or rational balance:—

"How shalt thou poise the courage
    That covets all things hard?
How pay the love unmeasured
    That could not brook reward?
How prompt self-loyal honour
    Supreme above desire,
That bids the strong die for the weak,
    The martyr sing in fire?
Why do I droop in bower
    And sigh in sacred hall?
Why stifle under shelter?
    Yet where, through forest tall,
The breath of hungry winter
    In stinging spray resolves,
I sing to the north wind's fury
    And shout with the coarse-haired wolves?

·   ·   ·   ·   ·   ·

What of thy priests' confuting
    Of fate and form and law—
Of being and essence and counterpoise
    Of poles that drive and draw?
Ever some compensation,
    Some pandering purchase still!
But the vehm of achieving reason
    Is the all-patrician Will!"

Mr. Blood must manage to re-write the last two lines; but the contrast of the two securities, his and the rationalist's, is plain enough. The rationalist sees safe conditions. But Mr. Blood's revelation, whatever the conditions be, helps him to stand ready for a life among them. In this, his attitude seems to resemble that of Nietzsche's *amor fati!* "Simply," he writes to me, "*we do not know. But when we say we do not know, we are not to say it weakly and meekly, but with confidence and content. . . . Knowledge is and must ever be secondary—a witness rather than a principal—or a 'principle'!—in the case. Therefore mysticism for me!*"

"Reason," he prints elsewhere, "is but an item in the duplex potency of the mystery, and behind the proudest consciousness that ever reigned, Reason and Wonder blushed face to face. The legend sinks to burlesque if in that great argument which antedates man and his mutterings, Lucifer had not a fighting chance. . . .

"It is given to the writer and to others for whom he is permitted to speak—and we are grateful that it is the custom of gentlemen to believe one another—that the highest thought is not a milk-and-water equation of so much reason and so much result—'no school sum to be cast up.' We have realized the highest divine thought of itself, and there is in it as much of wonder as of certainty; inevitable, and solitary and safe in one sense, but queer and cactus-like no less in another sense, it appeals unutterably to experience alone.

"There are sadness and disenchantment for the novice in these inferences, as if the keynote of the universe were low, but experience will approve them. Certainty is the root of despair. The inevitable stales, while doubt and hope are sisters. Not unfortunately the universe is wild—game flavored as a hawk's wing. Nature is miracle all. She knows no laws; the same returns not, save to bring the different. The slow round of the engraver's lathe gains but the breadth of a hair, but the difference is distributed back over the whole curve, never an instant true—ever not quite."

"Ever not quite!"—this seems to wring the very last panting word out of rationalistic philosophy's mouth. It is fit to be pluralism's heraldic device. There is no complete generalization, no total point of view, no all-pervasive unity, but everywhere some residual resistance to verbalization, formulation, and discursification, some genius of reality that escapes from the pressure of the logical finger, that says 'hands off,' and claims its privacy, and means to be left to its own life. In every moment of immediate experience is somewhat absolutely original and novel. "We are the first that ever burst into this silent sea." Philosophy must pass from words, that reproduce but ancient elements, to life itself, that gives the integrally new. The 'inexplicable,' the 'mystery,' as what the intellect, with its claim to reason out reality, thinks that it is in duty bound to resolve, and the resolution of which Blood's revelation would eliminate from the sphere of our duties, remains; but it remains as something to be met and dealt with by faculties more akin to our activities and heroisms and willingnesses, than to our logical powers. This is the anaesthetic insight, according to our author. Let *my* last word, then, speaking in the name of intellectual philosophy, be *his* word:—"There is no conclusion. What has concluded, that we might conclude in regard to it? There are no fortunes to be told, and there is no advice to be given.— Farewell!"

Notes

Notes

The William James Collection is housed in the Houghton Library of Harvard University. It can be identified by the call number 'MS Am 1092', with either 'b' or 'f' as a prefix and, sometimes, a decimal following the numeral '2'. Many books from James's library are also preserved there; many of these are sufficiently identified by their call numbers which begin with 'WJ'. Other books from his library are in Harvard's Widener Library and elsewhere, and in such cases their location is stated. Still others were sold and have not been located. However, Ralph Barton Perry made a list, noting markings and annotations; this unpublished list can be consulted at Houghton.

At present, the Houghton Library is reclassifying the James Collection. Some volumes of letters are being broken up and the 'WJ' call numbers eliminated. Since work on this edition began, several books have been moved from Widener into Houghton; others, reported by Perry as sold or not listed at all, have turned up in the Widener stacks. The concluding volumes of this edition will contain a complete account of James's library and will give the new call numbers and locations. Since the same volumes will contain James's annotations, extensively indexed, only those annotations are noted in the present volume which appear to have a direct bearing upon the text at hand.

James was a very active reader who filled his books with annotations and markings. The term 'markings' refers to underlining, vertical lines in margins, and the notation 'N.B.' His style is distinctive: the N.B.'s are usually written so that the same vertical stroke serves for both the 'N' and the 'B', while his underlining often has a distinctive waver. Furthermore, James habitually filled the flyleaves of his books with indexes, in some cases simply jotting down a page number or two, in others, noting numerous subjects and selecting passages for attention or quotation. Pages singled out in this fashion usually have markings. Thus, for books protected in Houghton, the risk of error in attributing a given marking to James is slight, except where there are signs that others had owned or handled the book. The risk is greater for materials in open stacks such as those in Widener, where the only claim made is that the book was owned by James and that there are markings. Any conclusions that might be drawn for these books are subject to error, although markings have been noted only where the evidence points to James. Where the books have been sold, we are totally dependent upon Perry's reports.

It was not always convenient, for major figures repeatedly mentioned in the text, to key the note to the first reference. In order to find such notes, the index should be consulted. The index is intended to serve in place of cross-references.

All references to *Pragmatism*, *The Meaning of Truth*, *Essays in Radical Empiricism*, and *A Pluralistic Universe* are to the volumes in the present edition (Cambridge, Mass.: Harvard University Press, 1975–), identified as WORKS, while others of James's works are cited in the original editions.

3.1 letter] Granville Stanley Hall (1844-1924), American psychologist, "College Instruction in Philosophy," *Nation*, 23 (September 21, 1876), 180. This is a letter to the editor initialled "G. S. H.," but Hall's authorship is not in doubt. In the fall of 1876, Hall became a graduate student at Harvard and in June of 1878, received the first doctorate granted by the Harvard philosophy department. The relations between James and Hall are studied in Dorothy Ross, *G. Stanley Hall: The Psychologist as Prophet* (Chicago: University of Chicago Press, 1972). James's letters to Hall are preserved in the Clark University Archives, Worcester, Mass., with copies at Houghton, while Hall's letters to James are at Houghton.

3.5 president] In his "Philosophy in the United States," *Mind*, 4 (January 1879), 89-105, an essay sharply critical of the teaching of philosophy, Hall states that there are some 300 non-Catholic colleges in the United States and that in most of them philosophy is taught by the president.

4.11 *Popular*] The first number of the *Popular Science Monthly* appeared in May 1872, edited by Edward Livingston Youmans (1821-1887), American editor and writer on science, a major promoter of the teachings of Herbert Spencer.

4.28 Touchstone's] One of James's favorite quotations, from Shakespeare's *As You Like It*, act 3, scene 2.

5.6 speaks] "The application of scientific methods in psychology by Spencer, Lewes, Lotze, Wundt, and others; the admirable text-books now accessible in the general history of philosophy; the application of philosophical systems to history, politics, law, and education, which have contributed to make these subjects centres of such fresh and eager interest under some of the great living German teachers, indicate how entirely our methods of instruction need to be remodelled" ("College Instruction in Philosophy").

6.4 Fechner's] Gustav Theodor Fechner (1801-1887), German philosopher, physicist, psychologist, *Elemente der Psychophysik*, 2 vols. (Leipzig: Breitkopf und Härtel, 1860). James's annotated copy (WJ 727.13) is dated Berlin, December 1867. Writing to Hall, January 16, 1880 (Clark University Archives), James stated that Fechner's psychophysics is as "moonshiny" as his other writings, but valuable for its rich detail. In *The Principles of Psychology*, 2 vols. (New York: Henry Holt, 1890), I, 534, James was again critical. James wrote an introduction to Fechner's *The Little Book of Life after Death* (Boston: Little, Brown, 1904). Ch. 4 of *A Pluralistic Universe*, WORKS, is devoted to a general assessment of Fechner's thought.

6.7 Helmholtz's] Hermann Ludwig Ferdinand von Helmholtz (1821-1894), German physiologist and physicist. James discusses unconscious inference in *The Principles of Psychology* (1890), II, 111-113, citing the *Handbuch der physiologischen Optik* (1867). In the *Principles* (1890), I, 169n, James cites Helmholtz's *Die Thatsachen in der Wahrnehmung* (Berlin: August Hirschwald, 1879) (WJ 737.51), p. 27, as evidence that Helmholtz modified his position.

6.15 writers] In the *Principles* (1890), I, 549, James concluded his discussion of Fechner's psychophysics as follows: "But it would be terrible if even such a dear old man as this could saddle our Science forever with his patient whimsies, and, in a world so full of more nutritious objects of attention, compel all future students to plough through the difficulties, not only of his own works, but of the still drier ones written in his refutation. Those who desire this dreadful literature can find it ... but I will not even enumerate it in a footnote."

6.23 Wundt] Wilhelm Wundt (1832-1920), German psychologist and philosopher. While Wundt began his career as a physiologist, he had published a number of works in psychology when in 1875 he went to Leipzig.

6.24 McCosh] James McCosh (1811-1894), Scottish-born philosopher, president of Princeton College from 1868 to 1888, *The Scottish Philosophy, Biographical, Expository, Critical, from Hutcheson to Hamilton* (New York: Robert Carter and Brothers, 1875), p. 458.

6.36 Harvard] In the academic year 1876-1877, George Herbert Palmer (1842-1933), American philosopher, taught a required psychology course for juniors with Locke's *Essay Concerning Human Understanding* as a text; Francis Bowen (1811-1890), American philosopher, used Kant's *Critique of Pure Reason*, Schopenhauer's *The World as Will and Idea*, and Eduard von Hartmann's *The Philosophy of the Unconscious* as texts in Philosophy 2 and Philosophy 3; Andrew Preston Peabody (1811-1893), American religious writer and philosopher, used Shadworth Hodgson's *The Theory of Practice: An Ethical Enquiry* in Philosophy 4. James himself used Spencer's *The Principles of Psychology* in his Natural History 2. In 1877-1878, James did not teach Natural History 2 and did not list Spencer as a text for Philosophy 4.

7.1 As]' The importance of Herbert Spencer (1820-1903) in the development of James's thought is made clear by the extremely extensive annotations, often sharply critical, in his copies of Spencer's works. Furthermore, the James Collection contains some 60 sheets of James's notes on Spencer (bMS Am 1092.9 [4484-4494]), to be reprinted in the manuscript volumes of the present edition. Perry includes excerpts dealing with Spencer from James's courses in *The Thought and Character of William James*, 2 vols. (Boston: Little, Brown, 1935), I, 474-493, and James's letter to Spencer, April 21, 1879, in which James asks whether an enclosed summary of Spencer's view of knowledge correctly represents Spencer's position. Spencer's reply, endorsing James's interpretation, is preserved at Houghton (Autograph File).

7.7 Voltaire] From the Conclusion of Voltaire's *Examen important de Milord Bolingbroke ou le tombeau du fanatisme*: "Que mettrons-nous à la place? dites-vous. Quoi! un animal féroce a sucé le sang de mes proches: je vous dis de vous défaire de cette bête, et vous me demandez ce qu'on mettra a sa place!" (*Œuvres complètes de Voltaire*, XXVI [Paris: Garnier Frères, 1879], 299). Perry reports that marked copies of vols. I and II of Voltaire's *Œuvres complètes*, dated 1815, were sold from James's library, but no edition which began publication in 1815 has been located.

7.14 *Nature*] *Nature: A Weekly Illustrated Journal of Science* was founded and edited by Joseph Norman Lockyer (1836-1920), British astronomer. The first issue is dated London, November 4, 1869.

7.23 *"adjustment"*] James's copy of Spencer's *The Principles of Psychology* was a reprint of the drastically altered second edition, 2 vols. (New York: D. Appleton, 1871-1873) (WJ 582.24.6). In 1876-1877, James taught Natural History 2, physiological psychology, among his first courses in psychology, using this book as a text. His copy is very heavily annotated. Spencer argues: "A generalization uniting two different but allied classes of facts, necessarily unites all the facts contained in either class. Hence, if we find a formula which along with mental evolution includes the evolution nearest akin to it, we shall, by implication, find a formula comprehending the entire process of mental evolution" (I, 292 [sec. 130]). Spencer holds that "The phenomena which those of Mind resemble in the greatest degree are those of bodily life" (I, 293 [sec. 130]). "So that from the lowest to the highest forms of life, the increasing adjustment of inner to outer relations is one indivisible progression" (I, 387 [sec. 173]). In James's copy, the first passage is marked with an exclamation point, apparently in James a sign of disagreement.

8.4 mental] "The presentation of Intelligence as an adjustment of inner to outer relations that gradually extends in Space and Time, that becomes increasingly special and complex, and that has its elements ever more precisely co-ordinated and more completely integrated, leaves us with a conception which obviously requires further development. The various degrees and modes of Intelligence known as Instinct, Memory, Reason, Emotion, Will, and the rest, must be translated in terms of this conception" (I, 392 [sec. 176]).

8.6 polyp's] The examples appear to be James's own, although like those Spencer gives. Concerning polyps, Spencer writes: "nor do the tentacles of polypes commonly behave in the same way when touched by inorganic bodies as when touched by organic bodies" (I, 308 [sec. 140]).

8.22 sentiments] Spencer argues that feelings are inseparable from intellectual processes: "If all mental phenomena are incidents of the correspondence between the organism and its environment; and if this correspondence passes insensibly from its lowest to its highest forms; then, we may be certain, *à priori*, that no orders of Feelings can be completely disentangled from other phenomena of consciousness. We may infer that they must arise gradually out of the lower forms of psychical action, by steps such as lead to the higher forms of psychical action already traced out; and that they must constitute another aspect of these" (I, 473 [sec. 209]).

9.28 Tylor] Edward Burnett Tylor (1832-1917), British anthropologist. While the sentence quoted has not been located, the thought is certainly very characteristic of Tylor. For example, among the concluding remarks of his *Primitive Culture*, 1st American ed., 2 vols. (Boston: Estes & Lauriat, 1874) , pp. 443-444, we find: "To establish a connexion between what uncultured ancient men thought and did, and what cultured modern men think and do, is not a matter of inapplicable theoretic knowledge, for it raises the issue, how far are modern opinion and conduct based on the strong ground of soundest modern knowledge, or how far only on such knowledge as was available in the earlier and ruder stages of culture where their types were shaped. It has to be maintained that the early history of man has its bearing . . . on some of the deepest and most vital points of our intellectual, industrial, and social state."

10.5 Unknowable] James's copy of Spencer's *First Principles of a New System of Philosophy* is a reprint of the revised edition (New York: D. Appleton, 1877) (WJ 582.24.4). It is very heavily annotated. Pt. I deals with the Unknowable.

10.20 biology] Perry reports that two annotated volumes of Spencer's *The Principles of Biology* were sold from James's library. He does not date the second volume, but gives 1864 as the date of the first, thus indicating the British edition, 2 vols. (London: Williams and Norgate, 1864-1867), and this edition will be used in the present notes.

10.23 synonyms] In *The Principles of Biology*, I, 74-77 (sec. 28), Spencer gives examples of correspondence between organisms and their environment. Most of the synonyms listed by James appear in this context. 'Adjusted' is used on p. 83 (sec. 32), 'meet', on p. 84 (sec. 32). 'Counteract' was not found.

10.38 moth] "The acts of animals exhibit countless failures of the internal order to parallel the external order. In the moth which flies at a candle-flame, there exists no relation of psychical states answering to the relation between light and heat in the environment" (*The Principles of Psychology*, I, 409 [sec. 184]). On pp. 409-410, attached by a guideline to the word 'moth', James has the following comment: "Correspondence of internal light & heat with external light & heat is a mere correspondence of *relations*. But unless we add to this some correspondence between external & internal *terms*, our account of intelligence is incomplete. If internal heat mirrors external heat the corresp. is purely *theoretic* & so is the intelligence. But the intelligence may exist in a *practical* shape, if without mirroring the outer heat, the inner heat produces a *fit* reaction (escape, e.g.) in the moth. This is the fact Spencer has in view, but he wont say it, because it absolutely neccessitates a teleological element in the conception of intelligence. The latter is incomplete without the notion of proper active tendency. Desire & aversion, as right or wrong, thus lie deeply involved in it. It is true that the rightness &c means at first mere self conservation—but psychically it is pleasure or striving, and thus the *interests* of the animal even away down at the beginning of the evolution are seen to be an independent co-factor of mental life, invalidating Spencer's definition of the mere correspondence. Later these interests become varied and divorced fm. mere conservation—(aesthetic, moral, ['theoretic' *del.*] interests) and form a vast flood of life relative to nothing in the environment. But the important point is that even in their earliest form they 'correspond' to nothing external whatever, but dominate & judge the correspondence, & decide whether it is of the sort called intelligent or not."

12.14 survival] In his *The Factors of Organic Evolution* (New York: D. Appleton, 1887) (WJ 582.24.2), p. 5, Spencer makes clear that before Darwin he himself had tried to explain evolution solely by reference to modifications of organisms induced by functional changes following upon changes in the environment. In *The Principles of Biology* (I, 449 [sec. 166]), Spencer recognizes Darwin to have shown the inadequacy of this explanation in many cases, but still insists that there are many phenomena "not explicable as results of natural selection."

15.35 Hodgson] Shadworth Hollway Hodgson (1832-1912), British philosopher, *Time and Space: A Metaphysical Essay* (London: Longman, Green, Longman, Roberts, and Green, 1865) (WJ 539.18.6). James's annotated copy is dated December 1875. Writing to Charles Renouvier, July 29, 1876, James recommended *Time and Space* and described Hodgson as the "most robust of English philosophic writers" (*The Letters of William James,* ed. Henry James, 2 vols. [Boston: Atlantic Monthly Press, 1920], I, 188). The relations between James and Hodgson, including excerpts from their correspondence, are treated by Perry, I, 611-653.

16.33 Talleyrand] Charles Maurice de Talleyrand-Périgord (1754-1838), French statesman, is the subject of numerous anecdotes. James's sources have not been located. The remark is also attributed to others, see Edward Latham, *Famous Sayings and Their Authors,* 2nd ed. (London: Swan Sonnenschein, 1906), p. 121.

17.12 Layard's] Austen Henry Layard (1817-1894), British archeologist and diplomat, concludes his *Discoveries Among the Ruins of Nineveh and Babylon* (New York: G. P. Putnam, 1853), with a letter from a Turkish Cadi to Layard's friend, in which the Cadi responds to questions about the history and economic life of his city: "I praise God that I seek not that which I require not. Thou art learned in the things I care not for; and as for that which thou hast seen, I defile it. Will much knowledge create thee a double belly, or wilt thou seek Paradise with thine eyes?" (p. 663).

17.40 Mill] John Stuart Mill (1806-1873) expresses this attitude in his *An Examination of Sir William Hamilton's Philosophy,* 4th ed. (London: Longmans, Green, Reader, and Dyer, 1872), p. 129: "I will call no being good, who is not what I mean when I apply that epithet to my fellow-creatures; and if such a being can sentence me to hell for not so calling him, to hell I will go." Perry reports that two editions of this work were sold from James's library, a copy of the 4th edition dated 1872, and an edition in two volumes dated 1865. Widener has a copy of vol. I from James's library (Boston: William V. Spencer, 1865) (Phil 2138.30 [1]). Some of the many markings appear to be by James, while the annotations are not. Vol. II of this edition, not annotated, from James's library, has been sold and is now in my possession.

18.17-18 Emerson's] Ralph Waldo Emerson, from the poem "Brahma," *Poems* (Boston: Houghton, Mifflin, 1885), pp. 170-171, vol. IX of *Emerson's Complete Works.*

20.39 Huxley] Thomas Henry Huxley (1825-1895), English biologist and essayist; William Kingdon Clifford (1845-1879), British mathematician and philosopher. James discusses Huxley's and Clifford's views concerning the motives of knowing in *The Will to Believe* (New York: Longmans, Green, 1897), pp. 7-11.

21.15 Moody] Dwight Lyman Moody (1837-1899), Ira David Sankey (1840-1908), American evangelists. In 1873-1877, Moody and Sankey conducted extensive revivals. Their partnership seems well characterized by a poster from their British campaign: "Moody will preach the Gospel | Sankey will sing the Gospel." James's copy of Paul Dwight Moody and Arthur Percy Fitt, *The Shorter Life of D. L. Moody*, 2 vols. (Chicago: Bible Institute Colportage Association, ᶜ1900) is preserved in Widener (US 13612.1.31), with a few markings possibly by James.

23.1 RÉDACTEURS] The editor of the *Critique philosophique* was Charles Renouvier (1815-1903), French philosopher. Perry (I, 654-710) gives a detailed account of the relations between James and Renouvier. Perry also edited the correspondence between them, in the *Revue de métaphysique et de morale*, "Correspondance de Charles Renouvier et de William James," 36 (1929), 1-35, 193-222, "Un Échange de lettres entre Renouvier et William James," 42 (1935), 303-318. Houghton preserves James's copies of Renouvier's *Esquisse d'une classification systématique des doctrines philosophiques*, 2 vols. (Paris: Bureau de la *Critique philosophique*, 1885-1886) (WJ 675.61), and of the *Essais de critique générale*, all three essays: *Traité de logique générale*, 2nd ed., 3 vols. (Paris: Bureau de la *Critique philosophique*, 1875) (WJ 675.61.2), *Traité de psychologie rationnelle*, 2nd ed., 3 vols. (Paris: Bureau de la *Critique philosophique*, 1875) (WJ 675.61.4), *Les Principes de la nature*, 2nd ed. (Paris: Félix Alcan, 1892) (WJ 675.61.6). Perry reports that three volumes of the first edition of the *Essais* were sold from James's library. One volume was dated by James, March 19, 1870, another, December 1871. Also sold were James's annotated copies of the *Critique philosophique*. Renouvier published a number of articles on James in the *Critique philosophique*: "La Question de la certitude. IX. — Le Pari de Pascal et le pari de M. W. James," 7th year, vol. 2 (September 12, 1878), 97-106; "De la Caractéristique intellectuelle de l'homme, d'après M. W. James," 8th year, vol. 1 (1879), 369-376, 394-397, 8th year, vol. 2 (1879) 17-26, 41-48; a note to the French translation of "The Sentiment of Rationality," 8th year, vol. 2 (1879), 136; "Quelques Remarques sur la théorie de la volonté de M. W. James," n.s. 4th year, vol. 2 (1888), 117-126; comments on a letter by James, "Quelques Mots sur la lettre qui précède," n.s. 4th year, vol. 2 (1888) 404-406.

23.3 Depuis] James is referring to a period of severe depression, particularly to the crisis recorded in his diary for April 30, 1870: "I think that yesterday was a crisis in my life. I finished the first part of Renouvier's 2nd *Essays* and saw no reason why his definition of free will — 'the sustaining of a thought *because I choose to* when I might have other thoughts' — need be the definition of an illusion. At any rate, I will assume for the present — until next year — that it is no illusion. My first act of free will shall be to believe in free will." This period of James's life is discussed by Perry (I, 320-332), with quotations from James's letters and diary, as well as in *Letters* (I, 140-164). James emphasized Renouvier's conception of freedom in his review of the *Essais*, "Bain and Renouvier," *Nation*, 22 (June 8, 1876), 367-369, reprinted in *Collected Essays and Reviews*, ed. Ralph Barton Perry (New York: Longmans, Green, 1920), pp. 26-35.

25.12 Huxley] James appears to be giving a loose translation of remarks made by Huxley in "A Modern 'Symposium'" on "The Influence upon Morality of a Decline in Religious Belief," *Nineteenth Century*, 1 (April 1877), 331-358; (May 1877), 531-546. Huxley claims that should a proof of religion not be forthcoming, "however bad our posterity may become, so long as they hold by the plain rule of not pretending to believe what they have no reason to believe because it may be to their advantage so to pretend, they will not have reached the lowest depths of immorality" (p. 539).

26.34 Il] This and the concluding note were presumably written by the editor of the *Critique philosophique*, Renouvier.

33.13-14 Whitman] James's copy of Whitman's *Leaves of Grass* has not been located. In *The Varieties of Religious Experience* (New York: Longmans, Green, 1902), p. 506n, he quotes Whitman and cites *Leaves of Grass*, 1872. This edition (Washington, D.C., 1872) is the one used here. James is quoting from "One Hour to Madness and Joy," in *Children of Adam*, p. 114 of 1872 edition.

34.33 Ueberweg's] Friedrich Ueberweg (1826-1871), German philosopher, *System of Logic and History of Logical Doctrines*, trans. Thomas M. Lindsay (London: Longmans, Green, 1871), p. 139: "The *essential* (essentialia) are those attributes which (a) contain the common and persistent basis for a multitude of others; and on which (b) the subsistence of the object, its worth and its meaning, depends."

35.7 Hartmann] Eduard von Hartmann (1842-1906), German philosopher, *Philosophie des Unbewussten*, 2nd ed. (Berlin: Carl Duncker, 1870), p. 249.

35.13 Schopenhauer] Arthur Schopenhauer (1788-1860), *Die Welt als Wille und Vorstellung*, 3rd ed., 2 vols. (Leipzig: F. A. Brockhaus, 1859), II, 83-84. James's annotated copy of this edition is preserved at Houghton (*AC 85.J2376.Zz859s).

36.33 D'Alembert's] Jean le Rond d'Alembert (1717-1783), French philosopher and mathematician, *Discours préliminaire de l'Encyclopédie*, in *Œuvres philosophiques, historiques et littéraires*, I (Paris: Jean-François Bastien, 1805), 211.

36.36 Spencer] "Can the oscillation of a molecule be represented in consciousness side by side with a nervous shock, and the two be recognized as one? No effort enables us to assimilate them. That a unit of feeling has nothing in common with a unit of motion, becomes more than ever manifest when we bring the two into juxtaposition" (*The Principles of Psychology*, I, 158 [sec. 62]). "The conditioned form under which Being is presented in the

Subject, cannot, any more than the conditioned form under which Being is presented in the Object, be the Unconditioned Being common to the two" (I, 162 [sec. 63]). On p. 162, after underlining 'common to the two', James asks: "What right has he to assert that it is common when he has said (p. 157) that their difference transcends all others?"

37.10 "nascent"] James returns to the same criticism in *The Principles of Psychology* (1890), I, 148-149, where he quotes the following from Spencer's *Psychology*, I, 435 (sec. 195): "And the quick succession of changes in a ganglion, implying as it does perpetual experiences of differences and likenesses, constitutes the raw material of consciousness. The implication is that as fast as Instinct is developed, some kind of consciousness becomes nascent."

37.12 girl] Frederick Marryat (1792-1848), British novelist, *Mr Midshipman Easy* (1836; London: J. M. Dent, 1896), p. 9: "'Good heavens! Dr Middleton, what can you mean by bringing this person here?' exclaimed Mrs Easy. 'Not a married woman, and she has a child!' 'If you please, ma'am,' interrupted the young woman, dropping a curtscy, 'it was a very little one.' " The girl is being questioned by the Easy family to establish her moral fitness for wet-nursing the newborn Jack Easy.

37.18 Lewes] George Henry Lewes (1817-1878), British philosopher. Perry reports, giving only dates of publication, that four volumes of the five making up the three series of Lewes's *Problems of Life and Mind* were sold from James's library. In his account of James's markings in *The Physical Basis of Mind* (1877) (2nd series of *Problems of Life and Mind*), Perry notes the following entry from the flyleaf: " 'aspects' 335, 341, 349, 383, 336, 359, 357." In the London edition (Trübner, 1877), on each of the pages indicated, we find a treatment of the relations of mind and body.

38.3 Cuvier] Georges Cuvier (1769-1832), Étienne Geoffroy Saint-Hilaire (1772-1844), French naturalists. In 1830, Cuvier insisted on the multiplicity of animal forms in a debate with Geoffroy Saint-Hilaire, who held that all living forms exhibit the same structure.

38.9 Mill] John Stuart Mill, *A System of Logic: Ratiocinative and Inductive*, 8th ed., 2 vols. (London: Longmans, Green, Reader, and Dyer, 1872) (WJ 555.51), II, 4 (bk. III, ch. 14, sec. 2): "It is therefore useful to remark, that the ultimate Laws of Nature cannot possibly be less numerous than the distinguishable sensations or other feelings of our nature; — those, I mean, which are distinguishable from one another in quality, and not merely in quantity or degree."

38.12 Bain] Alexander Bain (1818-1903), Scottish philosopher, "Mystery, and Other Violations of Relativity," *Fortnightly Review*, n.s. 4 (1868), 383-395. James is quoting from pp. 394 and 395.

39.15 Hume] The concluding remark of David Hume's *An Enquiry Concerning Human Understanding*, vol. II of *Essays Moral, Political, and Literary*, ed. T. H. Green and T. H. Grose (London: Longmans, Green, 1875) (WJ 540.54), p. 135 (sec. XII, pt. 3).

39.36 Luys] Jules Luys (1828-1897), French anatomist and physician, *Le Cerveau et ses fonctions* (Paris: Germer Baillière, 1876). Widener preserves James's marked copy (Phil 6121.7.3). On the back flyleaf, James lists a series of page numbers: "! 48, 72, 82,-4, 91-2, 115, 172, 204, 208." On most of these pages, as well as on some others, there are passages marked with an exclamation point.

39.38 Sièrebois] R. P. Sièrebois, pseudonym of Prudence Boissière (1806-1885), French writer, *Psychologie réaliste* (Paris: Germer Baillière, 1876). James is translating and paraphrasing fragments from pp. 9, 4, 5, 27-28.

40.13 Czolbe] Heinrich Czolbe (1819-1873), German physician and philosopher, *Grundzüge einer extensionalen Erkenntnisstheorie*, ed. Eduard Johnson (Plauen: A. Hohmann, 1875). James seems to have in mind the discussion in sec. 11 titled "Das Zurücksinken der Bewusstheit in die Unbewusstheit setzt als nothwending Elasticität, Continuität und Unendlichkeit der Empfindungssubstanz voraus, d. h. die Weltseele" (p. 78).

40.39 Taine] Hippolite Adolphe Taine (1828-1893), French psychologist and philosopher, *De l'Intelligence*, 2 vols. (Paris: Hachette, 1870) (WJ 684.41). On the back flyleaf of his copy of vol. I, James has the following: "Against spiritual acts + entities, 66-70, 412, 476, 458-60, 373-6." The words James attributes to Taine have not been located. James criticizes Taine's conception of the self in *The Principles of Psychology* (1890), I, 355.

41.8-9 Renouvier] "Examen des principes de psychologie de Herbert Spencer," *Critique philosophique*, 6th year, vol. I (July 12, 1877), 379-384, third in a series of examinations of Spencer. "Et quand l'évolutionniste emploie son idée favorite pour atteindre cette raison première des choses ou de leurs rapports qui se dérobe à tout effort de la pensée, il ne voit pas que la position logique qu'il prend est celle d'un homme à qui l'on demande:'Comment se fait-il que les choses soient ainsi?' et qui répond: 'C'est qu'elles ne *sont* pas ainsi, mais qu'elles se *font* ainsi; et voilà comment cela se fait!' L'harmonie est ainsi déplacée, transportée de l'*esse* au *fieri*. Est-elle pour cela moins postulée? et le *fieri* lui-même obtient-il seulement le moindre commencement d'explication, de cela qu'on suppose que tout ce qui se fait se fait peu à peu, par degrés insensibles, si bien qu'à regarder chacun de ces degrés, ce qui se fait se fait avec autant de facilité et de clarté que s'il ne se faisait point du tout?" (pp. 383-384). "Si l'on veut que ce soit là une production *ex nihilo* continue, il faut le dire, et alors abandonner franchement l'idée d'un 'passage' qui n'éclaircit rien" (p. 383). The article is unsigned. It is attributed to Renouvier by Louis Foucher, *La Jeunesse de Renouvier et sa première philosophie* (Paris: J. Vrin, 1927), p. xxi of the Bibliography.

42.10 Lotze] Rudolph Hermann Lotze (1817-1881), German philosopher, *Mikrokosmus*, 2nd ed., 3 vols. (Leipzig: S. Hirzel, 1869-1872) (WJ 751.88.6), I, 261: "Aber der Geist begnügt sich nicht damit, sich von dem Mechanismus der Wahrnehmung und Erinnerung Verbindungen der Vorstellungen aufbrängen zu lassen; als eine beständige kritische Thätigkeit sucht das Denken jede derselben auf die Rechtsgründe zurückzuführen, welche die Verbindung des Verbundenen bedingen und das Zusammenseiende als ein Zusammengehöriges erweisen. So trennt es von einander die Eindrücke, die ohne inneren Zusammenhang sich in der Seele zusammenfanden, und erneuert bestätigend die Verknüpfung derer, denen die innere Verbindung ihres Inhaltes ein Recht auf beständige Gesellung gewährt."

42.21 "All] *A Treatise of Human Nature*, ed. T. H. Green and T. H. Grose, 2 vols. (London: Longmans, Green, 1874) (WJ 540.54.2), I, 559 (Appendix): "In short there are two principles, which I cannot render consistent; nor is it in my power to renounce either of them, viz. *that all our distinct perceptions are distinct existences,* and *that the mind never perceives any real connexion among distinct existences.*"

42.28 Huxley] The passage has not been located. In a letter to Charles Kingsley, May 22, 1863, Huxley writes: "I know nothing of Necessity, abominate the word Law (except as meaning that we know nothing to the contrary), and am quite ready to admit that there may be some place, 'other side of nowhere,' *par exemple*, where 2 + 2 = 5, and all bodies naturally repel one another instead of gravitating together" (Leonard Huxley, *Life and Letters of Thomas Henry Huxley*, 2 vols. [London: Macmillan, 1900], I, 242).

42.32 Mill] *A System of Logic*, I, 549-550 (bk. III, ch. 12, sec. 6): "The word explanation is here used in its philosophical sense. What is called explaining one law of nature by another, is but substituting one mystery for another; and does nothing to render the general course of nature other than mysterious: we can no more assign a *why* for the more extensive laws than for the partial ones. The explanation may substitute a mystery which has become familiar, and has grown to *seem* not mysterious, for one which is still strange. And this is the meaning of explanation, in common parlance." James's concluding sentence is taken from the next paragraph: "The laws, thus explained or resolved, are sometimes said to be *accounted for;* but the expression is incorrect, if taken to mean any thing more than what has been already stated."

43.24 Bain] *Mental and Moral Science* (London: Longmans, Green, 1868) (WJ 506.41.2), p. 177.

43.33 "the] Alexander Bain, *Logic*, 2 vols. (London: Longmans, Green, Reader, & Dyer, 1870), II, 120: "When minor laws are thus merged in a greater law, the mind feels a peculiar and genuine satisfaction — the satisfaction of having burst a boundary to expatiate over a wider field. We rise from a statement bearing upon a small group of facts to a statement comprehending a much larger group; from a ten-fold condensation, we reach a thousand-fold condensation. The intellect, oppressed with the variety and multiplicity of facts, is joyfully relieved by the simplification and the unity of a great principle."

44.19 "The] Hermann Helmholtz, *Popular Lectures on Scientific Subjects*, trans. E. Atkinson (New York: D. Appleton, 1873), p. 47.

44.38-39 Agassiz's] Louis Agassiz (1807-1873), Swiss-born naturalist, professor at Harvard, one of James's teachers in the Lawrence Scientific School. Agassiz expresses this view in his *The Structure of Animal Life* (New York: Charles Scribner, 1866), pp. 5-6.

45.1 Owen's] James perhaps is referring to Richard Owen (1804-1892), British anatomist, and to the illustrations in his *On the Archetype and Homologies of the Vertebrate Skeleton* (London: printed for the author, 1848).

46.27 Lewes's] George Henry Lewes, *Problems of Life and Mind*, 1st series, 2 vols. (London: Trübner, 1874-1875), II, 376 (Problem V, sec. 31): "We habitually consider cause as change, and yet declare every change to have its cause. Hence the word sometimes means the action observed, and sometimes an antecedent of that action. But mere antecedence never suffices; nor even invariableness of antecedence, unless that invariableness means a *procession:* the antecedent must *enter into* and become *incorporated* in the consequent, otherwise we ought not to call it a cause. Hence every cause is efficient, and passes into its effect: the process and the product are one, viewed under two aspects."

46.33 "the] John Tyndall (1820-1893), British physicist, *Fragments of Science for Unscientific People*, 2nd ed. (London: Longmans, Green, 1871), p. 121: "Were our minds and senses so expanded, strengthened, and illuminated as to enable us to see and feel the very molecules of the brain . . . and were we intimately acquainted with the corresponding states of thought and feeling, we should be as far as ever from the solution of the problem, 'How are these physical processes connected with the facts of consciousness?' The chasm between the two classes of phenomena would still remain intellectually impassable."

46.38 Wundt's] Wilhelm Wundt, *Die physikalischen Axiome und ihre Beziehung zum Causalprincip* (Erlangen: Ferdinand Enke, 1866).

46.38 Riehl] Alois Riehl (1844-1924), Austrian philosopher, "Causalität und Identität," *Vierteljahrsschrift für wissenschaftliche Philosophie*, I (1877), 365-384.

46.40 Wright] Chauncey Wright (1830-1875), American philosopher, *Philosophical Discussions*, ed. Charles Eliot Norton (New York: Henry Holt, 1877), pp. 406-413, paper titled "A Fragment on Cause and Effect." For an account of the relations between Wright and James, see Perry, I, ch. 31.

47.2 Tyndall] *Fragments of Science*, p. 121.

47.28-29 Huxley] "A Modern 'Symposium,' " p. 337.

48.15 Butler's] Samuel Butler (1612-1680), *Hudibras*, ed. A. R. Waller (Cambridge: University Press, 1905), p. 7 (canto I).

48.28 Lewes] *The History of Philosophy from Thales to Comte*, 3rd ed., 2 vols. (London: Longmans, Green, 1867), I, xciv-cxiv, a section of the Prolegomena titled "Necessary Truths." Ch. 13 of Problem I of Lewes's *Problems*, 1st series, I, 390-414, is also titled "Necessary Truths."

49.11 Mill] James Mill (1773-1836), British philosopher and historian, *Analysis of the Phenomena of the Human Mind,* new edition, 2 vols. (London: Longmans, Green, Reader, and Dyer, 1869) (WJ 550.50), I, 249.

49.33 Taine] The first three chapters of Taine's *De l'Intelligence,* bk. I, have 'substitution' in their titles: "Of Signs in General and of Substitution," "Of General Ideas and Simple Substitution," "Of General Ideas and Repeated Substitutions." The titles are taken from the English translation by T. D. Haye, *On Intelligence* (New York: Holt & Williams, 1871). On the flyleaf in back of his copy of vol. I of the French, James has the entry "Nominalism 35-7, 66-8," indicating portions of chs. 2 and 3.

51.5 Spencer] In *The Principles of Psychology,* II, 59-60 (sec. 294), Spencer quotes Mill, including the passage quoted by James, 50.4 to 50.8, and continues the controversy between them on the subject of identity. Spencer concludes sec. 294 with a long footnote, pp. 62n-64n, in the course of which he claims to disagree with Mill's view than an attribute is " 'a particular mode of naming our sensations, or our expectations of sensation.' " Spencer asserts: "For the things named in the premises and conclusion of a syllogism, I conceive to be those objective existences which are the correlatives of my subjective states" (p. 63n).

52.34 Watson] John Watson (1847-1939), Scottish-born philosopher, taught in Canada, "The World as Force. [With Especial Reference to the Philosophy of Mr. Herbert Spencer.]," pt. 2, *Journal of Speculative Philosophy,* 13 (April 1879), 151-179. Watson writes: "But essential and unessential, like positive and negative, are purely relative distinctions; what from interest is now conceived as essential, is again rejected as unessential. It must, therefore, never be forgotten that, when we speak of the essence of a thing, we do not thereby limit reality for all time to the special group of properties we have in view for the time being" (p. 164).

53.17 Taine] In *The Principles of Psychology* (1890), I, 159n, in a list of defenders of the mind-stuff theory, James includes bk. III of Taine's *On Intelligence.* Pt. I, bk. III, ch. 1 is titled "Of Sensations of Hearing and their Elements" and in it Taine argues that the sensations of hearing at least can be reduced to simple elements. He writes: "Here we perceive the elementary sensation whose different combinations are sufficient to explain all the sensations of sound" (English translation, p. 109). Later Taine asserts that the "elementary sensations" must be combined before they can reach consciousness (p. 181 [pt. I, bk. IV, ch. 1]).

53.17 Spencer] In *The Principles of Psychology* (1890), I, 151-153, while discussing attempts to discover "psychic units," James quotes from Spencer's *The Principles of Psychology,* I, 148-152 (sec. 60), in which Spencer argues that musical sounds are reducible to simpler feelings.

53.30 Clifford] In *The Principles of Psychology* (1890), I, 159n, James cites Clifford's "On the Nature of Things-In-Themselves," *Lectures and Essays,* ed. Leslie Stephen and Frederick Pollock, 2 vols. (London: Macmillan, 1879), II, 71-88. Perry reports that both volumes of this edition were sold from

James's library. For Clifford, the continuity between "inorganic matter" and "ourselves" required by the theory of evolution can be achieved by supposing that both body and mind are composed of "mind-stuff."

53.30 Fechner] For James's interpretation of Fechner see "Concerning Fechner" in *A Pluralistic Universe*, WORKS.

53.31 Zöllner] Johann Carl Friedrich Zöllner (1834-1882), German astronomer and physicist. Zöllner speculates about consciousness in matter in "Ueber die allgemeinen Eigenschaften der Materie," *Über die Natur der Cometen. Beiträge zur Geschichte und Theorie der Erkenntniss*, 2nd ed. (Leipzig: Wilhelm Engelmann, 1872). James refers to this work in *The Principles of Psychology* (1890), I, 159n, citing pp. 320ff. of an unidentified edition.

53.31 Hall] James could be referring to Hall's "Notes on Hegel and His Critics," *Journal of Speculative Philosophy*, 12 (January 1878), 93-103, incorporated into Hall's doctoral dissertation on *The Perception of Space*, for which James served as one of the readers. On pp. 101-102, Hall discusses "psychic elements" and the identity of "mind and matter."

54.1-2 Laplace] Pierre Simon, Marquis de Laplace (1749-1827), French astronomer and mathematician. Emil Du Bois-Reymond (1818-1896), German physiologist, *Über die Grenzen des Naturerkennens*, 2nd ed. (Leipzig: Veit, 1872), pp. 3-4, quotes in German translation the following from Laplace: "Une intelligence qui pour un instant donné, connaîtrait toutes les forces dont la nature est animée, et la situation respective des êtres qui la composent, si d'ailleurs elle était assez vaste pour soumettre ces données à l'analyse, embrasserait dans la même formule, les mouvemens des plus grands corps de l'univers et ceux du plus léger atome: rien ne serait incertain pour elle, et l'avenir comme le passé, serait présent à ses yeux" (Introduction to *Théorie analytique des probabilités*, 3rd ed. [Paris, 1820], pp. ii-iii).

56.6 "Grau] Johann Wolfgang von Goethe, *Faust*, ed. Erich Trunz (Hamburg: Christian Vegner, 1963), p. 66 (lines 2038-2039). In Bayard Taylor's translation, 2 vols. (Boston: Houghton, Mifflin, ᶜ1870), the passage is as follows: "My worthy friend, gray are all theories, I And green alone Life's golden tree" (I, 81).

58.8 Bain] Alexander Bain, "Mystery, and Other Violations of Relativity." The first part of the quotation is taken from p. 393, the second, following the ellipsis, from pp. 393-394.

58.37 *fait*] See note to 36.33.

59.9 Hegel] James seems to have in mind the opening triad of Hegel's *Wissenschaft der Logik*, the identification of the categories of being and nothingness. Preserved are nine volumes from James's library of Hegel's *Werke*, 2nd ed. (Berlin, 1840-) (WJ 737.32), of which vols. 3-5 contain the *Wissenschaft der Logik*. There are few markings or annotations, none in vol. 3.

60.26 *reductive*] The term 'reductive' is probably taken from Taine's *On Intelligence*. It is used by Taine in ch. 1 of bk. II, "Nature et réducteurs de l'image," and elsewhere. In the English translation, 'réducteur' is translated as 'reductive'. James reviewed the translation in the *Nation*, 15 (1872), 139-141. For Taine, a reductive is a sensation which effaces an image so that the latter comes to be viewed as unreal.

61.36 author] George John Romanes (1848-1894), Canadian-born naturalist, using the pseudonym of Physicus, *A Candid Examination of Theism* (London: Trübner, 1878), p. 193: "Hence, if Existence is finite, No-existence becomes possible; and the doctrine of the indestructibility of Existence becomes, for aught that we can tell, of a merely relative signification. But, on the other hand, if Existence is infinite, No-existence becomes impossible; and the doctrine of the indestructibility of Existence becomes, in a logical sense, of an absolute signification. For it is manifest that if the universe of Existence is without end in space and time, the possibility of No-existence is of necessity excluded" (In the chapter "The Final Mystery of Things").

61.41 Renouvier] Renouvier discusses the antinomies in *Traité de logique générale*, III, 1-35. In James's copy, portions of this discussion are marked, but nothing was found linking the resolution of the antinomies with actuality and potentiality.

62.11 Carlyle] Carlyle has expressed this attitude often, for example in *Past and Present*, in the conclusion of bk. II, ch. 1: "For King Lackland *was* there, verily he; and did leave these *tredecim sterlingii*, if nothing more, and did live and look in one way or the other, and a whole world was living and looking along with him! There, we say, is the grand peculiarity; the immeasurable one; distinguishing, to a really infinite degree, the poorest historical Fact from all Fiction whatsoever" (*Thomas Carlyle's Collected Works*, XIII [London: Chapman and Hall, 1870], 59).

62.12 "Necessity,"] Eugen Karl Dühring (1833-1921), German philosopher and political economist, *Cursus der Philosophie* (Leipzig: Erich Koschny, 1875), p. 35.

62.32 Wordsworth] From "The Excursion," bk. I: "In such access of mind, in such high hour | Of visitation from the living God, | Thought was not; in enjoyment it expired" (*The Poetical Works of William Wordsworth*, ed. E. de Selincourt and Helen Darbishire, V [Oxford: Clarendon, 1949], 15 [lines 211-213]).

62.36 Whitman] From "Song of Myself," stanza 5: "I mind how once we lay, such a transparent summer morning; | How you settled your head athwart my hips, and gently turn'd over upon me, | And parted the shirt from my bosom-bone, and plunged your tongue to my bare-stript heart, | And reach'd till you felt my beard, and reach'd till you held my feet. | Swiftly arose and spread around me the peace and knowledge that pass all the argument of the earth" (p. 33).

63.12 Jacobi] Friedrich Heinrich Jacobi (1743-1819), German philosopher: "Licht ist in meinen Herzen, aber so wie ich es in den Verstand bringen will, erlicht es" (*Werke*, I [Leipzig: Gerhard Fleischer d. Jüng., 1812], p. 367), in a letter to Johann Georg Hamann, June 16, 1783.

63.24 Blood] Benjamin Paul Blood, see below note to 172.10. James is treating Blood's text loosely. The passage from 63.27 to 63.40 is taken from pp. 33-35 of *The Anæsthetic Revelation*; from 63.41 to 63.43, from p. 27; from 63.43 to the end, from p. 31. In the last sentence, the clause 'of Metaphysics' is supplied by James.

64.23 chapter] In "Reflex Action and Theism," *Unitarian Review*, 16 (November 1881), 389-416, reprinted in *The Will to Believe* (1897) without the note, on p. 389n, James describes "Reflex Action and Theism," "The Sentiment of Rationality," and "Rationality, Activity and Faith," *Princeton Review*, 2 (July 1882), 58-86, as fragments of a "larger essay on 'The Sentiment of Rationality'." A portion of the present "Sentiment of Rationality" together with "Rationality, Activity and Faith" constitutes "The Sentiment of Rationality" of *The Will to Believe* (1897). Other fragments of what probably was the same project survive in manuscript and are reprinted in the present volume as appendixes. Some of this material was published by Perry, I, 494-503.

65.1 Bradley] Francis Herbert Bradley (1846-1924), English philosopher, "On Professor James' Doctrine of Simple Resemblance," *Mind*, n.s. 2 (January 1893), 83-88, reprinted in *Collected Essays*, 2 vols. (Oxford: Clarendon, 1935), I, 287-294. For an account of the relations between James and Bradley see Perry, II, 485-493. James's letters to Bradley have been published by J. C. Kenna, "Ten Unpublished Letters from William James, 1842-1910 to Francis Herbert Bradley, 1846-1924," *Mind*, n.s. 75 (1966), 309-331. For James's other criticisms of Bradley see the essay "Bradley or Bergson?", reprinted herein, and the *Essays in Radical Empiricism*, WORKS.

65.1 "the] Bradley, p. 88; *Collected Essays*, I, 294.

66.12 theory] In ch. 6 of *The Principles of Psychology* (1890), I, 145-182, James discusses the mind-stuff theory and gives numerous references. See also above, notes to 53.17, 53.30, and 53.31.

66.13 Stumpf's] Carl Stumpf (1848-1936), German psychologist and philosopher. For relations between James and Stumpf see Perry, II, 173-204; the correspondence between them is preserved at Houghton (bMS Am 1092.9 [620-642] [3778-3811]). Stumpf has published "William James nach seinen Briefen. Leben. Charakter. Lehre," *Kant-studien*, 32 (1927), 205-241, reprinted as a pamphlet (Berlin: Rolf Heise, 1928). In *The Principles of Psychology* (1890), in ch. 13 on "Discrimination and Comparison," James quotes from vol. I of Stumpf's *Tonpsychologie*, 2 vols. (Leipzig: S. Hirzel, 1883-1890) (WJ 783.89).

66.24 abandon] According to Bradley, the illustrations used by James needlessly involve the notion of series, a notion much too difficult to be treated briefly. "I must therefore warn the reader that the instances, used in the arguments, involve a serious and (so far as I see) an irrelevant complication. I am hence forced to treat merely that part of them which seems to me to be essential" (p. 84; *Collected Essays*, I, 288).

66.28 *simplicity*] Bradley quotes (p. 87; *Collected Essays*, I, 292) the following from his *The Principles of Logic* (London: Kegan Paul, Trench, 1883) (WJ 510.2.2), pp. 307-308 (2nd ed., 2 vols. [Oxford: Clarendon, 1933], I, 332): "And that any actual presentation should be simple is quite impossible. Even if it had no internal characters, yet it must be qualified by the relations of its environment."

66.33 blunder] In *The Principles of Psychology* (1890), I, 492-493, James outlines two opposing views. According to one, associated with the mind-stuff theory, between two different things there are no degrees of resemblance but simply identity or lack of it in a given respect. For the other view, which James himself espouses, "unlikeness" is an "indecomposable relation amongst things," and one of which there are degrees. Identity is "the minimal degree of this unlikeness," the discernment of which is one of "our ultimate cognitive powers." The former theory seems to lead either to the view that all differences are merely differences in composition, the ultimate elements being in no way different from each other, or that simple elements are like or unlike each other, that is, to resemblance between simples. James's view, by contrast, says nothing about the composition of the two things compared, but simply insists that the resemblance between them is an ultimate fact, that is, simple resemblance.

66.36 accuse] "Simple impressions, in short, are mere abstractions, falsely taken to be facts. And I venture with great diffidence to add that this elsewhere seems to be the view held by Professor James himself. By simplicity he on other topics appears to mean a character which excludes not diversity, but only separability and partition" (p. 87; *Collected Essays*, I, 292).On November 23, 1909, James wrote to Bradley: "I never understood your references to me and 'identity' in our long ago discussion, and it has lately dawned on me that you probably thought I was denying sameness (à Mill) while I was only defending likeness. I believe that I maintained identity [long] before you did in your logic. Cf. Mind vol. iv, pp. 332-5 (1879) [above, pp. 49-51]" (Kenna, "Ten Unpublished Letters," pp. 326-327).

67.9 solution] "There is a view (Professor James must be well aware) which holds that identity and difference are complementary aspects, that the one aspect may be emphasised here, and the other aspect there, but that an attempt to isolate them leads everywhere to an infinite regress . . . . Now certainly a view may exist, and yet be so contemptible as to be treated fairly as non-existent. But then a man, who holds that view, is curious to know something of the ground for such contempt, at least in the case of a writer whom he has been led to respect" (p. 87; *Collected Essays*, I, 293).

67.15 Logic] On September 12, 1886, James wrote George Croom Robertson: "I have been off for a week in the White Mountains by myself and read Bradley's *Logic. What* a fresh book! How he ploughs up the black mould in

every direction! I don't know when I have read a more stimulating and exciting book. And in the style there is a *man*, though whether his sarcasms flow
from an acidulous and unsocial, or from a genially humorous temper, I
can't well make out. At any rate, it will be long ere I 'get over' the effects of
reading his book, and digest its results" (Perry, I, 604).

67.18   page]   *Collected Essays*, I, 289.

67.27   "our]   *Collected Essays*, I, 294.

67.31   dialectical]   "I am myself better acquainted with this dialectical way
of reasoning when used to arrive at a very different result. I know it better
when employed as a means to prove that we have not separable parts, but
inseparable aspects. But then it has not been picked up and applied for one
particular end, but has been worked systematically and in all directions" (p.
86; *Collected Essays*, I, 291-292).

67.34   Hegelian]   In his response to James's reply, in "Professor James on
Simple Resemblance," *Mind*, n.s. 2 (July 1893), 366-369 (*Collected Essays*, I,
295-300), Bradley wrote: "The 'Hegelian commonplace,' suggested by Prof.
James . . . is therefore, to me at least (whatever Hegel would have said of it),
in principle erroneous. It seems to contain the root of Prof. James' own
doctrine" (p. 366; *Collected Essays*, I, 296).

69.3   psychological]   "Or is the thesis idle psychologically, and is it as a
piece of ultimate metaphysical truth that Prof. James contends for it?"
(p. 368; *Collected Essays*, I, 298).

69.9   says]   "So far as the world or any part of it is to any degree intelligible,
so far as there is any knowledge which to any extent goes beyond the barest
feeling, this is the case solely because Identity, as I hold to it, is fact and truth.
Deny this principle and the world, as we have it, is destroyed. And immediate
Resemblance without identity seems to me on the other hand sheer nonsense"
(pp. 368-369; *Collected Essays*, I, 299).

69.20   identity]   "Identity and difference on this view are inseparable aspects
of one complex whole. They are not even 'discernible,' if this means that you
can separate them in idea, so as to treat one as remaining itself when the
other is excluded" (p. 366; *Collected Essays*, I, 295).

70.27   book]   "What opinions I have on this matter are in print and ready
to appear" (p. 368; *Collected Essays*, I, 298-299). Bradley is probably referring to *Appearance and Reality* (London: Swan Sonnenschein, 1893) (WJ
510.2).

70.30   ambiguity]   In *Mind*, n.s. 2 (October 1893), 510 (*Collected Essays*, I,
301-302), Bradley commented on James's second reply: "I should be glad to
accept Prof. James' conclusion that the question between us is about a word.
But to me both resemblance and identity, as he advocates them, are mere
self-contradictory ideas."

71.2 The] Below, 73.15-76.6, on the distinction between immediate and representative knowledge, was reprinted as "The Tigers in India" in *The Meaning of Truth*, WORKS. In a note added to this essay in James's *Collected Essays*, p. 371n, Perry writes: "The remainder of the present article, dealing with the problem of the unity of consciousness, should be read in the light of the earlier view maintained in the *Principles* (1890), Vol. I, pp. 177, 278, and *passim*, and the later view adopted in *The Pluralistic Universe* (1909), pp. 190, 205-212 [WORKS, pp. 87, 93-97]." In *A Pluralistic Universe*, WORKS, pp. 85-90, James surveys the development of his view of the problem.

71.21 Read] The Association met at Princeton, N.J., December 27-28, 1894.

72.21 Fullerton] George Stuart Fullerton (1859-1925), American philosopher. James perhaps has in mind Fullerton's "The Psychological Standpoint," *Psychological Review*, 1 (March 1894), 113-133, in which Fullerton claims that in *The Principles of Psychology* James never makes clear what he means by knowledge and consciousness. According to Fullerton, James's claim that mental states are simple and unanalyzable makes descriptive psychology impossible, but James's own practice differs from his theory. Fullerton remarks that he is using the *Principles* as a text at the University of Pennsylvania (p. 132). James refers to this essay below, p. 87n.

73.25 Hodgson's] In his pamphlet *The Method of Philosophy* (printed for private circulation, 1882), p. 19, Hodgson writes: "what do we know it as"; while in *Philosophy and Experience* (London: Williams and Norgate, 1885), p. 20, Hodgson has: "what Being is *known as*." In James's copies (WJ 539.18), there are markings in both places. On January 1, 1910, James wrote Hodgson that C. S. Peirce and Hodgson's question what things are "known-as" are the two sources of James's pragmatism (Perry, I, 635).

74.20 loose] From Hume's *An Enquiry Concerning Human Understanding* (sec. VII, pt. 2), *Essays Moral, Political, and Literary*, II, 61.

74.28 Miller] Dickinson Sergeant Miller (1868-1963), American philosopher, sometimes wrote under the pseudonym of R. E. Hobart. Miller studied at Harvard in 1892 and in 1893-1898 served as an associate in philosophy at Bryn Mawr College. Selections from James's letters to Miller are included in *Letters* and in Perry. Miller presented his "The Confusion of Content and Function in the Analysis of Ideas," at the second annual meeting of the American Psychological Association, at Columbia College, New York, December 27-28, 1893. This was published as "The Confusion of Function and Content in Mental Analysis," *Psychological Review*, 2 (November 1895), 535-550.

74.39 Miller's] "The Meaning of Truth and Error," *Philosophical Review*, 2 (July 1893), 408-425.

76.23 Hodgson] *The Philosophy of Reflection*, 2 vols. (London: Longmans, Green, 1878), I, 248-272, "Analysis of *minima* of consciousness" (bk. II, ch. 4, sec. 3). James wrote in back of his copy of vol. I (WJ 539.18.4): "Minima of Consciousness 251- ." Both volumes are marked, indexed, but without marginal annotations.

80.3 Mill] James Mill, *Analysis of the Phenomena of the Human Mind*, I, 71: "According to this order, in the objects of sense, there is a synchronous, and a successive, order of our sensations. I have SYNCHRONICALLY, or at the same instant, the sight of a great variety of objects."

80.5 Gurney's] Edmund Gurney (1847-1888), British aesthetician and psychical researcher. In *The Principles of Psychology* (1890), I, 209n, in reference to Gurney's notion of the secondary self, James cites Gurney's "Peculiarities of Certain Post-Hypnotic States," *Proceedings of the Society for Psychical Research* (English), 4 (May 1887), 268-323.

80.5 Binet's] Alfred Binet (1857-1911), French psychologist. In *The Principles of Psychology* (1890), I, 203n, in reference to the notion of a secondary consciousness, James cites Binet's articles in the *Open Court*: "Proof of Double Consciousness in Hysterical Individuals," 3 (July 25, 1889), 1739-1741; "The Relations Between the Two Consciousnesses of Hysterical Individuals," 3 (August 1, 1889), 1751-1754; "The Graphic Method and the Doubling of Consciousness," 3 (November 7, 1889), 1919-1922; and in the *Revue philosophique de la France et de l'étranger*, a series of articles in vols. 27-30 (1889-1890).

80.5 Janet's] Pierre Janet (1859-1947), French psychologist. In *The Principles of Psychology* (1890), I, 203n, in reference to the notion of a secondary consciousness, James cites Janet's *L'Automatisme psychologique* (Paris: Félix Alcan, 1889) (WJ 642.59).

80.17 Hartley] In *The Principles of Psychology* (1890), I, pages 594-604, in the chapter on association, are devoted to the history of the theory. James cites David Hartley (1705-1757), British philosopher, *Observations on Man* (1749); James Mill, *Analysis of the Phenomena of the Human Mind*; and Alexander Bain, *The Senses and the Intellect*, 3rd ed. (London: Longmans, Green, 1868) (WJ 506.41.4).

80.20 Attention] The article "Psychology" by James Ward (1843-1925), British philosopher and psychologist, in the 9th ed. (1886) of the *Encyclopædia Britannica*, is considered a major attack on associationism. Bain responded with two articles in *Mind*: "Mr. James Ward's 'Psychology'," 11 (October 1886), 457-477 and "On 'Association'-Controversies," 12 (April 1887), 161-182. On July 29, 1886, James wrote Ward that Ward's article "marks the transition of English psychology from one epoch to another" (Perry, II, 59). James's annotated cutting is preserved (WJ 592.75.2). Ward emphasized attention as a fundamental principle.

80.36 Wundt's] In "On 'Association'-Controversies," Bain represents Wundt as holding that while the lower mental processes can be stated in terms of association, a different principle, that of apperception, is needed for the higher functions. James's index to Wundt's *Grundzüge der physiologischen Psychologie* (Leipzig: Wilhelm Engelmann, 1874) (WJ 796.59.2), has no entry for apperception, but in the 2nd ed., 2 vols. (Leipzig: Wilhelm Engelmann, 1880) (WJ 796.59.4), James has the following in back of vol. II: "Apperception I, 492, II, 304." James's extensive comments on I, 492 indicate considerable perplexity. "Is this merely a statement of the conditions of feeling or is it an explanation of it as the pleasure of the Ap^{tgt} [Apperceptionsthätigkeit] rather than that of the man. Is the A. *that in* the man that feels the pleasure?" "This account seems to me to embody every defect. It is neither psychological nor physiological. One doesn't know whether the reaction d. Ap.thatgkt *is* the pleasure or is *followed* by the pleasure." Perry reports that both volumes of the 4th ed. (1893) were sold from James's library.

81.27 Herbart] Johann Friedrich Herbart (1776-1841), German philosopher. In *The Principles of Psychology* (1890), I, 603, James comments on Herbart's treatment of association in his *Psychologie als Wissenschaft* (1824).

81.27 Steinthal] Heymann Steinthal (1823-1899), German philosopher and linguist. In *The Principles of Psychology* (1890), II, 107, James states that in his *Einleitung in die Psychologie und Sprachwissenschaft*, 2nd ed. (Berlin: Ferd. Dümmler, 1881), pp. 166ff., Steinthal has "analyzed apperceptive processes with a sort of detail which is simply burdensome."

81.42 Nichols'] Herbert Nichols (b. 1852), American psychologist and philosopher, in 1892-1893 was in charge of the Harvard psychological laboratory. Perry reports that a marked copy of *Our Notions of Number and Space* (Boston: Ginn, 1894) was sold from James's library. Nichols formulates numerous laws on the basis of his experiments, for example: "Until successive stimulation of the combination occurs, the mental correspondent of the simultaneous stimulation of it will be one homogeneous qualitative whole" (p. 177).

82.27 Wundt] Wundt discusses his hypothesis concerning the location of the function of apperception in the brain in the *Grundzüge*, 2nd ed., I, 218-221.

82.33 Baldwin] James Mark Baldwin (1861-1934), American philosopher and psychologist. Of James's many letters to Baldwin, preserved at Houghton, eighteen are included in Baldwin's autobiography, *Between Two Wars: 1861-1921*, 2 vols. (Boston: Stratford Co., 1926). On December 1, 1894, while informing Baldwin that not a word of the presidential address had been written, James noted: "I have read the proof with the the greatest interest and admiration. If much of the book has the same originality and vigor, it will be epoch-making. It is all new to me. I had never thought of *synergy* as the condition of synthesis; and the whole thing is as yet so unassimilated by me that I can't tell whether I can make use of it or not" (*Between Two Wars*, II, 207). One may conjecture that James was reading Baldwin's *Mental Development in the Child and the Race* (New York: Macmillan, 1895) (WJ 406.49.4). In the Preface, James is listed among those who have read part of the manuscript (p. xi). Baldwin does not use the term 'synergy', while James's annotations provide no clear clues. James could have been thinking of the following doctrine: "*Motor-habit, then, is the measure of nervous and mental unity*" (p. 286). In James's copy the passage is marked.

82.33 Münsterberg] Hugo Münsterberg (1863-1916), German-born psychologist, James's colleague at Harvard. For relations between James and Münsterberg, including excerpts from letters, see Perry, II, 138-154. Münsterberg calls his view an "action theory." It is developed in his *Psychology and Life* (Boston: Houghton, Mifflin, 1899), pp. 91-99, and *Grundzüge der Psychologie* (Leipzig: Johann Ambrosius Barth, 1900) (WJ 757.62.2), pp. 525-562. Perry reports that a marked copy of the former work was sold from James's library.

82.40 Cattell] James McKeen Cattell (1860-1944), American psychologist, at that time serving as secretary of the American Psychological Association. Cattell has published many papers on the time taken up by mental operations. James could be referring to "The Time Taken up by Cerebral Operations," *Mind*, 11 (1886), 220-242, 377-392, 524-538. James's numerous letters to Cattell are preserved in the Library of Congress.

84.1 Ladd] George Trumbull Ladd (1842-1921), American philosopher and psychologist. In the back of his copy of Ladd's *Elements of Physiological Psychology* (New York: Charles Scribner's Sons, 1887) (WJ 448.17), James has the following: "Self-consciousness an action its unity 556, 558, 545, 683, 594, 630, 596, 612, 687." Ladd addressed the Princeton meeting of the American Psychological Association on "The Consciousness of Identity and So-called Double Consciousness." An abstract was published in the *Psychological Review*, 2 (March 1895), 159-161. Preserved at Houghton is James's copy of Ladd's *Philosophy of Mind: An Essay in the Metaphysics of Psychology* (New York: Charles Scribner's Sons, 1895) (WJ 448.17.2). On p. 406, in reference to a discussion of the self, James has written: "But what is *it*, all the while?" As if in reply to this question, in the back, we find: "An *activity* — this is L's intuition, tediously elaborated — see especially p. 406, 106."

84.39 Lotze's] In *The Principles of Psychology* (1890), I, 349n, James makes a similar claim about Lotze's development from the *Medicinische Psychologie oder Physiologie der Seele* (Leipzig: Weidmann, 1852) (WJ 751.88.4) to the *Metaphysik* (Leipzig: S. Hirzel, 1879) (WJ 751.88.8). James cites pp. 480-487 (sec. 243-245) of the *Metaphysik*.

87.4 psychology] See in particular *The Principles of Psychology* (1890), I, 182.

87.34 Meinong] Alexius Meinong (1853-1920), Austrian philosopher, "Beiträge zur Theorie der psychischen Analyse," *Zeitschrift für Psychologie und Physiologie der Sinnesorgane*, 6 (1894), 340-385, 417-455; "Ueber Begriff und Eigenschaften der Empfindung," *Vierteljahrsschrift für wissenschaftliche Philosophie*, 12 (1888), 324-354, 477-502; 13 (1889), 1-31.

87.36 Cornelius] Hans Cornelius (1863-1947), Monacan-born philosopher, "Ueber Verschmelzung und Analyse. Eine psychologische Studie," *Vierteljahrsschrift für wissenschaftliche Philosophie*, 16 (1892), 404-446; 17 (1893), 30-75.

90.1 It] Friedrich Paulsen (1846-1908). Preserved at Houghton are Paulsen's letters to James (bMS Am 1092, letters 651-654) and James's copies of

Notes

Paulsen's *Versuch einer Entwicklungsgeschichte der kantischen Erkenntniss-theorie* (Leipzig: Fues, 1875) (WJ 768.89.2), *Einleitung in die Philosophie* (Berlin: Wilhelm Hertz, 1892) (WJ 768.89), and *Introduction to Philosophy*, trans. Frank Thilly (New York: Henry Holt, 1895) (WJ 350.68). The copy of the *Einleitung* is dated Luzern, May 1893, with annotations primarily in the early sections. Inserted in the front of the *Introduction* is an examination paper, dated April 23, 1895, for Philosophy 3, 1894-1895, according to the *Annual Report of the President of Harvard College* for 1894-1895, the course in cosmology, a study of the fundamental conceptions of natural science with reference to evolution and materialism. Also inserted is an undated list of students in Philosophy D. According to the *President's Report* for 1906-1907, James taught the course that year to 133 students, approximately the number of names on the list. During the 1900's, James had several course syllabi printed, out of which *Some Problems of Philosophy* (New York: Longmans, Green, 1911) evolved. These show how extensively James used Paulsen in his teaching. James's copy is annotated primarily with teaching in mind.

90.13-14 publications] Paulsen's *System der Ethik* (1889) was translated by Frank Thilly, *A System of Ethics* (New York: Charles Scribner's Sons, 1899). His *Wesen und geschichtliche Entwicklung der deutschen Universitäten* (1893) was translated by Edward Delevan Perry, *The German Universities* (New York: Macmillan, 1895).

91.10 philosophy] Concerning philosophy, in the Preface to the first edition of the *Introduction*, Paulsen writes: "Modern science is its starting-point and precondition, while the universal reign of law in natural occurrences is its fundamental idea . . . . Its second fundamental conviction is that the teaching of natural science concerning reality is not all that can be said of it, that reality is something else and something more than a corporeal world moved according to the laws of mechanics" (p. xiii).

91.19-20 colleagues] Paulsen begins his criticism of materialism with references to Emil Du Bois-Reymond, *Über die Grenzen des Naturerkennens*, 7th ed. (1891) and *Die sieben Welträthsel* (published with the 5th ed. of *Über die Grenzen*; Leipzig: Veit, 1882), to the effect that scientists must confess themselves completely ignorant "as regards the riddle concerning what matter and force are and *how they can think*" (p. 77).

91.24 atomism] "Having once defined matter as an aggregate of atoms, of absolutely hard and rigid little blocks that are moved without being determined from within, by pressure and impact only, we naturally find it inconceivable that matter should be determined from within and should move by inner impulses. But what compels us to form such a concept? Surely not the facts. They show us none of those absolutely rigid, inert, passive atoms, awaiting an impact from without. On the contrary, they show us parts of matter with spontaneous activity issuing from within" (pp. 100-101).

91.33 Soul] "Is all striving and willing, as it confronts us in the thousand diverse forms of existence, finally combined into the unity of one being and will? Does a unity of inner life, in whose self-movement and self-realization all individual life and striving is included, correspond to the unity of the physical world in universal reciprocal action? The affirmation of this question gives us the conception of the universe called *Idealistic Pantheism*" (p. 232).

92.5 religious] Paulsen holds that science, philosophy, and religion, which were once one, in the course of time became differentiated. The aim of science is the "description and causal explanation of reality" (p. 11), while the essence of every religious belief "is the certainty that the good and perfect, towards which the deepest yearning of my will is directed, forms the origin and goal of all things" (p. 8).

93.19 Renouvier] *Traité de psychologie rationnelle*, II, 225. In the back of his copy of vol. II, James has: "Philosophie du certain = pur enfantillage 225."

94.1 The] While James is listed as a consulting editor of the *Dictionary of Philosophy and Psychology*, ed. James Mark Baldwin, 3 vols. (New York: Macmillan, 1901-1905), he was a reluctant contributor. To Baldwin he wrote on January 10, 1898: "I have a dim memory of agreeing to leave my name as consulting editor — though I am not sure" (*Between Two Wars*, II, 209). Following James's definition of 'Pragmatism', there is one by C. S. Peirce (*Dictionary*, II, 322) in which Peirce states that James has extended Peirce's pragmatism in a way to "give us pause." A similar remark is made by Baldwin (*Dictionary*, II, 323).

95.7 word] The fourth definition of 'phenomenon' is by John Dewey: "It is used in a colourless philosophic sense, as equivalent to 'fact,' or event — to any particular which requires explanation. And it may be questioned whether this practical, apparently non-philosophic sense is not in truth the most philosophic of all" (II, 289).

97.33 'Arry] According to the *Oxford English Dictionary*, " 'Arry' means a person who drops his h's, a low-bred fellow.

98.23 'Manners] "Manners and Fashion" is reprinted in vol. III of Spencer's *Essays: Scientific, Political, and Speculative*, 3 vols. (New York: D. Appleton, 1891). "The Origin of Laughter" has not been found; there is, however, "The Physiology of Laughter," reprinted in *Essays*, vol. II. "Illogical Geology" and "Bain on the Emotions and the Will" are reprinted in *Essays*, vol. I. "OWEN on the Homologies of the Vertebrate Skeleton," *British and Foreign Medico-Chirurgical Review*, 22 (October 1858), is an unsigned review of three works by Richard Owen.

98.27 Social] Social Statics: Or, the Conditions Essential to Human Happiness Specified, and the First of Them Developed (London: John Chapman, 1851).

98.28 The] The Man versus the State (New York: D. Appleton, 1884).

98.32 desultory] Spencer's biographers often point out that he read very little, for example, James Collier, one of Spencer's research assistants, in "Personal Reminiscences" published in Josiah Royce, *Herbert Spencer: An Estimate and Review* (New York: Fox, Duffield, 1904), pp. 210-215.

Notes

99.29 despises] James himself criticized Spencer on the role of great men in history in "Great Men, Great Thoughts, and the Environment," *Atlantic Monthly*, 46 (October 1880), 441-459, reprinted in *The Will to Believe* (1897).

100.1 *Sociology*] *The Principles of Sociology*, 3 vols. (New York: D. Appleton, 1880-1896).

100.5 *Data*] *The Data of Ethics* (New York: D. Appleton, 1879) (WJ 582.24). Incorporated into *The Principles of Ethics*, 2 vols. (New York: D. Appleton, 1892-1893).

101.6 Aristotle] When Spencer visited the United States in 1882, a banquet was held in New York, the proceedings of which were published as *Herbert Spencer on the Americans and the Americans on Herbert Spencer*, ed. Edward L. Youmans (1883; New York: Arno Press, 1973). Responding to a toast, John Fiske said: "It is work of the caliber of that which Aristotle and Newton did; though coming in this latter age, it as far surpasses their work in its vastness of performance as the railway surpasses the sedan-chair, or as the telegraph surpasses the carrier-pigeon" (p. 51).

102.10 Dewey] John Dewey (1859-1952). In a letter to James, November 13, 1898 (bMS Am 1092, letter 18), James Rowland Angell, at the time professor of psychology at the University of Minnesota, notes that Peirce's pragmatism is "surprisingly like what Dewey is driving at." But James seems not to have regarded Dewey as an ally until 1903; see his letter to Dewey, March 23, 1903 (Perry, II, 521-522). On November 15, 1903, James wrote to F.C.S. Schiller: "The best of the lot was reading up the output of the 'Chicago School of Thought,' and reporting it at a 'conference' which Royce has organized. It is splendid stuff, and Dewey is a hero. A real school and real thought . . . . Dewey needs a great deal of building out and following of his principles into all sorts of questions of detail. But it's a noble work. Pity that their style should be so dry and abstract; and lucky for the cause that you should be such a jolly splendid writer" (Perry, II, 501). Eighteen letters from Dewey to James are preserved at Houghton (bMS Am 1092.9 [128-144]), and five from James to Dewey (bMS Am 1092.9 [885-889]). Preserved is James's annotated copy of Dewey's *Studies in Logical Theory* (Chicago: University of Chicago Press, 1903), *The Decennial Publications of the University of Chicago*, 2nd series, vol. XI (WJ 417.93) and notes extracted from James's copy (bMS Am 1092.9 [4451]). The *Studies* carried the following dedication: "For both inspiration and the forging of the tools with which the writers have worked there is a pre-eminent obligation on the part of all of us to William James, of Harvard University, who, we hope, will accept this acknowledgment and this book as unworthy tokens of a regard and an admiration that are co-equal" (p. xi). To this James responded in a letter to Dewey, October 17, 1903: "On returning from the country yesterday, one of the first things that greeted my eyes was your *Logical Studies*, and the to me surprising words that close its Preface. What have I done to merit such a tribute? The Lord, who knoweth all things, knows doubtless about this too, but I accept it rather blindly, and most delightedly, as one of the good things that life sometimes strews in one's way. I feel so the inchoateness of all my publications that it surprises me to hear of anything definite accruing to others from them. I must do better, now that I am 'looked up to' so. I thank you from the bottom of my heart!" (Perry, II, 523-524).

102.11 disciples] Besides four articles by Dewey, the *Studies* contains the following: Helen Bradford Thompson Woolley (b. 1874), American psychologist, "Bosanquet's Theory of Judgment"; Simon Fraser McLennan (b. 1870), American philosopher, "Typical Stages in the Development of Judgment"; Myron Lucius Ashley (b. 1865), American educator, "The Nature of Hypothesis"; Willard Clark Gore, American psychologist, "Image and Idea in Logic"; William Arthur Heidel (1868-1941), American classical scholar, "The Logic of Pre-Socratic Philosophy"; Henry Waldgrave Stuart (b. 1871), American philosopher, "Valuation as a Logical Process"; Addison Webster Moore (1866-1930), American philosopher, "Some Logical Aspects of Purpose." All of the authors received their doctorates from the University of Chicago.

102.20 Mead] George Herbert Mead (1863-1931), American philosopher; James Rowland Angell (1869-1949), American psychologist. Moore's paper is titled "Existence, Meaning, and Reality in Locke's Essay and in Present Epistemology."

103.8 ethics] Preserved at Houghton is James's annotated copy of Dewey's "The Evolutionary Method as Applied to Morality," *Philosophical Review*, 11 (March 1902), 107-124 (WJ 400.5). For other articles on ethics by Dewey see *The Meaning of Truth*, WORKS, note to 71.30.

104.10 "In] Pp. 153-154, from "The Nature of Hypothesis" by Ashley.

106.5 Oxford] The Oxford group published a collective work, *Personal Idealism: Philosophical Essays by Eight Members of the University of Oxford*, ed. Henry Sturt (London: Macmillan, 1902) (WJ 583.89), which James reviewed in *Mind*, n.s. 12 (1903), 93-97, reprinted in part in *Collected Essays* (1920), pp. 442-444. Henry Sturt (b. 1863), British philosopher; Ferdinand Canning Scott Schiller (1864-1937), British philosopher, one of James's closest friends. For notes on the relations between James and Schiller see *Pragmatism*, WORKS, notes to 6.2, 37.24, 38.8; *The Meaning of Truth*, WORKS, note to 37.1.

107.18 "Aristotle] From the letter by F.A.P. Barnard, in *Herbert Spencer on the Americans*, p. 87.

108.2 "He] See above, note to 101.6.

110.18 Eliot] George Eliot met Spencer in 1851, the beginning of a life-long friendship (William Henry Hudson, *An Introduction to the Philosophy of Herbert Spencer* [New York: D. Appleton, 1894], p. 28).

111.40 "No] *An Autobiography*, 2 vols. (New York: D. Appleton, 1904), II, 512.

112.11 "Of] *An Autobiography*, II, 238-239.

113.36 Turner's] Spencer discusses Joseph Mallord William Turner (1775-1851), British painter, in *An Autobiography*, I, 267-270.

116.19 Mansel's] Henry Longueville Mansel (1820-1871), British philosopher and theologian, *The Philosophy of the Conditioned* (London: Alexander Strahan, 1866) (WJ 553.62.5).

116.19 Hamilton's] William Hamilton (1788-1856), Scottish philosopher. James seems to be referring to Hamilton's essay "On the Philosophy of the Unconditioned; in Reference to Cousin's Infinito-Absolute," *Discussions on Philosophy and Literature, Education and University Reform* (London: Longman, Brown, Green and Longmans, 1852).

117.20 first] The first edition was published in London by Williams and Norgate in 1862.

117.36 "redistribution"] "The law we seek, therefore, must be the law of *the continuous redistribution of matter and motion.* Absolute rest and permanence do not exist" (*First Principles* [1877], p. 277 [sec. 92]). In James's copy, parts of this passage are underlined and marked 'N.B.'

119.2 "Evolution,"] Spencer asserts: "We shall everywhere mean by Evolution, the process which is always an integration of matter and dissipation of motion, but which, as we shall now see, is in most cases much more than this" (p. 286 [sec. 97]).

123.3 Peirce] Charles Sanders Peirce (1839-1914), "How to Make Our Ideas Clear," *Popular Science Monthly*, 12 (1878), 286-302, reprinted in the *Collected Papers of Charles Sanders Peirce*, ed. Charles Hartshorne and Paul Weiss, V (Cambridge, Mass.: Harvard University Press, 1934), 248-271. James is quoting from V, 255-258 (secs. 396-402).

123.19 Union] The Philosophical Union of the University of California at Berkeley, founded by George Holmes Howison (1834-1916), American philosopher, before which James delivered in 1898 his "Philosophical Conceptions and Practical Results," of which "The Pragmatic Method" is a revised version.

126.37 Browning] Robert Browning, "A Lovers' Quarrel," *The Poetical Works of Robert Browning*, VI (London: Smith, Elder, 1889), 63: "Foul be the world or fair | More or less, how do I care? | 'T is the world the same | For my praise or blame, | And endurance is easy there."

128.22 Spencer] James is referring to Spencer's *The Principles of Psychology*, I, 616-627 (secs. 269-272).

129.7 Spencer's] According to Spencer, *First Principles*, p. 527 (sec. 181), the earth which is now undergoing evolution will eventually undergo dissolution, since the motion of the earth is being reduced by the resistance of the "ethereal medium" through which it passes. Spencer speculates, pp. 536-537 (sec. 183), that there will be an endless cycle of evolution and dissolution.

129.26 Balfour's] Arthur James Balfour (1848-1930), British philosopher and statesman, *The Foundations of Belief*, 1st impression (London: Longmans, Green, 1895) (WJ 506.49), p. 31 (pp. 30-31 of the 3rd [1895] impression).

129.38 cosmic] Chauncey Wright, *Philosophical Discussions*, p. 10: "Of what we may call cosmic weather, in the interstellar spaces, little is known."

131.30 theology] For a note on James's theological sources see *Pragmatism*, WORKS, note to 62.2.

132.20 Reid] Mayne Reid (1818-1883), Irish-born novelist. 'Closet naturalist', sometimes 'closet philosopher', seems a common expression in Reid. In *The Forest Exiles* (1854; New York: John W. Lovell, n.d.), p. 247, Reid writes: "There is one thing that is almost intolerable and that is the conceit of the 'closet naturalist,' who sneers at every thing as untrue that seems to show the least *design* on the part of the brute creation — who denies every thing that appears at all singular or fanciful."

134.38 Royce] Josiah Royce (1855-1916), American philosopher, James's colleague at Harvard. For an account of the extensive relations between James and Royce see Perry, I, chs. 49-51. Royce addressed the Union on August 30, 1895. His address, together with comments by Sidney Edward Mezes (1863-1931), American philosopher; Joseph LeConte (1823-1901), American naturalist; and Howison, was published by the Union as *The Conception of God* (Berkeley, 1895). This was reprinted with the addition of an introduction by Howison and an extensive supplementary essay by Royce (New York: Macmillan, 1897) (WJ 477.98).

135.3 'One] In the back of his copy of *The Conception of God*, James has: "Absolute a single instant, 210, 292." On p. 210, James marked the following: "Its unity is the unity of a single Instant." On p. 292, opposite Royce's "God's consciousness forms in its wholeness one luminously transparent conscious moment," James comments: "But how, if only a part of this luminous moment which as such can be conscious of it only *cum aliis*, does its being conscious *sine aliis* grow possible?"

135.6 Howison] Howison argues that in Royce's monistic idealism "no *manifold* of selves is provided for or can be provided for" (p. 104). But if individual selves are simply parts of the Absolute, Howison asks, "Is not He the sole real *agent*? Are we anything but the steadfast and changeless modes of his eternal thinking and perceiving?" (p. 99). For Howison, only persons can be moral agents, while persons are possible only in a community, each member of which is substantially independent of the others. On p. 99, opposite the passage quoted, James has: "Right & left wing hegelism."

135.16 One] For a more detailed pragmatic analysis of unity see *Pragmatism*, WORKS, pp. 64-79.

137.23 *known*] See above, note to 73.25.

137.26 Locke] James expanded these comments on Locke in *Pragmatism*, WORKS, pp. 47-48.

137.32 Berkeley] See *Pragmatism*, WORKS, p. 47 and note to 47.12.

138.1 Stewart] Dugald Stewart (1753-1828), Scottish philosopher. Perry reports that a marked copy of vol. I of Stewart's *Elements of the Philosophy of the Human Mind* (1818) was sold from James's library.

138.1 Brown] Thomas Brown (1778-1820), Scottish philosopher. Perry reports that a marked copy of Brown's *Philosophy of the Human Mind*, 10th ed., was sold from James's library.

140.1 Höffding] Harald Höffding (1843-1931), Danish philosopher, *Philosophische Probleme* (Leipzig: O. R. Reisland, 1903). Perry reports that a copy of this work was sold from James's library. Preserved are James's unannotated copies of *The Problems of Philosophy*, trans. Galen M. Fisher (New York: Macmillan, 1905) (Phil 182.36.5) in Widener, and in Houghton, a copy of the 2nd printing (1906) (WJ 350.39). The letters between James and Höffding are preserved at Houghton (bMS Am 1092.9 [226-234] [999-1013]). In the fall of 1902, Höffding gave some lectures on James's religious philosophy, published in English translation in Höffding's *Modern Philosophers*, trans. Alfred C. Mason (London: Macmillan, 1915). He also wrote a preface to the Danish translation of *Varieties*, *Religiøse erfaringer*, trans. E. Lehmann and C. Mønster (Copenhagen: V. Pios, 1906). Höffding visited James at Chocorua, N.H., in the summer of 1904.

140.2 *Psychology*] *Outlines of Psychology*, trans. M. E. Lowndes (London: Macmillan, 1891) (WJ 816.39); *A History of Modern Philosophy*, trans. B. E. Meyer, 2 vols. (London: Macmillan, 1900); *The Philosophy of Religion*, trans. B. E. Meyer (London: Macmillan, 1906). No English translations of Höffding's ethical works were located.

140.11 translated] The correspondence provides much information about James's role in the translation. On October 17, 1903, James thanked Höffding for a copy of the *Philosophische Probleme*, stating that he had read every word, for the most part "with adhesion," that he regarded it as a blow against absolutism. On January 22, 1905, James reported that no translator had as yet been found, but on March 9, 1905, that G. M. Fisher had translated about a third. In this letter, James offered a "short preface," since that "may help sales." The translation was finished on July 21, 1905, but when the proofs came, James was forced to rewrite about a fifth of the text (letter of October 4, 1905). Höffding indicated his pleasure over the results on November 11, 1905. In his letter of October 4, James stated that he planned to use the translation as a text in his metaphysics course.

140.22 radical] For an account of James's radical empiricism see *Essays in Radical Empiricism*, WORKS.

140.23 'ever] From Benjamin Paul Blood, *The Flaw in Supremacy*, p. 7, see below, note to 179.32.

141.14-15 continuities.'] Harald Höffding, *The Problems of Philosophy* (1905), p. 60: "All understanding is conditioned by the relation between continuity and discontinuity. The latter occasions the fulness and multiplicity of the content of the understanding, the former its connection and arrangement."

141.15 'irrational,'] "The empiricist and the sceptic will always be able to check the monistic metaphysician, because they can taunt him with the actual limitations of knowledge. We cannot even use *fact* as a criterion in a thoroughgoing manner, or carry out with strictness the distinction between dreaming and reality. With the same right with which we reason from the possibility of rational knowledge to a unifying force in Being, we might, apparently, reason to an irrational power in Being, to a cosmological principle that prevented the elements of Being from standing in a rationally determinable relation to one another" (p. 135).

141.21 'critical] "*Critical Monism*, as I call it, which asserts the reality of time, and hence the permanent unfinishedness both of Being and of knowledge . . . . It finds, then, in Being a force struggling towards unification, which, by progressive evolution, overcomes the sporadic and hostile elements" (pp. 136-137).

142.3 perfection] "Religion possesses a different character according as that which possesses highest worth is thought of as eternal and exalted above all becoming and all change, so that the temporal life is in the end only an illusion; or as that which possesses supreme worth is itself held to evolve in the course of ages and to battle for its own preservation during the changes which take place" (pp. 184-185).

142.8-9 'dynamic'] "The dynamic and symbolic notion of truth is here expressly put in the place of the naïf dogmatic concept to which the mechanical conception of nature formerly swore fealty. The problem reduces itself to finding a group of symbols which can be employed with entire *consistency*, and from which conclusions can be drawn that will be confirmed by new experiences which can themselves be again expressed by the same group of symbols. But by this method we never get rid of the possibility that another set of symbols might have expressed the actual experiences as well or better" (p. 90).

142.32 Whole] "But if analogy is employed metaphysically or cosmologically, it is not a *single* realm of Being serving to illuminate *another single realm*; it is a single realm that is used to express Being as a totality" (p. 122). "The phenomenon (the part or aspect of experience) on which the analogy is based may be called the *type-phenomenon* (Urphänomen)" (p. 124).

142.40 *intelligible*] "The first fact, whose consideration as a type-phenomenon of Being closely concerns philosophy, is that Being is to a great extent *intelligible*: we can recollect phenomena, infer from one phenomenon to another, and find continuity between them" (pp. 130-131).

143.8 Ethics] "As the discussion of the problem of Being showed, there is room for work being done by means of which Being develops itself. Such work is done in all human culture, but especially in ethical endeavor" (p. 158).

144.17 *Leonardo*] *Leonardo, rivista d'idee*, founded and edited by Papini, was published from 1903 to 1907. Preserved are seven issues from James's library (WJ 150.49), for 1906-1907, with a few annotations.

144.18 Papini] Giovanni Papini (1881-1956), Italian writer. Copies of some of James's letters to Papini are in Houghton (bMS Am 1092.1); the originals are in the possession of Signora Paolo Casini. Papini's letters to James are at Houghton (bMS Am 1092, letters 642-649). A few letters are in Perry, II, 571-573.

144.19 Prezzolini] Giuseppe Prezzolini (b. 1882), Italian writer.

144.20 Vailati] Giovanni Vailati (1863-1909), Italian philosopher, contributed " 'La concezione della coscienza' di William James" to the *Rivista di Psicologia*, I (1905), 242-245, and several reviews of works by James in vols. 1 and 3 of the same journal.

144.20 Calderoni] Mario Calderoni (1879-1914), Italian philosopher, together with G. C. Ferrari, translated *Varieties*, *Le varie forme della coscienza religiosa* (Turin: Fratelli Bocca, 1904).

144.20 Amendola] Giovanni Battista Amendola (1882-1926), Italian philosopher. Houghton preserves one letter from Amendola to James (bMS Am 1092, letter 14). Three letters from James to Amendola appear in Eva Amendola Kühn, *Vita con Giovanni Amendola* (Florence: Parenti, [1960]), primarily on never-realized plans for translating James.

144.23 JOURNAL] *Journal of Philosophy, Psychology, and Scientific Methods* was the main arena for controversies over pragmatism and radical empiricism.

145.23 pragmatist] Papini's articles on pragmatism, published in *Leonardo*, appeared in his *Sul pragmatismo (saggi e ricerche)* (Milan: Libreria Editrice Milanese, 1913); 2nd ed., *Pragmatismo: (1903-1911)* (Florence: Vallecchi, 1920).

145.24 *Leonardo*] Giovanni Papini, "Dall'Uomo a Dio," *Leonardo*, 4th year (February 1906), 6-15. Reprinted in both editions of *Pragmatismo*.

145.25 *Il*] *Il crepuscolo dei filosofi (Kant, Hegel, Schopenhauer, Comte, Spencer, Nietzsche)* (Milan: Società Editrice Lombarda, 1906). The present review by James was used as an introduction to the French edition, *Le Crépuscule des philosophes* (Paris: Chiron, 1922). The final chapter is titled "Licenzio la filosofia." The Widener copy (Phil 1715.2) was given by James, May 17, 1906. No other copy from James's library is known.

146.5 *Leonardo*] "Il pragmatismo messo in ordine," *Leonardo*, 3rd year (April 1905), 45-47, reprinted in both editions of *Pragmatismo*. James's six characteristics is a translation from *Sul pragmatismo*, pp. 77-78, *Pragmatismo*, p. 92.

146.23   corridor]   "Il pragmatismo messo in ordine," p. 47: "una *teoria corridoio*" (*Sul pragmatismo*, p. 82, *Pragmatismo*, p. 97).

146.37   "The]   *Il crepuscolo*, p. 266.

147.13   ideal]   *Il crepuscolo*, p. 270: "La formula generale di questi strumenti che l'uomo s'è fatti per accrescere il suo potere è questa: *la creazione di mondi immaginari capaci di servire per cambiare il mondo reale.*" Most of the present paragraph is a loose translation of p. 270.

147.29   'From]   On p. 9 of his copy of the February 1906 issue of *Leonardo*, James wrote: "Nietzsche tho't as well as style."

149.1   Gore]   Willard Clark Gore, "The Mad Absolute of a Pluralist," *Journal of Philosophy, Psychology, and Scientific Methods*, 3 (October 11, 1906), 575-577.

149.2   Schiller's]   F.C.S. Schiller, "Idealism and the Dissociation of Personality," *Journal of Philosophy, Psychology, and Scientific Methods*, 3 (August 30, 1906) 477-482.

149.6   *we*]   Gore speculates that a monist might reply to Schiller as follows: "Admit the derived nature of your pluralistic entity as thinkable, and on what must the tortoise of your universe rest? On a mad absolute? Mad, only in so far as pluralistic! Look again at the analogy of dissociated personality. Is it not true that alienists commonly locate the degree of insanity in the extent to which the personality of the patient is split off into inconsistent, conflicting or isolated selves, and that they attempt to effect a cure by sounding the depths of hypnotic reminiscence for the deeper and older bonds of association that have fallen out of the reach of voluntary recollection? Following out the implications of this analogy, what becomes of the madness ascribed to the absolute? Are not the tables completely turned? The quest for the absolute is the quest for sanity, for wholeness, health, that shall reunite and heal the isolated and insane elements, blindly pluralistic" (p. 577).

149.22   Sally]   Sally Beauchamp is the name given to one of the personalities described by Morton Prince (1854-1929), American physician and psychiatrist, *The Dissociation of a Personality* (New York: Longmans, Green, 1906) (WJ 471.41). Sally, who turns out to be not the real Miss Beauchamp, is the only one of the personalities who is aware of the others. Schiller's article was based upon Prince's book.

150.3   Renouvier]   Charles Renouvier and Louis Prat, French philosopher, one of Renouvier's collaborators, *La Nouvelle Monadologie* (Paris: Armand Colin, 1899). Section 134 is entitled "La chute du monde physique. Les causes psychologiques et morales de la chute."

150.27   logic]   For more detailed comments on the weakness of idealistic arguments see *A Pluralistic Universe*, WORKS, p. 96.

150.34   Fechner]   See "Concerning Fechner" in *A Pluralistic Universe*, WORKS.

150.36 Royce]   See *A Pluralistic Universe*, WORKS, pp. 83-84.

151.1 Bradley]   "Coherence and Contradiction," *Mind*, n.s. 18 (October 1909), 489-508, preceded by "On Truth and Coherence," *Mind*, n.s. 18 (July 1909), 329-342, followed by "On Appearance, Error and Contradiction," *Mind*, n.s. 19 (April 1910), 153-185. All three are reprinted in Bradley's *Essays on Truth and Reality* (Oxford: Clarendon, 1914). On December 23, 1909, while sending to Bradley a revised proof of "Bradley or Bergson?" James wrote: "I trust that you will not take offense, and that possibly the spirit may move you at some future time, when you feel very hearty, to say (in print) just why we *may* not use both perception and conception in philosophy as we use both blades of a pair of scissors" (Kenna, "Ten Unpublished Letters," p. 329).

151.3 Bergson's]   Henri Bergson (1859-1941). James discusses Bergson at length in *A Pluralistic Universe*, WORKS, "Bergson and His Critique of Intellectualism."

151.8 Bradley's]   In "A Disclaimer," *Journal of Philosophy, Psychology, and Scientific Methods*, 7 (March 31, 1910), 183, Bradley wrote: "The too flattering notice of myself by Professor James, in this JOURNAL (January 20), contains a statement which I think I should ask leave to correct. Professor James credits me with 'breaking loose from the Kantian tradition that immediate feeling is all disconnectedness.' But all that I have really done here is to follow Hegel. In this and in some other points I saw long ago that English psychology had a great deal to learn from Hegel's teaching. To have seen this, and to some extent to have acted on it, is all that common honesty allows me to claim. How far Hegel himself in this point was original, and how again M. Bergson conceives his own relation to post-Kantian philosophy, are matters that here do not concern me. I write merely to disclaim for myself an originality which is not mine. It belongs to me no more than does that heroical perversity or perverse heroism with which also I find myself credited."

151.14 'endosmosis']   See *A Pluralistic Universe*, WORKS, note to 114.37.

157.16 Fechner's]   James discusses Fechner's "wave-scheme" and the notion of "threshold," in connection with the view that the brain is an organ of transmission, a place through which the deeper reality of the universe can for a time shine through, in *Human Immortality* (Boston: Houghton, Mifflin, 1898), p. 23. In a note, pp. 59-66, he quotes at length from Fechner's *Elemente der Psychophysik*, II, 526-530.

158.40 Pierce]   Arthur Henry Pierce (1867-1914), American psychologist, in two articles in the *Journal of Philosophy, Psychology, and Scientific Methods*, "Should we Still Retain the Expression 'Unconscious Cerebration' to Designate Certain Processes Connected with Mental Life?", 3 (November 8, 1906), 626-630; "The Subconscious Again," 5 (May 7, 1908), 264-271; and in "An Appeal from the Prevailing Doctrine of a Detached Subconsciousness," in *Studies in Philosophy and Psychology*, ed. James Hayden Tufts and others (Boston: Houghton, Mifflin, 1906).

158.40-159.36 Münsterberg]   In his contribution to "A Symposium on the Subconscious," *Journal of Abnormal Psychology*, 2 (April-May 1907), 22-43, Münsterberg concludes that the "language of the subliminal self theory . . . flows over too easily into antiphilosophy" (p. 33).

159.36 Bergson]   James could be referring to the conclusion of ch. 3 of *L'Évolution créatrice* (Paris: Félix Alcan, 1907) (WJ 607.75.2), where Bergson compares life and consciousness to a current which subdivides itself into human individuals (pp. 292-293). The index in back of James's copy of this book has the following entry: "Consciousness, 120, 156+, 283, 293, 343." In his letter acknowledging receipt of James's article, Bergson does not comment upon this reference to himself (Perry, II, 632-633).

159.37 Myers]   Frederic William Henry Myers (1843-1901), British writer and psychical researcher, *Human Personality and Its Survival of Bodily Death*, 2 vols. (London: Longmans, Green, 1903). James's copy is preserved at Houghton (*AC 85.J2376.Zz903m). He reviewed it in the *Proceedings of the Society for Psychical Research* (English), 18 (1903), 22-33. To the same *Proceedings*, 17 (1901), 13-23, James contributed "Frederic Myers's Service to Psychology." This essay was reprinted in *Memories and Studies* (New York: Longmans, Green, 1911).

161.5 Stanford]   James spent the spring of 1906 teaching at Stanford University.

164.8 Hall]   Frederick Hall, "An Ether 'Vision'," *Open Court*, 23 (December 1909), 734-739. On p. 738n, Hall refers to a letter from James. "Ether-mysticism" was advocated by Benjamin Paul Blood, see herein, "A Pluralistic Mystic."

166.5 Boutroux]   Émile Boutroux (1845-1921), French philosopher. For relations between James and Boutroux, including some letters, see Perry, II, 560-569, and II, 766-768. Copies of James's letters to Boutroux are preserved at Houghton (bMS Am 1092.1); also at Houghton are the originals of Boutroux to James (bMS Am 1092, letters 43-51). James met Boutroux in London in late September, 1908 (*Letters*, II, 314). In his diary for March 1910 (MS Am 1092.9 [4559]), James recorded several social contacts with Boutroux while the latter was lecturing at Cambridge. Boutroux wrote the Introduction to the French translation of *Varieties*, *L'Expérience religieuse*, trans. F. Abauzit (Paris: Félix Alcan, 1906); "William James et l'expérience religieuse," *Revue de métaphysique et de morale*, 16 (1908), 1-27, reprinted in *Science et religion* (Paris: Flammarion, 1908); "William James," *Revue de métaphysique et de morale*, 18 (November 1910), 711-743, which served as the basis of his book, *William James* (Paris: Armand Colin, 1911), English translation by Archibald Henderson and Barbara Henderson (New York: Longmans, Green, 1912). Perry reports that a marked copy of *Science et religion* was sold from James's library.

166.18 lecture]   In his diary for March 7, 1910, James noted that the first lecture by Boutroux was "very fine" but that the audience was "wretched." On March 18, he characterized the lecture as "exquisite." Boutroux gave two series of lectures during his visit. The lectures titled "Contingence et liberté" were, according to the *Boston Evening Transcript*, March 8, 1910, p. 18, given in connection with G. H. Palmer's course in social ethics. There were eight of these, beginning on Monday, March 7, 1910. They were open to the general public. The second series, comprising four lectures, supported by a fund established by James Hazen Hyde, was given on March 8, 10, 17, 22. The *Boston Evening Transcript* published a report of each lecture on the day following its delivery. The lectures were titled "Pascal," "Auguste Comte," "L'Essence de la religion," and "Le Mouvement philosophique contemporain en France." The paper noted that the audiences were large and attentive. On March 11, p. 13, as part of its report of the second lecture, the *Transcript* quoted the following remark by James: "The word 'liberal' seems to have been coined especially to apply to him, so sympathetically has he entered into the most diverse states of mind interpreting scientific men, philosophers and religious men to each other. His own way of thinking has many points of resemblance to what is known as pragmatism in this country. His effort, since the publishing of his first book, has been to show that concrete life exceeds our powers of abstract formulation, that what we see, feel and think in the world of reality are only approximations which the intellect uses to make fact more amenable to its powers of treatment.

M. Boutroux's lectures on 'Contingence et Liberté,' are but an epitome of this, his whole method of thinking. By contingency he means the unforseeable novelties and variations which are constantly leaking into life, the real movement of which cannot be accurately confined within our intellectual formulas. This theory of M. Boutroux's, which he is now explaining, has radically influenced modern thought in France, yet the modification with which he applies it has made him the friend of men of the most diverse opinions."

167.10 Wagner]   Goethe, *Faust*, p. 40 (line 1105).

167.19 Institut]   Fondation Thiers, a learned foundation in Paris.

168.13 *La*]   *De la Contingence des lois de la nature* (Paris: Germer Baillière, 1874), Boutroux's doctoral dissertation.

169.6 Berthelot]   James probably means Marcelin Berthelot (1827-1907), French chemist.

169.6 Renan]   Joseph Ernest Renan (1823-1892), French philosopher and historian.

169.12 Fiske's]   John Fiske (1842-1901), American historian and philosopher, *Outlines of Cosmic Philosophy*, 2 vols. (London: Macmillan, 1874), I, 175-176: "There is one continuous process, which (if I may be allowed to invent a rather formidable word in imitation of Coleridge) is best described as a continuous process of *deanthropomorphization*, or the stripping off of the anthropomorphic attributes with which primeval philosophy clothed the unknown Power which is manifested in phenomena."

172.10 BLOOD]   Benjamin Paul Blood (1832-1919). Horace M. Kallen gives a brief biographical sketch in his Introduction to Blood's *Pluriverse: An Essay in the Philosophy of Pluralism* (Boston: Marshall Jones Co., 1920). Houghton preserves Blood's letters to James and a few from James to Blood (bMS Am 1092.9 [46-75] [751-762]; bMS Am 1452 [1] [3] [19-20]; bMS Am 1452.1 [14-15]), as well as newspaper clippings, pamphlets, printed poems, sent to James by Blood (bMS Am 1092.9 [4522] [4584-4585]). Excerpts from letters appear in Perry and in *Letters*.

172.13-14 occupation] On June 11, 1887, in a letter to James, Blood stated that he had inherited a farm and farmed it "in a way," that in his youth he had been a successful gambler, but had thrown the money away, that he had been a "fancy gymnast" and had had some "heavy fights." Blood accompanied the letter with a picture of himself taken after he had lifted 1160 lbs. (Perry, II, 227-228). Writing to James on June 7, 1896, Blood stated that he had been working ten hours a day in a mill (Perry, II, 230). In its notice of "A Pluralistic Mystic," the *Amsterdam Evening Recorder*, July 23, 1910, stated that few in the Mohawk valley "cared for a test of strength" with Blood in his youth.

172.15 author] Blood is the author of several larger works: *Napoleon I. A Historical Lecture* (Amsterdam, N.Y.: private edition, 1863), *The Bride of the Iconoclast. A Poem*, printed together with *Suggestions Toward the Mechanical Art of Verse* (Boston: James Munroe, 1854), *Optimism the Lesson of Ages* (Boston: B. Marsh, 1860), *The Philosophy of Justice Between God and Man* (New York: J. S. Taylor, 1851).

172.22 Harris] William Torrey Harris (1835-1909), American philosopher and educator, founder and editor of the *Journal of Speculative Philosophy*. Blood published in the *Journal* his "Philosophical Reveries," 20 (January 1886), 1-53, and a note, "What is Truth?", 10 (January 1876), 89-94.

173.2 poems] The following poems by Blood appeared in *Scribner's Magazine*: "In Egypt," 11 (1892), 627; "Lights and Shadows," 18 (1895), 201; "Nemesis," 26 (1899), 72-73; "Thoroughbreds," 27 (1900), 482; "Tithonus," 28 (1900), 603-604; "Thyreus," 30 (1901), 657-660; "Heraclitus," 36 (1904), 48. "The Lion of the Nile," *Scribner's Magazine*, 4 (1888), 707-711, was preceded by letters between James and Blood concerning revisions. Leaflet versions of "Nemesis" and "The Lion of the Nile," differing considerably from the published ones, survive in the James Collection. There is also a leaflet of a poem "Reveries of One." A collection of Blood's poems was published after his death, *Heirlooms, A Book of Poems*, (Albany, N.Y.: F. S. Hills, 1924).

173.6 *Anæsthetic*] *The Anæsthetic Revelation and the Gist of Philosophy* (Amsterdam, in New York, America, 1874). James's marked copy with portions cut out is preserved. James reviewed it in the *Atlantic Monthly*, 34 (1874), 627-629. In "The Secret of William James. And Anesthetic Revelation," *Springfield Sunday Republican*, October 16, 1910, Blood claimed that James's "real secret" was the anesthetic revelation, "which so far has failed of utterance. This was the bete noir of his latter years, that his 'unlucky heart' forestalled him from what he fully believed to be the secret of the world, which he as fully believed that I could articulate if I tried." In a note added to "On Some Hegelisms," *Mind*, 7 (April 1882) 186-208, reprinted in *The Will to*

Believe (1897), James gives an account of his own experiments with "nitrous-oxide-gas intoxication," experiments undertaken after reading Blood. In a passage left out of the published version of "A Pluralistic Mystic" (MS Am 1092.9 [4547], fol. 3), in reference to *The Anœsthetic Revelation*, James says that it has "remained as one of the cornerstones or landmarks of my own subsequent thinking."

173.26 met] James describes his visit to Blood in a letter to Mrs. Henry Whitman, June 16, 1895 (*Letters*, II, 20-22) and tells the anecdote on p. 173n.

174.4 simplify] On June 25, 1910, James wrote to Blood: "Of course I've used you for my own purposes, and probably misused you; but I'm sure you will feel more pleasure than pain, and perhaps write again in the *Hibbert* to set yourself right" (Perry, II, 660). James's quotations and paraphrases have not been corrected in the text and it has not seemed necessary as a rule to supply Blood's exact words in the notes.

174.28 "That] "Philosophical Reveries," p. 5: "Indeed, aside from Hegel's obscurity of claim, the philosophers are few who have come so close to the people as to declare: This is the question, and this is the answer; but of Hegel especially it may be well said that he philosophized for a conclusion which he never expressed. That he was pervaded by the great truth cannot be doubted; the eyes of the world, if not directly on him, are set toward the region which he occupied. Though he may not be the last of philosophers, pull him out and all the rest will be drawn into his vacancy. Yet something about him must be wrong while his results are so confessedly questionable."

174.36 "for] "Philosophical Reveries," p. 4.

174.37 The] "Paul's Sermon on Ideal Charity," *Amsterdam Evening Recorder*, December 24, 1908.

175.4 "a] *Tennyson's Trances and the Anœsthetic Revelation*, p. 9. This is a pamphlet without publisher or date, consisting of several introductory pages by J. I. Lexow, perhaps a pseudonym, and a letter by Blood to Lord Hallam Tennyson, son of the poet. In his *Alfred Lord Tennyson: A Memoir*, 2 vols. (New York: Macmillan, 1897), II, 158-159, Hallam Tennyson published a draft of a letter from the poet to an unnamed person, but clearly Blood, thanking that person for an essay on anesthetics. The actual letter received by him, Blood indicates, was quite different from the published draft and it was this fact which led Blood to write to Hallam Tennyson.

175.11 "Each] "Philosophical Reveries," p. 6.

175.17 "Popularly,"] "Philosophical Reveries," pp. 10-11.

176.10 "does] Not identified.

176.12 "to] "Philosophical Reveries," pp. 9-10.

176.27 "And] "Immortality of the Soul," *Albany Times*, written May 3, 1889, but date of publication unknown. The text quoted by James is directly preceded by the following: "As said William James, the philosopher of Harvard university, after being loaded to the muzzle with chloroform in the hope of expressing the anæsthetic revelation, 'There is no identity other than the identity of the difference between identity and difference.' If anybody sees any one thing in this description, he is welcome to it immortally." Blood appears to be referring to "On Some Hegelisms," p. 207 (*The Will to Believe* [1897], p. 297).

177.4 "Assume] *Tennyson's Trances*, pp. 7-8.

177.27 "To] "Philosophical Reveries," p. 8.

177.31 "but] The text from 177.31 to 178.11 was made up by James from "Philosophical Reveries," pp. 11-14.

178.6 'Thou] James is interpolating a passage, used by Blood in "Paul's Sermon on Ideal Charity," from Emerson's poem "The Sphinx," *Poems*, p. 13.

178.12 "Here] "Philosophical Reveries," p. 15.

178.25 "No] "Philosophical Reveries," pp. 49-50.

178.26 "How] "The Secret of the World," *Utica Morning Herald*, September 15, 1886.

179.14 "Such] "Philosophical Reveries," p. 32.

179.32 "As] *The Flaw in Supremacy: A Sketch of the Nature, Process and Status of Philosophy, as Inferring the Miracle of Nature, the Contingency of History, the Equation of Reason and Unreason, &c., &c.* (Amsterdam, N.Y.: B. P. Blood, 1893), p. 5.

179.37 "But] Not identified.

180.6 "A] *Tennyson's Trances*, p. 8.

180.6-7 Pleasure] "Paul's Sermon for Thanksgiving: 'The Shallows Murmur but the Deeps are Dumb'," *Amsterdam Evening Recorder*, November 24, 1909.

180.10 The] *The Flaw in Supremacy*, p. 2.

180.13 "being] *Tennyson's Trances*, p. 8.

180.16 "thenceforth] *The Anæsthetic Revelation*, p. 35.

180.30 "Experience] "The Justice of Eternity," *Amsterdam Evening Recorder*, November 29, 1905.

181.14 "Reason] "Paul Explains About Lawson," *Amsterdam Evening Recorder*, September 5, 1908.

181.17 'Is] "Nemesis," p. 72. Besides the *Scribner's Magazine* and leaflet versions of "Nemesis," James had available still different versions, since Blood quotes from it in his other writings and letters to James.

181.23 Go] Not identified.

181.29 "The] "After This, What? An Advancing Revolt from Monism to Pluralism," *Amsterdam Evening Recorder*, March 5, 1907.

181.33 "The] "Paul's Sermon for Thanksgiving."

182.19 "Whelped] James is using the leaflet version of "The Lion of the Nile." Lines 182.37 to 183.19 do not appear in *Scribner's*.

183.25 "There] *The Anæsthetic Revelation*, pp. 93-94.

183.27 No] *Tennyson's Trances*, p. 10.

183.32 "Whose] "Reveries of One."

184.1 "Repetition] *Tennyson's Trances*, p. 10.

184.9 "It] *The Anæsthetic Revelation*, pp. 34-35.

184.32 "This] *Tennyson's Trances*, pp. 10-11.

185.8 "The] Not identified.

185.15 "All] "After This, What?"

185.34 "Philosophy,"] From 185.34 to 186.6 is taken from Blood's letter to James of December 5, 1905; from 186.6 to 187.3, from letter of April 24, 1909 (fMS Am 1092.9 [61] [73]).

185.36 "Let] "Reveries of One."

187.6 "There] "After This, What?": "It were idle asking after Pluralism as a cult.... There is no where more about it consecutively, perhaps, than appears on this present page. It is the aroma, or the caviare, of occasional utterances of certain living men of genius — James, of Harvard; Howison, of California; Jastrow, of Wisconsin, and other subtle spirits, whose searching lights reveal the foreground of a new regime, a cosmical readjustment." Blood is referring to Joseph Jastrow (1863-1944), professor of psychology at the University of Wisconsin.

187.13 "Progress] "Paul's Sermon for Thanksgiving."

187.29 "Variety] "Herbert Spencer," *Amsterdam Evening Recorder*, December 15, 1903.

187.33 letter] Letter of May 6, 1910 (fMS Am 1092.9 [74]): "The *Nemesis* is all right enough, only the last of it is bad pluralism: 'a dream of life Ideal | That knows its own control —| Whose ends are at the centre, | And whose balance is the whole.' I think we are through with 'the whole', and with 'causa sui'."

188.5 "Contingency] *The Flaw in Supremacy*, p. 7.

188.12 "as] Not identified.

189.6 "Simply,"] Letter to James, January 20, 1908 (fMS Am 1092.9[68]).

189.11 "Reason,"] *The Flaw in Supremacy*, p. 6.

189.16 "It] *The Flaw in Supremacy*, p. 7.

190.14 "There] *The Flaw in Supremacy*, p. 8. In "The Secret of William James," Blood points out that James quotes these words at this point and asserts that they close James's "literary career."

I. K. S.

A Note on the Editorial Method

The Text of
Essays in Philosophy

Apparatus

Emendations
Textual Notes
Historical Collation
Alterations in the Manuscripts
Word-Division

A Note on the Editorial Method

These volumes of THE WORKS OF WILLIAM JAMES offer the critical text of a definitive edition of his published and unpublished writings (letters excepted). A text may be called 'critical' when an editor intervenes to correct the errors and aberrations of the copy-text[1] on his own responsibility or by reference to other authoritative documents, and also when he introduces authoritative revisions from such documents into the basic copy-text. An edition may be called 'definitive' (a) when the editor has exhaustively determined the authority, in whole or in part, of all preserved documents for the text; (b) when the text is based on the most authoritative documents produced during the work's formulation and execution and then during its publishing history; and (c) when the complete textual data of all authoritative documents are recorded, together with a full account of the edited text's divergences from the document chosen as copy-text, so that the user may reconstruct these sources in complete detail as if they were before him. When backed by this data, a critical text in such a definitive edition may be called 'established' if from the fully recorded documentary evidence it attempts to reconstruct the author's true and latest intention, even though in some details the restoration of intention from imperfect sources is conjectural and subject to differing opinion.

The most important editorial decision for any work edited without modernization[2] is the choice of its copy-text, that docu-

[1] The copy-text is that document, whether a manuscript or a printed edition, chosen by the editor as the most authoritative basis for his text, and therefore one which is reprinted in the present edition subject only to recorded editorial emendations, and to substitution or addition of readings from other authoritative documents, judged to be necessary or desirable for completing James's final intentions.

[2] By 'modernization' one means the silent substitution for the author's of an entirely new system of punctuation, spelling, capitalization, and word-division in order to bring

mentary form on which the edited text will be based. Textual theorists have long distinguished two kinds of authority: first, the authority of the words themselves—the *substantives*; second, the authority of the punctuation, spelling, capitalization, word-division, paragraphing, and devices of emphasis—the *accidentals* so-called— that is, the texture in which the substantives are placed but itself often a not unimportant source of meaning. In an unmodernized edition like the present, an attempt is made to print not only the substantives but also their 'accidental' texture, each in its most authoritative form. The most authoritative substantives are taken to be those that reflect most faithfully the author's latest intentions as he revised to perfect the form and meaning of his work. The most authoritative accidentals are those which are preferential, and even idiosyncratic, in the author's usage even though not necessarily invariable in his manuscripts. These characteristic forms convey something of an author's flavor, but their importance goes beyond aesthetic or antiquarian appreciation since they may become important adjuncts to meaning. It is precisely these adjuncts, however, that are most susceptible to compositorial and editorial styling away from authorial characteristics and toward the uniformity of whatever contemporary system the printing or publishing house fancied. Since few authors are in every respect so firm in their 'accidental' intentions as to demand an exact reproduction of their copy, or to attempt systematically to restore their own system in proof from divergent compositorial styling, their 'acceptance' of printing-house styling is meaningless as an indication of intentions. Thus, advanced editorial theory agrees that in ordinary circumstances the best authority for the accidentals is that of a holograph manuscript or, when the manuscript is not preserved, whatever

these original old-fashioned 'accidentals' of the text thoroughly up to date for the benefit of a current reader. It is the theory of the present edition, however, that James's turn-of-the-century 'accidentals' offer no difficulty to a modern scholar or general reader and that to tamper with them by 'modernization' would not only destroy some of James's unique and vigorous flavor of presentation but would also risk distortion of his meaning. Since there is every evidence that, in his books at least, James was concerned to control the texture of presentation and made numerous nonverbal as well as verbal changes in preparing printer's copy, and later in proof, for an editor to interfere with James's specific, or even general, wishes by modernizing his system of 'accidentals' would upset on many occasions the designedly subtle balances of his meaning. Moreover, it would be pointless to change his various idiosyncrasies of presentation, such as his increasing use of 'reform' spellings and his liking for the reduction of the capitals in words like *darwinism.* Hence in the present edition considerable pains have been devoted to reprinting the authoritative accidentals of the copy-text and also by emendation to their purification, so far as documentary evidence extends, from the housestyling to which they were subjected in print, which was not entirely weeded out in proof. For a further discussion, see below under the question of copy-text and its treatment.

typed or printed document is closest to it, so that the fewest intermediaries have had a chance to change the text and its forms. Into this copy-text—chosen on the basis of its most authoritative accidentals—are placed the latest revised substantives, with the result that each part of the resulting eclectic text is presented in its highest documentary form of authority.[3] It is recognized, however, that an author may be so scrupulous in supervising each stage of the production of a work that the accidentals of its final version join with the substantives in representing his latest intentions more faithfully than in earlier forms of the text. In such special cases a document removed by some stages from a preserved manuscript or from an early intermediary may in practical terms compose the best copy-text.

Each work, then, must be judged on its merits. In general, experience shows that whereas James accepted some journal styling without much objection even though he read proof and had the chance to alter within reason what he wished, he was more seriously concerned with the forms of certain of his accidentals in the books, not only by his marking copy pasted up from journal articles for the printer but more particularly when he received the galley proofs. Indeed, it is not too much to state that James sometimes regarded the copy that he submitted for his books (especially when it was manuscript) as still somewhat in a draft state, to be shaped by proof-alterations to conform to his ultimate intentions. The choice of copy-texts in this edition, therefore, rests on the evidence available for each document, and the selection will vary according to the circumstances of 'accidental' authority as superior either in the early or in the late and revised forms of the text. In this connection, the discussions in the textual analyses for other philosophical volumes of this edition give examples of the evidence and its application to the selection of copy-text that are pertinent to the present volume.

On the other hand, although James demonstrably made an effort to control the forms of certain of his accidentals in the proofs, even when he had been relatively careless about their consistency in his manuscript printer's copy, he was not always equally atten-

---

[3]The use of these terms, and the application to editorial principles of the divided authority between both parts of an author's text, was chiefly initiated by W. W. Greg, "The Rationale of Copy-Text," *Studies in Bibliography*, 3 (1950-51), 19-36. For extensions of the principle, see Fredson Bowers, "Current Theories of Copy-Text," *Modern Philology*, 68 (1950), 12-20; "Multiple Authority: New Concepts of Copy-Text," *The Library*, 5th ser., 27 (1972), 81-115; "Remarks on Eclectic Texts," *Proof*, 4 (1974), 31-76, all reprinted in *Essays in Bibliography, Text, and Editing* (Charlottesville: University Press of Virginia, 1975).

tive to every detail of the housestyling that printers imposed on his work. In some cases he simply did not observe anomalies even in his own idiosyncratic practices; in others he may have been relatively indifferent when no real clash of principles was involved. Thus, when an editor is aware that certain 'accidental' printing-house stylings have been substituted for James's own practices as established in manuscripts and marked copy, or have been substituted for relatively neutral journal copy that seems to approximate James's usual practice, he may feel justified in emending to recover by the methods of textual criticism as much of the purity of the Jamesian accidentals as of the substantives—both ultimately contributing to the most complete and accurate expression of James's meaning.

Except for the small amount of silent alteration listed below, every editorial change in the copy-text has been recorded, with the identification of its immediate source and the record of the rejected copy-text reading. An asterisk prefixed to the page-line reference (always to this edition) indicates that the alteration is discussed in a Textual Note. The formulas for notation are described in the headnote to the list of Emendations, but it may be well to mention here the use of the term *stet* to call attention in special cases to the retention of the copy-text reading. Textual Notes discuss certain emendations or refusals to emend. The Historical Collation lists all readings in the collated authoritative documents that differ from the edited text except for those recorded in the list of Emendations, which are not repeated in the Historical Collation. The principles for the recording of variants are described in the headnote to this Collation, including the special notation for cross-reference to the list of Alterations in the Manuscripts.

When manuscripts are preserved in the textual transmission, their rejected variants will be recorded in the Historical Collation according to the finally inscribed readings of the text. However, James's manuscripts are likely to be much rewritten both during the course of composition and in the process of review, creating variants while he struggled to give shape to his thought that are of particular concern to the scholar. Since this edition is bound to the principle that its apparatus should substitute for all authoritative documents, special provision is made by a list of Alterations in the Manuscripts for the analysis and description of every difference between the initial inscription and the final revision. Alterations which are included in the Historical Collation (set off by a special warning sign) as part of the final manuscript reading there recorded as a variant are not repeated in the list of Alterations in the Manuscripts.

A special section of the apparatus treats hyphenated word-compounds, listing the correct copy-text form of those broken between lines by the printer of the present edition and indicating those in the present text, with the form adopted, that were broken between lines in the copy-text and partake of the nature of emendations. Consultation of the first list will enable any user to quote from the present text with the correct hyphenation of the copy-text.

Manuscripts that are reproduced or are quoted in this edition are transcribed in diplomatic form,[4] without emendation, except for two features. As with many writers, James's placement of punctuation in relation to quotation marks was erratic, sometimes appearing within the marks as in the standard American system for commas and periods, sometimes outside according to the sense as in the British system, and sometimes carelessly placed immediately below the quotation mark. To attempt to determine the exact position of each mark would often be impossible; hence all such punctuation is placed as it would be by an American printer, the system that James in fact seems to have employed himself when he thought of it. Second, the spacing of ellipsis dots has been normalized. As part of this normalization the distinction is made (James's spacing usually being variable and ambiguous) between the closeup placement of the first of four dots when it represents the period directly after the last quoted word and the spaced placement (as in three dots) when the ellipsis begins in mid-sentence and the fourth dot thus represents the final period. According to convenience, manuscripts may be transcribed in their final, or clear-text, form, with all alteration variants recorded systematically in an appendix apparatus list, or on occasion they may be transcribed with a record of their alteration variants placed within the text. An abstract of the major features of the formulaic system for recording alterations, especially when they are described within the

---

[4] A diplomatic transcript reproduces exactly the final form of the original, insofar as type can represent script, but with no attempt to follow the lining of the original or visually—by typographical devices—to reproduce deletions, interlineations, additions, or substitutions. It follows that no emendation is attempted in such a transcript and all errors in the text are allowed to stand without correction, although a sparing use of square brackets for addition or clarification has been permitted. However, errors that clearly result from James's alterations are transferred to the list of Alterations in the Manuscripts, that, as necessary, may follow the particular transcript.

transcript of the text, may be found in the headnote to the Alterations in the Manuscripts.[5]

In this edition of THE WORKS OF WILLIAM JAMES an attempt has been made to identify the exact edition used by James for his quotations from other authors and ordinarily to emend his carelessnesses of transcription so that the quotation will reproduce exactly what the author wrote. All such changes are noted in the list of Emendations. On some occasions, however, James altered quotations for his own purposes in such a manner that his version should be respected. Such readings are retained in the text but recorded in the list of Emendations (with the signal *stet*), and the original form is provided for the information of the consulting scholar. The general principles governing the treatment of emendations are as follows. As a rule, the author's accidentals are inserted from the original to replace variants created in the normal course of James's copying without particular attention to such features, or of compositorial styling. For substantives, James faced the usual problem of a quoter in getting at the meat of the quotation by judicious condensation. He was likely to mark major omissions by ellipsis dots. On the other hand, he was by no means invariably scrupulous in indicating a number of his alterations. Thus to condense a quotation he might silently omit material ranging from a phrase to several sentences. Major omissions that would require excessive space to transcribe in the list of Emendations are indicated in the text by editorially added dots, recorded as emendations. For minor condensing omissions, James's text is ordinarily allowed to stand without the distraction of ellipsis dots, and the omitted matter is recorded as part of a *stet* entry in the list of Emendations. However, James's treatment of quotations could be more cavalier. Sometimes to speed up the quotation, but occasionally to sharpen its application to his own ideas, he paraphrased a word or phrase, or a major part of a sentence. Since alteration of this nature was consciously engaged in for literary or philosophic purposes, James's text in such cases is allowed to stand but the original reading is given as part of a *stet* entry in the Emendations. (Rarely, he paraphrased a whole quotation although enclosing it within quotation marks, in which case the marks are editorially removed as an emendation.) More troublesome are the minor variants in wording that seem to have no purpose ideologically or as condensations. When in the opinion of the editor these represent merely careless

[5] For full details of this system, see F. Bowers, "Transcription of Manuscripts: The Record of Variants," *Studies in Bibliography*, 29 (1976), 212-264.

or inadvertent slips in copying, on a par with James's sometimes casual transcription of accidentals, the originals are restored as emendations. Within James's quotations paragraphing that he did not observe in the original has not been recorded and final dots have not been added editorially when he ends a quotation short of the completion of a sentence. Variation from the original in James's choice whether to begin a quotation with a capital or lower-case letter has also not been recorded. Similarly, James's syntactical capitalization or use of lower case following ellipsis has been ignored whenever by necessity it differs from the original.

Although James's own footnotes are preserved in the text as he wrote them (the only footnotes allowed in the present edition), the citations have been expanded and corrected as necessary in Professor Skrupskelis' Notes to provide the full bibliographical detail required by a scholar, this ordinarily having been neglected in James's own sketchy notation. The Notes also provide full information about quotations in the text that James did not footnote.

References to McDermott (McD) are to the "Annotated Bibliography," *The Writings of William James*, ed. John J. McDermott (New York: Random House, 1967).

Silent alterations in the text concern themselves chiefly with mechanical presentation. For instance, heading capitals are normalized in the first line of any chapter or section, headings may have their final periods removed, the headlines of the originals may be altered for the purposes of the present edition, anomalous typographical conventions or use of fonts may be normalized including roman or italic syntactical punctuation, which here has been made to conform to a logical system. The minutiae of the accidentals of footnote reference have not been recorded as emendations or as rejected readings. For example, in the footnotes book titles are silently italicized from whatever other form present in the copy-text, as within quotation marks; periods are supplied after abbreviations and the forms of abbreviations are made consistent; the use of roman or italic fonts is normalized as is the general system of punctuating bibliographical references. In short, such matters involving the reference system have been silently brought into conformity with the printing practice of the time, and usually conform to that found in the styling of the period. When unusual features call for unusual treatment, special notice is always given.

All line numbers keyed to the text include section numbers and subheadings but do not include spaces. James's references to pages within the same essay are silently adjusted to the present edition;

references to other volumes already published in the WORKS are added in brackets after James's original page numbers.

The intent of the editorial treatment both in large and in small matters, and in the recording of the textual information, has been to provide a clean reading text for the general user, with all specialized material isolated for the convenience of the scholar who wishes to consult it. The result has been to establish in the wording James's latest intentions in their most authoritative form, divorced from verbal corruption whether in the copy-text or in subsequent printings or editions. To this crucial aim has been added the further attempt to present James's final verbal intentions within a logically contrived system of his own accidentals that in their texture are as close to their most authoritative form as controlled editorial theory can establish from the documentary evidence that has been preserved for each work.

The aid offered by this edition to serious scholars of William James's writings is not confined to the presentation of a trustworthy, purified, and established text. Of equal ultimate importance are the apparatuses and appendixes devoted to the facts about the progress of James's thought from its earliest known beginnings to final publication in journal and book, and continuing to annotation in his private copies by the record of alterations that were usually never made public except when practicable in a few plate-changes. Most of the materials here made available for close study of the development and refinement of James's ideas—almost literally in the workshop—have not previously been seen by scholars except in the James Collection of the Houghton Library, and then they could not be studied in detail without tiresome collation (here fully recorded in the apparatus). The refinements of thought between journal articles and book collection are of particular interest; but scholars may find more fascinating and fruitful for study the record of the manuscripts which—as they are reprinted in this edition or can be reconstructed from its apparatus—offer material for scholarly analysis of the way in which James shaped the thought itself as well as its expression, if the two can indeed ever be separated. As this edition progresses, the entire collection of manuscripts and of annotated journals and books at Harvard will be brought to philosophers, wherever they may live, for analysis and research in the privacy and convenience of their own studies.

It is the belief of the editors of the WORKS, and the Advisory Board, that this living historical record of the development of James's philosophical ideas and their expression, as found in the apparatus and appendixes, is as significant a part of the proposed 'definitive edition' for the purposes of scholarly research as is the establishment of a text closer to James's own intentions than is customarily represented by any single preserved document, including even his carefully worked-over books.

F.B.

The Text of *Essays in Philosophy*

In his Prefatory Note to the collection *Memories and Studies* that Henry James, Jr. (William's son), published in 1911, the following statement is made: "Professor William James formed the intention shortly before his death of republishing a number of popular addresses and essays under the title which this book now bears; but unfortunately he found no opportunity to attend to any detail of the book himself, or to leave definite instructions for others. I believe, however, that I have departed in no substantial degree from my father's idea, except perhaps by including two or three short pieces which were first addressed to special occasions or audiences and which now seem clearly worthy of republication in their original form, although he might not have been willing to reprint them himself without the recastings to which he was ever most attentive when preparing for new readers."[1]

The accuracy of this statement cannot be tested by any preserved evidence, but there is no need to doubt its general import. The mention of the title as authoritative is a detail likely to be a precise recollection. That James might propose to himself a collection of the sort described by his son is by no means improbable. So far as we can tell, however, mention of his plan may have been exclusively verbal, and perhaps correspondingly vague and unformed as to the precise list of contents, although their general popular nature could well have been indicated. It seems clear that James himself never made up a list—as he had for the abortive publication of *Essays in Radical Empiricism*—and thus that the actual selection in *Memories and Studies* is perhaps more of Henry James's responsibility than he preferred to acknowledge.

---

[1] *Memories and Studies* (New York: Longmans, Green, 1911), p. ix.

One does not need Henry James's testimony about his father's wishes for a collection to justify the present volume of the WORKS: any complete edition of James's writings requires the bringing together of his journal articles not reprinted as well as his more fugitive reviews and newspaper pieces. The WORKS will contain not only these *Essays in Philosophy* but also similar collections by subject in *Essays in Religion and Morality*, *Essays in Psychology*, and *Essays in Psychic Research*, as well as a more miscellaneous collection of reviews, eulogies, general addresses, and newspaper pieces planned as the final volume. In fact, the only question is whether *Memories and Studies* represents James's talked-of volume in sufficiently precise detail to have warranted its editing as a unit, despite the fact that its miscellaneous contents cut across the proposals of the present edition for convenient collections by subject matter. On the whole, the statement made by Henry James, Jr., does not seem to be so exact as to justify the re-editing of the *Memories and Studies* collection in the present edition on the analogy of *Essays in Radical Empiricism* for which William James did indeed draw up precise proposals. The present selection, therefore, is by subject matter, although admittedly it is sometimes difficult to draw a line between articles chiefly devoted to matters of philosophy or to psychology.

THE TEACHING OF PHILOSOPHY IN OUR COLLEGES (1876).

Copy-text: (P²⁵) "The Teaching of Philosophy in Our Colleges," *Nation*, 23 (Sept. 21, 1876), 178-179 (McDermott 1876:8). James's unsigned essay was suggested by the following letter to the editor by Dr. G. Stanley Hall, published in the same number on page 180:

SIR: I have often wished that the *Nation* would devote some space to the condition of philosophy in American colleges. Within the last few years I have visited the class-rooms of many of our best institutions, and believe that there are few if any branches which are so inadequately taught as those generally roughly classed as philosophy. Deductive logic, or the syllogism, is the most thoroughly dwelt upon, while induction, æsthetic and psychological and ethical studies, and especially the history of the leading systems of philosophy, ancient and modern, and the marvellous new developments in England and Germany, are almost entirely ignored. The persistent use of Hamilton, Butler's 'Analogy,' and a score of treatises on "moral science" which deduce all the ground of obligation from theological considerations, as text-books is largely responsible for the supposed unpopularity of the studies.

The application of scientific methods in psychology by Spencer, Lewes, Lotze, Wundt, and others; the admirable text-books now accessible in the general history of philosophy; the application of philosophical systems to history, politics, law, and education, which have contributed to make these subjects centres of such fresh and eager interest under some of the great living German teachers, indicate how entirely our methods of instruction need to be remodelled. I think the success which has attended the recent lecture courses at Cambridge on modern systems of philosophy and on æsthetic studies of literature and the fine arts, shows plainly how much might be accomplished in this direction by the proper method of instruction. This whole field of study is generally given into the hands of one of the older and "safer" members of the faculty, under the erroneous belief that it should be the aim of the professors of this department to indoctrinate rather than to instruct— to tell *what* to think, than to teach *how* to think. When we realize what educational impulses may be awakened in these departments, the loss of time and effort is sadly apparent. G. S. H.

Internal evidence suggests James's authorship of "The Teaching of Philosophy," but the presence of a clipping of the article in the scrapbook in MS Am 1092.9, #4563 (Box M), of the James Collection among other writings for newspapers which he preserved offers the strongest corroboration. The first sentence is at least in part the work of the editor of the *Nation*.

REMARKS ON SPENCER'S DEFINITION OF MIND AS CORRESPONDENCE (1878).

Copy-text: (P²¹) "Remarks on Spencer's Definition of Mind as Correspondence," *Journal of Speculative Philosophy*, 12 (Jan. 1878), 1-18 (McD 1878:1). The two emendations at 12.31 and 13.24 are accepted as found in the annotated copy of the offprint preserved in the James Collection in Box O, envelope 8. These two annotations are repeated in a copy of the journal (*AC85. J2376.LJ826) presented by James to the Harvard Library. A third is taken from a letter from James to the editor of the *Journal*. Substantive or significant accidental variants from the text in *Collected Essays and Reviews*, ed. R. B. Perry (1920), pp. 43-68 (McD 1920:2), have been recorded in the Historical Collation and the list of Emendations.

On December 6, 1877, James sent an undated letter, dictated to his brother Henry, to William Torrey Harris, editor of the *Journal*:

I send you by this mail an article on Spencer's definition of Mind, which I hope *you [*over* 'to'] may not find unworthy to be printed in your Journal of Speculative Philosophy. If you decide to accept it, I wish you let me know promptly, and also inform me at what date it will appear. I have important practical reasons for wishing to publish several articles in different journals as early as possible (Harris correspondence from Hoose Library of Philosophy, University of Southern California).

Another dictated letter signed by James was sent on December 11:

> Mr. G. S. Hall has just told me of your application to him for "copy" for the Jan. No of your review. This makes me think that my article on Spencer which I recently mailed to you will appear in that number. The time will of course be too short to send me a proof—or may this not be the case? I want to make three or four emendations. If you cannot send me a proof, I must beg you to alter the text in these three places: first, instead of saying that Spencer's chapters on the emotions are the *"only admirable,"* make me say that they form the *"most admirable"* part of the book—second after the allusion to his chapter on the associability of relations I use the words *"operose ineptitude"*; pray alter these into *"artificiality*[.]*"* In the last sentence of the article, instead of saying *"barren as such a formula" is" "utterly barren and indeterminate &c*[.]*"*
>
> I have a feeling that part of my account of survival &c in physical terms lacks clearness, but I enclose a sentence on a slip of paper which you may possibly see where and how to work in to advantage, with or without some alteration on your part.
>
> But if ['this' *del.*] it be not immediately obvious to you where or how to insert it, print the matter just as it stands.
>
> I should be very sorry were the article to appear with the harshness of the first two places mentioned above unmitigated as I propose [.]

The final correspondence about the article is contained on a post-card dated December 13, in answer to some lost note from Harris:

> Your note rec'd. I hope you will put the article in your Jany No. The practical reasons I spoke of had nothing whatever to do with the *sacra auri fames*—& I never supposed that the J. of Sp. Ph. *paid* you, far less anyone else.

Either James received a proof or his request for changes reached Harris in time to alter the proof, for the change to 'most admirable' was made at 9.8-9, and at 22.4 to 'utterly barren and indeterminate'; however, the alteration of 'operose ineptitude' was overlooked. The sentence that James enclosed on a slip of paper cannot be identified.

QUELQUES CONSIDERATIONS SUR LA MÉTHODE SUBJECTIVE (1878).

Copy-text: (P⁹) "Quelques Considérations sur la methode subjective," *Critique philosophique*, 2 (Jan. 24, 1878), 407-413 (McD 1878:2). The communication is subscribed November 20, 1877, and is followed by a paragraph of appreciation, presumably by the editor. Reprinted in *Collected Essays and Reviews*, ed. R. B. Perry

(1920), pp. 69-82. An unannotated offprint is preserved in the James Collection, bMS Am 1092.9, #4565 (Box O, envelope 2).

The Collection also contains the manuscript of a translation into English by an unknown hand (bMS 1452.1 [23]), but this was not part of the bequest of James's papers and was bought on June 9, 1945, from Walter R. Benjamin Autographs, Inc., of Hunter, New York, its previous history unknown. This manuscript is transcribed in the present volume as Appendix I. It consists of a quired note-book of twenty leaves of paper, ruled in blue, made from ten folded full sheets, foliated [3] 1-17, the first three leaves being blank. In the first and last three leaves and the mid-section (fols. π1-3, 4-11, 15-17) the paper is laid, with vertical chainlines, watermarked J. L. F. & Co., the leaves measuring 256 x 200 mm. The intervening leaves (fols. 1-3, 12-14) are on unwatermarked ruled wove paper measuring 256 x 211 mm., thus slightly wider than the laid paper. The rules are 13 mm. apart, with a heading space of 26 mm. and a tail space of 8 mm. On fols. 1-3 (the first three leaves of the wove paper) beginning the text the ink is black except that the heading on fol. 1 has a slightly bluish tone. This bluish toned ink is used to inscribe the rest of the manuscript starting with fol. 4, the laid paper mid-section. On the verso of fol. 12, reversed, is a pencil notation in a different hand dated 9 April 1884 and giving a list of names and positions on a baseball team identified as 'Hopkinson's 2ᵈ Nine'. Its placement on the leaf may indicate that the note was made after the manuscript had been quired and inscribed; if so, it may set a provisional terminus ad quem but is not otherwise helpful in dating the exact writing-out of the manuscript. The paper is not found anywhere in the James Collection, a fact that may indicate that the translation did not originate within the family.

James was sufficiently fluent so that no question can obtain that he wrote this essay in French. Some touching up was given it by Renouvier, the editor, however. In a letter of December 14, 1877, acknowledging receipt of the article, Renouvier promises to "m'occuper d'en faire disparaître les anglicismes . . . . Il va sans dire que je respecterai vos expressions propres et originales, autant qu'elles seront compatibles avec la correction grammaticale." In an important post-publication letter of May 14, 1878, Renouvier discusses first James's "Remarks on Spencer's Definition of Mind," refers to James's compliments on the improvements he had made in "Quelques Considérations" "que vous avez bien voulu m'envoyer en français pour la *Critique philosophique*," and finally engages in a lengthy discussion of its ideas (bMS Am 1092.9, #485 and

#486, quoted from "Correspondance de Charles Renouvier et de William James," ed. R. B. Perry, *Revue de métaphysique et de morale*, 36 [1929], pp. 8-11).

THE SENTIMENT OF RATIONALITY (1879).

Copy-text: (P²⁴) "The Sentiment of Rationality," *Mind*, 4 (July 1879), 317-346 (McD 1879:7). Reprinted in *Collected Essays and Reviews*, ed. R. B. Perry (1920), pp. 83-136. In his file set of *Mind* (Phil 22.4.6*) James encloses 54.19-23, 56.36-57.8, and 59.22-33 in pencil brackets. An offprint in bMS Am 1092.9, #4565 (Box O, envelope 15), is partly mutilated by a small cut out piece in one page, and has a few of James's annotations in ink and in pencil.[2] A portion of the text of this article was combined with "Rationality, Activity and Faith," *Princeton Review*, 2 (July 1882), 58-86 (McD 1882:2) to form a new essay "The Sentiment of Rationality" in the collection *The Will to Believe* (1897), pp. 63-110, but despite its title this later essay has little in common with the original article in *Mind*; hence collations of the small portion of parallel text are not recorded in the present volume but will be found in *The Will to Believe* in the WORKS.

Under the pressure of "publish-or-perish," in an undated letter, probably of early January 1878[3] (bMS Am 1092.9, #3536), James wrote to G. Croom Robertson, the editor of *Mind*:

> I enclose herewith the first part of a MS. which I hope you may not find ['it' *del.*] unworthy of insertion in Mind. I am one of several candidates for a psychological chair which is to be filled in June. It is therefore of great practical consequence to me that this paper, if accepted by you at all, should appear in your April number. May I beg of you therefore to read the MS. promptly, and if you find it unfit for your Review, or incapable of so early a publication as I would like, to return it to me forthwith, so that I may get in time to offer it to a journal here. In case however that the MS is accepted, let me inform you that the second part of it is about half as long as the first

---

[2]The text excised comes on the verso of a leaf, page 16 in the repaged offprint corresponding to p. 332 of the original. The text from *Every colour* to *mystical* is cut out (49.16-23), for some unknown purpose. The first ink addition at the end of the first section, 'Discarding ... alone.' (34.13-14) and the simultaneous deletion of the first sentence in section II is discussed in the text below. Otherwise, *material* is deleted before *substratum* at 53.26; *almost* is inserted in pencil in the margin with a caret between *an* and *infinity* (now emended to *an immense number*) (54.19-20); after *Such* a pencil *latter* is inserted but deleted in pencil (54.31); *every* is substituted for deleted *is a* in ink and then *moment is a* is added after *every* (56.4); in the footnote at 61.40 the error *impresses* is altered in pencil to *expresses*; at 62.38 *around* is substituted in ink for deleted *over*. See the emendations for these changes.

[3]In the upper right corner, in Robertson's hand, is the date '17.1.78.', presumably that of receipt.

part, and will be forwarded to you in ample time for your July no.[4]

I would send you a neater copy of this first part, but the shortness of the time, and a temporary affliction of my eyesight force me to mail it as it stands.

Trusting that you will read it with indulgent eyes, I am with great respect

Yours truly

Wm. James M.D.

(Asst Prof. of Physiology)
Harvard University

P.S. On second tho'ts I send the MS. separately to Williams and Norgate's care. It is entitled "the Sentiment of Rationality."

Inserted below James's address is Robertson's memorandum, 'Cannot either in next or one after next. therefore return at once to H. James 3 Bolton St. Piccad. W. as [ied] on envelope'. The note of declination must have cited the inability to publish within James's limits, for James seems to have returned the manuscript. After this second view Robertson wrote to James on May 13, 1878:

I am sorry not to have been able till now to read your Ms. carefully through: I had read it but partially when it was first in my hands. It interests me much (taken in connexion with your remarks in Renouvier's journal ["Quelques Considérations sur la méthode subjective"] and your article in the St. Louis J. of S. P. ["Brute and Human Intellect"]), and I shd. really be glad to have your view stated in *Mind*, but I cannot *judge [*intrl.*] how far it may be practicable to admit the paper wholly or in part, till I know your mind about the second article (in continuation) to which you refer in the present one and wrote of originally, but about which you say nothing in your last note. If the second article is written, it were best that I should see it, before I say anything more about the present one. I can however say that if your *whole* view could have been put in one article not longer than the present considerable one, the chance of publication wd. have been greater, in view of the quantity of matter I have in hand or in prospect to publish (#504).

The succeeding correspondence is not preserved so that we do not know what difficulties developed. However, James must eventually have despaired of publication in *Mind* and on November 26, 1878, he addressed W. T. Harris, editor of the *Journal of Speculative Philosophy*, in a dictated letter:

I have just completed the first two parts of a psychological essay, ['enti' *del.*] (to be completed in four parts) entitled "The Sentiment of

---

[4]This second part appeared, with a considerable delay after acceptance, as "Rationality, Activity and Faith," in 1882 in the *Princeton Review*. The little that is known of the publication of this article is detailed in WORKS, "The Text of *The Will to Believe.*"

Rationality." It seems to me much more important than anything I have yet written, and I wish now to ask you (supposing you accept it at all) how early it can begin to appear. The first installment will fill about thirty of your pages. If the delay is too great I must publish it as an independent pamphlet (Hoose Library of Philosophy, University of Southern California).

The nature of Harris' response is not known but he seems to have warned of a delay, for on December 13 in another dictated letter James wrote:

> Since receiving your reply to my last note of inquiry, ideas have occurred to me which may lead me to make of the essay I have in hand a much larger work than I had at first intended. I beg you therefore not to retain a place for me in your July number. I am heartily delighted at what you say of the number of your new contributions. I hope it means a resur[r]ection of American philosophizing.
>
> Should I hereafter determine to publish part of my work in a review I think I shall send it to *Mind*. A long article which I sent to Robertson in November will, he assures me, appear in the January number. *Mind* too, has a wider public, and I am sorry to say that the pay it offers for articles tempts me even against the voice of patriotism (Hoose).

The arrangement that James ultimately made with *Mind* is not known, but he must have negotiated it very shortly after his last letter to Harris, for on January 24, 1879, Robertson wrote to him:

> I shall like to print your paper and will, if I can, do so in July, though it may *possibly* have to stand over till October. Perhaps you will not mind looking again at the two pages I enclose. The passage I have bracketed—first because of the use of the word *canaille*, and then because of the succession of gustatory metaphors from 'table-sweepings' onwards—strikes me as rather overstrained. If you could convey your feeling in some other terms, it might be more in the way of such a very sober journal as *Mind*. I should be quite as ready to make the like remark on anything proceeding from the other camp; and I hope you will understand that I am only, as there is time for reconsideration, suggesting to you that you might reconsider these expressions. *I don't object to 'Sunday School' & 'Catechism' and recognise their application. [*instd.*] (bMS Am 1092.9, #506).

The last letter preserved about this article is Robertson's of March 23, 1879:

> I am very sorry that a letter and two postcards of yours have remained unanswered for a number of weeks. I have been extremely busy with my April number & college work, so that I have not yet had time to read the last instalment you have sent of the 'Rationality' article. In a few days I hope to do so, and to be able to decide how & when the whole may best appear. At present I am on the eve of a journey to Scotland which will cause me a little delay; & therefore I write this line at once rather than wait longer. I promise

to do my best to find room for you early and will see, if it be at all possible, that you have proofs. Considerations of economy make it less easy for me, than it is for editors of larger & more popular reviews, to have a large number of articles set up long beforehand. But I like authors to be responsible for their own correcting, and will hit your wishes if I can (#507).

The first ink annotation in the offprint in bMS Am 1092.9, #4565, seems designed to replace the note found at the end of the article (64.23-26) since it reads 'Discarding for the present both custom and congruity, the *present essay [*insrtd.for del.* 'following pages'] will deal with the theoretic way alone.' James simultaneously deleted the first sentence of section II, 'It will be best to take up first the theoretic way.', to avoid repetition. This sounds as though James were contemplating some form of republication, but whether to precede "Rationality, Activity and Faith" in a series of chapters implementing the promise of the concluding note in 1879 or in some other manner is not clear. The possibility is not to be overlooked, of course, that James may originally have planned to reprint the present "Sentiment of Rationality" in some shortened form in *The Will to Believe* (1897) but then saw the need to popularize and condense it more drastically by joining it to "Rationality, Activity and Faith" in a single essay for the 1897 collection. The notes made in the offprint must have been preliminary only, if active republication had been in James's mind, for they by no means represent the thoroughness of his usual revision for book publication and are confined to six additional, trifling changes, including the correction of a misreading or strained expression, and the correction of a quotation.

What appears to be a second round of revisions are represented by nine changes written in James's hand in another file of *Mind* (Phil 22.4),[5] two of which deal in different ways with readings that James had found unsatisfactory in his annotation of the offprint in #4565. The P[24] text at 54.19-20 reads, *In short, a plurality of categories and an infinity of primordial entities*, which in #4565 James qualified by inserting *almost* before *infinity* but in the subsequent revision he preferred *immense number* to the hyperbolic *infinity*. Correspondingly, at 54.31-32 James began the P[24] sentence as *Such attempts do but postulate unification*. In #4565 he showed that he was concerned to relate *Such attempts* to the sentence at 54.23-25 by adding marginal *latter* but then deleting it. In the file set, however, the altered reading is *Such attempts as these latter*. Two other changes at 61.40 and 62.38 duplicate

[5] These nine appear at 48.5, 50.11, 51.19, 53.31, 54.17-18, 54.20, 54.31, 61.40, and 62.38.

annotations made in the #4565 offprint. In his reprint in *Collected Essays and Reviews* R. B. Perry included these nine revisions from the file set but added six more substantive changes at 47.20, 51.21, 53.18, 54.32, 57.37, and 62.9 that are more likely to represent his stylistic tinkering than his possession of a now lost offprint in which James had marked the six changes now found in the file set plus additional ones. These minor variants in Perry have been ignored in the present text, therefore, whereas the nine annotations in the file set have been incorporated.

In the present text British spellings in *Mind* are silently Americanized according to James's own characteristics, and the position of punctuation in relation to quotation marks is also silently adjusted to conform to American usage.

Two sets of manuscript notes made in preparation for "The Sentiment of Rationality" are transcribed in Appendix II. The more elementary set is found in bMS Am 1092.9, #4465 (Box E, envelope 5), in the James Collection and is miscellaneous in its constitution. The second, preserved in bMS Am 1092.9, #4464 (Box E, envelope 1), represents a mixture of notes with a serious attempt at a draft of the text. On a scrap of paper in this envelope is found a note by Alice James: 'Keep[.] W.J.'s notes for The Sentiment of Rationality. He burned most of his manuscripts.'

MR. BRADLEY ON IMMEDIATE RESEMBLANCE (1893).

Copy-text: (P^{24}) "Mr. Bradley on Immediate Resemblance," under the heading of Discussions in *Mind*, n.s. 2 (April 1893), 208-210 (McD 1893:2a). In James's file set of *Mind* (Phil 22.4.6*) he wrote five corrections and revisions, adopted in the present text. This note was reprinted from P^{24} (unannotated) in *Collected Essays and Reviews*, ed. R. B. Perry (1920), pp. 333-338. James was writing in reply to F. H. Bradley's "On Professor James' Doctrine of Simple Resemblance," *Mind*, n.s. 2 (Jan. 1893), 83-88.

IMMEDIATE RESEMBLANCE (1893).

Copy-text: (P^{24}) "Immediate Resemblance," under the heading of Discussions in *Mind*, n.s. 2 (Oct. 1893), 509-510 (McD 1893:2b), reprinted without substantive variation in *Collected Essays and Reviews* (1920), pp. 339-341. This note was a reply to Bradley's "Professor James on Simple Resemblance," *Mind*, n.s. 2 (July 1893), 366-369. To the end of James's note, on p. 510, Bradley added a reply. The controversy was not continued.

THE KNOWING OF THINGS TOGETHER (1895).

Copy-text: (P³⁴) "The Knowing of Things Together," *Psychological Review*, 2 (March 1895), 105-124 (McD 1895:4).

On December 1, 1894, James wrote to J. Mark Baldwin, "I haven't written a line yet, and imagine that nothing may come at all. Of course there need be no presidential address—it isn't part of the to be Constitution, I hope, but a free gift if it comes, any year, and I am disposed to think, if my paper does materialize, that since it will be wholly technical in form, it will be better to give it as one of the common communications and not as a presidential address. The latter should be some rather broadly zusammenfassend review of the situation, I should say" (bMS Am 1092.1, typescript copy). Whatever the literal truth of the sentiments in this statement, the paper was delivered as the President's Address before the American Psychological Association, meeting at Princeton, New Jersey, on December 27, 1894. Copy must have been ready very soon, since it appeared in the March number of the *Psychological Review*, although this journal had a bad reputation for being late in its issue, and the actual date of publication may well have been later.

It would seem that at some comparatively late stage of the preparation of copy for *The Will to Believe* (1897), James had proposed to include "The Knowing of Things Together" in the collection, although in the end he changed his mind. In bMS Am 1092.9, #4565 (Box O, envelope 14ª), is preserved a curious form of the article, which appears to have been part of the original copy assembled for *The Will to Believe*. Pages 105 and 106, 114-124 are pasted with reduced margins that cut off the running-heads on sheets of typewriter paper watermarked MERCHANTS PURE BOND. Between pages 106 and 114 appears a typescript numbered 1-10, with an additional sheet, unnumbered, after page 5, headed by a note in James's hand, 'note to typewritten sheet No 5.' This typescript, on paper watermarked WARD'S TRIMOUNT BOND—a paper found nowhere else in the James Collection—is a (probably professional) copy of the missing article pages 107-113, sometimes a line-for-line transcript. The first two pages of the pasted-up article are numbered in James's hand 247 and 248 at top center; pages 114-124 are 257-267. The gap in the pasted-up leaves is one more than the pages of the article, but it may be that (as in the typescript) footnote 4 on 110.23-34 (75.37-39–76.24-32) with its diagram was given a separate leaf, or there may have been some slip in the numbering. The date of the typescript is unknown, but it must have been made after April 17-18, 1908, when the two leaves numbered 254 and 255 containing pages 111-112 of the article were abstracted and used as fols. 10-11 of Lecture VII in the manuscript of *A Pluralistic Universe*. (What happened to leaves 249 to 253 is not known; leaf 256 was probably removed along with 254 and 255 but not used.) It is clear, then, that the typescript part of this prepared copy of the article is materially later than the pasting up and numbering of the leaves. The date for making up this pasted copy, as during the preparation of copy for *The Will to Believe*, seems to be settled by the preservation in the same envelope of the article "The Hidden Self" (McD 1890:1), which was partly utilized in *The Will to Believe*. This article is also pasted on sheets of the Merchants Bond paper (a paper used in the manuscript for "The Will to Believe") and similarly numbered starting with 280. In fact, only the first two pages of the original article (pp. 361-362), which would have been pasted on 278-279 before the text on preserved 280 (pasting up p. 363) were used to help make up "What Psychical Research Has Accomplished" as printed in *The Will to Believe*; hence their absence from the made-up copy of "The Hidden Self" is sufficient evidence that they were detached when the final form of *The Will to Believe* copy was being prepared.[6]

In the made-up copy of "The Knowing of Things Together" only one annotation appears in the printed text, the transfer at 72.10-11 of *simply* from after *phenomenon* (72.12) to follow *as* (for a discussion of this variant, see the Textual Note). The typescript part has a few trifling variants in the accidentals and four mistakes in the substantives,[7] evidence that its printed copy had not been annotated before the typing. However, in James's file set of the *Psychological Review* (WJ 110.72) thirteen holograph alterations appear in this article. On the first page is James's pencil note, 'Philosophy 3 ['3' *over* '9'] men may also refer to my article on the function of cognition in Mind, vol X p 27 (1885) W.J.' In the space before section III he wrote, 'Philosophy 9 men can stop here. W.J.' These instructions seem to go back to the articles he assigned to his class in Philosophy 9 (Metaphysics), which he taught in the

---

[6]On the verso of p. 267 of "The Knowing of Things Together" are pencil calculations by which 38 is multiplied by 21 for a total of 798, this then being multiplied by 50 for a total of 39,900. "The Hidden Self" has similar calculations ending in a total of 40,128. What these figures refer to is not entirely clear, or how they were arrived at; it does seem, however, that they are probably word counts for *The Will to Believe* at different stages.

[7]These are 74.35 no one] one TMs; 74.35 [2]one] no one TMs; 75.11 till] will TMs; 76.27 other] *omit* TMs.

first semester of the academic year 1904-1905,[8] and were made on at least two occasions, in ink and in pencil.[9] Although not designed for publication, they revise the text to readings that clearly represent James's latest preserved intentions, and hence they have been accepted as authoritative emendations in the copytext. Another offprint is preserved in bMS Am 1092.9, #4565 (Box O, envelope 11), with two notes in a strange hand referring to *A Pluralistic Universe* and, probably in a different hand, a guideline transposing *simply*, originally after *phenomenon* at 72.12, to an impossible position before *already* (72.11), with the marginal circled note *tr.* This reading has no apparent authority, and is inferior to the two other alterations of the position of the same word.

The article was reprinted in *Collected Essays and Reviews*, ed. R. B. Perry (1920), pp. 371-400, with four substantive variants of no ascertainable authority: necessary corrections at 81.28 and 81.36 and seeming sophistications at 81.26 and 84.21.

In his autograph list of May 1907 for the contents of a proposed collection of essays on radical empiricism (bMS Am 1092.9, #4426 [Box F, envelope 7]) James placed "The Knowing of Things Together" as second, but added to the title '(partly)'. This intention bore fruit later when in 1909 he excerpted pp. 73.15-76.6 of the article in revised form as "The Tigers in India" in *The Meaning of Truth* (WORKS, pp. 33-36). The present text does not take account of these revisions but offers the original article, altered only in respect to James's 1904 annotations in his file set of the *Review*.[10]

In a letter to James E. Creighton, editor of the *Psychological Review*, of March 20, 1895 (bMS Am 1092.9, #829), James gave permission to print 'my summary' referring to an abstract of his address given at Princeton appearing in the same issue of the *Review* as the article but on pages 152-153. It was reprinted later without change in the *Philosophical Review*, 4 (May 1895), 336-337. Appendix III of the present volume reprints the *Psychological Review* text since it seems to be authenticated as written by James.

PREFACE TO PAULSEN'S *INTRODUCTION TO PHILOSOPHY* (1895).

Copy-text: (P) *Introduction to Philosophy*, by Friedrich Paulsen, translated by Frank Thilly from the third German edition (New

---

[8] For this matter see the correspondence with editors of journals about getting his articles into print in time for this class quoted in "The Text of *Essays in Radical Empiricism*," *Essays in Radical Empiricism*, WORKS, pp. 201-202.

[9] Those in pencil occur at 75.24, 84.39, 86.10, 87.12, 88.3. The rest are in ink.

[10] The variants in *The Meaning of Truth* excerpt from "The Knowing of Things Together" are recorded in the apparatus of *The Meaning of Truth*, WORKS, p. 249.

York: Henry Holt, 1895), pp. iii-vii (McD 1895:13).[11] Five other printings followed in James's lifetime in 1898, 1899, 1902, 1904, and 1906, and the volume continued to be reprinted at least as late as 1930. Collation reveals that no changes were made within James's preface in the plates of the later printings. James's preface is headed 'PREFACE.' and is subscribed 'WILLIAM JAMES. | HARVARD UNIVERSITY, April, 1895.' Henry Holt entered the book for copyright under no. 9445 on February 14, 1895; two copies were deposited in the Library of Congress on February 15. However, the original entry had not mentioned James's Preface. To protect this, one assumes, Holt recopyrighted the book with the Preface under no. 38315 on July 25, 1895, with the two statutory copies deposited on the same day.

On September 20, 1894, James wrote to Frank Thilly:

I have the highest opinion of the execution of Paulsen's book, but a low opinion of the simple naturalism there propounded as a philosophy. If you care for a page and a half of preface in which I should say that, I will gladly

[11] The title-page reads: 'INTRODUCTION TO PHILOSOPHY | BY | FRIEDRICH PAULSEN | *Professor of Philosophy in the University of Berlin* | TRANSLATED WITH THE AUTHOR'S SANCTION | BY | FRANK THILLY | *Professor of Philosophy in the University of Missouri* | WITH A PREFACE | BY | WILLIAM JAMES | *Professor of Psychology in Harvard University* | *FIRST AMERICAN FROM THE THIRD GERMAN EDITION* | [device] | NEW YORK | HENRY HOLT AND COMPANY | 1895. The text of James's own copy (WJ 350.68) is not annotated, but the copy does show some signs of use. Pasted inside the front cover is an hour's examination for Philosophy 3 dated April 23, 1895. Pasted on the front free endpaper is a list of students for Philosophy D (no date), beginning with Andrews, R. E. and ending with Zabriskie, G. G. Since the classes after the names run from 1907 to 1910, it is evident that this is a list for the course in 1907. On the recto of the front flyleaf is James's note in pencil 'Not by a specially dignified *principle* or *entity* can you rescue the world from materialism, but by its bearing spiritual fruits.' After a short rule, he continues 'Convert "cause" into "reason." Things mutually determinant like elements of triangle. Lotze Aesthetik i. D.' On the verso of the front flyleaf is written in ink, 'Prag^m | Parallel^m'. On the recto of p. i (which contains advertisements on its verso) James has written his name and address in pencil; he also writes his name and address in ink on the title page. Another note by James appears on the verso of the back flyleaf: '*determinism 221 [*pencil*] | *immortality of pastness 243 234 | We can free God of evil etc "only at the price of dualism" 265— awful price! & characteristic saying. [*ink*]' On the recto of the back endpaper James has written in ink:

Make *the [*over* 'thes'] following distinctions in P.'s text quite plain to the Class.

panpsychism (mental & physical are co extensive)	{	epiphenomenalism	{	monistic
		psychic activity or causality		pluralistic.

Interactionism = mental & physical not coextensive, mental interpolated between links of physical.

write you one. I really think that as a statement of simple naturalism it should be held to supersede all other books.

*I congratulate ['I con' *over* 'Sin'] you on so speedy a conclusion of your task. Such things are so apt to drag. I wish that I could hear you speak of the work yourself now that you are so intimate with it. I hope to be able to use it in my class on "Cosmology" but am not quite sure yet (Frank Thilly Papers, Dept. of Manuscripts and University Archives, Cornell).

Two letters to Thilly reveal James's care to read the translation before beginning the preface. On October 14, 1894, he wrote: "Will you kindly tell me just when you would like the preface? And would it be possible to let me have ['the' *del.*] copies of the plate proofs? I should be more 'inspired' by a re-reading of the ['tra' *del.*] book in its english dress. Nevertheless if this is going to make trouble at publishers or printers, let it pass." After a delay, he wrote again on December 1: "I get no proofs of Paulsen, and don't know whether they mean to send any. It would certainly help me with the preface to have them to look over. I shall assume that you are looking out for me—I don't want to be notified abruptly some day, that my preface is expected on the morrow, the presses waiting etc." The period of uncertainty was over on April 20, 1895, when in a letter to Henry Holt, the publisher, he formally agreed to write the preface (bMS Am 1092.1, copy). The preface was thereupon written promptly, as indicated by a letter from Thilly of May 22, 1895: "I thank you very much for the *Introduction* which you have been kind enough to write for my translation of Paulsen's *Einleitung* and for the complimentary way in which you speak of my humble efforts to render *Paulsen* accessible to English readers." He then disagrees with James's use of 'hylozoist' as applied to Paulsen (bMS Am 1092, #1136). To this James replied on May 26, 1895:

I am glad you approve my preface (barring the word hylozoism) and thank you for calling me the "greatest *philosopher ['er' *over* 'y'] of our country"—I trust you are willing to join me thereupon in saying "God help the country," when scraps and fragments are its best. But what do you think of my colleague Royce, who is *not* scraps and fragments? Or *of [*intrl.*] Bowne, whose philosophy of Theism is a really able book?

As to hylozoism, I used the word undiscriminatingly and shall be delighted to write "monistic idealism" in its stead when it comes to printing the thing. I dare say that P. himself, to whom I have sent the MS. will also suggest the alteration. P's whole *view of the [*intrl.*] relation between finite minds and *the [*intrl.*] All-mind seems to me sadly deficient in distinctness. He has n't distinctly realized any *of the [*intrl.*] difficulties of the problem, and after showing that all the ends in nature are partial and that the larger things come by "heterogony" etc immediately in the twinkling of a page passes over to an all inclusive mind. I think a good fight can still be made for pluralism, although monism is doubtless an unconquerable idol. Nevertheless Paulsen's is a beautiful book.

Despite the discussion, *hylozoism* was retained in the text at 91.25.

"PRAGMATISM": FROM BALDWIN'S *DICTIONARY* (1902).

Copy-text: (D) *Dictionary of Philosophy and Psychology,* edited by J. M. Baldwin (New York and London: Macmillan, 1902), II, 32 (McD 1902:2). This section of a larger definition is signed '(W. J.)'.

"EXPERIENCE": FROM BALDWIN'S *DICTIONARY* (1902).

Copy-text: (D) *Dictionary of Philosophy and Psychology,* edited by J. M. Baldwin (New York and London: Macmillan, 1902), I, 361-362 (McD 1902:3). This second section of a larger definition is signed '(W. J.)'.

According to a typed copy of a letter to Baldwin in the James Collection (bMS Am 1092.1) dated August 25 (1896?), James had reluctantly agreed to do some articles for the *Dictionary*: "Replying to yours of date Munich 10th inst. would say 'Barkis is willing but damns you all the same.'" In a similar letter of October 9, 1896, he declined to do a suggested article for the dictionary. Finally, on January 10, 1898, James wrote to Baldwin that he wanted no proofs.

HERBERT SPENCER DEAD (1903).

Copy-text: (NYP) "Herbert Spencer Dead," *New York Evening Post,* December 8, 1903, pp. 1, 5 (McD 1903:8). Reference is also made to (MS) an incomplete manuscript in the James Collection (bMS Am 1092.9, #4485 [Box B, envelope 1]); to (P25) "Herbert Spencer," *Nation,* 77 (Dec. 10, 1903), 460-461; and to (Cr) "Herbert Spencer Born 1820 Died 1903," *Critic,* 44 (January 1904), 21-24. James's Scrapbook in MS Am 1092.9, #4563 (Box M) has two autograph alterations in the clipping of NYP.

The manuscript consists of six cut-down leaves of L. L. Brown laid typewriter paper (averaging 251 x 192 mm.), written and revised in ink, with a few final pencil alterations, foliated 1-6, the 1 in the upper right corner and the others centered. It is headed 'Herbert Spencer' double underlined. Folio 6 ends with deleted *for he would* after *would have failed:* at 97.25, probably not a natural stopping point, so that we may take it that the rest of the leaves of what had been a complete manuscript are not preserved. The differences between this manuscript and the NYP text that derives ultimately from it are so normal for James as to encourage the theory that when he had the manuscript typed, he revised it and sent it to the *Post* without further attention.

The *New York Evening Post* obituary is headlined 'HERBERT SPENCER DEAD| [short rule] | PASSING OF ONE OF ENG-LAND'S| GREATEST THINKERS. |[short rule] | His Health Had Been Failing for Sev-|eral Months, but His Illness Became| Critical Only a Few Days Ago—An| Appreciation of the Eminent Phi-|loso-pher by Prof. William James| of Harvard University—The Enor-|mous Popular Success of His Works| Due to the Incomparable Superior-|ity of His Constructive and Critical| Methods—His Direct Influence | Greater Even than Darwin's. | [short rule]'. Under-neath this headline is the simple announcement of Spencer's death at Brighton, datelined London, December 8, then the paragraph 'The newspapers to-day all publish long appreciations and anec-dotes of Mr. Spencer, whom they universally describe as the"last of the great thinkers of the Victorian age."', this followed by James's signed appreciation. The news account concludes with a brief biography by some other hand.

Without acknowledgment, the *Nation* reprinted the *Post* appre-ciation by James but unsigned. The closeness of the accidentals to those of NYP, especially in such variable matters as the use of single and of double quotation marks, indicates a direct derivation. The essay is slightly cut in two places, and no independent sub-stantive readings suggest that James himself sent a corrected copy of NYP to the *Nation*: the correction of several NYP errors in P^{25} although judicious do not include 99.14 which James had marked in his scrapbook clipping. *The Critic* lists James as the writer and footnotes its derivation: 'Reprinted from the *Evening Post* by arrangement'. In this case some of the accidental variants might be argued for as evidence that Cr was set from a carbon of the type-script that was the copy for NYP, but others support more strongly the quite natural line of descent as acknowledged in the footnote, which there is no reason to challenge.

The textual situation, then, works out as follows. Since NYP derives directly from some authoritative copy supplied by James (perhaps a typescript and not a fair-copy manuscript) made from the manuscript as represented in its incomplete state in #4485, and since this later copy certainly contained James's final altera-tions, NYP is to be chosen as copy-text. Both P^{25} and Cr radiate independently from NYP and neither singly nor collectively can be taken to have any authority. In certain accidentals the manuscript may preserve James's characteristics more faithfully than the NYP print, in which case the copy-text has been corrected by reference to MS. The two authorial alterations in the scrapbook in #4563 are adopted and appear in the text for the first time.

THE CHICAGO SCHOOL (1904).

Copy-text: (P³³) "The Chicago School,"*Psychological Bulletin*, 1 (Jan. 15, 1904), 1-5 (McD 1904:3). A truncated version was reprinted by R. B. Perry in *Collected Essays and Reviews* (1920), pp. 445-447. An annotated offprint of P³³ is preserved in the James Collection, bMS Am 1092.9, #4565 (Box O, envelope 11).

James wrote to Schiller on April 8, 1903:

Has one A. S. Moore of Chicago sent you a paper of his? It tickled me hugely, and I wrote urging him to send to you and to Sturt. It seems to me a masterly pragmatic production, and it appears now that under Dewey's inspiration, they have at Chicago a flourishing school of radical empiricism of which I for one have been entirely ignorant, having been led to neglect its utterances by their lack of "terseness," "crispness," "raciness" and other "newspaporial" virtues,ˣ [*in margin* 'You yourself, by the way, reviewed, *in Mind [insrtd.]* I believe *the [over 'a'] previous paper on Locke by *Moore.[period aft. del. comma][' in Mind' del.]*'] though I could discern that Dewey himself was laboring with a big freight, towards the light. They have started from Hegelianism, and they have that temperament (that is, such *men [alt. fr. 'mean'] as Mead and Lloyd have it strongly) which makes one still suspect that if th[e]y do strike Truth eventually, they will mean some mischief to it after all, but still the fact remains that from such opposite poles minds are moving towards a common centre, that old compartments and divisions are breaking down, and that a very inclusive new school may be formed. Once ['at' del.] admit that experience is a river which made the channel that now, in part, but only in part, confines it, and it seems to me that all sorts of realities and completenesses are possible in Philosophy, hitherto stiffened & cramped by the silly littlenesses of the upper and the lower dogmatisms *alternating [ab. del. 'with'] their petty rationalistic and materialistic idols of the shop (Manuscripts Division, Stanford).

On October 21, 1903, James wrote to J. Mark Baldwin: "I don't know whether you or Cattell is in charge of the Psych. Rev. this year, but I think 'tis you. If no one else is in view I should not be unwilling to write a review of Dewey's studies in Logical Theory, or possibly still better, a general article on the Chicago School of Thought, whose recent collective manifestations loom up so massively and harmoniously. I can't tell which I should prefer till I have read more of this book. Don't let me displace you, or anyone else whom you may have been thinking of, however. I am not itching for the job" (bMS Am 1092.1, typed copy). Then in a letter of November 15, 1903, to Schiller once more:

I have had all sorts of outside things shoved upon me since my return a month ago to Cambridge, things for other people, and they *have ['v' *over* 'd'] taken all my energy & tired me out. The best of the lot was reading up the output of the Chicago School of Tho't and reporting it at a "Conference" which Royce has organized. It is splendid stuff, and Dewey is a hero. A real school & real thought. At harvard we have plenty of tho't, but not school. At Yale & cornell, the other way about. . . . Dewey needs a great deal of building out and following of his principles into all sorts of questions of detail. But it's a noble work. Pity that their style should be so dry and abstract . . . I must write a notice of Dewey for the ['Phil' *del.*] Psych. Rev., two other hack *magazine [*ab. del.* 'book'] affairs which I have had to promise to interested parties, etc, etc (bMS Am 1092.9, #3702).

The notes that James made for the conference organized by Royce have been preserved in the James Collection as bMS Am 1092.9, #4451, and have been transcribed in Appendix IV. It would seem that he referred to these notes when writing "The Chicago School."

On November 29, 1903, in a postscript to a letter to James McKeen Cattell, James added: "How late can stuff for the Jan. Psych. Rev. be sent in? I promised Baldwin to review Dewey's Studies in Logical Theory, but haven't been able to touch the article yet. Can begin writing to morrow. But I fear that by this time your Jany. N°. is made up. [¶] I regard these Chicago Decennial Contribs. to Phil. as something extremely important" (Library of Congress, Cattell Papers). Without knowing it, James had involved the article in a split between Baldwin and Cattell in which Cattell left the *Review* to start the *Psychological Bulletin*. Baldwin evidently had not received James's article, which Cattell must have taken with him for the opening number of the *Bulletin*. In a letter to Baldwin of December 5, 1903, James showed he was as yet unaware of Cattell's proposal for the article, since he still assumed it would appear in the *Review* despite the schism: "What do you mean by my paper on pragmatism? I never offered one. Possibly you may be thinking of my review of Dewey and disciples. That was sent to Cattell 3 days ago, and may even now be in your hands" (bMS Am 1092.1, typed copy). The rest of the letter discusses his plan to provide the *Bulletin* with a review of Schiller's *Humanism* to balance the Dewey in the *Review* unless Baldwin would take his writing for the *Bulletin* as an unfriendly act. No record seems to be preserved of his acquiescence in the publication of "The Chicago School" in the *Bulletin* instead of the

Review. These letters set the date of composition, however, between November 29 and December 2 of 1903.

HERBERT SPENCER (1904).

Copy-text: (P⁶) "Herbert Spencer," *Atlantic Monthly*, 94 (July 1904), 99-108 (McD 1904:8). Henry James, Jr., reprinted this essay with the title "Herbert Spencer's Autobiography" in *Memories and Studies*, pp. 107-142 (McD 1911:2), dropping the footnote, correcting an error in the copy-text at 120.28, and correcting the Spencer quotation at 110.40; otherwise, no substantive variants appear. In the James Collection, bMS Am 1092.9, #4565 (Box O, envelope 1, no. 8), is an offprint. A single ink marginal addition of *that* at 116.20 to make the text read *and that has hardly raised its head* is not definitely to be attributed to James. Nevertheless, it is required by the sense and could be his, the more especially since the addition does not appear in *Memories and Studies* and so cannot be attributed to an editorial hand, which in pencil may have written '7000-7500 words' in the upper right corner of the first page.

In a postcard of March 4, 1904, to Bliss Perry, the *Atlantic's* editor, James agreed to review Spencer's autobiography, and on May 10 he wrote:

My review of Spencer has *trainé en longeur*. I send you the first 2 3rds of it. It ought to be finished by Sunday P.M. in a dozen more pages at most.

I fear it will please Sp.'s enemies more than his disciples, but the last couple of pages will be very sympathetic.

There is a good deal of quotation, which if put into finer type *will [ab. del. 'may']* make the article print shorter. I mark ['Truly' *and start of* 'y' *del.*] the same in blue pencil to attract your notice. . . .

[P.S.] May I, if need be, take a little longer than Sunday? *College [intrl.]* Business is pressing just now, & I am very tired (bMS Am 1343, #282).

THE PRAGMATIC METHOD (1904).

Copy-text: (P²⁰) "The Pragmatic Method," *Journal of Philosophy, Psychology, and Scientific Methods*, 1 (Dec. 8, 1904), 673-687 (McD 1904:13). Reference is also made to (TMs) a typescript carbon preserved in the Philosophical Union files of the University Archives of the University of California at Berkeley; to (PC) "Philosophical Conceptions and Practical Results," (Berkeley: The University Press, 1898); and to (Pr) Lecture III "Some Metaphysical Problems Pragmatically Considered," *Pragmatism* (New York and

London: Longmans, Green, 1907) (McD 1907:11), edited in the
WORKS.

On August 26, 1898, James delivered a major address "Philo-
sophical Conceptions and Practical Results" before the Philosophical
Union at the University of California at Berkeley, the opening gun
of his discourses on pragmatism.[12] As early as April 16, James in
Cambridge was discussing the lecture in a letter to his friend
G. H. Howison, at Berkeley:

> But how I dread the fantastic public lecture before your Union! What is
> this new sort of Californian philosophizing which you have organized, to the
> accompaniment of brass bands, yellow journal capitals & caricatures etc., etc?
> I note that it is to be on the 26th., but I see plainly that I must arrive 10 days
> beforehand, and work hard at its composition after conferring with you and
> ascertaining what sort of a thing you want. I will therefore (subject to later
> different advice) turn up about August 15th. . . .
> I should be glad *to read [*ab. del.* 'of'] the insolent attacks which the
> members of the Union have been indulging in through the winter, in order to
> prepare my defence. . . .
> I will answer Mr. Garlick, when I get his letter, naming date, etc. I say for
> clearness sake that you are to pay me $200 for my services (?) to the Union,
> he $400 for my 6 + 1 (=7) lectures (Howison letters in bMS Am 1092.9,
> #1048).

On July 24 James wrote again:

> Your kind letter greeted me on my arrival here three days ago—but I have
> waited to answer it in order to determine just what my lecture's title should
> be. I wanted to make something entirely popular, and as it were emotional,
> for technicality ['in philosophy' *del.*] seems to me *to spell [*ab. del.*
> 'tantamount to'] "failure" in philosophy. But the subject in the margin of
> my consciousness failed to make connexion with the centre, and I have
> fallen back on something less vital, but still, I think, sufficiently popular &
> practical, which you can advertize under the rather ill chosen title of
> "Philosophical conceptions and ['classical' *del.*] practical results," if you
> wish (#1049).

The preserved typescript at Berkeley appears to have been made
up professionally from James's handwritten manuscript. Its title-
page reads:

---

[12]On January 14, 1897, James had initiated the proposal that he give a course of
lectures on psychology to teachers in California. For an account of the negotiations and
the final results, considerably modified, see Frederick J. D. Scott, "William James' 1898
Visit to California," *San Jose Studies*, 3 (Feb. 1, 1977), 7-22. The schedule for the discussion of *The Will to Believe* by members of the Philosophical Union, planned as part
of the visit and the Union lecture, is reprinted as Appendix V in *The Will to Believe*,
WORKS.

[rule] | PHILOSOPHICAL CONCEPTIONS AND PRACTICAL RESULTS |
[rule] | An Address Delivered by | WILLIAM JAMES, M.D., LLD., | At
Berkeley, August 26, 1898, | Before | THE PHILOSOPHICAL UNION. |
[short rule]

The thirty-two pages, including the title, are on wove paper watermarked Crane's Japanese Linen, the date 1897 appearing between
the outline of a crane. One may conjecture that the ribbon copy
was used for the printer of the *University Chronicle*, 1 (September
1898), 287-310, moderately revised both in substantives and in
accidentals. The standing type of the *Chronicle* printing was
thereupon utilized for a pamphlet of twenty-four pages with the
title:

PHILOSOPHICAL UNION OF THE UNIVERSITY OF CALIFORNIA | [short
rule] | PHILOSOPHICAL CONCEPTIONS | AND PRACTICAL RESULTS |
THE ANNUAL PUBLIC ADDRESS BEFORE THE UNION | *AUGUST 26,
1898* | BY | WILLIAM JAMES | PROFESSOR OF PSYCHOLOGY IN HAR-
VARD UNIVERSITY | [short rule] | [Reprinted from THE UNIVERSITY
CHRONICLE for September, 1898.] | [short rule] | BERKELEY | THE
UNIVERSITY PRESS | 1898

In the copy of this pamphlet in the Bancroft Library of the
University of California at Berkeley the title-page is variant: under
'WILLIAM JAMES' instead of 'PROFESSOR OF PSYCHOLOGY
IN HARVARD UNIVERSITY' the reading is 'M.D., Ph.D., Litt.D.,
LL.D., Corresponding Member of the French Institute, | Professor
of Psychology in Harvard University.' Two seemingly authoritative
changes appear in the standing type between *Chronicle* and pamphlet, both on page 18. At 18.12 (133.37) a comma after *life* has
been removed to agree with its absence in the typescript, and at
18.21 (134.5) the necessary word *you*, omitted in typescript and
in *Chronicle*, is added before *yourselves*.

Four copies of the pamphlet are preserved in the James
Collection under AC85.J2376.898p. Copy A is unannotated. Copy
B, like the rest, has on its title James's rubber stamp '*William
James,* | *95 Irving St.,* | *Cambridge, Mass.*' prefixed by his auto-
graph 'Return to', but in this copy with the addition 'who owns
only three copies.' It has a single autograph marking—the ink
marginal addition of *is exerted* at 12.26 (129.4) with a caret after
and. On its title Copy C has the deleted presentation 'E. D. Starbuck
| from W. J.' The note 'Annotated Copy' as well as the note
'Keep' (this latter written on all other copies) are not in James's
hand. Copy C appears to have been marked with some idea of
publication in mind. At 4.36-37 (omitted in P[20]) James added in

ink the word *most* with a caret and guideline before *evident*, inserted a period, and deleted the end of the printed sentence *to our eyes.* On page 8.17 a marginal short horizontal line marks the start of a paragraph (125.19). The local allusion 'The verbal . . . care for." ' (127.21-25) is marked for skipping at 10.31-37, and so is the passage 'The common man . . . really absurd.' (127.29-34) on page 11.3-8. On page 15.5 (131.7) a horizontal marginal line marks the end of the paragraph. It is probably no accident that these marginal lines enclose something close to the material later abstracted for Lecture III of *Pragmatism.* Possibly they have some reference to the entry in the outline for the second Wellesley lecture on fol. 6 of bMS Am 1092.9, #4512 (notebook O in Box L) (see *Pragmatism*, WORKS, Appendix III) 'Cal. address 1898', a direction for reading or for summary. In the left margin of page 18.11-30 (133.36-134.13), against the text 'These direct experiences . . . pragmatism works.', James wrote the note 'Theol. is secondary on religious exp., just as grammar is secondary on the function of language.' This refers to the two lines 26-27 on the page marked in the right margin by a vertical stroke, 'But they are certainly the originals of the God-idea, and theology is the translation' (134.9-10). Finally, on page 24.18 (139.10) the error *hypothesis* is corrected to *hypotheses.* Copy D is inscribed 'C. C. Everett from W. J.' Its revised and condensed version of the text, all in James's hand, was the actual printer's copy for "The Pragmatic Method."

James wrote on September 10, 1904, to F. J. E. Woodbridge, editor of the *Journal of Philosophy, Psychology, and Scientific Methods*, opening the question of publication of "The Pragmatic Method":

Dear Woodbridge

The "Pragmatic Method" was first made public in an address which I made at the U. of California 5 or 6 years ago "Philosophical Conceptions & Practical Results.["] I applied it to the Theistic question—it having slumbered since Chas. Peirce first formulated it about 1870.

That address of mine was printed in the Cal. University Magazine which has absolutely no circulation outside. I had 30 reprints which I distributed. Apart from that it can hardly be said to be published. It is interesting reading and not technical. It has occurred to me, since "pragmatism" is so much talked about to day, and I am named, that it would be well for *me* to have my exact words on the subject published again. I wonder if it wd. be *infra dig* in your Journal to print something already printed,[x] omitting of course 2 or 3 pp. of California palaver.

If you like, I will send you one of my two remaining copies, to enable you to decide.

Truly yours,
Wm James

[x]I will gladly pay for composition (Columbia University).

On September 25, James wrote: "Thanks for yours of the 18th. I send you the California lecture, of which I find only the 1st. three pp. can be omitted. Some of the stuff has been worked in to my chapter on Philosophy in the Varieties of Rel. Exp., but not much. If you conclude *not* to reprint it, please let me have this copy back. I *can [*ab. del.* 'only'] lay my hand on only two others. If you print it I will add nothing, but let it go with its own date, etc. I should like in that case 200 reprints" (Columbia University). James kept his word, for although the first three pages of the copy are marked for deletion, and the next two pages have a few substantive alterations, he contented himself for the rest chiefly with substituting single for double quotation marks. On October 12 he jogged Woodbridge: "I suppose you got the California lecture which I sent you *10 [*over* '8 or'] days or so ago. If you think best not to print it, pray send it back. Take your time!" Proofs seem to have arrived on November 16, according to a letter of that date. The *Journal* was received on December 11, and James wrote on a postcard: "Hurrah for the 'Pragmatic Method' in the Journal! Will it now be possible to send me the 200 desideratio off-prints *promptly?*" On December 18: "No signs of reprints as yet! I waited more than 3 weeks for the last ones. [¶] Is it too much for me to ask for a revise of the proof which I mailed you last night ["The Thing and Its Relations"]? The printers made havoc of one of my corrections in the last proof ["The Pragmatic Method"]—so much so that I think an erratum had better be inserted. Of course ['it wil' *del.*] this will come too late for the next number, but it might well appear in the form of a P.S. to the article I sent last night. I write it on the opposite page." The note was:

ERRATUM. In my *recent [*intrl.*] article on the Pragmatic method, page 684, last line of third paragraf, read 'further,' instead of 'logical.' On the next line above, read 'insignificant' instead of 'significant' and 'a' instead of 'the.' To the line above that, after 'abstract' add the following words: 'noetic unity, as we may call it is a very.' W.J.

The requested alterations of *the noetic* to *a noetic* (136.18) and of *further* for *logical* (136.19) occasion no difficulty. The printer, however, had dropped a whole line of type *noetic unity (as one might call it) is practically an extremely in-* so that the next line began with the nonsense *significant.* In repairing the damage it is not wholly clear that James had before him the original text so that he was aware of what had been lost. If he had, his change to *noetic unity, as we may call it*[,] *is a very insignificant* might be debatable, but the partial recovery of the line seems to indicate that he knew what was wanting and was deliberately changing the expression. These requested variants, therefore, have been adopted in the present edition. Since the offprint found in #4565 is unannotated, no further guides to James's final intentions about the text have been preserved except for the alterations he made when he utilized a portion in Lecture III of *Pragmatism*. These variants were for another occasion, however, and though recorded in the Historical Collation, along with the variants in TMs and in PC, have not been introduced into the text. "Philosophical Conceptions and Practical Results" will be found reprinted as Appendix I of *Pragmatism* in the WORKS in a reading text emended by reference to TMs and to the annotated copies in the James Collection, with an Historical Collation of variants from the typescript.[13]

As late as February 7, 1906, James was still concerned to secure extra copies of "Philosophical Conceptions" despite his reworking in "The Pragmatic Method." On that date he wrote to Howison, from Stanford: "I wish to ask seriously if you cannot give me *one* (or two?) of the remaining reprints of my address 'Philosophical

---

[13] Dr. Scott, *ibid.*, p. 20, has cast doubt on the authority of the differences between the typescript and the printed text by a blanket statement that they were all the work of Howison, the evidence being James's letter of October 22, 1898, after publication: "A word to tell you that the reprints have arrived and look very well. I commend all your changes and wish you had made more. I revere your self-control in not re-writing the passage about Kant."(For the point of this reference to Kant, see Scott, below on p. 20.) Since the printer's copy, the ribbon of the preserved typescript, is wanting, we cannot tell whether Howison made his alterations in this copy or in proof after James had marked in the proof what he wanted. The terms of the letter might suggest the latter. However, that James had himself read proof and was responsible for the major differences between TMs and the printed pamphlet can scarcely be doubted when the list of variants is analyzed in connection with his known habits of perfecting his work in proof. For instance, it is quite impossible to conceive that Howison would have altered TMs *my colleague at Harvard* to printed *whose colleague at Harvard I am proud to be* (134.37), or would have tinkered with TMs *has contributed absolutely nothing serious* to printed (UC) *has really contributed nothing serious* (129.12), or would have italicized *nothing* for the roman of TMs (130.3) or for that matter reduced to roman the italic emphasis as at 125.2 and 125.3 or rearranged the position of James's joke about the escaped Berkeley student at 127.23-25, and so on and so on. The implication is easy to draw from Dr. Scott's statement that James never read proof, but the evidence is strong to the contrary. This being so, James may be thanking Howison for minor stylistic tinkering (perhaps such as marks the change from the prefix *in-* to *un-* at 132.9,39) and other minor 'improvements' such as what may be the sophistication *philosophical* for TMs *philosophic* (127.20) (compare 51.21 in the Historical Collation for "The Sentiment of Rationality" and Perry's similar change). That Howison would rewrite TMs as illustrated by the numerous variants after James had sent in his marked proof is too fantastic a proposition to be credited. That James had indeed read proof is certain and should have been more strongly emphasized in the account of the text in *Pragmatism*. In short, the printed text is authoritative less by reason of James's approval of whatever changes Howison had made than by James's own proofreading changes from TMs.

Conceptions' etc? Papini, of Florence, who is about publishing a book on *Il Prammatismo* has just written to me supplicating me to find him a copy. If any one deserves it, he does—therefore pray send it hither, and deeply oblige yours affectionately" (bMS Am 1092.9, #1060). On February 9 Howison replied that the Union had just twenty-five copies left, from which the Secretary was sending James twelve. On February 14 James acknowledged to Howison the receipt of the copies.

PREFACE TO HÖFFDING'S *PROBLEMS OF PHILOSOPHY* (1905).

Copy-text: (HP) *The Problems of Philosophy*, by Harald Höffding, translated by Galen M. Fisher (New York: Macmillan, 1906), pp. v-xiv (McD 1905:12, *wrongly listed as* 1906:6). The book was copyrighted by Macmillan under A 129530, October 24, 1905, and two copies were deposited in the Library of Congress on the same day. The publication date was October 26, 1905. A second printing appeared in October 1906; collation discloses that the plates for James's Preface are invariant between the two. The title-page reads: 'THE PROBLEMS OF | PHILOSOPHY | BY | HARALD HÖFFDING | TRANSLATED BY | GALEN M. FISHER | WITH A PREFACE BY | WILLIAM JAMES | 𝔑𝔢𝔴 𝔜𝔬𝔯𝔨 | THE MACMILLAN COMPANY | LONDON: MACMILLAN & CO., LTD. | 1905 | *All rights reserved*'. James's copy (WJ 350.39) is of the second printing.

The story of James's making arrangements for the translation and publication of *The Problems of Philosophy*, and then his involvement in revising the translation in proof and furnishing the index, begins in a letter he wrote to Harald Höffding on October 17, 1903: "I thank you most heartily for sending me your philosophische Probleme. I have read every word of it with the intensest interest, and for the most part with adhesion. It is a luminous little *multum in parvo*—why don't more philosophers succeed in writing themselves down ['so' *del.*] in so brief a compass. [¶] I admire immensely your making of 'continuity' the centre of gravity of everything, and the way in which you work to it and from it. I take great pleasure in your willingness to admit a real discontinuity, and to treat absolute unity as *the ['t' *over* 'a'] goal of a real process by which the tendency to unity gets fulfilled. [¶] I regard the book as a very strong blow to Absolutism" (bMS Am 1092.9, #1000). Höffding visited James in the summer of 1904. On January 22, 1905, James wrote: "I haven't yet laid my hand on a translator ['of' *del.*] for your Phil. Prob. I ought to do it myself, but my working powers are too small, decidedly, for me to undertake any translation at all. We shall see" (#1003). On March 9 James reports that "A young man named Fisher (G. M.) 31 Sacramento Street, Cambridge, has translated about one third of your philosophische Probleme, *very well*, and in the summer, I must try to find a publisher. I shall be happy to contribute a short preface, if you dont object. It may help sales. But if we cannot find a publisher to take it at his own risk, should you feel like putting any money of your own into it? I am myself willing to *do ['d' *over* 's'] something, but not all, I will write to you again about it when I return in June" (#1004).

The promised letter was written on July 21, 1905:

> I have waited to write the letter till I should be able to give you news of the translation of your Philosophische Probleme. It is finished (by one Galen Fisher, now gone to Japan) and the Macmillan Company agree to publish it, paying you 15% of the price of each copy sold *above 1000*. This leaves you nothing until 1000 copies are sold, but I am sure it would be vain to seek anything more favorable from another publisher; so, to save time, I am sending them the MS., leaving a few specifications to be settled later, and asking for 50 dollars outright for Mr. Fisher.
>
> I am to revise the proof, and write a preface. Do you care to write a new preface[?] The translation is, I think, good, and I imagine that I shall be following your wishes if I sacrifice verbal literality to ['easy en' *del.*] clear english sentences, in my proof correcting (#1005).

On August 15 Höffding replied from Denmark thanking James for his interest in the book, accepting the terms, and adding: "I am glad also that you will revise the translation and write a preface, which will certainly be a very good thing for the success of the book. Perhaps you will accentuate the points, where we disagree, and this would give the book a peculiar interest.—I myself do'nt wish to write a preface.—" (bMS Am 1092.9, #227).

James's diary notes on August 27, 1905, "Proofs of Höffding's book came," and on September 6 he wrote on a postcard to Höffding: "I am sending you the 1st 78 pp. of paged proof of the problems—not the last revision—as a specimen. It will be too late for alterations suggested by you. I have had to do a *great deal* of proof-revision, the translator having done his work less well than I expected, and the bill will be heavy—leider Gottes!" (#1006). On September 12 James recorded in his diary, "I write preface to Hoffding" and followed this entry with the word "Proofs." The next day, the 13th, he noted once again "Proofs" and in the line below, "Index," an entry that indicates he himself made up the index, as he had expected. On September 21 appears "Proof of preface of Höffding," and on the 22nd, "Proofs of *last pages [*ab. del* 'preface'] & index." A letter to Höffding on October 4 reads:

This is to let you know that the last proof (stereotype) has gone off—title, index, & all, and that the book ought now to appear in a couple of weeks.

I regret to say that the corrections are very *heavy, [*comma over period*] ['Mr.' *del.*] and that the bill for them will be very large. Mr. Fisher has a good command of idiomatic english, but his knowledge of german was insufficient and he made many mistakes. Besides his translation was too literal—preserving all the german *words*—words which *lubricate* in german, but which complicate & obstruct in English. I had to *re-write ['r' *over* 'w'] about a 5th. of the whole[.] I am sorry for the expense entailed. I could n't do it on the closely written MS.—it had to be done on the proof.[14] You will receive ½ a dozen copies soon, and I shall receive ½ a dozen which I will place where they can do most service. The publisher will of course supply the Journals with copies for review.

I am going to use it as a text in my course in Metaphysics. And that reminds me that I promised a student that I would ask you if you could send a Danish copy. Send it to me; I will give it to our Harvard Library; and he can read it thus (#1007).

On October 26 the diary records, "Hoffdings Problems published." On October 12, after expressing regret that "the correction of the proof-sheets has been so toilsome," Höffding insisted, "As to the bill, it is to be put exclusively on my account" (#228). On October 17 he insisted again, on a postcard, that he be sent the bill for the corrections. After receiving copies of the book, Höffding wrote on November 11 thanking James for his care with the translation, with which he professes himself much pleased, praising the "masterly exposition of my views" in the preface, and again requesting a bill. James replied from Stanford on January 28, 1906:

I have been expecting to ['gett' *del.*] get a bill for extra proof corrections from Macmillan. Not getting it yet, the idea has occurred to me that you may have written to them to pass over my head and send it directly to you. If so, it was very delicate on your part, and I thank you. I was expecting to pay it, and *to [*intrl.*] have an auseinandersetzung with you—for I really feel as if I ought to have paid some of it, since instead of making corrections *in [*over* 'on'] the MS. I did it on the proof. However, the former course was impossible. The bill must be a heavy one. Will you kindly tell me if my hypothesis is a correct one, and gratify my curiosity by letting me know the size of the bill. I have just received a letter from Mr. Fisher, who is in charge of "Young Men's Xian Association" work in Japan, expressing satisfaction with the 50 dollars that Macmillan allowed him, and saying that I have practically rewritten the

[14]In a letter of February 6, 1906, to Giovanni Papini, James remarked, "I recently got a little book ('the Problems of philosophy,' by Harald Höffding translated; but I had to rewrite the thing almost when I came to revise the proofs, which made the job very expensive" (courtesy of Signora Paolo Casini).

work. I regret extremely now that I did not print, as an appendix, your splendid little summarizing paper in the Journal of Philosophy. I thought of it too late, & I wish that you had reminded me (#1008).

If Höffding answered this request for information, the letter has not been preserved.

G. PAPINI AND THE PRAGMATIST MOVEMENT IN ITALY (1906).

Copy-text: (P[20]) "G. Papini and the Pragmatist Movement in Italy," *Journal of Philosophy, Psychology, and Scientific Methods,* 3 (June 21, 1906), 337-341 (McD 1906:3). Reprinted in *Collected Essays and Reviews,* ed. R. B. Perry (1920), pp. 459-466, without substantive alteration save for the correction of a misprint at 144.12.

On April 27, 1906, from Del Monte, California, James sent a letter to Papini that not only announces his intention to write about Papini's work but also refers to it in terms close to those of the article, which—according to his diary—was composed on May 15, 1906 ("I write article on Papini"):

My dear friend and master, Papini,
I have just been reading your Crespuscoli dei Filosofi, and the February number of Leonardo, and great is the resultant fortification of my soul. What a thing is genius! and you are a real genius! Here have I, with my intellectual timidity and conscientiousness, *been [*intrl.*] painfully trying to clear a few steps of the pathway that leads to the systematized new Weltanschauung, and you with a ['single' *del.*] pair of bold strides, get out *in a moment [*intrl.*] beyond the pathway altogether into the freedom of the whole system, into the open country. It is your *temper of carelessness,* quite as much as your particular formulas, that has had such an emancipating effect on my intelligence. You will be accused of extravagance, and *correctly* accused; you will be called the Cyrano de Bergerac of Pragmatism, etc; but the abstract program of it *must* be sketched extravagantly. "Correctness" is one of the standards of the older way of philosophizing, that looks in the particular fact for the ghost of some "principle" that legitimates its being, and takes *creation* out of reality. If creation takès place in particulars, as I have always "seen reasons for believing" but now "believe," "correctness" is not a category for judging anything real, and to ['be entire' *del.*] show a temper entirely careless of it as you do, is of edifying example and of good augury. I myself suspect that you are hoping too much from telepathy, mediumship, etc:, but no matter, we can all gather from you the example of courage, and I have done so. I wish that I could stop lecturing and begin writing, but for one year more, at least, I must continue. I shall soon write a notice of the Crepuscolo & Leonardo for Woodbridge's journal, and call you the master of the movement now. You're such a brilliant, humorous and witty writer! It is splendid to see old Italy renovating *us all [*ab. del.* 'herself'] in this way (courtesy of Signora Paolo Casini).

THE MAD ABSOLUTE (1906).

Copy-text: (P²⁰) "The Mad Absolute," *Journal of Philosophy, Psychology, and Scientific Methods*, 3 (Nov. 22, 1906), 656-657 (McD 1906:4). Reprinted in *Collected Essays and Reviews*, ed. R. B. Perry (1920), pp. 467-469, without substantive variation except for a misprint at 149.6.

BRADLEY OR BERGSON? (1910).

Copy-text: (P²⁰) "Bradley or Bergson?" *Journal of Philosophy, Psychology, and Scientific Methods*, 7 (Jan. 20, 1910), 29-33 (McD 1910:1). Reprinted without substantive variation except for the correction of a misprint at 153.33 in *Collected Essays and Reviews*, ed. R. B. Perry (1920), pp. 491-499. A complete draft manuscript (MS) is preserved in the James Collection as the first item in a Partridge and Cooper hardbound notebook, blue wove un-watermarked paper, 245 x 198 mm., catalogued as bMS Am 1092.9, #4519 (Box L, notebook Nᵛⁱⁱⁱ). The inscription, in pencil, begins on the first leaf of the notebook after a stub marking a cut-out leaf, and continues unfoliated on the rectos to fol. 20. A pencil note appears on fol. 13ᵛ relating to the text of fol. 14 but otherwise all versos are blank. Some notes on Bergson appear in Box F, envelope 9, but they are not so directly related to the present article as to be reproduced here. An unannotated offprint of P²⁰ is found in bMS Am 1092.9, #4565 (Box O, envelope 6).

James's diary records on November 28, 1909, "Wrote article 'Bergson or Bradley?' " and on the 29th "Type-wrote & mailed my article." It was promptly accepted, according to a reference in a letter to Schiller of December 4 in which James congratulates him on his own article on Bradley: "In a later part *(IV) [*intrl.*] I'm not quite sure that you do justice to B's having broken away from the Greenian crew by having asserted the unity of feeling. He keeps asserting it in his October article, on which I myself have made a brief comment which Woodbridge has accepted & of which I'll send you proof" (Stanford). On December 23 James addressed Bradley (presumably enclosing the revised proofs):

> The momentum acquired by my pen in its last note to you was so great that it overflowed into an article which I sent to the J. of P., and of which I now send you a revised proof, just in.
>
> I trust that you will not take offense, and that possibly the spirit may move you at some future time, when you feel very hearty, to say (in print) just why we *may* not use both perception and conception in philosophy as we use both blades of a pair of scissors. I find myself more and more satisfied by

taking them both up *tels quels* (or *telles quelles?*!) and letting the trans conceptual region vigorously alone. I hope at any rate that you may be struck by ['the' *del.*] some pregnancy in the parallel between you and Bergson which I draw.[15]

In a letter of December 31, 1909, Schiller acknowledged receipt of a set of proofs and discussed various points, making a number of suggestions. James responded on January 16, 1910:

'Tis a great letter that comes from you this morning. Your tho't is far finer grained than mine, and I wish it were not too late to incorporate some of your marginalia on the proof into my article on B^y & B^n. But I understand it to appear this week, so it must ['go ap-' | *del.*] go *in [*intrl.*] without them. As regards Bergson, it is barely possible that I am overdoing his rôle as a pragmatist. I confess *that there is much that I fail to un[*ab. del.* 'I don't un-'|] derstand ['much' *del.*] in his way of thinking, in particular, *I don't understand [*ab. del.* 'not'] how much his *'intuition' [*final* 'ism' *del.*] as the philosofic attitude, differs from the usual 'mystical' ['el' *del.*] enlargement of immediate perception. But I don't *understand [*ab. del.* 'take'] him *(as you seem to) [*parens over commas*] to treat that same intuition as in any sense *copying* reality—it is, I think, *an [*del., then insrtd.*] immediate['ly' *del.*] experience [*final* 'e' *over* 'ing'] *of reality, [*ab. del.* 'it,'] only in a wider form ['that' *del.*] than ['is n' *del.*] the naif man uses (Stanford).

On January 10 the *Journal* queried James, "Did you receive revised galley proof of your article on Bradley and Bergson, and if you did have you returned it?" At the foot of the letter James responded: "The 2 revises I asked for were rec'd all right, and I sent them to Bradley & Bergson respectively. They needed no correction, and *I [*intrl.*] didn't know that you usually wated *for ['f' *over* 'b'] revises. Print without them!" (Columbia University). On January 20, the diary noted that the article had appeared.

The draft state of the manuscript, combined with the fact that James made his own typescript and read both proofs and revises, leads to the choice of the *Journal* article as copy-text. It would appear to represent James's final intentions with relatively greater faithfulness than the manuscript, since James usually considered his manuscripts, as well as any intermediate typescripts, as drafts to be worked over in proof.

In response to James's sending of proofs, Bergson replied on March 31, 1910:

Je ne vous ai pas encore parlé de votre très intéressant article "Bradley or Bergson?" Le cas Bradley y devient tout-à-fait instructif et frappant. C'est

[15] J. C. Kenna, "Ten Unpublished Letters from James to Bradley," *Mind*, n.s. 75 (July 1966), 329. The reference to the origin of the article is found in the preceding letter no. 8.

celui d'un penseur qui retrouve, aiguisées et subtilisées en problèmes dialectiques insolubles, les réalités toutes simples qu'il n'a pas voulu accepter bonnement sous leur forme naturelle, sous prétexte qu'elles ne comptent pas pour la philosophie. Il était piquant de montrer que Bradley envisage les concepts absolument comme le ferait un non-intellectualiste. Et il était non moins piquant de montrer en lui un esemple de ce que peut le Will to believe! (bMS Am 1092.9, #39).

A SUGGESTION ABOUT MYSTICISM (1910).

Copy-text: (P²⁰) "A Suggestion about Mysticism," *Journal of Philosophy, Psychology, and Scientific Methods,* 7 (Feb. 7, 1910), 85-92 (McD 1910:2). Reprinted without substantive change, other than the correction of a misprint at 158.3, in *Collected Essays and Reviews,* ed. R. B. Perry (1920), pp. 500-513.

The incomplete start of the essay is preserved in manuscript (MS), in the James Collection, bMS Am 1092.9, #4519 (Box L, notebook N^viii). This notebook is from Partridge and Cooper, London, hardbound, the leaves of blue wove unwatermarked paper 245 x 198 mm. The first item is the draft, in pencil, of "Bradley or Bergson?," fols. 1-20, followed by fols. 21-26, the start of a draft of "The Moral Equivalent of War." After a cut-out leaf marked by a stub, "A Suggestion about Mysticism" begins, written in pencil with a few ink alterations added to the copious pencil changes, headed "A suggestion about mysticism," foliated 1-9 and inscribed on fols. 27-34 of the notebook rectos, including a brief addition on fol. 6ᵛ (fol. 33ᵛ) and fol. 9 written on the verso of fol. 33. On the verso of fol. 34 is a blank paste-over covering a reversed page of pencil notes for *Some Problems of Philosophy.* The final part of the text, numbered 9, continues the text of fol. 8 onto 8ᵛ, first horizontally about halfway down the leaf and then vertically in the upper half. Following this truncated draft, which was intended to end where it does, is a series of 86 stubs for missing leaves. When the notebook continues, with a page on Perry and then a number of leaves of drafts for *Some Problems,* the book has been reversed and the inscription is from the back forward.

The diary entries for December 16-17, 1909, indicate the speed with which the notebook draft was written on the first day, carrying the text up to the end of the paragraph at 159.27: a brief entry for December 16 notes, "Write on Mysticism"; and the next day, the 17th, "Copy & mail mysticism article." The autobiographical memorandum on his dreams, on February 12-13, 1906, at Stanford, has not been preserved. Since all the material in this notebook dates from 1909, it is not at all likely that the dreams had been recorded among the leaves represented now in notebook N^{viii} only by stubs. Possibly the description had been preserved in some written-up loose leaves, close to their final form, so that when James copied the article on December 17 he merely added these to the fair copy of the notebook draft. If this is so, the journal article was set from an authorial fair copy (typescript or holograph) of the notebook draft and then continued with un-known copy, probably holograph but possibly dictated or typed. On December 20, 1909, a letter to Woodbridge, editor of the *Journal*, announces briefly, "Here goes another applicant for a place in the J. of P. I hope you may look kindly on it" (Columbia University).

A GREAT FRENCH PHILOSOPHER AT HARVARD (1910).

Copy-text: (P^{25}) "A Great French Philosopher at Harvard," *Nation*, 90 (March 31, 1910), 312-314 (McD 1910:4). On March 26, 1910, James wrote to Dickinson S. Miller, "Boutroux, who is a regular angel, has just left our house. I've written an account of his lectures which the 'Nation' will print on the 31st. I should like you to look it over, hasty as it is" (*Letters*, II, 332).

A PLURALISTIC MYSTIC (1910).

Copy-text: (P^{17}) "A Pluralistic Mystic," *Hibbert Journal*, 8 (July 1910), 739-759 (McD 1910:5). Reprinted without substantive variation by Henry James, Jr., in *Memories and Studies* (1911), pp. 369-411.

The James Collection (bMS Am 1452.1[23]) contains a set of galley-proofs (P^{17}[p]) stamped in blue SECOND PROOF and dated by the printer May 31, 1910. The lower left corner of the first galley, corresponding to 'practically . . . named.' (173.17-29, 37-40) has been torn off. James's markings in the master copy of these second proofs returned to the *Hibbert Journal* are recoverable by collation of the proofs against the *Journal* text, recorded in the Historical Collation. In making these late revisions, James filled in a missing part of a date (173.1), altered four words (176.8, 181.24, 182.8, 190.10), omitted a sentence (190.12-13), put a roman word into italic (181.17), added two hyphens in compounds (178.12, 179.39), and changed four punctuation marks (176.6, 177.23, 177.23-25, 188.4). He did not transfer these mark-ings to the duplicate proofs, and since the three changes noted there are not found in the *Journal* text they appear to have been made too late to incorporate. Some of the markings in the preserved proofs are no more than notes to himself, like the *Self-relation* he wrote in the margin opposite 177.31-33 and presumably the brackets he drew in the margin opposite three passages.[16] But at 174.33 he deleted *means* and in the margin wrote *should say*, at 176.2 he deleted the comma after *ground*, and at 177.24 he first queried and then deleted *yet* after *while*. Since these three post-proof alterations appear to represent true final intentions, they have been adopted as emendations in the present text.

In MS Am 1092.9, #4547, is preserved a collection of early notes and the broken-off start of a draft of the article. The notes start with three leaves of a thick light-blue wove paper (250 x 200 mm.), unwatermarked. The first two leaves, written in pencil by James, are unnumbered, but the third, also in pencil, is foliated 3 in ink in the upper right corner. The fourth leaf, foliated 4 in ink at the upper right, is a sheet of heavy white wove typewriter paper (253 x 203 mm.) watermarked with a wheat sheaf between the hollow letters THE HEDLEY | NOTE, and in script, Waterlow & Sons | Limited. This fourth leaf begins with two words in pencil by James continuing fol. 3, followed by a quotation written in ink by James's wife Alice, and concludes with James's inscription in ink. Its text completes the page in mid-sentence but the rest of the text, whatever it was, on the next and perhaps other leaves is missing. The notes conclude with four leaves, each containing a quotation from Blood, written in ink on the Waterlow paper by Alice James.

In the same folder is an incomplete draft manuscript (MS[1]) consisting of eleven leaves of L. L. Brown wove typewriter paper foliated [1] 2-4, 6(5), 7(6), 8(7), 9(8), 10-11. The inscription is in ink and stops on fol. 11, which is only about three-quarters filled with text. Folio 4 is a part-page substitute for a discarded leaf but its text does not link with fol. 6, renumbered from 5. Evidently reworked leaves 4 and 5 (fol. 5 now lost) substituted for an original fol. 4, with consequent renumbering, the expansion being made before fol. 10 was written, or at least before it and fol. 11 were numbered. The notes and this draft text are transcribed in Appendix V, a record of their alterations being added in Appendix VI.

The final manuscript (MS[2]) completes this folder. It is marked

---

[16]Marginal brackets appear opposite 174.6 *sometimes dialectic ... proceed.* 174.11; 174.37 *The beginning ... signifies.* 175.2 (in which *the stare of being at itself, in the* appears to be underlined); and 178.32 *So ... philosophy.* " 178.42 (in which a later marking seems to set off *in the clear perception ... philosophy.*"). At the head of the seventh galley beginning *I have spoken* (182.13) James marked a space.

by compositors and was the printer's copy for the *Hibbert Journal* (P^{17}) text. The manuscript, written in ink, is foliated 1-11, 12(5), 13(6), 14(7), 15(8), 16(9), 17(10), 18(11), 19(12), 20(13), 21(14), 22(15,22^a), 23(22^b), 24, 25(16,23), 26(24), 27^a(25,26), 27^b, 28(26^a), 29(26^b), 30(26^c), 31(27), 32(28), 33(29), 34(30), 35(31), 36(32), 37(33), 38(5,34), 39(35), 40(36), 41^a(37), 41^b, 42(38), 43(39), 44(40), 45(41), 46(42), 47(43), 48(44), 49-50. Folios 1-2, 6-11 are numbered in pencil; fols. 3-5 are in ink; fol. 12 is renumbered in pencil from pencil 5, 13 in pencil from ink 6, 14-21 renumbered in pencil from pencil originals, 22 in pencil from ink 15 and an added 'a' in ink, 23 in ink from ink 22^b, 24 in ink, the 5 of 25 in ink from pencil 23 and ink 16, the 6 of 26 in ink over pencil 24. From fol. 27^a to the end the original numbering and all altered foliation is in ink. Folio 1, headed 'A Pluralistic Mystic | William James' (the former triple underlined and the latter inserted and double underlined), is written on the Waterlow paper, but fol. 2 starts the sequence of blue wove paper (250 x 200 mm.) water-marked PARTRIDGE AND COOPER | CHANCERY LANE. The only variation from this blue paper is an inserted footnote on fol. 4 on a Waterlow sheet and an added leaf, fol. 38, with a clipping from Blood pasted on a leaf of L. L. Brown typewriter paper. The versos of fols. 27^b, 34, and 44 contain rejected text. That on fol. 27^{bv} was originally a trial for the start of fol. 30; that on fol. 34^v was the original continuation of fol. 27^a; that on fol. 44^v was a trial for the start of fol. 28. On fol. 50^v is the editor's pencil note to the printer marking the copy 'urgent'.

The use of the Waterlow paper for fol. 1 and for the inserted leaf containing footnote 4 indicates that fol. 1 (172.1 *Not . . . name of* 172.8) is a revision of a lost original on Partridge and Cooper paper; but this is a revision of a revision, for fols. 1-11 (172.1 *Not . . . distinguished from* 175.8) are manifestly an expanded version of original lost leaves 1-4 on the evidence of the renumbered fol. 12 from 5 and the part-page of text on linking fol. 11. The lower half of fol. 19 (originally 12) below an opening ink inscription consists of a pasted-in clipping (177.12 ᴧ *Sameness . . . well.* 177.22), the first of several such pieces of verbatim quotation from Blood. At first, original fol. 15 was renumbered as 22, continued on renumbered 23. However, James added footnote 2 on a leaf that he first foliated 22^b, renumbering 22 as 22^a; but when he continued the footnote with fol. 24, he went back, deleted the 'a' from 22, changed 22^b to 23, and altered the original continuation of text from 23 to 25. The original sequence stops with this original fol. 16, renumbered first 23 and then 25 (178.24

... *of criticism.* [plus deleted text]). Its lower third was deleted; but that the sequence originally continued beyond 16 is shown by the fact that the excised text joins with no preserved leaf. Instead, a rewriting starts with fol. 26 (originally 24)(178.25 *But Mr. Blood*), and this sequence continues to the end with only a few interruptions, although how much was rewritten beyond lost original fol. 17 cannot be known. Originally fol. 27^a was 25 altered to 26. Its foot was deleted and a revision started on what is now fol. 34^v, which in turn was deleted and fol. 28 (originally 26) (180.3 *There...remains.'* 180.18) was written. The direction for a paste-on clipping for footnote 5 on fol. 29, first numbered 26^b, places this note on fol. 26^a, later altered to 28. The addition with references to a fol. 26 in existence shows that fol. 28, first numbered 26 and then 26^a, originally followed the undeleted text of present 25 (originally 16 and then 23). However, the clipping for footnote 4 was inserted on 27^b with a direction placing it on 'p. 27^a'. Thus original 25 having been changed to 26, was then made 27^a, followed by 27^b, its continuation, and then by renumbered 28. On fol. 37(33) appears a mixture of handwritten text and clippings, but fol. 38 (34) is entirely a paste-on clipping (184.9 *'It is ... soul.'* 185.3) with its head and foot deleted, an extra clipping pasted over the excised text at the foot. The interesting point here is that this leaf was originally numbered 5 (centered), now deleted. This must have been the numbering of a preparatory series of leaves of clippings pasted on L. L. Brown sheets, for in no way could this text precede original fol. 6, renumbered 13, on Partridge and Cooper paper. Another footnote, the seventh, was added by a clipping on fol. 41^b, an expansion that made fol. 41(37) become 41^a. Thereafter no detectable revisions of the manuscript appear except for the necessary renumbering for the final foliation.

Although the authority of the printer's-copy MS^2 is very high indeed, James as usual worked over the proofs for correction and extensive revision particularly in the lost first proofs. Thus the choice of the *Hibbert Journal* (P^{17}) as copy-text accepts the document with the final overall authority but one that requires correction on occasion to replace some features of its housestyling with James's familiar accidental characteristics as they appear in the printer's-copy MS^2.

On April 30, 1910, James's diary records, "During these last days, in addition to *writing & [*intrl.*] mailing an article on Blood to Jacks, I have read ... " and on May 26, "Proofs of Hibbert J. article."

The letter of acceptance on May 2, 1910, from Lawrence Piersall

Jacks, editor of the *Hibbert Journal*, reads in part:

Let *facts* tell you what I think of your article. During the past year I have turned back over a thousand; there are forty accepted ['artic' *del.*] in my drawer & quarrels proceeding, *re* postponement, with most of their authors; there is a basketful waiting examination; but I had no sooner finished your last page than I placed the whole, without interrupting volition, in an envelope & sent it to the printer. Q.E.D.

How I rejoice when the cataracts of sawdust cease for a moment & the living waters of vision fall on my aching head! I splash, and wallow & think.

Your man Blood is great: and the world will thank you for digging him out. "Full many a gem" etc. I want to read about him again & again (bMS Am 1092, #441).

At the start of a letter of May 24, 1910, Jacks wrote: "I send herewith the proof & Ms of your article & I shall be glad to have the latter back as soon as possible. Thanks also for the Blood literature which is delightful and tonic—and great" (#443). Since James was in Germany, he was able to return the proofs promptly so that the printer dated the second proofs May 30, 1910. On May 29, James wrote from Nauheim to his daughter Peggy:

The very *first* thing I want you to do is to look in the drawer marked "Blood" in my tall filing case in the library closet, and find the *date* of a number of the Journal of Speculative philosophy there that contains an article called *"Philosophic Reveries."* Send this *date* *not the article [*intrl.*] to the Revd Prof. L. P. Jacks, 28 Holywell, Oxford, if you find it, *immediately*. He will understand what to do with it. If you don't find the article, do nothing! Jacks is notified. I have just corrected the proofs of an article on Blood for the Hibbert J. which, I think, will make people sit up and rub there eyes at the apparition of a new great writer of english. I want Blood himself to get it as a surprise (bMS Am 1092.9, #3113).

From England on June 25, 1910, James wrote to Blood a most characteristic letter (bMS Am 1092.9, #761), known only in a copy made by James's daughter Margaret after his death, his son noting at the head: 'Copy made by M. M. J. Blood would not part with the original. (H. J.)':

My dear Blood— About the time you will receive this, you will also be surprized by receiving the Hibbert Journal for July, with an article signed by me, but written mainly by yourself. Tired of waiting for your final synthetic pronunciamento, and fearing I might be cut off ere it came I took time by the forelock, & at the risk of making ducks and drakes of your thought, I resolved to save at any rate some of your rhetoric, and the result is what you see. Forgive! forgive! forgive! It will at any rate have made you *famous*, for the circulation of the H. J. is *choice* as well as large (12,000 or more, I'm told) and the print and paper the best ever yet. I seem to have lost the editor's letter, or I ['wld' *del.*] wd. send it to you. He wrote in accepting the article in May

"I have already 40 articles accepted, and some of the writers threaten lawsuits for non-publication, yet such was the exquisite refreshment Blood's writing gave me, under the cataract of sawdust in which editorially I live, that I have this day sent the article to the printer. Actions speak louder than words! Blood is simply *great*, and you are to be thanked for having dug him out. L. P. Jacks."

Of course I've used you for my own purposes, and probably misused you, but I'm sure you will feel more pleasure than pain, and perhaps write again in the Hibbert ['Journal' *del.*] to set yourself right. You're sure of being printed, whatever you may send.

How I wish that I too *cd. ['d' *over* 'o'] write poetry, for pluralism is in its *Sturm und drang* period and verse is the only way to express certain things. I've just been taking the "cure" at Nauheim for my unlucky heart, no results so far! Sail for home again on August 12th. Address always Cambridge, Mass. Things are forwarded. Warm regards, fellow pluralist! Yours ever,

Wm. James

Pasted in Henry James, Jr.'s, private corrected copy of *Memories and Studies* (*AC85.J2376.911m) is a proof of a poem entitled "Reverie" with Henry's comment on its back, 'Evidently by B. P. Blood'. In black ink William James had written 'Reason namely!' opposite lines 10-12, had underlined text in lines 4-12, and drawn a marginal line at 4-16.

FREDSON BOWERS

Emendations

Every editorial change from the copy-text is recorded for the substantives, and every change in the accidentals as well save for such silent typographical adjustments as are remarked in A Note on the Editorial Method. The reading to the left of the bracket, the lemma, represents the form chosen in the present edition, usually as an emendation of the copy-text. (A prefixed superior [1] or [2] indicates which of any two identical words in the same line is intended.) The sigil immediately following the bracket is the identifying symbol for the earliest source of the emendation, followed by the sigla of any later agreeing documents. Readings in parentheses after sigla indicate a difference in the accidental form of the source from that of the emended reading to the left of the bracket. A semicolon follows the last of the sigla for emending sources. To the right of this semicolon appear the rejected readings of the copy-text and of any other recorded documents, followed by their sigla; a plus sign is used after a sigil when all later documents agree with its reading. When emendations need to be made that are not drawn from any authoritative document, for convenience R. B. Perry's *Collected Essays and Reviews* (1920) or Henry James, Jr.'s, *Memories and Studies* (1911), in which a number of the essays in this volume were reprinted, have been utilized, and failing that, the editor's own alterations marked as H (Harvard). However, CER and M&S are not noted in the list of Emendations except when they are emending agents or rejected substantives. The word *stet* after the bracket calls special attention to the retention of a copy-text reading. It may be employed to key a Textual Note, as marked by an asterisk before the page-line number. In a quotation it may indicate that James's version (differing from the source in some respect) has been retained in the edited text. It may also be used in rare instances to indicate that a possibly questionable or unusual reading has been retained in the text.

For convenience, certain shorthand symbols familiar in textual notation are employed. A wavy dash (~) represents the same word that appears before the bracket and is used exclusively in recording punctuation or other accidental variants. An inferior caret (ᴧ) indicates the absence of a punctuation mark (or of a footnote superscript) when a difference in the punctuation constitutes the variant being recorded, or is a part of the variant. A vertical stroke (|) represents a line ending, sometimes recorded as bearing on the cause of an error or fault. A hand symbol (☞) before a page-line reference draws attention to the parenthetical listing of additional lines where the forms of emendation are identical. Quotations within the text are identified in Professor Skrupskelis' Notes. The sigil WJ/ followed by the appropriate symbol (as WJ/P[20]) indicates James's autograph revisions, usually found in his file sets or private copies of journal articles, and in books, proofs, or clippings.

Emendations

THE TEACHING OF PHILOSOPHY IN OUR COLLEGES

The copy-text is P²⁵, "The Teaching of Philosophy in Our Colleges," *Nation*, 23 (September 21, 1876), 178-179 (McDermott 1876:8).

5.6-7 philosophical] Hall; philosophic P²⁵
5.7 and] *stet* P²⁵; *omit* Hall
6.28 any thing] McCosh; anything P²⁵

6.29 their] *stet* P²⁵; the McCosh
6.38-39 *Essay ... Psychology*] H; *all roman in sg. qts.* P²⁵

REMARKS ON SPENCER'S DEFINITION OF MIND AS CORRESPONDENCE

The copy-text is P²¹, "Remarks on Spencer's Definition of Mind as Correspondence," *Journal of Speculative Philosophy*, 12 (January 1878), 1-18 (McD 1878:1). Emendations are accepted from WJ/P²¹, the annotated reprint in Box O, envelope 8, and from a letter of December 11, 1877, to the editor of the *Journal*, for which see the section on the text. Reference is made to the reprint in CER, *Collected Essays and Reviews*, edited by R. B. Perry, pp. 43-68 (McD 1920:2), which has been collated for substantives only.

7.8 *je*] Voltaire, CER; *jé* P²¹
7.19-20 *Principles of Psychology*] CER; *roman* P²¹
12.31 tribal] WJ/P²¹; *omit* P²¹, CER
*13.24 things,] WJ/P²¹, CER; things ∧ non-existent, P²¹

15.35-36 *Time and Space.*] H; "∼∼∼." P²¹
16.3 artificiality] WJ/*letter*; operose ineptitude P²¹, CER
17.12 Nineveh] H; Ninevah P²¹
18.22 pass,] Emerson; ∼ ∧ P²¹

QUELQUES CONSIDÉRATIONS SUR LA MÉTHODE SUBJECTIVE

The copy-text is P⁹, "Quelques Considérations sur la méthode subjective," *Critique philosophique*, 2 (January 24, 1878), 407-413 (McD 1878:2). Reference is made to the reprint in CER, *Collected Essays and Reviews*, edited by R. B. Perry, pp. 69-82 (McD 1920:2).

27.31 réponds] CER; répond P⁹

THE SENTIMENT OF RATIONALITY

The copy-text is P²⁴, "The Sentiment of Rationality," *Mind*, 4 (July 1879), 317-346 (McD 1879:7). Reference is made to WJ/P²⁴ᵃ, the annotated offprint preserved in Box O, envelope 15 (bMS Am 1092.9, #4565), of the James Collection, to WJ/P²⁴ᵇ, the annotated article found in the Widener stacks (Phil 22.4), and to the reprint in CER, *Collected Essays and Reviews*, edited by R. B. Perry, pp. 83-136 (McD 1920:2), from which emendations are drawn. An emendation is also adopted from the revised form of "The Sentiment of

Rationality" appearing in WB, *The Will to Believe* (McD 1897:3). British spellings in *Mind* are normalized silently to their Americanized form as is the placement of punctuation in respect to quotation marks.

32.3;47.25 everyone] H; every one P^{24}

34.13-14 Discarding . . . alone.] WJ/P^{24a}; *omit* P^{24},CER

34.16 The] WJ/P^{24a}; It will be best to take up first the theoretic way. The P^{24},CER

36.10 More] WB; Mere P^{24},CER

36.34 L'univers,] d'Alembert; $\sim$ $_\wedge$ P^{24}

36.34 sauroit] d'Alembert; saurait P^{24}

36.35 vue,] d'Alembert; $\sim$ $_\wedge$ P^{24}

36.35 seroit] d'Alembert; serait P^{24}

36.36 vérité] d'Alembert; verité P^{24}

*36.37-39 $_\wedge$no . . . common,$_\wedge$] H; "$\sim$ . . . $\sim$," P^{24}

36.40 Unconditioned] Spencer; Unconditional P^{24},CER

38.13 with,] Bain; with, or P^{24},CER

38.13 of,] Bain; $\sim$ $_\wedge$ P^{24}

38.14-15 are, . . . resort, two,] Bain; $\sim$ $_\wedge$ . . . $\sim$ $_\wedge$ $\sim$ $_\wedge$ P^{24}

38.15 one. . . .] H; $\sim$ . . . P^{24}

38.15 'unfortunate'] *stet* P^{24}; "unfortunate," as is sometimes said, Bain

38.17 union;] Bain; $\sim$, P^{24}

38.17 rather] *stet* P^{24}; *omit* Bain

38.18 do] *stet* P^{24}; do or may Bain

39.16 make?] Hume; $\sim$! P^{24}

39.17-18 volume; . . . instance;] Hume; $\sim$ $_\wedge$ . . . $\sim$, P^{24}

39.17 metaphysics] Hume; metaphysic P^{24},CER

39.18-19 *Does . . . number?*] Hume; *roman* P^{24},CER

39.19-20 *Does . . . existence?*] Hume; *roman* P^{24},CER

39.20 *and*] Hume; *omit* P^{24},CER

39.21 For] Hume; for P^{24}

40.10 "rhinoceros"] H; '$\sim$' P^{24}

41.10;55.12 *critique*] H; *Critique* P^{24}

41.13,38 *philosophique*] H; *Philosophique* P^{24}

42.21-23 All . . . existences] *stet* P^{24}; *italic* Hume (*except* 'and')

42.21 existences,] Hume; $\sim$ $_\wedge$ P^{24}

42.21 and] *stet* P^{24}; and *that* Hume

42.39 *Mikrokosmus*] H; *Microcosmus* P^{24}

43.39 177] H; 107 P^{24},CER

44.21 leaf] *stet* P^{24}; leaf-like organ Helmholtz

44.24 the wider] Helmholtz; this wider P^{24},CER

44.26 the flower] Helmholtz; a flower P^{24},CER

46.38 *Physikalischen*] H; *Physikalische* P^{24}

46.39 365] H; 265 P^{24},CER

47.31 our] *stet* P^{24}; the Huxley

47.31 in] Huxley; of P^{24},CER

47.33 another,] Huxley; $\sim$ $_\wedge$ P^{24}

47.34 billiard ball] Huxley; $\sim$ – $\sim$ P^{24}

47.40 'Symposium,'" *Nineteenth*] H; $_\wedge$ $\sim$, $_\wedge$" *XIXth* P^{24}

48.5 act; and on] H; $\sim$, & On WJ/P^{24b}; $\sim$. On P^{24}

48.44 is;] *stet* P^{24}; is, and cannot be other than what it is; Lewes

49.18 ^{2}common,] Mill; $\sim$; P^{24}

50.11 not always] WJ/P^{24b},Mill,CER; always P^{24}

51.19 let him] WJ/P^{24b},CER; *omit* P^{24}

52.19 "Thought$_\wedge$"] H; "$\sim$," P^{24}

53.26 substratum] WJ/P^{24a}; material substratum P^{24},CER

53.31 given] WJ/P^{24b},CER; given given P^{24} (*error*)

54.17-18 are . . . laws] WJ/P^{24b}, CER; is for us an empirical law P^{24}

54.20 immense number] WJ/P^{24b},CER; infinity P^{24}; almost infinity WJ/P^{24a}

54.31 attempts . . . latter] WJ/P^{24b},CER; attempts P^{24}; ['latter' *del.*] attempts WJ/P^{24a}

56.4 every moment] WJ/P^{24a}; *omit* P^{24},CER

58.11-12 contradiction;] Bain; $\sim$: P^{24}

58.16 science,] Bain; $\sim$ $_\wedge$ P^{24}

59.25 act),] H; $\sim$,) P^{24}

61.40 expresses] WJ/$P^{24a\text{-}b}$,CER; impresses P^{24}

62.38 around] Whitman, WJ/$P^{24a\text{-}b}$,CER; over P^{24}

62.38 him] *stet* P^{24}; me Whitman

63.27-44 "There . . . answer."] *stet* P^{24} (*free treatment of* Blood)

Emendations

MR. BRADLEY ON IMMEDIATE RESEMBLANCE

The copy-text is P[24], "Mr. Bradley on Immediate Resemblance," under the heading of Discussions in *Mind*, n.s. 2 (April 1893), 208-210 (McD 1893:2a). Reference is made to WJ/P[24], the annotated article in James's file set of *Mind* (Phil 22.4.6*), and to the reprint in CER, *Collected Essays and Reviews*, edited by R. B. Perry, pp. 333-338 (McD 1920:2). British spellings in *Mind* are normalized silently to their Americanized form as is the placement of punctuation in respect to quotation marks.

67.3 like, be] WJ/P[24]; like, are P[24],CER
67.12-13 "the . . . students."] H; *sg. qts.* P[24]
67.13 philosophical] Bradley; philosophic P[24],CER
67.15 *Logic*] H; Logic P[24]
67.17-18 "in . . . point"] H; *sg. qts.* P[24]

67.28 inseparable,] Bradley; ~ ∧ P[24]
67.35 since] WJ/P[24]; whereas P[24],CER
67.38 seems] WJ/P[24]; seems to me P[24], CER
68.6 coalescence∧] WJ/P[24]; ~, P[24]
68.11 "in . . . point,"] H; *sg. qts.* P[24]
68.14 but] WJ/P[24]; and P[24],CER

IMMEDIATE RESEMBLANCE

The copy-text is P[24], "Immediate Resemblance," under the heading of Discussions in *Mind*, n.s. 2 (October 1893), 509-510 (McD 1893:2b). British spellings in *Mind* are normalized silently to their Americanized form as is the placement of punctuation in respect to quotation marks.

69.10-11 "sheer nonsense,"] H; *sg. qts.* P[24]
*69.11-12 [1] ∧to . . . world,∧] H; *sg. qts.* P[24]
69.12 "state the principle"] H; *sg. qts.* P[24]

69.13 I "object] *stet* P[24]; he objects Bradley
69.13 "object to identity."] H; *sg. qts.* P[24]

THE KNOWING OF THINGS TOGETHER

The copy-text is P[34], "The Knowing of Things Together," *Psychological Review*, 2 (March 1895), 105-124 (McD 1895:4). Reference is made to MT, the extract of the article (73.15-76.6) printed as "The Tigers in India," Chapter II of *The Meaning of Truth* (New York and London: Longmans, Green, 1909) (McD 1909:8), pp. 43-50 (WORKS, pp. 33-36). James's annotations in his file set of the *Review* (WJ 110.72) are noted as WJ/P[34]. The annotation in his private offprint of the article, preserved in Box O, envelope 14[a], of the James Collection at Harvard, is discussed in the textual note to 72.10-12 as is the unauthoritative annotation found in another offprint in Box O, envelope 11. Reference is also made to the reprint in CER, *Collected Essays and Reviews*, edited by R. B. Perry, pp. 371-400 (McD 1920:2), which has been collated for substantives only.

*72.10-12 simply as . . . phenomenon.] WJ/P[34]; as . . . phenomenon simply. P[34],CER
[*begin* MT]
75.19,21 may be] WJ/P[34]; is P[34],MT,CER

75.24 again, for,] WJ/P³⁴; again— P³⁴,MT,
CER
75.37 experience] MT,CER; experienee
P³⁴
[*end* MT]
77.21 sense] WJ/P³⁴; sense of ideal presence of what is absent in fact, P³⁴,CER
77.21 absent,] WJ/P³⁴; absent, in a word,
P³⁴,CER
81.28 foundations] CER; foundation P³⁴
81.36 give] CER; gives P³⁴
84.39 ∧ as Lotze's did∧] WJ/P³⁴;
,∼∼∼, P³⁴

85.3 whom] WJ/P³⁴; which P³⁴,CER
86.10 illusorily] WJ/P³⁴; spuriously and
illusorily P³⁴,CER
87.12 to ascertaining] WJ/P³⁴; ascertaining and tracing P³⁴,CER
88.3 describing] WJ/P³⁴; expressing P³⁴,
CER
88.17 psychology-books] WJ/P³⁴; ∼ ∧ ∼
P³⁴
88.18 then,] WJ/P³⁴; ∼ ∧ P³⁴
*88.26 'fields'] WJ/P³⁴; 'contents' P³⁴,
CER

PREFACE TO PAULSEN'S *INTRODUCTION TO PHILOSOPHY*

The copy-text is P, *Introduction to Philosophy*, by Friedrich Paulsen, translated by Frank Thilly from the third German edition (New York: Henry Holt, 1895), pp. iii-vii (McD 1895:13). A second printing from the same plates appeared in 1922 without variation in the preface.

90.16 Professor] H; Prof. P
93.21 incertitudes,] Renouvier; ∼ ∧ P
93.21 variations,] Renouvier; ∼ ∧ P

93.21-22 philosophie] *stet* P; philosophie,
historiques et actuelles Renouvier
93.23 disons-le] Renouvier; ∼ ∧ ∼ P
93.24 s'arrêter] Renouvier; s'arrêtér P

"PRAGMATISM": FROM BALDWIN'S *DICTIONARY*

The copy-text is D, *Dictionary of Philosophy and Psychology*, edited by J. M. Baldwin (New York and London: Macmillan, 1902), II, 32 (McD 1902:2).

No emendations

"EXPERIENCE": FROM BALDWIN'S *DICTIONARY*

The copy-text is D, *Dictionary of Philosophy and Psychology*, edited by J. M. Baldwin (New York and London: Macmillan, 1902), I, 361-362 (McD 1902:3).

No emendations

HERBERT SPENCER DEAD

The copy-text is NYP, "Herbert Spencer Dead," *New York Evening Post*, December 8, 1903, pp. 1, 5 (McD 1903:8). Reference is made to MS, an incomplete manuscript in the James Collection at Harvard (bMS Am 1092.9, #4485 [Box B, envelope 1]), to P²⁵, "Herbert Spencer," *Nation*, 77 (December 10, 1903), 460-461, and to Cr, "Herbert Spencer Born 1820 Died 1903," *Critic*, 44 (January 1904), 21-24. James's autograph alterations in the clipping found in the Box M Scrapbook are noted as WJ/NYP.

[*begin* MS]
96.4 ways,] MS; ~— NYP,Cr
96.4 immediate,] MS; ~ ∧ NYP,Cr
96.5 influence,] MS; ~ ∧̇ NYP,Cr
96.9 "Public"] MS; "public" NYP,Cr
96.11-12 contrariwise,] MS,Cr; ~ ∧ NYP
96.12 wide∧] MS,Cr; ~, NYP
*96.12 direct] MS; *direct* NYP,Cr
†96.21 over] MS,WJ/NYP; and NYP,Cr
97.3 "Pantheon of Philosophy,"]P25,Cr;
    ∧~~~,∧ MS; '~~~,' NYP
*97.12 at . . . suddenly] MS; suddenly at
    some time NYP+
97.15 whilst] MS; while NYP+
97.24 Carlyle∧] MS,Cr; ~, NYP,P25
[*end* MS]
98.22 *Essays*] H; "Essays" NYP+
☛ 98.27 *Social Statics*] H; *sg. qts.*
    (roman) NYP,P25; *db. qts. (roman)* Cr
    (This emendation of the form of the
    title in NYP,P25, *and* Cr *is also made*

by H *at* 98.28, 39; 99.17; 100.5, 12, 14
    [*twice*], 20, 25, 34)
98.39 'The Unknowable'] H; "~ ~"
    NYP+
99.14 foci] WJ/NYP; facts NYP+
*99.22 collections] P25; collection NYP;
    a collection Cr
99.27 always gives] P25; always given
    NYP; has always given Cr
100.1 *Biology*, . . . *Sociology*,] H; *no qts.*
    (roman) NYP,Cr; *all sg. qts. (roman)*
    P25
100.6-7 *Synthetic Philosophy*,] H; '~~,'
    (roman) NYP; "~~," *(roman)* P25,Cr
100.15 attempts] H; attempt NYP+
100.27 *System of Philosophy*,] H;
    '~~~,' *(roman)* NYP; "~~~,"
    (roman) P25; "~~~ ∧" *(roman)* Cr
100.36 *Synthetic Philosophy*]H; '~~'
    (roman) NYP; "~~" *(roman)* P25,Cr

THE CHICAGO SCHOOL

The copy-text is P33, "The Chicago School," *Psychological Bulletin*, 1 (January 15, 1904), 1-5 (McD 1904:3). A truncated version of the article, in which the text from 103.3-105.22 is omitted, was reprinted in CER, *Collected Essays and Reviews*, edited by R. B. Perry, pp. 445-447 (McD 1920:2).

102.19-22 "The . . . Philosophy,"] H;
    titles all ital. P33
102.20 Meaning,] H; ~∧ P33
102.22 Structural . . . Psychology] CER
    (ital.); *Philosophy* P33

104.10 terms,] Dewey; ~ ∧ P33
104.13 thus] Dewey; *omit* P33,CER
104.16 adequate] *stet* P33; longer an
    adequate stimulus Dewey

HERBERT SPENCER

The copy-text is P6, "Herbert Spencer," *Atlantic Monthly*, 94 (July 1904), 99-108 (McD 1904:8). Reference is made to the reprint entitled "Herbert Spencer's Autobiography," in M&S, *Memories and Studies*, edited by Henry James, Jr., pp. 107-142 (McD 1911:2), and to an offprint contained in Box O, envelope 1, no. 8 (bMS Am 1092.9, #4565), of the James Collection at Harvard assigned the sigil WJ/P6.

107.16-17 powerful thinker] *stet* P6;
    most powerful intellect Barnard
107.18 ''Arry'] H; 'Arry' P6

110.25 thoughts] Spencer; thought P6,
    M&S
110.30 application] *stet* P6; application
    than I had before perceived Spencer

110.31 Again$_\wedge$] Spencer; $\sim$, P[6]
110.34 pages 462-464] H;
 page 464 P[6],M&S
110.40 others'] Spencer,M&S; other's P[6]
111.2 within . . . .] H; $\sim$. $_\wedge$ P[6]
111.3 organized] *stet* P[6]; organized, or
 re-organized, Spencer
111.3-4 structure] *stet* P[6]; structure in
 course of elaboration Spencer
111.6 indifference$_\wedge$] Spencer; $\sim$, P[6]
☛111.8 from. . . .] H; $\sim$.$_\wedge$ P[6] (*The*
 addition of three ellipsis dots in P[6] *is*
 also made by H *at* 112.11,18,33;113.2)
111.8 [2]I] *stet* P[6]; I, without thinking
 much about the matter, Spencer
111.11 books] *stet* P[6]; works Spencer
111.13 all$_\wedge$ . . .] H ($\sim$ $_\wedge$ Spencer); $\sim$,$_\wedge$ P[6]
112.2 those] *stet* P[6]; the views Spencer
112.3 And,] Spencer; $\sim$ $_\wedge$ P[6]
112.5 in speech] Spencer; speech P[6],M&S
112.6 around,] Spencer; $\sim$ $_\wedge$ P[6]
112.11 late] *stet* P[6]; late, however,
 Spencer
112.15 But,] Spencer; $\sim$ $_\wedge$ P[6]
112.19 almost universal] *stet* P[6];
 prevailing—indeed almost universal—
 Spencer

112.20 use,] Spencer; $\sim$ $_\wedge$ P[6]
112.20 cone,] Spencer; $\sim$ $_\wedge$ P[6]
112.26 for] Spencer; *omit* P[6],M&S
112.34 composition:] Spencer; $\sim$, P[6]
113.1 'my . . . afternoon.'] *stet* P[6]; *db. qts.*
 Spencer
113.3 excuse] Spencer; an excuse P[6],M&S
113.3 for] Spencer; to P[6],M&S
113.12 devil-worship] Spencer; $\sim$$_\wedge$$\sim$ P[6]
113.13 on] Spencer; upon P[6],M&S
114.37 enough] *stet* P[6]; *omit* Spencer
116.20 that] WJ/P[6]; *omit* P[6],M&S
119.2 "Evolution,". . . "is] *stet* P[6]; existences of all orders *do* exhibit Spencer
 (*First Principles*, p. 307)
119.2-3 the . . . [1]matter] *stet* P[6]; the integration of matter Spencer (*First Princi-*
 ples, p. 285); a progressive integration
 of Matter Spencer (*First Principles*,
 p. 307)

119.3 dissipation of motion] *stet* P[6]; concomitant dissipation of motion Spencer
 (*FP*, p. 285); concomitant loss of
 Motion Spencer (*FP*, p. 307)
*120.28 triggers] M&S; trigger P[6]

THE PRAGMATIC METHOD

The copy-text is P[20], "The Pragmatic Method," *Journal of Philosophy,
Psychology, and Scientific Methods*, 1 (December 8, 1904), 673-687 (McD
1904:13), which derives from PC, "Philosophical Conceptions and Practical
Results" (Berkeley: The University Press, 1898); James's annotations of the
PC copy he sent to the *Journal* are noted as WJ/PC. Reference is also made to
TMs, "Philosophical Conceptions and Practical Results," the typescript carbon
of James's address to the Philosophical Union of the University of California
at Berkeley, preserved in the University Archives, and to Pr, Lecture III of
Pragmatism, "Some Metaphysical Problems Pragmatically Considered" (New
York and London: Longmans, Green, 1907) (McD 1907:11), pages 97.12-
108.14 (WORKS, 51.4-56.5) of which were a revision of P[20] 675.36-680.18
(*ed.*, 126.13-131.20). Two proof corrections are made from WJ/*letter*, a
letter of December 18, 1904, from James to F. J. E. Woodbridge, editor of
the *Journal*.

124.1-2 develope] TMs; develop PC,P[20]
125.20-21 $_\wedge$ therefore$_\wedge$] TMs; , $\sim$, PC,
 P[20]
125.32 us$_\wedge$] TMs; $\sim$, PC,P[20]
[*start* Pragmatism]

126.24 being] TMs; Being PC,P[20],Pr
126.36 "the . . . blame,"] TMs,PC;
 sg. qts. P[20],Pr
126.36 same$_\wedge$] Browning; $\sim$, TMs+
126.36 our] *stet* TMs+; my Browning

128.23 *Psychology*] H; Psychology TMs
(psychology), PC,P[20]

128.34,35;129.11;130.14 aesthetic] TMs;
æsthetic PC,Pr; esthetic P[20]

129.26 *et seq.* cannot] TMs,PC; can not
P[20],Pr

129.31 consciousness,] Balfour; ~ ∧
TMs+

129.35 though] Balfour; if TMs+

129.35 never] Balfour; not TMs+

129.35 *is*] Balfour, TMs; is PC,P[20],Pr

129.36 be worse] Balfour; worse TMs+

129.36 labour] Balfour, TMs; labor PC,
P[20],Pr

129.36 devotion,] Balfour, TMs,PC,Pr;
~ ∧ P[20]

129.37 generations] Balfour; ages TMs+

129.40 *The Foundations of Belief,*] TMs,
Pr; The Foundations of Belief, PC; 'The
Foundations of Belief,' WJ/PC; 'The
Foundation of Beliefs,' P[20]

130.14 motion'] H; ~,"] TMs,PC;
~,'—WJ/PC,P[20]; ~,'∧ Pr

130.15 philosophy—] TMs; ~,—PC,
P[20]; ~,∧ Pr

130.28 him] TMs,Pr; Him PC,P[20]

130.30 he] TMs,Pr; He PC,P[20]

131.13 chimaeras] TMs; chimæras PC+
[*end* Pragmatism]

131.35 deity] TMs; Deity PC,P[20]

132.27;133.10,21;134.25 deity] H;
Deity TMs+

132.34 living∧] TMs,PC; ~, P[20]

133.29 *saecula saeculorum*] TMs; *sæcula
sæculorum* PC,P[20]

134.28 so called] TMs,PC; ~-~ P[20]

*135.14 principle] TMs,PC; principles
P[20]

*136.17 noetic . . . insignificant]
WJ/*letter*; noetic unity (as one might
call it) is practically an extremely insignificant TMs,PC; significant P[20]

136.17 it,] H; ~) TMs,PC; ~∧ WJ/*letter*

136.18 a noetic] WJ/*letter*; the noetic P[20]

136.19 further] WJ/*letter*; logical P[20]

137.3-4 half way] TMs,PC; ~-~ P[20]

*137.16+ *space*] PC,WJ/PC; *no space*
TMs,P[20]

137.34 ∧ therefore∧] TMs,PC; ,~, P[20]

138.24 ∧ as . . . fact∧] TMs; ,~...~,
PC,P[20]

138.40 bric-a-] TMs,PC; bric-à- P[20]

139.14 fulness] TMs,PC; fullness P[20]

PREFACE TO HÖFFDING'S *PROBLEMS OF PHILOSOPHY*

The copy-text is HP, *The Problems of Philosophy,* by Harald Höffding,
translated by Galen M. Fisher (New York: Macmillan, 1906), pp. v-xiv (McD
1905:12, *wrongly listed as* 1906:6).

140.2-5 *Psychology, . . . Religion*] II;
all db. qts. (roman) HP

140.23 'ever not quite'] H; *db. qts.* HP

G. PAPINI AND THE PRAGMATIST MOVEMENT IN ITALY

The copy-text is P[20], "G. Papini and the Pragmatist Movement in Italy,"
Journal of Philosophy, Psychology, and Scientific Methods, 3 (June 21, 1906),
337-341 (McD 1906:3). Reference is made to the reprinted article in CER,
Collected Essays and Reviews, edited by R. B. Perry, pp. 459-466 (McD
1920:2).

144.12 always] CER; aways P[20]

☛145.11 *Studies . . . Theory*] CER;
sg. qts. (roman) P[20] (*This emendation of the form of the title in* P[20]

is also made by CER *at* 145.25-26,
28; 146.31)

145.25-26 *crepuscolo . . . filosofi*] H;
init. caps. P[22]

145.30-31 Nietzsche] H; Neitzsche P[20]

Emendations

THE MAD ABSOLUTE

The copy-text is P[20], "The Mad Absolute," *Journal of Philosophy, Psychology, and Scientific Methods,* 3 (November 22, 1906), 656-657 (McD 1906:4). Reference is made to the reprint in CER, *Collected Essays and Reviews*, edited by R. B. Perry, pp. 467-469 (McD 1920:2).

No emendations

BRADLEY OR BERGSON?

The copy-text is P[20], "Bradley or Bergson?" *Journal of Philosophy, Psychology, and Scientific Methods*, 7 (January 20, 1910), 29-33 (McD 1910:1), which derives from MS, the holograph manuscript preserved in the James Collection at Harvard (bMS Am 1092.9, #4519 [Box L, notebook N[viii]]). Reference is made to CER, the reprint in *Collected Essays and Reviews*, edited by R. B. Perry, pp. 491-499 (McD 1920:2).

151.9 kantian] MS; Kantian P[20]

151.10 *Logic . . . Appearance*] CER;
'~' . . . '~' (roman) MS; "~" . . .
"~" (roman) P[20]

☛151.14 'endosmosis'] MS; *db. qts.* P[20]
(*This punctuation emendation of* P[20] *is
also made from MS at* 151.14;152.39
[*three words*] ,40;153.10,11-12,36;
154.2,17 [*last phrase*] ,18 [*first two*] ;
155.17)

151.15 french] H; French P[20]

152.15 bradleyan] H; Bradleyan P[20]

152.19;154.3 developes] MS; develops P[20]

153.2 'truth.'] H; ∧Truth,∧ MS; "truth."
P[20]

153.3 that] Bradley,MS; the P[20],CER

153.4,6 cannot] Bradley,MS; can not P[20]

153.5 Real] Bradley; real MS,P[20]

153.6 judgment .] H; ~ ∧ Bradley,MS;
~, P[20]

153.6 For] Bradley; for MS,P[20]

153.14 where] Bradley; at which MS,P[20],
CER

153.15 On] *stet* MS,P[20] ; on Bradley

153.16 nothing else] *stet* MS,P[20]; that
nothing else here Bradley

153.16 If] *stet* MS,P[20]; if Bradley

153.16 here,] Bradley; ~ ∧ MS,P[20]

153.18 a delusion,] Bradley; MS (~~;);
delusion; P[20],CER

153.23 from,] Bradley; ~ ∧ MS,P[20]

153.25 unintelligible . . . .] H; ~ . . . MS;
~. P[20]

153.26-27 recognise] Bradley; recognize
MS,P[20]

153.31 onesided] Bradley; ~- ~MS,P[20]

153.33 importing] Bradley,MS,CER;
imparting P[20]

153.34 mine,] Bradley; MS (~∧);
thine, P[20],CER

153.38 develope] MS; develop P[20]

154.4-5 *Appearance and Reality*] CER;
∧~~~ ∧ (roman) MS; "~~~"
(roman) P[20]

☛154.12 'suprarelational'] H; ∧~ ∧
MS; *db. qts.* P[20] (*This punctuation
emendation of* MS,P[20] *is also made by
H at* 154.18 [*last phrase*] ,39;155.8-9)

154.12 transconceptual] H; ~- ~P[20]

154.17 'way of ideas,'] H; "~~~," P[20]

154.36 anyone] MS; any one P[20]

155.15 'philosophy'] MS ('philosophic');
"~" P[20]

155.18 onesided] MS (onsided); ~- ~P[20]

155.24 'philosophy∧'] MS (' ~,') ; "~ ∧"
P[20]

155.30 non-'transmuted'] H; ∧untrans-
muted∧ MS; ~- "~" P[20]

156.2 english] MS; English P[20]

156.4 -kantian] MS (∧ ~); -Kantian P[20]

Emendations

A Suggestion about Mysticism

The copy-text is P[20], "A Suggestion about Mysticism," *Journal of Philosophy, Psychology, and Scientific Methods*, 7 (February 17, 1910), 85-92 (McD 1910:2), which derives from MS, the incomplete holograph manuscript, corresponding to 157.1-159.25 of P[20], preserved in the Houghton Library (bMS Am 1092.9, #4519 [Box L, notebook N[viii]]). Reference is also made to the reprint in CER, *Collected Essays and Reviews*, edited by R. B. Perry, pp. 500-513 (McD 1920:2).

157.11 'field∧ of consciousness,'] H;
'∼' ∼∼.∧ MS; "∼∧∼∼." P[20]

☛ 157.16 'wave-scheme'] MS; *db. qts.*
P[20] (*This punctuation emendation of
P[20] is also made from MS at 158.36,37;
159.37*)

157.19 'threshold,'] H; ∧∼, ∧ MS;
"∼, " P[20]

158.2 again∧] MS; ∼, P[20]

158.3 others] MS,CER; other P[20]

158.6 lowers∧] MS; ∼, P[20]

158.8 centre] MS; center P[20]

*158.16 sensation,] *stet* P[20]; sensations∧ MS

158.37 transmarginal] MS;
trans-marginal P[20]

[*end* MS]

160.29-30 'fall . . . threshold'] H;
"∼ . . . ∼" P[20]

164.12 causes . . . . But] H; ∼, but P[20]

164.12 *didn't*;] Hall; ∼, P[20]

164.13 mental] *stet* P[20]; mental effort or Hall

164.14 The] *stet* P[20]; But the Hall

164.16 *was*] Hall; was P[20],CER

164.16 was] *stet* P[20]; this was Hall

164.17 of] Hall; of the P[20],CER

164.20 Or] *stet* P[20]; Or (another figure) Hall

164.20,24 fog∧] Hall; ∼, P[20]

164.26 'skips'] *stet* P[20]; "∼" Hall

164.27 Thus] *stet* P[20]; Yet thus Hall

164.27 discover,] Hall; ∼ ∧ P[20]

164.40-165.3 'emotion . . . rubbish.'] H;
all *db. qts.* P[20]

A Great French Philosopher at Harvard

The copy-text is P[25], "A Great French Philosopher at Harvard," *Nation*, 90 (March 31, 1910), 312-314 (McD 1910:4).

166.4 Professor] H; Prof. P[25]

167.19 Académie] H; Academie P[25]

168.13 *La Contingence . . . nature*] H;
"La Contingence . . . nature" P[25]

168.14 1874] H; 1867 P[25]

A Pluralistic Mystic

The copy-text is P[17], "A Pluralistic Mystic," *Hibbert Journal*, 8 (July 1910), 739-759. Reference is made to MS[2], "A Pluralistic Mystic," the holograph printer's copy in the Houghton Library (MS Am 1092.9, #4547), and to P[17](p), a set of second proofs with a few markings by James (bMS Am 1452.1 [23]), indicated as WJ/P[17](p). When P[17](p) is not separately noted it is to be taken as agreeing with P[17] except at 173.17-29,37-40 where P[17](p) has been cut out. Reference is made to the reprint in M&S, *Memories and Studies*,

edited by Henry James, Jr., pp. 371-411 (McD 1911:2). Owing to the freedom with which James treated the pieces by Blood from which he quoted, no
attempt has been made to restore Blood's text by emendation or to record its
differences here. The British spellings of P^{17} (including all but one occurrence
of the characteristic form 'Mr') have been silently emended chiefly by reference
to MS^2. A few printer's or editorial stylings of James's marked characteristics
in other of the accidentals are also emended by reference to MS^2. References
to quotations from Blood pasted into MS^2 are given the sigil MS^2 (*clipping*),
and James's annotations of these clippings are noted as WJ/MS^2 (*clipping*).

172.19 *Utica Herald,*] M&S ($\sim\sim_\wedge$);
   'Utica Herald,' MS^2; $_\wedge$*Utica Herald*$_{\wedge\wedge}$
   P^{17}

☛173.8 'weirdly'] MS^2; *db. qts.* P^{17}
   (*This punctuation emendation of* P^{17} *is*
   also made from MS^2 *at* 173.18,20,28,
   39;174.3;182.4;185.5,6,7,33;188.8
   [*both*], 15;190.1,6[*second word*])
173.14 fichtean] H; Fichtean MS^2, P^{17}
*173.14 hegelian] H; Hegelian MS^2, P^{17}
173.16 anaesthetics] MS^2; anæsthetics
   P^{17}
173.16 world!—] MS^2; $\sim$ $_\wedge$— P^{17}
*173.28 developes] MS^2; develops P^{17}
173.33 Monism] MS^2; Morrison P^{17},M&S
173.37 Amsterdam$_\wedge$] MS^2; $\sim$, P^{17}
174.9 *meâ*] MS^2; *mea* P^{17}
174.14; 177.2-3 hegelian] MS^2; Hegelian
   P^{17}
174.25 'fie'] H; "fie" MS^2,P^{17}
174.26 anyone] H; any one MS^2,P^{17}
174.33 should say] WJ/P^{17}(p); means
   MS^2,P^{17},M&S
174.38 Mr.] M&S; $\sim$ $_\wedge$ MS^2,P^{17}
*175.24 would),] MS^2; $\sim$); P^{17}
176.2 ground$_\wedge$] WJ/P^{17}(p); $\sim$, MS^2,P^{17}
177.23 enquires] MS^2; inquires P^{17}
177.24 while] WJ/P^{17}(p); while yet MS^2,
   P^{17},M&S
*178.14 here] MS^2; there P^{17}, M&S

178.33;183.26;184.28;188.8-9 anaesthetic]
   MS^2; anæsthetic P^{17}
178.33 exhilaration$_\wedge$ . . .] H; $\sim$, ...
   MS^2; $\sim$ $_\wedge$ . . . . P^{17}
179.14 inures] MS^2(*clipping*); enures P^{17}
*179.19 That alien] WJ/MS^2(*clipping*);
   The MS^2(*clipping*); The alien P^{17},M&S
*180.2 the] *stet* P^{17}; *del.* MS^2
*180.4 much fact] MS^2; fact P^{17},M&S
180.42 insures] MS^2(*clipping*); ensures P^{17}
180.43 settlement;] MS^2 (*clipping*);
   $\sim$: P^{17}
181.7-8 philistine] MS^2; Philistine P^{17}
181.16 ever-more] MS^2; evermore P^{17}
183.19 love . . . ."] H; $\sim$.' . . MS^2;
   $\sim$." . . P^{17}
183.21 english] MS^2; English P^{17}
185.1 Existence:] MS^2(*clipping*); $\sim$; P^{17}
186.38 forever] MS^2(*clipping*); for ever
   P^{17}
187.19 bonfires$_\wedge$] MS^2; $\sim$, P^{17}
187.25 Spain$_\wedge$] MS^2; $\sim$, P^{17}
*188.13 6] *stet* P^{17}; — MS^2
*188.24 martyr] MS^2; martyrs P^{17},M&S
188.33 confuting$_\wedge$] MS^2; $\sim$, P^{17}
188.34 law—] MS^2; $\sim$, P^{17}
188.35 counterpoise$_\wedge$] MS^2; $\sim$, P^{17}
190.6 'inexplicable,'] H; $_\wedge$$\sim$, $_\wedge$ MS^2,
   P^{17}(p); " $\sim$," P^{17}
190.12 anaesthetic] H; anæsthetic P^{17}

Textual Notes

13.24 things,] In the annotated copy of P[21] found in Box O, envelope 8, James deleted 'non-existent' in pencil but not the comma following it, which was thus—presumably—intended to apply to 'things', in the same construction. Although not aware of the Box O reprint, Perry in *Collected Essays and Reviews* removed the word (retaining the comma also) as making no sense.

36.37-39 ∧no . . . common,∧] This sentence is not a true quotation from Spencer but instead only a paraphrase; hence James's quotation marks are improper and have been removed. For Spencer's text, see the Notes.

69.11-12 ¹∧to . . . world,∧] The P[24] single quotation marks have been removed since the sentence is a paraphrase, not a quotation, of Bradley's 'Deny this principle and the world, as we have it, is destroyed.'

72.10-12 simply as . . . phenomenon.] In James's file set of the *Psychological Review*, one of the thirteen revisions is the deletion of 'simply' in its original position at the end of the sentence and its marginal addition with a caret placed after 'thus'. On the other hand, in the copy of this article prepared abortively for publication in *The Will to Believe* (Box O, envelope 14[a]), the single annotation is the positioning of 'simply' after 'as' by a guideline. Oddly, the copy in Box O, envelope 11, transposes 'simply' by a guideline and marginal 'tr' in an impossible manner after 'is', but this marking is not James's. The order of the annotation of the file set and of the copy marked-up for *The Will to Believe* is not known. However, it may be suggested that on the evidence of its cover, James had lent the O11 offprint to someone, who had returned it with the transposition of 'simply' marked as a suggestion, and that it was this note that triggered James's sole annotation of the copy in O14[a]. If so, the position in the file set would perhaps be more authoritative since it was obviously part of a general review of the article which might have been later than the single annotation of the O14[a] copy. The virtue of the alternate positioning after 'as' in the O14[a] copy is that it uses the word 'simply' in the sense of *merely*, as in the immediately preceding sentence beginning 'Common sense simply says'. However, if this had been James's initial intention, it is difficult to justify the placement of 'simply' at the end of the sentence. Instead, it would seem that the alteration in the file-set copy 'simply' to follow 'thus' further refines on the use of 'simply' in 72.6-9 and deepens it to mean *in a simple manner*, a meaning, we may guess, intended in the original form of the text as printed. The alteration in the file set, therefore, has been adopted in the present edition.

88.26 'fields'] James deleted the word 'contents' but left the quotation marks standing. Thus it may be taken that he intended the marks to apply to his marginal substitute 'fields'.

96.12 direct] The use of italics for this word in NYP may well go back to a typist's error, mistaking a very long cross stroke on a deleted 'it' in the original line in the manuscript for an underline of 'direct'.

96.21 over] The appearance of 'and' in NYP seems to be a misreading of a rather scrawled 'over' in MS. It is confirmed by the correction in the NYP clipping in the Box M Scrapbook to 'over'.

97.12 at . . . suddenly] In MS 'at some time | suddenly | grown' are added in the left margin ('at some time' just possibly later) as a substitute for deleted text, for which see the Alterations list. The intent seems clearly to read in order downwards, but the transcriber of MS misinterpreted 'at some time' as an interlineation after 'suddenly', and this wrong syntax therefore got into the printed texts.

99.22 collections] NYP 'collection' is a misprint, and the P25 'collections' is only a guess. However, it appears to be a better one than Cr's 'a collection', after the analogy of 100.15-16 where the NYP mistake 'attempt . . . are' is more simply explained as another lost plural 's' than as a contaminated plural 'are'. On the other hand, perhaps incorrectly, the editor, in context, takes it that at 99.27 the NYP error 'given' is somewhat more likely to be a mistake for 'gives', as guessed by P25, than a dropped 'has' as emended by Cr.

120.28 triggers] The P6 reading 'trigger' appears to represent an error. Henry James's alteration to the plural in *Memories and Studies* (1911) may have derived from some note he had seen, but it may, as well, have been merely a guess. As a guess, it is the more probable emendation given the sometimes ambiguous nature of William James's final 's', even though normal sense and idiom might suggest the alternative, 'a trigger'.

135.14 principle] The use of the singular 'principle' at 134.22, and such singulars as 'principle' at 131.23, 27, and especially at 124.13 ('the principle of Peirce, the principle of pragmatism.'), as well as at 124.19 and 124.25, all suggest that this use of the plural at 135.14 is wrong, perhaps an inadvertent contamination from 'results' in the next phrase.

136.17 noetic . . . insignificant] In P20 a line seems to have dropped out, since on its page (136.17) the line begins with 'significant' and the preceding line ends with 'abstract'. The spacing is exact, and 'significant' was undoubtedly hyphenated in the original typesetting. In his letter of December 18, 1904, to Woodbridge, editor of the *Journal*, James closes with an Erratum list that corrects the omission but in a different way from that found in TMs and PC. One cannot know whether the variant results from intention or because James did not have a copy of PC at hand for reference. The PC text is slightly awkward, and so the present edition adopts James's final instructions for the passage, even though the question remains whether he altered the wording while in full knowledge of the lost text, as in PC. See the textual introduction for a discussion.

137.16+ *space*] Despite the presence of a one-line white space in PC and James's marking for the space to be observed, P20 does not observe the request and prints no space.

173.14 hegelian] James's later custom, as in 'hegelian' 174.14 and 177.2-3 in MS2, was to reduce capitals to lower case in adjectives made of proper nouns. Thus the emendations to 'fichtean' and 'hegelian' make the text conform to his usual custom.

173.28 developes] This is James's invariable spelling, almost always altered by compositors to 'develops'.

175.24 would),] The MS² comma is found in Blood; the P¹⁷ semicolon, although more emphatic, is but a sophistication—whether by the compositor or by James cannot be known.

178.14 here] The P¹⁷ misreading of MS² 'here' as 'there' was caused by James's writing 'h' over 'th' in revision and the compositor mistaking the final intention. Blood reads 'here'.

179.19 That alien] James altered in ink the clipping utilized here for the quotation by writing 'at' over final 'e' of 'The' and interlining 'alien' with a caret. The possibility should not be overlooked that the compositor set 'That' from copy and James returned to 'The' in proof (a reversal he was perfectly capable of making), but probably the 'The' is a compositorial misreading or misunderstanding of James's inscription.

180.2 the] This word is clearly deleted in MS², and though it is possible the compositor somehow misread it, the odds favor the hypothesis that James changed his mind and restored the deleted word in proof. This was by no means an unusual practice with him.

180.4 much fact] The P¹⁷ omission of 'much' seems to be an error, either of compositorial eyeskip or else of inadvertent dropping out if there had been trouble in reworking some other error in proof at this point.

188.13 6] The reference in P¹⁷ (and in P¹⁷ [p]) is to galley 6 in P¹⁷ (p), this galley reference not being changed to page reference, in error, when the galleys were paged.

188.24 martyr] A semi-detached stroke in the final 'r' in MS² might have been misread by the compositor as a final 's'. Blood's "Nemesis" itself reads 'martyr'. On the evidence of the restoration in proof of the correct punctuation of "Nemesis" in lines 188.22,23,30, but especially in 188.38, it is evident that James read the first (lost) proof back against Blood's poem, even though he also added some quite wrong punctuation at the same time in 188.33, 34, 35. Whether he tinkered with 'martyr', however, is not to be determined. The plural is very clearly a misunderstanding, perhaps fostered by its being taken as the subject of a plural verb 'sing' instead of the object of 'bids' followed by an infinitive.

Historical Collation

This list comprises the substantive and accidental variant readings that differ from the edited text in the authoritative documents noted for each essay but including for their intrinsic interest the substantive variants (less bibliographical additions and cross-references) in two collections of James's essays in which a number of the essays in this volume were reprinted: *Collected Essays and Reviews* (CER), edited by R. B. Perry (1920) and *Memories and Studies* (M&S), edited by Henry James, Jr. (1911). The reading to the left of the bracket is that of the present edition. The rejected variants in the noted documents follow in chronological order to the right of the bracket. Any collated texts not recorded are to be taken as agreeing with the edition-reading to the left of the bracket: only variation appears to the right, except for the special case of emphasis when the origin of an accepted reading to the left is a James annotation in his private marked copies at Harvard, indicated as WJ/ followed by the sigil for the periodical, book, proofs, or clipping. The noting of variant readings is complete for the substantives and for the accidentals. To save space, however, both substantive and accidental variants are omitted in the Historical Collation whenever the copy-text has been emended and thus when the details may be found recorded in the list of Emendations. Otherwise the noting of variant readings is complete for the substantives save for the special cases of the editorial references and other strictly editorial changes (found almost entirely in Perry) in CER and M&S, and save for the rejected readings of the sources for James's quotations (all other *stet* readings from the Emendations are listed), which are also confined to the Emendations list. The rejected accidental variants in collated texts are also complete except for one special circumstance: trivial differences in the accidental bibliographical details of footnotes such as in the typography, punctuation, abbreviation, and forms of references and dates are ignored. The only exception is the recording of James's occasional use of lower case instead of capitals in titles, an occasional characteristic that may be of interest to the reader, and the normalizing of French titles to standard usage. Finally, James's occasional inscription in manuscript of more than the usual three or four dots indicating ellipsis (unless the manuscript is the copy-text and is emended, in which case the emendation is accidental and confined to the Emendations list) and such purely typographical matters as the use of an asterisk instead of a number for a footnote are not recorded.

The headnote to the Emendations list may be consulted for general conventions of notation. One special feature appearing in the Historical Collation, as in the Emendations, is the use of *et seq*. When this phrase occurs, all subsequent readings within the essay are to be taken as agreeing with the particular feature of the reading being recorded (save for singulars and plurals and inessential typographical variation, as between roman and italic), unless specifically noted to the contrary by notation within the entry itself, or by the use of *stet* within the apparatus. Other arbitrary symbols employed in the Historical Collation when a document other than the manuscript is the copy-text include the § and the ‡. The mark § indicates that the variant is included wholly or in part in an alteration in the manuscript, the description of which has been removed to the Historical Collation from the list of Alterations in the Manuscripts. The double dagger (‡) indicates that the variant in the MS is part of a larger alteration not easily transferable to the Historical Collation, the details of which can be found in the Alterations in the Manuscripts. When used together, the two symbols show that the variant occurs both in a unique alteration and as part of a larger alteration. To find the details of the larger alteration the reader should consult the Alterations in the Manuscripts. In those cases when another document agrees with a revised manuscript variant, a semicolon separates that document's sigil from the listing of MS; this emphasizes the agreement of the document(s) with the final reading of the MS.

Occasionally a variant reading between the copy-text and MS occurs because James has made a simple error, as in putting a caret in the wrong position to indicate an interline, or in failing to omit a word or punctuation mark in an otherwise deleted passage, or in deleting a word or punctuation mark in error and not restoring it. Such mistakes, if linked to an alteration, are recorded as part of the entry for the passage in the Alterations list instead of in the Historical Collation.

For conventions of description in alterations see the headnote to the list of Alterations in the Manuscripts.

REMARKS ON SPENCER'S DEFINITION OF MIND AS CORRESPONDENCE

The copy-text is P^{21}, "Remarks on Spencer's Definition of Mind as Correspondence," *Journal of Speculative Philosophy*, 12 (January 1878), 1-18 (McD 1878:1), with reference to unique substantive variants contained in the reprint in CER, *Collected Essays and Reviews*, edited by R. B. Perry, pp. 43-68 (McD 1920:2).

18.6 no] not CER	20.17 norm-ative] normative CER
19.1 noway] no way CER	

THE SENTIMENT OF RATIONALITY

The copy-text is P^{24}, "The Sentiment of Rationality," *Mind*, 4 (July 1897), 317-346 (McD 1879:7). Substantive variants appearing in the reprint in CER, *Collected Essays and Reviews*, edited by R. B. Perry, pp. 83-136 (McD 1920:2), which do not originate with James's annotations in WJ/P^{24b} (see the headnote to the Emendations), are listed below.

47.20 bottom] the bottom CER	54.32 effect it] effect CER
51.21 *philosophic*] *philosophical* CER	57.37 mind] minds CER
53.18 for an instant waive] waive for an instant CER	62.9 doubt that] doubt CER

THE KNOWING OF THINGS TOGETHER

The copy-text is P^{34}, "The Knowing of Things Together," *Psychological Review*, 2 (March 1895), 105-124 (McD 1895:4), with reference to MT, the extract of the article (73.15-76.6) printed as "The Tigers in India," Chapter II of *The Meaning of Truth* (New York and London: Longmans, Green, 1909) (McD 1909:8), pp. 43-50 (WORKS, pp. 33-36). Collation with the reprint in CER, *Collected Essays and Reviews*, edited by R. B. Perry, pp. 371-400 (McD 1920:2) revealed two unique substantive variants.

71.21-23 ¹Read . . . notes.] ¹Extracts from a presidential address before the American Psychological Association, published in the *Psychological Review*, vol. ii, p. 105 (1895). MT
[*begin* MT]
73.17 Although] Altho MT
74.16 taken by themselves] *italic* MT
74.17 physical] phenomenal MT
74.18 physical] intra-experiential MT
74.18-19 if . . . there] *italic* MT
74.28 Miller, of Bryn Mawr,] D. S. Miller MT
74.36,38 may] *may* MT

74.39-40 ³See . . . 1893.] ²See Dr. Miller's articles on Truth and Error, and on Content and Function, in the *Philosophical Review*, July, 1893, and Nov., 1895. MT
75.10 being∧] ∼, MT
75.21 ∧ again∧], ∼ , MT
76.6 common . . . philosophers.∧] philosophers and of common men.¹ | ¹[The reader will observe that the text is written from the point of view of *naïf* realism or common sense, and avoids raising the idealistic controversy.] MT
[*end* MT]
81.26 dynamic] of dynamic CER
84.21 do] to do CER

HERBERT SPENCER DEAD

The copy-text is NYP, "Herbert Spencer Dead," *New York Evening Post*, December 8, 1903, pp. 1, 5 (McD 1903:8), with reference to MS, an incomplete manuscript in the James Collection at Harvard (bMS Am 1092.9, #4485 [Box B, envelope 1]). Reference is also made to P²⁵, "Herbert Spencer," *Nation*, 77 (December 10, 1903), 460-461, and to Cr, "Herbert Spencer Born 1820 Died 1903," *Critic*, 44 (January 1904), 21-24. Manuscript ampersands and variant spacing (as sometimes appears in words like *is n't*) are not recorded in this collation.

[*begin* MS]
96.0 Herbert Spencer Dead] Herbert Spencer MS (*double underlined*); *HERBERT SPENCER* P²⁵; Herbert Spencer Born 1820 Died 1903 Cr
96.1 Spencer,] Spencer, which the telegraph reported last [*space*], MS
96.3-97.1 Influences . . . there.] *omit* P²⁵
96.6 even] either Mill or MS
§96.6 Darwin's . . . was] Both Mill's influence and Darwin's *were [ab. del.* 'have been'] MS
§96.7 he] they ['have' *del.*] MS
96.8 (*twice*),9 his] their MS
96.9 has] has in the main MS
§96.10 Darwinism,] *Mill & Darwin∧ [ab. del.* 'these two philosophers,'] MS

§96.11 has] ['into' *del.*] have [*alt. fr.* 'has'] MS
96.11 of it] them MS
‡96.11 influence] influence on the public MS
96.15 system] picture MS
96.18 somewhat] *omit* MS
96.20 of Spencer's works] *omit* MS
97.1 And in] In P²⁵
97.4 this] the P²⁵
§97.5-6 as . . . any] one of the rarest and greatest ['of qualities' *del. intrl.*] MS
97.6 belongs] belong P²⁵
97.8 fire mist] ∼ – ∼ Cr
97.11 ever-changing] ∼ ∧ ∼ MS
97.12 "environment"] ∧ ∼ ∧ MS
97.13 parents'] parent's MS

97.13   or] and MS
97.16   When] Whan [*error*] MS
‡97.16   Herbert] Mr. MS
97.19   man;] ∼, MS
97.22-23   pluses and minuses] *pluses* and *minuses* MS
§97.23   Mr. Spencer's] *such a [*in pencil ab. del.* 'Mr. Spencer's'] MS
97.23   embodied,] ∼; MS
§97.23   but a] *that **of [*insrtd. bef. del.* 'but'] a [*ab. del.* 'a common'] MS
§97.25   failed.] ∼ : [*colon over possible semicolon*] ['for he would' *del.*] MS
[*end MS*]
97.29   thrill∧] ∼, P25
97.33-98.3   "The ... these.] *omit* P25
97.39   ∧still∧] , ∼, Cr
98.3   Yet∧] Nevertheless, P25
98.6   flesh,] ∼; Cr
98.6   2and∧] ∼, P25
98.8   had] *omit* P25
98.11   Moreover (*no* ¶)] ¶ P25
98.12,18   à priori] *a priori* Cr
98.20   à priorist] *a priorist* Cr; apriorist P25

98.23-24   'Manners ... Geology,'] *all db. qts.* P25,Cr
98.25-26   'Bain's ... Skeleton,'] *all db. qts.* Cr
98.25   'Bain's ∧Emotions ... 'Owen's ∧Archetype] ∧∼' ∼ ... ∧∼' ∼ P25
98.29   Yet∧] ∼, P25
98.38   sincere∧] ∼, Cr
99.4-5   system;] ∼, P25
99.8   good-by;] ∼–∼ P25
99.9   away,] ∼; P25
99.12   state] State P25
99.15   The (*no* ¶)] ¶ P25
99.29   free-will] ∼∧∼ P25, Cr
100.9   singular] single Cr
100.11   inclusive∧] ∼, P25, Cr
100.16   are] is Cr
100.20   ¶Of] *no* ¶ P25
100.20   too,] *omit* P25
100.20   be] be further P25
100.25   larger] longer P25
101.2   well nigh] ∼–∼ Cr
101.2   flight,∧] ∼;∧ P25; ∼, – Cr

HERBERT SPENCER

The copy-text is P[6], "Herbert Spencer," *Atlantic Monthly*, 94 (July 1904), 99-108 (McD 1904:8). Reference for unique substantives only is made to the reprint entitled "Herbert Spencer's Autobiography," in M&S, *Memories and Studies*, edited by Henry James, Jr., pp. 107-142 (McD 1911:2).

107.0   Herbert Spencer] Herbert Spencer's Autobiography M&S

108.40   *An* ... 1904.] *omit* M&S

THE PRAGMATIC METHOD

The copy-text is P[20], "The Pragmatic Method," *Journal of Philosophy, Psychology, and Scientific Methods*, 1 (December 8, 1904), 673-687 (McD 1904:13), with reference to TMs, "Philosophical Conceptions and Practical Results," the typescript carbon of James's address to the Philosophical Union of the University of California at Berkeley, preserved in the University Archives. Reference is also made to PC, "Philosophical Conceptions and Practical Results" (Berkeley: The University Press, 1898), and to Pr, Lecture III of *Pragmatism*, "Some Metaphysical Problems Pragmatically Considered" (New York and London: Longmans, Green, 1907) (McD 1907:11), pages 97.12-108.14 (WORKS, 51.4-56.5) of which were a revision of P[20] 675.36-680.18 (*ed.*, 126.13-131.20). The marked up copy of PC which James sent to the *Journal* is noted in this collation as WJ/PC, and a correction in the typescript is designated as WJ/TMs.

123.0 The Pragmatic Method[1]] WJ/PC
(*triple underlined*); PHILOSOPHICAL
CONCEPTIONS AND PRACTICAL
RESULTS. TMs,PC

123.1 The ... pragmatism,] The principle
of *pragmatism, ['p' over 'P'] WJ/PC;
Peirce's principle, TMs,PC

123.2-3 *Popular Science Monthly*] roman
TMs

123.3 Mr. ... Peirce] WJ/PC; he TMs,PC

123.9 belief] a belief TMs

123.10 subject] object TMs

123.17 but] mere TMs,PC

123.19-23 [1]The ... EDITOR.] Editor/PC
(here, with a few changes); *omit* TMs,PC

124.1 significance.] WJ/PC; significance.
"Please open the door," and, "*Veuillez
ouvrir la porte,*" in French, mean just
the same thing; but "D――n you, open
the door," although in English, *means*
something very different. PC,TMs
("Veuillez ouvrir la porte," mean ...
door" *means*)

124.3 produce;] ∼: TMs

124.19 prefer] WJ / PC,P[20]; prefer, for our
purposes this evening, TMs,PC (prefer∧
... evening∧)

124.30 discussion.] WJ/PC; discussion. So
I shall devote the rest of this precious
hour with you to its elucidation, because I sincerely think that if you once
can grasp it, it will shut your steps out
from many an old false opening, and
head you in the true direction for the
trail. [¶] One of its first consequences
is this: TMs,PC (once grasp ... this.)

124.30-31 , in fact, that] WJ/PC; *omit*
TMs,PC

124.33 assuming] WJ/PC; supposing
TMs,PC

124.36 assumed] WJ/PC; supposed TMs,
PC

124.37 real] WJ/PC; *omit* TMs,PC

124.37-38 difference—] ∼,— TMs,PC

125.2-3 *be ... make*] WJ/PC; be ...
make PC

125.6 somewhere∧] ∼, TMs,PC

125.11 *y*'s∧] ∼, TMs,PC

125.13 *b*'s∧] ∼, TMs,PC

125.13 *c*'s;∧] ∼: – TMs; ∼ ; – PC

125.16 what ... difference] *italic* TMs

125.26 with] *omit* TMs,PC

125.26 for either] either for TMs

☛ 125.29-30 'Is ... too?'] WJ/PC;
"∼ ... ∼?" TMs,PC (*This punctuation
variation from* P[20] *also occurs in* TMs,
PC *at* 127.40; 128.24; 130.14 [*word
and phrase*]; 132.23; 133.10-11
[*phrase*]; 134.2; 135.3-4, 4-5, 8-9, 25, 29
[*two words*], 30; 136.11; 137.23-26, 32;
138.7; 139.5)

126.3 But] Now TMs

126.4 , as ours now is,] *omit* TMs

126.5 irrational] senseless and irrational
TMs,PC

[*start* Pragmatism]

126.14 such] *omit* Pr

126.17 attain,] ∼∧ Pr

126.20 passing,] ∼ ∧ TMs

126.22-23 draws) ... come; –] ∼, ... ∼;);
TMs; ∼) ... ∼ ; ∧ PC,Pr

126.26 namely,] *omit* TMs

126.27 'laws'] WJ/PC; "∼" PC; ∧ ∼ ∧ Pr

126.27-28 *should ... them?*] roman TMs,
PC,Pr

126.30 the] any Pr

126.30 'crassness∧'] WJ/PC (*comma not
del.*); '∼,' TMs; "∼," PC

126.30-31 'crassness' and ghastliness] or
∧crassness,∧ Pr

126.31 it] *omit* Pr

☛ 126.32 'living,'] WJ/PC; "∼," PC
(*This punctuation variation from* P[20]
also occurs in PC *at* 130.19; 132.16, 18,
19; 133.4-5, 10 [*first word*]; 135.19,
19-20, 20-21; 136.15; 137.7)

126.32-33 'living,' ... sight?] ∧ living∧∧
or richer? Pr

126.34 any] an TMs

126.37 indefeasibly;] ∼: Pr

126.40 God∧ ... respectively,] God, the
atoms∧ TMs

127.2-3 do— ... speak—] ∼, ... ∼, TMs

127.6 absent,] ∼ ∧ TMs

127.9 just ... it] *omit* TMs

127.13-14 in that event] then TMs

127.14 exactly] practically exactly TMs

127.15 can] could Pr

127.15-16 mixed ... yet] *omit* Pr

127.17-18 Accordingly,] ∼ ∧ TMs,PC

127.18-19 instinctively— ... deliberately—]
∼, ... ∼ ∧ TMs; ∼, ... ∼, Pr

127.18-19 a large . . . scientists,]
  positivists and scientists ∧ Pr
127.20 philosophical] philosophic TMs
127.21 future] practical future TMs
127.22 our studies] your studies TMs;
  philosophy Pr
127.22-23 you . . . Union] we Pr
127.23 Philosophical] philosophical TMs
127.23 sadly] *omit* Pr
127.23-25 A . . . for.'] WJ/PC; "Words . . .
  for," said an escaped Berkeley student
  to me at Harvard not long ago. TMs; An
  escaped Berkeley student said to me at
  Harvard the other day—he had never
  been in the philosophical department
  here—"Words . . . for." PC; *omit* Pr
127.25-26 We . . . of] If Pr
127.25 ²philosophers] *omit* TMs
127.26 the] our TMs
127.27 metaphysical . . . investigation]
  theories under fire Pr
127.30 ¹can] say they Pr
127.30 outcomes. And] ∼ , and Pr
127.31 common . . . scientist] others Pr
127.34 something really absurd] silly Pr
127.36 conjectural and] *omit* TMs,PC
127.36 is] is really TMs,PC
127.37 the . . . theism;] our question, Pr
127.38 real] *omit* Pr
127.38 ²the] in the Pr
127.39 has] *has* Pr
127.40 world ∧] ∼ , TMs
128.2 how . . . case] that it is so Pr
128.3 program] programme TMs,PC
128.5 atoms] blind atoms Pr
128.5 elementary] *omit* Pr
128.7 indeed ∧] ∼ , Pr
128.7 These] Those Pr
128.9 atoms ∧] ∼ , TMs
128.17 a term] terms TMs,PC
128.18 connotations,] ∼ ∧ TMs,PC
128.18 hand;] ∼ , TMs
128.19 ignobility,] ∼ ∧ TMs
128.22-23 us . . . *Psychology*.] us; and if
  philosophy were purely retrospective,
  he would thereby proclaim himself an
  excellent pragmatist. Pr
128.23-37 In . . . dislikes.] [¶] But
  philosophy is prospective also, and,
  after finding what the world has been
  and done, and yielded, still asks the

further question 'what does the world
  promise?' Pr
128.28 exquisite] exquitite TMs
128.28 complexity] immensity TMs
128.28 nature's] WJ/PC; Nature's TMs,PC
128.31 eloquent] elegant TMs
128.31-32 even noble] noble even TMs
128.35;129.1 has] *has* TMs
128.37-38 Give . . . *forever*] Give us a
  matter that promises *success*, that is
  bound Pr
128.38 *forever*] forever TMs,PC
128.38 nearer and nearer] ever nearer Pr
129.4 is exerted] *omit* TMs,PC,Pr
129.5 now] *omit* TMs,PC,Pr
129.6 missed.] missed. 'Cosmic emotion'
  would here be the right name for
  religion. Pr
129.9 cosmically] *omit* TMs
129.10 is tragedy] is foretold by science
  to be death tragedy Pr
129.12 really contributed] contributed
  absolutely TMs
129.13 results,] ∼ ∧ TMs
129.17 point, . . . prospectively,]
  ∼ ∧ . . . ∼ ∧ TMs,PC
129.18 practical . . . opposite] *omit* Pr
129.23 and] *omit* TMs
129.25 foreseeable . . . dead] state of the
  Pr
129.25-26 as . . . forth] which evolutionary science foresees Pr
129.33 know] no TMs
129.35 is ∧] is, TMs; is ∧ PC,P²⁰; is, Pr
129.39 jeweled] jewelled TMs,PC,Pr
130.3 gone,] ∼ ∧ TMs
130.3 *nothing*,] ∼ ∧ TMs (*roman*), PC,Pr
130.3 remains,] ∼ ∧ TMs
130.8 final] utter final TMs,PC,Pr
130.12 which] through which TMs
130.12 see] foresee TMs
130.13;131.4 anyone] any one Pr
130.15-16 in it] *omit* Pr
130.16 its ulterior practical] all its ultimate TMs
130.19 is] *is* TMs
130.20 that] that TMs
130.20 , on the contrary,] ∧ ∼ ∼ ∼ ∧
  TMs
130.24 those] *omit* TMs
130.24 so] *omit* TMs

130.39;131.2,9 theism] spiritualism Pr
131.1 means simply] simply means TMs
131.3 an] *omit* TMs
131.5 serious] a serious Pr
131.6-7 Concerning ... wrong.] *omit* Pr
131.6 , at any rate,] ∧~~~∧ TMs
131.7 -poohers] -pooh-ers TMs,PC
131.8 defense] defence Pr
131.10 yourselves] *omit* TMs
131.14 Well ... if] If TMs
131.18 concern] concerns Pr
131.20 more] most TMs
[*end* Pragmatism]
131.21 However] Still TMs
131.22 ultimate,] ~∧ TMs
132.2 orthodox] Catholic TMs
132.3,4 *se*,] ~∧ TMs
132.8 attribute] attributes TMs,PC
132.9 unalterable] inalterable TMs
132.14 if ... then] *omit* TMs
132.15 active] *omit* TMs
132.21 hunters∧] ~, TMs
132.21-22 field-observers] ~ ∧ ~ TMs
132.25 that] *omit* TMs
132.27 are] *are* TMs
132.31 word] name TMs
132.31 'God'] WJ/PC; ∧~∧ TMs; " ~ "
  PC
132.34-35 , indeed,] *omit* TMs
132.39 do] *omit* TMs
132.39 unalterability] inalterability TMs
132.40 banish] banishes TMs
133.3-4 himself ... 'By] himself. For by
  TMs
133.5 appeased?'] ~?∧ TMs
133.7 creation;] ~, TMs
133.7 that] the TMs
133.8;134.9 certainly] *omit* TMs
133.10 'court'] WJ/TMs,WJ/PC; '~∧ TMs;
  " ~ " PC
133.10 pomp] pomps TMs
133.15 on theology] *omit* TMs
133.19 fish] a fish TMs,PC
133.24 systems] a system TMs
133.26 professors] professor TMs
133.26 after-effects] afterthoughts TMs
133.28 conduct,] WJ/PC; ~∧ TMs,PC
133.39 primary] *omit* TMs
134.1 God∧] ~, TMs,PC
134.2 unreal] unreal and PC
134.3 means] *means* TMs

134.5 you] *omit* TMs
134.7 experiences,] ~ ∧ TMs
134.7-8 too certainly] must TMs
134.8 general] *omit* TMs
134.8-9 They ... infallible.] *omit* TMs
134.11 now] *omit* TMs
134.11-12 not ... only] *omit* TMs
134.12 show] show you TMs
134.18 stayed] staged TMs
134.19 enough] enough then, TMs
134.23 this ... idea] the idea of the
  Diety TMs
134.31 heresy,—] ~,∧ TMs
134.31 mean] mean of TMs
134.32 God, ... creator,] ~∧...~∧
  TMs
134.34 whole,] whole, a TMs
134.36 California] Californian TMs,PC
134.37 (whose ... be),] , my colleague at
  Harvard, TMs
134.38-39 *The* ... *God*] the ... God
  (*roman*) TMs
135.1 address] first address TMs,PC
135.6 , in particular,] ∧~~~∧ TMs
135.8 monistic] Monistic TMs
135.14 out,] ~∧ TMs
135.21 ¹and ... in] *and ... in* TMs
135.27 mere number] *mere number* TMs
135.28 'one,'] WJ/PC; "One," TMs; "~,"
  PC
135.30 *practically* mean by] practically
  mean by TMs
135.31 One,] ~? TMs
135.36 ²and ... up,] *omit* TMs
136.11 Now,] ~∧ TMs
136.17-19 Chaos ... all.] *omit* TMs,PC
136.36 hand,] ~∧ TMs
136.40;137.4 monism] Monism TMs
137.5 still more] *still more* TMs
137.8 long,] ~; TMs,PC
137.13 Many ... One] many ... one
  TMs
137.23-24 *known as ... cash-value*]
  roman TMs
137.24 *-value*∧] -~, PC
137.27 mean] *mean* TMs
137.35 'matter'] WJ/PC; ∧~'∧ TMs;
  " ~ " PC
138.5 negations;] ~ — TMs
138.5 Hume,] ~ ∧ TMs
138.6 Mill∧] ~, TMs,PC

138.15 come,] ~∧ TMs
138.20 ponderous] ponderour TMs
138.35 much–] ~,– TMs
138.37-38 intellectually, . . . morally,]
    ~∧ . . . ~∧ TMs
138.38 sounder∧] ~, TMs,PC
138.40 museums;] ~, TMs,PC
139.5 thing:] ~. TMs
139.10 hypotheses] WJ/PC; hypothesis
    PC
139.15 lines.] WJ/PC; lines. [¶] May I

hope, as I now conclude, and release your attention from the strain to which you have so kindly put it on my behalf, that on this wonderful Pacific Coast, of which our race is taking possession, the principle of practicalism, in which I have tried so hard to interest you, and with it the whole English tradition in philosophy, will come to its rights, and in your hands help the rest of us in our struggle towards the light. TMs,PC

THE MAD ABSOLUTE

The copy-text is P[20], "The Mad Absolute," *Journal of Philosophy, Psychology, and Scientific Methods*, 3 (November 22, 1906), 656-657 (McD 1906:4), with reference to the reprint in CER, *Collected Essays and Reviews*, edited by R. B. Perry, pp. 467-469 (McD 1920:2). No substantive variants exist other than the misprint listed below.

149.6 mad] made CER

BRADLEY OR BERGSON?

The copy-text is P[20], "Bradley or Bergson?" *Journal of Philosophy, Psychology, and Scientific Methods*, 7 (January 20, 1910), 29-33 (McD 1910:1), with reference to MS, the holograph manuscript preserved in the James Collection at Harvard (bMS Am 1092.9, #4519 [Box L, notebook N[viii]]). Manuscript ampersands and variant spacing (as sometimes appears in words like *is n't*) are not recorded in this collation.

§151.1 Dr.] Mr∧ ['r' *over* 'i'] MS
☛151.1 *Weltanschauung*] roman MS
    (*This emphasis variation from* P[20]
    also occurs in MS *at* 152.40; ‡154.11;
    155.4,17)
151.1-2 in . . . article] in an article in last
    October's *Mind*, MS
151.2 for] *omit* MS
151.4 last∧] ~, MS
151.5 knife-edge∧] ~∧~, MS
§151.6 leans to one side] ['goes' *del.*]
    takes one way MS
§151.7 the . . . choice] *the conse-
    quences of [*ab. del.* 'what he was
    about.'] his act MS
151.8 in . . . his] was in MS
§151.9 immediate . . . all] in [*intrl.*] im-
    mediate feeling *we have ['forms a' *del.*]
    sheer [*ab. del.* 'is pure'] MS

§151.10 insisted] urged ['d' *over* 's'] MS
§151.11 reality,] ['a' *del.*] Reality, ['R'
    over 'r'] MS
151.12 , as thus encountered,] ∧~~~~∧
    MS
§151.12-13 the . . . of a] that of continu-
    ity and ['unity' *del.*] union, *that of a
    [*ab. del.* '–it is a tran'] MS
151.13 This (*no* ¶)] ¶ MS
151.15 the french writer] he MS
§151.17-18 feelings . . . discontinuous,]
    discontinuous [*ab. del.* 'the chaos of']
    aboriginal feelings MS
151.20 flatly;] ~, MS
151.20 battle] strategy MS
§151.21-22 destroy . . . process] *smash
    the notion that [*ab. del.* 'discredit'] the
    ['whole' *del.*] conceptual process *is
    ['i' *over* 'a'] a unifying agent MS

151.22 discrete;] ∼, MS
§151.23 get] cut [*ab. del.* 'get'] MS
151.23 continuous,] ∼; MS (*semicolon doubtful*)
152.1 construct] reconstruct MS
152.1-2 , moreover,] ∧∼∧ MS
152.2 static,] ∼∧ MS
§152.3-4 inalienable features] ['inalienable' *del. ab. del.* 'the essential'] features, *inalienably [*ab. del.* 'as it is directly'] felt MS
‡152.4 Bergson,] B.∧ MS
152.4 more,] ∼∧ MS
§152.4-5 intelligible,] ∼∧ [*comma del.*] MS
§152.5 when ... radically] *when ever we [*ab. del.* 'as is usually supposed. It makes them less intelligible as soon'] ['as we' *undel. in error*] *use ['take' *del.*] them [*ab. del.* 'make'] radically ['ly' *added*] *and seriously [*ab. del.* 'use of them'] MS
§152.5-6 They ... theoretically.] Their ['ir' *added*] service [*ab. del.* 'good they do us'] is *more [*intrl.*] practical ['more' *del.*] than theoretical. MS
152.7 experience,] ∼∧ MS
152.7 show] reveal MS
152.10 thoroughgoing] thorough going MS
§152.11 realities] Reality ['R' *over* 'r'] MS
§152.11-12 intellect ... becomes] *intellects the conceptual translation is [*ab. del.* 'concepts, ['we make it incomprehens' *del.*] what we substitute *for it [*ab. del.* 'for it'] is ['incom' *del.*] contradictory and'] incomprehensible through & *through: [*colon over period*] ['Change is in' *del.*] activity ['a' *over* 'A'] becomes [*ab. del.* 'is'] MS
152.13 contradictory] self-contradictory MS
152.15 the bradleyan] from the MS
152.18 first] *omit* MS
152.19 conception;] ∼, MS
152.19 then] *omit* MS
152.20 and more contradictory] *omit* MS
§152.20 comes] soon [*intrl.*] comes MS
152.20-21 of its usefulness] *omit* MS
152.22 Arrived ... conviction,] At this point∧ MS

§152.22 *drops* conception—] drops [*ab. del.* 'gives up'] ∼, MS
§152.23 and, turning] &∧*turning ['ing' over 's'] MS
§152.24 towards] to [*ab. del.* 'towards'] MS
152.24 perception∧] ∼, MS
152.24 multiplicity-in-union] ∼∧∼∧∼ MS
§152.25 philosophy, as] ∼∧ as *yielding [*insrtd.*] MS
152.25 material] knowledge MS
§152.26-30 The ... *bounds*] Their fault is ['one' *del.*] of extent and not of nature; and ['*Bergson ['son' *undel. in error*] thinks sets us thinks that' *del.*] the *only [*intrl.*] way to *get at [*ab. del.* 'understand'] Reality ['R' *over* 'r'] intimately is ['by' *del.*] to *let our [*ab. del.* 'try by'] sympathetic imagination ['to en'*del.*] enlarge their bounds MS
152.32 , on the one hand,] ∧∼∼∼∼∧ MS
152.32 old-fashioned] ∼∧∼ MS
152.32 mysticism,] ∼∧ MS
152.33 possibly] *omit* MS
152.35 thorough∧] ∼, MS
‡152.35 its] his MS
152.36 form] immediate form MS
152.36-37 an ... which] a revelation of something that MS
§152.38 understanding; they] ∼: [*colon over period*] they ['t' *over* 'T'] MS
152.40 Bradley] Mr. Bradley MS
153.2-9 view," ... found."] *all sg. qts.* MS
153.3 must] *must* MS
153.5 ideally] *ideally* MS
153.10 , in sooth,] ∧∼∼∧ MS
153.13-35 "At ... spot."] *all sg. qts.* MS
153.14 says,] ∼∧ MS
153.18 may be] is MS
§153.19 [*i.e.*, to feeling]] *[i.e.∧ feeling] [*insrtd.*] MS
153.21 oneself] ones self MS
153.25 For] And against this *poition∧ ['position,' Bradley] while [*ab. is del.* '[so long as]'] it is true to itself, I have nothing to *say, [∼; Bradley] though I regret that to be true to itself is ['a thing' Bradley] so seldom within its power. For MS

153.30 philosophy] phil. MS
153.33 'this'] *'this'* MS
153.36 only] *omit* MS
153.39 October . . . 498.] NS. 72, p. 498. Italics mine. MS
153.40 ²*Ibid.*, pp. 500-502.] *omit* MS
154.2 , however,] *omit* MS
‡154.3 point,] ∼ ∧ MS
154.5 at this point] *omit* MS
§154.6-8 drop . . . hark] *drop ['our' *del.*) truth, ['ideas' *del.*] as an ['the' *del.*] improvement on reality, and hark [*ab. del.* '['treat the ideas irreligiously' *del.*] go'] MS
154.9 upon] on MS
154.10 forward,] ∼ ∧ MS
154.12 and transconceptual] *omit* MS
154.14 feeling,] ∼ ∧ MS
154.14 backs] back MS
154.17 ∧philosophy,∧] '∼ ∧' MS
154.17 with . . . ideas,'] *omit* MS
154.17 ∧absolute∧] 'Absolute' MS (*cap. doubtful*)
§154.19 to belief;] to [*over* 'th'] mind, MS
154.21-22 obvious? Or] ∼, or MS
§154.22 factor of] moment ['of' *del. in error*] ['person' *del.*] MS
154.24 *The* . . . admits,] The way of philosophy for Mr. Bradley is not the way of life, MS (*roman*)
154.25 for the philosopher] *italic* MS
154.25 he continues,] *omit* MS
§154.25 seems . . . *is*—] *seems in spite of all its drawbacks to be the only ['way' *del.*] possible way [*ab. del.* 'is the way to follow']— MS
‡154.26 life,] ∼ ∧ MS
154.27 starveling] starver MS
§154.27-29 all . . . appear.] the *only [intrl.*] way. *['left.' *del. bef. del.* 'possible.'] [*ab. del.* 'to follow.'] *Granted! yet [*ab. del.* 'But why is it better to be either starver or philosopher?'] Why ['W' *unreduced in error*] ['on these terms' *del.*] should one *choose* *['to be' *del.*] either ['a' *del.*] [*insrtd. for del.* 'eith starvation'] starvation [*alt. fr.* 'starver'] or ['a' *del.*] philosophy ['y' *over* 'er']? MS
154.29 possibly] *omit* MS

154.29-31 for . . . intellectualist] *for **choosing [*ab. del.* 'being a'] philosophy ['y' *over* 'er'] ***on these terms [*ab. del.* 'as thus defined'] is ['the' *del.*] old intellectualist [*ab. del.* 'is the *old [*ab. del.* 'ancient'] ['greek prejudice' *del.*] inherited greek'] MS
154.34-35 Not . . . view.] *omit* MS
154.36 is] is simple, MS
154.37 ∧philosophy,∧] '∼,' MS
§154.38 slides,] ['falls' *del. ab. del.* 'goes'] ∼ ∧ [*intrl.*] MS
‡155.1 suprarelational] supra-relational MS
‡155.2 will-to-believe;] ∼ ∧ ∼ ∧ ∼. MS (*error*)
‡155.2-3 Bradley, . . . -empiricists,] ∼ ∧ . . . ∧ ∼ ∧ MS
§155.4 thought: . . . him] thought. *The one for['m' *del.*] him [*ab. del.* 'Feeling, *he confesses, [*intrl.*]'] reveals MS
§155.4-5 reality perfectly,] *reality ['ity' *del. in error*] perfectly [*dash del.*] only it is [*poss.* 'pur' *del.*] concrete not ideal reality [*insrtd. for del.* 'its manyness in oneness, [*illeg. word*] perfectly' *ab. del.* '['ity, its transparent union' *del.*] ity, for Mr. Bradley, shows how ['oneness' *del.*] manyness can be transparently *convincing way [*ab. del.* 'one.']'] MS
§155.5 the . . . ¹it] *the other breaks down [*ab. del.* 'Thought breaks down ['up' *del.*] ['up' *del.*]'] MS
155.5 utterly∧] ∼, MS
§155.6-7 committed∧ . . . reverse,] committed, [*comma added*] [*bef. del.* 'to [*undel. in error*] thought ['th' *del.*] forward mo' *ab. del.* 'we can never go back'] we [*intrl.*] can't reverse our movement, MS
‡155.7 save . . . only] only save ourselves MS
155.8 absolute] Absolute MS
§155.8 will . . . and] [', as' *del.*] realizes ['s' *over* 'd'] ['by it' *del.*] unintelligibly MS
155.9 etc.,] etc∧, MS
155.11 , on . . . hand,] *omit* MS
155.13 clear] still MS
155.13 sensible] *omit* MS
§155.14 manyness-in-oneness] ∼ ∧ *∼ ['i' *over* 'a'] ∧∼ MS

§155.14 so] so [*ab.del.* 'a'] perfectly MS

‡155.15 , if you will,] ∧ if you like∧ MS

§155.15-17 from ... *of*] *from the knowledge of them but recognize it as at least the only [*ab. del.* 'knowledge if you like, *but [*undel. in error*] let it be called ['the' *del.*]'] the [*undel. in error*] *complete ['['highest' *del.*] complete kind of' *del.*] [*ab. del.* 'fullest'] MS

155.20 full ... and] *omit* MS

§155.21 *me's ... here's*] mes & thees and nows and *heres, [*ab. del.* 'thises,'] MS

155.21 on ... hand,] *omit* MS

§155.22 like ... other] *& abstraction [*intrl.*] MS

155.23 knowledge merely] *omit* MS

155.25 But if] If MS

155.25 rather] *omit* MS

§155.28-29 find ... side] *find no possible excuse for not falling in the [*ab. del.* '['take no other course.' *del.*] do no otherwise than follow'] *Bergsonian side. [*alt. fr.* 'Bergson.'] MS

‡155.31 confidence] unlimited confidence MS

155.33 alternative∧] ~, MS

§155.34 one's] one∧s [*ab. del.* 'one's'] MS

§155.34 must ... told.] *must be **told∧ [*period omitted in error*] [*insrtd. for del.* '*['have to become explicit.' *del.*] cannot remain concealed. [*ab. del.* '['cannot' *del.*] ['must' *del.*] ['must be plain.' *del.*] must plainly appear.']'] MS

155.35 an empiricist∧] empiricist, MS

155.35 a] *omit* MS

155.35 whichever you please,] *omit* MS

155.36 why!] ~ . MS

§155.36 sincerely believe] sometimes [*ab. del.* 'have taken the liberty to *think [*ab. del.* 'assign'] inveterate'] think MS

155.37 choice; for at] choice. At MS

§155.39 sensible reason] ['rational' *del.*] *reason* MS

§155.39 should ... takes] ['does' *del.*] falls ['s' *added*] the way he does MS

156.1 ever] *omit* MS

156.1 *revoke,* and] *omit* MS

156.3 extinguished] extinguisht MS

156.4 , between them,] ∧ ~ ~ ∧ MS

§156.4 might lay] would *['lay' *del.*] have laid [*ab. del.* 'put'] MS

156.5 permanently] *omit* MS

A SUGGESTION ABOUT MYSTICISM

The copy-text is P20, "A Suggestion about Mysticism," *Journal of Philosophy, Psychology, and Scientific Methods,* 7 (February 17, 1910), 85-92 (McD 1910:2), with reference to MS, the incomplete holograph manuscript, corresponding to 157.1-159.25 of P20, preserved in the Houghton Library (bMS Am 1092.9, #4519 [Box L, notebook Nviii]). Manuscript ampersands and variant spacing (as sometimes appears in words like *is n't*) are not recorded in this collation.

157.0 A ... Mysticism] A suggestion about mysticism MS

§157.4 spoken as] ['taken part' *del.*] ventured to speak as one MS

157.5 an] a complete MS

157.6 say] have to say MS

157.6 will prove] may publish MS

§157.6 readers] the [*ab. del.* 'any'] reader MS

157.7 since∧ ... outsiders∧] as, ... ~, MS

157.11-12 extensions] extension MS

157.12-13 , if ... correct,] *omit* MS

§157.15 would become] became ['a' *in ink over* 'o'] MS

‡157.15 would grow] grew MS

157.17 as ... it,] *omit* MS

157.18 steep] very steep MS

§157.19 below ... gradually] ['in all directions,' *del.*] very gradually [*comma del.*] below it MS

158.3 narrow,] ~ ∧ MS

158.11-12 exceptionally extensive] extreme MS

§158.12   paroxysm,$_\wedge$] $\sim$, – [*dash intrl.*] MS

§158.14   remarks] general [*intrl.*] remarks MS

§158.16   sensation,] sensations$_\wedge$ [*final 's' del. and restored*] MS

§158.17   emotions, concepts, etc.] emotions$_\wedge$ [*intrl.*] and *concepts ['s' *over* 'ions']. ['is added.' *intrl. and ink del.*] MS

§158.24   *present*] present['ness' *del.*] MS

‡158.26   perspective$_\wedge$] $\sim$, MS

158.28   , now,] *omit* MS

§158.29   mass of *sensation*;] ['*sensation*' *del.*] *mass* *of *sensation*, [*intrl.*] MS

158.34   But with] With MS

§158.35   are] are *normally [*intrl. in ink*] MS

158.36   at ordinary times] *omit* MS

158.40   example,] $\sim$ $_\wedge$ MS

‡158.40-159.36   Münsterberg] Munsterberg MS

159.6   subconscious] hidden MS

§159.7   feelings,] $\sim$ [*final 's' added over doubtful comma*]$_\wedge$ MS

159.16-17   circumstances; . . . enhanced.] circumstances. MS

159.19   singly,] $\sim$ $_\wedge$ MS

159.21   separately,] $\sim$$_\wedge$ MS

§159.25-27   do . . . precise.] point out its shortcomings or errors with definite ness, it will have amply served its *purpose. [*period added in ink*] ['in psychological literature' *del. in ink*] MS

159.36   *e.g.*,] e.g.$_\wedge$ MS

§159.37   the] *del.* MS

[*end* MS]

A Pluralistic Mystic

The copy-text is P[17], "A Pluralistic Mystic," *Hibbert Journal*, 8 (July 1910), 739-759. Reference is made to MS[2], "A Pluralistic Mystic," the holograph printer's copy in the Houghton Library (MS Am 1092.9, #4547) and to P[17](p), a set of second proofs with a few markings by James (bMS Am 1452.1[23]), indicated as WJ/P[17](p). When P[17](p) is not separately noted it is to be taken as agreeing with P[17]. Collation establishes that no substantive variants occur in the reprint in M&S, *Memories and Studies*, edited by Henry James, Jr., pp. 371-411 (McD 1911:2). References to quotes from Blood pasted into MS[2] are noted as MS[2](*clipping*), and James's annotations of these clippings are indicated as WJ/MS[2](*clipping*). Unless noted otherwise by *stet* readings, double quotes in P[17] correspond to single quotes in MS[2], and single quotes in P[17] are double quotes in MS[2]. Manuscript ampersands and variant spacing (as sometimes appears in words like *is n't*) are not recorded in this collation.

172.9   the readers] any reader MS[2]

172.16   , moreover,] $_\wedge$ $\sim$ $_\wedge$ MS[2]

§172.18   *Gazette*$_\wedge$] 'Gazette,' [*first sg. qt. over db. qt.*] MS[2]

172.18   *Recorder*] 'Recorder' MS[2]

172.19   *Albany Times.*] 'Albany Times.' MS[2]

172.21   Once,] $\sim$ $_\wedge$ MS[2]

§172.22   W. T. Harris$_\wedge$] *W. T. $\sim$, [*ab. del.* 'editor'] MS[2]

172.22   *Journal . . . Philosophy*$_\wedge$] Journal of speculative philosophy, MS[2]

173.1   1889).] 18)$_\wedge$ MS[2]; 18). P[17](p)

§173.2-3   *Scribner's Magazine*] Scribner's *Magazine ['M' *over* 'm'] MS[2]

173.3   1888, . . . 1899).] 18 , . . . 18)$_\wedge$ MS[2]

173.6   the *Anæsthetic Revelation*,] 'the Anaesthetic Revelation,' MS[2]

173.9   stepping-stones] $\sim$ $_\wedge$ $\sim$ MS[2] (*This punctuation variation from* P[17] *also occurs in* MS[2] *at* 178.12 [*first*], 21; 180.29; 185.19-20)

173.13   precision,] $\sim$; MS[2]

173.14   an] *omit* MS[2]

173.16   wrought] developed MS[2]

173.17-29,37-40 practically . . . has |
  ¹"Yes! . . . named.] *cut out* P¹⁷(p)
§173.21-22 made . . . hesitate,] given
  pause to *other [*intrl.*] pluralistic-minded *students∧ [*ab. del.*
  'persons'] MS²
173.40 journals] Journals MS²
‡174.2 philosophy,] ∼ ∧ MS²
§174.2 in . . . resort] *at last [*intrl.* | MS²
☞ 174.5 rather;] ∼ , MS² (*This punctuation variation from* P¹⁷ *also occurs in*
  MS² *at* 174.11;177.5;180.3)
174.7 monistic] monistic (as it seems)
  MS²
174.12 I] *omit* MS²
174.19 reason,] ∼∧ MS²
175.18 think,] ∼ ∧ MS²
175.29 no-thing] nothing MS²
175.30;178.31 , then,] ∧ ∼ ∧ MS²
175.37 spirit. . . .] ∼ . MS²
175.40 cheap∧] ∼ , MS²
176.5 Indeed,] ∼ ∧ MS²
176.6 which,] ∼ ∧ MS², P¹⁷(p)
176.8 making] makings P¹⁷(p)
176.8 so,] ∼ ∧ MS²
§176.19 , forsooth,] ∧ ∼ ∧ [*intrl.*] MS²
176.22 'picture'] *stet* MS²
§176.34-35 , as . . . platform,]
  *∧ ∼ . . . ∼ ∧ [*intrl.*] MS²
176.37+;177.30+;178.18+;185.3+;189.33+
  space] *no space* MS²,M&S
‡176.39;177.2 paragraphs] paragrafs MS²
177.3 thoroughly] thoroly MS²
177.3 idealistic:—] ∼ : ∧ MS²
177.5 difference,] ∼ ∧ MS²
177.8,9-10 question,] ∼ ∧ MS²
177.8 What] what MS²
177.10 proposition,] ∼ ∧ MS²
177.11 other. . . .] ∼ . MS²
177.12 "Sameness] ∧ ∼ MS²(*clipping*)
177.15 other—] ∼ , —ⁱ MS²(*clipping*)
177.16 subjective,] ∼— MS²(*clipping*)
177.17 limit∧] ∼ , MS²(*clipping*)
177.17 field. . . .] ∼ . MS²(*clipping*)
177.18 "We]] ∧ ∼ MS²(*clipping*)
177.20 -distinction—] - ∼ , — MS²
  (*clipping*)
177.23 ∧ but] — — MS²
177.23 *time?*∧] ∼ ?' " P¹⁷(p)
177.23 logician.] ∼ : MS²
177.23-25 ∧A . . . understanding."]

"∼ . . . ∼ ." MS² ; "∼ . . . ∼ . ∧P¹⁷(p)
  (*opposite marginal WJ pencil qst. mk.
  del. in pencil*)
177.25 distinction:] ∼ , MS²
177.26 ∧But] ' ∼ MS²
177.27 "To] ∧ ∼ MS²
177.29 ¹lie,] ∼ ∧ MS²
177.31-33 Philosophy . . . object.] *in*
  P¹⁷(p) *opposite WJ pencil note*
  'self-relation'
177.35 object,] ∼ ; MS²
177.35 cannot . . . that;] cannot, MS²
177.35 as] taken as MS²
177.36 'universe'] *stet sg. qts.* MS²
177.39 utmost,] ∼ ∧ MS²
178.1 a] a contrast of the MS²
178.2 conjecture,] ∼ ∧ MS²
178.12 bed-rock] ∼ ∧ ∼ MS²,P¹⁷(p)
178.14 is,] ∼ ∧ MS²
‡178.19 nineteenth-] XIXth∧ MS²
§178.25 note:] *[' 'timeless' ' del.*] note.
  [*ab. del.* 'monistic ['rat' *del.*]
  transcendental-idealistic tone:'] MS²
178.25 "No] *stet db. qt.* MS²
178.28 ¹and∧] ∼ , MS²
178.31 other∧] ∼ , MS²
178.36 once—astounding] ∼ . Astounding MS²
179.2 *is*] is MS²
§179.6 was, not] ∼ * — ∼ [*ab. del.
  comma*] MS²
§179.8 waif,] ∼ — [*dash ab. del. comma*]
  MS²
179.10 ¹not] no MS²
179.14 "Such idealism] WJ/MS²(*clipping*); idealism MS²(*clipping*)
179.20,32-36 side.³] ∼ . ∧ (*omit fn.*)
  MS²(*clipping*)
179.31 show."⁴] WJ/MS²(*clipping*)
  (∼ .ˣ); ∼ . ∧∧ MS²(*clipping*)
179.37 Elsewhere∧] ∼ , MS²
179.38 answer∧] ∼ , MS²(*clipping*)
179.38 Nothing,] ∼ , — MS²(*clipping*)
179.39 air-drawn] ∼ ∧ ∼ P¹⁷(p)
179.39 no such] nosuch MS²(*clipping*)
  (*error*)
180.19 but it] but MS² (*clipping*)
180.28 time.' "] ∼ . "∧ MS²(*clipping*)
180.29 essay] Essay MS²
§180.29 Emerson. For] Emerson [*colon
  del.*]—for MS²

180.30 "Experience] *stet*
    WJ/MS² (*clipping*); ∧ ~ MS² (*clipping*)

180.32 himself for] *omit* MS² (*clipping*)

180.36 "It] *stet* WJ/MS² (*clipping*);
    ∧ ~ MS² (*clipping*)

180.36 cannot] can not MS² (*clipping*)

180.37 ²every] WJ/MS² (*clipping*); the
    MS² (*clipping*)

180.40-41 'Though ... Him.'] *stet*
    WJ/MS² (*clipping*); "~ ... ~." MS²
    (*clipping*)

180.42-45 "This ... worst."] *stet* WJ/MS²
    (*clipping*); ∧~ ... ~.∧ MS² (*clipping*)

181.1 II] *omit* MS²

181.7 him,] ~ ∧ MS²

‡181.13 these:−] ~.∧ MS²

181.17;188.14 heaven] Heaven MS²

§181.17 *justice*] justice [*underline del.*]
    MS²; P¹⁷(p)

181.23 fact, nothing more−] ~−~~,
    MS²

181.24 given-ness] given MS²; giver P¹⁷(p)

§181.28-32 Yea." ... will."] *stet* MS²
    [*db. qts. alt. fr. sg. qts.*]

181.33 ¶Or] *no* ¶ MS²

181.34 standstill] stand-still MS²

‡182.2 catch:] ~− MS²

182.8 running] run MS²; ran P¹⁷(p)

§182.10 pardon;∧] ~,− [*dash intrl.*]
    MS²

182.12+ space] *no space* MS²; WJ *marked
    for space top of galley* P¹⁷(p)

182.16 Lion] lion MS²

182.17 incarnations.] ~ : MS²

§182.19 "Whelped] *stet* MS² [*db. qts.
    alt. fr. sg. qts.*]

182.35 life.∧ ..."] ~.' ... .∧ MS²

182.36 Again:∧] ~:− MS²

§182.37 "Naked] *stet* MS² [*db. qts.
    alt. fr. sg. qts.*]

183.1 gazed−] ~,− MS²

183.2 Isles] isles MS²

183.27 'coming to,'] *stet sg. qts.* MS²

183.27 No] WJ/MS² (*clipping*); But no
    MS² (*clipping*)

183.29 primordial∧] ~, MS² (*clipping*)

183.32 lairs,] ~ ∧ MS² (*clipping*)

183.35 *them*;] them, MS² (*clipping*)

183.43 ever,] ~ ∧ MS² (*clipping*)

183.43 again.] ~? MS² (*clipping*)

184.1 "Repetition] ∧ ~ MS² (*clipping*)

184.4 but] WJ/MS² (*clipping*); only
    MS² (*clipping*)

184.9 "It] WJ/MS² (*clipping*) (*opp.
    marginal* ¶); ∧it MS² (*clipping*); WJ *del.
    pencil note* ' .... I think most' *at
    top of clipping*

184.22 low,∧] ~,− MS² (*clipping*)

184.23 man,] ~ ∧ MS² (*clipping*)

184.26 peace,] ~ ; MS² (*clipping*)

184.33 declared:∧] ~:− MS² (*clipping*)

185.1 know, ... known,] ~− ... ~.−
    MS² (*clipping*)

185.3 soul."] WJ/MS² (*clipping*); ~− ∧
    MS² (*clipping*)

185.5-6 philosophy] *omit* MS²

185.9 a *name*,] *omit* MS²

185.12 overcoat.] ~ ∧ MS²

185.12 this,] *omit* MS²

185.30 fast,] ~ ∧ MS²

185.34 Philosophy,] ~ ∧ MS²

185.34 Mr.] *omit* MS²; ~ ∧ P¹⁷

185.35 freedom:∧] ~:− MS²

185.36-186.8-46 "Let ... free."] *stet*
    WJ/MS² (*clipping*); ∧~ ... ~.∧ MS²
    (*clipping*)

‡186.1 letter,] ~: MS²

186.7 final,] ~ ∧ MS²

186.10 [ermined]] WJ/MS² (*clipping*);
    purpled MS² (*clipping*)

186.11-14 Ah ... Calvary] *omit* MS²
    (*clipping*)

186.16 themselves:] ~ ; MS² (*clipping*)

186.20 orbs] orbits MS² (*clipping*)

186.22 nor] or MS² (*clipping*)

186.30 gonfalon,] ~ ∧ MS² (*clipping*)

186.40 torch∧] ~, MS² (*clipping*)

187.1 pragmatically,] ~ ∧ MS²

187.2 remains,] ~ ∧ MS²

187.3,33-41 Mystery."⁰] ~.'∧ (*omit fn.*)
    MS²

187.6 ¹fact∧] ~, MS²

187.6 uninvolved] unincluded MS²

§187.8 is,] ~ ∧ [*caret over orig. comma*]
    MS²

187.13 author. "And] ~, 'and MS²

187.17 be,] ~ ∧ MS²

187.29 "Variety] *stet db. qt.* MS²

§188.4-5 from ... thinking] this ['vision
    is one' *del.*] vision, intellectually con-
    sidered, MS²

188.4 view∧] ~, P¹⁷(p)

188.7 pieces."$_\wedge$] $\sim$.'— MS^2

188.9 revelation,] $\sim _\wedge$ MS^2

188.10 father—] $\sim$, MS^2

188.13 6] — MS^2

§ 188.17-40 "How . . . Will!"] *stet db. qts.* MS^2 ['W' *over* 'w']

188.22 desire,] $\sim _\wedge$ MS^2

188.23 That] The MS^2

188.23 weak,] $\sim _\wedge$ MS^2

188.30 resolves,] $\sim _\wedge$ MS^2

188.36 draw?] $\sim$! MS^2

188.38 still!] $\sim$, MS^2

189.3-4 conditions . . . revelation,] conditions; Mr. Blood, MS^2

§ 189.4 whatever] ['feels that w' *del.*] whate'er [*alt. fr.* 'whatever'] MS^2

§ 189.4 helps . . . stand] stands [*ab. del.* 'is'] MS^2

189.5-6 In . . . *fati!*] *omit* MS^2

189.10 'principle'!] $_\wedge \sim _\wedge$! MS^2

189.18-19 milk-and-water] $\sim _\wedge \sim _\wedge \sim$ MS^2 (*clipping*)

§ 189.34 "Ever not quite!"] *stet* MS^2 [*db. qts. alt. fr. sg. qts.; opp. marginal* '¶']

189.34 panting] *omit* MS^2

‡ 189.35 philosophy's mouth] philosophy MS^2

§ 189.38 verbalization,] verbalization$_\wedge$ [*alt. fr.* 'verbality [*alt. fr.* 'verbals'] '] and MS^2

189.38-39 and discursification,] *omit* MS^2

190.2 means] *omit* MS^2

190.4 burst into] burst,' Mr. Blood quotes, 'into MS^2

§ 190.7-10 the intellect . . . met and] *Blood's anesthetic 'revelation' ['mysticism' *del.*] [*ab. del.* 'the anaesthetic revelation'] finally *eliminates [*ab. del.* 'disposes of'], is the *intellect's [*intrl.*] claim to *reason out [*ab. del.* 'logicize'] reality; and *his [*insrtd. for del.* 'the'] mystical insight is *that [*intrl.*] reality ['['can be' *del.*] is dealt with, and can be dealt with, and' *del.*] can ['only' *del.*] be MS^2; P^{17}(p) (anæsthetic "revelation" . . . eliminates from the sphere of our duties)

§ 190.10 by] only [*ab. del. comma*] by ['a non-int' *del.*] MS^2; P^{17}(p)

190.12-13 This . . . author.] *omit* MS^2, P^{17}(p)

Alterations in the Manuscripts

All alterations made during the course of writing and of revision are recorded here except for strengthened letters to clarify a reading, a very few mendings over illegible letters, and false starts for the same word. The medium is the black ink of the original inscription unless otherwise specified. It is certain that many of the alterations were made *currente calamo* but others as part of one or more reviews. The two are ordinarily so indistinguishable in the intensity of ink or in the kind of pen, however, as not to yield to systematic recording by categories on the physical evidence. In the description of the alterations, when no record of position is given the inference should be that the change was made in the line of the text and during the course of the original writing. *Over* means inscribed over the letters of the original without interlining; *above* (*ab.*) always describes an independent interlineation. When an addition is a simple interlineation either with or without a caret, the description *intrl.* is used; when an interlineation is a substitute for one or more deleted words, the formula reads, instead, *ab. del.* 'xyz'. The word *inserted* (*insrtd.*) ordinarily refers to marginal additions or to squeezed-in letters, syllables, and words that also cannot properly be called interlines but are of the same nature. When reference is made to one or the other of two identical words in the same line of the present edition, some preceding or following word or punctuation mark is added for identification, or else the designated word is identified with a superscript [1] or [2] according as it is the first or second occurrence in the line. A superscript is also used to indicate which of more than one identical letter in the same word is referred to. A vertical stroke | signifies a line ending.

In order to ease the difficulty of reading quoted revised material of some length and complexity, the following convention is adopted. The quoted text will ordinarily be the final version in the manuscript, whereas the processes of revision are described within square brackets. To specify what words in the text are being affected by the description within square brackets, an asterisk is placed before the first word to which the description in brackets applies; thus it is to be taken that all following words before the square brackets are a part of the described material. For example, in *A Pluralistic Universe* (see the WORKS) at 26.28-29, James first wrote 'One must have lived longer with this system, to appreciate its advantages. I might now undertake to describe them, but they will appear more intelligibly after the details of the system have been worked out, and can be dealt with then', which took him to the bottom of the page. He then decided to revise, first writing 'merits.' above deleted 'advantages.' and interlining with a caret 'ingratiate my audience by exhibiting the latter seriatum, but' after 'undertake to'; at the same time he inserted 'its advantages' in the margin of the next line. He then revised the insertion by writing 'the' over 'its' and interlining with a caret 'of the system will be' after 'advantages' and at the same time deleted 'describe [to which he had added an 'ing' at some point] them, but they will appear'. He revised the remainder of the sentence by altering the 'y' of 'intelligibly' to 'e', writing 'its' above 'the' before 'details', and deleting the following 'of the system'. Finally, he seems to have changed his mind about the passage altogether and returning to the beginning of the first sentence, interlined 'But' with a caret before 'One', inserted 'some time' for deleted 'longer', and wrote 'such a' above deleted 'this', and then deleted 'such'. At the same time he deleted 'its merits. . . . with then' and substituted 'its merits.' for the deletion on the next page. In formulaic terms this series of alterations is transcribed as 'But [*intrl.*] One [*unreduced in error*] must have lived *some time [*insrtd. for del.* 'longer'] with *a [*aft. del.* 'such' *ab. del.* 'this'] system, to appreciate [*del.* 'its *merits. [*ab. del.* 'advantages.'] I might now undertake to *ingratiate my audience by exhibiting the latter seriatum, but **the [*over* 'its'] advantages ***of the system will be [*intrl.*] [*ab. del.* 'describing ['ing' *over* 'e'] them, but they will appear'] more *intelligible ['e' *over* 'y'] after *its [*ab. del.* 'the'] details ['of the system' *del.*] have been worked out, and can be dealt with then'] '.

In the above formulaic transcription double asterisks are used to set off subsidiary alterations occurring between the single asterisk and the bracketed description that applies to this single asterisk. Inferior brackets clarify subsidiary bracketed descriptions within or before the main bracketed entry, with or without the use of asterisks according to circumstances.[1]

The lemmata (the readings to the left of the bracket) are ordinarily drawn from the present edition and represent the agreement of book and manuscript. To permit condensed entries, in some cases a single dagger prefixed to the page-line reference warns the user to refer to the Historical Collation for the exact manuscript reading in simple situations when the precise form of the alteration in words or accidentals is (a) not printed in the lemma, or (b) not specified in the descriptive part of the entry. For instance, at 10.12 in *A Pluralistic Universe*, the edition text reads 'leaving the disorderly parts out;' whereas the MS interlineation is 'leaving the disorder out;'. The daggered entry †10.12 leaving . . . out;] *intrl.* saves space by referring the user to the Historical Collation which reads 10.12 disorderly parts] disorder MS. On the contrary, twin daggers warn the user that the lemma is not (as in every other circumstance) the reading of the edition text but is instead that of the manuscript. This convention is employed only when the two readings are so similar that a user following the edition text in the Alterations list will be able to identify with certainty the reading that is intended, without recourse to the Historical Collation. A simple example of an accidental difference occurs in *A Pluralistic Universe* at 15.14 where the edition text punctuates the phrase 'in the zenith' with a following comma which is missing in the MS phrase inscribed over a deletion. The condensed entry reads ††15.14 in the zenith‸] *ab. del.* 'makes witchery'. A simple substantive example comes at 17.26 where the edition text reads 'a character of' and the MS 'and a character of' is inscribed above a long deletion. The alteration is noted as ††17.26 and a character of] *ab. del.* '['If we are good theists' *del.*] ['The externality' *del.*] Their mutual'. In some cases daggers may refer the reader to the Emendations list. This will occur when a source other than the MS has been used as the emending agent in an emendation. In such cases, the MS reading and the emended text reading will diverge, and because emendations are not repeated in the Historical Collation the reader must check the Emendations list for the details of variation. It is worth emphasizing that whereas the device of twin daggers saves the reader from consulting any other part of the apparatus, the

---

[1] The full details of this system may be found in F. Bowers, "Transcription of Manuscripts: The Record of Variants," *Studies in Bibliography*, 29 (1976), 212-264.

details of all such variants will nevertheless appear in the Historical Collation and in the Emendations list should he wish to check them there. One instance in which a twin-daggered variant cannot be found in the Historical Collation is when James has made an obvious error in MS; in this case the error is cited in the Alterations entry and is not repeated in the Historical Collation. Finally, when the manuscript reading used in the lemma corresponds to a variant in the edition text which has been silently emended or is not recorded in the Historical Collation (as indicated in A Note on the Editorial Method or in the headnotes to the list of Emendations or the Historical Collation), twin daggers refer to no other section of the apparatus but merely draw attention to the easily construed variant between text and MS.

Whenever practicable, alterations in the manuscript that also comprise textual variants complete in themselves appear in the Historical Collation instead of in the list of Alterations. For the details of these entries, see the headnote to the Historical Collation.

The use of three dots to the right of the bracket almost invariably indicates ellipsis rather than the existence of dots in the manuscript. This is the only violation of the bibliographical rule that material within single quotes is cited exactly as it appears in the original document.

Deleted versos not apparently relating to the revision described within the main body of the Alterations list are transcribed in a separate section following the list of alterations for each essay.

HERBERT SPENCER DEAD

96.2　loss] *ab. del.* 'death'

96.2　one of] *intrl.*

96.2　two or three] *intrl.*

96.2　most] *bef. del.* 'widely'

96.2　thinkers whom] 's' *added*; 'whom' *ab. del.* 'which'

96.3　to our] *insrtd. for del.* 'to the present'

96.3　Influences] *aft. del.* '['Mill's influence was great, the remoter' *del.*] ['We may widely *rather* [*initial* 'r' *over* 't'] than deeply, for it may be doubted whether' *del.*] Philosophic [*insrtd.*] influences ['i' *over* 'I'] are of two kinds, wide *or* [*ab. del.* 'and'] deep, immediate or remote, and it is the'

96.5　For] *aft. del.* 'It is an'

96.6　Darwin.] *bef. del.* 'Mill's influence was technical, more over other thinkers than over *non technical [ab. del.* 'common'] readers,'

96.7　circles,] *bef. del.* 'and only remotely over the educated public,'

96.7　students] *insrtd. for del.* 'readers'

96.7　touched] *ab. del.* 'affected [*bef. pencil del.* 'have']'

96.8　owed as much to] *ab. del.* 'valued the example of'

96.8　theoretic] *intrl.*

96.8　as to] *ab. del.* 'quite as much as'

96.10　who] *intrl.*

†96.11-12　Spencer's ... direct.] ('contrariwise,' *in pencil ab. pencil del.* 'on the other hand,'); *ab. del.* '['But' *del.*] Spencer's influence, was no less direct than it *is [ab. del.* 'was'] wide.'

96.12　Thousands of readers] *ab. del.* '['Untechnical' *del.*] Readers ['R' *over* 'r']'

96.12-13　who ... students] *insrtd.*

96.13　original;] *bef. del.* 'and what they value more than [*start of illeg. letter del.*] either his method or his temper,'

96.13-14　and ... given] *ab. del.* 'and he gives them'

96.14-15　(what ... temper)] *parens over commas*

96.14　either] *intrl.*

96.15 theoretic] *intrl.*

96.15 a simple,] ('simple,' *ab. del.* 'vast,'); *aft. del.* '*a a vast, simple, utilizable [*ab. del.* 'a set of easily apprehensible'] result['s' *del.*], a vast and simple way and to many a sublime, result, in the'

96.16 which] *aft. del.* 'the light of'; *bef. del.* '[*del.* 'they can live, *in [*insrtd.*] with a patient and hopeful ['tempera ['a' *doubtful*]' *del.*] attitude of soul, seeing in all things *corroboration [*ab. del.* 'illustrations'] of an explanatory [*illeg. letter del.*] formula so elastic as to fit almost any conceivable phenomenon'] ['view all things' *del.*] all'

96.16 whose] *ab. del.* 'and the'

96.17 formula] *ab. del.* 'formula of which'

96.17 to] *intrl.*

96.17 every] *aft. del.* 'elastically [*ab. del.* 'itself to']'

96.18 the] *bef. del.* '['hopeful' *del.*] patient and hopeful'

96.18 vague] *final* 'ly' *del. in pencil*; *bef. pencil del.* 'religious'

96.18-19 optimism which is] *ab. del.* 'hopefulness is'

96.19 so] *insrtd.*

96.19 important] *in pencil ab. pencil del.* 'characteristic'

96.19 a tendency in] *ab. del.* 'of the'

96.19 life.] *aft. del.* 'mind.'; *bef. del.* 'In *this ['t' *over* 'T'] immediate efficacy of Mr. Spencer's writings'

96.20 popular success] *ab. del.* 'direct influence'

96.21 constructive] *aft. del.* '['the' *del.*] the'

96.22 already] *intrl.*

96.22 man] *bef. del.* 'who comes'

††96.22 has an] 'n' *added to* 'a', *then undel. in error*; *bef. del.* 'intelligible [*intrl.*]'

96.22 propound.] *period insrtd. bef. del.* '; and'

96.23 waste] *aft. del.* 'clear the ground of'

96.23 in] *ab. del.* '['by' *del.*] in attacking errors or'

96.23 old] 'o' *alt. fr.* 'a'

96.23 views; his view] *semicolon alt. fr. period*; 'his' *insrtd.*; 'view' *ab. del.* 'His system'

96.23-97.1 simply] *bef. del.* 'substitutes itself for previous ones and'

97.1 others] *alt. fr.* 'them'

97.1 there. And] *period insrtd. bef. del. semicolon or comma*; 'A' *over* 'a'

97.1-2 awarding] *ab. del.* 'reckoning up the'

97.2 "points"] *bef. del.* 'which are to be credited'

97.4 on] *ab. del.* 'for'

97.4 score of] *aft. del.* 'merit' *ab. del.* 'point of'

97.4 positive and systematic] *tr. by guideline fr.* 'systematic and positive'

97.5 greatness this] |'ness this' *over* | 'ness goes with that'

97.5 imports—] (*dash aft. del.* 'signifies—'); *intrl.*

97.6 measure] *aft. del.* 'degree'

97.7 vividly] *ab. del.* 'fully'

97.8 evolved] *alt. fr.* 'evolving'

97.9 heterogeneity and] *aft. del.* 'coher'; *bef. del.* 'organic cohere'

97.9-10 coherence] *alt. fr.* 'coherent'

97.10 of texture and] *insrtd.*

97.10 can] *aft. del.* 'does n't not realize both'

97.11 a set of] *ab. del.* 'an'

97.11 ways] 's' *added*

†97.12 at . . . grown] *insrtd. for del.* '['thought of the' *del.*] ['pondered over the' *del.*] found him-|['self ethically sobered' *del.*] self morally made'

††97.13 parent's] *bef. del.* 'fruits of the'

††97.13 sinful and virtuous] *alt. fr.* 'sins and virtues'

97.13 habits] *ab. del.* '['ac' *del.*] acts'

97.14 destined to] *intrl.*

97.15 whilst] *ab. del.* 'so long as'

†97.16-17 of . . . genius,] *intrl.*

97.17 appraisal] *ab. del.* 'assessment'

97.17 his] *ab. del.* 'Mr. Spencer's'

97.18 a hard] *ab. del.* 'most delicate'

97.18 one,] *intrl.*

97.19 was] *alt. fr.* 'is'; *ab. del.* 'was'

97.19 temperament] *aft. del.* 'man,'

97.20 the] *alt. fr.* 'his'

97.20 ground] *aft. del.* 'his'

97.20 his work covered] ('his' *bef. del.* 'the'; 'covered' *alt. fr.* 'covers,'); *ab. del.* 'his studies covered'

97.20   narrow] *aft. del.* 'angular'

97.21   was] *alt. fr.* 'is'; *intrl.*

97.21   he . . . showed.] *ab. del.* '*this
author's [*insrtd. for del.* 'his [*insrtd.*]
['his [*alt. fr.* 'he']' *del.*]'] personality
[*alt. fr.* 'personally'] presents'

97.21   A] *over* 'a'; *aft. del.* '['One should
have the *pen brush [*ab. del.* 'pen'] of a
Carlyle to adequately breathe upon' *del.*]
Only'

97.22   might] *ab. del.* 'could adequately
*convey [*insrtd. for del.* 'give'] the impression'

97.24   like the] *insrtd.*

97.24   present critic] (*bef. del. insrtd.
doubtful* 'one'); *pencil insrtd. for del.
intrl.* '['present' *del.*] *author of the
present lines [*pencil del.*]'

97.24   indeed,] *intrl. with caret over
comma*

BRADLEY OR BERGSON?

[*The inscription is in pencil.*]

151.10   In] 'I' *over* 'i'; *aft. del.* 'Both'

151.10   as well as in] *ab. del.* 'and'

151.10   he] *ab. del.* 'and Reality he not
only confesses but'

151.11   of] *bef. del.* 'conceptualized [*ab.
del.* 'uninterpreted']'

151.11   directly] *intrl.*

151.11   and] *aft. del.* 'of which the continuity and'

151.15   of] *bef. del.* 'immediate'

151.17   idealist] *ab. del.* 'kantian'

151.18   continuity] *ab. del.* 'unity'

151.19   which] *aft. del.* 'or categories'

151.20   tactics] *aft. del.* 'manner of spe'

152.2   be] *bef. del.* 'equivalents for a
perce'

††152.4   Concepts, says B.ᴧ] *ab. del.* 'The
use of concepts, Bergson says, is not
what ['ration' *del.*] intellectualism has
always assumed it to be, to'

152.4   less, not] *insrtd.*

152.9   is just as] *ab. del.* 'shows a similar'

152.9   independent of] *alt. fr.* 'independence of the'

152.10   still] *ab. del.* 'than Bergson'

152.10   criticism of the] *ab. del.* 'demonstration that'

152.10-11   function] *aft. del.* 'makes the'

152.11   felt] *aft. del.* 'the ['pe' *del.*] pr'

152.13   change inadmissible,] *intrl.*

152.14   impossible] *bef. del. comma*

152.16   make] *alt. fr.* 'have made'

152.16   with] *bef. del.* 'all'

152.18   up] *aft. del.* 'upo'

152.20   an] *aft. del.* 'and'

152.23   do;] *ab. del. semicolon*

152.24   its] *bef. del.* 'much-at-once-ness is'

152.24   transparent] *bef. del.* 'type of
union'

152.24   he] *insrtd. for del.* 'I'

152.25   its data] 's' *added*; 'data' *intrl.*

152.25   kind] *ab. del.* 'type'

152.26   replace.] *bef. del.* 'Its data must
remain there untransformed, just as
old-fashioned empiricism has always
claimed.'

152.30-31   mediated,] *comma added*

152.31   , but of the immediate] *moved fr.
aft.* 'is [152.30]' *to aft.* 'mediated'

152.31   type.] *period insrtd. bef. del.*
', just as the mystics have always said.'

152.31   with] *bef. del.* 'both'

152.33   could] *aft. del.* 'is complete.'

152.34   thorough] *bef. del. comma*

†152.35   in . . . steps.] *insrtd. bel. del.* 'so
[*ab. del.* 'as'] far as what is concrete in
it goes.'

152.36   in] *bef. del.* 'immediate'

152.36   is] *bef. del.* 'something that even
the absolute must'

152.37   must preserve] 'must' *intrl.*; *final*
's' *of* 'preserves' *del.*

152.40   is] *aft. del.* 'anti-empir'

††153.1-2   Crude . . . ᴧTruth,ᴧ] ('u' *in*
'unmediated' *over* 'a'; 'shall' *over* 'can';
'T' *over* 't'); *ab. del.* 'We'

153.3   he] *aft. del.* 'transcends &'

153.4   upon] 'up' *intrl.*

††153.7   . . . . . . The] *aft. del.* '*, [*comma
undel. in error*] ['and yet jud' *del.*] and
yet judgment seeks in vain to escape
from this foregone method'

153.8   has] *bef. del.* 'not'

153.10-11   nothing] *aft. del.* 'the ['dut'
del.] rationalist duty of keeping data of
immediate feeling'

153.11-12 'untransformed'] *insrtd.*

153.12 into] *aft. del.* 'naive [*doubtful*] *tel quel*'

153.12 explain] *ab. del.* 'justify'

153.13 here onwards] *ab. del.* 'this point onwards'

153.17 [This]] *ab. del.* 'Our'

153.19 permitted. . . .] *sg. qt. del. aft. period*

153.23 feeling.] *bef.* ' . . . . . [*intrl.*]'

153.36-37 doggedly . . . a] ('a' *aft. del.* 'the') ; *ab. del.* 'never giving up a'

153.37 entered on] *ab. del.* '['struck' *del.*] started on but pursuing it'

153.37 We] *bef. del.* 'start'

153.38 and . . . ideas] ('and' *bef. del.* 'but'); *ab. del.* 'and for good reason find that'

154.1 more intelligible] *intrl.*

154.1 respects.] *period insrtd. bef. del.* 'more 'intelligible' when we *judge it by [*ab. del.* 'turn it into'] ideas.'

†154.2-3 which . . . the] ('point' *ab. del. illeg. word*); *ab. del.* 'and pursuing this still *farther [*doubtful*] find *ourselves [*alt. fr.* 'ourself' '] landed in the'

154.3 bog] *aft. del.* 'q'

154.4 through] *intrl.*

154.5 wades.] *ab. del.* 'sets forth.'

154.6 seem to] *intrl.*

154.8 there . . . that] *insrtd.*

154.9-10 not do sooner] *ab. del.* 'do anything but rather'

154.10 this.] *bef. del.* '['There must be' *del.*] An ['A' *over* 'a'] ultimate reality [*illeg. word*] while the wholeness and certainty and unity of feeling'

154.10 let us] *ab. del.* 'must he'

154.10 He] *ab. del.* 'His mind'

154.11 desperate] *bef. del.* 'transperceptual and'

††154.11-12 beyond . . . perspective] ('ideal' *aft. del.* 'id'; 'perspective' *aft. del.* 'conceptual'); *ab. del.* 'the Absolute is that something in which somehow this'

††154.12 ultimate ⌃suprarelational⌃] *sg. qts. del. fr.* 'ultimate'; 'suprarelational' *ab. del.* 'and transfigured'

154.13 somehow] *sg. qts. and preceding comma del.*

154.14 forever] *intrl.*

154.15 are . . . to] *ab. del.* '['are' *del.*] shall'

††154.18 ²be⌃] *intrl.*

154.18 only candid] *ab. del.* 'only sincere'

154.19 statement] *ab. del.* 'way'

154.21 of a] ('a' *aft. del.* 'the'); *ab. del.* 'be made'

154.22 bring] *aft. del.* 'better show the point of arbitrary choice?'

154.22 the] *bef. del.* 'psychological'

154.22 choice] *bef. del.* '?'

††154.24 life,] *comma over period bef. del.* 'which is the superior way? and the'

154.25 but] *ab. del.* 'yet'

154.26 not] *intrl.*

††154.26-27 life⌃ but to] *ab. del.* 'being [*ab. del.* 'getting'] fed, yet for'

154.29 motive] *insrtd. for del.* 'reason'

154.31 universals.] *period insrtd. bef. del.* 'and'

154.31 They are] *alt. fr.* 'Theirs is'; *bef. del.* 'the [*ab. del.* 'the']'

154.32 objects] *aft. del.* 'way'

154.32 than . . . sense] ('than' *bef. del.* 'are'); *ab. del.* ', ['for' *del.*] of attention'

154.33 In] *ab. del.* 'To [*over* 'In']'

154.33 feeling,] *intrl. bef. del.* 'the other' *ab. del.* 'sense-particulars,'

154.33 a] *ab. del.* 'the'

154.34 high] *intrl. aft. del.* 'true' *ab. del.* 'calling turn'

154.34 always turn] *ab. del.* 'keep'

154.34 face.] *period insrtd. bef. del.* '['turned' *del.*] always turned'

154.37 thin] *alt. fr.* 'thinnest' *bef. del.* 'possible'

154.38 dry] *intrl. aft. del.* 'waterless' *ab. del.* 'dry unwatered'

††154.39 ⌃absolute⌃] *insrtd. for del.* 'the Absolute, the *habitation [*ab. del.* 'home'] of every'

154.39 nests] *final* 's' *added*

154.39 abstractions,] *bef. del.* '['rather than which he c' *del.*] ['which' *del.*] in which he'

†154.39-155.1 fictitious . . . being] *ab. del.* 'imaginary absolute' *ab. del.* 'fictitious resurrected reality'

155.1 his will prefers.] 'his will' *ab. del.* 'he'; *period insrtd. bef. del.* 'to *invoke.

[*ab. del.* 'the given reality that feeling gives *us, [*intrl.*] *a reality whose union, [*ab. del.* 'and the unity and'] wholeness and transparency of which it can only incomprehensibly pretend to ape.']'

†155.2 there . . . -believe;] *ab. del.* 'choice made with wider open eyes,'

155.2 Mr.] 'M' *over* 'm'

†155.2-3 unlike . . . deludes] ('anti∧ empiricists∧' *aft. del.* 'rationalists'; 'deludes' *alt. fr.* 'deceives'); *intrl.*

155.3 feeling] *aft. del.* 'the insufficience'

155.5 as soon] *aft. del.* '['as soon' *del.*] disintegrating all things,'

155.5-6 carry . . . few] *ab. del.* 'let it go further than a few simple'

155.6 Yet] *bef. del.* 'truth is more than reality, so'

155.7 ²we] *insrtd. for del.* 'be'

†155.7-8 save . . . that] ('by' *aft. del.* 'by that'); *ab. del.* 'backing ['b' *over* 'p'; 'ing' *added*] into'

155.9 so] *bef. del.* 'intelligibly gave.'

155.10 made] *ab. del.* 'makes ['s' *added*]'

155.13 always] *aft. del.* 'are.'

155.13 reality] *aft. del.* 'we encounter'

155.13 reveals] *ab. del.* '['& are' *del.*] reveals its ['com' *del.*] ['manifo' *del.*] inner nature as'

†155.15 then . . . of] *ab. del.* 'let th the knowledge of *particulars [*ab. del.* '['them' *del.*] them [*insrtd.*]'] not be called'

155.18 in . . . sense] *ab. del.* 'pass'

155.18 which] *aft. del.* 'imperfect knowledge'

155.18 he candidly] *insrtd. for del.* 'Mr. Bradley'

155.19 lies] *ab. del.* 'is'

155.19 knowing] *ab. del.* 'knowledge of'

155.20 in] *bef. del.* 'all'

155.20 activity,] *ab. del.* 'mes and thees and nows and theres, and'

155.21-22 knowing a] *bef. del.* '['spectral' *del.*] conceptual evap'

155.24 it . . . named] 'it' *insrtd.*; 'has been named' *ab. del.* 'it is called'

155.24 to be] *bef. del.* 'loyal'

155.25 names are] *aft. del.* 'that [*ab. del.* 'th']'; *alt. fr.* 'name is'

155.25-26 give . . . to] ('to' *aft. del.* 'call'); *ab. del.* 'reserve it for'

155.26-27 , the kind in which] (', the' *aft. del.* 'philosophy'); *ab. del.* 'and let'

155.27 mix] *aft. del.* 'intermingle their indispensable parts.'

155.28 can] *aft. del.* 'can'

155.30 confirmed] *ab. del.* '['confirm' *del.*] re-established'

155.30 my] *bef. del.* 'nature'

††155.30 untransmuted] *intrl.*

†155.31 my . . . down] ('unlimited' *insrtd.*); *ab. del.* '['the credit of the conceptual' *del.*] method of *turning of ['con' *del.*] them into concepts [*insrtd. for del.* 'conceptual translation down']'

155.32 their . . . converged] *ab. del.* 'working together they have brought ['things' *del.*] us'

155.33 sharp] *ab. del.* '['perfectly' *del.*] clear'

155.33 which now . . . in which] ('and' *bef. del.* 'everyone's'); *ab. del.* 'in which'

155.34 reasons] *ab. del.* 'motives'

155.35 be] *intrl.*

155.36 at least say] 'at least' *intrl.*; 'say' *ab. del.* 'know the reason'

155.37 accounts] *alt. fr.* 'can account'

156.1 take] *aft. del.* 'fall into the ['Bergsonia' *del.*] other valley'

††156.2 thought∧] *period omitted in error*; *insrtd. for del.* 'philosophy. Bergson & he together would make ['put h' *del.*] have put the whole'

156.3 previous forms of] *ab. del.* 'pre kantian'

156.5 underground.] *bef. del.* 'out of date.'

DELETED VERSOS FOR "BRADLEY OR BERGSON?" MANUSCRIPT

[*undel. fol.* 13ᵛ: *in pencil; corresponds to text at* 154.24] 'The way of phil. is not the way of life'

A Suggestion about Mysticism

[The inscription is in pencil unless otherwise noted.]

157.1 religious] *intrl.*
157.2 Most] *aft. del.* 'I have not read many of the'
157.2 writings] *ab. del.* 'articles'
157.3 subject] *ab. del.* 'matter'
157.5 views.] *ab. del.* 'contentions.'
157.6 possibly] *intrl.*
157.8 unexpressed.] *aft. del.* 'unprinted.'
157.9 The] *over* 'My'
157.9 stated] *ab. del.* 'is exprest'
157.10 may be] *ab. del.* 'are'
157.10 the] *over* 'a'; *aft. del.* 'what psychologists call the ordinary f* ['in *vast* [*doubtful*]' *del.*] ['psychology is known' *del.*]'
††157.11 'field'] *qts. added in ink*
157.11 Concerning] *ab. del.* 'Of'
††157.12-13 would consist['s' *del.*]] 'would' *intrl.*
157.13 an] *aft. del.* 'a [*ab. del.* 'the'] flattening, so to speak, of the centre of the field, and'
157.13 immense spreading of] *ab. del.* 'extension of'
157.14 margin] *bef. del.* 'such at'
157.14 so] *ab. del.* 'such'
157.14 knowledge] *intrl. aft. del.* 'consciousness' *ab. del.* 'objects'
157.15 and] *bef. del.* '*what under [*ab. del.* 'the'] ordinary *conditions is the **margin [*undel. in error*] [*ab. del.* 'margin grows [*illegible*]']'
†157.15 the . . . grow] ('margin grew' *aft. del.* 'grew'); *ab. del.* 'quickly grows'
157.16 Fechner's] *bef. del.* 'willin [*doubtful*]'
157.16-17 alteration] 'l' *over* 't'
157.17 wave] *aft. del.* 'consciousness [*ab. del.* 'horizontal lines']'
157.17-18 of present awareness,] ('of present' *insrtd. bef. del. intrl.* 'of'); *intrl.*
157.18-19 plane of the] *ab. del.* 'ordinary th'
157.19-20 in all directions.] *ab. caret formed fr. orig. period*
157.21 produce] *aft. del.* 'do what *a

spring's [*bef. del.* 'the *ebb [*intrl.*]']' tide does *when it ebbs [*intrl.*] on an unusually flat beach. It would uncover vast tracts ordinarily covered, but'
157.22 shore] *ab. del.* 'beach ['when' *del.*]'
157.23 then] *intrl.*
158.1 few] 'f' *over* 'v'
158.1-2 are submerged again] *ab. del.* '['are' *del.*] go under water'
158.3 Some] *alt. fr.* 'Sub [*doubtful*]'
158.3 narrow] *aft. del.* 'latter'
158.4-5 an unusually] *alt. fr.* 'in unusual'
158.5 form of the] *intrl. bef. del. intrl.* 'w'
158.5 wave.] *period insrtd. bef. del.* 'above the threshold.'
158.5 any] *intrl.*
158.6 direct] *ab. del.* 'my own'
158.8 come] *final* 's' *del.*
158.8 view,] *comma insrtd. bef. del.* 'all at once,'
158.9 perceived] *intrl.*
158.10 experience; and] *semicolon added;* 'and' *ab. del.* 'which'
158.10 now] *intrl.*
158.11 it] *intrl.*
158.11 an] *intrl.*
158.12 to give us] *ab. del.* 'and we get'
158.12 such] *bef. del.* 'term'
158.13 allowed.] *insrtd. for del.* 'not impertinent.'
158.15 definiteness] 'd' *over doubtful* 'l'
158.15 The field] *ab. del.* 'It'
158.16 mass] *ab. del.* 'nucleus'
158.16 in a] *insrtd. in ink for ink del.* 'to which' *ab. pencil del.* 'plus'; *precedes* 'a' *undel. in error*
††158.17 Yet These] 'Yet' *insrtd.*; 'T' *unreduced in error*
158.17 ingredients,] *comma insrtd.*
158.17-18 which . . . separately] 'which . . . named' *ab. del.* 'are not atomistically'; 'ly' *over* 'd'
158.18 are] *aft. pencil and ink del.* '*are not sepa [*ab. del.* 'but coalesce'] and interpenetrate, and *are dissolved. [*ab. del.* 'melt into one another.'] The present field *melts. [*period del.*] in the field's unity.'

158.19 in . . . ²the] *ab. del.* 'and'

158.20 sensations,] *comma added in ink*

158.20 concepts,] *aft. del.* '&'; *bef. del.* '['are' *del.*] and'

158.20 etc.,] *insrtd.*

158.20 coalesce] *bef. del.* 'and interpenetrate'

158.20-21 dissolved.] *period insrtd. bef. del.* 'in the fields unity.'

158.21 present] *aft. del.* 'whole [*intrl.*]'

158.21 as] 'a' *over* 'i'

158.21 a . . . continuously] *ab. del.* 'similarly ['dissolv' *del.*] melted'

158.22 will] *aft. del.* 'melts *a [*undel. in error*]'

158.22 as . . . again,] *alt. fr.* 'with similar continuity,'

158.23 one] *aft. del.* 'one sensa'

158.23 giving] *ab. del.* 'yielding'

158.24 a gradually changing] *intrl.*

158.26 place] *intrl. aft. pencil del.* 'envelope [*in ink*]' *ab. del.* '*surround ['round' *ink del.*] the'

158.26 whatever] 'ever' *intrl.*

158.26 in a] 'in' *ab. del.* 'with'; 'a' *bef. ink del.* 'sphere of'

††158.26-27 perspective, . . . vast.] (*comma over period*); *ab. del.* 'vastness and remoteness.'

158.29 for sensation] ('sensation' *insrtd. in ink aft. ink del.* 'that'); *ab. del.* 'or if that comes ['at all' *del.*] into view at all it is only in'

158.29-30 stimulations] *final* 's' *added*

158.30 purely] *ab. del.* 'psychi'

158.31 physical] *second* 'l' *del.*

158.31 were] 'wire' *in error ab. del.* 'are'

158.32 subliminally] *ab. del.* 'marginally'

158.32 next] *ab. del.* 'new'

158.32 would] *aft. del.* 'wd'

158.32-33 whatever] *ab. del.* 'the'

158.33 was] *intrl.*

158.33 reveal] *alt. fr.* 'report'

158.34-35 conational states,] 'conational' *in ink ab. ink del.* 'relational'; *comma insrtd. in ink*

158.35 is] *ab. del.* 'seems to be'

158.35 exactly] *in ink ab. ink del.* 'just'

158.37 thought] *bef. del.* 'we'

158.38 of them] *intrl.*

158.38 set] *intrl.*

158.39 or] *intrl.*

158.39 terms] 'e' *over doubtful* 'a'

158.40 such] *ab. del.* 'subliminal'

††158.40-159.36 & Munsterberg apparently).] '& . . . apparently.' *intrl.*; *second period insrtd. bef. del. semicolon and first period written in error*

159.4 that always stood] ('stood' *insrtd. aft. del.* 'standing'); *ab. del.* 'that were always'

159.5 hypothesis] *ab. del.* 'idea'

159.5 movement] *ab. del.* 'fall'

159.5 downwards] *ab. del.* 'produces on this mental field an enlargement'

159.5 will] *bef. del.* 'bring'

159.6 memories] 'ies' *over* 'y'

159.6 conceptions] 's' *added*

159.7 and perceptions] *ab. del.* 'sense'

159.8 this] ('s' *in ink*); *alt. fr.* 'the'

159.8 nimbus] *aft. del.* 'material'

159.9 no one of the] *intrl. aft. del.* 'none of the' *ab. del.* 'the *sing [*doubtful*]'

159.10 attracts our] *ab. del.* 'are none of them raised high above the threshold, [*illeg.*] hold of'

159.10 singly,] *ab. caret formed fr. orig. comma*

159.10 shall] *intrl.*

159.11 in . . . respects] *intrl.*

159.13 of reality,] 'of' *aft. del.* 'rapturously'; 'reality,' *intrl. in ink*

159.13 enlargement,] *comma insrtd. in ink*

159.15 coalesces in it] ('o' *over* 'a'; *final* 's' *added*); *aft. del.* 'is made to'; 'in it' *intrl.*

159.15 its] *intrl.*

159.18 remembered . . . objects] *ab. del.* 'ingre-|dients of memory & conception'

159.19 only] *ab. del.* 'only'

159.20 a] *insrtd. for del.* 'of'

159.20 suddenly revealed.] 'suddenly ['re' *del.*] revealed.' *ab. del.* '['only' *del.*] come to view.'

159.23 suggestion.] *bef. del. note* 'Real mys'

159.23 mystical] *aft. del.* 'the'

159.24 will no doubt] *intrl. in ink bef. ink del.* 'may' *ab. del.* 'will doubtless'

159.24-25 any such shall] *ab. del.* 'they criticize'

159.36   Others] 'O' *over* 'o'
159.36   make] 'a' *over* 'i [doubtful]* '
159.36   exist and carry] *in ink ab. ink del.*
　　　　　'contain'
159.37-38   mode of] *ab. del. paren*
159.38   one] *bef. del.* 'mind in'

159.38   another's] ''s' *added in ink*
159.39   its existence;] 's' *of* 'its'
　　　　　added in ink; 'existence;' *in ink ab.*
　　　　　ink del. doubtful semicolon
159.40   set] *ab. del.* 'suppose'

Deleted Versos for "A Suggestion about Mysticism" Manuscript

[fol. 8ᵛ(34ᵛ); reversed page of pencil notes for Some Problems of Philosophy *(relates to 75.18-21 of Longmans, Green edition), covered by blank paste-over]* 'be to make students who are beginners in filosofy get a clearer notion of what the distinction means.

Wallace says that we are here to *know [*ab. del.* 'understand'] the world, not to make it better. This is the intellectualist position. Not to enter the world is the condition of loftiest being. But how does entering keep one from knowing? And *may [*ab. del.* 'does'] one not by entering learn something that *to [*intrl.*] outsiders remains unknown. Passive *onlooking [*ab. undel.* 'contemplation'] loses part of the experience.'

A Pluralistic Mystic

††172.0   A Pluralistic Mystic. | William James.] 'A . . . Mystic.' *triple underl.;* 'William James' *insrtd. with guideline and double underl.*
172.3   higher] *aft. del.* 'the'
172.3   metaphysics.] *ab. del.* 'philosophy.'
172.9   so I] *ab. del.* 'and I can'
172.11   city] *ab. del.* 'town'
172.12   situated] 's' *over* 'o'; 'ed' *over* 'ion'
172.15   him] *over* 'his'
172.15   short spurts] *ab. del.* 'brief fits'
172.17   as] *ab. del.* 'upon'
172.17   tracts,] *ab. del.* 'leaflets,'
172.20   such] *over* 'his'
172.20   subtile efforts] *ab. del.* 'dialectics'
172.20   creditable] *alt. fr.* 'a credit'
172.21   editors] *alt. fr.* 'editorship'
172.22   old] *intrl.*
172.23   these] *aft. del.* 'some of'
173.2   were] *ab. del.* 'got'
††173.5   days.*] *refers to marginal* '*Note on next page'
††173.6   ˄Anaesthetic] *initial sg. qt. alt. fr. db. qt. then del.*
173.9   been] *ab. del.* 'remained'
173.10   shows] *intrl.*
173.11   albeit . . . it] ('albeit' *bef. del.*

'although'); *ab. del.* 'save [*doubtful comma del.*] that in it one finds'
173.12   ²felicity] *intrl.*
173.13   metaphoric ['flight' *del.*] reach;] *ab. del.* 'extravagance'
173.14   of] *intrl.*
173.14   type,] (*comma alt. fr. semicolon*); *ab. del.* 'in character;'
173.15   trumpet-] *intrl.*
173.15   straight from] *ab. del.* 'appealing for its authority to'
173.16   −of . . . world!−] *intrl.*
173.17   heard] *ab. del.* 'read'
173.18   'regular'] *ab. del.* 'past'
173.18   unquestionably] *intrl.*
173.18   *monistic;*] *semicolon added bef. del.* 'in its tendency;'
173.19   characteristic] *aft. del.* 'habi'
173.20   there ˄] *comma del.*
173.21   manner] *aft. del.* '& authoritative'
173.21   have] *aft. del.* 'often'
173.23   often] *intrl.*
173.24   but . . . accept]('accept' *aft. del.* 'but'); *ab. del.* 'only bow to'
173.24-25   having . . . weight.] ('having some amount of' *insrtd. for del.* 'authoritative on'; 'evidential' *alt. fr.* 'evidence,'

bef. del. 'wrong to disregard.'); *ab. del.* 'else [*over* 'or'] pass it by.'

173.27 if] *aft. del.* 'be,'

173.27 be understood] *ab. del.* 'taken'

173.28 the] *ab. del.* 'his'

173.28 ones] *ab. del.* 'writings'

173.28-29 voice of defiance['s' *del.*],] *ab. del.* 'quality,'

173.29 has] *ab. del.* 'is'

173.30 sound] *ab. del.* 'tone'

173.31 made] *ab. del.* 'caused'

173.31 depart.] *ab. del.* 'to disappear.'

173.31 now] *intrl.*

173.32 kind of support] *insrtd. for del.* 'value' *ab. del.* 'sort of credential'

173.33 corroboration may confer['s' *del.*].] *ab. del.* 'insight may confer. experience may lend.'

173.33 claim] *aft. del.* 'flatter itself'

173.34 beneficiary . . . right['s' *del.*]] *ab. del.* 'heir of'

173.34 may . . . lend] ('to' *aft. del.* 'right'); *ab. del.* ' 's power and place.'

173.35 *prestige.*] *insrtd.*

††173.37-40 'Yes! . . . named.] *aft. circled* 'Note to page 2'

173.39 sought] 'o' *over* 'a'

173.39 by calling him] *ab. del.* 'as'

173.40 thought of him] *ab. del.* 'knew'

173.40 as . . . of] *ab. del.* 'of his'

174.1-2 more . . . audience:] *ab. del.* 'wider reading circle.'

174.2 his] 'h' *over* 'H'

††174.2 philosophy∧ however mystical,] *ab. del.* 'evolution from monism to pluralism'

174.3 must] *ab. del.* 'will'

174.4 certainly] *ab. del.* 'possibly'

174.4-5 consecutive] *aft. del.* 'very'

174.5 aphoristic] *bef. del.* ', syllogistic,'

174.5 oracular∧] *comma del.*

174.6 sometimes poetic,] *intrl.*

174.9 I . . . unprepared] 'I am ['to be' *del.*] not quite un-' *ab. del.* 'am quite'

174.10 missed] *aft. del.* 'mys'

174.10 his] *insrtd. for del.* 'the'

174.13 pure] *intrl.*

174.15 ²which] *ab. del.* 'of'

174.23 other] *ab. del.* 'any'

174.23 reports.] 's' *and period insrtd. bef. del.* 'from the same region.'

174.25 popular understanding] *moved by guideline fr. bef.* 'operations'; *guideline del.* ' 's' *of orig.* 'understanding's'

174.27 Blood] *alt. fr.* 'Blood's mind'

174.28 tribe.] *ab. del.* 'family.'

174.35 ²fact] *final* 's' *del.*

††174.37 for . . .] *sg. qt. del. aft. first period*

174.38 again] *ab. del.* 'elsewhere'

175.1 itself,] *bef. del.* 'as at itself,'

175.2 this] *intrl.*

175.2 signifies.] *ab. del.* 'means.'

175.5 our] *aft. del.* 'the'

175.5 rebound] *ab. del.* 'shall'

175.7 separate] *aft. del.* 'sp'

175.8 specific] *ab. del.* 'particular'

175.9 being—] *dash ab. del. comma*

175.9-10 imaginary background.] *in pencil ab. del.* 'foil. Being and the negative thereof thus ['form' *del.*] make an inseparable couple in our understanding.'

175.10 but] *ab. del.* 'save'

175.11 form] *aft. pencil del.* 'arc correlative and'

175.11 pair.] *aft. del.* 'couple.'

175.13-14 (where . . . itself)] *parens over commas*

175.14 the position . . . nothing.] *intrl. ab. del. period*

175.21 immediately] *aft. del.* '['limited' *del.*] simple—assumes knowledge as an'

††175.23 we assume['s' *del.*]] 'we' *reduced in error ab. del.* 'It'

175.24 we forget['s' *del.*]] 'we' *ab. del.* 'it'

175.25 if] *ab. del.* 'for'

175.25 were] *intrl.*

175.25 ²that] *insrtd.*

175.27 just as] *in pencil ab. del.* 'alike'

175.28 useless] *aft. del.* 'unintelligible and'

175.30 were] *bef. del.* 'alike'

175.34 evolving,] *intrl.*

175.38 ²of] *intrl.*

176.3 those] *aft. del.* 'all'

176.3 make] *ab. del.* '['are re-' | *del.*] ['makes' *del.*] give'

176.3 in] *ab. del.* 'to'

176.6 things] *underline del.*

176.6-7 simply owning entity,] *ab. del.* 'complete entities,'

176.7 background] *aft. del.* 'p'

176.8 holes] 's' *added*
176.10 indispensable in] *intrl.*
176.16 there for] *ab. del.* '['real in thought' *del.*] real in'
176.16-17 as . . . ¹its] *ab. del.* 'its'
176.18 By *its* absence] 'By' *intrl.*; 'its' *ab. del.* '"*Its*"; 'absence' *bef. del. sg. or db. qt.*
176.19 how] *aft. del.* '['ho' *del.*] now'
176.20 these] *ab. del.* 'any'
176.20 absences] *final* 's' *added*
176.20 save] *ab. del.* 'or from absence in general? We answer: It differs'
176.21 picture? The] *qst. mk. over colon*; 'T' *over* 't'
176.22 our] *insrtd.*
††176.23-24 what . . . conception.'] *alt. fr.* 'preserves in one sense what it destroys [*period and sg. qt. del.*] in a'
176.25 The] *opp. marginal* '¶'
176.25 it be] *ab. del.* 't'
176.25 or] *bef. del.* 'whether'
176.26 which] *intrl.*
176.26 not∧] *comma del.*
176.27 or] *ab. del.* 'and'
176.27 the process,] *intrl.*
176.28 doubleness] 'ness' *added*
176.28 endures] ('es' *ab. del.* 'ing'); *aft. del.* 'is proposed as'
176.30 ¹the] *aft. del.* 'the'
176.31 this] *alt. fr.* 'the'
176.31 ²now] *intrl.*
††176.39 paragrafs, since] *ab. del.* 'p utterances, for'
176.39 place] *ab. del.* 'part of a *ring [*ab. del.* 'circle']'
176.39 as another for] *ab. del.* 'to'
176.39 entering] 'ing' *added*
176.39-177.1 a ring by,] *ab. del.* 'as another,'
177.1 expert] *intrl.*
177.1 will discern] *ab. del.* 'who has been there feels'
177.1 authentic] *intrl.*
177.2 circling.] *period insrtd. bef. del.* 'of the thought.'
177.8 twin] *bef. del.* 'fool['s' *del.*]'
177.9 difference?] *qst. mk. aft. del. db. qt.*
177.10 each] *ab. del.* 'afford as much *of [*intrl.*] sameness as they do of difference. Each'

††177.23 time?"] *qst. mk. over db. qt.*
††177.27 You] 'Y' *over* 'y'
††177.29 lie,'] *sg. qt. insrtd. bef. del. sg. qt.*
177.30 not.∧] *sg. qt. del.*
177.31 Philosophy] *aft. del.* 'The power of gra'
177.31 of] *aft. del.* 'to'
177.34 as] *aft. del.* ', but su'
177.34 topic,] *bef. del.* 'but such a taking would be vain as assuming that a ,totality can be immediate'
177.34 just an] *ab. del.* 'all'
177.35 but] *ab. del.* 'whereas'
177.35-36 or opposite,] *ab. del. comma*
177.36 within] *underline del.*
177.37 contain] *underline del.*
178.3 the subjective] *aft. del.* 'but such as carries with it'; *bef. del.* 'which'
178.3 it;] *semicolon aft. del.* 'as a status'
††178.6-7 . . . . "Thou . . . eye." . . .] *intrl.*
178.9 somewhat] 'what' *ab. del.* 'thing'
††178.11 relations.∧ˣ] *sg. qt. del.*; *opp. marginal* 'ˣ | Note on next page'
178.14 here] 'h' *over* 'th'
178.17 and identically] *ab. del.* 'the experience which we find.'
178.18 which] *bef. del.* '*is." [*possible sg. qt.*]'
178.18 fact∧] *comma del.*
178.19 This] ('T' *over* 't'); *aft. del.* 'All'
††178.19 XIXth∧ . . . of] ('development' *ab. del.* 'rendering'); *ab. del.* 'post-kantian outcome of'
178.20 idealistic vision.] *ab. del.* 'form of idealism.'
178.20 To me] *bef. del.* '[¶]It s'
178.20 monistic] 'mo' *added aft. del.* 'unquestionably mo-' |
178.20 enough] *aft. del.* 'yet in the sequel it gets pluralistic enough.'
178.22 circling] *second* 'l' *del.*
178.22 on] *ab. del.* 'in'
178.23 listens] *final* 's' *added*
178.23 under the pines] *intrl.*
178.23 to ∧the] *initial db. qt. del.*
178.23 leaves and insects,] (*insrtd. for del.* 'the flies under the pines,'); *ab. del.* 'bees in immemorial elms,'
178.24 criticism.] *bef. del.* '['But [*ab. del.*

'When']'*del.*] ['¶' *insrtd. in margin*]
[Mr. Blood *then [*ab. del.* 'then'] asks:
'If the things I see do not exist without
intelligence, whose intelligence is it?'
*He [*ab. del.* 'and'] replies: 'Certainly
not mine;' and goes on: '*Then ['T'
over 't'] how can *I* *hold that I [*intrl.*]
make or contribute to the things I see;'
and answers again: 'There is certainly a
difficulty in so holding—a difficulty'

178.25 But] *ab. del.* 'Then'

178.25 Blood] *bef. del.* 'then [*intrl.*]
proceeds,'

178.25 ['to' *del.*] strikes] (*final* 's'
added); *ab. del.* 'striking'

††178.26-37 *'How . . . mystery] *under*
'Note to previous page' *marked off by*
horiz. line

178.26 is] *aft. del.* 'I'

178.32 them] *aft. del.* 'itself'

178.32 in] *aft. del.* 'when,'

††178.33 exhilaration, ...] *dots intrl.*

178.33 we] *aft. del.* 'we ask ourselves
what is this life . . . '

178.35 (*twice*) one's] *ab. del.* 'his'

178.36 one.] *aft. del.* 'him.'

††178.37-42 of . . . philosophy.?] *under*
'Note continued.' *marked off by horiz.*
line

179.1 rationally] *aft. del.* 'actually is'

179.8 might] *ab. del.* 'shall'

179.9 could] *ab. del.* 'can'

179.11 a ground] *aft. del.* 'a tendency to,
or'

179.11 for‸] *comma del.*

179.12 bare] *intrl.*

††179.13 go. . . . .] *del. sg. qt. aft. first*
period

††179.14 'Such] *opp. marginal* '¶'

††179.31 show.'ˣ] *opp. marginal* 'ˣ| Note
on next page'

††179.37-180.19-28 Elsewhere, . . .
time.'"] *under* 'ˣnote to p. 27ª' *marked*
off by horiz. line

180.2 our] *aft. del.* 'Mr. B'

180.2 thought] *ab. del.* 'deliverances'

180.2 it] *ab. del.* 'them'

180.3 rationalism.] *period alt. fr. colon;*
bef. del. '[*on fol.* 27ª] ['There must be
a reason for everything and so much
reason, so much thing.' *del.*] ['The

monism is of th' *del.*] The mystical
pronouncements *also [*intrl.*] are of
the most radical monistic strife. His |
[*fol.* 34ᵛ] first account of the ether-
revelation is that 'thenceforth each is all,
in God. The One remains, the many
change and pass; and each and every one
of us is the One that remains.' There
must be a reason for everything, and so
much reason, so much thing. The whole
['backgr' *del.*] of its background, its
negation, its remainder, is the reason
['for everything' *del.*] ['sought;' *del.*]
of it.'

180.5 foil and] *intrl.*

180.5 ²and] *over comma*

180.5 of . . . whole] *intrl.*

††180.6-10 . . . . Pleasure . . . more.]
added in margin and moved by guide-
line to replace three periods after
'better.'

180.11-12 Thus do truth's] 'Thus do'
insrtd.; initial 't' *over* 'T' *in* 'truth's'

180.12 seem to] *intrl.*

180.13 cost,] *comma alt. fr. semicolon*

180.14 in their] *intrl.*

††180.14 terms.'ˣ] *refers to marginal*
'ˣ Note on p. 26ᵇ'

180.15 also] *aft. del.* 'sounds'

180.15 is] *intrl.*

180.16 in] *intrl.*

180.18 One] 'O' *over* 'o'

††180.18 remains.'] *bef. del.* 'The'

180.29-45 There . . . worst."] *under* 'Note
to p. *28 [*in pencil ab. pencil del.* '26ª']'
marked off by horiz. line

181.4 note] *aft. del.* 'dialectic'

181.4 what . . . dialectic] *ab. del.* 'true'

181.7 not] *aft. del.* 'as a'

181.8 renegade] *aft. del.* 'traitorous relapse and'

181.8 and relapse.] *ab. del. period*

181.9 known] 'kn' *over* 'no'

181.9 or] *intrl.*

181.10 is . . . blind.] *ab. del.* 'has never
seen the light.'

181.11 explain . . . may,] *intrl.*

181.12 Just] *ab. del.* 'But'

181.12-13 for . . . such] *ab. del.* 'now to
what the'

181.13 deliverances] (*aft. del.* 'phase';

bef. del. 'like these:—'); ab. del. 'side of
Mr. Blood:—'

††181.13 on . . . these.$_\wedge$] insrtd.

††181.14 'Reason] aft. circled '¶'

181.33 again:] bef. del. 'Pluralism'

181.33 $_\wedge$philosophy$_\wedge$] sg. qts. del.

181.35 contradiction] aft. del. 'self'

181.36 faith] aft. del. 'vision'

181.36 dialectic] aft. del. 'a'

181.36 like] aft. del. 'which I am too dull
to | to ['apprehend' del.] catch,'

181.36 the] intrl.

††181.37 disc$_\wedge$] aft. del. 'stationary';
bef. del. 'or *wheel, [comma del. in
error]'

181.38 one another] aft. del. 'each'

182.1 uses] 'u' over 'c'

182.2 pure] ab. del. 'deep'

††182.2 —a . . . must] ('a' insrtd. bef. del.
'A'); ab. del. ': I am not the man to'

182.3 my] aft. del. '*Mr Blood [intrl.]
['him' del.] chastise'

182.3-4 be . . . if] ('castigated' over
'chastized'); ab. del. 'if ['he' del.] its'

182.4 my 'Subject'] ('my' insrtd.; 'S'
triple underl.); insrtd.

182.6 the rest of] 'the rest' intrl.; 'of'
omitted in error

182.6 to some] ab. del. 'that I'

182.6 ³of] insrtd. bef. del. 'a little'

182.7 In] alt. fr. 'I'

182.7-8 making . . . have] ('so far' intrl.;
'him,' bef. del. intrl. 'so far,'); ab. del.
'have'

182.9 inverting] ('ing' over 'ed'); aft. del.
'often in'

182.9 their] intrl.

182.9 altering] 'ing' over 'ed'

182.9 words—] dash intrl.

182.10 for] aft. del. 'in making him'

182.10 all] intrl.

182.10 beg] bef. del. 'his'

182.10 my author] '*['Mr. Blood' del.]
my author [ab. del. 'him']'

182.11 pluralist] alt. fr. 'pluralistic
mystic'

182.11 interpretation] ab. del. 'the [illeg.
del.] exegesis'

182.12 (if . . . stained)] intrl.

182.12 exegetic blood.] ab. del. '['crime.'
del.] philologic crime.'

182.13 ¹his] insrtd. for del. '*my

Subject's [ab. del. 'Mr. Blood's']'

182.13 poetry.] ab. del. 'verses.'

182.14 Before] alt. fr. 'In'

182.14 mystic] aft. del. 'plu'

182.14 refresh] ab. del. 'give'

182.15 (doubtless . . . dialectic)] parens
over commas

182.15 now] intrl.

182.15 by] aft. del. 'a specimen of'

182.15 his] ab. del. 'quite unphilosophic'

182.17 its] intrl.

182.25 And] 'A' over 'a'

182.25 laughed] insrtd.

182.30,31 That] 'T' over 't'

183.16 grew] 'e' over 'o'

183.20 less than] ab. del. 'about'

183.20 poem,] comma insrtd. bef. del.
period

183.20-21 ²of . . . all] ab. del. 'If Mr.
Blood knows not the english language,
who does *know ['k' over qst. mk.] it
better *and ask [ab. del. qst. mk.]
which living writer'

††183.30 or] intrl.; 'o' reduced in error

183.31 Gods—] dash over qst. mk.

185.4 rather] ab. del. 'more'

185.4 return] aft. del. 'must'

185.4 Blood's] '*['the' del.] Blood's
[intrl.]'

185.5 its] '*['his' del.] its [ab. del.
'Mr. Blood']'

185.6 its] ab. del. 'his'

185.7 parodizes] ab. del. 'criticizes'

185.7 demand] intrl.

185.9 There] aft. del. 'They need some-
thin'

185.9 I] alt. fr. 'It'

185.10 that] ab. del. 'who'

185.12 —No bad] ab. del. '['This is' del.]
Good ['G' over 'g']'

185.12 surely,] intrl.

185.13 putting] ab. del. 'putting'

185.32 Blood's] (bef. del. 'last'); ab. del.
'the'

185.32 his own] ab. del. 'the'

††185.34 thing.ˣ] refers to marginal
'ˣNote on next page.'

185.35-186.8-46 I . . . free."] under
'ˣNote to page 41ᵃ'

††186.1 to . . . letter:] ab. del. 'elsewhere,'

186.2 in] bef. del. 'men'

186.6 philosophy.$_\wedge$] *sg. qt. and three periods del.*

187.4 the] *aft. del.* 'Mr.'

187.5 native] *aft. del.* 'own'

187.5 realized] *intrl.*

187.7 upon] 'up' *added*

187.8 indeed . . . otherwise,] *intrl.*

187.8 more] *intrl.*

187.9 fact] *aft. del.* 'or all generating'; *bef. del.* 'any more'

187.11 in]'*in ['into' *del.*] [*ab. del.* 'out of']'

187.11 converging] 'ing' *ab. del.* 'ent'

187.12 ends.] *ab. del.* 'grows.'

187.12 Hegel's] *aft. del.* ' 'There is no purpose of eternity,' Mr. Blood repeats. 'Progress? and to what? Time'

187.12 belongs to] *ab. del.* 'is in'

187.12 ^{2}to] *over* 'in'

187.13 line] *aft. del.* 'straight'

††187.13 'Progress?'] *aft. del.* 'There is no purpose of eternity'

187.20 banners?] *qst. mk. over sg. qt.*

187.25 also] *intrl.*

187.25 day.] *period insrtd. bef. del.* 'too.'

188.4 Of] *aft. del.* 'In this exceedingness of life over reason,'; *opposite marginal* '¶'

††188.8 mystical . . . sufficiency'] *insrtd. for del.* 'serenity, triumphant *tic [*intrl.*] peace, and assurance'

188.9 very] *ab. del.* '['of a a' *del.*] widely'

188.10 can claim] *aft. del.* 'seeks'; *bef. del.* 'to produce,'

188.10 ^{1}more] *ab. del.* 'The is The anaesthetic *More ['M' *over* 'm']'

188.10 prouder,] *intrl.*

188.11 heroic.$_\wedge$] *db. qt. del.*

188.11 From] *aft. del.* 'I quoted on page 000 above ['a' *del.*] some lines from Blood's poem of Nemesis. The writer'

188.11 feel towards] *ab. del.* 'turn on'

††188.12 'as] *sg. qt. insrtd.*

188.12 felt towards] *ab. del.* 'did *on '[*sg. qt. undel. in error*]'

188.12 millions of] *intrl.*

††188.13 $_\wedge$in . . . part.'] *surrounding db. qts. del.; sg. qt. added*

188.13 above,] *intrl.*

188.14 from] *aft. del.* 'some verses'

188.14 "Nemesis"—] *dash over comma*

188.14 Is] *over* 'is'

188.15-16 or rational balance:—] *insrtd. for del. colon*

189.2 securities] *aft. del.* 'moods'

189.4 the conditions] 'the' *alt. fr.* 'they'; 'conditions' *intrl.*

189.4-5 for . . . them.] ('for a life among' *ab. del.* 'to be with'); *ab. del.* 'for them.'

189.6 to] *intrl.*

189.7 weakly] *alt. fr.* 'meekly'

189.8 meekly] *aft. del.* 'weakly'

189.11 prints] *ab. del.* 'writes'

189.13 Reason] 'R' *over* 'r'

189.34 "Ever"] *opp. marginal* '¶'

189.34 wring] *ab. del.* 'be'

†189.34-36 very . . . device.] *insrtd. for del.* 'motto [*ab. del.* 'root-principle'] of the pluralistic philosophy.'

189.36 complete] *ab. del.* 'all-embracing'

189.37 total] *ab. del.* 'all-seeing'

189.37 pervasive] (*alt. fr.* 'pervading'); *insrtd. for del.* 'compelling [*ab. del.* 'upgathering']'

189.37 everywhere] 'where' *intrl.*

189.37 some] *alt. fr.* 'something'

189.38 residual resistance] *ab. del.* 'rebellion [*alt. fr.* 'rebellious']'

189.38 formulation,] *alt. fr.* 'formulas,'

189.39 some] *alt. fr.* 'something'

189.39 genius . . . that] *ab. del.* 'that'

189.39 pressure] *ab. del.* 'dash'

190.1 that] *aft. del.* '['to' *del.*] something exceeding and private'

†190.1-2 and claims . . . be] ('privacy,' *alt. fr.* 'private$_\wedge$' *aft. del.* 'is'); *ab. del.* 'that can only be'

190.3 somewhat] *aft. del.* 'something'

190.3 original and novel.] *ab. del.* 'and originally new.'

190.5 reproduce] *aft. del.* 'only'

190.5 but] *ab. del.* 'the'

190.5 itself,] *intrl.*

190.6 gives] *ab. del.* 'greets [*doubtful*]'

190.11 our activities] 'our' *intrl.*; 'ies' *over* 'y'

190.12 ^{1}to] *insrtd. for del.* 'by'

190.13 in the name of] *ab. del.* 'for'

DELETED VERSOS FOR "A PLURALISTIC MYSTIC" MANUSCRIPT

[*del. fol.* 27ᵇᵛ: *trial for start of fol.* 30, *corresponds to text* 181.2-5] 'It seems to me that *any [*ab. del.* 'every'] transcendental idealist ought to *['hear find' *del.*] discern [*ab. del.* 'greet'] in these fragments which I ['have' *del.*] quote['d' *del.*] the dia-|*lectic [*ab. del.* 'rare accent'] note of true *profundity. [*period aft. del. comma*] ['and to extend a' *del.*]'

[*del. fol.* 44ᵛ: *trial for start of fol.* 28, *corresponds to text* 180.3-14] 'There must be a reason for everything, & so much reason, so much thing. The reason is the whole background, negation, remainder, of *['the' *del.*] reality. ['reality.' *del.*] [*ab. del.* 'the thing.'] [' . . .' *del.*] A man may feel good only by feeling *better,' [*sg. qt. aft. del. sg. qt.*] *& [*intrl.*] 'The [*sg. qt. insrtd. bef. del. sg. qt.*] black and yellow gonfalon of Lucifer is indispensable **in [*ab. del.* 'to'] any spiritual picture. [*period insrtd.; sg. qt. del.*] [*all circled opp. marginal circled* 'tr' *and moved by guideline from after* 'reality.'] The two components of reality balance; across the line of indifference truth vibrates; 'and being and not-being have equal value and cost . . . The couples which make this duplexity are mainly convertible in their terms.'

Word-Division

The following is a list of actual or possible hyphenated compounds divided at the end of the line in the copy-text but which were not confirmed in their forms as printed in the present edition either because the copy-text did not derive from a journal or a manuscript (or the manuscript gave the form as two separate words which was not adopted as an emendation). In a sense, then, the hyphenation or the non-hyphenation of possible compounds in the present list is in the nature of editorial emendation. When the compounds were divided in the copy-text at the ends of lines but their probable form was evidenced in the source, this edition prints the reading of the source (unless emended by record), and no list is provided here.

4.13 textbooks	79.14 cologne-water
5.33 willy-nilly	80.18-19 anti-associationists
7.13 hard-headed	82.18 *knowing-together*
9.11 all-sufficing	86.12 over-soul
12.20 all-embracing	86.24 psycho-physical
20.9 non-mental	88.5 soul-theory
22.1 *should-be*	90.9 Schleswig-Holstein
27.30 existât-elle	95.11 question-begging
28.1 elle-même	99.30 hero-worship
37.22 nerve-process	109.16 world-formula
39.31 thinghood	109.29 noonday
40.16 india-rubber	113.32 horse-breaking
43.21 custom-bred	113.40 non-rendering
46.32 brain-tremors	115.11 sleuthhound
47.3 double-aspect	116.10 textbook
57.1 Sunday-school	116.34 ninety-nine
67.39 *quasi*-miracle	151.5 knife-edge
73.8 thought-stuff	168.37 bugbear
73.25 *known-as*	178.12 twenty-five
74.33 thing-stuff	

The following is a list of words divided at the ends of lines in the present edition but which represents authentic hyphenated compounds as found within the lines of the copy-text. Except for this list, all other hyphenations at the ends of lines in the present edition are the modern printer's and are not hyphenated forms in the copy–text.

11.9 well-|being	50.5 to-|day
13.5 self-|approbation	51.29 sand-|heap
14.26 good-|natured	52.5 choke-|damp
19.19 non-|mental	54.26 pseudo-|principle
27.26 *n'est-|il*	58.40 never-|resting
28.10 eux-|mêmes	63.6 first-|rate
34.30 to-|morrow	66.11 Mind-|dust
45.10 back-|bone	78.11 -known-|together

79.20	cologne-|water	132.29	dictionary-|adjectives
82.23	infra-|cortical	133.5	self-|love
86.7	soul-|theory	159.21	steep-|waved
90.10	extraordinary-|professor	167.27	Anglo-|Saxon
95.8	subject-|matter	168.28	common-|sense
104.37	experience-|material	169.12	de-|anthropomorphization
105.28	object-|world	171.8	non-|human
112.14	salt-|spoon	184.37	twenty-|seven
113.31	well-|greaved	185.19	well-|set-
115.38	second-|rateness	187.38	self-|determination
121.18	attitude-|taking	189.18	-and-|water
121.26	truth-|telling	189.22	cactus-|like
127.18	so-|called		

The following are actual or possible hyphenated compounds broken at the end of the line in both the copy-text and the present edition.

81.34,35	brain-|processes (*i.e.*, brain-processes)	132.21	field-|observers (*i.e.*, field-observers)
87.39	non-|recognition (*i.e.*, non-recognition)	163.16	dream-|experiences (*i.e.*, dream-experiences)
132.20	-of-|door (*i.e.*, -of-door)	174.33	Non-|dialectic (*i.e.*, Non-dialectic)

Appendixes

Appendix I

Translation of "Quelques Considérations
sur la méthode subjective"

The James Collection at Harvard contains an anonymous English translation of "Quelques Considérations," which appears in its original French form
as the third essay in this volume. The manuscript (bMS 1452.1 [23]) was
not part of the bequest of James's papers and was bought on June 9, 1945,
from Walter R. Benjamin Autographs, Inc., of Hunter, N.Y., its previous
history unknown. For a description of the manuscript see The Text of *Essays
in Philosophy*, p. 248.

Translation

"Quelques considérations sur la methode subjective"

Some reflections on the subjective method

To the Editors of the Revue Philosophique.

Gentlemen,

It has long been my custom when haunted by gloomy *ideas,
[*intrl.*] by *pessimism[² 'm' *over* 'tic'] and fatalism, to rid myself
of them by means of a very simple process of reasoning *which
[*over* 'one'] agrees so well with the principles of the philosophy to
which your review is dedicated, that I wonder at having never
found it, *totidem verbis*, in some of your hebdomadal pages. I
venture to lay it before you.

The question in point is, to decide, *whether one [over 'if it'] be
['right to reject' del.] justified in rejecting a theory which many
objective facts apparently confirm, solely because it does not in
any way respond to our inward preferences.*

One is not so justified, we are told by nearly all the *scientists
[¹ 's' *over illeg. letter*] of the day, and by all the positivists. To reject
a conclusion on the sole ground that it clashes with our innermost
feelings, & with our desires is to make use of the subjective
method, *and the subjective method [*intrl.*] according to their
creed, is the original sin of science, the root of all scientific
mistakes. According to them, so far from going whither his desires
lead him, the man who is searching for truth ought to reduce himself to a mere recording machine, to make his *scientific consciousness* ("conscience de savant") a sort of blank page—a dead surface,

331

on which external reality will write itself without change or deflection.

I absolutely deny the legitimacy of such a *foregone conclusion* ("parti pris") on the part of those who pretend to lay it down as an *unvarying* rule of method. This rule is good as applied to investigations of a certain kind, it is utterly worthless, it is absurd indeed, in the search for truths of a different kind.

To reject, unsparingly, the subjective method in every case when the truth exists wholly apart from my action, and is determined with certainty independantly [i.e., 'independently'] of all I can desire, or dread, is perfectly reasonable. Thus past facts of history, the future movement of the stars, are already determined whether I like them or not. My preferences here are powerless to produce or to modify things, and could only serve to confuse my judgment. I ought to silence them, resolutely. ['But' *del.*]

But there is a class of facts whose matter is not thus constituted, fixed, beforehand—facts which are not (given facts?) (fixed quantities?) "*donnés.*" ['Suppose' *del.*] I am making an Alpine ascent. I find myself in a hard place from which I can only get out by means of a bold dangerous leap. I may wish to make the leap, but I am ignorant from lack of experience whether I have the strength for it. Let us suppose I make use of the subjective method. I believe what I desire. My confidence gives me strength, & makes possible something which without it, perhaps might not have been. So I leap the chasm, and am out of danger. But suppose I am inclined to disbelieve in my ability for the reason that it has never been proved by exploits of the sort: then I waver, I hesitate, till at last weakened and trembling, compelled to take the leap by sheer despair, I miss my aim & fall into the crevasse. In a case like that, whatever may come of it, I should be a fool if I did not believe what I wished, as my belief happens to be a preliminary condition which is essential to the accomplishment of the end which it affirms (or of its object.) Believing in my powers, I leap. The result puts my belief in the right, verifies it. It is then only that it becomes true; but then, one may say, it *was* true. Thus, there are cases in which my belief creates its own verification. Believe not! you will be right—in fact—you will fall into the chasm. Believe! You will be equally right, for you will save yourself. The only difference in the two cases is, that the latter is much to your advantage.

From the moment I admit that a certain alternative exists and option is only possible for me on condition of my making a personal contribution, from the moment I admit that this personal contribution depends on a certain degree of subjective energy which itself can only become *real [*alt. fr.* 'a reality'] through a certain degree of faith in the result and that this possibility of the future rests on a belief of the present, I must see how absurd it would be to will away the subjective method, the faith of the intellect (intelligence) (foi de l'esprit). On the actual existence of this faith the possibility of the future is based. This faith may mislead, easily. The effort it induces me to make may not result in creating the state of things it foresees, & would fain bring to pass. Granted, [*false start of letter del.*] my life pays the forfeit unquestionably. But would not the life of M. Huxley, for instance—of M Huxley who recently wrote "To believe, because one would like to believe would evince the last degree of immorality—," would not *this [*over* 'that'] life be equally forfeited, if it should chance to be that the belief he would proscribe were right after all?

The case is always possible. Whatever one may do in this game called life, or believe, or doubt, or deny, there is always the possibility of losing. Is that a reason for not playing? No—clearly; but since what one loses is always a fixed quantity (after all one can only forfeit *one's self [*ab. del.* 'oneself' *over* 'himself']) ("payer de sa personne") is a reason for making sure by all legitimate means that in event of winning the gain shall be a maximum. If, for instance, through believing, one can increase the great good sought after, the possible prize[,] that is reason good for believing.

Moreover it is exactly thus in regard to *the [*intrl.*] various questions of universal import which are the problems of philosophy. Let us take up that of pessimism. Without having, indeed *everywhere [*intrl.*] reached the condition of a philosophic *dogma['s' *over poss.* 'n' *del.*] such [*intrl.*] as we see it in Germany, pessimism presents a serious problem to every thinker: Is life of any value? (what is life good for?) ("a quoi bon la vie?") or in colloquial phrase, is the game worth the candle? If one decides in favor of the pessimistic answer what does one gain in event of being right? Not much assuredly. On the other hand, a maximum is gained in event of being right, after having decided in favor of the opinion that the world is good. What can we do to make the world good? Contribute something of our own (out of ourselves), to it. ("Y contribuer de notre part—") *And [*over* '&'] how can such a minute contribution alter the worth of such an immense *or of *so* great a whole [*intrl.*] sum-total? *in [*alt. fr.* 'In'] that its *quality* is immeasurably superior[.] Such is the quality of the *acts [*alt. fr.* 'facts'] of the moral life.

Let M represent the mass of facts outside of myself and let R be my individual reaction, the contingent of facts that derive from (originate in) *([*over comma*] "*dérive de—*") my personal activity. M contains as we know an immense mass of phenomena of want, of misery, pain, old age,—things calculated to excite fear and loathing. It might be that R would manifest itself as a reaction of despair—as an act of suicide for instance. M + R—the sum total of every thing I have to do with, would then ['represent' *del.*] stand for a state of things bad from every point of view. No gleam of light in the darkness. Pessimism in this hypothesis receives its finishing touch from my act itself, (a derivative) (a result) "dérive de" of my belief. The thing is done, and I was right in asserting it. Let us suppose on the other hand that the feeling of the evil contained in M instead of disheartening me does but increase my inward resistence [i.e., 'resistance']. This time my reaction will be the opposite of despair. R will contain patience, courage, devotion, faith in the invisible, all the heroic virtues, and all the joys that spring from them. Moreover it is a fact of experience and empiricism cannot dispute it that such joys are of incomparable worth *by the [*over* 'beside'] side of those merely passive satisfactions which are excluded *through [*ab. del.* '['because' *del.*] by the fact *of [*over* 'that']'] the ['moral' *del.*] nature of the M *being [*over* 'is'] what it is. If it be true then, that moral happiness is the greatest happiness known, if on the other hand, the nature of the M by means of the evil it contains & the resistence [i.e., 'resistance'] it provokes be the condition of this happiness, is it not clear that M is at least *susceptible* ("susceptible") of belonging to the best of worlds? I say *susceptible* only, because everything depends on the character of R. *M [*over poss.* 'B'] in itself is ambiguous, capable, according to the complement it will receive, of ['belonging' *del.*] taking part in either a moral pessimism or a moral optimism.

It will hardly make part of an optimism if we lose our moral energy; it may make part of one, if we keep it. But how shall we keep it unless we believe in the possibility of a success, unless we reckon on the future and say to ourselves—The world *is good*, since, *from [*over* 'in'] a moral point of view, it *is what I make it*, and I will make it good? In a word, how can we exclude the *subjective ['ive' *added*] method from the *knowledge* of fact, since this method is the *rightful ['ful' *added*] instrument with which to produce the fact?

In all questions of universal bearing, the acts of the subject and their endless consequences must be contained in the formula (statement) "formule." Such should be the extension of the formula M + R, when it is made to stand for the world. This granted[,] our vows, our wishes, being real coefficients of the term R whether in themselves or through the beliefs they inspire in us, or (if we prefer so to state it) by *means ['m' *over poss.* 'r'] of the hypotheses they suggest to us[,] it ought to be confessed that these beliefs beget a portion at least of the truths they assert. Such, and such convictions, such and such results. Other convictions—other results. And let us note carefully that all this is independant [i.e., 'independent'] of the *question [*intrl.*] of absolute freedom or of absolute necessity, ("determinism.") If our facts *are necessitated [*intrl.*] so [*over* 'ou'] also are our beliefs; but *whcthcr [*intrl.*] ncccssitated ("determined") or not as the latter may be, they are the phenomenal condition necessarily preliminary to the "results" "facts," ("faits"), and consequently a necessary component of the truth we seek to know.

So here we have the subjective method logically justified provided its use be properly restricted. It can only be harmful, one might even say "immoral" if applied to cases where the facts to be stated do not include the subjective term R as a factor. But wherever this factor enters the application is legitimate. Let us again consider this problem, as an example.

Is the inward nature of the world moral, or is the world nothing but a simple fact, a mere actual existence. This is at bottom the question of materialism[.] The positivists will object that such a question is unanswerable, *or [*over* '&'] indeed irrational in asmuch as the inward nature of the world if it exist, is not a phenomenon and therefore cannot be proved. I answer that every question is significant and is propounded with propriety, ['whi' *del.*] from which an obvious practical alternative results in such sort that *accordingly ['ly' *added*] as it be answered in the one way or the other, one, or other line of conduct should be followed. Now this is the case here. The materialist, & the man who ascribes a moral character to the world ought to act differently *in [*ab. del.* 'under'] many circumstances. The materialist whcn facts do not suit his moral sentiments is always at liberty to sacrifice the latter. The verdict he passes on a fact as good or bad is relative to his *psychical [*ab. del.* 'psychological'] constitution & depends upon it, but this constitution being itself nothing but a fact[,] a (given quantity,? datum?) ("*donnée ['ée' *over* 'es']") is not in itself either good or bad. It is then permissable [i.e., 'permissible'] to modify it, to stifle ['for instance by all sorts of means' *del.*] the moral sentiment for instance in all sorts of ways, & thus to change the verdict ("jugement—") by transforming the datum (donnée) in which it originates. On the other hand, he who believes in the inward moral nature of the world, holds that the attributes of good & evil pertain to all phenomena and belong to psychical ['phenomenon' *del.*] data, ("données") as well as to the facts that relate to them. He would not dream of falsifying these sentiments as if it were a perfectly simple thing so to do. The sentiments themselves must according to him, be of the one sort or the other.

On the one side then we should have resistence [i.e., 'resistance'] of evil, poverty accepted, martyrdom if needs be, in a word—tragic life. On the other, concessions[,] compromises, capitulations with conscience[,] epicurean life—such are the portions of the two beliefs. Be it observed however that their divergence is ['only' *del.*] strongly emphasized at the critical & decisive moments of life only, when the insufficiency of everyday maxims compels a resort to great principles[.] Then the contradiction is ['conspicuous.' *del.*] striking. The one says: "The world is a *solemn [*ab. del.* 'grand'] thing everywhere and always, and there are bases for the moral judgment." The other, the materialist replies, "What matters is how I decide, since vanitas vanitatum is the bottom of it all?" Wisdom's watchword for the one, when pushed to extremity is Anaesthesia; for the other, Energy.

It is evident that the problem is a significant one since it admits of conclusions so opposite in the conduct of life. How can [we] know now which solution is the right one? But how can the scientist know whether his hypothesis be correct? He assumes that *it [*intrl.*] is correct & proceeds to deductions. He acts according to what he has assumed. Sooner or later the effects of his actions will undeceive him if his starting point have been falsely assumed. Is it not the same here? We always have to do with M + R. If M in its inner nature is moral, & the R be furnished by a materialist, these elements are in disaccord and will go on diverging more & more from one another. The same *divergence [*over doubtful* 'cha'] should convict itself in event of the agent governing his conduct on the assumption that the world is *a [*intrl.*] moral fact —when in reality the world is mere brute fact, just an aggregate of ['merely' *del.*] utterly material phenomena. On both sides there is ['futile effort' *del.*] hope deceived; whence the ['subs' *del.*] necessity for subsidiary hypotheses becoming more & more complicated like those of which the history of astronomy furnishes example in the multiplicity of epicycles which had to be imagined in order to make facts as more & more closely observed, square with the system of Ptolemy. If then the partisan of a moral world has chosen the false hypothesis in his assumption, he will experience a succession of disappointments & will not attain to peace of

heart in the end. His tragic choice will not be justified[.] In the
*other case [*ab. del.* 'opposite example'], M + R being in harmony
& no mere collection of discrepant elements time will go on con-
firming the hypothesis and the agent who has adopted it will have
increasing grounds for congratulating himself on his choice. He will
sail so to speak, under full canvas in the lot he has made for himself.

Thus the method of proving whether an opinion be well founded
is the same here as in Science and we know of none other. Let us
observe however, that the time required for verification varies
according to the question. A given hypothesis in Physics may be
verified in an hour—another like transformation will need more
than a generation to become firmly established; & hypotheses of
universal order like those of which we are speaking may remain
subjects of doubt for many centuries to come. But while waiting
we must act, & to act, we must choose a hypothesis. Often indeed,
doubt itself is equivalent to active choice. From the moment when
one is compelled to choose, nothing can be more rational than to
give the preference to that one of the sides offered, which is felt to
be the *more [*alt. fr.* 'most'] attractive, at the risk of finding
*one'sself [*apostrophe doubtful*] condemned & distracted by the
nature of things if the decision have been erroneous. To sum up,
faith and *working hypothesis* are here one and the same. In time
the truth will reveal itself.

I may go farther, I may ask, why materialism and belief in a
moral universe may not be *equally verifiable* in the manner I have
just suggested? In other words why may it not be that M is
essentially ambiguous and dependant [i.e., 'dependent'] on its
complement R for the ultimate determination which will make it
either take its place in a moral order, or reduce it to a system of
brute *fact? ['?' *alt. fr. period*] The case is conceivable. A given
line may make part in an infinite number of curves, a given word
may enter ['in [*over* 'to'] ' *del.*] many different sentences. *In
[*over* 'If we'] connection with matters of this sort it might lie
with R to weight the scale in either direction. Suppose that in
acting we draw inspiration from the belief in a moral world. This
truth will become more striking day by day. *On [*over poss.* 'At']
the other hand, act with the materialist, and the lapse of time will
show more & more that the world is a frivolous thing, and that
vanitas vanitatum is indeed at the root of everything. Thus, the
world will be what we make it.

And let no one tell me that such a trifling thing as R could
*not [*intrl.*] change the character of the enormous mass M. A
simple negative particle reverses the meaning of the longest sen-

tences. If one had to explain the universe from the point of view of sensibility one would be obliged to look at the animal kingdom alone, although so meagre a fact *quantitatively [*alt. fr.* 'quantitively']. The moral definition of the world may depend on even fewer phenomena. Believe in such a world; the results of our belief will remedy the defects that hinder it from being such. Believe that it is but an empty notion; and empty it will prove. Thus the subjective method is legitimate in both theory & practice.

I have already observed that it is not a question of *absolute* freedom in the illustrations I have used. This freedom may or may not really be. But if free acts are possible they may be brought forth and become more & more frequent by favor of the subjective method. In fine faith in their possibility increases the moral energy that gives them rise. But to talk of freedom in the Critique Philosophique is to carry gold to California. Rather let me conclude by saying once more that I think I have shown the Subjective method to be something different from the process characterized as "shameful" by a strange abuse of the selftermed scientific spirit. We must pass beyond this sort of proscription, this absurd veto, which, were we to ['submit' *del.*] conform to it could paralyze two of our most essential faculties—that namely, of setting ourselves a task in virtue of an act of faith which can be accomplished only by our own effort; and that of entering boldly into action in circumstances when success cannot be assured in advance.

Wm. James.

Harvard Coll. Cambridge Mass. Etats-Unis-d['] Amerique[,]

20 nov. 1877.

Appendix II

Notes for "The Sentiment of Rationality"

A: Box E, Envelope 5 (bMS Am 1092.9, #4465)

Fifty-six leaves, loose.

Leaves 1-2 compose a fold of laid paper, unwatermarked, each leaf measuring 222 × 158 mm., horizontal chainlines 17 mm. apart. The text of leaf 1 continues on the verso; leaf 2 is blank, recto and verso. The writing is in ink.

Leaves 3-6 are made up from two quired folds of the same paper. Leaf 3 is blank, recto and verso. The text is written in ink from leaf 4 to 6^v.

Leaf 7 is a single sheet, the right-hand corner torn off, of wove unwatermarked paper 215 × 187 mm. It is headed '*Faith*' in ink followed by a large arabic 3, this heading partly written over a pencil note 'bring it about.' Below the heading to the left is a diagram, a semicircular arrow joining the left-hand letter 'O' to the right-hand letter 'S', above, and another semicircular arrow, below, joining the 'S' to the 'O'. To the right is the deleted profile drawing of a man's head and upper torso. The text begins beneath a horizontal line. The verso is blank.

Leaf 8 is written in pencil on a sheet of paper like that of leaves 1-6, the text concluding on 8^v.

Leaves 9-11, foliated 1-3, are written in ink on sheets of light-weight wove paper, unwatermarked, measuring 215 × 187 mm., the versos blank. The same heading '*Ontologic knowledge*' is found on each leaf.

Leaves 12-28 consist of a series of two-leaf folds, except for the single-leaf 20, of the same laid paper as in leaves 1-6, 8. On leaf 12 the heading 'Rationality' is in ink but the text follows in pencil until ink begins about three-fifths of the way down on leaf 13 with 'nameless' altered from 'Nameless'. The ink text ends with the part-page 13^v; pencil resumes with leaf 14 and except for an ink inserted '3' for an unwritten item on 14^v it continues on rectos and versos through 15^v. Ink then starts on fol. 16 and continues, rectos and versos, to end on part-page 18^v. Leaf 19, the second leaf of a fold, is blank recto and verso except for a trial, reversed, at the foot of 19^v. Leaf 20^v is blank. Leaf 20 had been foliated 1 and 21 is foliated 3. Since 20 is a single leaf, it seems clear that its conjugate (foliated 2) has been removed and is lost. From leaf 21 the ink text proceeds on rectos and versos to end on part page 27^v. The second leaf of this fold, leaf 28, is blank recto and verso.

Leaf 29, consisting of notes in ink on the recto only, is a sheet of unwatermarked laid paper 250 × 200 mm., horizontal chainlines 18 mm. apart.

Leaves 30-37 are quired folds to make a little notebook. The paper is an unwatermarked laid 242 × 195 mm., horizontal chainlines 18 mm. apart. All text is in ink. The versos of 30 and 31 are blank, these leaves being followed by completely blank leaves 32-37 to end the notebook.

Leaf 38 is a single sheet of the same paper as leaves 30-37, its ink text ending partway on 38^v.

Leaf 39 is the same paper, its text also ending partway on 39^v.

Leaves 40-43 are quired folds of the same paper. All are blank, recto and verso, except for the start of a note at the head of leaf 41.

Leaf. 44 starts a sequence of unwatermarked wove sheets (which are the same as leaves 9-11) 215 mm. tall but varying in width although chiefly 188 mm. wide. The writing is in ink and the versos blank except for a trial word on 44ᵛ, foliated 3 centered. Leaf 44 is foliated 1 at top center. Leaves 46-51 have a running head 'Metaphysics' and are foliated II–VII (leaf 45 has only a roman numeral 'I'); the numbers I-III are in the upper right corner but IV-VII are centered after the running head, which is underlined for these last four pages. Leaf 45 (I) has a deleted arabic 8 centered, which may be written over some indistinguishable number; on leaf 47 (III) the heading 'Metaphysics' has been added to the left of a centered deleted 10. The sequence ends on leaf 51.

Leaves 52-53 compose a conjugate fold of the same laid paper as leaves 1-6, 8, 12-28. The writing is in a very black ink and continues on 52ᵛ, but 53 is blank recto and verso save for a pencil doodle. The heading *'Magnolia 2'* and the start of the text in mid-sentence indicates that a preceding leaf has been abstracted.

Leaves 54-55 also compose a conjugate fold but of a different paper, a cream-white unwatermarked laid with vertical chainlines, 224 × 158 mm., the writing in ink on rectos and versos.

The final leaf 56 is of the same laid paper as 52-53 and is written in ink on both sides.

Errors which are caused by alterations in the manuscripts can be found in their uncorrected form in Appendix VI; for ease of reading they are corrected in the following transcripts. Only errors of omission of words or punctuation marks linked to alterations are allowed to stand. All other errors unrelated to alterations are also transcribed as they appear.

[*leaf* 1]

Explanation

1   is logical, by deduction from an element (Taine)

2)   ontological, by reference to entity (substance, God)

3)   practical, when expectation is fully determined.

1 & 2 look backward, 3 forward. The sentiment of rationality is satisfied when the datum furnished by 1 or 2 is such as at the same time provides for 3; and the ideal of explanation is when in part 3 expectancy coalesces with desire. This case is that of final and efficient cause involving each other. Only the efficient cause (element or entity) leaves room for a discussion. It is *datum*. Contrasted with a possible nothing it itself demands explanation. To get over this one must either prove that it takes up the nothing; or exorcise the nothing (give it "apodal sufficiency"); or else exorcise the question.

[*leaf* 1ᵛ]

4 ways. of treating metaphysic *need [*doubtful*].

1. The question impertinent, (Blood) This seems to refer us for a

model to the brutes who assume all with out question or wonder.
2 The question legitimate and the answer a really existing thing
but removed beyond our horizon. (Spencer's unknowable.)
3 The question applicable only within the phenomena we know.
Beyond them inapplicable. Though a beyond exist, it wd. not
contain an answer to our question. (Kantian noumenalism)
4 The question soluble (Hegel.) By showing a logical connexion
between your first datum and *nothing*, you exclude all other
possibilities of determined being except that particular first datum.
Being then is explained as to the particularity of that first datum;
for the only alternative to it, is nothing; if anything there must be
it.

[*leaf* 4]

Explanation——

A matter is "explained"
1) when it is *deduced* fm. some other matter allready admitted or
   known
2) when referred to a class already known
3) when so familiar as to be "taken for granted" we say it "needs
   no explanation" or "versteht sich von selbst."
Now there are two momenta to be discriminated here. In 1) the
explanation (whatever its ultimate nature may be) seems superficially and practically at any rate to be more essential and intimate
than in 2) & 3.) Call it the *logical* explanation and the 2 other
sorts may be called *psychical* since their sufficiency seems due to a
peculiarity of the [*leaf* 4ᵛ] Subject rather than to an intrinsic
relation of the topics to each other.
   Psychical explanation. 2) by reference to the Evident—simply
carries us on to 3 the Evident itself. By what is this constituted?
By our ability to receive it unquestioningly; to rest in its presence,
at home so to speak. What is not evident—the unexplained &c, on
the contrary produces a state of discomfort in us; of uneasiness
without definite issue. So that the criterion of the Evident is
psychically a negative one—the absence of this unrest. Now
familiarity *per se* with a subject produces repose in its presence and
sofar forth makes us take it for granted. On the other hand novelty
per se acts as an irritant to the mind; which is only assuaged when
the novel thing has become [*leaf* 5] classified or when it has grown
so familiar, that "we dont mind it." This last fact means that we
are so used to it that we know what to *expect* from it. And seems
to point to a practical genesis for curiosity überhaupt, and for the

irritant quality of the unexperienced. It is of course vitally important that we should have prevision of the properties of the objects that surround us, not go to sleep on powder mines &c—and the mingled curiosity & fear of dogs and horses in presence of the strange objects calculated to strike their attention seems to point to this element of conscious insecurity or perplexed expectation as the irritant in what is novel.

The explanations which religious & mystical philosophies offer of the universe all meet this practical need. They define [*leaf* 5ᵛ] the sum of things by a term the quality of which is familiar to us— so that we rest in the assurance that whatever the future may harbor, it can be nothing essentially incompatible with the character of this term, God, Love, perfection or what not. We feel secure against the unexpected. The notion of immortality which seems in the minds of most people to be the touchstone of religion & the essence of their creed is a strong proof of the part expectation has in causing the craving for explanation. Till we know what to expect from a thing we seek to explain it; when we know, we take it for granted.

Explanation *per substantiam* i.e. the immutable, seems to gratify the same want. The indignation of Spencer against free will and the rationalistic and scientific objection to the reign of miracle appeals to the same root—dislike of the incalculable & uncertain.

[*leaf* 6]

Explanation

Beale complains (Biopl. 207) of physicists that they are unable to explain the phenomena of living matter; his "explanation" apparently being that it is "vital."
1. First the fact.
2. Then an abstract name descriptive of the fact in its vague totality
3. Then an abstract ingredient or element of the fact, named.
4. Then an element of the fact, concrete & analyzed out.
5. Then another fact involved in the existence of such an element. Such is the scale of explanation from the weakest to the highest. Beale's is 2 or at best 3—it is a sham explanation, really no explanation at all; but as against pure positivists who take their stand on 1. it is right because it is a *postulate* of explanation überhaupt. Cuvier is 1, St. Hilaire 2 & 3.
[*leaf* 6ᵛ] Beale's vitality is a mere pointing to *something other* than the fact *with which* the fact is connected—The only definition

of *this other* being that it is able to produce *this fact.* In other words it is saying that this fact as such is meant, intended—beside its brute existence it has a rational existence or an ideal duplicate. Now this process of the mind is so constant a phenomenon, it foists itself in so often under the garb of explanation and is nevertheless so easily trampled out by *nüchtern* nominalism & positivism that one is tempted to ask whether as a *postulate* it may not be right in the sense in wh. G. St. H. was right against Cuvier. If so the problem is: what is the *fact* involved in the *something other* and in what sense may it be called an ideal presupposition or duplicate of *this fact* which we have to explain.

[*leaf* 7]

Faith

From the point of view of the man of affairs on the one hand and of the moralist & religious man on the other there seems s'thing monstrously petty & morbid and unmanly in the eager thrashing of abstractions and champing the jaws over fine spun distinctions which constitutes the activity of the metaphysician. The living healthy man tends to action, and only needs as much thought as will give him a sufficiently secure practical basis to start upon. The sufficiency of the basis is measured by the willingness of the man to accept it and take the risks, and as in the affairs of life we esteem

[*leaf* 8]
Morals

Elements which help make an act or state moral
———————————

1 association with material interests.
2 approbation of others
4 consistency as a mental delight.
3 gratification of sympathetic passion.
5 pleasure of energetic volition (ft just. pt. mundus)
6 Independence of the external—stoic apathy or serenity, (probably connected with 5)
7 Self esteem or the pleasure more or less reflectively derived from the consciousness of one's worth.
8 The self-blighting gravity which comes from the thought of one's personal transitoriness against the permanance [*leaf* 8ᵛ] of

wider interests; and the metaphysical intuition of a common substance:tat tivam asi. These certainly count for much in the Schopenhauerian criterion of neminem laede.

[*leaf* 9]
Ontologic knowledge.
So far as a thing can be discriminated from an *other*, it can lay no claim to be a universal form of being. That can be discriminated only, if at all, from *nothing*. It is questionable whether this act wd. mean anything different from the act of discrimating between the absence of feeling and feeling *überhaupt*. However that may be, it can be plausibly maintained, that the Universe considered as Being must always be inexplicable to us, we must simply find it, take it for granted, remain Empiricists. For the Universal being, having nothing to be discriminated from cannot be consciously realized in any quale. It is an eternal tastelessness or monotony, only discriminated in our logic from Nothing—but that is not another *quale*.
[*leaf* 10]
Nor is it *explicable* in the usual sense of explanation viz. the being referred to another genus already known—for by the hypothesis there is no such.

Therefore the "Relativity of Knowledge" is no imbecillity of our understanding, but results from the essence of being. But it don't follow at all that because we can't know being in this old sense, that we are any the worse off, or excluded from anything, that it is opaque to us. If it is *upon* us all the while, if we are of it, why seek to pour it in to the form of the known and understood. We all admit that the sphere of understanding is not all in us, that were complete knowledge attained we should still be dissatisfied, *life* wd. assert itself, will, action and the rest.
[*leaf* 11]
Why is not this will, this blind substance of the living man, that seems to be his backing his third dimension extending from the painted surface of the intelligible world into the deep of ontology, and in which he rests, at home, & feels him*self*, (though when he looks *at* it it vanishes) why is not this absolute being? Only not understood because above understanding, and not needing to be understood? (see Blood)

[*leaf* 12]
Rationality

That character of a mental experience which I have called its rationality is according to the empirical school nothing but an effect of habit. Habitual sequences, customary feelings breed an acquiescence in us leave us in repose, we feel at home in them. This feeling is agreeable, as mere ease or rest and is opposed to that unpleasant uneasiness which incongruous i.e. uncustomary representations excite, the distress of doubt, misunderstanding, irrationality. But *all* pleasure cannot be explained by habit. And it may be that not every form of this pleasure of rationality is equivalent to the mere ease of habit [*leaf* 12ᵛ] The admission by idealism that there are true and false representations seems at first sight to contradict its professed principles in as much as true to most minds neccessarily conveys the notion of conformity with something independent of the representation. But idealism explains this "truth" to be merely a general name for certain classes of representations which are distinguished by the possession of certain marks which are not *tokens* of the truth as common sense thinks, but its *essence*. It thus denies that there is any contradiction. Nominalism says that the "truth" of common sense, like its "substance," "cause," &c, are not representations at all, but pseudo-ideas.
[*leaf* 13]

A man is a match for the universe actively or on the emotional side when it becomes as a whole so qualified to his thought as to bring forth in him what I call a *rational* reaction; like fortitude, resignation, rapture, pious gratitude or any other state which is felt as pleasant and as worthy, and unlike fear, despair, doubt, or that nameless Unheimlickkeit which comes over one at thought of there being nothing objective either in the sense of existence or of End. These latter emotional reactions are all unpleasant and uneasy; the mind does not *rest* in them, but is agitated yet without definite direction.
[*leaf* 13ᵛ]

The Objective both as End and Existence has the common character of being effective, of constraing in some way our consciousness. In all the emotions I mentioned on the preceding page the feeling of an *object* becomes a very strong ingredient; in fear quite as much as in rapture, only in the latter we recognize a *ratio* between us and it, a mutual harmony, in the other the reverse.

Is this sense of harmony, the *eu-* a primitive element of feeling?

[*leaf* 14]

"Rationality"

According to idealistic empiricism can have no other meaning than habit; and if there be a true quale of emotion corresponding to the recognition of it, this can only be explained as an additional original form of representation the law of which is to arise with such representations as have frequently been experienced before. Habit as such in this school can have no effect, mental any more than physical. It supposes a substratum upon which each repetition leaves its impress in a way that alters the mode of appearance of the next repetition. But as each repetition in the Bain Hume school is a wholly distinct being, with no element in common with any other, it can in no way affect the next, or add to it an emotion of ease, rationality or anything else. These must be considered as wholly separate atoms superinduced [*leaf* 14ᵛ] in a definite order of juxtaposition.

For H. Spencer, on the contrary, what we call rationality in thought has an outward test viz. "correspondence" with the Real; and so far as it is a conscious *quale* of emotion, it may have been produced by several causes:

1 Natural selection
2 Habit as modifier of the nervous substratum
3

Admitting it as a *quale*, does it in this school of tho't play the part wh. it does in common sense? does it "testify" to an "inward" congruity in the ideas who by their conjunction produce it? Or does the only conceivable "inwardness" in the matter belong to the Unknowable cause to the arrangement (one must bring in some such [*leaf* 15] word and so far make it knowable) of whose parts or terms corresponds the arrangemement of the terms of representation, so that each term of representation has a causal connection with each of the unknowable, but no qualitative union with its successor in representation, only a growth together.
Rationality is a mark of truth
Verification its test.

Neither representation a or b are separately *true*. But the proposition a is b or a & b are inseparable may be true if the Unknowable's terms to which a & b correspond are themselves inseparable. Thus the truth of "*a* is *b*" depends on the [*leaf* 15ᵛ] possibility of our *verifying b* whenever we have got *a*. If term for term the

Unknowabe produced in us a qualitative determinations B quite diff.ᵗ fm. *b*, *a is B* wd. be as true as *a* is *b* and we should feel it to be as rational, although the only ground of rationality between the two qualities wd be the inaccessible one of union between their several unknowable causes. *Unless* we admit that what is united by essence in the unknowable is united also by essence in its conscious effects; & that two terms which are continuous in the unknowable must produce terms in conscious nature of equal *intrinsic* continuity.

[*leaf* 16]

Active Element in Thought I

According to the naturalistic empiricism the mind is a product of experiences, & nothing is in it but what has been caused *ab extra* except such re-arrangements of the elements derived ab extra as are possible.

4 degrees:
1 Memory
2 repeated memory, rational tho't.
3 fancy, reverie, nonsense, chaos
4 ideal tho't

Experience gives directly only 1 & 2; and them only by the cooperation of the subjective factor of active interest. If the mind were the purely passive tabula which the early essays of this school affirmed, *chaos* wd. be the only possible result of experience, for the *whole* mass of impressions falling on any individual are chaotic, and become orderly only [*leaf* 16ᵛ] by selection. And the selection is in the first instance surely very restricted, the vast majority of impressions remaining ignored because the subject takes no interest in them.

If the mental life were ruled by the purely physiologic law of association of ideas, we should be without that deep discrimination in our thought between the rational & the irrational. Following the physiologic law we shd think as rivers flow and that wd. be an end of the matter. But together with this sort of thinking in us we find an activity which keeps interfering with it and regulating it, accusing it of error & checking it, ordering it in short with reference to Ends or purposes [*leaf* 17] which are operative as *interests* of the subject, and set by the emotional nature.

Cf. *Windelband* in Steinth. & Laz. Ztschr. 1874

Bain's rush of expectation or whatever he calls it, the assumption that the future will be like the past; Mill's inference fm. analogy, from one particular to another; Spencer's test of truth; Huxley's standing by truth even if materialistic, are all cases of belief leading to action which proves the belief true, and yet incapable of rational defense. They rest on a physical basis. We can't prove [*leaf* 17ᵛ] | (vide Deunett on Geo. Eliot.) rational tho' not logical | them but we yield ourselves to them. And the act is an equivalent of so much reason, though it is not reasoned itself. It is right, though not yet stamped so by critical reflexion. What can this add? In the Mill case as above it ascends to the general in one particular and then sees the other particular to be also a case of that general. (see Taine.) wh. *proves* it, but only by referring it to a given ground, Which ground itself may also be doubted and have to refer to another ground & so on, until some ground is found wh. is evident or taken for granted—that is i.e. our *reason* for believing it or being satisfied by it is physical rather than logical.—In any case [*leaf* 18] | Active Element in Thought. II | [*short rule*] | then, our reasoning is based on and surrounded by a margin of mental *life* which is active, productive, and (judged by its results) true and practically therefore rational. Nevertheless it is not logical.——Faith.

Pure sensation is the Vague. It has to be discriminated or analyzed into different qualities. For this *attention* seems neccessary, and *re*cognition of what we attend to as identical with or different from qualities already experienced, i.e. the application of universals. And a discriminating attention does not seem possible without some discriminating interest on the subjects part; i.e some [*leaf* 18ᵛ] quality strikes him more than others as pleasant or unpleasant. Thus for any distinct sensation to occur there must be discriminating reaction on the subject's part, and apperception involving the use of concepts.

[*leaf* 20]
Is this a *moral universe*?
If so, Emotion is a legitimate factor in theory.
If not, the mind must register as passively as possible, to be right.

What is meant by a moral Universe? One in which not only the judgments *is* or *is not* are truly applicable to the things that occur, but one in which the judgments *should be or should not be* are also really, objectively pertinent; one in which the element of fitness, preferability, betterness or worseness is to be considered as an essential element of things, making [*leaf* 21] | Moral Universe II | [*short rule*] | our emotional judgment of them "right" or "wrong," in the same way that their existence or non existence proves our intellectual judgment of them "true" or "false."

All past events and all actual existing facts are wholly subject to the intellectual judment, without being at the same time withdrawn from the emotional judgment. Only in both spheres, the judgment we make today of what is to day, is liable to be rectified by what we may learn tomorrow.

All future events are not only subject to the emotional judgment but are products of emotional factors so far as they depend on the actions of sentient beings. Whether they are wholly subject to the intellectual [*leaf* 21ᵛ] judgment,—that is whether we may (supposing the perfect ideal of intellectual theory to have been realized) say of *any* & every supposed future fact whatever that it either *shall* or or *shall not be*—depends upon whether determinism is or is not true. Practically at least for us it is untrue, the future is partly contingent, and pro tanto withdrawn from the intellectual judgment.

Now, you and I do not yet dogmatize so far as either to affirm or deny that this is a moral world, but admit that it perhaps is so perhaps not.

If not, what are the conditions of true theory? Simply to ascertain accurately and formulate distinctly all that has been and is, and all that will be, so far as prediction is possible. Even in this case the future may be contingent, and since moral quality is as irrelevant to its [*leaf* 22] particulars as to its sum, its unpredictable contingencies may be called absolute accidents. So that in any event, every sort of assumption by the theorizing mind is out of place, notoriously so in extant matter, but in contingent matter equally so; for if the Mind should assume something which it was in the power of his future action to make true and then, having acted say that the assumption was justified by the result and thus legitimate,—if, I say, the mind should thus make truth it wd still do a superfluous & therefore unphilosophical thing. Instead of *this* assumption, you may make a different one and verify it as well, and thus produce a different philosophy which will be equally true with the first. Admitting assumption, there are many truths and no [*leaf* 22ᵛ] criterion to judge them. Or in other words truth is accidental. Why therefore assume anything or go beyond the data that can be passively ascertained to be determined? Why not leave the contingent aside simply as such.

If on the contrary, it *is* a moral world, the laws of theorizing become widely different. So far as facts are already determined of course the intellectual judgment is adequate and is best performed without the assistance of emotion. But so far as they are contingent, and contigent on the action of the philosopher, and so far as that action is a subject for the moral judgment,—why so far any theoretic assumption he may provisionally make as a basis for action, becomes a factor in the moral complexion of [*leaf* 23] | Moral Universe III | [*short rule*] | the future. And between two assumptions (I speak only of such as our action may help verify) equally verifiable in this way, we have a criterion in the moral judgment. Of equal truth, one is right—the other wrong, for it is better that one should be true than the other.

Such assumptions as those of optimism and pessimism, belief or disbelief that this is a moral world, belief or disbelief in immortality so far as the belief motives moral action and so far again as the fact of immortality may possibly depend on the fact of moral action—all these are clear cases in point. Any belief which affects [*leaf* 23ᵛ] action is thus right if it gives rise to right action.

Suppose that there is no God but that belief in one furthers right action—can the belief be called right, true, or legitimate?
Suppose apart from verification we say it were better a certain belief should be than not be, it being untrue but subjectively noble,— could we call it true or right or anything eulogistic? To this it might be replied that truth is essential to the excellence of a belief —and that the moral judgment is only a criterion to decide between beliefs that may be either true. The antimoralists can't even say absolutely that a belief should be true. Their judging of the excellence of beliefs proceeds on the hypothetic and conventional of belief by truth.

—— Still, suppose human beings so constituted that a belief in God be neccessary to keep the moral world going, and yet [*leaf* 24] that God does not exist. Could the success of the moral world make the existence of God in any sense a truth? No!

There is a triple alternative.
1° It may be better for the moral world to admit the truth of atheism and then expire. This wd. show adhesion to truth to be the chief moral duty.
2° Or to go on believing a lie, which wd. make truth a subordinate moral value.
3 Or maybe the hypothesis is contradictory and not to be entertained at all. But in saying this, we abandon the formal ground of *method* in which we have hitherto been moving and take account

of the material part in our examples. I don't know whether this is permissible.
[*leaf* 24ᵛ]

The subjective method in theorizing is justifiable when and only when into the verification of the theory a subjective factor neccessarily enters. Where verification is objective theory must be wholly produced by the objective method.

Philosophy only dealing with facts so far as general, may be said not to recognize at all the emotions or actions of any individual unless they can prove themselves to be typical. On an empirical basis typicalness is proved by universality or generality of occurrence. On a moral scheme, it is claimed to belong to whatever is excellent or desirable. So that the world should on this scheme be supplemented by *the desirable excellent products of the Subject* before it can be considered as forming a complete object for philosophical research.
[*leaf* 25]
Moral world one in which the "should be" judgment is valid.
What constitutes the *truth* of the moral world, its test and its warrant?
Of course subjectively the "shd. be" judgment is always possible. And if we adopt it—true or false—the result is the same we shall never be the wiser as to the soundness of our theoretic faith unless there is some way of testing or verifying. We must distinguish too between the empirical "judged by its results" of *particular* moral judgments—mistake is there shown by disastrous consequences and just as much so on an empirical as on a moral hypothesis. What we want here is a test as to the objective [*leaf* 25ᵛ] validity of the total class of judgments. In the first place as the *shd. be* is not a *fact*, it can neither be established nor refuted by a fact. The "by your fruits shall ye know them" test may be applicable, the whole harmony of life on the moral basis turning out superior to that on the mechanical. But this harmony being a general complex result may be ignored as evidence—

Does the simple presence of the "shd be" constitute a moral world; or need we also a power to warrant the should be and con-[*leaf* 26] vert its doubters and reward the faithful by a blazing proof? Not neccessarily the latter. The world may be moral but a pessimism.

351

The "should be's of common life are hypothetical that is based on certain assumed conditions e.g. A. being what it is, B should be thus, or harmony between B and A is lost. The event proves this shd. be by a fact—for the particular harmony or discord is easy to ascertain.

Now a universal should be has no such fact to refer itself to and be judged (unless one appeal to the will of a deity, or the in some way expressed [*leaf* 26ᵛ] meaning of the cosmos.) The harmony here can only be an internal organic harmony. The proof that the moral philosophy is right can only lie in the satisfactoriness of its results as a whole—by which the truth or rightness acquires a sort of self evidence.

The general principle of pragmatism proves every thing by its result, but the results of an absolute "should be" in things are not determinable beforehand as to their quality. If the universe is a pessimism the results are tragic—the soul cleaving to its ideal and defying the actual by wh. it perishes. If on the other hand it is an optimism, the results are satisfactory—most satisfactory when the *should be* is followed—and may have an internal evidence as above. But in either [*leaf* 27] case the actual is no stringent proof of the a priori existence of the ideal. One may still deny & disbelieve.

Has the moral character of the world an *existence* at all? Can we say: it *is* a moral world? or is there any *is*-ness to the *should*? may it not be *should be's*—all the way down? "It *should be* a moral world," not "it *is* one?"

Such an assumption seems to contravene an irresistible tendency of the mind to rest only in existences actual or essential as the ultimate ground of explanation and reality. to which tendency the assumption of a God and Providence by those who believe the world to be moral, is due.

Quoad existentiam nothing is more comprehensible than anything else. The ultimate explanatory existence is a simple datum, [*leaf* 27ᵛ] something which we come upon and find.

A moral world is one in wh *rightness* as well as actuality has to be considered in regard to all the incidents—among the incidents being our beliefs.

[*leaf* 29]

I maintain that there is an absolute of excellent *being just as there is an absolute of true being.* That "this" is *meant* to be so— not accidental—a mere happening wh. might *equally well* have been otherwise. Equally well for what? of course not for the present accidents—Equally well then with other accidents. But this involves a total change, & when we speak of "well" at all or "equally well" we are supposed to refer to some *constant criterion.* Good is then essentially relative—continuity again comes in.

[*leaf* 30]   *A*

List of complex notions whose factors are taken up into them so to speak, i.e. never afterwards conceived barely, or as they may be supposed to have existed in the mind previous to the formation of the complex. This latter may then be said to be explanatory of them, it may be called an hypothesis whose historic origin in the mind is posterior to that of the factors but whose logical function is prior, forming a basis for their intelligibility.

1 Space, evolved out of innumerably *gradated* muscular & tactile sensations. These afterwards even when separately conceived are arranged [*leaf* 31] according to the spatial order.

2 Externality,

3 The Substantial Identity in things as a ground for our belief in the "Uniformity of Nature."

[*leaf* 38]   B

List of complex notions from which the tributary factors may still be abstracted & used separately by the mind, so that the complex notion seems a luxury so to speak, convenient as a summarizing sign, but not conferring intelligibility.

Under {1 Excellence as a product of utility
C.   {2 Reality

"Love" as distinct from the several particular impulses, propensities, & emotions that characterize it. Impulse to be near her as often and as close as possible, to make her notice me, to kiss and the rest of it. Joy when I believe she [*leaf* 38ᵛ] depends on me, values me &c. All the manifestations of love or hatred may be expressed in other language perfectly well.

[*leaf* 39]   C

List of complex notions equivalent to a certain set of simple ones, but of different felt quality, so that the mind with difficulty is able to "cash" the former by the latter. These differ fm. those in lists A & B in that intercouse between factors & product is so to speak arrested after the formation of the latter; it being not used to explain the former, nor they clothing themselves in its quality.
1 Excellence as a product of utilities [*leaf* 39ᵛ]
2. Such a notion as that of *reality*, in most people's minds, which means neither exactly breath of relation, intensity of sensation, persistence in one mind, nor coexistence in all. It comes nearest to Objectivity as we feel it. It ought perhaps to be placed under B, as it *explains* the marks of it given above.

[*leaf* 41]
Books wh. I should

[*leaf* 44]
middle beginnings & ends gone
If mind Constituted a la Kant then knowledge essential qua knowledge
Remains the notion of noumena. Whence? By extension of the empiric distinction of thought (ie erroneous, imperfect tho't) versus thing (i.e. source of perfect complete thought) Thing here is a limit
Überhaupt if noumena are limits towards wh. we may swing, and which thus determine our orientation in the universe, we need not repine at the limitations of our knowledge.
An object logically essential.
But its *quale* determined by a long experience
Philosophies seek to say what is the most real quale.

[*leaf* 45]
Metaphysical ideas like substance, absolute, infinite real, objective, &c, are intelligible and valid as *used*—they function well. It is only when reflected on, that they grow suspicious. One may define the metaphysical as the not yet criticised, or reflected on. And in this sense the *living*, in tho't, takes its place beside the real in being, as being both entitled to pass muster until challenged by critical

reflection, but both liable as soon as they are challenged, to collapse into semblances, or idols branded "subjective." The Real in being in fact is but incident to one species of the genus which criticism calls metaphysical illusion," but which it is best to call living tho't, and whose other species generate such qualities as Absolute, substance &c &c [*leaf* 46] The instant tho't *is* always living in this sense, and only potentially matter of reflection. While we are *in* it we believe in it as implying, revealing, *meaning* some object, while we think *of* it we believe in it as being itself an object. Metaphysical illusion cleaves to the instant, and only quits it when the instant has become the past, and an object to the next instant. Then what seemed *its* Real, its objective, &c drop into its subjectivity, become encapsulated by it, so to speak or pocketed as its incidents; as the magic lantern image returns into the stede when the lamp passes from behind the latter. And we define the world as purely representational—meaning to include by anticipation the instant,—which however we can't practically do. If we did that would encapsulate all things concentrically into one subjective moment, just as the projection of an interminable perspective is a boundary line [*leaf* 47] (a window frame e.g.) surrounding circles including smaller circles ad' infinitum. This is egoistic or pyrrhonic idealism.) (But this is impossible; for every subjectivity once recognized as such is *objectively such.* sophism?)

[*leaf* 48]

I call essentially metaphysical, every affirmation of a *transcendency* on the part of any discriminable thing, idea, or representation. An idea has its instant, subjective, "*as-such*" existence, which is absolutely simple, a mere discriminable quality, a "first intention," whatever you please to call it; and this may be called its *physical existence*. Now every admission that *this* existence is not the absolute whole of the idea; that in addition the idea is *related* to others, is *operative, effective,* forms *part* of an organism, is *recognized* as it were where it physically is not—every such admission is that of a transcendency of its physical existence, and leads in its different applications to the categories [*leaf* 49] of *cause, meaning, purpose substance,* (both in the noumenal & in the phenomenal sense,) *nature,* Essence and *objective* reality—which are metaphysical.

Ordinary usage classes also as metaphysical, notions of the *absolute,* the *infinite,* & and the *noumenon.*

The *absolute* is certainly the contradictory of the metaphysical in the sense above given for it signifies that which in no way refers beyond itself. Nevertheless it is tabooed by the same men who taboo the former notions. The fact is that all cognitions are practically absolute until *reduced* by a further reference to a relation. *The* Absolute is simply an ideal abstraction from this familiar experience, and is logically on a par with *The* Metaphysical, which postulates the infinite or unfathomable transcendency [*leaf* 50] of the Essence or nature of each thing to the physical or phenomenal existence of the thing.

The Metaphysical as an ideal is identical with the Infinite and the noumenon, both of which are mere postulates—not adequate concepts—and point to the fact that our knowledge is true only as far as it goes, that we come upon truth & find it, as a datum,—and that it exists where we have not yet found it. This is the lasting truth of "Empiricism."

The Metaphysical & *the* Absolute are thus poles between which all our thought oscillates. In each item of thought there is an absolute and a metaphysical element. The absolute is its "first" the metaphysical its "second, intention," or its sensational quality & its logical "position," or its phenomenal existence [*leaf* 51] and its real meaning &c &c &c, its *self* & its relations in a word.

When Nihilists say knowledge is non-metaphysical do they include (see above II [*leaf* 46]) by anticipation the instant consciousness?

They can't, for that being essentially metaphysical, can't commit suicide in that way.

When on the other hand Substantialists reflectively corroborate the verdicts of the instant, & when, taking the relations under which we in our several perceptions, thought the objects, they affirm them to be permanently true of them, thus spreading the affection of the instant *into* what has ceased to be the living instant but

[*leaf* 52] | *Magnolia 2* |
seems to be connected with the material content of the affair, and independent of its relations with other representations.

Idealism meets with reception from minds whose motives are very dissimilar. It is discriminated from materialism (rudely tho't) and noumenalism. Ontologic repose throws people upon it from noumenalism. Ontologic passion makes noumenalists. But ontologic passion is an emotion of the tender (self subordinating) class which is usually associated with other refined emotions that make men averse to materialism. So that it too makes idealists tender being often found in those souls whose tender nature makes them crave a warrant for safety &c. These people are therefore noumenalists [*leaf* 52ᵛ] by their intellect, and absolutists by their heart.

Anti substantialist idealism is recruited from the ranks of those who like a short story, hate ontologic mystery, and enjoy clear and simple thought. (Wright & Co) on the other hand by those who on the positive side love mystery, but on the negative are liable to fear uncertainty, unsafety, alienation, and who find in the material content of Being as idealistically defined a warrant for their peace. The motive of the first class is logical, that of the second moral. And the disagreements between the two are of the nature of personal antipathy rather than of rational disagreement.

[*leaf* 54]

The conclusions of common sense, or of any given opinion, are *reduced* by criticism to inferior grades of absoluteness or certainty to those which their maintainers assign to them. What is held for *reality* is shown not to possess absolute reality, subjective certainty is shown not to give *the right* to objective affirmation, the *explanations* of the vulgar are shown not to be explanations at all but habitual coherences, *causal* connexion is not truly such,

In all these cases where the predicate ordinarily affirmed is simply exploded by criticism (cause, explanation, objectivity) [*leaf* 54ᵛ] instead of being shoved simply along to a more restricted application (as in the confining of reality to an unknowable substance) we have a right to ask of criticism what its *reductive* then is. To say that the cases we call causation are not truly such, that our explanations and deductions of neccessary truth are not such in reality, wd. seem to presuppose the existence in the critic of a positive standard of causality & explanation compared with which our cases prove deficient. If causality & explanation are simply meaningless words they cannot be *denied* of the ordinary instances, but only declared superfluous—but by critics [*leaf* 55] they are denied. *Substance* it is true is often simply exploded, and may serve to show by contrast what the critical procedure is in the case of deduction, causation, and the reduction of reality to "phenomena." In the critics' mind there is an intelligible ideal of what these words mean. If an empiricist, he therefore stands in the dilemma of having to locate the ideals somewhere out of experience, or of showing how the experience to which he says they don't apply, has none the less generated them. He usually shows them to be of anthropomorphic origin.

[*leaf* 55ᵛ]
That to which we attribute a quality is the seat of the quality unless we can show the quality to have been transferred to it by a mental confusion from something else. In the latter case this s'thing else is its real seat and the reductive of the first thing. In other words an *intelligible* quality cannot be exploded *schlechthin*. When common sense says: immediate certainty gives us the right to affirm objective truth, and we deny it, we must show in what that right can inhere better; for if it inhere in nothing even hypothetically better than in immediate certainty, it must be either nonsense, or be left with that. The best *there is*, must be good. The truest we can conceive must be the real truth for us

[*leaf* 56]
Common sense says it has the marks *because* it is real; nominalism, it simply has the marks, and we group it with other things that have the marks by calling the whole class *realities*.

The common run of theories of consciousness, external perception &c, commit the fallacy of postulating an object capable of producing certain representations, wh. latter become its marks and lead the mind to *infer* it when it feels them.

[*leaf* 56ᵛ]
By *reality* common sense means a something which explains its marks, and which the marks merely help us to infer.

Nominalism says the reality is exhaustively constituted of the marks, and that what we infer from some mark or marks is but the presence of the others.

Kantism might say that the reality was produced by the mind to simplify the marks into one bundle.

Taine that it was a character common to all the marks, which their collocation enabled us to abstract.

REJECTED VERSOS

[*leaf* 19ᵛ]   ['middle|Emotional'|*del.*] Objective Implication of Emotions
[*leaf* 44ᵛ]   a nether e

B: Box E, Envelope 1 (bMS Am 1092.9, #4464)

Thirty-three sheets of paper, punched to make up a form of notebook. The manuscript contains certain pencil markings which were probably inserted by Ralph Barton Perry. All text is in ink unless specifically noted to the contrary.

Leaves 1-2 are written on a wove paper (222 × 172 mm.), unwatermarked, foliated 1, 1 *bis*, their versos blank. Folio 1 is headed 'The Sentiment of Rationality' double underlined with the section heading I inserted below the title.

Leaf 3, laid paper (222 × 157 mm.), unwatermarked, vertical chainlines 18 mm. apart, foliated 4 in upper right corner, now heavily smudged—whether as deletion is not certain. The text is continued on the verso where it ends about two-thirds down the page.

Leaves 4-5, same paper as leaf 3 but joined in a fold, their versos blank.

Leaf 6 starts new text on a sheet of laid paper (202 × 127 mm.), watermarked with a crown below 'Royal' in script; the text continues on the verso.

Leaf 7 is written in pencil on wove paper (253 × 202 mm.), unwatermarked, with blank verso.

Leaves 8-11 are on wove paper (215 × 188 mm.), unwatermarked, foliated 1-4 (4 in pencil) in the center of each leaf, the text ending about a third of the way down on the last page. The versos are blank except for leaf 11, which has two brief notes in pencil, reversed.

Leaf 12 begins in mid-sentence on the same paper, originally foliated 6, centered, but the number deleted and 9 written in the upper left corner. On its verso is the single word 'Rationality'.

Leaf 13 starts fresh text on an irregularly torn piece of light-weight wove paper (242 × 190 mm.), unwatermarked; the text continues on the verso, ending about halfway down the page.

Leaf 14 contains separate text on a light-weight wove paper (212 × 186 mm.), unwatermarked; a short pencil passage appears on the verso.

Leaf 15 is written in Alice James's hand, headed 'Plan of Essay.' on a piece of laid paper (221 × 160 mm.), unwatermarked, the vertical chainlines 15 mm. apart, verso blank.

Leaves 16-17 are written in James's hand in pencil on light-weight laid paper (253 × 198 mm.), unwatermarked, the horizontal chainlines 17 mm. apart, versos blank, the text ending about halfway down the second page.

Leaves 18-33 contain continuous text headed 'The sentiment of rationality.' written on slightly coated wove paper (217 × 177 mm.), unwatermarked, ending at the foot of leaf 33. Leaf 18 has been foliated with a pencil 1, centered, and leaf 19 with a pencil 2, also centered. Leaves 20-33 have been foliated in ink 1-14, respectively. All versos are blank.

[*leaf* 1]

THE SENTIMENT OF RATIONALITY

I

"The Psychology of Philosophizing" would perhaps be a better title for this Essay than the one which it bears. For it arose in the attempt to discover in an analysis of the motives wnich prompt men to philosophic activity, some facts which might help us to decide between the conflicting claims to authority of the different systems to which that activity gives birth.

In the following pages, then, I treat systems of truth as purely subjective creations, invented for the satisfaction of certain aesthetic needs; and I seek by defining the needs to discover what conditions a system must satisfy in [*leaf* 2] order to obtain universal acceptance. If universal acceptance be, as it surely is, the only mark of truth which we possess, then any system certain not to get it, may be deemed false without further ceremony, false at any rate for us, which is as far as we can inquire.

There is no doubt that a vast deal of the confusion hitherto prevalent in philosophy has been due to the fact that the real motives to an opinion were concealed rather than explicitly avowed—that the reasons ostensibly put forward by a philosopher formed but a small portion of his real premisses.* For not to speak on the one hand of reverence for authority and of purely polemic or iconoclastic bias on the other, how much obscurity has resulted from the mingling of analytical with sentimental considerations, from the

---

*See on this subject the masterly remarks of Ch. Renouvier in the *Critique Philosophique*, for Novem 29th, 1877

[*leaf* 3]
Givenness of Cosmos the only problem of the Absolute.
Brute datum indistinguishable from pure accident.
We have to try to make it seem less of an accident, less of an arbitrary fact.
[Metaphysic entity as cause wd. help us only if self existence were comprehensible of *them,* which is really not the case.]
1 We may resign ourselves, and accept givenness—of the Cosmos as the all. Positivism. Neccessity of counting in *all* the laws of the Kosmos. Ordinary materialistic positivism mutilates. Must define world as representations. Clearnessı with a certain suspense or fortitude. Being *as* related. Free-will. moral laws.—God, immortality etc. phenomenally conceived.
2.) Try to show question irrelevant. Limit of logical reduction when unity has been reached. Absurd to say given world lacks comprehensibility. Blue. Contradiction alone incomprehensible. Desire to understand has 3 roots. Unity. Expectancy. Activity. In point of fact [*leaf* 3ᵛ] when these three are answered men always

have been satisfied, the world has seemed rational, altho' after all, as so defined, it was still a mere datum. It was a datum that on could react upon. We were acquainted with it through & through— no foreignness. subject a match for object. Subject-object the Absolute. Question then becomes frivolous. *rightness* exorcises. teleologic answer alone possible. Simple adoration mystical position

3 Hegelism, tries after the datum being has been found to intermediate between it & nothing. Possibly infinite pro- or regress in the way of answering.

[*leaf* 4]
You have now an itching on the point of your nose. For me to know that, you say, is a very poor kind of knowledge; but when I know a nebula full of mind stuff, you say that is a sublime kind of knowledge. Really one is as incomplete as the other. The mere mind-stuff nebula as such, what is it, what is it worth? It is a fact like the itching. Only when determined as the nebula *destined to produce* that itching in your nose here and now [*leaf* 5] can it be complete knowledge. Only when the itching itself is felt as the result of the nebula does *it* become complete. And then, no matter which way you start, you get the same whole. Both are stumps, taken apart.

[*leaf* 6]
Royce's formula
But how would such a mind act?
So as to lose as little as possible,
So as to get the best possible whole.
But how decide conflicts? Which wills sympathize with?
Follow the common traditions. Sacrifice all wills which are not
　organizable, and which avowedly go against the whole. No
　one pretends in the main to revise the decalogue, or to take
　up offenses against life, property, veracity or decency into
　the permanent whole. If those are a man's goods, the man is
　not a member of the whole we mean to keep, and we sacri-
　fice both him & his goods without a tear. [*leaf* 6ᵛ] When the
　rivalry is between real organizable goods the rule is that the
　one victorious should so far as possible keep the vanquished
　somehow represented. Find some innocent way out.
Examples:
Savage virtues preserved by athletics;

Warlike by organized warfare; constitutional government, excitement remains.

Aristocratic love of art and splendor with democratic equality; Variety of races with supremacy of the best; Humanity with Darwinism; Romantic love with breeding.

These reconciliations still come before us as problems. The worlds trial better than the *closet solution*

[*leaf* 7]
Competition wd. not account for the prevalence of a *better* (or fitter to live) except on the supposition that the better is stronger too; and a universe in wh. this rule holds already indicates its divine constitution   Contemp. XIX 619
Hartmann on externality.
Brentano on Bain's belief.
I. H. Fichte w
Empiricist account to have been once is a reason for repetition

Is it that rational order
The postulation of a *truth* is equivalent to that of a rational order ante rem which as such we recognize. That is the *actual* expects always further determination, protends, refers beyond itself. But in as much as such reference has a retroactive force, we by anticipation place its deliverance in the present actual. Everett's insistence that we do suppose s'thing extra rem—we certainly suppose it in making our sensibles to be due to atoms & vibrations etc; or is that merely equivalent to saying that if something could happen, we know not what we shd. see those latter.

[*leaf* 8]
Cause, meaning, *plus ultra* the phenomenon
Ideal matrix, rational order, existence *ante rem*, transcendent existence, potentiality, Substance, Ding an sich are all expressions which have no meaning according to the theory that phenomenal actuality is the all. On that theory there is no existence but plenary existence, i.e. the fully determinate here & now. All else is verbal sign, only justified by its capacity for translation into full particulars. Beyond or behind the instant *fact*, Nothing! and inasmuch as to that fact cleaves always the incident of *being known*, we may add: beyond representation, nothing! There is no *nature* in phenomena whereby they are as they are and not other wise. When from a certain no. of marks we are ordinarily said to infer a ground of those marks, (as according to common sense truth according to

Hartmann externality, according to others reality, coerciveness as mark of reality according to Brentano belief, according to Martineau goodness) this theory maintains that so far from inferring a ground we are only providing a collective name [*leaf* 9] for the marks. When indeed, the inferred thing is a separate representation that may be concretely experienced, it has real existence, but then it is not a ground for the marks but is a mere associate of them, and they may be called its ground as well as it theirs. But in other cases, the ground is wholly devoid of real existence has purely verbal being. Its being postulated to bind the marks together is a superfluity if the marks actually are together. If the marks are *not* together of course we shd. never say it existed. But if they may exist not together without the aid of a special principle of disunion, surely they are competent to exist together without a principle of union. The vulgar theory supposes that whatever happens, happens through the overcoming of its negation; through the raising of an inhibition which raising is of course the act of a special cause. Instead of simply one thing, the happening, it assumes three [*leaf* 10] things, the matrix or potentiality of the happening, the non actuality or negation of it, the negation of that or the ground. Thus if the visual appearance of a peach be followed by other marks, flavour, odour, juiciness etc, the vulgar suppose it neccessary to posit a peach nature there as a reason why they came together, if the same visual marks were followed by coldness, hardness, great weight etc. they wd. posit a stone nature. The theory I am attempting to describe wd. on the other hand say that both stone nature and peach nature so far from preceding the collocation of marks and making it to be such and not otherwise, followed it, was a name for it. If the marks fall out one way, they make a peach, if another a painted stone. Neither "peach" nor "stone" exist until the additional marks *have* occurred. The first visual marks are truly am-[*leaf* 11]biguous and have no a priori connexion with what follows. *Something* must follow however, and according as it is juiciness & flavor, or cold and hardness, it has a retroactive force on what preceded and we say the visual marks already belonged to a peach, i.e. the "peach" existed in some sort ante rem before it was plenary etc.

[*leaf* 12]
to reflect and call subjective the one elapsed, we in the instant anticipate this verdict of the future and call all subjective. Always able to criticize or doubt the deliverance of consciousness we only affirm the instant as liable to this potentiality. Always experienc-

ing a plus ultra of being we suppose all being thus flanked. Relative we suppose the whole can have no moral quality. Constantly able to conceive of the instant having a different quality from that which it does have, we, we always infect it with this *aliter possibile*. Finding that a given thing's existence is contradictory of other existences, we generalize this contradiction and hypostatize it in the form of non-entity which is the contradiction of *all* being.

[*leaf* 13]
Says Mill, we shd. never be able to contrast the outer with the inner world unless there existed, *ab initio* some distinguishable peculiarities in the two experiences. *What* d. p.? "*Outness*," says the vulgar; "intensity, coerciveness, connexion of a certain kind with other phenomena, &c, &c," say the empirical philosophers,— only *not* outness. That comes in posteriorly as a summarizing sign for the preceding list, a heading merely under which to class, having no *quale* of its own in feeling, or at most such a *pseudo-quale* as results from the coalescence of the blurred and "nascent" peculiarities mentioned above.
The principle of "pragmatism," which allows all assumptions to be of identical value so long as they equally *save the appearances* will of course be satisfied with this empiricist explanation, (supposing it complete.) But common sense is not assuaged. She says, yes, I get all [*leaf* 13ᵛ] the particulars, am cheated out of none of my expectations. And yet the principle of *intelligibility* is gone. Real outness makes everything as simple as the day, but the troops of ideas marching and falling perpetually into order, which you now ask me to adopt, have no *reason* in them—their whole existence is *de facto* not *de jure*.
These ideas do in the Kantian sense confer rationality to the particulars of thought.

[*leaf* 14]
a prior :
   All the men being in doors *keeps* the yard empty
a post
   All ″   ″   ″   ″   ″ *is* the yard empty.
_____

"relations presupposed in association" Murphy ii, 74

_____

a priori: "The action of all forces is governed by the laws of motion, and yet the laws of motion will not account for orgin

of force &c." Murphy ii, 156.
a post.: the laws of motion *are* the realized motions and there is
no force.

---

a priori: the habitual in tho't is *because* rational
a post: the habitual in tho't *is* and means the rational

[*leaf* 15]
Plan of Essay.

Ineffable demands
Constancy of point of view—if you change it for one item you
must change for all.
The HUME-HODGSON "metaphysic" surface contrasted with the
FICHTE-HARTMANN duplicating ontologism.
The latter explained à la WRIGHT and LIEBMANN.
Rational order preexistent to fact seems the only upshot. Psycho-
logical deduction of this.
Leading to conclusion in accord with ordinary theism.

[*leaf* 16]
Potential—ideal—rational—a priori all designate a matrix so to call
it in which reality lies embedded as it lies embedded in space. Into
this preappointed receptacle the matter of reality fits and derives
its logical or systematic form. It is the world of essences of logical
relations, of universals, of meanings, of reasons, of "Universalia ante
rem." It is indeed almost impossible to conceive of the universe
with this abolished, for every act of aperception by which we assign
its particular thinghood to a thing assumes the separation & then
the reception of the matter into its particular pigeon hole of the
rational system. To deny it is the very extreme and climax of
skepticism. So extreme in fact that perhaps the majority of those
who call themselves empiricist have never even conceived it, and
the greatest difficulty which a priorists have in vindicating their
view arises perhaps from the stupidity of unimaginative opponents
who *think* they have thrown overboard everything but the world
of absolute fact [*leaf* 17] but who are so far from having lapsed
from the paradise of primeval philosophic innocence into which all
men are born, as still to conceive of their derationalized world of
fact, as thoroughly saturated with the a priori nature. What wonder
then, if swearing there is no a priori ground they still stand with
one foot upon it; they are the chief obstacles to clear discussion of
principles, and the great dogs on philosophic advance. Real acute-

ness, of whatever school brings fruit and hope. Muddle headedness brings nothing.

[*leaf* 18]

The sentiment of rationality.

Before starting in quest of a philosophy, t'is well to frame a notion of what the phil. might be like if attained—so as to recognize it; to state in other words what is the exact subjective demand which the philosophy shd. satisfy and what the subjective conditions of its being satisfied.

1. Aesthetic Unity in thought, leading to deductive explanation or explanation by *elements* (Taine.) These elements however are merely logical and have no neccessary connexion with existence, that is many consistent elementarily deduced systems might be conceived, none of wh. were real The principle wh. tells why *if* a thing be, it shd. be *so*, is diff! fm that wh. tells why it should *be* überhaupt

2 The element of reality or existential neccessity is thus left unaccounted for. This the stronghold of Empiricism. (Fitz. J. Stephen).

3 Empiricism tainted by uncertainty as to future. Warrant for fixed expectation a further motive for philosophizing.

4 *Substance* viewed in this light. (Absolute *being* more rational to us than absolute *happening.*)

5 The nihilistic objection that the substance adds nothing to the phenomenon, having no other connotation that that of being substance to *this phenomenon*, does not exactly hit the mark; for the essence of the substantial judgment added [*leaf* 19] by us to our apprehension of the phenomenon is, "*It is meant so. This being meant* is, that which separates "real" phenomena fm. figments & fancies.

What exactly it portends is uncertain. The most spontaneous answer is the theistic:—an intelligence behind the phenomenon which ours meets in the phenomenon. (Berkeley) Or it may mean only the absolute circular coherence of phenomena. Whatever it signify, if we allow it to stand, there results the stability of the present system, and consequently practical peace. The theoretic insight into the neccessity of things is not vouchsafed us, and the Empiricists so far are right. But this practical stability constitutes the most important part of the philosophic quest. The intellect is really built up of practical interests. Helmholz, teaching dog, match for the world. Emotion of rationality present where facts are such as to call for rational reaction on our part. [*leaf* 20] This mode of expressing the facts leave assuredly no fact out. Everything can be verified. Principle of parcimony, expectation, & adequacy to action are all there. What more is wanted. Something, certainly, though at first sight it may be hard to define it. To human nature there is something uncanny, unheimlich in the notion of a universe stripped so stark naked, brought down to its fighting weight so to speak. Men have at all times believed in something over and above bare actuality, have allowed to the phenomenon a form of being other than that which immediately impressed the senses. Whether they have called this *other*, universalia ante rem, or noumenon or substance, or the Unknowable, or idea in the platonic sense, or whether they have hypostatized its "possibility" like John Mill,— thoughts of God, meaning, purpose, nature, a rational order like the stoics, the absolute thought in wh the phenomenon forms [*leaf* 21] a moment of the hegelians, or the mere nature of the phenomenon of common sense,—under each and all of these formula-- tions lurks the same mental act, that of insisting that things do not exist so to speak only once, but are in a manner duplicated, appointed, called for, recognized at other places and moments than those of their plenary actuality. As ours is a psychological study, we are bound, as soon as we observe so universal a mental tendency as this to inquire into its causes. If they should prove to be permanent and neccessary factors of our mental constitution why then of course it would appear that a consistently nominalistic account of things could never be generally accepted as the truth— the craving for a plus ultra the instant phenomenon, shut off to day, would reassert itself tomorrow [*leaf* 22] in some new mode of formulation and breed an everlastingly self-renovating protest against the reduction of all reality to actuality.

The first and perhaps strongest reason why the instant phenomenon does not seem self sufficing lies in the fact that it is always cognized or interpreted by us through some general notion which we already have. Apperception is the admirable word, which should be naturalized in english by which modern germans denote the act by which the mind goes out to meet the phenomenon and receive it into a pre existing bed. Here is something before me. What is it? a small thing, a round thing, a pink thing, a fragrant thing, a peach. Until the successive pre existent concepts have been projected upon it, the thing is wholly indeterminate. Now we are con- [*leaf* 23] scious throughout this performance of *identifying* the thing with the concepts—it *is* round, it *is* pink. Checked, it *is* a peach etc. But as we are also conscious of the concepts as possible forms of being before experiencing this actual peach, we get to regard the world of concepts as a sort of permanent ideal matrix with an order of its own into which concrete particulars may upon occasion come and fit or settle into their appropriate places. It makes no difference that a nominalist may say that so long as a concept is ampliative of the impression it is not yet verified and so is untrue, and that the only truly applied concepts are only names for the actual impression which is what it is as much without as with the names—this I say makes no difference to our spontaneous feeling which always will posit, just as it does now a recognition of things rather than a cognition of them, a rational order with which the mind communes and upon [*leaf* 24] which actuality settles here and there by a sort of accident, and in settling acquires its specific determinations.

Thus then, the familiar logic of predication contradicts to our spontaneous sensibility the nominalistic account, and if an other account can be critically established gives to that other the palm. If I seek a phrase for the logical protest, I should say it was made in favor of an all enveloping "rational order." So deep and wide is this feeling that probably very few readers of empiricist accounts of mental development even catch a glimpse of their full import. Their imagination is not trained to a sufficient power of abstraction. Take for example Spencer's well known account of Mind as measured by the increase in range of the correspondence between inward & outward relations. The outward facts [*leaf* 25] occur in a certain order, the mental representatives of those facts must occur in the same order, or the mind in question will be proved incompetent. The sense of neccessity or appropriateness that the mind feels in the habitual order is its sentiment of rationality; but, once having the right order and the sentiment, it feels when next it recognizes a case of the order in the outward world as if there too the order obeyed the same sort of rational neccessity, which thus objectively exists *a priori* to the fact. The fact, of course, and the order of fact have in the empiricist view nothing rational about them. Rationality is a wholly derivative and secondary affair pertaining exclusively to the subjective realm, not a sort of middle kingdom to wh. mind and fact alike pay tribute & in which mind may meet fact and learn, fact meet mind & be judged. There is no essential and general reason dominating all. Nature does not even *happen* to be rational, but what [*leaf* 26] ever *is* together in nature comes to have the subjective comment "rationally compatible" tagged on to it in our minds by pure gratuity. To talk of Reasonableness in the objective nature of things is as absurd as to call a kind "obedient" because his presence awakens impulses to obedience in his retainers. The antithesis is well stated by C. S Peirce:

Chance is the only name we have for such a world Now it is certain that most of the scientific readers of Mr Spencer wholly fail to catch the destructive import of his theory in this respect. They are willing to believe with the Master that the deepest reality is the absolutely irrational, because that reality is unknowable, but few of them intimately realize that the knowable of their philosophy forms a world of Chance pure and simple. If they did, they would feel uncomfortable and cast [*leaf* 27] about them for a more congenial guide.

But there are still other forces at work in the mind which lead it to suppose something over and above the mere actuality of things. The sense of futurity, the power of expectation, which we have already seen to play so important a part again comes in here. We prolong a line of experience hitherto habitual into the future we make it envelope by anticipation the present just as it hitherto enveloped the past. Just as according to empiricism we supply a spatial *beyond* to the space we now think of merely because all the spaces we ever have had to do with proved to have such a beyond. Always having been able in the subsequent moment to look back and see that the *thing* we had in [*leaf* 28] mind was only the thing *as we thought it*, we learn to anticipate this future reflection on the instant and say that *all* our "things" are representations. Always able to criticize, expand or rectify a deliverance of our mind a few moments after we have made it, we grow to affirm the instant only as liable to this potential doubt, in other words to bear in mind that the truth which now appears to us may possibly be *other* than it appears. The experience of error in expectation conspires also to the same result. Our notion of a future time with its material content forms a sort of matrix *ante rem* into which in its time the *res* fits, but when instead of the *res* we [*leaf* 29] thought of, a different one comes in, we feel that our expectation not only is wrong now, but *was* wrong, and this involves the notion that all the while the expectation was alive, the *res* previous to its plenary existence enjoyed some sort of existence sufficient to invalidate my expectation. In other words the thing I expect may even now before its actuality be other than my expectation. Desires, again, and judgments that things would be better thus than so, involve the feeling that apart from their actuality things have a certain coercive hold on being. The hold an ideal thing has on my desire seems the instrument by which its realization is bro't about.

Our moral judgments, that reflective approbation of our present states of mind which tells us now that we are right and now wrong [*leaf* 30] also involves the notion of something related to the instant representation and yet lying beyond its mere actuality. We feel not simply so, or so but in addition believe that we should feel so that we are meant to feel so, that here again there is an ideal rational matrix into which our bare fact of feeling if it be true, fits, while if false, the feeling finds no foothold upon it and becomes detached and lost.

From all these different sources there grows up round about the actually present in consciousness an atmosphere of reference to something more which haunts it. This "more" may be the margin of otherness in time and space; it may be the truer determination of the instant, whether as the real which [*leaf* 31] is to correct instant expectation, the rectification which is to correct instant perception, the desireable end which coerces instant feeling, the mere doubt which corrects instant dogmatism, or the reflection this is subjective which corrects instant ontology. The present cannot move unaccompanied by this escort, this ontologic sphere in which it lies embedded, and which prevents us from accepting it schlechthin as asbolutely given. Here and now might be, may be otherness, says the sphere—in other words the here and now, in addition to being the seat of actual feelings become a sort of locus of intersection of the network of ideal relations arising from association anticipation, reflection, desire, &c in the way I have described and the actual feeling which occupies the locus gets to be regarded as a sort of accidental intruder which may or may not remain. Our acceptance of it is infected [*leaf* 32] with an *aliter possibile*. The actuality of the feeling does not exhaust the matter. All this extra-ness belongs there too. Abolish the actuality and the extra-ness remains as a sort of matrix or at least a a postulate of another possible order.

Now each these feeders of the notion of an order other than the actual may be criticized and deprived of validity, but as a whole their massive effect is too great to be overpowered. Even the criticisms of a Hume himself did not lead him further than to *doubt* the existence of a rational order. I for one must confess that if by an effort of abstraction I am able for a moment to conceive of the world in Humian terms, of representation sprouting upon representation by absolute happening [*leaf* 33] of everything being only once, of evolution with nothing involved, of our mental life for example as having come to be with no ideal preexisting determinant of it, I feel as if the breath was leaving my body. But so long as only the general form is present of an order additional to the actual, that order may act simply as a reductive to the actual making it appear unstable and unreal. Such is the function of the plus ultra in many philosophies—in Mr Spencer's and in Kant's e.g. the noumenon is a dog in the manger, it does nothing for us itself but merely stands and blasts with its breath the actual. Liebmann in his work on Kant has well explained in psychological terms how the mind comes to furnish such a reductive to all that it posi-

Rejected Versos

verso of [11]   A picture does not "wear" because it is good but
(reversed)   ['Not' *del.*] its wearing is its goodness.
                 Virtue does not ditto.

verso of [12]   Rationality

verso of [14]   Bain's postulate of uniformity of nature = all the
                 unifying categories of others. It amounts to undoing
                 what the Hume school does with time. They say it
                 is a mere ground of division—this *not* a pure ground
                 of division

Appendix III

Abstract of "The Knowing of Things Together"

James's abstract in the *Psychological Review*, 2 (March 1895), 152–153, of his presidential address to the American Psychological Association on December 27, 1894, at Princeton University, printed as "The Knowing of Things Together" in the *Psychological Review*, 2 (March 1895), 105–124. The abstract, subscribed Author's Summary, was reprinted without substantive change in the *Philosophical Review*, 4 (May 1895), 336–337.

Abstracts of Papers.

(I.) *The Knowing of Things Together.*
Address by the President,
Prof. WILLIAM JAMES, Harvard University.

The synthetic unity of consciousness is one of the great dividing questions in the philosophy of mind. We know things singly through as many distinct mental states. But on another occasion we may know the same things together through one state. The problem is as to the relation of the previous many states to the later one state. It will not do to make the mere statement of this problem incidentally involve a particular solution, as we should if we formulated the fact to be explained as *the combination of many states of mind into one*. The fact presents itself, in the first instance, *as the knowing of many things together*, and it is in those terms that the solution must be approached.

In the first place, *what is knowing?* 1. *Conceptual* knowing is an external relation between a state of mind and remote objects. If the state of mind, through a context of associates which the world supplies, leads to the objects smoothly and terminates there, we say it knows them. 2. *Intuitive* knowing is the identity of what, taken in one world-context, we call mental content and in another object. In neither 1 nor 2 is there involved any mysterious self-transcendency or presence in absence. 3. This mystery does, however, seem involved in *the relation between the parts of a mental content itself*. In the minimum real state of consciousness, that of the *passing moment*, past and present are known at once. In desire, memory, etc., earlier and later elements are directly felt to *call for* or *fulfil* each other, and without this sense of mutuality in their parts, such states do not exist. Here is presence in absence; here knowing together; here the original prototype of what we *mean* by knowledge. This ultimate synthetic nature of the smallest real phenomenon of consciousness can neither be explained nor circumvented.

We can only trace the particular conditions by which particular contents come thus to figure with all their parts at once in consciousness. Several attempts were then briefly passed in review. Mere synchronical sense-impression is not a sufficient condition. An additional inner *event* is required. The event has been described: *physiologically* as 1) 'attention;' as 2) ideational processes added to the sensorial processes, the latter giving unity, the former many-ness; as 3) motor synergy of processes; *psychologically* as 4) the thinking of relations between the parts of the content-object; as 5) the relating of each part to the self; *spiritually* as 6) an act of the soul; *transcendentally* as 7) the diminution (by unknown causes, possibly physiological) of the obstruction or limitation which the organism imposes on the natural knowing-of-all-things-together by an Absolute Mind. For transcendentalism the problem is, 'How are things known separately at all?'

The speaker dealt with these opinions critically, not espousing either one himself. He concluded by abandoning the attempt made in his Principles of Psychology to formulate mental states as integers, and to refer all plurality to the objects known by them. Practically, the metaphysical view cannot be excluded from psychology-books. 'Contents' have parts, because in intuitive knowledge contents and objects are identical; and Psychology, even as a 'natural science,' will find it easier to solve her problem of tracing the conditions that determine what objects shall be known together, by speaking of 'contents' as complex unities.

[The address is printed in full in the *Psychological Review* for March, 1895.]

Appendix IV
Notes for a Report on the Chicago School

In preparation for a conference on the Chicago School initiated by Josiah Royce (see "The Text," p. 262), James made a few notes to guide his own report, transcribed here. These were written in ink, with a couple ink additions, on a sheet of wove typewriter paper, watermarked L. L. Brown (266 X 204 mm.) after folding across its shorter axis to form a little booklet of two leaves. The manuscript is preserved in the James Collection at Harvard, bMS Am 1092.9, #4451.

[p. 1] Chicago! School of Thought.
Dewey—Moore repeats.
Long-necked.
Monotonous, but important; & *true.*
Characterize generally:
    Like Spencer, an *Evolutionism.* ['E' over 'e']
    Unlike Sp., does n't apply to details.
    The *Real ['R' over 'r'] changes. No term static. Nothing
      ready-made. (no Absolute)
    Ante rem vs. *in re* [*insrtd. in pencil vertically in mrgn.*]
    An *Empiricism.*
      Biology & psychol. continuous.
      "*Situations*" involve *Adjustments, [*comma over period*]
        Reconstructions.

[p. 2] [Doubt as to whether *monistic*?—He talks of Experience as one process. *But ['B' over 'b'] all his particular statements make for pluralism—and I will report him in pluralistic terms]

'Situations' involve many factors—reduce to E. & *O [*over* 'S']. for simplicity's sake.
They *interact*, *& develope **each [*over poss.* 'one'] other, so that [*ab. del.* 'and'] readjustment continues. (Each reaction makes new environment, etc.) Two variables
Biological
Ethical (Monist, vol VIII.) *Phil. R., XI) [*added*]
Psychological.
    (I confine myself to *this.*)
In *perfectly* 'adapted situation, we need no ['(consciousness or?)' *del.*] judgment

[p. 3] All conscious *determination* of anything has reference to change in experience. *Conflict essential. [*insrtd.*]

Habit won't *run—[*dash over period*] Hesitation.—[*intrl.*] situation must be re-constructed. Problematic object.

Read 153-5-6 *([*paren over poss. sg. qt.*]*resumption*)

S. a "stimulus."

P. an *"hypothesis" [*comma prob. del. bef. end quote*] in response.

Complete definition *passes into [*ab. undel.* 'means'] *action.*

"Knowing" is thus only one use of consciousness. (Read 253-5)

Fact & theory continuous: (Read 163)

S. & P. = *that* & *what.*

D. claims to escape *paradoxes ['p' *over* 'e'] of epistemology.

[p. 4] 'Functional' terms. Fall *within* experience, within activity.

Truth an *immanent [*alt. fr.* 'imme Re'] character, not a "correspondence." ['Flux' *del.*]

Nothing ready-made.

Empiricism *hypostatizes [*final* 's' *over* 'd'] the abstraction S. Rationalism the abstraction *P [*over poss.* '1'].

*Results in concrete individualism, [*ab. del.* 'Panta rei Flux | Read 126 Read 126 | Results'] in treating value & fact together, ['in making everything genetic' *del.*] in using genetic method, in opposition to dogmatism, & *finality, [*comma over period*; *insrtd. for del.* 'Continuity | Flux! Read 126.'] in continuity. Coherence, not inherence. *Concrete not abstract. [*insrtd. in pencil*] Flux! *Read ['R' *over* 'r'] 126. Calif. Address p. 19-22.

Appendix V

Notes for MS¹, and MS¹, of "A Pluralistic Mystic"

Notes for MS¹ of "A Pluralistic Mystic"

[*fol.* [1]] Dialectic thought is a whirlpool into which some persons are sucked out of the stream of the straightforward understanding. Once in the eddy naught but rotary motion can go on. All who have been in it know the feel of its swirl—they know thereafter that thinking unreturning on itself is but one part of reason, and that rectilinear mentality is insufficient.

Though each one may report in different words of his rotational experience, the experience itself is [*fol.* [2]] almost childishly simple, and whosoever has "been there' instantly recognizes any authentic report from the same region. To know that eddy is a freemasonry, of which the common password is a "fie," on all the operations of the popular understanding.

In Hegel's thought the vortex was at its liveliest, and anyone who has once had a taste of Hegel, will recognize Mr. Blood's mind [*fol.* 3] to be of the same family. "That Hegel was pervaded by the great truth," Blood writes, "cannot be doubted. The eyes of philosophy, if not set directly on him, are set towards the region which he occupied. Though he may not be the final philosopher, yet pull him out and all the rest will be drawn into his vacancy."

Drawn into the whirlpool, Mr. Blood means. Non-dialectic thought takes "facts" as positively given and accounts for one fact by another. But when we think of 'all' fact we see that nothing of the nature of fact can explain it—"for that were but one more added to the list of things to be accounted for." 'The beginning of curiosity in the philosophical . . . sense,' Mr. Blood [*fol.* 4] writes elsewhere: "is the stare of being itself, as at itself, in the wonder why anything is at all, and what being means. Naturally we first assume the void, and then wonder how, with no ground and no fertility, anything should come into it or out of it.'—We treat it as a positive nihility beyond all *things*, like a barrier from which 'all our batted balls of being shall rebound.' Upon this idea Mr. Blood passes the usual transcendentalist criticism. There *is* no such separate opposite to being; yet we never think of Being as such—pure Being as distinguisht from

[*fol.* [5]] "Of the usual postulate that for any fact to be there must be an adequate reason for the fact behind it, he says it is like not being satisfied with goods which we receive, but complaining

376

that they come without an invoice. I think, he writes, of Dickens is horse that always fell down when they took him out of the shafts, or of the fellow who felt weak when naked but strong in his overcoat."

[*fol.* [6]] "One can never feel good until he feels better. Pleasure is ever in the company and contrast of pain: for instance in thirsting and drinking, the pleasure of the one is the exact measure of the pain of the other, and they cease precisely together—or else the patient would drink more.

But if the two are equal in this experience there is no profit thereby."

[*fol.* [7]] "The insight that mystery—The Mystery—as such, is the final, the hymnic word. You are tearing Reason to pieces—you name it oftenest in quotation marks; you use it pragmatically, and deny it "absolutely"—you cant be beaten be assured of that; but the Fact remains and of course the Mystery."

[*fol.* [8]] "I find myself growing clearer as to the relations of the Anaesthetic Revelation to Philosophy. Philosophy is past; it was the long endeavor to logicise what practically (although not necessarily) we can realize only in mental experience. I am more and more impressed that Heraclitus insists on the equation of reason and unreason, or chance, as well as of being and not-being, positive and negative, etc. This throws the Secret beyond logic, and makes Mysticism, as Experience, outclass philosophy."

MS¹ of "A Pluralistic Mystic"

[*fol.* [1]]

AN UNUSUAL TYPE OF MYSTIC.

I hold that one of the duties of a good reader is to call the attention of other readers to any neglected author of rare quality whom he may discover in his explorations. For years past both my thought and my literary taste have been exquisitely titillated by a writer the very name of whom I venture to say is unknown to any of my present readers; and the time has come when I can no longer abet the general conspiracy of silence concerning the merits of Benjamin Paul Blood.

Mr. Blood inhabits the modest town of Amsterdam, on the New York Central Railroad. What his regular or bread-winning "business" is I know not, but it can't have made him super-wealthy. He is [*fol.* 2] an author only when the fit strikes him and for short flights at a time—shy moreover to the point of publishing what he may have to say or sing, only in privately printed tracts or leaflets, or in letters to such far-from-reverberant organs of publicity as the Amsterdam Gazette, the Amsterdam Recorder, the Utica Herald, or the Albany Times. "Yes! Paul is quite a correspondent," said a good citizen of Amsterdam from whom I inquired the way to Mr. Blood's dwelling many years ago, after alighting from the train. I had sought to particularize him as an 'author' but his neighbor particularized him still more, apparently, thinking only of those letters to the Journals I have named. Odd places for his subtle dialectics to appear in! Once indeed, D.ʳ Harris, the lamented Editor of the old Journal of Speculative philosophy got wind of these epistles, and the result was a revision of some [*fol.* 3] of them for that Review under the name Philosophic Reveries (   ). Once a poem by Mr. Blood, "the Lion of the Nile" was reprinted from its leaflet by the Editor of Scribner's Magazine. But apart from these two dashes before the footlights, Mr. Blood's Muse has kept behind the curtain all her days.

Just how I first met her, I have now forgotten, but the document I met was 'the anaesthetic revelation,' the author's maiden adventure, a pamflet printed privately at Amsterdam in 1874. It fascinated me both by its matter and its form, and has I think, remained as one of the cornerstones or landmarks of my own subsequent thinking. After thirty pages of a dialectic introduction decidedly hegelese in tenor Mr. Blood avows [*fol.* 4] that his personal avenue to deeper truth is ether-intoxication! 'After experiments ranging over nearly fourteen years,' he says, 'I affirm—what any man may prove at will—that there is an invariable and reliable condition (or uncondition) ensuing about the instant of recall from anaesthetic stupor to sensible observation or "coming-to," in which *the genius of being is revealed*; but because it cannot be remembered in the normal condition it is lost altogether through the infrequency of anaesthetic treatment in any individual's case and ordinarily buried, amid the hum of returning common sense, under that epitaph of all illumination "this is a queer world." ' . . . . . . I think most

[*fol.* 6] Unable to decide whether this passage was sublime or ridiculous, I recollect reading it to the late Edwin L. Godkin, and putting him the question. He laughed, and said "I can't be sure, but on the whole it strikes me as rather funny."

Godkin was more of a *Verstandesmensch* than of a mystic. To genuinely dialectic eyes the noonday-light of the understanding hides depths even more than it shows surfaces, and its exclusive use unfits one for profounder insight. Your metaphysician born and bred revolves, in close company with mystics, in that vespertilian gloom—where [*fol.* 7] day and darkness mix, where, to use our author's words, 'for the light to go out or for the darkness to go out were equally calamitous,' and where the one thing not to be done is to 'fixate' clearly or part aught from its background. Even to seek to do this is, according to mystic-dialectic thought, to doom oneself to superficiality forever. This crepuscular region Mr. Blood's mind seems always to inhabit. Most mystic-dialectic writers fly like bats, as if attached to some invisible centre—all our anglo-hegelians are good examples. Mr. Blood also zigzags & circles like a bat, when he expounds dialectics, [*fol.* 8] but when the wind of mysticism catches and swings him loose he glides and soars as if he were a sea gull.

It is because I find in his writings a development which, it seems to me, may well be typical that I am devoting these pages to them. When he reasons he is a decided monist, of the hegelian type, and so he was in his first statements of the ether-mysticism. 'Thenceforth,' as I just quoted, 'each is all, he says, 'in God.... The One remains, the many change & pass; and each and every one of us is the One that remains.' But his later mystical dicta are distinctly pluralistic in sound: 'The monistic notion of a Oneness, a centered wholeness, ultimate purpose [*fol.* 9] or climacteric result of the world, has utterly given way.... Thought evolves no longer a centered whole, a One, but rather a numberless many, adjust it how we may.' Or again: 'Pluralism has talked rationalistic philosophy to a stand-still.'

Mystical tradition has usually been monistic in the extreme; and in asmuch as it is the habit of mystics to speak not as the scribes, but with authority, as men who have 'been there' & seen with their own eyes, I think this fact must have given pause to some who, like myself, have been led by reasoning about monism, to regard its pretensions to absolute authority as vain, and to treat it as [*fol.* 10] an hypothesis merely, like any other one might frame. The mystical consciousness, inarticulate tho' it be, has great prestige, and comes to monism's support. But Mr. Blood's mysticism, tho' it has the full authentic ring, breaks the tradition altogether by coming out with pluralistic results. It is extreme left-wing mysticism, if so you please to call it; but whatever it be, monism can now no longer claim to be the only heir of mysticism's wealth. I confess that the existence of a brand of mysticism like Mr. Blood's has caused a certain cowering mood of my own before the earlier mystics to evaporate. [*fol.* 11] I feel as if my pluralism also had the higher kind of credential.

The region which dialectic thought frequents, altho' prodigious wordiness has emanated from it, is hard to make report of, from its very simplicity. The more you talk of it, the more you darken the air, and the more ineffable you must confess it. This is why it ever tempts you to sink back into feeling only, and why the dialectic-verbal tends so often to pass into the dialectic-mystical. I know of no one who on the whole has verbalized the matter less objectionably than Mr. Blood, or who has more simply effected the mystical transition.

Appendix VI

Alterations in:
  (1) Notes for "The Sentiment of Rationality":
    a. Box E, Envelope 5
    b. Box E, Envelope 1
  (2) Notes for MS¹, and MS¹, of "A Pluralistic Mystic"

Alterations in Notes
for "The Sentiment of Rationality":
Box E, Envelope 5

340.29 deduction from an] *ab. del.* 'enl'
340.30 reference to] *intrl.*
340.33 satisfied] *aft. del.* 'best'
340.34 for] *bef. del.* 'th'
340.34 explanation] *aft. del.* 'the'
340.34 part] *intrl.*
340.35 expectancy] *aft. del.* 'mere'
340.37 element] *aft. del.* '1 or 2'
340.37 leaves] 's' *added; aft. del.* 'give'
340.37 It is] *ab. del.* 'They'
340.37 *datum*] *alt. fr.* 'data'; *aft.* 'are' *undel. in error*
340.38 it itself] *alt. fr.* 'they themselves'
340.38 demands] 's' *added*
340.39 it] *ab. del.* 'they'
340.39 takes] 's' *added*
340.39 or] *bef. del.* 'that'
340.40 it] *ab. del.* 'them'
340.43 4] *over* '3'
340.43 of . . . need] ('of' *bef. del.* 'metaphysic'); *intrl.*
340.44 1.] *aft. del.* 'Either'
341.5 inapplicable. Though] *period over* semicolon; 'T' *of* 'Though' *over* 't'
341.7 By] *alt. fr.* 'Bef'
341.15 A] *aft. del.* 'I'; *bef. del.* 'phenomenon'
341.19 we] *over* 'it'
341.25 to] *bef. del.* 'the'
341.26 Subject] 'S' *over* 's'
341.27 of] *alt. fr.* 'as'
341.28 Evident] 'E' *over* 'e'
341.30 unquestioningly;] *semicolon over* period; *bef.* 'To ['T' *unreduced in error*]'
341.35 familiarity] *aft. del. doubtful* 'as'

341.35 in] 'n' *over* 't'
341.36 us] *aft. del.* 'it ne'
341.41 ¹for] *alt. fr.* 'of'
341.41 ²for] *intrl.*
342.2 properties] *aft. del.* 'qualit'
342.4 in] *over* 'a'
342.5 strange] *intrl.*
342.6 element] *aft. del.* 'notion of'
342.10 a] 't' *of* 'at' *wiped out*
342.15 touchstone] *ab. del.* 'essence'
342.16 ²of] *bef. del.* 'this'
342.16 expectation] *underline del.*
342.17 explanation] 'na' *over* 'ain'
342.17 Till] *ab. del.* 'When'
342.21 The . . . will] *insrtd. for del.* 'Logical explanation'
342.21 ²the] *ab. del.* 'of'
342.30 abstract] *alt. fr.* 'abstraction'; *bef. del.* 'of the more general ingredients of the fact.'
343.9 ²in] *aft. del.* 'how'
343.13 *Faith*] *in ink over pencil* 'bring it about.'
343.17 the] 't' *over false start of letter*
343.19 healthy] *aft. del.* 'man'
343.19 ²as] 's' *over* 'I'
343.22 as] *intrl.*
343.36 self-] *aft. del.* 'reflective'
344.8 this] *alt. fr.* 'that'
344.19 usual] *intrl.*
344.20 another] 'a' *over* 'o'; *aft. del.* 'a wider'
344.24 old] 'o' *over* 's'
344.28 understanding] *ab. del.* 'knowledge'
344.29 dissatisfied] 'dis' *intrl.*

344.36 vanishes)] *paren over comma*
344.36 absolute] *aft. del.* 'real and'
345.7 as] *aft. del.* 'often'
345.7 rest] *bef. del.* '; but in the higher'
345.8 uncustomary] *alt. fr.* 'unaccustomary'
345.11 not] *intrl.*
345.11 is] *bef. del.* 'not'
345.12 the] *intrl.*
345.12 habit] *alt. fr.* 'habitual'; *moved fr. bef. to aft.* 'ease of'
345.12 by idealism] *moved fr. aft.* 'representations' [345.13]
345.14 contradict] *aft. del.* 'be'
345.16 this] *alt. fr.* 'the'
345.19 are] *bef. del.* 'signs of'
345.21 of] *ab. del.* 'in the'
345.24 is] *bef. del.* 'ade'
345.24 actively] 'a' *over* 'o'
345.24 ²the] 't' *over false start of letter*
345.26 like] *aft. del.* 'that is, a reaction'
345.29 nameless] 'n' *over* 'N'
345.29 Unheimlickkeit] 'U' *over* 'u'
345.30 either] 'ei' *over* 'in'
345.35 End] 'E' *over* 'e'
345.35 Existence] 'E' *over* 'e'
345.36 being] *aft. del. doubtful* 'co'
345.38 a] *intrl.*
345.39 recognize] 're' *over* 'c' *and illeg. letter*
346.1 a] *alt. fr.* 'an'
346.1 primitive] 'pri' *over* 'ani'; *intrl.*
346.4 idealistic] *aft. del.* 'Mill'
346.5 true] *intrl.*
346.5 emotion] 'e' *over* 're'
346.8 representations] *final* 's' *added*
346.10 substratum] *bef. del.* 'of sameness'
346.13-14 with any other] *intrl.*
346.14 or] *intrl.*
346.16 separate] *bef. del.* 'und'
346.19 the Real] *alt. fr.* 'some real'
346.20 ²it] *intrl.*
346.23 modifier] *alt. fr.* 'modify'
346.23 nervous] *aft. del.* 'physical'
346.27 who] *alt. fr.* 'whose'
346.27 by their] *intrl.*
346.27 produce] *final* 's' *del.*
346.28 does] *alt. fr.* 'is'
346.28 only] *bef. del.* 'inn'
346.29 Unknowable] 'U' *over* 'u'

346.29 to] *bef. del.* 'whose'
346.29 bring] *aft. del.* 'p'
346.31 arrangemement] ¹'n' *over* 'g'
346.32 so] *aft. del.* 'without'
346.32 each] *intrl.*
346.32 causal] *ab. del.* 'true'
346.33 but] *aft. del.* 'these'; *bef. del.* 'only a'
346.35 Rationality] *aft. del.* 'Verification is the criterion of truth,'
346.36 its] *alt. fr.* 'is'
346.37 the] 't' *over* 'a'; *aft. del.* 'if the'
346.40 ²the] *over* 'one'
347.1 a] *intrl.*
347.1 determinations] *bef. del.* 'quite'
347.2 B] *over* 'b'
347.2 ²b] *over* 'B'
347.4 wd] *intrl.*
347.7 &] *intrl.*
347.8 terms] *aft. del.* 'conscious'
347.16 4] *over* '3'
347.17 Memory] *aft. del.* 'Reverie'
347.23 tabula] *ab. del.* 'factor'
347.24 possible result of] *intrl.*
347.27 majority] *ab. del.* 'bulk'
347.30 ¹the] *intrl.*
347.30 life] 'li' *over* 't' *and false start of letter*
347.34 together] *ab. del.* 'co ordinate'
347.36 ³it] *alt. fr.* 'in'
347.37 as] *bef. del.* 'all'
347.38 set by] *ab. del.* 'belong to'
348.3 test of] *del. and reinstated by underdotting*
348.3 truth] *ab. del.* 'universal postulate'
348.7 (vide . . . logical] *marg. addition*
348.9 It] *aft. del.* 'Taking for example the inference from analogy, we are'
348.10 so] *intrl.*
348.13 to] *bef. del.* 'a something already understood in the sen-'|
348.15 & so on] *ab. del.* '&c'
348.16 is] *bef. del.* 'which belongs to the realm of physical not logical cogency'
348.17 case] *bef. del. short rule and* 'See II'
348.18 Thought] *alt. fr.* 'Thout'
348.20 practically] *aft. del.* 'as' *or* 'ap'
348.22 Vague] 'V' *over* 'v'
348.22 or] *aft. del.* 'by'
348.27 discriminating] *intrl.*

348.31 concepts.ᴧ] *db. qts. del.*

348.34 Emotion] 'E' *over* 'e'; *aft. del.* 'the'

348.36 which] *bef. del.* 'the categories of existence and non existence are not alone valid, but in which the *judg ments ['s' *doubtful*] Better ['B' *over* 'b'] or *Worse ['W' *over* 'w'] is ['absolut' *del.*] should'

348.37 applicable] 'b' *over* 'p'

348.39 pertinent;] *semicolon over period; bef.* 'One ['O' *unreduced in error*]'

349.1 making] *bef. del.* 'them right'

349.3 proves] *ab. del.* 'makes'

349.5 actual] *alt. fr.* 'actually'

349.8 rectified] *aft. del.* 'modified by and'

349.9 what] *ab. del.* 'things'

349.9 tomorrow] *aft. del.* 'hereafter ['rea' *over illeg.*]'

349.10 not only] *intrl.*

349.11 but] *aft. del.* 'and are'

349.11 products] *bef. del.* 'to a'

349.11 far] *final* 'e' *wiped out*

349.11 on] *intrl.*

349.15 & every] *intrl.*

349.15 fact] *ab. del.* 'event'

349.17 untrue,] *bef. del.* 'and'

349.17 partly] *intrl.*

349.20 far] *alt. fr.* 'fare'

349.21 perhaps] *ab. del.* 'possibly'

349.21-22 so perhaps] *ab. del.* 'one, possibly the'

349.26 contingent,] *bef. del.* 'but'

349.26 since] *ab. del.* 'in so far as rea'

349.26 as] *intrl.*

349.27 as] *ab. del.* 'and'

349.27 unpredictable] *intrl.*

349.29 theorizing] *intrl.*

349.30 extant] *aft. del.* 'continge'

349.31 assume] *aft. del.* 'suppose'

349.31 something] *ab. del.* 'a truth to act upon, and having acted'

349.32 future] *intrl.; placement doubtful*

349.32 action] 'ion' *intrl.*

349.32 make true] *ab. del.* 'verify'

349.32 having] *aft. del.* 'say tha'

349.33 thus] *ab. del.* 'is'

349.34 legitimate,] *bef. del.* 'one could reprove it by saying'

349.34 should] *aft. del.* 'could'

349.34-35 still do a] *ab. del.* 'yet be'

349.35 & . . . thing.] *intrl.*

349.36 well,] *comma over period; bef. del.* 'Why therefore assume anything? or go beyond'

349.37 thus produce a] *ab. del.* 'your'

349.37 which] *intrl.*

349.38 truths] *aft. del.* 'thr'

349.41 ascertained] *bef. del.* '? So far as you a'

349.41 ²be] *bef. del.* 'independently of your'

349.41 determined?] *qst. mk. over comma*

349.41 Why not leave] *ab. del.* 'leaving'

350.2 ²is] *bef. del.* 'pe'

350.3 emotion] *aft. del.* 'the moral nature'

350.4 contigent] *alt. fr.* 'contigency'; *aft. del.* 'so far as their'; *bef. del.* 'is conditional'

350.6 theoretic] *alt. fr.* 'theory'; *bef. del.* 'he'; *aft. del. intrl.* 'th'

350.6 assumption he] *intrl.*

350.6 make] *aft. del.* 'form'; *bef. del.* 'in asmuch becomes'

350.8 between] *ab. del.* 'of'

350.11 Of equal] 'Of' *intrl.*; 'Equally' *alt. to* 'Equal ['E' *unreduced in error*]'

350.11 truth] *alt. fr.* 'true'

350.13 Such] 'u' *over* 'h'; *bef. del.* 'judgments'

350.14 belief] 'b' *over* 'd'

350.15 the belief] *ab. del.* 'it affects one's'

350.17 Any] *aft. del.* 'Belief in God in the usual sense of a creative cause &c, does not seem clearly to fall'

350.20 right,] *comma insrtd. bef. del.* 'or'

350.20 true,] *comma over qst. mk.*

350.25 judgment] 'ju' *over* 'cri'

350.26 either] *aft. del.* 'both'

350.26 antimoralists] *aft. del. poss.* 'anit'

350.27 absolutely] *intrl.*

350.27 Their] *alt. fr.* 'There'

350.28 conventional] *alt. fr.* 'convential'; *bef. del.* 'basis of *test [poss. 'last']'

350.30 God] *final* 's' *del.*

350.31 that] *bef. del.* '(the intellectual judgment concerning God show)'

350.33 in any sense] *moved fr. aft.* 'world' [350.32]

350.34 alternative.] *bef. del.* 'lo the'

350.35 better] *aft. del.* 'morally'

350.40 maybe] *aft. del.* 'poss'

350.40-41 entertained] *aft. del.* 'allowed'

351.4 The] *aft. del.* '[*poss. false start of* 'W' *del.*] Where the ['subject' *del.*] matter is such that'

351.4 method] *aft. del.* 'is leg'

351.9 recognize] *ab. del.* 'concern itself with'

351.10 prove] *aft. del.* 'show the'

351.12 scheme] *ab. del.* 'basis'

351.14 desirable] *poss. undel. in error; ab. is intrl.* 'excellent'

351.14 *Subject*] 'S' *over* 's'

351.15 a] *alt. fr.* 'as'

351.31 applicable,] *comma insrtd. bef. del.* 'by' *over* 'to'

351.33 mechanical] *alt. fr.* 'phys'

351.35 simple] *intrl.*

351.35 constitute] *aft. del.* 'alone'

351.37 its] *aft. del.* 'its subjective uncertainty into a'

352.1 The] *aft. del.* 'The proof ['that a given should be is right' *del.*] is in.'

352.2 B] *over* 'be'

352.3 proves] *alt. fr.* 'proofs'

352.7 ²the] *intrl.*

352.9 that] *ab. del.* 'of'

352.10 moral] *aft. del.* 'should be'

352.11 the] *alt. fr.* 'the' *to* 'their' *to* 'the'

352.11 acquires] *aft. del.* 'becomes self evident,'

352.14 results] *ab. del.* 'proof'

352.16 defying] *aft. del.* 'perishing'

352.23 say] *over doubtful* 'is'

352.25 it] 'i' *over* 'a'

352.31 *Quoad*] 'uo' *over doubtful* 'ia'

352.34 wh] *intrl.*

353.9 essentially] *aft. del. illeg. letters*

353.11 taken] 't' *over* 's'

353.12 conceived] *bef. del.* 'al'

353.13 supposed] *aft. del.* 'have'

353.13 in the mind] *intrl.*

353.14 then] *alt. fr. doubtful* 'be'

353.16 but] *aft. del.* 'w'

353.18 innumerably] *aft. del.* 'gra'

353.22 ¹in] *ab. del.* 'of'

353.25 factors∧] *comma del.*

353.26 still] *intrl.*

353.28 a] *alt. fr.* 'an'

353.29-30 Under C.] *insrtd. in marg.*

353.32 propensities] *aft. del.* '&'

353.32 Impulse] 'I' *over* 'i'

354.5 of] *aft. del.* 'of t'

354.5 with] *intrl.*

354.6 These] 'T' *over* 't'; *aft. del.* 'In'

354.8 latter;] *semicolon over period; bef.* 'It ['I' *unreduced in error*]'

354.9 they] *alt. fr.* 'tha'

354.10 utilities] *alt. fr.* 'utility'; *bef.* '2 S' *undel. in error*

354.13 persistence] *aft. del.* 'nor'

354.14 ²as] *alt. fr.* 'is'

354.27 thus] 'h' *over* 'a'

354.27 determine] *alt. fr.* 'determines'

354.31 say] 's' *over* 'f'

354.33 real, objective,] *intrl.*

354.35 grow suspicious] *alt. fr.* 'grew suspect'

354.37 as] *ab. del.* 'as both'

355.2 Real] 'R' *over* 'r'

355.3 incident to] *intrl.*

355.3 which] *aft. del.* 'living ['liv' *over* 'bei'] tho't of'

355.4 ∧metaphysical] (*db. qt. del. in error*); *aft. del.* 'living thought or'

355.5 generate] *aft. del.* 'as such'

355.8 in] *aft. del.* 'it is'

355.9 itself] *intrl.*

355.17-18 If . . . would] *insrtd. for del.* 'Idealists'

355.18 things] *aft. del.* 'concen'

355.20 (a . . . g.)] *intrl.*

355.21 including] *aft. del.* 'infinitely'

355.22 once] *intrl.*

355.23 sophism?)] *bef. del.* 'Idealists have 3 grades of being to decide between. *1 Simply—[intrl.] Objective being which they deny, *2 [insrtd.] subjective being having the "objective" character, *3 [insrtd.] subjective being not having this. They exclude the former. 2 is illusive, but intelligibly illusive. ['It don't keep' del.] Its ['I' over 'i'] promises are not kept but we can understand what they are'

355.25 of] *aft. del.* 'that th'

355.33 were] *aft. del.* 'whe'

355.34 in] *aft. del.* 'to the'

355.34 ²its] *intrl.*

355.35-36 meaning, purpose∧] *intrl. for del. intrl.* 'Zwecke'; *comma aft.* 'purpose' *omitted in error*

355.36 (both] *ab. del.* 'either'
355.36 &] *over* 'or'
355.37 sense,)] *paren insrtd.*
355.37 Essence] *intrl.*
355.40 absolute,] *bef. del.* '&'
356.3 men] *alt. fr.* 'man'
356.5 practically] *intrl.*
356.6,17 Absolute] 'A' *triple underl.*
356.7 Metaphysical] 'M' *triple underl.*;
   bef. del. 'or *Transcendent['T'*
   triple underl.]'
356.8 unfathomable] *aft. del.* 'bottom'
356.9 Essence] 'E' *over* 'e'
356.11 is identical with] *ab. del.* 'leads
   then to'
356.13 point] 'i' *over* 's'
356.15 yet] *intrl.*
356.17 Metaphysical] 'M' *triple underl.*
356.18 oscillates] 'ci' *over* 'sc'
356.18 item of] *ab. del.* 'several'
356.24 (see above II)] *moved fr. aft.*
   'Nihilists' [356.23]
356.28 when, taking] ('a' *of* 'taking' *over*
   false start of letter); *ab. del.* 'affirm
   objective'
356.28 under] *aft. del.* 'of'
356.29 perceptions] *aft. del.* 'acts of
   thought'
356.31 into] *aft. del.* 'over'
356.33 to] *bef. del.* 'relate h'
356.36 dissimilar.] *bef. del.* 'Ontologic
   rest & ontologic passion, or the desire
   of the absolute & the love of the immense and mysterious are often, perhaps usually, connected in the same

mind. Or, makes *one like [*intrl.*]
idealism [*alt. fr.* 'idealists'] *for its [*ab.
del.* 'by its'] denial [*alt. fr.* 'denying']
of [*intrl.*] a plus ultra, where ontologic
passion would affirm'
356.37 throws] *alt. fr.* 'through'
356.38 But] *ab. del.* '['But' *del.*] And'
357.2 averse] *aft. del.* 'maler'
357.2-3 it ... often] *ab. del.* 'the ontologic nature of a man makes him
   doubly an idealist. But on the other
   hand the ontologic passion is'
357.6 Anti substantialist] ('a' *of* 'anti' *l.c.*
   in error); *intrl. bef.* 'Idealism ['I' *unreduced in error*]'
357.14 disagreement.] *bef. del.* 'The
   mind a product of experiences'
357.17 certainty] *bef. del.* 'than'
357.18 held] 'h' *over* 'r'
357.19 shown] 's' *over* 'n'
357.23 is] 'i' *over paren*
357.24 objectivity)] *alt. fr.* 'objective';
   bef. del. 'we have a perfect right to'
357.27 then] *alt. fr.* 'is'
357.32 our] *alt fr.* 'ours'
357.38 what] 'w' *over* 'm'
358.12-13 even hypothetically] *intrl.*
358.14 must be good.] *ab. del.* 'is
   enough.'
358.20 external] 't' *over* 'p'
358.22 marks] *alt. fr.* 'make'
358.25 By] *aft. del.* 'Are'
358.25 means] *aft. del.* 'thinks of'
358.31 marks] *aft. del.* 'bundle'

Alterations in Notes
for "The Sentiment of Rationality":
Box E, Envelope 1

359.43 THE ... RATIONALITY] *double*
   underl. bef. del. 'I'
359.44 I] *insrtd.*
359.46 in] *bef. del.* 'the needs'
360.1 motives] *aft. del.* 'mental needs
   which'
360.4 to] *intrl.*
360.4 which] *bef. del.* 'are products of'

360.7 seek ... needs] *insrtd. for del.* 'try'
360.7 discover] *bef. del.* 'from the constitution of our aesthetic nature'
360.8 conditions] *ab. del.* 'points'
360.11 may] *bef. del.* 'immediately'
360.12 us,] *insrtd. for del.* 'all'
360.14 due] *aft. del.* 'solely'
360.15 rather] *aft. del.* 'tr'

360.16 by a philosopher] *intrl.*
360.17 his] *ab. del.* 'the'
360.18 authority] 'ity' *insrtd. for del.* 'ity'
360.22 See] 'S' *over* 's'; *bef. del.* 'a mas'
360.23 for] *ab. del.* '['for' *del.*] 29'
360.32 Positivism.] *bef. del.* 'Renouvier.'
360.33 Ordinary] 'O' *over* 'o'
360.34 Clearness∧] *(period undel. in error); moved fr. aft.* 'Kosmos.' [360.31] *to bef.* '['Clearne' *del.*] with'
360.35-36 moral . . . conceived.] *insrtd.*
361.2 still] *intrl.*
361.13 kind] 'i' *over* 'n'
361.14 know] *bef. del.* 'it as the result of'
361.14 sublime] *bef. del.* 'way of knowing'
361.15 incomplete] *ab. del.* 'poor or as good'
361.16-17 It . . . itching.] *intrl.; aft. del.* 'nothing!'
361.17 Only] 'O' *over* 'o'
361.17 determined] *aft. del.* 'th'
361.19 is] 's' *over* 't'
361.28 sympathize] *aft. del. illeg. letter*
361.29 all] 'a' *over false start of letter*
361.30 organizable] 'i' *insrtd.*
361.34 not] 'n' *over doubtful* 'a'
361.36 real] *bef. del.* 'goods'
361.37 keep] *aft. del.* 'preserve'
361.38 Find . . . out.] *insrtd.*
361.39 Examples:] *insrtd.*
362.2 excitement remains.] *insrtd.*
362.6 still] 's' *over* 'a'
362.9-10 (or fitter to live)] *intrl.*
362.19 ante rem] *intrl.*
362.31 the] 't' *over* 'a'
362.31 theory] *bef. del.* 'of'
362.32 existence] *bef. del.* 'p'
362.33 the] *intrl.*
362.34 translation] *aft. del. false start of* 'th'
362.40 according . . . truth] *intrl.*
363.1-2 coerciveness . . . reality] *intrl. without caret to indicate position*
363.9 is] *aft. del.* 'has'
363.9 has] *aft. del.* 'is' *and false start of letter*
363.13 special] *intrl.*
363.14 disunion] *aft. del.* 'not'
363.16 ²through] *aft. del.* 'it thus posits the'
363.21 ²the] 't' *over* 'a'
363.22 juiciness] *aft. del.* 'etc'
363.30 they] *aft. del.* 'th'
363.31 until] *alt. fr.* 'unless' *to* 'untill' *to* 'until'
363.33 a priori] *intrl.*
363.34 according as] *ab. del.* 'if [*alt. fr.* 'it']'
363.34 is] *ab. del.* 'be'
363.35 it] *aft. del.* 'we'
363.35 what] *aft. del.* 'the'
363.39 to reflect] *aft. del.* 'quent moment'
363.42 liable] 'l' *over* 's'
363.42-364.1 Always ['aw' *del.*] . . . flanked.] *insrtd. for del.* '[¶] Now how does the notion of enveloping nonentity arise—'
364.1 Relative] *aft. del.* 'Always finding the moral quality of things to be'; 'r' *l.c. in error*
364.2 Constantly] *aft. del.* 'Always'; 'c' *l.c. in error*
364.6 contradiction] ²'i' *over* 't'
364.16 at] *aft. del.* 'if it have any'
364.20 so long as they] *ab. del.* 'which'
364.23 the] *insrtd.*
365.2 realized] 'ized' *insrtd.*
365.7 Plan] 'P' *over* 'p'
365.11 HUME-HODGSON] *double underl.*
365.12 FICHTE-HARTMANN] *double underl.*
365.13 WRIGHT . . . LIEBMANN] *double underl.*
365.14 seems] *insrtd.*
365.24 every] *aft. del.* 'to deny it'
365.29 empiricist] *ab. del.* 'skeptics [*reinstated by underdotting, then del.*]'
365.29 even] *intrl.*
365.29 conceived] ¹'c' *over poss.* 'd'; *bef. del.* 'of'
365.34 paradise of] *ab. del.* 'state of'
365.36 the] 't' *over* 'a'
365.37 swearing] *aft. del.* 'standing themselves with one foot on a priori ground they swear'
365.39 advance. Real] *period insrtd.*; 'Real ['R' *over* 'r']' *aft. del.* 'with'
366.1 school] *bef. del.* '—there is—'

366.4   The . . . rationality.] *aft.* 'that [*undel. in error*] [*ab. del.* 'what']'

366.8   ¹the] 'th' *over* 'ph'

366.10   Aesthetic] *intrl.*

366.14-16   The . . . überhaupt] *moved fr. marg. by guideline wh. is over period aft.* 'real' [366.14]

366.15   ¹be] *over poss.* 'is'

366.20   Empiricism] *alt. fr.* 'Empirical'

366.21   expectation] *bef. del.* 'the'

366.28   by] *alt. fr.* 'to'

366.29   is] *aft. del.* 'it'

366.29   that] *intrl.*

366.32   theistic:—an] *colon insrtd.*; 'an' *alt. fr.* 'and'

366.33   (Berkeley)] *aft. del.* 'This'

366.34   phenomena.] *bef. del.* 'In any event its practical upshot is important.'

366.35   signify] *aft. del.* 'mean ['m' *over* 'p']'

366.37-38   us, and . . . right.] (*comma over period*; 'are' *aft. del.* 'But this'); 'and . . . right.' *insrtd.*

366.40   match] 't' *over* 'c'

366.41   facts] *aft. del.* 'one'

367.4   wanted] 'a' *over* 'h'

367.10   they] *aft. del.* 'they have with the ancients'

367.11-12   substance] *bef. del.* 'or God,'

367.15   absolute] *intrl.*

367.15   in] *ab. del.* 'of'

367.20   places] *ab. del.* 'times'

367.20   moments] *aft. del.* 'mome'

367.20   than] *alt. fr.* 'that'

367.21   As ours] 'as [*l.c. in error*]' *intrl. bef.* 'Ours ['O' *unreduced in error*]'

367.21   is] *bef. del.* 'only'

367.22   ¹we] *aft. del.* 'but'

367.24   permanent] *aft. del.* 'such as are'

367.26   generally] *intrl. bef. del. intrl.* 'universally'

367.26   truth] *aft. del.* 'th'

367.33   general] *intrl.*

367.34   word] *aft. del.* 'german'

367.35   modern] *ab. del.* 'the'

367.38   a small] *aft. del.* 'A cherry-peach. Until the the pre-existing concept has been cast over it, it is'

367.42   thing] *ab. del.* 'peach'

367.43   also] |'so' *ab. del.* |'ways'

368.1   get to] *intrl.*

368.2   permanent] *aft. del.* 'pre existing m'

368.5   nominalist] ²'n' *over* 'l'

368.7   untrue] *bef. del. doubtful* 'in'

368.7   truly] *alt. fr.* 'true'

368.7   applied] *intrl.*

368.15   Thus then,] *insrtd. bef.* 'The ['T' *unreduced in error*]'

368.15   contradicts] *ab. del.* 'then'

368.17   critically] *intrl.*

368.19   an] 'n' *added*

368.19   all enveloping] *intrl.*

368.20   empiricist] *ab. del.* 'nominalistic'

368.23   Mind] *ab. del.* 'mental development'

368.24   range] *aft. del.* 't'

368.25   relations.] *bef. del.* 'Rightness of a thought is tested by its'

368.25   facts] *insrtd. for del.* 'relations'

368.30   feels] 'f' *over false start of letter*

368.31   there] *alt. fr.* 'the'

368.31-32   too the] *intrl.*

368.32   obeyed] *aft. del.* 'there'

368.33   exists] *alt. fr.* 'existed'

368.35   them] *alt. fr.* 'it'

368.36   pertaining] *aft. del.* 'not a com-'|

368.37   to . . . &] *intrl.*

368.40   together] *intrl.*; *bef. marg. addition* 'subvert the order, you subvert the terms but not the sentiment'

368.41   "rationally] *bef. del.* 'tagged'

368.42   To talk of] ('To' *over* 'the'); *intrl.*; *bef.* 'Reasonableness ['R' *unreduced in error*]'

369.6   They are] *intrl.*; *aft. del.* '['They do not think *that [ab. del.* 'of'] the knowable world *in its essence is [ab. del.* 'as'] one of pure *Chance ['C' *over* 'c'] as the unknowable' *del.*] Although'

369.6   willing] 'ing' *added*

369.7   ¹is] *bef. del.* 'unkno'

369.14   things.] ('s' *added*); *aft. del.* 'a'; *bef. del.* 'These forces are given in the general capacity for *reflection* which we possess.'

369.16   hitherto] *bef. del.* '['c' *del.*] uninte [*doubtful*]'

369.16   future] *bef. del.* 'make *u [*doubtful*]'

369.18   according] *aft. del.* 'from always'

369.20   proved to] *intrl.*

369.20 ²have] *alt. fr.* 'had'
369.21 beyond.] *period aft. del. comma*
369.21 moment] *bef. del.* 'to' *and illeg.*
369.23 learn] *ab. del.* 'are able'
369.23 future] *intrl.*
369.25 expand] *intrl.*
369.25 a] *ab. del.* 'the'
369.25 deliverance] *final* 's' *del.*
369.25 mind] *bef. del.* 'some moments back we are'
369.27 bear] *ab. del.* 'keep'
369.28 be] *underline del.*
369.29 appears.] *bef. del.* 'Erroneous expectations likewise'
369.30 a] *insrtd. for del.* 'the'
369.31 matrix] *aft. del.* 'ideal'; *bef. del.* 'which'
369.32 instead] *aft. del.* 'we expect wrongly and a different res'
369.34 ¹wrong] *intrl.*
369.37 invalidate] *aft. del.* 'nullify'
369.38 be] *aft. del.* 'have as'
369.41 thing] *intrl.*
370.1 that] *ab. del.* 'our'
370.8 if] *ab. del.* 'the'
370.8 the] *intrl.*
370.9 becomes] *aft. del.* 'is lost'
370.12 haunts] *aft. del.* 'nevertheless is in a sense the same, ['the' *del.*] be ['it' *del.*]'
370.14 whether] *bef. del.* 'the i'

370.14 is to correct['s' *del.*]] 'is to' *insrtd.; aft.* 'cor-'|*undel. in error*
370.15 is to] *insrtd.; bef.* 'corrects ['s' *undel. in error*]'
370.16 desireable] *intrl.*
370.16 feeling,] *aft. del.* 'fel'; *bef. del.* '['or' *del.*] or'
370.17 mere] *intrl.*
370.19 ontologic] *alt. fr. doubtful* 'ontogeny'
370.20 us] *alt. fr.* 'is'
370.21 schlechthin] *alt. fr.* 'schlectthin'
370.21 as] *bef. del.* 'purely'
370.25 arising] *aft. del.* 'given'
370.25 association‿] *intrl.; comma omitted in error*
370.31-32 a sort] *aft. del.* 'its matrix, or as the possible'
370.33 each] *ab. del.* 'all'; *following* 'of' *omitted in error*
370.35 Even] *bef. del.* 'Hume himself'
370.38 am able] *ab. del.* 'can'
370.38 to] *intrl.*
371.4 philosophies—] *dash over period; bef.* 'In ['I' *unreduced in error*]'
371.4 Spencer's] *bef. del.* 'philosophy'
371.6 Liebmann] *aft. del.* 'To exorcise this'; *bef. del.* 'has'
371.7 has] *bef. del.* 'pithily'
371.7 explained] *bef. del.* 'this'

Alterations in Notes for MS¹, and in MS¹, of "A Pluralistic Mystic"

[*begin* 8 *leaves of notes preceding* MS¹, "An unusual type of Mystic"]
[*in pencil*]
376.2 stream] *aft. del.* 'onflowing'
376.3 naught] *aft. del.* 'there is'
376.3-4 can ['occur.' *del.*] go on.] *ab. del.* 'is possible any more.'
376.4 it] *ab. del.* 'the eddy'
376.5 thereafter] *intrl.*
376.5 thinking‿] *aft. del.* 'straight'; *comma del.*
376.5 one] (*over* 'a'); *bef. del. insrtd.* 'small'

376.6 reason,] *alt. fr.* 'reason's *opera-tions, [comma over period*]'
376.6 that rectilinear] *insrtd. for del.* '['harbor a' *del.*] preserve a disdain for all *the [*ab. del.* 'that'] simpler *popu-lar [*intrl.*]'
376.6 insufficient.] *ab. del.* 'superficial.'
376.7 ¶Though] *aft. del.* '[¶] Character-istic as ['their' *del.*] feel of ['dialecti' *del.*] the dialectic eddy is, every'
376.7 each one may] *ab. del.* 'every one'
376.7 report] *final* 's' *del.*
376.8 almost] *aft. del.* '['so' *del.*] specific

*enough to [*ab. del.* 'that it'] found['s *del.*] a freemasonry. All dialecticians recognize one another as having also 'been *there.' [*period insrtd. for del. comma; bef. del.* 'and as brothers'] They feel like brothers of one family, and repudiate alliance with'

376.9 and . . . recognizes] *ab. del.* 'and'

376.10 authentic] *intrl.*

376.10 from . . . region.] *insrtd. in ink for del.* ', *of it [*insrtd.*] is recognizable ['as authen' *del. intrl.*] by ['those who have' *del.*] any one *whosoever ['ever' *intrl.*] has also 'been there.''

376.10 To . . . is] *ab. del.* 'To [*ab. del.* 'The experience founds']'

376.11 of] *aft. del.* 'the members of which ['unite in' *del. ab. del.* 'unite in'] warmly agree in their ['conviction that' *del.*] disdain of the ordinary'

376.11 common] *intrl.*

376.11 a . . . all] ('fie,' *aft. del.* 'simple' *and bef. del.* '['on' *del.*] passed'); *ab. del.* 'contempt for'

376.12 operations] *aft. del.* 'shallow['er' *del. insrtd.*]'

376.12 popular] *aft. del.* 'pori [*doubtful*]'

376.13 was at its liveliest,] (*comma over period*); *ab. del.* 'showed its ['biggest' *del.*] widest, [*comma over period*]'

376.13 and] *ab. del.* 'but'

376.14 had . . . of] *intrl. bef. del.* '*looked at [*ab. del.* 'tasted of']'

376.14 recognize . . . mind] 'recognize [*insrtd.*] Mr. *Blood's [' 's' *aft. del.* ' 's'] mind' *ab. del.* 'see the consanguinity. of Mr. Blood's dialectic.'

376.15 by] *bef. del.* 'a'

376.20 Non] ('N' *in ink over* 'n'); *aft. del.* 'Rectilinear or' *del. in ink*

376.21 takes] 's' *added*

376.21 positively] *ab. del.* 'simply'

376.22 another.] *period insrtd. for del.* ', when it thinks of'

376.22 'all' fact] *alt. fr.* ' "all fact" '

376.22 nothing of] *aft. del.* 'its *ground [*ab. del.* 'conse'] can be'; 'of' *over* 'an'

376.23 can explain it] *insrtd.*

376.23 but] *aft. del.* 'to be'

376.25 curiosity] 'sity' *over* 'us'

376.25 . . .] *ab. del. comma*

[*begin* Alice James *in ink*]

376.26 "is] *aft. del.* ' "Let me at first presume that the beginning of human curiosity, in the philosophical sense,'

376.29 ¹it . . . ²it] WJ *insrtd. in ink for del.* 'it." The ancients'

[*end* Alice James; *begin* WJ *in ink*]

376.29 We] *aft. del.* 'There is as yet no question of content, ['but' *del.*] of what is or has being, but only of being itself"—and Mr. Blood's first answer is the regular'

376.29 treat] *ab. del.* 'assume'

376.29-30 a positive] *ab. del.* 'an ['n' *added*] ['positive' *del.*]'

376.30 like . . . from] ('like' *over* 'a'; 'barrier' *aft. del.* 'wall *against [¹'a' *over* 'y']'; *aft. del.* '*something from [*ab. del.* 'a limit upon']'

376.30 'all] *sg. qt. over db. qt.*

376.30 our] *ab. del.* 'the'

376.31 of being] *ab. del.* 'of being'

376.31 Upon] *ab. del.* 'Th To'

376.31 idea] *ab. del.* 'assumption'

376.32 passes] *ab. del.* 'makes'

376.32 criticism.] *ab. del.* 'objection.'

376.33 separate] *intrl.*

376.33,34 Being] 'B' *over* 'b'

[*end* WJ; *begin* Alice James *in ink*]

376.37 not] *aft. del.* 'demanding'

377.15 ²be] *aft. del. illeg. letter*

377.18 ¹Philosophy] 'P' *over* 'p'

377.23 Secret] 'S' *over* 's'

[*end* Alice James]

[*end preliminary notes for* MS¹; *begin* "An unusual type of Mystic"]

377.27 AN . . . MYSTIC.] *double underl.*

377.28 the . . . reader['s *del.*]] *ab. del.* 'a writer's duties'

377.29 neglected author] *ab. del.* 'writer'

377.29 quality] *del. intrl.* 'but' *ab.* 'quality'

377.30 discover] *alt. fr.* 'have discovered'

377.30 in his explorations.] *ab. del.* 'vegetating in obscurity.'

377.31 literary taste] *ab. del.* 'capacity for verbal enjoyment'

377.31 exquisitely titillated] *ab. del.* 'nourisht'

377.31-32 writer . . . whom] *ab. del.* 'writer of whom I feel'

377.32 say] *ab. del.* 'think'

377.33 readers; and the] *semicolon over period;* 't' *over* 'T'

377.33-34 abet . . . silence] ('abet' *bef. del.* 'abet'); *ab. del.* 'hold my peace'

377.36 Blood] *bef. del.* 'is'

377.36 modest] *ab. del.* 'small'

377.37 regular . . . -winning] *ab. del.* 'regular'

378.2 when . . . him] ('fit' *ab. del.* 'mood'); *ab. del.* 'on occasions'

378.2-3 short flights] *ab. del.* 'rare *fits [*insrtd.*] ['flights' *del.*]'

378.3 moreover . . . of] *ab. del.* 'enough *usually [*ab. del.* 'sometimes'] to'

378.3 publishing] 'ing' *added*

378.4 may] *intrl.*

378.4 or sing,] *intrl.*

378.5 reverberant] *ab. del.* 'megatonic ['t' *over* 'f']'

378.6 ²the . . . Recorder,] *intrl.*

378.10 particularize] *ab. del.* 'specify'

378.10-11 as ['the' *del.*] an 'author'] *ab. del.* 'as ['an' *del.*] [' "a My' *del.*] a "writer," '

378.11 neighbor particularized] *ab. del.* 'townsmen specified'

378.11 apparently,] *intrl.*

378.13 for] *aft. del.* 'of appearance'

378.13 to appear in!] *ab. caret formed fr. orig. period*

378.13-14 DF . . . lamented] *ab. del.* 'the late'

378.14 old] *intrl.*

378.15 these] *aft. del.* 'some of'

378.16 Review] *ab. del.* 'Journal'

378.17 by Mr. Blood,] *ab. del.* 'of his'

378.19 two dashes] *ab. del.* 'emergences'

378.20 Muse] *ab. del.* 'literature'

378.20 her] *ab. del.* 'its'

378.21 Just how] 'Just' *insrtd.;* 'h' *over* 'H'

378.21 met her] *ab. del.* 'met [*ab. del.* 'made acquaintance with it']'

378.22 I met] *intrl.*

378.22 maiden] *ab. del.* 'first'

378.23 a] *intrl. aft. del.* 'a [*ab. del.* 'printed private']'

378.23 at] *aft. del.* 'in 1874'

378.23-24 fascinated] *aft. del.* 'struck'

378.24 ¹its] *aft. del.* 'its *reasonin [*ab.

del. 'contents'] and its style, and has, I think,'

378.24-25 remained as] *ab. del.* 'formed'

378.26 of a] *intrl. aft.* 'of [*undel. in error*]'

378.26-27 decidedly . . . tenor] ('in tenor' *ab. del.* 'introduction'); *moved by guideline fr. aft.* 'of a'

378.27 personal] *intrl.*

378.28 deeper] *ab. del.* '['truth is' *del.*] philosophic'

378.28 is] *bef. del.* 'by the'

378.28 'After] *aft. del.* ' "By the anaesthetic revelation I mean'

378.29 he says,] *intrl.*

378.35 and ordinarily] *aft. del.* 'ordinarily'; 'ordinarily' *intrl.*

378.38 Unable . . . whether] ('U' *over* 'u'); *ab. del.* 'I recollect ['when' *del.*] reading'

378.38-39 was . . . it] ('I' *aft. del.* 'reading it'); *intrl.*

378.39 the late] *intrl.*

378.39 Godkin,] *bef. del.* 'of the *N. Y. [*intrl.; undel. in error*] Nation and *Evening ['E' *over* 'e'] Post,'

378.41 rather] *aft. del.* 'more comic." '

378.42 To] *aft. del.* '['Blood inhabited' *del.*] Mr. Blood's mind steadily inhabits that region of'; *bef. del.* 'the'

378.43 eyes] *insrtd. for del.* 'minds'

378.43 noonday-light] 'noonday ['high' *del.*] ['meridian' *del.*]-light' *ab. del.* 'noon-day'

379.1 hides] *ab. del.* 'conceals [*aft. del. illeg. letter*]'

379.1 even more than] *ab. del.* 'as much as'

379.1 its] ('s' *added*); *aft. del.* '[*del.* '*is thought to [*ab. del.* 'is disdained as'] unfit['ting' *del.*] its possessor ['for profounder' *del.*] for profounder'] ['is deemed to' *del.*] its [*over* 'is'] use'

379.2 unfits] ('s' *added*); *aft. del.* 'is deemed to'

379.2 profounder insight] *aft. del.* 'profoun the'; 'insight' *ab. del.* 'metaphysical achievement.'

379.2 Your] *aft. del.* 'To [*intrl.*]'; *bef. del.* '['genuine' *del.*] purely blooded'

379.2-3 metaphysician . . . revolves,] 'ian'

ab. del. 'cal [over 'cian']' *and* 'c'*not re-*
instated in error; 'born' *ab. del.* 'that';
'and bred revolves' *insrtd. for del.* '*and
bread [*insrtd.*] of pure blood [*ab. del.*
'vespertilian mind lives']'

379.3　company] *ab. del.* 'partnership'

379.3　mystics] 's' *over* 'ism'

379.3　vespertilian] *aft. del.* 'vesyp'

379.4　gloom] *ab. del.* 'twilight'

379.4　²where] *aft. del.* 'and the one *impossible thing [*ab. del.* 'urgent need']
is to distinguish ['the' *del.*] aught from
its own other,'

379.5-6　'for . . . calamitous,'] *sg. qts.*
over db. qts.

379.7　to] *aft. del.* 'stably'

379.7　'fixate' clearly or] *insrtd.*

379.7　background] *ab. del.* 'own other'

379.7　Even] *ab. del.* 'Even obstinately'

379.9　doom oneself to] ('doom' *intrl.*
bef. del. '['tre' *del.*] espouse'); *ab. del.*
'doom ones['s' *del.*] to'

379.9　superficiality‸] *sg. qt. del.*

379.9　crepuscular region] *ab. del.* 'is the
region which'

379.10　always to] *ab. del.* 'steadily to
have'

379.10　inhabit['ed' *del.*].] *bef. del.*
'steadily. [*intrl.*]'; *period insrtd.*

379.10　Most] 'M' *triple underl.*; *aft. del.*
'['All this' *del.*] His later writings
hardly do more than vary the *expressions [*final* 's' *added*] of the ['thought'
del.] anaesthetic revelation. But but
like as the region is, ['his wings' *del.*]
the motion of his wings'

379.11　fly] *bef. del.* 'round in circles'

379.11-12　all . . . -hegelians] *ab. del.* 'the
english hegelian'

379.12　examples.] *period insrtd. bef. del.*
dash

379.12　zigzags &] *insrtd.*

379.13　¹when] *aft. del.* 'and with the
same flittering motion'

379.13　wind] *aft. del.* 'mystic'

379.14　and . . . loose] '['him' *del.*] *and
swings him loose [*intrl.*] ['his wings
more like a sea gull's and' *del.*]'

379.16　his writings a] *ab. del.* '*Mr.
Blood [*ab. del.* '['his' *del.*] ['the development of his mind' *del.*] ['his writings

a' *del.*]']'

379.16　it] *intrl.*

379.17　may well] *ab. del.* 'as if it might'

379.17　them.] *ab. del.* '['Mr. Blood.' *del.*]
his writings.'; *bef.* 'when' *l.c. in error*

379.19　was] *ab. del.* 'is'

379.19　first] *aft. del.* 'original st'

379.19-20　'Thenceforth] *sg. qt. over db.*
qt.

379.20　'each] *sg. qt. over db. qt.*

379.20,22,26　One . . . One . . . One] 'O'
triple underl. in each

379.22　remains] 's' *added*

379.22　dicta] *aft. del.* 'asser'

379.23　'The] *aft. del.* '*'Pluralism [*sg. qt.*
over db. qt.] has talked *Philosophy
['P' *over* 'p'] to a stand-still . . . ''

379.23　notion] *ab. del.* 'conception'

379.25　way. . . .] '. . .' *intrl. aft.* 'way.'

379.27　may.'] *bef. del.* ' . . .'

379.27　'Pluralism] *sg. qt. over db. qt.*

379.29　Mystical tradition] *alt. fr.* '*Mysticism traditional [*alt. fr.* 'The traditional
mysticism']'

379.29　usually] *ab. del.* 'always'

379.29　monistic] *aft. del.* 'in favor'

379.29　extreme;] *semicolon alt. fr.*
doubtful colon

379.30　it . . . of] *intrl.*

379.30　to] *aft. del.* 'always'

379.30-31　not . . . but] *intrl.*

379.31　men] *ab. del.* 'those'

379.31　'been] *sg. qt. over db. qt.*; *aft.*
del. 'personally [*intrl.*]'

379.31-32　& . . . eyes,] ('seen' *ab. del.*
'felt truth'; 'own eyes,' *aft. del.* '['flesh
personally,' *del.*] themselves,'); *ab. del.*
'and not as the scribes,'

379.32　think] *ab. del.* 'am sure that'

379.32　this fact] *ab. del.* 'their authority'

379.32　have] *aft. del.* 'often sometimes
*often [*intrl.*]'

379.32　some who,] *ab. del.* 'those [*ab.*
del. 'persons']'

379.33　have] *ab. del.* 'who had'

379.33　led] *bef. del.* ', to pluralism'

379.33　its] *aft. del.* 'its'

379.34　absolute authority] *ab. del.*
'necessity'

379.35　one might] *ab. del.* '['one [*ab. del.*
'on']' *del.*] may *be [*intrl.*] frame['d'

del. insrtd.]'

379.35 The] *bef. del.* 'prestige of the'

379.36 great] *ab. del.* 'its'

379.37 Mr.] *aft. del.* 'in'

379.37 full] *ab. del.* 'genuine'

379.38 out with] *insrtd. for del.* '*round to [*ab. del.* 'out with']'

379.40 it be,] *ab. del.* '['it' *del.*] you call it,'

379.40 now no] 'w' *added*; 'no' *insrtd.*

379.41 only heir of] *ab. del.* 'exclusive *beneficiary [*insrtd.*] ['heir' *del.*] of monism'

379.41 wealth.] *insrtd. for del.* 'prestige. credit.'

379.42 caused] *ab. del.* 'dissipated'

380.3 frequents,] *ab. del.* |'inhabits,'

380.4 wordiness] *ab. del.* 'verbality'

380.5 simplicity] *aft. del.* 'child-|like'

380.5 of it,] *insrtd.*

380.6 air,] *bef. del.* 'of it, & that is why'

380.6 you . . . it.] *(period aft. del. semicolon); ab. del.* 'grows what you feel, and that'

380.6 This] *intrl.*

380.7 ever tempts] *insrtd.*

380.7 to] *intrl.*

380.8 -verbal] *intrl.*

380.8 so often] *ab. del.* 'ever'

380.10 simply] *aft. del.* 'effectively'

Index

This index is a name and subject index for the text of *Essays in Philosophy* and Appendixes I and II. References to Appendix I, the English translation of "Quelques Considérations sur la méthode subjective," are placed in parentheses immediately after the parallel reference to the French original.

It is an index of names only for the "Notes," "A Note on the Editorial Method," "The Text of *Essays in Philosophy*," and Appendixes III, IV, and V. Names of persons, localities, and institutions and titles of books, articles, lectures, and periodicals, where discussed, are indexed. Such items are not indexed if no information about them is provided, if they are only part of an identification of a discussed item or are used merely to indicate the location of such an item.

References to William James and to *Essays in Philosophy* are not indexed. Also not indexed is Professor McDermott's Introduction.

Index

Index

Analyse" (A. Meinong), 214
Belief: and verification, 24 (332); value
  of, 25 (333); in science, 29 (337); and
  ultimate data, 75; Peirce's view of,
  123-124; and action, 348, 350
Benjamin Autographs, Inc., Walter R.,
  248, 331
Bergerac, Cyrano de, 272
Bergson, Henri: on concepts, 151-152;
  and life, 155; and rationalism, 156;
  notes on, 225, 226; quoted, 274-275;
  mentioned, 159n, 171, 273
Berkeley, George, 72, 137, 366
Berkeley, Cal., 219, 263, 264, 265, 268n
Berlin, 90, 194
Berthelot, Marcelin, 169, 227
Between Two Wars (J. M. Baldwin), 213,
  216
Binet, Alfred, 80; note on, 212
Biology, Spencer's, 100
Bioplasm (L. S. Beale), 342
Blood, Benjamin Paul: on anesthetics,
  63n; his personality, 172-173; and
  dialectic, 174-175; on being, 175-
  176; on sameness, 177; on totality,
  177-178; his idealism, 178-179, 181;
  and monism, 180; and irrationalism,
  181, 185-189; and pluralism, 181-182,
  185; his style, 182-185; on progress,
  187-188; on metaphysics, 340; notes
  on, 208, 227-232; mentioned, 221,
  226, 277, 278, 279, 280, 344, 376,
  377, 378, 379, 380
Boissière, Prudence: note on, 202; quoted,
  39-40
"Bosanquet's Theory of Judgment" (H.
  B. T. Woolley), 218
Boston, Mass., 166
Boston Evening Transcript, 227
Boutroux, Émile: his lectures, 166-167;
  his influence, 167-168; on reality,
  169-171; his originality, 171; notes
  on, 226-227; mentioned, 276
Bowen, Francis, 195
Bowers, Fredson, 237n, 240n
Bowne, Borden Parker, 258
Bradley, Francis Herbert: on resemblance,
  65-68, 69-70; and concepts, 151; and
  rationalism, 152, 156; on judgment,
  153; on philosophy, 153-155; notes
  on, 208-211, 225; mentioned, 116,
  253, 273, 274, 275
"Bradley or Bergson?" (W. James): textual
  documents, 273-275; mentioned, 208,
  225
"Brahma" (R. W. Emerson), 18, 198
Brentano, Franz, 362-363

Bride of the Iconoclast, The (B. P. Blood),
  228
Brighton, England, 260
Brown, Thomas, 138; note on, 221
Browning, Robert, 126, 219
Brown Paper Co., L. L., 259, 277, 278,
  374
"Brute and Human Intellect" (W. James),
  250
Bryn Mawr College, 74, 211
Buddhism, 16-17
Butler, Joseph, 245
Butler, Samuel, 204; quoted, 48

Calderoni, Mario, 144; note on, 223
California, 30 (338), 134
California, University of, 123n, 219, 231,
  263, 264, 265, 266, 267
Cambridge, Mass., 30 (338), 166, 226,
  246, 262, 270, 281
Canada, 205
Candid Examination of Theism, A (G. J.
  Romanes), 61n, 207
Carlyle, Thomas, 62, 97; note on, 207
Cash-value, 137
Casini, Signora Paolo, 223, 271n, 272
Cattell, James McKeen, 82-83, 261, 262;
  note on, 214
"Causalität und Identität" (A. Riehl),
  46n, 204
Causality, 38, 357
Causation, 137-138
Cause, 340
Cerveau et ses fonctions, Le (J. Luys),
  39, 202
Chance, 369
Change, 147
Chaos, 43, 54, 136
Chicago, Ill., 217, 261, 262
Chicago, University of, philosophy at,
  102-106, 218, 374-375
"Chicago School, The" (W. James): tex-
  tual documents, 261-263; James's
  notes for, 374-375
Children of Adam (W. Whitman), 200
Chocorua, N.H., 221
Christianity, 4, 7, 17, 37, 90
Churches, 3-4
Clark University Archives, 194
Classicism, 168-169
Classification, 43-45
Clearness, 38
Clifford, William Kingdon, 20-21, 53;
  notes on, 199, 205-206
Clive, Robert, 188
Closet-naturalists, 132
Cogitandum, law of the, 15, 20

396

Index

Index

on, 146; encounter of, 151; Bradley
on, 152-153; and feeling, 153-154;
and truth, 154; and concepts, 169;
Boutroux on, 169-171; common sense
on, 358
Reason, 169-170
Recognition, 83, 348
Reductive, 60-61
Reflex action, 101
"Reflex Action and Theism" (W. James),
208
Reid, Mayne, 132; note on, 220
Relating, 83
Relations, 39, 68
"Relations Between the Two Conscious-
nesses of Hysterical Individuals, The"
(A. Binet), 212
"Relations of Structural and Functional
Psychology to Philosophy, The" (J.
R. Angell), 102n
Relativity of knowledge, 344
Religion: and philosophy, 3-6; evolution
of, 9; Paulsen on, 92; Spencer on, 98-
99; and science, 116; and practice,
132; and experience, 133-134; and
idealism, 134; Höffding on, 143; and
mysticism, 157; and explanation, 342
Religiøse erfaringer (W. James), 221
"Remarks on Eclectic Texts" (F. Bowers),
237n
"Remarks on Spencer's Definition of
Mind as Correspondence" (W. James):
textual documents, 246-247; men-
tioned, 248
Reminiscence, 81-82
Renan, Joseph Ernest, 169; note on, 227
Renouvier, Charles: on unity, 41; on
wholeness, 62; notes on, 199-200,
202, 207, 216, 224; quoted, 93, 248;
mentioned, 55, 61, 150, 171, 198,
200, 250
Representation, 38
Resemblance, 65-68, 69-70, 88n
Result, 352
"Reveries of One" (B. P. Blood), 228,
231
*Revue philosophique de la France et de
l'étranger*, 212
Riehl, Alois, 46n; note on, 204
Rivista di Psicologia, 223
Robertson, George Croom, 209, 249, 251;
quoted, 250, 251-252
Rockefeller, John Davison, 171
Romanes, George John, 61n; note on, 207
Rome, 187
Roosevelt, Theodore, 167, 171
Ross, Dorothy, 194

Royce, Josiah: on unity, 134-135; and
analogy, 150; his formula, 362-363;
notes on, 220; mentioned, 216, 217,
225, 258, 262, 374
Ruskin, John, 110

Saint-Hilaire. *See* Geoffroy Saint-Hilaire,
Étienne
Sameness, 49-51, 136, 177
San Francisco, 161
Sankey, Ira David, 21; note on, 199
Sartor Resartus (T. Carlyle), 64
Schiller, Ferdinand Canning Scott: on
truth, 148; on the absolute, 149-150;
note on, 218; mentioned, 106, 171,
217, 224, 261, 262, 273, 274
Schleswig-Holstein, 90
Scholasticism, 74, 93, 168
Schopenhauer, Arthur: note on, 200;
quoted, 35, 58-59; mentioned, 6, 41,
145, 195
Science: and speculation, 5; passivity of,
16; and teleology, 18-19; and subjec-
tive method, 23-24 (331-332); and
belief, 29 (337); and classification,
44-45; and things, 72-73; and psy-
chology, 87-88; and philosophy, 91;
and religion, 92, 116; classic view of,
169; on miracle, 342
Science et religion (É. Boutroux), 226
Scotland, 251
Scott, F. J. D., 264n, 268n
Scottish Philosophy (J. McCosh), 195
Scribner's Magazine, 173, 228, 231, 378
"Secret of William James, The" (B. P.
Blood), 228, 230, 232
Self, the, 135
Selincourt, E. de, 207
Sensation: and reality, 21; and things, 72;
and field of consciousness, 158; pure,
348; and space, 353
Senses and the Intellect, The (A. Bain),
212
"Sentiment of Rationality, The" (W.
James): textual documents, 249-253;
James's notes for, 339-340, 359; title
for, 359-360; mentioned, 199, 208,
268n
Sentiments, 8
Series, 66
Shakespeare, William, 15, 169, 194
Shorter Life of D. L. Moody, The (P. D.
Moody and A. P. Fitt), 199
Should be, 351-352
"Should we Still Retain the Expression
'Unconscious Cerebration'?" (A. H.
Pierce), 225

James, William, 1842-1910.
    Essays in philosophy / William
James ; [edited by Frederick H.
Burkhardt, Fredson Bowers, Ignas K.
Skrupskelis ; introd. by John J.
McDermott]. -- Cambridge, Mass. :
Harvard University Press, 1978.
    xxxv, 410 p. ; 25 cm. -- (The works
of William James)
    Includes bibliographical references
and index.
    ISBN 0-674-26712-5

    1. Philosophy--Addresses, essays,
lectures. I. Burkhardt, Frederick
Henry, 1912-   II. Bowers, Fredson
                    (Cont. on next card)

James, William, 1842-1910.   Essays in
    philosophy. 1978   (Card 2)

    Thayer. III. Skrupskelis, Ignas K.,
1938-   IV. Title.